Index

Introduction

The carrying of concealed weapons by civilians is regulated by state law. Nevada State Law provides that all persons not specifically prohibited from obtaining a permit will be granted a Concealed Firearm Permit.
The law requires issue of a permit if the applicant:

Is 21 years of age or older

Can legally possess firearms*

Has completed an approved firearms safety course

Has no outstanding arrest warrants

Has not been convicted of Driving While Intoxicated during the past five years

Has not been convicted of a misdemeanor crime involving violence during the past three years

Has no criminal cases in progress that upon conviction would prohibit issuance of the permit

Has not been admitted to a mental health facility <u>voluntarily or involuntarily</u> during the past five years

Has completed the application process and paid the required fees

*Eliminates felons, domestic violence perpetrators, illegal aliens, adjudicated mental incompetents, drug abusers, etc.

This book is intended to provide some basic information to private citizens on the safe handling of firearms, the reasonable use of force in self-defense and regulations pertaining to legally carrying a concealed firearm in Nevada. It should be understood by the reader that this information can only act as a supplement to actual hands on, in person instruction from a qualified instructor. The subject matter is for informational purposes only and should not be construed as legal advice or rendering legal opinions. The law is an ever evolving thing with court opinions and legislative changes modifying it on a daily basis. Readers are encouraged to consult competent legal counsel for advice and interpretation of laws in relation to any specific actual fact incident.

The commentary within is based on my 25 years experience in law enforcement and civilian firearms instruction as well as interviews, investigations and court testimony on numerous firearm incidents.

The "Case in Point" examples used herein as examples are all based on actual cases but names and places are eliminated to protect the privacy of those involved. I acknowledge the many instructors, investigators, attorneys, victims and criminals who have knowingly and unknowing contributed the information herein.

Bob Irwin 2008

FORWARD

This book is dedicated to two very important subjects, firearm safety and the use of force in self-defense by private citizens. It has been my experience as a plaintiff's attorney in literally hundreds of cases that individuals often place themselves in precarious legal positions with clearly questionable actions. Many of the events that generate years of litigation, simply should have never taken place. Clearly some simple instruction in safety procedures with firearms and common sense principles to be applied in self-defense situations is necessary. The instruction here, in many cases could have saved those involved tremendous amounts of stress, time and money. Unfortunately, with today's quick media coverage of events, the public gets most of it's information in sound bite form. The reality of the never ending investigations, second guessing and litigation in the aftermath of a shooting rarely reaches the public. Most citizens have a very limited education as to the legal complexity of real events. By studying the advice contained herein, citizens who keep and carry firearms for self-defense will be better prepared to defend themselves during as well as after an attack.

Victor Lee Miller, Esq.

Permits are processed and issued by each County Sheriff and are valid in any county of the state. Many Sheriffs will not issue to a resident of different Nevada county and will ask such applicants to apply in their county of residence. An out of state resident may apply in any Nevada county.

Nevada issues permits only for concealed firearms not for other weapons such as knives and batons.

Federal Law contains provisions for active Law Enforcement Officers and those honorably retired from active law enforcement to carry within all states under certain conditions and restrictions. Under provisions of "The Law Enforcement Officers Safety Act of 2004" honorably retired officers with at least 15 years service may provide evidence of a current firearms qualification with a revolver, semi-automatic pistol or both and submit that along with a proof of service letter from their department and their retired officer identification to the Sheriff in their county of residence. That Sheriff will then issue an identification card showing compliance with the federal statute which in turn allows concealed carry in any state as if they had a concealed firearm permit for that state. These cards must be renewed with a re-qualification yearly. Sheriffs usually do not charge any fees to the retired officers for this program.

Firearms Safety

Firearm safety encompasses three things:

The knowledge of how to safely handle firearms
The physical ability to use those safety procedures
The attitude to put the first two into constant use

With a Concealed Firearm Permit, the increased amount of contact with your gun carries with it a greatly increased probability of accidents.

Remember:

None of us are perfect.
We all make mistakes.
Accidents can always happen.

If the firearms safety rules are faithfully followed, when you have an accident, it will be embarrassing but not fatal. Lots of noise but no one is injured! The National Rifle Association has embraced three main safety rules for years and years and if followed, they work!

1 Keep firearms pointed in a safe direction.

If your firearm is pointed in a direction where there are no people, no one can be hurt. Whatever mistake you may make, it will only be embarrassing, not fatal. Injuries can only happen when a firearm is pointed toward a person. That of course includes those on the other side of thin walls or doors as well as those in range of a direct hit or deflected bullet (ricochets). Generally, it is a fairly safe practice to point firearms either upward or downward. Common sense should dictate what direction is the safest depending on your specific location and circumstances.

It is not surprising that when a person is hit with an accidentally fired bullet, 65% of the time the victim is the person holding the gun. When you are handling a firearm there is always someone nearby, you! Never point the gun at yourself. During manipulation of the firearm the muzzle should never "sweep" your own body or limbs. When people accidentally shoot themselves it is almost always in their "offside" (non-gun) hand or their "onside" (gun hand) leg. Commonly people place their hand or fingers in front of the muzzle when loading, cocking or otherwise manipulating a handgun. If a slip happens, they naturally shoot their hand or their fingers . When drawing or re-holstering their handgun, something catches the trigger and fires a round into their leg. Sometimes that thing is part of the holster or safety strap. On rare occasions it is clothing that is around the holster entangled in the trigger but most often it is the shooters finger.

Case in Point: A gun knowledgeable friend helpfully reassembles a hard to assemble pistol his buddy brought over in pieces. While handing it back to the owner, he pulls the trigger. Naturally, both sides blame the other for the gun being loaded. The litigation correctly resulted with fault assigned to the guy who pointed the gun and pulled the trigger.

2 Keep your finger off the trigger.

In virtually every firearm accident, the trigger was pulled. Careless trigger manipulation is the number one cause of accidents. Never "play" with firearms. Never pull the trigger if you did not check the gun yourself to be absolutely sure it is unloaded. There is a natural tendency to place your finger across the trigger when handling a gun. Try to avoid that. The stress of a threatening situation usually causes unintended trigger pressure. The adrenaline rush will add unexpected strength to your fingers. If you are startled or bumped off balance, your fingers will grasp by reflex. That frequently causes unintended trigger pulls. Try to develop a constant habit of placing your trigger finger along the flat of the gun frame above the trigger unless you are actually trying to fire your gun. Only place your finger on the trigger when you are bringing the muzzle on target, not as you draw it. Always get your finger clear of the trigger before re-holstering. You may need to draw quickly but always have lots of time to re-holster, slow down and think.

Case in Point: During a police academy range training session, a cadet tried to return a Glock pistol to the holster with his finger still across the trigger, firing a .40 caliber round into his thigh. Medical repairs were handled as a Workman's Comp Claim.

3 Keep firearms unloaded unless necessary.

For maximum safety, firearms should be stored unloaded. Personal defense guns kept in the home may need to be an exception to this rule depending on your home situation. Firearms carried on your person pursuant to your Concealed Firearm Permit will certainly be carried loaded. This planned "violation" of the third safety rule for self-defense guns makes constant practice of the first two rules absolutely critical. Always keep the gun pointed in a safe direction and keep your fingers as well as other objects away from the trigger.

Case in Point: A 16 year old brings his 17 year old friend over after school. No one else is home, so he decides to show off with his dad's single action revolver. After "unloading" it, they pass it back and forth playfully pointing and dry firing the gun. After a few snaps a missed round in the cylinder indexed to the barrel and the gun fired, killing the 16 year old instantly. The resulting litigation targeted the homeowner.

Notes:

Additional Safety Considerations

Whenever you come into contact with a firearm, if you don't know how to operate it, don't handle it! Find some one who knows how it works and let them show you. Whenever you pick a gun up, immediately point it in a safe direction. After you have done that, check to see if it's loaded. Safe direction is always first.

⌐he mechanical safeties built into firearms should always be used but never relied upon. All things break, including firearm safeties, The most important "safety" is your dedicated practice of the firearm safety rules. Use the safeties built into your firearm, just don't trust them with your life. Never let any "expert" talk you into disconnecting a safety device to make your gun "better" It won't be better, it will be dangerous. The engineers at the manufacturer's plant know a bit about guns too. Trust them. The same generally applies to any add on improvement parts available on the internet and at gun shows. If it was really that much better, don't you think Colt or Smith & Wesson or whoever would install it at the factory? On an almost daily basis, we have guns come in to the shop that are malfunctioning and the cause is some after-market part the customer installed to make it better. Don't risk it with your self-defense guns! Use factory parts and factory magazines. If it works, don't fix it.

Use only ammunition designated for use in your firearm. The proper type for your gun is usually marked on the firearm's barrel. Compare that with the information on the ammunition box or stamped on the back end of the cartridges themselves. Some manufacturers (most foreign countries) use different names for the same cartridges. Particularly if you are using foreign made ammunition or a firearm not marked in English, be sure that you have the right cartridges for that firearm. If you are not sure, don't try finding out by firing the combination. Go to your local gun shop with the firearm and the ammunition and ask! The fact that the cartridges will fit in the gun does not give you reliable information. Fingers have been lost by people who guessed wrong.

Maintain your guns in safe operating order. If there is any doubt as to the firearm's safe working condition, have it checked by a competent gunsmith.

When shooting, know what is beyond your target. Most self-defense type pistols are powerful enough to drive their bullets well over one mile. When shooting for practice or recreation, be sure to consider where your projectiles are going to land. Never shoot over a hill, through brush or in any direction where you cannot see the background clearly.

Case in Point: A family out shooting in the desert accidentally fires a single handgun round over the hill they were using as a backstop. That bullet killed an individual riding a dirt bike almost a mile away.

Always wear eye and ear protection. Guns emit debris and hot gases that can cause injury, especially to the eyes. Many outdoor and some indoor shooting facilities have some small degree of danger from ricochets as well. Usually bullets bouncing back do not have sufficient energy to do more than cause a welt but there have been cases, especially when hit in the eye, that people have been killed. The high decibel level of gunshots will cause hearing loss. Ear plugs are mandatory. However, plugs alone are insufficient to stop all damage. Even though you barely hear the shots, sound waves still travel into your inner ear through bone conduction. If you shoot on a regular basis, get yourself a set of ear muffs rated to stop at least 25 decibels. If you shoot a lot of high powered pistols or rifles, wear the muffs over a set of ear plugs. If you don't protect your hearing, a high dollar surround sound stereo will sound just like a cheap radio in a few years, at least to you.

Never use alcohol or drugs when shooting or before going shooting. Anything that might impair your judgment or restrict your physical ability should be avoided when handling firearms. Self-induced diminished capacity is not a strong defense for an accidental shooting.

Notes:

Children and Guns

Where children or irresponsible adults and guns may come into contact some special safety concerns come into effect. Children are naturally curious. They will explore anything and everything in your home. Did your parents tell you to stay out of their room when they left the house? Did you obey that rule? Of course not! When the parents leave, the kids search through everything with special emphasis on areas that are "off limits". They will find your gun. If it's not loaded, they will load it. They learned how by watching all those "cop" shows on TV. Ammunition should be stored separately from your firearms and both items locked up. Firearms and ammunition mixed with children is a recipe for disaster.

Through your guidance, your children may become "gun safe" but the friends they invite over may not be.
When an adult is not there to supervise, guns as well as ammunition must be locked away. More than one child has been injured by hitting a cartridge with a hammer to "see what happens". Avoid locks that open with some trick turning or heavy hand pressure, kids can usually open those given enough time. Obtain a gun safe or a trigger lock that takes a key to open it and take the key with you. Young children do not comprehend the dangers of firearms. They will take foolish risks to impress their peers.

Case in Point: A parent goes out to run errands leaving a twelve year old girl and a thirteen year old neighbor boy in her home without adult supervision. The boy attempts to impress the girl by retrieving an unsecured high powered air rifle and shooting himself. He survived after emergency surgery to remove the BB from his chest. The lawsuit against homeowner for negligent storage was settled for a high dollar amount.

Be both a responsible parent and safe gun owner. Set a positive example when you handle firearms and never fail to lock your guns and ammunition out of children's reach, including air guns. The National Rifle Association publishes the "Eddie Eagle" program designed for young children.

Program educational material, a cartoon safety video and children's workbooks are available in some local gun shops or by calling the N.R.A. at 1-800-231-0752

The Eddie Eagle Gun Safety Message

When you find a gun:

STOP
    DON'T TOUCH
        LEAVE THE AREA
            TELL AN ADULT

Good rules for children to remember!

A Gun In The Home

If you are going to carry a firearm pursuant to a Concealed Firearm Permit, obviously it will be in your home at least some of the time. In fact, a huge number of Nevada residents keep at least one firearm in their home while a lot fewer get permits to carry one on the street. That is probably as it should be. There are considerably more home burglaries than street robberies. If you need a gun, the event will statistically be more likely to take place in your home than away from your home.

The decision to keep a home defense firearm is not necessarily a simple one. Consideration must be given to the details of your personal situation. Is everyone living in or with access to the home responsible enough to be around firearms? If they are not, do you have the facilities to keep your firearm secured? Homes that include individuals with poor emotional control or lack of ability to contain their anger, should not be homes with firearms. People who make irrational choices due to alcohol or substance abuse are never safe around firearms.

If your home is a safe place for a firearm, you should have one. Some will say that they do not want to own a firearm because they don't want to shoot anyone. A noble thought, but having a gun does not require that you use it. That attitude simply indicates that you have chosen not to defend yourself no matter what the circumstances. When the home invader is stabbing you or a loved one, you just might change your mind about shooting someone. The availability of a firearm simply gives you that option. Remember, the gun in the home is to protect the people there from physical harm, not to protect the objects kept there.

If you choose to maintain a firearm in your home, you must be physically and mentally competent to use it. Have you practiced with your gun enough to handle it smoothly under stressful conditions? Can you load it, reload it and operate it safely in limited light? Manipulating even simple mechanical devices can be very difficult under panic conditions. Practicing these physical motions can quite literally save your life.

Do you possess the mental toughness to use your firearm for self-defense if that becomes necessary? Using deadly force is always a difficult decision. If you are not comfortable with using deadly force, a pepper spray, a Taser or some other less lethal deterrent would certainly be a better choice for you.

Firearms kept in your home for immediate self-defense use should be stored in the same place all the time. When you are suddenly awakened by an intruder, trying to remember where you left your gun may be impossible. You must know where it is. If the firearm is locked up, you must remember where you put the key. If your home situation does not permit keeping a self-defense firearm loaded, you must also be able to find the ammunition quickly. A number of companies manufacture small, one gun safes that open by pressing buttons in a particular sequence. Most have holes that allow you to bolt them onto a wall or the floor and provide just enough room inside for your handgun and a small flashlight. These are a great solution for most home situations. If you have curious children however, buy one that locks with a key and take the key with you when you leave the house.

In order to prevent mistakes, don't keep an unlocked, loaded firearm within immediate reach of your bed. This is to make sure you are fully awake before using your gun. Your imagination may mix the sounds you hear while sleeping into a fantasized scenario if you are disturbed while dreaming. Keeping your firearm away from the bed requires you move to obtain it. That in turn will help you become more aware of your actual situation and perhaps prevent a tragic error.

Case in Point: A woman is asleep in an upstairs bedroom when she hears noises that sound like an intruder entering the downstairs living room. In her sleepy state she retrieves a .357 magnum from the headboard cabinet and aims it at the closed bedroom door. While she is waiting for the burglar to try to enter the bedroom, she hears the television come on. Now she realizes that it is her husband coming home late from work. Fortunately, he decided to watch the television news before coming to bed.

Notes:

Choosing a Home Defense Firearm

In picking a home firearm, there are many things to consider. First, as with any self defense firearm, it must function flawlessly every time. This means a quality gun with quality ammunition in it. Tools used for protecting your life are not the place to be "saving a few bucks". A lot of self appointed experts will tell you here that the best tool for home defense is a shotgun. The sight and sound of such a gun will cause the intruder to take flight. If you have to fire it, you can't miss as the pattern will cover the entire room. Reality check time. Shotguns are way to large and long to manipulate in tight places and move with when going around corners. Long guns can be slapped away from you if your opponent is anywhere close to you. Pistol grip versions are extremely difficult to aim and all shotguns require use of both hands to operate. The pattern, even from an 18 inch barreled riot gun, is only 1 inch in diameter for each three feet of distance. Your 12 gauge will shoot into a 4 inch circle across your bedroom and that assumes you and the intruder are at extreme opposite ends of the room at the time. More likely he will be closer, a lot closer.

The far better choice is a handgun. You can point it and fire it with one hand. The other hand is free to use the phone, hold the door shut or deflect his attack. Try to get one that can mount a flashlight if possible as most home intrusions take place at night. The burglar may have disconnected your power before breaking in so a flashlight is really helpful. If it is already attached to your pistol, even better! What type of handgun and what caliber are the areas of great debate. It should be double action so there is no manipulation needed under the stress of the incident. Both revolvers and automatics are available with double action triggers.

The caliber should be the heaviest that you can shoot accurately but not so powerful that it over penetrates, goes through the intruder, the wall and injures your child in the next room. Try to avoid 10mms, 44 Magnums, Desert Eagle 50's or similar cannons that your well meaning, macho buddies recommend. Try to find something you like in .380, .38 Special, 9mm, .40 S&W or .45 ACP. All have decent power but still reasonably controllable recoil and muzzle blast so they won't disorient you. Buy some quality hollow point ammunition and test it to be sure it functions in your firearm. Hollow points are less likely to pass through the interloper and hit something or someone you don't want to hit. If you find the mid level calibers too difficult to shoot, pick a .22, .25 or 32 instead. Despite the conventional wisdom, they all work pretty well. A hit with a .22 is far more effective than a miss with a .45.

Case in Point: A local gangbanger got in a shouting match with another motorist over a traffic altercation. He pulled out his brand new, unfired, inexpensive (low quality) 9mm pistol and tried to shoot his opponent. Despite numerous attempts, the gun failed to fire so he was only charged with attempted murder. Sometimes not testing your equipment results in a good thing.

Notes:

The Decision to Carry

Having the ability to defend yourself and your family against criminal attack anywhere you go is a truly comforting thought. Law enforcement cannot be and never will be everywhere at once. Police respond to incidents and may on rare occasions arrive in time to help. More often however, they arrive to late to prevent the crime. Their function becomes one of finding and arresting the perpetrator in order to punish him and perhaps prevent future crimes. Unfortunately, that leaves the potential victims to provide for their own immediate safety and defense. The availability of Concealed Firearm Permits to private citizens allows them to protect themselves from attacks that could otherwise result in injury or death.

The ability to legally carry a firearm in public comes with some awesome responsibilities. First the reader must understand that firearms cannot be used as an argument tool in the low level disagreements we all have every day. Threats serious enough for you to consider displaying or firing your carry gun, even in today's violent society really happen quite rarely. Statistical studies indicate that firearms are used by civilians in self-defense situations between two and three million times a year in the United States. Many of these incidents go unreported and most don't make the papers. In 95% of these confrontations, the firearm is only alluded to or pointed as a threat and the incident ends. So you might display your gun for self-defense once every 10 years or actually fire it toward an attacker once in a lifetime. Your personal situation, employment or neighborhood will of course, drastically alter these averages. Again, having a firearm does not require it's display or use, but only provides the options.

Case in Point: A young man is approached in front of his residence by another individual with whom he has a long running feud. Over the previous few years they had engaged in several fistfights. As his enemy walks toward him across the lawn, the resident pulls out his pistol and shoots the trespasser dead. While he was not the original aggressor in the confrontation, he was still convicted of voluntary manslaughter. His belief that any intruder on private property can be legally killed was, of course, wrong.

Notes:

Choosing a Carry Gun

Which firearm and what type of ammunition is best for self defense carry? As with your home defense gun, the very first thing to look for is safety and reliability. This gun must be safe to carry loaded and work absolutely every time. Your ability to operate it smoothly and shoot it accurately are extremely important considerations. Look for a model that you can conceal easily and carry comfortably. Most manufacturers offer several models that may fit your needs. Examine and test fire several before making a choice if possible. A firearm too large to carry comfortably might be left at home on the day you need it most. One so powerful that the blast and recoil make it difficult to shoot straight may prove nearly useless in a real confrontation.

Many people settle on one of the medium sized semi autos or short barreled revolvers now made specifically for concealed carry. These models usually have low profile controls and sights to prevent snagging on your clothing and are constructed of lighter weight materials like titanium or aluminum and a lot of plastic. Try to find one that fires double action so you don't have to manipulate levers or cock hammers but has a long or fairly heavy trigger pull to prevent accidents. Remember you will probably be a lot stronger under the stress of the confrontation which may make it a good deal easier to inadvertently fire your gun.

Again the recommended calibers are .380, 9mm, .38 Special, .40 S&W and 45 ACP. Some of these can be very difficult to shoot in the smaller, light weight guns. If you have problems with the recoil, opt for a smaller caliber that you can shoot comfortably and accurately. The smaller calibers still work. Rarely will the attacker say "I see you only have a .22 so I don't care if you shoot me". When they perceive the danger of being shot, most criminals will withdraw rather quickly.

Notes:

Methods of Carry

There are three main things to consider when deciding how to carry your concealed firearm. They are that the firearm is secure, that it is not visible and that it is available relatively quickly.

Having your gun secure means carrying in a manner that it will not inadvertently fall out. Most street robberies and assaults start with the application of some impact on the victim to get them off balance or disorient them. If your firearm is carried loosely it can become dislodged and fall to the ground just when you need it most. Many modern holsters have a safety strap or some mechanism that grabs the trigger guard to prevent the firearm from falling out. A holster without such features may release the gun when you skip down the stairs or get in or out of your car. Certainly the gun will detach from you when you are bounced off a wall or knocked forcefully to the ground in a fight. Test your holster. Unload your firearm, put it on and jump up and down. Try falling to the ground and rolling around. If the gun comes loose, get a better holster. When you are fending off a criminal attack, you cannot afford to have the your gun come free and fall away from you.

In addition, your firearm must not be unintentionally exposed. Occasionally a private citizen seeing a firearm carried by another private citizen reacts by calling the police. Certainly a bank teller or convenience store clerk will make that call. If reaching for your wallet in your back pocket exposes your gun, move your wallet or move the holster. The operative word in Concealed Firearm Permit is concealed. Inadvertently exposing your firearm may start a really embarrassing sequence of events.

If you accidentally expose your firearm in some situation where it is obvious that someone has called the authorities, you should call them also. Explain who you are, that you have a permit and what happened. Then the responding officers will be aware of both sides and not assume you are a criminal. A firearm that is well concealed and secured by a safety strap may be a bit slower to employ. Practicing your draw, with an unloaded firearm, will go a long way toward solving this problem.

For self-defense, it is generally better to use a holster that securely retains you firearm even if it results in a slightly slower draw. Firearm carry devices that are not securely attached to you are another problem. Guns carried in purses can easily be lost during a theft or pulled away during an attack. Often stealing the purse is the reason for the attack. Fanny packs can be quickly ripped off your waist. Try to carry your firearm hidden on your body, not in something that can be ripped away or is itself the target of a theft.

Purses and fanny packs carry another drawback. In most cases they require two hands to retrieve the gun. One to hold the device and one to open the device. Any method of carry that requires both hands to get your weapon can be a huge mistake. When under attack usually one of your hands is busy deflecting an incoming weapon or fist. You may need to open a door to escape or hold one closed to keep the attacker at bay. If that's the case, you must draw your firearm with one hand. Carry your firearm in a manner that it is at least possible to draw it using only one hand.

Case in Point: A young man is attacked by a person slashing and stabbing at him with a kitchen steak knife. Trying to deflect the knife with one hand he tries to pull the snap on his fanny pack only to have the whole rig move up under his arm. Pulling the zipper caused the fanny pack to slide around to his back still unopened. Fourteen stab wounds later he finally got his gun out and shot his attacker dead. He had never tried to draw his fanny pack gun with one hand before this incident.

Although they offer great concealment, ankle holsters are another poor choice. While law enforcement officers commonly carry these, it is for a back-up gun, their primary self-defense gun is carried somewhere on their waist. Picture a thug with an impact tool attacking and you have your gun strapped to your ankle. As he tries to beat your brains in, how do you retrieve your firearm? Bend down to reach it? Pull one leg up so you are standing on one foot? Kneel down? None of those are practical when under immediate physical attack. Can you back away from the attack while drawing your gun? Is it possible to draw it while he is chasing after you? Leave the ankle rigs for the TV shows and carry your defense tools where you can reach them.

Law Enforcement Contact

You're carrying your gun and are stopped by the police. Most of these are traffic stops. The officer will not magically know that you have a permit. He may run the license plate to see if the car is stolen or cold plated, but he will not know who is driving. Stay in the car and if it's dark outside, turn on the interior light. Before the officer approaches, place your hands on the top of the steering wheel. As he asks for your license, registration and insurance, tell him you have a firearm in the vehicle and where it is. Thousands of citizens in Nevada have Concealed Firearm Permits and many others simply carry a firearm in their cars as that is legal most places in Nevada. The officer will not find it unusual when you announce that there is a firearm in your automobile. He hears that quite frequently. Just be sure to have your hands in plain view when you advise him of that fact and follow his directions. If you are stopped while on foot, use the same pattern. Show the officer your empty hands as you tell him you have a firearm with you. Remember, the officer will have no idea who you are. He may be looking for a violent criminal with a description similar to yours. Show your hands, explain that you are armed and don't reach for your license or identification until he asks you to do so. Contact between law enforcement and armed citizens can be dangerous at times so be very careful in your actions.

Avoiding Criminal Attack

The best solution to any confrontation is, of course, not to have one at all. While it is impossible to make your self attack proof, there are some simple things that can reduce the probability.

In your home, your risk of burglary or worse, a home invasion, is fairly high. Reduce that risk by using quality dead bolt door locks. Have a peephole or metal grill that allows you to see who's there before opening your door. Use lots of lighting outside at night, display beware of dog signs and if possible, alarm company logos. Having a burglar alarm system is the best single method to reduce your risk of intruders. If at all possible get one installed. Look over the other homes in your immediate neighborhood and upgrade your home to make sure it is not the easiest target.

In your vehicle you are usually safe as long as you are moving. As long as you remain mobile, you will be very difficult to attack. If a situation appears threatening, just drive away. Stopping to argue with another motorist or a pedestrian usually solves nothing and can be extremely dangerous. Keep your doors locked and windows rolled up. If you are followed, drive to someplace with lots of people. Casino valet parking facilities are great for this, they are always open and security is nearby.

To be safe on the street, try to avoid isolated areas and walking alone. Don't flash your valuables. If a situation or area appears dangerous, trust your instincts and walk another direction. It is easy in a street confrontation to let your ego get in the way. Nobody wants to let the criminal element determine where we are allowed to stroll. However, common sense dictates that you should avoid obviously dangerous places when you can do so even if you have a firearm.

Suppose you are confronted by a thug with a knife who demands your watch. If he is at sufficient distance you might try throwing your watch past him so he must turn to recover it. When he moves to pick it up, run away. It is foolish to risk your life to save a watch or a credit card that you can cancel with a quick phone call. It is even more foolish to kill someone over such items. In street robberies, there are few winning options for victims. You can lose your valuables, be seriously injured or shoot someone. None of these outcomes are happy ones. If you can safely withdraw, that is always the prudent decision to make.

If withdrawing is not a viable option, it may be appropriate to display or use your firearm. Remember however that carrying a weapon never requires it's use, it only provides an option.

Threat Response

When you need to use force to protect yourself, a number of possible options may be available depending on the circumstances of the threat. The amount of force used must meet a rather simple standard, must be reasonable and it must be necessary. Reasonable force means the action taken is within bounds dictated by the danger level of the attack. While it may be reasonable to shoot someone who is trying to stab you, it would not be reasonable to shoot someone who is yelling at you. Necessary force means that you had no other safe options available. Suppose the circumstances allowed you to safely withdraw but you chose instead to shoot your opponent. Such a shooting would not be considered necessary. Force can only be used when needed for self-defense, not to punish the attacker or to get revenge. There are other options:

Evasion of Danger
The best solution, of course, is not to be attacked at all. If you can avoid the situation by not entering the threat area or escape by prudently withdrawing, that is always the best solution. Letting your macho image get in the way of common sense can result in injury and often results in huge legal bills. By avoiding the confrontation you can drastically reduce your risk of injury, criminal charges or lawsuits.

Verbal Warnings

If you cannot escape, the next best option is to use a verbal warning. A shouted threat will often cause an opponent to rethink his position. Use a warning that tells him he is free to go rather than trying to detain him. Try "Get away from me or I'll shoot!" rather than "Put up your hands and don't move." If a criminal realizes you are armed but he has a chance to flee, he probably will do just that. Let him go. If you attempt to hold him for the police, he may decide to violently attack you in order to escape. It is not unusual for suspects to fight rather than submit to arrest. Sometimes people just don't want to go to jail. Warning shots, while loud, are non-specific. He may think you are shooting at him and react by shooting you. The other problem with warning shots is that they all hit something. Where is your bullet going? Remember, any warning may not work as expected, be prepared for an unusual reaction.

Case in Point: During an interrogation, an attempted rape suspect (who had been shot several times by his intended victim) was asked why he continued forward when the lady pointed a gun at him. He said "I didn't think she would really shoot me".

Physical restraint

If escape and warnings are not effective, available or practical, the next step up is use of "soft hands" techniques. Here we are talking about non-impact physical techniques designed to make you safe but still not seriously injure your opponent. If you have sufficient training in Judo or similar control techniques, this is the spot for their use. Most people don't have the training or the physical agility to use this type of defense but if you do, so much the better.

If you can make yourself safe from the attack without the legal risks of injuring the other party, that's a fine solution. If you are accosted by a slobbering drunk in a parking lot, gently set him on the ground and walk away. These are the same techniques you might use on an unruly child. Get control but don't injure him.

Chemical and electronic weapons

Bear in mind that all "less lethal" weapons have been accused of causing deaths under odd conditions. The Star Trek "Phaser set on stun" does not exist, at least not yet. In the vast majority of cases however, the use of pepper spray, stun guns or Tasers offer viable solutions.

Pepper spray (Oleoresin Capsicum or O.C. spray) is now civilian legal almost everywhere and has racked up an remarkable 85% stop rate in field use. A pair of one second bursts directed toward the opponents eyes will bring most confrontations to an abrupt conclusion. Buy the key ring size so that you will always have it with you. The larger units tend to be left at home as they are to big to comfortably carry. Look for a brand that carries an SHU (heat rating) of 1.5 million or greater on the label and has an expiration date. The compressed propellant will last no more than two years before it leaks out to zero pressure. As it nears expiration, toss it and get a new one. They also come in stream, cone spray, foggers and foam versions. The stream ones will spray 20 feet or so but have a narrow spread hence requiring aiming. That may be hard to do in a wrestling match. The foggers are very effective but short ranged, perhaps 5 feet or so. The general use best choice is the cone spray version, reasonable range, usually around 10 feet, but still a wide enough pattern to very reliably get into the opponent's eyes.

The foam types are for indoor use to avoid contamination of the surrounding area but carry the danger of being wiped off by your opponent and then applied to you. Avoid those types. When you use your pepper spray you will certainly catch some of the spray yourself. It will be substantially worse for the person directly sprayed but be prepared, it stings! The key ring size units usually cost less than $5. Cheap insurance indeed!

Hand held electronic stun guns are a little less effective than pepper sprays but a lot easier to clean up after. They are however, not legal everywhere so you must check before you travel. The other down side is you must keep it in physical contact with a large muscle (thigh or stomach works best) on your opponent for two to three seconds for it to take effect. That may prove impossible in a physical fight. While they are certainly useful in areas where pepper sprays are unlawful for civilians, stun guns are a second tier choice. A decent brand stun gun, rated at 100,000 volts or better costs about $50.

Tasers are the "king of the hill" in the less lethal arena. Law enforcement has had an amazing success rate when these devices are used against combative subjects. There are several potential downsides to Tasers. First is cost, the current civilian versions start at nearly $300.00. Second, there is considerable litigation against Taser International over alleged deaths cause by use (or misuse) of the devices. Should these deaths be laid at the feet of Taser or were from other causes is the question. On the positive side, there is now available a recording camera that mounts on the X26 police and X26c civilian versions that records the action when the safety is flipped off. A real advantage when you are accused of misuse of force. As usual with any new technology, you may expect improved yet cheaper versions to be developed as was the pattern with chemical sprays and stun guns.

Use of Impacts

Punches, kicks and karate strikes can certainly be useful self-defense tools in some situations. Impacts with fists, elbows, feet or objects at hand may stun your attacker long enough for you to effect an escape. The usefulness of these techniques will depend on your physical agility, training and the particular circumstances. If you are capable of controlling the opponent with a short fight, it is certainly an option to consider. There is little good that can come from using more force than you need to use. Again, this level of force will not apply to many readers, but if it will work for you, it may be a viable solution.

Use of Deadly Force

The use deadly force in self defense presents some complex issues. First the reader must understand that "deadly force" legally means force that is reasonably likely to cause death <u>or substantial bodily harm.</u>

Nevada law note:
NRS 0.060 "Substantial Bodily Harm" defined.
Unless the context otherwise requires, "substantial bodily harm" means:
1. Bodily injury which creates a substantial risk of death or which causes serious, permanent disfigurement or protracted loss or impairment of the function of any bodily member or organ; or:
2. Prolonged physical pain.

While some of the "less lethal" tools and techniques above can on occasion cause death or serious injury, it is usually an unexpected or unpredictable result. Gunfire always carries the risk of death or serious injury as a probable result. In other than very rare cases, those who use firearms in self-defense will always be considered to have been using deadly force. There are two popular street theories where firearms are not deadly force. One is "I only fired a warning shot past him to scare him away" When you fire your gun near someone is there a danger of you missing and actually hitting him? Could he actually move into the bullets path while trying to evade the shot? Could he be struck by a ricochet? Given those possible outcomes, might it then reasonably likely that he could be injured or killed?

The second street theory is even more bizarre, "I'm only going to wound him". The attempt is to shoot the opponent in the arm or leg to just disable him. If an intended miss is considered use of deadly force, where does that leave an intended hit? Reality of gunshot wounds is of course, that they are quite unpredictable. People die from "non-lethal" wounds and survive "lethal" wounds all the time. In real gunfights, marksmanship is usually terrible. National averages for police show that they hit their silhouette targets around 97% of the time in training. In real life, with hostile opponents as the target, that hit ratio drops to 18% or less. Consider also that the average police gunfight takes place at a bit less than ten feet. Although we keep no such statistical averages on civilian shootings, anecdotal evidence suggests similar results. Stress, fear and the adrenaline rush take terrible toll on shooting skills. When you fire because your life depends on it, you will probably miss. Slow down, use the sights and press the trigger. The first shot does not usually win, the first hit usually does!

In 1985, the United States Supreme Court handed down a landmark decision in use of deadly force. The Court reviewed the shooting of Edward Garner by an Officer of the Memphis Tennessee Police Department in 1974. Garner had committed a burglary and was attempting to evade the pursuing officers. Ignoring orders to halt, he was going over a fence behind the victim's home when shot by an officer. Tennessee law said that police may use deadly force to prevent escape of a felony suspect and as he had been warned, the officer met the legal standard for shooting. Garner's parents sued in civil court for the wrongful death of their 15 year old, unarmed son. They argued that the killing was outrageous considering the relatively minor crime committed and low danger level presented to the officer. The Court agreed with them.

The Justices ruled that the shooting was unreasonable because Garner presented no physical danger to the officer or anyone else at the time he was killed. The Court decision said that deadly force could only be used to protect a human being who is in danger of death or great bodily harm. No human in serious danger means no gunfire. The Garner case and hundreds of others since, eliminated the use of deadly force to prevent property crimes. If someone is stealing your car or breaking your windows, gunfire is not an option. Deadly force cannot be used to protect objects, it may only be used for protection of human beings.

The threat must also present a serious danger. The Court said "danger of death or substantial bodily harm". The details of the incident must show the victim has a "reasonable fear" of being seriously injured or killed. Reasonable fear is fear aroused by circumstances that would cause a rational person to believe that they were in danger. A fear that is based on emotional overreaction rather than a discernable danger, is not sufficient to justify use of deadly force. To make a determination if use of deadly force is reasonable and necessary, consider the following parameters:

Ability
Does the attacker's physical strength or weapon present a serious danger to you or others? Is he realistically capable of causing great bodily harm or death?

Opportunity
Is he close enough to carry out an attack? Give consideration to his distance from you or another potential victim. With the type of weapon he is trying to use, is he actually near enough to cause harm?

Imminent Jeopardy
Are you or others in immediate danger? Is the attack actually in progress right now? Shooting someone because you think there may be an attack later is not legal. The actual attack must be in progress at the time the defensive shots are fired.

Preclusion

Is there another safe way out of this situation? Are there other solutions available that will allow you to control the situation safely? Is it necessary to use deadly force or would a less lethal option be an effective choice?

As discussed earlier, there are often a number of responses available to a given problem. Evaluate the various force options you have. Can you evade the attack by running away? Are you able to simply warn him off? Does your size and speed allow you to wrestle him to the ground? Will your pepper spray slow him down, allowing you to escape? Could you fight him off with kicks or other impacts? Should there be no other available safe options, gunfire might be the only viable solution. The details of the particular attacker, the distance, his weapons and the number of opponents versus your physical ability, weapons and usable options will determine the most reasonable solution.

Remember, your response to any particular threat is not required to be perfect, it is only required to be reasonable.

Case in Point: Two friends walking to their cars in a night club parking lot are in the path of an SUV that is leaving the lot. After some name calling and posturing as to who is in who's way, the two step aside allowing the SUV to pass. As they near their cars, they see the SUV coming back. Both friends run to their cars and retrieve pistols. The SUV pulls up behind their cars, blocking them in. Two passengers start to exit the SUV, one is holding a knife, the other appears unarmed. One of the intended victims fires several shots, killing the knife wielder. The driver of the SUV moves it away and the friends get in their cars and leave the scene. A foolish mistake. The arriving police have only the stories of the dead guy's associates (who had hidden the knife) as to what happened. The shooter and his friend are arrested for murder. After all the evidence is introduced, the trial jury finds the shooter and his friend not guilty.

Post Shooting Problems

Today's gun magazines frequently carry stories relating to self-defense with firearms. There are short examples of incidents showing how armed citizens were able to use a firearm to protect themselves or their family when confronted by a criminal. While the vast majority of these incidents in real life end with only a warning, the gun magazines tend to report the more note worthy cases wherein the would be criminal gets himself shot. Unfortunately, these articles rarely tell the entire story. There 3 an unreported addition to these cases of self-defense that the magazines don't report. These incidents rarely actually end when the criminal is transported to the jail, hospital or morgue.

There are three major areas of concern here. First there is the possibility of criminal charges being filed against the citizen because the shooting did not meet the state's legal standard for the justifiable use of deadly force. Then there is the probability of a civil lawsuit from the criminal or his family to gain monetary compensation for his loss of life or injuries. The third potential problem area is the mental and moral anguish many individuals suffer after taking a human life no matter how justified.

To understand civilian use of force, we first must separate out law enforcement incidents from the explanation. A great deal of what civilians "know" about the legal use of deadly force is incorrect. The problem is that most of the publicized shootings of criminals are those done by law enforcement. That causes many citizens to believe that they can do the same thing. In most cases that belief is incorrect.

Police intervene in violent situations because they are required to. They cannot ignore a cry for help. Unlike law enforcement officers, private citizens have no legal duty to protect anyone from anything.

Because law enforcement officers are required to intervene in dangerous situations, they carry in the law a protection called "qualified immunity". That legal principle provides that if they acted reasonably based on whatever information they knew (or should have known) at the time of the shooting, they cannot be held to answer in court. That principle applies even in cases when additional information discovered after the fact shows that the police were wrong. The law recognizes that law enforcement officers sometimes must make quick decisions often based on incomplete information. The typical instance is the "later we discovered it was a toy gun" type of case. Civilians carry no such immunity as they are acting because they choose to, not because the law requires it. Civilians can run away from dangerous situations, police cannot. A law enforcement officer's rules of engagement are very different from those applying to a private citizen. In most instances, civilians simply cannot legally take the same actions that we expect of a police officer.

The reader should understand that there are rarely perfect shootings by the police or by civilians. The potential victims react to what they perceive as an imminent threat and take immediate defensive action. Investigators, judges and juries all understand that. Remember from the previous chapter, the force applied in self-defense must be reasonable, not perfect, reasonable.

Some direct advice here. Don't lie about what happened! In the immediate moments after the event, you will look around as you start to regain your composure and make a discovery. You will find that things are not exactly as they seemed when you made the decision to fire. The attacker was at greater distance or the knife is smaller than it seemed. Your shooting was not "perfect". What do you do now? The police have arrived and are asking questions. What you do is tell the truth as you remember it. Never exaggerate and don't purposely leave things out. Your memory of the event will be full of gaps. When reacting under stress, people rarely have a clear idea of all of the events or the correct sequence of events. Don't guess, if you don't remember, you don't remember. It may come back to you later, it may not. If you guess and the evidence shows you are wrong, you will appear to be lying about what "really" happened. Give the officers the basic information about the shooting and then politely request time to speak to an attorney. There will be legal issues that you don't know about, plus a short delay will give you time to collect your thoughts before making an official statement.

That being said, lets look at what the post shooting dangers are to civilians. First consider the possibility of criminal liability. What if it turns out the use of gunfire was actually illegal? Juries can vary quite a bit in what they consider justifiable use of deadly force. Nevada generally does allow you to stand your ground when confronted whereas some states actually require retreating or exhausting all other options before using your firearm. If you really had no other way out, the District Attorney or a criminal jury will likely understand that.

In general terms there must be surrounding circumstances indicating the situation was so dangerous that gunfire was actually a reasonable solution and was only used in order to save yourself or another person. Remember, nothing in the law allows shooting of people who you think deserve to be shot, only those that actually need to be shot.

Case in point: During a domestic dispute over who's turn it was to baby sit, the ex-wife slaps her ex-husband. He responds to that attack by shooting her several times in "self-defense". A jury convicted him of first degree murder after a very short deliberation which then resulted in a life without the possibility of parole sentence.

Case in point: After a short road rage chase, two drivers pull into a shopping center parking lot. One gets out and walks toward the other vehicle screaming obscenities. Instead of driving away, the first driver points a pistol out the window and shoots his inebriated opponent dead. A claim of self-defense at trial resulted in a voluntary manslaughter conviction and a sentence of up to 20 years.

Notes:

Case in point: A bar/restaurant patron was quietly eating his dinner when an old antagonist entered the establishment. The interloper charged across the room and punched the victim in the side of the head, knocking him into his dinner plate. The victim pulls his legally carried gun and strikes the his attacker in the side of the head with it, ending the fight. He was later charged with assault with a deadly weapon for striking an opponent with his handgun (an action that is not recommended for safety reasons), He did not fire his gun but rather used it as an impact tool to ward off the attack. It took the jury only 31 minutes to return a not guilty verdict.

A much more common addendum to self-defense shootings are civil lawsuits. The fact that you were not criminally charged in a shooting does little to prevent lawsuits. In a criminal case the jury question is "could you legally shoot?" In a civil case the jury question is "should you have shot?" There have been several high profile cases recently where a criminal jury found the shooter "not guilty" but a civil jury still awarded substantial monetary damages. Basically the criminal jury looks at what action you took, was it legal or not? The civil jury looks at what action you took and what else you could have done instead. Civil court is where you are asked "Why didn't you just run away or point your gun to warn him off". Was there a safe solution you chose to ignore? The confrontation sometimes unfolds in a manner that you could legally shoot, but wasn't actually necessary. Gunfire was one choice out of several options. It is those types of cases where you see the criminal case dismissed and the civil lawsuit take your home and savings.

A separate word here about court cases. If you get involved in a shooting, hire an attorney and follow their advice. When you speak to investigators or testify in court, tell the truth about what happened. Juries understand fear and panic, they don't understand lying about the incident. Your memory of the event will be poor at best. People acting quickly in stressful situations rarely remember the events clearly and in the right sequence.

Case in point: An armed homeowner investigates a noise downstairs in the middle of the night. As he enters his home office, a surprised burglar spins toward him with a pry bar in his right hand. The homeowner fired several shots, killing the intruder. A reasonable self-defense shooting but more reasonable than he knew. In his panic he had failed to notice the small pistol in the burglar's left hand and the two shots the burglar fired that missed the homeowner.

Don't add to the facts or testify as to what you think may have happened. If you don't remember, you don't remember. If you guess and are wrong, you will appear to be a liar. If the jury thinks you are lying, you will lose.

The third problem is post traumatic stress. Over the years I have had the opportunity to interview more than 80 individuals that have shot and killed someone in a self-defense type situation. These include police and security officers who shot suspects, merchants shooting robbers, homeowners shooting burglars and potential victims who shot rapists and muggers. All in all I would guess about 20% of the shooters are mentally fine with the incident and go on with their lives as before. Another 40% have some emotional problems over it and take a few months or more to get themselves back together.

The other 40% have serious life changes because of the experience. They commonly become alcoholics, addicted to pain killers, end up divorced, lose their jobs or in extreme cases, commit suicide. Taking the life of another human is not an easy thing for most of us. You were taught from childhood that killing is wrong. That lesson was correct, killing is wrong. Unfortunately, life occasionally presents scenarios where you have no other option. Should you or a loved one become involved in one of these traumatic events, even if you think you're emotionally OK, get some professional counseling.

The ability of Americans to possess firearms in their homes and businesses has saved countless lives. Almost all states are now allowing issue of Concealed Firearm Permits. Nationally in the last few years, the addition of these armed citizens has caused at least part of a statistical drop in the rate of street crime. We can expect these types of crimes to continue to decline as rape and robbery become more risky professions. That being said, the use of deadly force in self-defense is rarely a completely winning situation. I would suggest that even if your state law allows you to stand your ground, you evade the attack instead.

If you are able to escape, you are safe from the attacker, safe from criminal charges, safe from civil lawsuits and probably don't need the psychiatrist.

The only way to really win a gunfight: don't have one!

Notes:

Firearm Laws

Some other states honor Nevada Concealed Firearm Permits while others do not. Information about the laws in the various states is available at: www.handgunlaw.us. For the reader's verification, a list of each state's Attorney General's Office telephone number is included on the last page of this book. It is suggested that you call to confirm the current law before traveling.

For the reader's information, the following section contains parts of various Nevada Revised Statutes, Clark County Ordinances and some county and city codes that apply to firearms, other weapons and use of force by private citizens. In order to save space some sections of statutes that are less commonly applicable have not been printed here or have been greatly abbreviated.

The reader must be aware that the law is a fluid thing, often changed by lawmakers and constantly modified by court decisions.

This section is an informational reference tool only. It is not a complete statement of the law, nor is it intended to be. In order to determine if a particular statute even applies to an actual situation or incident, the entire statute, case law variations and competent legal opinions must be considered. Readers are again encouraged to consult professional legal counsel for information and advice on how any law may apply in their individual case circumstances.

United States Code

Federal firearms laws affect citizens primarily in two areas, Who can't legally possess a firearm and "Interstate Commerce" in firearms. The who can't possess a firearm is covered on the form when you purchase a gun and duplicated by Nevada State Law. It includes felons, illegal aliens, domestic violence perpetrators, drug addicts, those adjudicated mentally incompetent and the like. Interstate commerce is the change of control of a firearm from a resident of one state to a resident of a different state. These laws can be complex depending on the laws in the receiving parties state. I would strongly suggest having a licensed gun dealer handle any interstate transaction for you. Traveling with your gun through other states is fine under federal guidelines. If you stop or stay in another state for any length of time you become subject to their laws.

TITLE 18, PART I, CHAPTER 44 § 926A
Interstate transportation of firearms

Notwithstanding any other provision of any law or any rule or regulation of a State or any political subdivision thereof, any person who is not otherwise prohibited by this chapter from transporting, shipping, or receiving a firearm shall be entitled to transport a firearm for any lawful purpose from any place where he may lawfully possess and carry such firearm to any other place where he may lawfully possess and carry such firearm if, during such transportation the firearm is unloaded, and neither the firearm nor any ammunition being transported is readily accessible or is directly accessible from the passenger compartment of such transporting vehicle: Provided, That in the case of a vehicle without a compartment separate from the driver's compartment the firearm or ammunition shall be contained in a locked container other than the glove compartment or console.

Law note: This law to allow transportation of your firearms when passing through one jurisdiction to get to another may not apply when you exit the highway. It certainly will not protect you from local regulations when you are well away from the highway to visit something and are no longer on your " traveling through the state" route.

Notes:

Nevada State Law

200.010. "Murder" defined.
Murder is the unlawful killing of a human being:
      1. With malice aforethought, either express or implied.

200.020. Malice: Express and implied defined.
1. Express malice is that deliberate intention unlawfully to take away the life of a fellow creature, which is manifested by external circumstances capable of proof.
2. Malice shall be implied when no considerable provocation appears, or when all the circumstances of the killing show an abandoned and malignant heart.

200.040. "Manslaughter" defined.
1. Manslaughter is the unlawful killing of a human being, without malice express or implied, and without any mixture of deliberation.
2. Manslaughter must be voluntary, upon a sudden heat of passion, caused by a provocation apparently sufficient to make the passion irresistible, or, involuntary, in the commission of an unlawful act, or a lawful act without due caution or circumspection.

200.050. "Voluntary manslaughter" defined.
1. In cases of voluntary manslaughter, there must be a serious and highly provoking injury inflicted upon the person killing, sufficient to excite an irresistible passion in a reasonable person, or an attempt by the person killed to commit a serious personal injury on the person killing.

200.060. When killing punished as murder.
The killing must be the result of that sudden, violent impulse of passion supposed to be irresistible; for, if there should appear to have been an interval between the assault or provocation given and the killing, sufficient for the voice of reason and humanity to be heard, the killing shall be attributed to deliberate revenge and punished as murder.

200.120. "Justifiable homicide" defined.
Justifiable homicide is the killing of a human being in necessary self-defense, or in defense of habitation, property or person, against one who manifestly intends, or endeavors, by violence or surprise, to commit a felony, or against any person or persons who manifestly intend and endeavor, in a violent, riotous, tumultuous or surreptitious manner, to enter the habitation of another for the purpose of assaulting or offering personal violence to any person dwelling or being therein.

Wording note: This statute may be misread to condone shooting in defense of personal property (as in objects), but in this context the word "property" actually refers to real estate.

200.130. Bare fear insufficient to justify killing; reasonable fear required.
A bare fear of any of the offenses mentioned in NRS 200.120, to prevent which the homicide is alleged to have been committed, shall not be sufficient to justify the killing. It must appear that the circumstances were sufficient to excite the fears of a reasonable person, and that the party killing really acted under the influence of those fears and not in a spirit of revenge.

200.150. Justifiable or excusable homicide.
All other instances which stand upon the same footing of reason and justice as those enumerated shall be considered justifiable or excusable homicide.

200.160. Additional cases of justifiable homicide.
Homicide is also justifiable when committed:

    1. In the lawful defense of the slayer, or his or her husband, wife, parent, child, brother or sister, or of any other person in his presence or company, when there is reasonable ground to apprehend a design on the part of the person slain to commit a felony or to do some great personal injury to the slayer or to any such person, and there is imminent danger of such design being accomplished; or

    2. In the actual resistance of an attempt to commit a felony upon the slayer, in his presence, or upon or in a dwelling, or other place of abode in which he is.

200.200. Killing in self-defense.
If a person kills another in self-defense, it must appear that:

    1. The danger was so urgent and pressing that, in order to save his own life, or to prevent his receiving great bodily harm, the killing of the other was absolutely necessary; and

    2. The person killed was the assailant, or that the slayer had really, and in good faith, endeavored to decline any further struggle before the mortal blow was given.

Case note: A killing in necessary self-defense is justifiable and not punishable in any manner.
Kelso v. State, 95 Nev. 37

200.275. Justifiable infliction or threat of bodily injury not punishable.
In addition to any other circumstances recognized as justification at common law, the infliction or threat of bodily injury is justifiable, and does not constitute mayhem, battery or assault, if done under circumstances which would justify homicide.

202.255. Setting spring gun or other deadly weapon: Unlawful and permitted uses; penalties.

1. A person who sets a so-called trap, spring pistol, rifle, or other deadly weapon shall be punished:

(a) If no injury results therefrom to any human being, for a gross misdemeanor.

(b) If injuries not fatal result therefrom to any human being, for a category B felony

(c) If the death of a human being results therefrom:

(1) Under circumstances not rendering the act murder, for a category B felony

(2) Otherwise, for murder which is a category A felony as provided in NRS 200.030.

202.257. Possession of firearm when under influence of alcohol, controlled substance or other intoxicating substance; administration of evidentiary test; penalty; forfeiture of firearm.

1. It is unlawful for a person who:

(a) Has a concentration of alcohol of 0.10 or more in his blood or breath; or

(b) Is under the influence of any controlled substance, or is under the combined influence of intoxicating liquor and a controlled substance, to a degree which renders him incapable of safely exercising actual physical control of a firearm, to have in his actual physical possession any firearm. This prohibition does not apply to the actual physical possession of a firearm by a person who was within his personal residence and had the firearm in his possession solely for self-defense.

202.265. Possession of dangerous weapon on property or in vehicle of school; exceptions.

1. Except as otherwise provided in this section, a person shall not carry or possess, while on the property of the Nevada System of Higher Education, a private or public

school or child care facility or while in a vehicle of a private or public school or child care facility:

(a) An explosive or incendiary device;

(b) A dirk, dagger or switchblade knife;

(c) A nunchaku or trefoil;

(d) A blackjack or billy club or metal knuckles;

(e) A pistol, revolver or other firearm ; or

(f) Any device used to mark any part of a person with paint or any other substance.

3. This section does not prohibit the possession of a weapon listed in subsection 1 on the property of :

(a) A private or public school or child care facility by a:

(1) Peace officer;

(2) School security guard; or

(3) Person having written permission from the president of a branch or facility of the Nevada System of Higher Education or the principal of the school or the person designated by a child care facility to give permission to carry or possess the weapon.

(b) A child care facility which is located at or in the home of a natural person by the person who owns or operates the facility so long as the person resides in the home and the person complies with any laws governing the possession of such a weapon.

4. The provisions of this section apply to a child care facility located at or in the home of a natural person only during the normal hours of business of the facility.

5. For the purposes of this section:

(a) "Childcare facility" means any child care facility that is licensed pursuant to chapter 432A of NRS or licensed by a city or county.

(b) "Firearm" includes any device from which a metallic projectile, including any ball bearing or pellet, may be expelled by means of spring, gas, air or other force.

(c) "Nunchaku" has the meaning ascribed to it in NRS 202.350.
(d) "Switchblade knife" has the meaning ascribed to it in NRS 202.350.
(e) "Trefoil" has the meaning ascribed to it in NRS 202.350.
(f) "Vehicle" has the meaning ascribed to "school bus" in NRS 484.148

202.273. Unlawful manufacture or sale of certain metal-penetrating bullets: Exceptions; penalty.
1. It is unlawful to manufacture or sell any metal-penetrating bullet capable of being fired from a handgun.
4. As used in this section, "metal-penetrating bullet" means a bullet whose core:
     (a) Reduces the normal expansion of the bullet upon impact; and
     (b) Is at least as hard as the maximum hardness attainable using solid red metal alloys, and which can be used in a handgun. The term does not include any bullet with a copper or brass jacket and a core of lead or a lead alloy, or a bullet made of lead or lead alloys.

202.275. Possession, manufacture or disposition of short-barreled rifle or short-barreled shotgun:
1. Except as otherwise provided in subsection 3, a person who knowingly or willfully possesses, manufactures or disposes of any short-barreled rifle or short-barreled shotgun is guilty of a category D felony and shall be punished as provided in NRS 193.130.
2. For purposes of this section:
     (a) "Short-barreled rifle" means:
          (1) A rifle having one or more barrels less than 16 inches in length; or
          (2) Any weapon made from a rifle, whether by alteration, modification or other means, with an overall length of less than 26 inches.

(b) "Short-barreled shotgun" means:

(1) A shotgun having one or more barrels less than 18 inches in length; or

(2) Any weapon made from a shotgun, whether by alteration, modification or other means, with an overall length of less than 26 inches.

3. This section does not prohibit:

(b) The possession of any short-barreled rifle or short-barreled shotgun by a person who is licensed as a firearms importer, manufacturer, collector or dealer by the United States Department of the Treasury, or by a person to whom such a rifle or shotgun is registered with the United States Department of the Treasury; or

(c) The possession of any short-barreled rifle or short-barreled shotgun that has been determined to be a collector's item pursuant to 26 U.S.C. Chapter 53 or a curio or relic pursuant to 18 U.S.C. Chapter 44.

202.277. Changing, altering, removing or obliterating serial number of firearm prohibited; possession of firearm with serial number changed, altered, removed or obliterated prohibited

1. A person shall not intentionally change, alter, remove or obliterate the serial number upon any firearm. Any person who violates the provisions of this subsection is guilty of a category C felony.

2. A person shall not knowingly possess a firearm on which the serial number has been intentionally changed, altered, removed or obliterated. Any person who violates the provisions of this subsection is guilty of a category D felony.

202.280. Discharging firearm in or upon public streets or in places of public resort; throwing deadly missiles; duties of civil, military and peace officers; penalties.

1. Unless a greater penalty is provided in NRS 202.287, a

person, whether under the influence of liquor, a controlled substance or otherwise, who maliciously, wantonly or negligently discharges or causes to be discharged any pistol, gun or any other kind of firearm, in or upon any public street or thoroughfare, or in any theatre, hall, store, hotel, saloon or any other place of public resort, or throws any deadly missile in a public place or in any place where any person might be endangered thereby, although no injury results, is guilty of a misdemeanor.

2. All civil, military and peace officers shall be vigilant in carrying the provisions of subsection 1 into full force and effect. Any peace officer who neglects his duty in the arrest of any such offender is guilty of a gross misdemeanor.

Law note: Law Enforcement Officers are required to intervene under NRS 202.280 but civilians have no legal duty to do the same.

202.285. Discharging firearm at or into structure, vehicle, aircraft or watercraft; penalties.

1. A person who willfully and maliciously discharges a firearm at or into any house, room, apartment, tenement, shop, warehouse, store, mill, barn, stable, outhouse or other building, tent, vessel, aircraft, vehicle, vehicle trailer, semitrailer or house trailer, railroad locomotive, car or tender:

    (a) If it has been abandoned, is guilty of a misdemeanor unless a greater penalty is provided in NRS 202.287.

    (b) If it is occupied, is guilty of a category B felony.

202.287. Discharging firearm within or from structure or vehicle; penalties.

1. A person who is in, on or under a structure or vehicle and who maliciously or wantonly discharges or maliciously or wantonly causes to be discharged a firearm within or

from the structure or vehicle:

(a) If the structure or vehicle is not within an area designated by city or county ordinance as a populated area for the purpose of prohibiting the discharge of weapons, is guilty of a misdemeanor.

(b) If the structure or vehicle is within an area designated by city or county ordinance as a populated area for the purpose of prohibiting the discharge of weapons, is guilty of a category B felony

3. The provisions of this section do not apply to:

(a) A person who lawfully shoots at a game mammal or game bird pursuant to subsection 2 of NRS 503.010.

(b) A peace officer while engaged in the performance of his official duties.

(c) A person who discharges a firearm in a lawful manner and in the course of a lawful business, event or activity.

4. As used in this section:

(a) "Structure" means any temporary or permanent structure, including, but not limited to, any tent, house, room, apartment, tenement, shop, warehouse, store, mill, barn, stable, outhouse or other building.

(b) "Vehicle" means any motor vehicle or trailer.

202.290. Aiming firearm at human being; discharging weapon where person might be endangered.
Unless a greater penalty is provided in NRS 202.287, a person who willfully:

1. Aims any gun, pistol, revolver or other firearm, whether loaded or not, at or toward any human being; or

2. Discharges any firearm, air gun or other weapon, or throws any deadly missile in a public place, or in any place where any person might be endangered thereby, although an injury does not result, is guilty of a gross misdemeanor.

202.300. Use or possession of firearm by child under age of 18 years; unlawful to aid or permit child to commit violation; penalties; child 14 years of age or older authorized to possess firearm under certain circumstances.

1. Except as otherwise provided in this section, a child under the age of 18 years shall not handle or have in his possession or under his control, except while accompanied by or under the immediate charge of his parent or guardian or an adult person authorized by his parent or guardian to have control or custody of the child, any firearm of any kind for hunting or target practice or for other purposes. A child who violates this subsection commits a delinquent act and the court may order the detention of the child in the same manner as if the child had committed an act that would have been a felony if committed by an adult.

3. A person does not aid or knowingly permit a child to violate subsection 1 if:

      (a) The firearm was stored in a securely locked container or at a location which a reasonable person would have believed to be secure;

      (b) The child obtained the firearm as a result of an unlawful entry by any person in or upon the premises where the firearm was stored;

      (c) The injury or death resulted from an accident which was incident to target shooting, sport shooting or hunting; or

      (d) The child gained possession of the firearm from a member of the military or a law enforcement officer, while the member or officer was performing his official duties.

5. Except as otherwise provided in subsection 8, a child who is 14 years of age or older, who has in his possession a valid license to hunt, may handle or have in his possession or under his control, without being accompanied by his parent or guardian or an adult person authorized by his parent or guardian to have control or custody of him:

    (a) A rifle or shotgun that is not a fully automatic firearm, if the child is not otherwise prohibited by law from possessing the rifle or shotgun and the child has the permission of his parent or guardian to handle or have in his possession or under his control the rifle or shotgun; or

    (b) A firearm capable of being concealed upon the person, if the child has the written permission of his parent or guardian to handle or have in his possession or under his control such a firearm and the child is not otherwise prohibited by law from possessing such a firearm, and the child is traveling to the area in which he will be hunting or returning from that area and the firearm is not loaded, or the child is hunting pursuant to that license.

6. Except as otherwise provided in subsection 8, a child who is 14 years of age or older may handle or have in his possession or under his control a rifle or shotgun that is not a fully automatic firearm if the child is not otherwise prohibited by law from possessing the rifle or shotgun, without being accompanied by his parent or guardian or an adult person authorized by his parent or guardian to have control or custody of him, if the child has the permission of his parent or guardian to handle or have in his possession or under his control the rifle or shotgun and the child is:

    (a) Attending a course of instruction in the responsibilities of hunters or a course of instruction in the safe use of firearms;

    (b) Practicing the use of a firearm at an established firing range or at any other area where the discharge of a firearm is permitted;

    (c) Participating in a lawfully organized competition or performance involving the use of a firearm;

    (d) Within an area in which the discharge of firearms has not been prohibited by local ordinance or regulation and he is engaging in a lawful hunting activity in accordance with chapter 502 of NRS for which a license is not required;

(e) Traveling to or from any activity described in paragraph (a), (b), (c) or (d), and the firearm is not loaded;

(f) On real property that is under the control of an adult, and the child has the permission of that adult to possess the firearm on the real property; or

(g) At his residence.

7. Except as otherwise provided in subsection 8, a child who is 14 years of age or older may handle or have in his possession or under his control, for the purpose of engaging in any of the activities listed in paragraphs (a) to (g), inclusive, of subsection 6, a firearm capable of being concealed upon the person, without being accompanied by his parent or guardian or an adult person authorized by his parent or guardian to have control or custody of him, if the child:

(a) Has the written permission of his parent or guardian to handle or have in his possession or under his control such a firearm for the purpose of engaging in such an activity; and

(b) Is not otherwise prohibited by law from possessing such a firearm.

8. A child shall not handle or have in his possession or under his control a loaded firearm if he is:

(a) An occupant of a motor vehicle;

(b) Within any residence, including his residence, or any building other than a facility licensed for target practice, unless possession of the firearm is necessary for the immediate defense of the child or another person; or

(c) Within an area designated by a county or municipal ordinance as a populated area for the purpose of prohibiting the discharge of weapons, unless he is within a facility licensed for target practice.

202.310. Sale of firearms to minors; penalty.
Any person in this state who sells or barters to a child who is under the age of 18 years, with reckless disregard of whether the child is under the age of 18 years, or with knowledge or reason to know that the child is under the age of 18 years, a pistol, revolver or a firearm capable of being concealed upon the person is guilty of a category B felony.

202.320. Drawing deadly weapon in threatening manner.
1. Unless a greater penalty is provided in NRS 202.287, a person having, carrying or procuring from another person any dirk, dirk-knife, sword, sword cane, pistol, gun or other deadly weapon, who, in the presence of two or more persons, draws or exhibits any of such deadly weapons in a rude, angry or threatening manner not in necessary self-defense, or who in any manner unlawfully uses that weapon in any fight or quarrel, is guilty of a misdemeanor.
2. A sheriff, deputy sheriff, marshal, constable or other peace officer shall not be held to answer, under the provisions of subsection 1, for drawing or exhibiting any of the weapons mentioned therein while in the lawful discharge of his duties.

202.350. Manufacture, importation, possession or use of dangerous weapon or silencer; carrying concealed weapon without permit; penalties; issuance of permit to carry concealed weapon; exceptions.
1. Except as otherwise provided in this section and NRS 202.355 and 202.3653 to 202.369, inclusive, a person within this State shall not:
    (a) Manufacture or cause to be manufactured, or import into the State, or keep, offer or expose for sale, or give, lend or possess any knife which is made an integral part of a belt buckle or any instrument or weapon of the kind commonly known as a switchblade knife, blackjack, slungshot, billy, sand-club, sandbag or metal knuckles;

(b) Manufacture or cause to be manufactured, or import into the State, or keep, offer or expose for sale, or give, lend, possess or use a machine gun or a silencer, unless authorized by federal law;

(c) With the intent to inflict harm upon the person of another, possess or use a nunchaku or trefoil; or

(d) Carry concealed upon his person any:

(1) Explosive substance, other than ammunition or any components thereof;

(2) Dirk, dagger or machete;

(3) Pistol, revolver or other firearm, or other dangerous or deadly weapon; or

(4) Knife which is made an integral part of a belt buckle.

3. Except as otherwise provided in this subsection, the sheriff of any county may, upon written application by a resident of that county showing the reason or the purpose for which a concealed weapon is to be carried, issue a permit authorizing the applicant to carry in this State the concealed weapon described in the permit. The sheriff shall not issue a permit to a person to carry a switchblade knife. This subsection does not authorize the sheriff to issue a permit to a person to carry a pistol, revolver or other firearm.

4. Except as otherwise provided in subsection 5, this section does not apply to:

(a) Sheriffs, constables, marshals, peace officers, correctional officers employed by the Department of Corrections, special police officers, police officers of this State, whether active or honorably retired, or other appointed officers.

(b) Any person summoned by any peace officer to assist in making arrests or preserving the peace while the person so summoned is actually engaged in assisting such an officer.

(c) Any full-time paid peace officer of an agency of the United States or another state or political subdivision thereof when carrying out official duties in the State of Nevada.

(d) Members of the Armed Forces of the United States when on duty.

5. The exemptions provided in subsection 4 do not include a former peace officer who is retired for disability unless his former employer has approved his fitness to carry a concealed weapon.

6. The provisions of paragraph (b) of subsection 1 do not apply to any person who is licensed, authorized or permitted to possess or use a machine gun or silencer pursuant to federal law. The burden of establishing federal licensure, authorization or permission is upon the person possessing the license, authorization or permission.

7. This section shall not be construed to prohibit a qualified law enforcement officer or a qualified retired law enforcement officer from carrying a concealed weapon in this State if he is authorized to do so pursuant to 18 U.S.C. § 926B or 926C.

8. As used in this section:

(a) "Concealed weapon" means a weapon described in this section that is carried upon a person in such a manner as not to be discernible by ordinary observation.

(b) "Honorably retired" means retired in Nevada after completion of 10 years of creditable service as a member of the Public Employees' Retirement System. A former peace officer is not "honorably retired" if he was discharged for cause or resigned before the final disposition of allegations of serious misconduct.

(c) "Machine gun" means any weapon which shoots, is designed to shoot or can be readily restored to shoot more than one shot, without manual reloading, by a single function of the trigger.

(d) "Nunchaku" means an instrument consisting of two or more sticks, clubs, bars or rods connected by a rope, cord, wire or chain used as a weapon in forms of Oriental combat.

(e) "Qualified law enforcement officer" has the meaning ascribed to it in 18 U.S.C. § 926B(c).

(f) "Qualified retired law enforcement officer" has the meaning ascribed to it in 18 U.S.C. § 926C(c).

(g) "Silencer" means any device for silencing, muffling or diminishing the report of a firearm, including any combination of parts, designed or redesigned, and intended for use in assembling or fabricating a silencer or muffler, and any part intended only for use in such assembly or fabrication.

(h) "Switchblade knife" means a spring-blade knife, snap-blade knife or any other knife having the appearance of a pocket knife, any blade of which is 2 or more inches long and which can be released automatically by a flick of a button, pressure on the handle or other mechanical device, or is released by any type of mechanism. The term does not include a knife which has a blade that is held in place by a spring if the blade does not have any type of automatic release.

(i) "Trefoil" means an instrument consisting of a metal plate having three or more radiating points with sharp edges, designed in the shape of a star, cross or other geometric figure and used as a weapon for throwing.

202.360. Ownership or possession of firearm by certain persons prohibited; penalties.
1. A person shall not own or have in his possession or under his custody or control any firearm if he:

(a) Has been convicted of a felony in this or any other state, or in any political subdivision thereof, or of a felony in violation of the laws of the United States of America, unless he has received a pardon and the pardon does not restrict his right to bear arms;

(b) Is a fugitive from justice; or

(c) Is an unlawful user of, or addicted to, any controlled substance.

2. A person shall not own or have in his possession or under his custody or control any firearm if he:

(a) Has been adjudicated as mentally ill or has been committed to any mental health facility; or

(b) Is illegally or unlawfully in the United States.

3. As used in this section:

(a) "Controlled substance" has the meaning ascribed to it in 21 U.S.C. § 802(6).

(b) "Firearm" includes any firearm that is loaded or unloaded and operable or inoperable.

202.362. Sale or disposal of firearms or ammunition to certain persons prohibited; penalty; exceptions.

1. Except as otherwise provided in subsection 3, a person within this state shall not sell or otherwise dispose of any firearm or ammunition to another person if he has actual knowledge that the other person:

(a) Is under indictment for, or has been convicted of, a felony in this or any other state, or in any political subdivision thereof, or of a felony in violation of the laws of the United States of America, unless he has received a pardon and the pardon does not restrict his right to bear arms;

(b) Is a fugitive from justice;

(c) Has been adjudicated as mentally ill or has been committed to any mental health facility; or

(d) Is illegally or unlawfully in the United States.

3. This section does not apply to a person who sells or disposes of any firearm or ammunition to:

(a) A licensed importer, licensed manufacturer,

licensed dealer or licensed collector who, pursuant to 18 U.S.C. § 925(b), is not precluded from dealing in firearms or ammunition; or

(b) A person who has been granted relief from the disabilities imposed by federal laws pursuant to 18 U.S.C. § 925(c).

202.3653. Definitions.
As used in NRS 202.3653 to 202.369, inclusive, and sections 2 and 3 of this act unless the context otherwise requires:

1. "Concealed firearm" means a loaded or unloaded pistol, revolver or other firearm which is carried upon a person in such a manner as not to be discernible by ordinary observation.

2. "Department" means the Department of Public Safety.

3. "Permit" means a permit to carry a concealed firearm issued pursuant to the provisions of NRS 202.3653 to 202.369, inclusive, and sections 2 and 3 of this act.

4. "Revolver" means a firearm that has a revolving cylinder with several chambers, which, by pulling the trigger or setting the hammer , are aligned with the barrel, placing a bullet in a position to be fired. The term includes, without limitation, a single or double derringer.

5. "Semiautomatic firearm" means a firearm which:

(a) Uses the energy of the explosive in a fixed cartridge extract a fixed cartridge and chamber a fresh cartridge with each single pull of the trigger; and

(b) Requires the release of the trigger and another pull of the trigger for each successive shot.

202.3657. Application for permit; eligibility; denial or revocation of permit.

1. Any person who is a resident of this State may apply to the sheriff of the county in which he or she resides for a permit on a form prescribed by regulation of the Department. Any person who is not a resident of this State may apply to the sheriff of any county in this State for a permit on a form prescribed by regulation of the Department. Application forms for permits must be furnished by the sheriff of each county upon request.

2. Except as otherwise provided in this section, the sheriff shall issue a permit for revolvers, for semiautomatic firearms, or for revolvers and semiautomatic firearms, as applicable, to any person who is qualified to possess the firearm or firearms to which the application pertains under state and federal law, who submits an application in accordance with the provisions of this section and who:

(a) Is 21 years of age or older;
(b) Is not prohibited from possessing a firearm pursuant to NRS 202.360; and
(c) Demonstrates competence with revolvers, semiautomatic firearms, or revolvers and semiautomatic firearms, as applicable, by presenting a certificate or other documentation to the sheriff which shows that the applicant:
(1) Successfully completed a course in firearm safety approved by a sheriff in this State; or
(2) Successfully completed a course in firearm safety offered by a federal, state or local law enforcement agency, community college, university or national organization that certifies instructors in firearm safety. Such a course must include instruction in the use of revolvers, semiautomatic

firearms, or revolvers and semiautomatic firearms and in the laws of this State relating to the use of a firearm. A sheriff may not approve a course in firearm safety pursuant to subparagraph (1) unless the sheriff determines that the course meets any standards that are established by the Nevada Sheriffs' and Chiefs' Association or, if the Nevada Sheriffs' and Chiefs' Association ceases to exist, its legal successor.

3. The sheriff shall deny an application or revoke a permit if the sheriff determines that the applicant or permittee:

(a) Has an outstanding warrant for his or her arrest.

(b) Has been judicially declared incompetent or insane.

(c) Has been voluntarily or involuntarily admitted to a mental health facility during the immediately preceding 5 years.

(d) Has habitually used intoxicating liquor or a controlled substance to the extent that his or her normal faculties are impaired. For the purposes of this paragraph, it is presumed that a person has so used intoxicating liquor or a controlled substance if, during the immediately preceding 5 years, the person has been:

(1) Convicted of violating the provisions of NRS 484C.110; or

(2) Committed for treatment pursuant to NRS 458.290 to 458.350, inclusive.

(e) Has been convicted of a crime involving the use or threatened use of force or violence punishable as a misdemeanor under the laws of this or any other state, or a territory or possession of the United States at any time during the immediately preceding 3 years.

(f) Has been convicted of a felony in this State or under the laws of any state, territory or possession of the United States.

(g) Has been convicted of a crime involving domestic violence or stalking, or is currently subject to a restraining order, injunction or other order for protection against domestic violence.

(h) Is currently on parole or probation from a conviction

obtained in this State or in any other state or territory or possession of the United States.

(i) Has, within the immediately preceding 5 years, been subject to any requirements imposed by a court of this State or of any other state or territory or possession of the United States, as a condition to the court's:

(1) Withholding of the entry of judgment for a conviction of a felony; or

(2) Suspension of sentence for the conviction of a felony.

(j) Has made a false statement on any application for a permit or for the renewal of a permit.

4. The sheriff may deny an application or revoke a permit if the sheriff receives a sworn affidavit stating articulable facts based upon personal knowledge from any natural person who is 18 years of age or older that the applicant or permittee has or may have committed an offense or engaged in any other activity specified in subsection 3 which would preclude the issuance of a permit to the applicant or require the revocation of a permit pursuant to this section.

5. If the sheriff receives notification submitted by a court or law enforcement agency of this or any other state, the United States or a territory or possession of the United States that a permittee or an applicant for a permit has been charged with a crime involving the use or threatened use of force or violence, the conviction for
which would require the revocation of a permit or preclude the issuance of a permit to the applicant pursuant to this section, the sheriff shall suspend the person's permit or the processing of the person's application until the final disposition of the charges against the person. If a permittee is acquitted of the charges, or if the charges are dropped, the sheriff shall restore his or her permit without imposing a fee.

6. An application submitted pursuant to this section must be completed and signed under oath by the applicant. The applicant's signature must be witnessed by an employee of the sheriff or notarized by a notary public. The application

must include:

(a) The name, address, place and date of birth, social security number, occupation and employer of the applicant and any other names used by the applicant;

(b) A complete set of the applicant's fingerprints taken by the sheriff or his or her agent; (c) A front-view colored photograph of the applicant taken by the sheriff or his or her agent;

(d) If the applicant is a resident of this State, the driver's license number or identification card number of the applicant issued by the Department of Motor Vehicles;

(e) If the applicant is not a resident of this State, the driver's license number or identification card number of the applicant issued by another state or jurisdiction;

(f) Whether the application pertains to semiautomatic firearms;

(g) Whether the application pertains to revolvers;

(h) A nonrefundable fee equal to the nonvolunteer rate charged by the Central Repository for Nevada Records of Criminal History and the Federal Bureau of Investigation to obtain the reports required pursuant to subsection 1 of NRS 202.366; and

(i) A nonrefundable fee set by the sheriff not to exceed $60.

202.366. Investigation of applicant for permit; Issuance or denial of permit: expiration of permit.

1. Upon receipt by a sheriff of an application for a permit, including an application for the renewal of a permit pursuant to NRS 202.3677, the sheriff shall conduct an investigation of the applicant to determine if the applicant is eligible for a permit. In conducting the investigation, the sheriff shall forward a complete set of the applicant's fingerprints to the Central Repository for Nevada Records of Criminal History for submission to the Federal Bureau of Investigation for its report concerning the

criminal history of the applicant. The investigation also must include a report from the National Instant Criminal Background Check System. The sheriff shall issue a permit to the applicant unless the applicant is not qualified to possess a handgun pursuant
to state or federal law or is not otherwise qualified to obtain a permit pursuant to NRS 202.3653 to 202.369, inclusive, or the regulations adopted pursuant thereto.

2. To assist the sheriff in conducting the investigation, any local law enforcement agency, including the sheriff of any county, may voluntarily submit to the sheriff a report or other information concerning the criminal history of an applicant.

3. Within 120 days after a complete application for a permit is submitted, the sheriff to whom the application is submitted shall grant or deny the application. If the application is denied, the sheriff shall send the applicant written notification setting forth the reasons
for the denial. If the application is granted, the sheriff shall provide the applicant with a permit containing a colored photograph of the applicant and containing such other information as may be prescribed by the Department. The permit must be in substantially the following form:

NEVADA CONCEALED FIREARM PERMIT

County.......................... Permit Number........................

Expires.......................... Date of Birth............................

Height.......................... Weight.....................................

Name .... Address...................................

City.............................. Zip...

Photograph
Signature ....
Issued by.......................
Date of Issue.................
Semiautomatic firearms authorized.............. Yes...............No
Revolvers authorized.......................Yes............................No

4. Unless suspended or revoked by the sheriff who issued the permit, a permit expires 5 years after the date on which it is issued.

5. As used in this section, "National Instant Criminal Background Check System" means the national system created by the federal Brady Handgun Violence Prevention Act, Public Law 103-159.

202.3662. Confidentiality of Information;

1. Except as otherwise provided in this section and NRS 202.3665 and 239.0115:

(a) An application for a permit, and all information contained within that application;

(b) All information provided to a sheriff or obtained by a sheriff in the course of the investigation of an applicant or permittee;

(c) The identity of the permittee; and

(d) Any records regarding the suspension, restoration or revocation of a permit are confidential.

2. Any records regarding an applicant or permittee may be released to a law enforcement agency for the purpose of conducting an investigation or prosecution.

202.3665. Duties of sheriff upon receiving notification that applicant or permittee has been charged with or convicted of crime involving use or threatened use of force or violence.

1. If a sheriff who is processing an application for a permit receives notification pursuant to NRS 202.3657 that the applicant has been:

(a) Charged with a crime involving the use or threatened use of force or violence, the sheriff shall notify any victim of the crime of the fact that the sheriff has, pursuant to NRS 202.3657:

(1) Suspended the processing of the application until the final disposition of the charges against the applicant; or

(2) Resumed the processing of the application following the dropping of charges against the applicant or the acquittal of the applicant.

(b) Convicted of a crime involving the use or threatened use of force or violence, the sheriff shall notify any victim of the crime of the fact that the sheriff has, pursuant to NRS 202.3657, denied the application.

2. If a sheriff who has issued a permit to a permittee receives notification pursuant to NRS 202.3657 that the permittee has been:

(a) Charged with a crime involving the use or threatened use of force or violence, the sheriff shall notify any victim of the crime of the fact that the sheriff has, pursuant to NRS 202.3657:

(1) Suspended the permit of the permittee until the final disposition of the charges against the permittee; or

(2) Restored the permit of the permittee following the dropping of charges against the permittee or the acquittal of the permittee.

(b) Convicted of a crime involving the use or threatened use of force or violence, the sheriff shall notify any victim of the crime of the fact that the sheriff has, pursuant to NRS 202.3657, revoked the permit of the permittee.

3. The sheriff shall notify a victim pursuant to subsection 1 or 2 not later than 10 days after the date on which the sheriff performs one of the actions listed in subsection 1 or 2 concerning an application or a permit.

202.3667. 1. Each permittee shall carry the permit, or a duplicate issued pursuant to the provisions of NRS 202.367, together with proper identification whenever the permittee is in actual possession of a concealed firearm. Both the permit and proper identification must be presented if requested by a peace officer.

202.367. Duplicate permit; notification to sheriff of recovered permit; penalty.

1. A permittee shall notify the sheriff who issued his permit in writing within 30 days if:

    (a) His permanent address changes; or

    (b) His permit is lost, stolen or destroyed.

2. The sheriff shall issue a duplicate permit to a permittee if he:

    (a) Submits a written statement to the sheriff, signed under oath, stating that his permit has been lost, stolen or destroyed; and

    (b) Pays a nonrefundable fee of $15.

3. If any permittee subsequently finds or recovers his permit after being issued a duplicate permit pursuant to this section, he shall, within 10 days:

    (a) Notify the sheriff in writing; and

    (b) Return the duplicate permit to the sheriff.

202.3673 1. Except as otherwise provided in subsections 2 and 3, a permittee may carry a concealed firearm while he is on the premises of any public building.

2. A permittee shall not carry a concealed firearm while he is on the premises of a public building that is located on the property of a public airport.

3. A permittee shall not carry a concealed firearm while he is on the premises of:

(a) A public building that is located on the property of a public school or a child care facility or the property of the Nevada System of Higher Education, unless the permittee has obtained written permission to carry a concealed firearm while he is on the premises of the public building pursuant to subparagraph (3) of paragraph (a) of subsection 3 of NRS 202.265.

(b) A public building that has a metal detector at each public entrance or a sign posted at each public entrance indicating that no firearms are allowed in the building, unless the permittee is not prohibited from carrying a concealed firearm while he is on the premises of the public building pursuant to subsection 4.

4. The provisions of paragraph (b) of subsection 3 do not prohibit:

(a) A permittee who is a judge from carrying a concealed firearm in the courthouse or courtroom in which he presides or from authorizing a permittee to carry a concealed firearm while in the courtroom of the judge and while traveling to and from the courtroom of the judge.

(b) A permittee who is a prosecuting attorney of an agency or political subdivision of the United States or of this State from carrying a concealed firearm while he is on the premises of a public building.

(c) A permittee who is employed in the public building from carrying a concealed firearm while he is on the premises of the public building.

(d) A permittee from carrying a concealed firearm while he is on the premises of the public building if the permittee has received written permission from the person in control of the public building to carry a concealed firearm while the permittee is on the premises of the public building.

6. As used in this section:

(a) "Childcare facility" has the meaning ascribed to it in paragraph (a) of subsection 5 of NRS 202.265.

(b) "Public building" means any building or office space occupied by:

(1) Any component of the Nevada System of Higher Education and used for any purpose related to the System; or

(2) The Federal Government, the State of Nevada or any county, city, school district or other political subdivision of the State of Nevada and used for any public purpose. If only part of the building is occupied by an entity described in this subsection, the term means only that portion of the building which is so occupied.

202.3677. Application for renewal of permit......

1. If a permittee wishes to renew his or her permit, the permittee must :

(a) Complete and submit to the sheriff who issued the permit an application for renewal of the permit ; and

(b) Undergo an investigation by the sheriff pursuant to NRS 202.366 to determine if the permittee is eligible for a permit.

2. An application for the renewal of a permit must:

(a) Be completed and signed under oath by the applicant;

(b) Contain a statement that the applicant is eligible to receive a permit pursuant to NRS 202.3657;

(c) Be accompanied by a nonrefundable fee equal to the nonvolunteer rate charged by the Central Repository for Nevada Records of Criminal History and the Federal Bureau of Investigation to obtain the reports required pursuant to subsection 1 of NRS 202.366; and

(d) Be accompanied by a nonrefundable fee of $25. If a permittee fails to renew his or her permit on or before the date of expiration of the permit, the application for renewal must include an additional nonrefundable late fee of $15.

3. No permit may be renewed pursuant to this section unless the permittee has demonstrated continued competence with revolvers, with semiautomatic firearms, or with revolvers and semiautomatic firearms, as applicable, by successfully completing a course prescribed by the sheriff renewing the permit.

202.3678 Application for certification as qualified retired law enforcement officer; fee.

1. A retired law enforcement officer who is a resident of this State may apply, on a form prescribed by regulation of the Department, to the sheriff of the county in which he resides for any certification required pursuant to 18 U.S.C. § 926C(d) to become a qualified retired law enforcement officer. Application forms for certification must be provided by the sheriff of each county upon request.

2. The sheriff shall provide the certification pursuant to subsection 1 to a retired law enforcement officer who submits a completed application and pays any fee required pursuant to subsection 3 if the sheriff determines that the officer meets the standards for training and qualifications.

3. The sheriff may impose a nonrefundable fee in the amount necessary to pay the expenses in providing the certification.

4. As used in this section, "qualified retired law enforcement officer" has the meaning ascribed to it in 18 U.S.C. § 926C.

202.3687. Temporary permits.

1. The provisions of NRS 202.3653 to 202.369, inclusive, and sections 2 and 3 of this act do not prohibit a sheriff from issuing a temporary permit. A temporary permit may include, but is not limited to, provisions specifying the period for which the permit is valid.

2. Each sheriff who issues a permit pursuant to the provisions of NRS 202.3653 to 202.369, inclusive, and sections 2 and 3 of this act shall provide such information concerning the permit and the person to whom it is issued to the central repository for Nevada records of criminal history.

NRS 202.3688. Circumstances in which holder of permit issued by another state may carry concealed firearm in this State; holder of permit issued by another state subject to same restrictions and requirements as holder of permit issued in this State.

1. Except as otherwise provided in subsection 2, a person who possesses a permit to carry a concealed firearm that was issued by a state included in the list prepared pursuant to NRS 202.3689 may carry a concealed firearm in this State in accordance with the requirement set forth in NRS 202.3653 to 202.369, inclusive.

2. A person who possesses a permit to carry a concealed firearm that was issued by a state included in the list prepared pursuant to NRS 202.3689 may not carry a concealed firearm in this State if the person:

(a) Becomes a resident of this State; and

(b) Has not been issued a permit from the sheriff of the county in which he resides within 60 days after becoming a resident of this State.
3. A person who carries a concealed firearm pursuant to this section is subject to the same legal restrictions and requirements imposed upon a person who has been issued a permit by a sheriff in this State.

NRS 202.3689, Department to prepare list of states that meet certain requirements concerning permits; Department to provide copy of list to law enforcement agencies in this State; Department to make list available to public.

1. On or before July 1 of each year, the Department shall:

(a) Examine the requirements for the issuance of a permit to carry a concealed firearm in each state and determine whether the requirements of each state are substantially similar to or more stringent than the requirements set forth in NRS 202.3653 to 202.369, inclusive.

(b) Determine whether each state has an electronic database which identifies each individual who possesses a valid permit to carry a concealed firearm issued by that state and which a law enforcement officer in this State may access at all times through a national law enforcement telecommunications system.

(c) Prepare a list of states that meet the requirements of paragraphs (a) and (b). A state must not be included in the list unless the Nevada Sheriffs' and Chiefs' Association agrees with the Department that the state should be included in the list.

(d) Provide a copy of the list prepared pursuant to paragraph (c) to each law enforcement agency in this State.

2. The Department shall, upon request, make the list prepared pursuant to subsection 1 available to the public.

244.364 1. Except as otherwise provided by specific statute, the Legislature reserves for itself such rights and powers as are necessary to regulate the transfer, sale, purchase, possession, ownership, transportation, registration and licensing of firearms and ammunition in Nevada, and no county may infringe upon those rights and powers.

As used in this subsection, "firearm" means any weapon from which a projectile is discharged by means of an explosive, spring, gas, air or other force.
2. A board of county commissioners may proscribe by ordinance or regulation the unsafe discharge of firearms.
3. If a board of county commissioners in a county whose population is 400,000 or more has required by ordinance or regulation adopted before June 13, 1989, the registration of a firearm capable of being concealed, the board of county commissioners shall amend such an ordinance or regulation to require:
        (a) A period of at least 60 days of residency in the county before registration of such a firearm is required.
        (b) A period of at least 72 hours for the registration of a pistol by a resident of the county upon transfer of title to the pistol to the resident by purchase, gift or any other transfer.

4. Except as otherwise provided in subsection 1, as used in this section:

(a) "Firearm" means any device designed to be use as a weapon from which a projectile may be expelled through the barrel by the force of any explosion or other form of combustion.

(b) "Firearm capable of being concealed" includes all firearms having a barrel less than 12 inches in length.

(c) "Pistol" means a firearm capable of being concealed that is intended to be aimed and fired with one hand.

Law note: Identical regulations (NRS 268.418.1 and NRS 269.222.1 prohibit cities and towns from regulating firearms in the same manner.

407.0475 Administrator: Regulations; penalty for violation of regulations.

1. The Administrator shall adopt such regulations as he or she finds necessary for carrying out the provisions of this chapter and other provisions of law governing the operation of the Division. Except as otherwise provided in subsection 2, the regulations may include prohibitions and restrictions relating to activities within any of the park or recreational facilities within the jurisdiction of the Division.

2. Any regulations relating to the conduct of persons within the park or recreational facilities must:

(a) Be directed toward one or both of the following:

(1) Prevention of damage to or misuse of the facility.

(2) Promotion of the inspiration, use and enjoyment of the people of this State through the preservation and use of the facility.

(b) Apply separately to each park, monument or recreational area and be designed to fit the conditions existing at that park, monument or recreational area.

(c) Not establish restrictions on the possession of firearms within the park or recreational facility which are more restrictive than the laws of this State relating to:

(1) The possession of firearms; or

(2) Engaging in lawful resistance to prevent an offense against a person or property. Any regulation which violates the provisions of this paragraph is void.

3. Any person whose conduct violates any regulation adopted pursuant to subsection 1, and who refuses to comply with the regulation upon request by any ranger or employee of the Division who has the powers of a peace officer pursuant to NRS 289.260, is guilty of a misdemeanor.

503.165. Carrying loaded rifle or shotgun in or on vehicle on or along public way unlawful; exceptions.

1. It is unlawful to carry a loaded rifle or loaded shotgun in or on any vehicle which is standing on or along, or is being driven on or along, any public highway or any other way open to the public.

2. A rifle or shotgun is loaded, for the purposes of this section, when there is an unexpended cartridge or shell in the firing chamber, but not when the only cartridges or shells are in the magazine.

3. The provisions of this section do not apply to paraplegics, persons with one or both legs amputated or who have suffered a paralysis of one or both legs which severely impedes walking, or peace officers and members of the armed forces of this state or the United States while on duty or going to or returning from duty.

Law note: Some of these older local statutes for Clark County and the cities of Las Vegas, Henderson, North Las Vegas, and Mesquite are out of date, or overturned by case law. These entities cannot update their laws due to a mid 1980's state pre-empition law (NRS 244.364) forbidding any government entity other than the State of Nevada making "new" firearms laws.

Clark County Code

12.04.050 Persons prohibited from purchasing or owning pistols.

It is unlawful in the unincorporated area of Clark County, for any person to receive from another by loan, gift, purchase, or in any manner, or attempt to obtain in any manner or have in his possession or control, a pistol as defined by this chapter who:

(a) Has been convicted of a felony in the state of Nevada, or in any state or territory of the United States or any political subdivision thereof;

(b) Is a fugitive from justice;

(c) Is an unlawful user or seller of narcotics;

(d) Is a habitual drunkard;

(e) Is a member of an organization advocating criminal syndicalism as defined in NRS 203.160 through 203.190;

(f) Has been adjudged insane in the state or any other state and has not subsequently been adjudged sane;

(g) Is seventeen years of age or under.

12.04.060 Prohibited sales and transfer of a pistol.

It shall be unlawful for any person or a dealer in pistols to sell, lease, lend, or otherwise transfer a pistol to any person whom he knows or has reasonable cause to believe:

(a) Is under the influence of intoxicating beverages;

(b) Is mentally ill or disturbed;

(c) Is seventeen years of age or under;

12.04.070 Certain persons prohibited from purchasing or owning pistols.

It shall be unlawful for any person who is included in any one or more of the categories set forth in Section 12.04.050 of this chapter, to receive from another by loan, gift, purchase or in any other manner, or in any manner whatsoever, to attempt to obtain, or have in his or her possession or control, any pistol; provided, however, that a person under the age of eighteen years may have a pistol in his or her possession, or under his or her control, while accompanied by or under the immediate charge of his or her parent, guardian, or other responsible adult, and while engaged in hunting or target practice or other lawful purpose.

12.04.080 Time between sale and delivery of pistol. When any sale of a pistol is made by a dealer under this chapter, seventy-two hours must elapse between the time of sale and the time of delivery to the purchaser. When delivered, all pistols must be securely wrapped and be unloaded, and must be accompanied by a receipt signed by the dealer, setting forth the name, address, and description of the purchaser or transferee, a complete description of the pistol (including the manufacturer, model and manufacturer's serial number thereof), the date and time of sale, and the date and time of delivery, of such pistol, and advise to the purchaser or transferee that the pistol must be registered with the sheriff within seventy-two hours.

12.04.090 Exceptions to Section 12.04.080. The aforesaid seventy-two hour waiting period shall not apply to the sale of a pistol to any person who, at the time of such sale, produces bona fide documentary evidence that he is a member of a federal law enforcement agency; or a peace officer of the state of Nevada or any political subdivision thereof, regularly employed for pay by the state or such subdivision; or that he currently owns a pistol which is duly registered in his name with any law enforcement agency in Clark County; or that the pistol is an unfinished kit which is designed to fire black powder of the cap and ball or flintlock variety. And said waiting period shall not apply to any person who requires the use of a pistol in connection with his employment, and who receives written permission from the sheriff with express waiver of the waiting period; however, all of the other provisions herein shall apply to any such sales.

12.04.110 Registration of pistols within seventy-two hours. Any resident of the county receiving title to a pistol, whether by purchase, gift, or any other transfer, and whether from a dealer or from any other person, shall, within seventy-two hours of such receipt, personally appear at the county sheriff's office, together with the pistol, for the purpose of registering the same with the sheriff. It shall be the duty of the sheriff to register the pistol, and he may, and is hereby authorized to cooperate in any manner he sees fit with other law enforcement agencies, and with licensed dealers, relative to registration of pistols, so that efficient registration shall be secured at minimum cost and duplication.

12.04.120 Sale or possession of certain pistols prohibited. It shall be unlawful to purchase, sell, or in any manner to transfer, or have in possession or control, any pistol on which the name of the manufacturer, or the model, or the manufacturer's serial number has been removed, obliterated, concealed, or altered.

12.04.170 Unlawful to permit persons under eighteen years to have possession or control of pistol. It shall be unlawful within the unincorporated area of Clark County, for any person to aid, or knowingly permit, another under eighteen years of age to handle, or have in his or her possession, or under his or her control, any pistol, except while accompanied, by or under the immediate charge of, his or her parent, guardian, or other responsible adult and while engaged in hunting, target practice or other lawful purpose.

12.04.180 Concealed weapons prohibited without permit.
It is unlawful, within the unincorporated area of Clark County, for any person to carry upon his person a concealed weapon of any description, including a knife with a blade of three inches or more, a gun, pistol, revolver or other firearm, capable of being concealed, without first having received written permission therefor from the sheriff.

12.04.200 Registraion of firearms capable of being concealed. It is unlawful for any person with at least sixty days of residency in the county to own or have in his possession, within the unicorporated area of Clark County, a pistol or other firearm capable of being concealed, unless the same has first been registered with the sheriff or with a police department of any of the incorporated cities of Clark County.

12.04.210 Unlawful transfer of firearms capable of being concealed.
It is unlawful for any person to sell, give away or permanently pass possession to another person of any pistol, revolver or other firearm capable of being concealed, unless the transferor thereof first registers, or causes the weapon to be registered to the transferee and new owner thereof, either with the sheriff, or with a police department of one of the incorporated cities of Clark County.

Las Vegas City Code

10.66.060 Sale-delivery waiting period--Manner of delivery.
(A) When any sale of a pistol is made by a dealer under this Chapter, seventy-two hours must elapse between the time of sale and time of delivery to the purchaser, and when delivered, all pistols must be securely wrapped, must be unloaded and must be accompanied by a receipt, signed by dealer, setting forth:
(1) The name, address and description of the purchaser or transferee;
(2) A complete description of the pistol, including the manufacturer, model and manufacturer's serial number thereof;
(3) The date and time of sale and the date and time of delivery of such pistol; and
(4) A statement notifying the purchaser or transferee that said pistol must be registered with the Sheriff or his designee within twenty-four hours.
(B) The aforesaid seventy-two-hour waiting period shall not apply to the sale of a pistol to any person who, at the time of such sale, produces bona fide documentary evidence that he is a member of a Federal law enforcement agency, that he is a peace officer of the State or any political subdivision thereof who is regularly employed for pay by the State or such subdivision, or that he currently owns a pistol which is duly registered in his name with any law enforcement agency in the County, nor shall said waiting period apply to any person who requires the use of a pistol in his employment and receives written permission from the Sheriff.

10.66.070 Notice to Police of delivery.

A dealer making a sale of a pistol shall, within twenty-four hours after the delivery thereof, deliver to the Sheriff of the Metropolitan Police Department or his designee a duplicate copy of the receipt referred to in Section 10.66.060, signed by the dealer and by the purchaser or transferee of such pistol.

10.66.080 Altered or removed identification marks.

It shall be unlawful to purchase, sell, or to transfer in any manner or to have in possession or control any pistol on which the name of the manufacturer, model or manufacturer's serial number has been removed or altered.

10.66.140 Registration of ownership required.

(A) Any person receiving title to a pistol, whether by purchase, gift or other transfer, and whether from a dealer or any other person, shall within seventy-two hours of such receipt personally appear, together with such pistol, and register the same with the Sheriff of the Metropolitan Police Department or his designee. It shall be unlawful to possess a pistol which is not so registered.

10.68.010 Required.

No person, except a peace officer, shall wear or in any manner carry concealed upon his person any loaded or unloaded gun, pistol or revolver, or any other dangerous or deadly weapon permitted to be carried by law without having, at the same time, actually in his possession and upon his person, an unexpired permit so to do issued by the Sheriff of the Metropolitan Police Department or his designee. The requirement to possess a permit does not apply to:

    (1) A person who has not been a resident of the City for at least sixty days; or

    (2) A firearm during the seventy-two hour period within which a person is allowed to register that firearm.

10.72.010 Limited to galleries.

It shall be unlawful within the City limits, except in a regular licensed shooting gallery to willfully discharge any pistol, firearm, air gun, musket, or instrument of any kind, character or description which throws a bullet or missiles for any distance by means of the elastic force of air or any explosive substance.

10.70.030 Fighting or disorderly conduct while possessing.

It shall be unlawful for any person who has concealed upon his person or who has in his immediate physical possession any dangerous or deadly weapon to engage in any fight or to participate in any other rough or disorderly conduct upon any public place or way or upon the premises of another.

North Las Vegas City Code

7.22.050 Person with concealed weapon not to loiter. It shall be unlawful for any person, while carrying concealed upon his person any dangerous or deadly weapon, to loaf or loiter upon any public street, sidewalk or alley, or to wander about from place to place with no lawful business thereby to perform, or to hide, lurk, or loiter upon or about the premises of another. It shall be unlawful for any who has concealed upon his person any dangerous or deadly weapon to loiter about any place where intoxicating liquors are sold or any other place of public resort.

7.22.060 Person with concealed weapon not to be disorderly. It shall be unlawful for any person who has concealed upon his person or who has in his immediate physical possession any dangerous or deadly weapon to engage in any fight or to participate in any rough or disorderly conduct or to participate in any rough or disorderly conduct upon any public place or way or upon the premises of another.

7.22.070 Deadly weapon prohibited in car-exceptions. It shall be unlawful for any person to have in his possession in any automobile any dangerous or deadly weapon, but this restriction shall not be deemed to prohibit the carrying of ordinary tools or equipment carried in good faith for uses of honest work or trade or business, or for the purpose of legitimate sport or recreation.

Henderson City Code

8.98.010 Concealed Weapons Prohibited Except by Permission
It is unlawful for any person to carry upon his person a concealed weapon of any kind or description including a knife with a blade of three inches or more, a gun, pistol, revolver, or other firearm, within the city of Henderson without first having received written permission from the chief of police.

8.98.030 Concealable Weapons to be Registered
It is unlawful for any person to own or have in his possession a gun pistol revolver or other firearm capable of being concealed without first having registered it with the chief of police.

8.98.050 Concealable Weapon Defined
For the purposes of this chapter, a weapon capable of being concealed is defined as any gun or firearm with a barrel whose length is fourteen inches or less or whose overall length is eighteen inches or less.

Boulder City Code

7-1-3: Discharging Firearms, Air Guns. No person shall fire or discharge any firearms or air guns of any description within one thousand (1000) yards of any building, street, sidewalk, alley, highway or other public place or to have any firearms or air gun in his possession within one thousand (1000) yards of any building, street, sidewalk, alley, highway or public place unless it is unloaded and knocked down or enclosed within a carrying case, provided that this section shall not prevent the maintenance and the use of duly supervised rifle or pistol ranges or shooting galleries authorized by the City Council. This section shall not prohibit the stocking of firearms by duly authorized dealers in the same.

Mesquite City Code

5-1-10: FIREARMS AND WEAPONS:

A. Concealed And Dangerous Weapons:

1. Carrying Concealed Weapons Restricted: It is unlawful for any person within the city to wear, carry or have concealed upon his person any dirk, dirk knife, pistol, sword in case, slingshot, brass knuckles or other dangerous weapon without first obtaining permission from the city council.

2. Issuance Of Permit: The city council may, upon application in writing showing the reason or purpose for which a concealed weapon is to be carried, grant a permit under its seal and attested by the city clerk to the person making the application authorizing him to carry the concealed weapon described in the permit.

B. Discharging Firearms:

1. Discharge Prohibited: Except as provided in subsection B2 of this section, any person discharging any gun or pistol within the city is guilty of a misdemeanor.

2. Exceptions: The provisions of subsection B1 of this section do not apply to:

    a. Necessary self-defense or the defense of one's family or property.

    b. A civil officer in the discharge of his duty.

    c. A licensed shooting gallery or a lawful breastwork for target shooting.

    d. Legal hunting of animals.

Attorney General
Telephone Numbers:

Alabama	(334) 242-7300	Nebraska	(402) 471-2682
Alaska	(907) 465-2133	Nevada	(702) 486-3420
Arizona	(602) 542-4266	New Hampshire	(603) 271-3658
Arkansas	(501) 682-2007	New Jersey	(609) 292-4925
California	(916) 324-5437	New Mexico	(505) 827-6000
Colorado	(303) 866-4500	New York	(518) 474-7330
Connecticut	(860) 808-5324	North Carolina	(919) 716-6400
Delaware	(302) 577-8400	North Dakota	(701) 328-2210
Florida	(850) 414-3990	Ohio	(614) 466-4320
Georgia	(404) 656-4585	Oklahoma	(405) 521-3921
Hawaii	(808) 586-1282	Oregon	(503) 378-6002
Idaho	(208) 334-2400	Pennsylvania	(717) 787-3391
Illinois	(312) 814-2503	Rhode Island	(401) 274-4400
Indiana	(317) 232-6201	South Carolina	(803) 734-3970
Iowa	(515) 281-3053	South Dakota	(605) 773-3215
Kansas	(785) 296-2215	Tennessee	(615) 862-5500
Kentucky	(502) 696-5300	Texas	(512) 463-2191
Louisiana	(225) 326-6000	Utah	(801) 366-0300
Maine	(207) 626-8800	Vermont	(802) 828-3171
Maryland	(410) 576-6300	Virginia	(804) 786-2071
Massachusetts	(617) 727-2200	Washington	(360) 753-6200
Michigan	(517) 373-1110	Washington D.C.	(202) 727-6248
Minnesota	(651) 296-3353	West Virginia	(304) 558-2021
Mississippi	(601) 359-3692	Wisconsin	(608) 266-1221
Missouri	(573) 751-3321	Wyoming	(307) 777-7841
Montana	(406) 444-2026		

Notes:

About the Author

Bob Irwin is certified by the National Rifle Association as a civilian handgun, shotgun, home defense and firearms safety instructor as well as a Training Counselor (instructor trainer). Nevada Peace Officer Standards and Training as a law enforcement firearms instructor and instructor trainer. In addition, Bob holds instructor certificates from the Nevada Attorney Generals Office and the Utah Department of Public Safety.

Bob currently operates The Gun Store in Las Vegas, Nevada and trains Concealed Firearm Permit applicants for the states of Nevada, Utah and Florida. He has taught firearms and use of force in 28 police academies over his 35 year career as well as training thousands of Security Officers in those subjects. Bob actively trains law enforcement and civilian firearms instructors.

Bob is the author of more than eighty published articles addressing firearms safety, training, tactics and use of force issues. He holds a lieutenant's commission with the Constable's Office in Boulder Township, Nevada and is a Bailiff for Clark County Justice Courts. Bob has testified as an expert witness in numerous criminal & civil cases.

Be a Fodor's Correspondent

Your opinion matters. It matters to us. It matters to your fellow Fodor's travelers, too. And we'd like to hear it. In fact, we *need* to hear it.

When you share your experiences and opinions, you become an active member of the Fodor's community. That means we'll not only use your feedback to make our books better, but we'll publish your names and comments whenever possible. Throughout our guides, look for "Word of Mouth," excerpts of your feedback.

Here's how you can help improve Fodor's for all of us.

Tell us when we're right. We rely on local writers to give you an insider's perspective. But our writers and staff editors—who are the best in the business—depend on you. Your positive feedback is a vote to renew our recommendations for the next edition.

Tell us when we're wrong. We're proud that we update most of our guides every year. But we're not perfect. Things change. Hotels cut services. Museums change hours. Charming cafés lose charm. If our writer didn't quite capture the essence of a place, tell us how you'd do it differently. If any of our descriptions are inaccurate or inadequate, we'll incorporate your changes in the next edition and will correct factual errors at fodors.com *immediately.*

Tell us what to include. You probably have had fantastic travel experiences that aren't yet in Fodor's. Why not share them with a community of like-minded travelers? Maybe you chanced upon a beach or bistro or bed-and-breakfast that you don't want to keep to yourself. Tell us why we should include it. And share your discoveries and experiences with everyone directly at fodors.com. Your input may lead us to add a new listing or highlight a place we cover with a "Highly Recommended" star or with our highest rating, "Fodor's Choice."

Give us your opinion instantly at our feedback center at www.fodors.com/feedback. You may also e-mail editors@fodors.com with the subject line "Norway Editor." Or send your nominations, comments, and complaints by mail to Norway Editor, Fodor's, 1745 Broadway, New York, NY 10019.

You and travelers like you are the heart of the Fodor's community. Make our community richer by sharing your experiences. Be a Fodor's correspondent.

Happy traveling!

Tim Jarrell. Publisher

CONTENTS

MAPS

ABOUT THIS BOOK

Our Ratings

Sometimes you find terrific travel experiences and sometimes they just find you. But usually the burden is on you to select the right combination of experiences. That's where our ratings come in.

As travelers we've all discovered a place so wonderful that its worthiness is obvious. And sometimes that place is so unique that superlatives don't do it justice: you just have to be there to know. These sights, properties, and experiences get our highest rating, Fodor's Choice, indicated by orange stars throughout this book.

Black stars highlight sights and properties we deem Highly Recommended, places that our writers, editors, and readers praise again and again for consistency and excellence.

By default, there's another category: any place we include in this book is by definition worth your time, unless we say otherwise. And we will.

Disagree with any of our choices? Care to nominate a place or suggest that we rate one more highly? Visit our feedback center at www.fodors.com/feedback.

Budget Well

Hotel and restaurant price categories from ¢ to $$$$ are defined in the opening pages of each chapter. For attractions, we always give standard adult admission fees; reductions are usually available for children, students, and senior citizens. Want to pay with plastic? AE, D, DC, MC, V following restaurant and hotel listings indicate whether American Express, Discover, Diner's Club, MasterCard, and Visa are accepted.

Restaurants

Unless we state otherwise, restaurants are open for lunch and dinner daily. We mention dress only when there's a specific requirement and reservations only when they're essential or not accepted—it's always best to book ahead.

Hotels

Hotels have private bath, phone, and TV and operate on the European Plan (aka EP, meaning without meals), unless we specify that they use the Continental Plan (CP, with a Continental breakfast), Breakfast Plan (BP, with a full breakfast), or Modified American Plan (MAP, with breakfast and dinner) or are all-inclusive (including all meals and most activities). We always list facilities but not whether you'll be charged an extra fee to use them, so when pricing accommodations, find out what's included.

Many Listings
- ★ Fodor's Choice
- ★ Highly recommended
- ⊠ Physical address
- ‡ Directions
- ⌂ Mailing address
- ☎ Telephone
- 🖷 Fax
- ⊕ On the Web
- ✍ E-mail
- ☑ Admission fee
- ☉ Open/closed times
- ► Start of walk/itinerary
- Ⓜ Metro stations
- ▭ Credit cards

Hotels & Restaurants
- ⊡ Hotel
- ⤸ Number of rooms
- ⟁ Facilities
- ¡○¡ Meal plans
- ✕ Restaurant
- ⟀ Reservations
- ⌾ Dress code
- ⚲ Smoking
- ₿₽ BYOB
- ✕⊡ Hotel with restaurant that warrants a visit

Outdoors
- 🏌 Golf
- ⛺ Camping

Other
- ☺ Family-friendly
- ⚐ Contact information
- ⇨ See also
- ⊠ Branch address
- ☞ Take note

NORWAY

8th Edition

Where to Stay and Eat
for All Budgets

Must-See Sights
and Local Secrets

Ratings You Can Trust

Fodor's Travel Publications   New York, Toronto, London, Sydney, Auckland
www.fodors.com

FODOR'S NORWAY

Editor: Emmanuelle Alspaugh

Editorial Production: Tom Holton
Editorial Contributors: Daniel Cash, Mike Nalepa, Norman Renouf, and Lars Ursin
Maps: David Lindroth *cartographer*; Rebecca Baer and Bob Blake, *map editors*
Design: Fabrizio La Rocca, *creative director*; Guido Caroti, *art director*; Moon Sun Kim, *cover designer*; Melanie Marin, *senior picture editor*
Production/Manufacturing: Colleen Ziemba
Cover Photo (cruise ship in Magdalenenfjord, Spitsbergen, Svalbard Islands): Gräfenhain Günter/ Fototeca 9x12

Eighth Edition

ISBN: 1–4000–1614–2

ISBN-13: 978–1–4000–1614–3

ISSN: 1073–6603

SPECIAL SALES

This book is available for special discounts for bulk purchases for sales promotions or premiums. Special editions, including personalized covers, excerpts of existing books, and corporate imprints, can be created in large quantities for special needs. For more information, write to Special Markets/ Premium Sales, 1745 Broadway, MD 6-2, New York, New York 10019, or e-mail specialmarkets@ randomhouse.com.

AN IMPORTANT TIP & AN INVITATION

Although all prices, opening times, and other details in this book are based on information supplied to us at press time, changes occur all the time in the travel world, and Fodor's cannot accept responsibility for facts that become outdated or for inadvertent errors or omissions. So **always confirm information when it matters,** especially if you're making a detour to visit a specific place. Your experiences—positive and negative—matter to us. If we have missed or misstated something, **please write to us.** We follow up on all suggestions. Contact the Norway editor at editors@fodors. com or c/o Fodor's at 1745 Broadway, New York, New York 10019.

PRINTED IN THE UNITED STATES OF AMERICA

10 9 8 7 6 5 4 3 2

	Norway, roughly 400,000 square km (155,000 square mi), is about the same size as California. Approximately 30% of this long, narrow country is covered with clear lakes, lush forests, and rugged mountains. Western Norway, bordered by the Norwegian Sea and the Atlantic Ocean, is home to Jotunheimen, Norway's highest, wildest mountain region and land of fjords—few places on Earth can match its power and splendor.
OSLO	A capital city of stunning natural beauty, Oslo sits amid lush forested woodlands, called *marka,* to its north, and the Oslofjord with its islands and beaches to the south. It's one of the few major European cities with subway service to the forest, or lakes and hiking trails within the city limits. Holmenkollen, a ski resort northwest of town, has a famous ski jump, visible from the city, and has stunning views over the city and its surrounding fjords. Oslo has its share of glass-and-steel skyscrapers and architectural monstrosities, but it is still one of the most attractive European capitals. Karl Johans Gate forms the backbone of downtown Oslo, and around it are the neoclassical buildings of Norwegian royalty and the city government, and several wonderful museums. Southwest of downtown is Gamlebyen, a beautiful medieval historic district. The neighborhoods of Frogner and Majorstuen to the northwest are filled with trendy boutiques and art galleries.
OSLO SIDE TRIPS	Surrounding Oslo are landscapes to suit all tastes and interests, and they're easily accessible from the city, by bus and train. If you want beaches and maritime activities, you can hop on a ferry and head to the islands of the Oslo Fjord with their windswept beaches, swimming, and boating. The towns lining the east of the fjord are where many Norwegians spend their summer vacations in cabins along the water. Here you will find Viking archaeological sites and bohemian artists' colonies, and many places to swim. Along the western side of the Oslo Fjord, Sandefjord is known as the "Bathing City" because of its many beaches, islands, and archipelago. To the north of the Oslo fjord, northwest of Oslo, is green, hilly countryside, with small towns of historic and cultural interest.

SOUTHERN NORWAY	The interior region of southern Norway, Telemark and the Setesdal Valley, lies in the shadow of the famed beaches and fjords of the coast, but certainly doesn't lack majestic scenery—forested hills meet deeply etched valleys, and lakes stretch across the serene countryside.
	If you follow the coast south, you'll come to Sørlandet (the Southland), known for its long stretches of unspoiled, uncrowded beach. The region has a mild summer climate and terrain that varies from coastal flatland to inland mountains and forests. Oslo's residents migrate here every summer to soak up the sunshine. The North Sea Road winds along the coastline, starting at the resort town of of Kristiansand, the "Summer City," with its sunny beaches and beautiful harbor. From here the road winds west through the Sørlandet region to Stavanger, a bustling and vibrant city that enjoys the riches brought by the discovery of North Sea oil in the 1960s.
BERGEN	Bergen, on the west coast, is often hailed as the Fjord Capital of Norway. Although it's the second-largest city in the country, its cobblestone streets and well-preserved buildings at Bryggen (the quay) add to its storybook charm. It is surrounded by fjords and has seven forested mountains, providing a natural setting of which its residents are justifiably proud. The large harbor that has ensured Bergen's importance as a commercial center lies at the heart of the city. At night the historic Hanseatic wooden buildings on Bryggen are illuminated, giving visitors a view of one of the most dramatic cityscapes in northern Europe.
THE WEST COAST	The Norwegian fjords snake inland from the Russian border in the far north all the way to Norway's southern tip. The magnificent Sognefjord, the longest inlet in western Norway, is only one of many fjords found here, including the Hardangerfjord, Geirangerfjord, Lysefjord, and Nordfjord.
CENTRAL NORWAY	Halfway between Oslo and Bergen lies Hardangervidda (Hardanger plateau), Norway's largest national park. If you take Route 7 from Drammen towards the Hardanger plateau you'll pass through the Hallingdal Valley, known for its ski resorts and well-preserved log buildings. To get to Hardan-

gervidda, you can continue along Route 7 or take the train from Oslo to Bergen, which passes through the spectacular countryside of Europe's largest mountain plateau. At the foot of the plateau is Geilo, one of the country's most popular ski resorts.

Colorful farmhouses dot Norway's interior countryside, bordered by Sweden to the east, and Finland and Russia to the north. Here rivers run wild through abundant valleys, and mountains reach up to the sky. The main town is Lillehammer, known for its ski slopes and trails; just north is Gudbrandsdalen (Gudbrands Valley), one of the most beautiful valleys in Norway, which extends from Lake Mjøsa, just north of Oslo, to Åndalsnes.

TRONDHEIM TO THE NORTH	From Trondheim, a thin expanse of land stretches up to the Nordkapp (North Cape). Known as the Land of the Midnight Sun (the display of the northern lights in winter is amazing too), this region is marked with exquisite landscapes: glaciers, fjords, islands, and rocky coasts. Narvik, a major arctic port, is the gateway to the Lofoten Islands, where puffins and penguins march about. Even farther north is one of Norway's major universities, Tromsø, the lifeline to settlements and research centers at the north pole.
SAMILAND TO SVALBARD	At the very top of Norway, on the roof of Europe, is the vast, windswept county of Finnmark (Finnmarksvidda), where the continent's only nomadic indigenous people, the Sami, live. They recognize no national boundaries, and Samiland stretches from the Kola Peninsula in Russia through Finland, Sweden, and Norway. Norwegian Samiland is centered around the communities of Karasjok and Kautokeino. At its top, Norway hooks over Finland and touches Russia; a good way to visit this part of the country is to go to Kirkenes and explore the region by car from there.

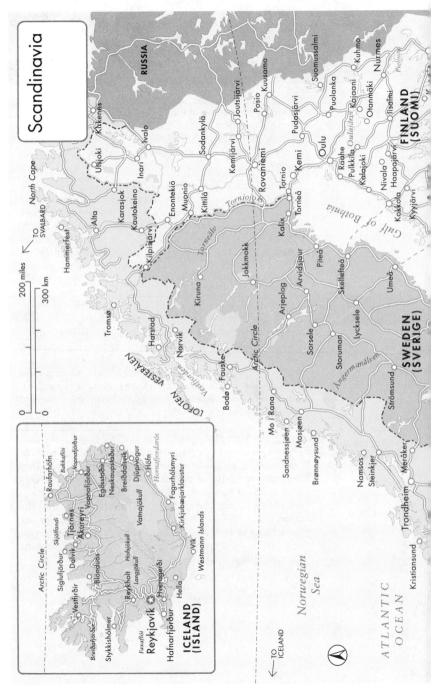

Scandinavia

RUSSIA

North Cape

TO SVALBARD

200 miles

300 km

Hammerfest

Tromsø

VESTERÅLEN

LOFOTEN

Harstad

Narvik

Bodø

Fauske

Mo i Rana

Sandnessjøen

Brønnøysund

Norwegian
Sea

Namsos

Steinkjer

Trondheim

Kristiansund

ATLANTIC
OCEAN

TO
ICELAND

Alta

Karasjok

Kautokeino

Kilpisjärvi

Kiruna

Enontekiö

Muonio

Kittilä

Jokkmokk

Arjeplog

Arvidsjaur

Sorsele

Storuman

lycksele

Strömsund

Meråker

SWEDEN
(SVERIGE)

Ångermanälven

Arctic Circle

Umeå

Skellefteå

Piteå

Kalix

Torneå

Luleå

Kirkenes

Ivalo

Inari

Utsjoki

Sodankylä

Kemijärvi

Rovaniemi

Tornio

Kemi

Posio

Joutsijärvi

Kuusamo

Suomussalmi

Kuhmo

Nurmes

Puolanka

Pudasjärvi

Oulu

Raahe

Pulkkila

Kajaani

Otanmäki

Kalajoki

Nivala

Haapajärvi

Kokkola

Kyyjärvi

Iisalmi

Pielinen

FINLAND
(SUOMI)

Oulujärvi

Torniojoki

Torneälv

Gulf of Bothnia

ICELAND (ISLAND)

Arctic Circle

Breiðafjörður

Stykkishólmur

Vestfirðir

Siglufjörður

Dalvík

Blönduós

Reykholt

Langjökull

Reykjavík

Hafnarfjörður

Hella

Hvergerði

Westmann Islands

Vík

Faxaflói

Raufarhöfn

Bakkaflói

Vopnafjörður

Skjálfandi

Tjörnes

Akureyri

Vopnafjörður

Egilsstaðir

Neskaupstaður

Breiðdalsvík

Hofsjökull

Vatnajökull

Djúpivogur

Höfn

Hornafjarðarós

Fagurhólsmýri

Kirkjubæjarklaustur

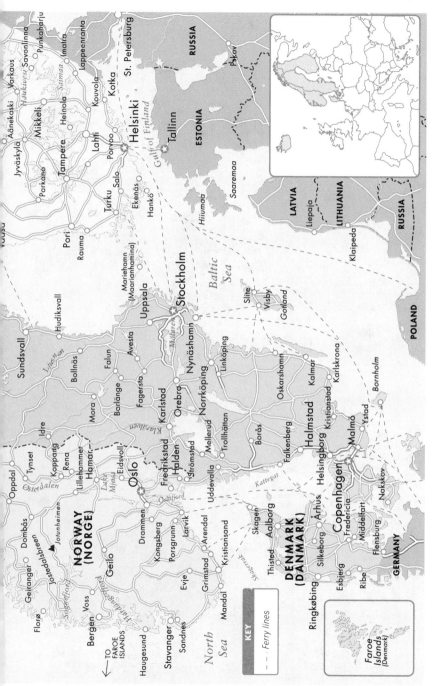

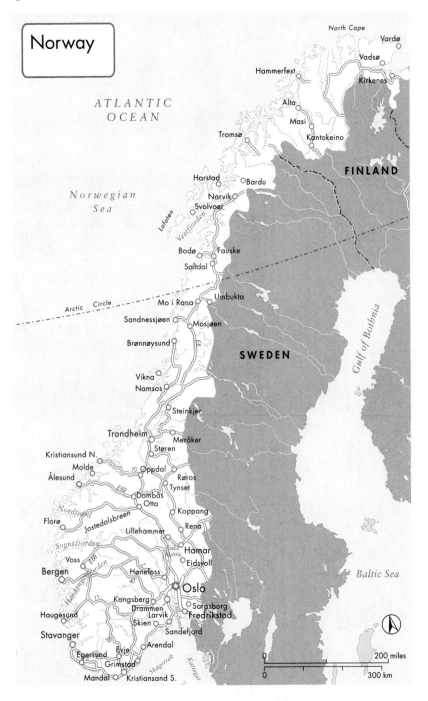

Norway

ATLANTIC
OCEAN

Norwegian
Sea

North Cape

Vardø
Vadsø
Hammerfest
Kirkenes
Alta
Masi
Tromsø
Kantokeino

FINLAND

Harstad
Bardu
Narvik
Svolvoer
Lofoten
Vestfjorden
Bodø
Fauske
Saltdal

Arctic   Circle
Mo i Rana
Umbukta
Sandnessjøen
Mosjøen
Brønnøysund

SWEDEN

Gulf of Bothnia

Vikna
Namsos
Steinkjer
Trondheim
Meråker
Kristiansund N.
Støren
Molde
70
Oppdal
Ålesund
Røros
Tynset
E69
Dombås
Otta
Nordfjord
Floro
Jostedalsbreen
Koppang
Lillehammer
Rena
Sognefjorden
Hamar
Voss
Eidsvoll
Bergen
E68
Hønefoss
Baltic Sea
40
Hardangerfjorden
Oslo
Haugesund
11
Kongsberg
Sarpsborg
Drammen
Fredrikstad
Larvik
Stavanger
Skien
Sandefjord
Evje
Arendal
Egersund
Grimstad
Skagerrak
Mandal
Kristiansand S.
Kattegat

0   200 miles
0   300 km

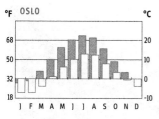

The tourist season peaks in June, July, and August, when daytime temperatures are often in the 70s°F (21°C–26°C) and sometimes rise into the 80s°F (27°C–32°C). In general, the weather is not overly warm, and a brisk breeze and brief rainstorms are possible anytime. Nights can be chilly, even in summer.

Visit in summer if you want to experience the endless days of the midnight sun; the best time to visit is mid-May to late July. Hotels, museums, and sights have longer opening hours and the modes of transportation run on more frequent schedules. If you decide to travel in May, try to be in the country on the 17th, or Syttende Mai, Norway's Constitution Day, when flag-waving Norwegians bedecked in national costumes, or *bunader,* fill the streets. Fall, spring, and even winter are pleasant, despite the Nordic reputation for gloom. The days become shorter quickly, but the sun casts a golden light not seen farther south. On dark days, fires and candlelight will warm you indoors.

The Gulf Stream warms the western coast of Norway, making winters there similar to those in London. Even the harbor of Narvik, far to the north, remains ice-free year-round. Away from the protection of the Gulf Stream, however, northern Norway has cold, clear weather that attracts skiers.

Winter Norway is a wonderland of snow-covered mountains glowing under the northern lights, and few tourists are around to get in your way (although many tourist attractions are also closed). The days may seem perpetually dark, and November through February can be especially dreary. If it's skiing you're interested in, plan your trip for March or April, as there's usually still plenty of snow left. Take note that during Easter Week many Norwegians head for the mountains, so it's hard to get accommodations—cities are virtually shut down, and even grocery stores close.

🎦 **Forecasts Weather Channel Connection** ☎ 900/932-8437 95¢ per min from a touch-tone phone ⊕ www.weather.com.

QUINTESSENTIAL NORWAY

Fjords

Whether you cruise, drive, or hike the shoreline, you are sure to be treated to incomparable views of Norway's majestic fjords. Among the world's most spectacular geological formations, a typical fjord consists of a long narrow inlet of the sea, with steep mountainsides stretching into mountain massifs. Fjords were created by glacier erosion during the ice ages. In inlets like Sognefjord and Geirangerfjord, walls of water shoot up the mountainsides, jagged snowcapped peaks blot out the sky, and water tumbles down the mountains in an endless variety of colors. Along the dramatic coastline you'll find some of Norway's most vibrant cities, including Bergen, the gateway to the fjords, and Ålesund, the art nouveau city.

Mountain Hiking

One of the most common expressions in the Norwegian language is *gå på tur*, or "go

for a walk." Naturally, in the country's mountainous landscape, Norwegians have been *fjellfolk* (mountain people) for thousands of years. Today it's never far to the well-marked mountain trails where many Norwegians spend their *fritid* (free time) hiking and strolling. One of the best places for hiking is on the Hardangervidda plateau, where the gently sloping terrain is perfect for beginners. Experienced hikers can head to the steeper terrain in Hemsedal. About 320 km (200 mi) farther north you'll find both the rounded mountains of Rondane National Park and the jagged peaks of Jotunheimen National Park. One of Norway's classic mountain trips is *hytte til hytte* (cabin to cabin) in Jotunheimen.

The Midnight Sun

There's nothing quite like basking in the glow of the midnight sun. Travel north from Trondheim anytime between early June and mid-July to experience a day when the

If you want to get a sense of contemporary Norwegian culture, start by familiarizing yourself with the rituals of daily life. These are a few highlights—things you can take part in with relative ease.

sun doesn't set. Bodø, Narvik, and Nord-kapp (North Cape) are some of the prettiest places to watch this phenomenon. If you take the *Hurtigruten* coastal mail boat cruise, you'll have beautiful views of the midnight sun dipping to the water's edge, then rising back up again.

Viking History

The Vikings' travels and conquests took them west to Iceland, England, Ireland (they founded Dublin in the 840s), and North America, and east to Kiev and as far as the Black Sea. Though they were famed as plunderers, their craftsmanship, fearlessness, and ingenuity have always been respected. Some of the most impressive examples of Viking shipbuilding expertise can be viewed at the Vikingskiphuset, or Vikings Ship Museum, in Oslo. Imagine yourself at sea as you walk around the well-preserved ships and other relics that tell the story of these seafaring warriors.

Skiing

Norwegians are "born with skis on their feet" goes the popular saying. Skiing dates back thousands of years in Norway, where it was first used for transportation. The word "ski" actually comes from the Old Norse *skid,* which means a board or piece of split wood. Cross-country or Nordic skiing is a perfect way to experience Norway's nature, either on pristine prepared trails through forests, or off-trail. Popular cross-country skiing areas are in Rondane, Peer Gynt Ski Region, Lillehammer, Beitostolen, Midt-Valdres, Hallingdal, and Dovrefjell. Downhill or alpine skiing and snowboarding are offered at more than 500 ski centers, including Hafjell, Trysil, Hemsedal, and Kvitfjell. There's also traditional telemark skiing and newer hybrid sports such as kite-skiing and ski-sailing. The ski season lasts from November to Easter, after which there is summer skiing on select glaciers through August.

IF YOU LIKE

Communing with Nature

Norwegians are an active lot, especially in summer, when they spend their time hiking, biking, fishing, cruising, and swimming. From the beaches in the south to the incredibly steep fjords of the west to the land of the midnight sun in the north, Norway's mountains, plains, and coastline present some of the most beautiful scenery in the world. You can witness some of this beauty from the train between Oslo and Bergen, but the best way to truly experience it is to take part in an activity that brings you in direct contact with the landscape.

- **Hiking in Jotunheimen or Rondane national parks.** The jagged peaks of Jotunheimen and the rounded mountains of Rondane offer countless wonderful hiking opportunities for all skill levels.

- **Biking the Rallarvegen.** The most popular bike trek in Norway is the 80-km (50-mi) Rallarvegen, which follows the Bergen Railway, westbound over the Hardangervidda, from Haugastøl to Flåm.

- **Riding horseback across Hardangervidda plateau.** Half a dozen outfitters in Geilo will organize horseback-riding trips for you across Europe's largest mountain plateau. If you're lucky, you'll catch a glimpse of Hardangervidda's wild reindeer herds.

- **Fishing inland and off the coast.** Some 200 species of saltwater fish live and breed along the coast, particularly cod, pollack, and the smeltlike capelin. Near Geilo and Lillehammer are rivers and lakes well stocked with salmon, trout, Arctic char, pike, grayling, whitefish, and perch.

The Arts

No one can deny that Norway has produced its fair share of influential artists in every field, from music and the visual arts to literature and architecture. One of the best ways to get to know Norway is to see it through the eyes of such artists as painter Edvard Munch, sculptor Gustav Vigeland, writer Henrik Ibsen, and composer Edvard Grieg.

- **Pay homage to Edvard Munch.** Take a trip to the Munchmuseet in Oslo to see the 20th-century icon, *The Scream.* Munch bequeathed thousands of his works to Oslo upon his death in 1944.

- **Check out some original Norwegian architecture.** You can get an overview of Norwegian history with a trip to one of Europe's largest open-air museums, the Norsk Folkemuseum in the Bygdøy neighborhood of Oslo. An original stave church, sod houses, and other buildings span the country's past.

- **Edvard Grieg's salon, frozen in time.** See where the composer played for European luminaries at his home, Troldhaugen, outside Bergen. The name means Hill of the Trolls.

- **Vigeland's monumental sculptures.** If you only have one day in Oslo, don't miss the chance to take a stroll through Vigelandsparken, named for famous sculptor Gustav Vigeland. Also known as Frognerparken, the park is home to 212 bronze, granite, and wrought-iron sculptures depicting the stages of life.

Winter Activities

When winter comes and the light fades, Norwegians don't simply hole up and hibernate. Rather, they take part in many different winter activities to keep the blood circulating and the spirit high. Skiing, kite-skiing or ski-sailing, snowboarding, and, up north, dogsledding and reindeer sledding are just some of the activities that bring out the natives, especially around Christmas and Easter.

- **Skiing in the birthplace of the sport.** Norway's ski slopes are the stuff of legend. If you're brave enough to visit Norway in winter, you'll definitely want to plan a trip to Lillehammer, Geilo, Rondane, or Hallingdal.

- **Dogsledding up the side of a misty glacier on Svalbard.** Consider an overnight dogsledding tour with Sven Engholm, an 11-time winner of the Finnmarksløpet (Europe's longest dogsledding race) and a top-10 finisher in the Iditarod. Several other tour companies, including Spitsbergen Travel (SPITRA) and Svalbard Polar Travel (SPOT), also organize dogsledding tours.

- **Eating dinner in a Sami tent,** with your reindeer parked outside. Karasjok Opplevelser A/S organizes reindeer sledding trips, and restaurants in Karasjok offer meals under traditional Sami tents.

- **Viewing the northern lights.** It is said that the northern lights, or aurora borealis, decorate the nighttime skies over Tromsø more than over any other city in Norway.

Shopping

It's hard to leave Norway without a hand-knit sweater and something troll-related. Norway's crafts and outdoor wear make excellent gifts and souvenirs. Wood boxes, bowls, and platters are often carved or painted with images of trolls, Norway's enduring mythical characters. Oslo has the best selection and often the best prices of anywhere in the country.

- **Sweaters.** The prices for hand-knit sweaters may seem high, but the quality is outstanding and they're much more expensive outside the country. Although the classic knitting designs, with snowflakes and reindeer, are still best sellers at *husfliden* (home-craft) outlets, gift stores tend to sell more contemporary, fashionable designs.

- **Outdoor wear.** Given Norwegians' affection for the outdoors, it's not surprising that an abundance of high-quality sports gear and outerwear is available. Good buys include Helly Hansen rain gear, insulated boots, and the *supertrøye,* a gossamer-thin insulated undershirt.

- **Crafts.** Look for embroidered cloth; pewter and wrought-iron candlesticks; candles; glass; and wood bowls, spoons, and platters made of birch roots, decorated with rosemaling. Other, more offbeat, items include *ostehøvler* (cheese slicers) and *kransekakeformer,* graduated forms for making almond ring cakes.

- **Music.** Norwegian music, traditional to popular, classical to jazz, sung in English and Norwegian, can be a lasting memento.

GREAT ITINERARY

NORWAY IN A NUTSHELL

The famous Norway in a Nutshell tour was devised by Norwegian State Railways (⊕ www.nsb.no), or NSB, in the 1960s, and has since become the most popular way to see Norway, both for independent travelers and those taking part in a guided trip. Tickets can be purchased through myriad agencies, including NSB's own tour company, **Fjord Tours AS** (⊕ www.norwaynutshell. com), and tourist information offices throughout the country.

Essentially a highlights tour, you can complete the trip in one whirlwind day, but we suggest taking a more leisurely six-day tour. You can start from either Oslo or Bergen and do a one-way or round-trip tour. Below we've outlined the most popular route, one way from Oslo to Bergen.

Days 1 & 2: Oslo

Norway's capital makes a good starting point since most flights to Norway arrive here. Spend your first two days exploring the city. Take it easy on the first day by exploring the downtown area—meander on Karl Johans Gate, see Akershus Castle and the Kvadraturen, and walk through Vigelands (Frogner) Park. On your second day, head out to Bygdøy and visit the area's museums.

Day 3: Oslo to Flåm

On your third day, start early and take the Bergen train line to Myrdal. When you make your reservations, book your trip all the way to Flåm, a good town in which to stop for the night. When you reach Myrdal, you have to transfer to the Flåm railway. The five-hour trip across Norway's interior between Oslo and Bergen passes over the Hardangervidda plateau and is con-sidered one of the most spectacular train rides in the world. It only gets better on the Flåm railway, which winds between towering mountains and immense fjords, passing cascading waterfalls and tiny villages. The trip from Myrdal to Flåm covers 20 km (12 mi) and takes 53 minutes. You should reach Flåm by late afternoon, giving you enough time to relax in an outdoor café, do a little souvenir shopping, and perhaps see the Flåmsbanemuseet, or Flåm Railway Museum, which gives you a look at how the Flåm railway was engineered.

Day 4: Flåm to Voss

This leg of your journey begins with a boat trip from Flåm through Aurlandsfjord and into the Nærøyfjord, the narrowest fjord in Europe. Both inlets are part of the larger Sognefjord, one of Norway's most famous fjords and, at 204 km (127 mi), its longest. The ride lasts two hours and ends at Gudvangen, at which point you board a bus for the one-hour trip to Voss up the Nærøyfjord Valley and along the old Stalheimskleivane Road with its dramatic hairpin bends. If you can, try to book your stay at the 18th-century Stalheim Hotel, 36 km (22 mi) outside Voss.

Days 5 & 6: Bergen

From Voss, the train to Bergen takes one hour. When you get to Bergen, check into your hotel and head to Bryggen for dinner. Here along Bergen's wharf are some of the city's oldest and best-preserved buildings. Spend your sixth day exploring Bergen. If you have time, visit Troldhaugen, which was composer Edvard Grieg's house for 22 years; it's a half-day trip from Bergen's center.

ON THE CALENDAR

WINTER	
December 10	The **Nobel Peace Prize** is awarded in Oslo.
January	The **Tromsø International Film Festival**, Norway's largest and the world's most northerly such festival, presents a cutting-edge program of features and short films from around the world.
February	The **Winter Arts Festival** in Lillehammer has music, theater, and art exhibitions. The **Røros Fair** has been an annual tradition since 1854.
SPRING	
March	The **Finnmarksløpet** (Finnmark Race), Europe's largest dogsledding competition, follows old mail routes across Finnmarksvidda. The **Birkebeiner Race** commemorates a centuries-old cross-country ski race from Lillehammer to Rena. The **Holmenkollen Ski Festival** has skiing events as well as breathtaking ski-jumping feats.
March–April	The **Karasjok Easter Festival** has concerts, theater performances, art exhibits, snowmobile rallies, and husky and reindeer races.
May	The **Grete Waitz Race** is a 5-km (3-mi), women-only race in Oslo. The **Bergen International Festival** is customarily opened by the king; festivities include dance, music, and theater performances.
May 17	**Constitution Day** brings out every Norwegian flag and crowds of marchers for parades and celebrations throughout the country.
SUMMER	
June 23	**Midsummer Night,** called Sankt Hans Afton, is celebrated nationwide with bonfires, fireworks, and outdoor dancing. The **Emigration Festival** in Stavanger is the place to meet fellow Norwegian-Americans and Norwegians. The **Festspillene i Nord-Norge** (North Norway Cultural Festival) in Harstad features a feast of cultural activities, including performance art, exhibitions, music, theater, and youth events.
July	The **Kristindagene** (Kristin Festival) puts on plays, exhibitions, concerts, and historic walking tours that pay tribute to *Kristin Lavransdatter,* the novel by Nobel Prize–winning Sigrid Undset. It is held at Jørund Farm, the site of Liv Ullmann's movie adaptation of the novel.

	The **Molde International Jazz Festival,** one of the longest-established in Europe, draws jazzaholics and international stars to Norway's west coast. There are theater performances, art exhibitions, and more than 50 free concerts.
	The **ExxonMobil Bislett Games** attract leading track-and-field athletes to the Bislett Stadium in Oslo.
August	The **Telemark International Folk Festival** in the town of Bø draws Scandinavian and international folk music performers, and has folk dancing and folk singing concerts, as well as jazz and blues shows.
	The **Peer Gynt Festival** in Gudbrandsdalen brings art exhibits, children's activities, and open-air theater performances of Henrik Ibsen's *Peer Gynt*—as well as Edvard Grieg's music.
	The **International Chamber Music Festival** stages classical concerts at venues in and around Stavanger.
	Near the end of the month the **Ibsen Stage Festival** gets underway in Oslo, with stars from overseas participating. The festival is held in even-number years.
FALL	
September	The **Oslo Marathon** is run over a distance of 42 km (26 mi) through the streets of Oslo.
	The **Høstutstillingen** (Fall Exhibition), held annually at Kunstnernes Hus (Artists' House) is worth a visit for art lovers.

SMART TRAVEL TIPS

AIR TRAVEL

CARRIERS

From North America to Oslo Gardermoen, Air Canada has flights via London and Frankfurt; American Airlines has flights via London and Brussels; Continental has direct flights; Finnair has flights with connections through Helsinki; Iceland Air has flights with connections through Reykjavík, Amsterdam, Copenhagen, and Stockholm; Lufthansa has flights with connections through Frankfurt and Munich; and Scandinavian Airlines System (SAS), partnering with United, has flights via Copenhagen and Stockholm.

From the United Kingdom, British Airways and British Midland have direct flights to Oslo; Norwegian flies to Oslo, Bergen, and Trondheim; Ryan Air has direct flights to Oslo Torp Sandefjord and Haugesund; and SAS has direct flights to Oslo, Bergen, and Stavanger.

Within Norway, Braathens, Norwegian, and SAS connect many of the cities by regular flights, and Widerøe connects smaller towns and cities that are usually along the coast.

⚐ To & from Norway **Air Canada** ☎ 888/247-2262 in Canada and the U.S. ⊕ www.aircanada.ca. **American** ☎ 800/433-7300 ⊕ www.aa.com. **British Airways** ☎ 0870/850-9850 ⊕ www.british-airways.com. **British Midland** ☎ 0870/607-0222. **Continental** ☎ 800/523-3273 ⊕ www.continental.com. **Finnair** ☎ 800/950-5000 ⊕ www.finnair.com **Iceland Air** ☎ 800/223-5500 ⊕ www.icelandair.com. **Lufthansa** ☎ 800/645-3880, 86-90-98-00, Ext. 2 in Sweden ⊕ www.lufthansa.com ☎ 800/399-5838, 23-35-54-00 in Norway. **Ryan Air** ☎ 0871/246-0000 in the U.K. ⊕ www.ryanair.com. **SAS** ☎ 800/221-2350 ⊕ www.scandinavian.net. **United** ☎ 800/241-6522 ⊕ www.united.com.

⚐ Within Norway **Braathens** ☎ 91-50-54-00 in Norway ⊕ www.sasbraathens.no. **Norwegian** ☎ 815-21-815 in Norway ⊕ www.norwegian.no. **SAS** ☎ 800/221-2350 in the U.S. ⊕ www.scandinavian.net. **Widerøe** ☎ 810-01-200 in Norway ⊕ www.wideroe.com.

CHECK-IN & BOARDING

Always **find out your carrier's check-in policy.** Plan to arrive at the airport about

2 hours before your scheduled departure time for domestic flights and 2½ to 3 hours before international flights. You may need to arrive earlier if you're flying from one of the busier airports or during peak air-traffic times. To avoid delays at airport-security checkpoints, try not to wear any metal. Jewelry, belt and other buckles, and steel-toe shoes are among the items that can set off detectors.

Assuming that not everyone with a ticket will show up, airlines routinely overbook planes. When everyone does, airlines ask for volunteers to give up their seats. In return, these volunteers usually get a several-hundred-dollar flight voucher, which can be used toward the purchase of another ticket, and are rebooked on the next available flight out. If there are not enough volunteers, the airline must choose who will be denied boarding. The first to get bumped are passengers who checked in late and those flying on discounted tickets, so get to the gate and check in as early as possible, especially during peak periods.

Always **bring a government-issued photo ID** to the airport; even when it's not required, a passport is best.

CUTTING COSTS

The SAS Visit Scandinavia/Europe Air Pass offers up to eight flight coupons for one-way travel between Scandinavian cities (and participating European countries). Most one-way tickets for domestic travel within each Scandinavian country cost $69; one-way fares between the Scandinavian countries usually cost $80, unless you are venturing into the far north, Lapland, Iceland, or Greenland (these flights range from $122 to $200); and fares to other European destinations range from $65 to $165. These passes can be bought only in conjunction with a round-trip ticket between North America and Europe on SAS and must be used within three months of arrival. SAS also provides family fares—a spouse and children ages 2 to 17 can each get 50% off the full fare of business-class tickets with the purchase of one full-fare business-class ticket. Contact SAS for information.

Widerøe Airline offers two types of bargain fare plans. The Fly Norway plan, available

year-round, offers standard-rate tickets at either NKr 58 or NKr 82 and, for extra-short flights, NKr 47 or NKr 69. The Explore Norway by plane plan, available between late June and mid-August, divides Norway into three parts with boundaries at Trondheim and Tromsø, and you can fly as much as you like within a 14-day period. This costs €480 for the whole country; €329 for one zone and €414 for two zones. An extra week costs €220.

It's smart to call a number of airlines and check the Internet; when you are quoted a good price, book it on the spot—the same fare may not be available the next day, or even the next hour. Always check different routings and look into using alternate airports. Also, price off-peak and red-eye flights, which may be significantly less expensive than others. Travel agents, especially low-fare specialists (⇨ Discounts & Deals), are helpful.

Consolidators are another good source. They buy tickets for scheduled flights at reduced rates from the airlines, then sell them at prices that beat the best fare available directly from the airlines. (Many also offer reduced car-rental and hotel rates.) Sometimes you can even get your money back if you need to return the ticket. Carefully read the fine print detailing penalties for changes and cancellations, purchase the ticket with a credit card, and confirm your consolidator reservation with the airline.

🛈 **Consolidators** AirlineConsolidator.com ☎ 888/468-5385 ⊕ www.airlineconsolidator.com; for international tickets. **Best Fares** ☎ 800/880-1234 ⊕ www.bestfares.com; $59.90 annual membership. **Cheap Tickets** ☎ 800/377-1000 or 800/652-4327 ⊕ www.cheaptickets.com. **Expedia** ☎ 800/397-3342 or 404/728-8787 ⊕ www.expedia.com. **Hotwire** ☎ 866/468-9473 or 920/330-9418 ⊕ www.hotwire.com. **Now Voyager Travel** ☎ 212/459-1616 ⊕ www.nowvoyagertravel.com. **Onetravel. com** ⊕ www.onetravel.com. **Orbitz** ☎ 888/656-4546 ⊕ www.orbitz.com. **Priceline.com** ⊕ www.priceline.com. **Travelocity** ☎ 888/709-5983, 877/282-2925 in Canada, 0870/111-7061 in the U.K. ⊕ www.travelocity.com.

🛈 **Discount Passes** FlightPass, EuropebyAir, ☎ 888/387-2479 in the U.S. ⊕ www.europebyair. com. **SAS Air Passes**, Scandinavian Airlines,

☎ 1300/727-707 in Australia, 0870/6072-7727 in the U.K., 800/221-2350 in the U.S ⊕ www. scandinavian.net. **Widerøe Airline** ☎ 810-01-200 in Norway ⊕ www.wideroe.no.

ENJOYING THE FLIGHT

State your seat preference when purchasing your ticket, and then repeat it when you confirm and when you check in. For more legroom, you can request one of the few emergency-aisle seats at check-in, if you're capable of moving obstacles comparable in weight to an airplane exit door (usually between 35 pounds and 60 pounds)—a Federal Aviation Administration requirement of passengers in these seats. Seats behind a bulkhead also offer more legroom, but they don't have under-seat storage. Don't sit in the row in front of the emergency aisle or in front of a bulkhead, where seats may not recline. SeatGuru.com has more information about specific seat configurations, which vary by aircraft.

Ask the airline whether a snack or meal is served on the flight. If you have dietary concerns, request special meals when booking. These can be vegetarian, low-cholesterol, or kosher, for example. It's a good idea to pack some healthful snacks and a small (plastic) bottle of water in your carry-on bag. On long flights, try to maintain a normal routine, to help fight jet lag. At night, get some sleep. By day, eat light meals, drink water (not alcohol), and **move around the cabin** to stretch your legs. For additional jet-lag tips consult *Fodor's FYI: Travel Fit & Healthy* (available at bookstores everywhere).

FLYING TIMES

A flight from New York to Oslo takes about 8 hours. From London, a nonstop flight gets to Oslo in 1¾ hours; it's about 1½ hours to Stavanger. From Sydney and major cities in New Zealand, the flight to Oslo will be over 20 hours, and will require at least one transfer.

HOW TO COMPLAIN

If your baggage goes astray or your flight goes awry, complain right away. Most carriers require that you **file a claim immediately.** The Aviation Consumer Protection Division of the Department of Transporta-

tion publishes *Fly-Rights*, which discusses airlines and consumer issues and is available online. You can also find articles and information on mytravelrights.com, the Web site of the nonprofit Consumer Travel Rights Center.

🛈 **Airline Complaints Aviation Consumer Protection Division** ✉ U.S. Dept. of Transportation, Office of Aviation Enforcement and Proceedings, C-75, Room 4107, 400 7th St. SW, Washington, DC 20590 ☎ 202/366-2220 ⊕ airconsumer.ost.dot.gov. **Federal Aviation Administration Consumer Hotline** ✉ For inquiries: FAA, 800 Independence Ave. SW, Washington, DC 20591 ☎ 800/322-7873 ⊕ www.faa.gov.

RECONFIRMING

Check the status of your flight before you leave for the airport. You can do this on your carrier's Web site, by linking to a flight-status checker (many Web booking services offer these), or by calling your carrier or travel agent. Always confirm international flights at least 72 hours ahead of the scheduled departure time.

AIRPORTS

Gardermoen Airport, about 53 km (33 mi) northeast of Oslo, is the major entry point for most visitors to Norway. Other international airports are in Bergen, Kristiansand, Sandefjord, Stavanger, and Trondheim.

🛈 **Airport Information Gardermoen Airport** ☎ 815-50-250 or 64-81-20-00 ⊕ www.osl.no/english. **Oslo Torp** ✉ Sandefjord ☎ 33-42-70-02 ⊕ www.torp.no.

BOAT & FERRY TRAVEL

Taking a ferry isn't only fun, it's often necessary in Norway, as they remain an important means of transportation along the west coast. More specialized boat service includes hydrofoil (catamaran) trips between Stavanger, Haugesund, and Bergen. There are also fjord cruises out of these cities and others in the north. Møre og Romsdals Fylkesbåter (MRF) and Hardanger Sunnhordalandske Dampskipselskap (HSD) are two of the most important ferry companies, and Route Information Norway is a company that has comprehensive links to all forms of transport within Norway.

The famous Norwegian Coastal Voyage *Hurtigruten* sailings are covered in more detail under the Cruise Travel heading.

From the United Kingdom, DFDS Seaways has services departing from Newcastle at 3 PM and arriving in Kristiansand, southern Norway, at 9:15 AM. Fjord Line sails from Newcastle to Stavanger, Haugesund, and Bergen, with crossings taking about 22 hours. Smyril Line operates between Bergen, Tórshavn (Faroe Islands), and Lerwick (Shetland) on Monday from mid-May to mid-September.

🚢 **Boat & Ferry Information DFDS Seaways** ✉ DFDS Seaways Travel Centre, Scandinavia House, Parkeston, Harwich, Essex CO12 4QG ☎ 8705/333-111 ⊕ www.dfdsseaways.co.uk. **Fjord Line** ✉ Norway House, Royal Quays, near Newcastle, NE29 6EG North Shields ☎ 0870/143-9669 ⊕ www.fjordline.co.uk. **Hardanger Sunnhordalandske Dampskipselskap (HSD)** ✉ Sundtsgt. 36, 5817 Bergen ☎ 55-23-87-00 ⊕ www.hsd.no. **Møre og Romsdals Fylkesbåter (MRF)** ✉ Gotfred Lies Plas 2, Molde ☎ 71-21-95-00 ⊕ www.mrf.no. **Route Information Norway** ⊕ www.ruteinfo.no. **Smyril Line** ✉ J. Broncks gøta 37, FO-110 Torshavn ☎ 298/34-59-00 ⊕ www.smyril-line.com.

BUSINESS HOURS

BANKS & OFFICES

Standard bank opening hours are weekdays 8:15–4. On Thursday many banks stay open until 5. Offices are generally open weekdays 9–4, but normally close one hour earlier in summer.

SHOPS

Most shops are open from 9 or 10 to 5 weekdays, Thursday until 7, Saturday from 9 to 2 or 4, and are closed Sunday. In some areas, especially in larger cities, stores stay open later on weekdays. Large shopping centers, for example, are usually open until 8 weekdays and 6 on Saturday. Supermarkets are open until 9 or 10 weekdays and until 6 on Saturday. In summer, and especially in rural areas, most shops close weekdays at 4 and at 1 on Saturday.

BUS TRAVEL

Bus tours can be effective for smaller regions within Norway, but the train system is excellent and offers much greater coverage in less time. Buses do, however, tend to be less expensive.

Every end station of the railroad is supported by a number of bus routes, some of which are operated by the Norwegian State Railway (NSB), others by local companies. Long-distance buses usually take longer than the railroad, and fares are only slightly lower. Virtually every settlement on the mainland is served by bus, and for anyone with a desire to get off the beaten track, a pay-as-you-go, open-ended bus trip is the best way to see Norway.

Most long-distance buses leave from Bussterminalen close to Oslo Central Station. Nor-Way Bussekspress, a chain of 50 Norwegian bus companies serving 500 destinations, can arrange any journey. They offer a bus pass that provides 10 consecutive days of unlimited travel on all domestic lines for NKr 1,300, and another that provides 21 consecutive days for NKr 2,400.

CUTTING COSTS

🚌 **Bus Information Ruteinformasjonen** ☎ 177; for timetables and fares for the area you are situated in [except Finnmark and Svalbard]. **Bussterminalen** ✉ Galleriet Oslo, Schweigaardsgt. 10 ☎ 23-00-24-00 bus information. **Nor-Way Bussekspress** ✉ Bussterminalen ☎ 820-21-300 ⊕ www.nbe.no. **Norwegian State Railway (NSB)** ☎ 815-00-888 ⊕ www.nsb.no.

CAMERAS & PHOTOGRAPHY

The *Kodak Guide to Shooting Great Travel Pictures* (available at bookstores everywhere) is loaded with tips.

📷 **Photo Help Kodak Information Center** ☎ 800/242-2424 ⊕ www.kodak.com.

EQUIPMENT PRECAUTIONS

Don't pack film or equipment in checked luggage, where it is much more susceptible to damage. X-ray machines used to view checked luggage are extremely powerful and therefore are likely to ruin your film. Try to ask for hand inspection of film, which becomes clouded after repeated exposure to airport X-ray machines, and keep videotapes and computer disks away from metal detectors. Always keep film, tape, and computer disks out of the sun. Carry an extra supply of batteries, and be prepared to turn on your camera, camcorder, or laptop to prove to airport security personnel that the device is real.

CAR RENTAL

Rates in Oslo begin at $75 a day and $284 a week. This does not include 24% tax and a $15 to $25 service charge.

Alamo ☎ 800/522-9696, 020/8759-6200 in the U.K. ⊕ www.alamo.com. **Avis** ☎ 800/331-1084, 800/879-2847 in Canada, 09/526-2847 in New Zealand, 0870/606-0100 in the U.K., 02/9353-9000 in Australia, 815-33-044 in Norway ⊕ www.avis.com. **Budget** ☎ 800/527-0700, 0870/156-5656 in the U.K., 800-30-210 in Norway ⊕ www.budget.com. **Dollar** ☎ 800/800-6000, 0800/085-4578 in the U.K., 02/9223-1444 in Australia ⊕ www.dollar.com. **Hertz** ☎ 800/654-3001, 800/263-0600 in Canada, 0870/844-8844 in the U.K., 02/9669-2444 in Australia, 09/256-8690 in New Zealand, 67-16-80-00 in Norway ⊕ www.hertz.com. **National Car Rental** ☎ 800/227-7368, 020/8680-4800 in the U.K., 815-22-466 in Norway ⊕ www.nationalcar.com.

CUTTING COSTS

For a good deal, book through a travel agent who will shop around. Do look into wholesalers, companies that do not own fleets but rent in bulk from those that do and often offer better rates than traditional car-rental operations. Prices are best during off-peak periods. Rentals booked through wholesalers often must be paid for before you leave home.

Wholesalers Auto Europe ☎ 207/842-2000 or 800/223-5555 🖷 207/842-2222 ⊕ www.autoeurope.com. **Destination Europe Resources** (DER) ✉ 9501 W. Devon Ave., Rosemont, IL 60018 ☎ 800/782-2424 🖷 800/282-7474.

INSURANCE

When driving a rented car you are generally responsible for any damage to or loss of the vehicle. Collision policies that car-rental companies sell for European rentals typically do not cover stolen vehicles. Before you rent—and purchase collision or theft coverage—see what coverage you already have under the terms of your personal auto-insurance policy and credit cards.

REQUIREMENTS & RESTRICTIONS

Ask about age requirements: the minimum driving age in Norway is 18, but some car-rental companies require that drivers be at least 25. Your driver's license is acceptable for a limited time; check with the Norwegian Tourist Board before you go. An international driver's permit is a good idea; it's available from the American or Canadian Automobile Association, or, in the United Kingdom, from the Automobile Association or Royal Automobile Club.

SURCHARGES

Before you pick up a car in one city and leave it in another, ask about drop-off charges or one-way service fees, which can be substantial. Also inquire about early-return policies; some rental agencies charge extra if you return the car before the time specified in your contract while others give you a refund for the days not used. Most agencies note the tank's fuel level on your contract; to avoid a hefty refueling fee, return the car with the same tank level. If the tank was full, refill it just before you turn in the car, but be aware that gas stations near the rental outlet may overcharge. It's almost never a deal to buy a tank of gas with the car when you rent it; the understanding is that you'll return it empty, but some fuel usually remains.

CAR TRAVEL

You can drive in Norway with your valid U.S., Canadian, U.K., Australian, or New Zealand driver's license.

Excellent, well-marked roads make driving a great way to explore Norway, but it can be an expensive choice. Ferry costs can be steep, and reservations are vital. Tolls on some major roads add to the expense, as do the high fees for city parking. Tickets for illegal parking are painfully costly.

If you're planning to drive around Norway, call or check the Web site of Vegmeldingsentralen, an information center for the Statens Vegvesen (Public Roads Administration). The center monitors and provides information about roads and road conditions, distances, and ferry timetables. Phones are open 24 hours a day.

The southern part of Norway is fairly compact—all major cities are about a day's drive from each other. The distances are felt on the way north, where Norway becomes narrower as it inches up to and beyond the Arctic Circle and hooks over Sweden and Finland to touch Russia. It's virtually impossible to visit the entire country from one base.

In a few remote areas, especially in northern Norway, road conditions can be unpredictable, so plan carefully for safety's sake. Should your road trip take you over the mountains in autumn, winter, or spring, make sure that the mountain pass you're heading to is actually open. Some high mountain roads are closed as early as October due to snow, and do not open again until June. When driving in remote areas, especially in winter, let someone know your travel plans, **use a four-wheel-drive vehicle,** and **travel with at least one other car.**

There are toll charges to enter Oslo, Bergen, Trondheim, Stavanger, and Kristiansand. Costs range from NKr 10 to NKr 20, and full details of all tolls for roads and tunnels can be found at the Vegmeldingsentralen Web site listed below.

🚗 **Vegmeldingsentralen (Road Information Center)** ☎ 175 in Norway, 815–48–991 from abroad ⊕ www.vegvesen.no.

AUTO CLUBS

🚗 In Australia **Australian Automobile Association** ☎ 02/6247-7311 ⊕ www.aaa.asn.au.
🚗 In Canada **Canadian Automobile Association (CAA)** ☎ 613/247-0117 ⊕ www.caa.ca.
🚗 In New Zealand **New Zealand Automobile Association** ☎ 09/377-4660 ⊕ www.aa.co.nz.
🚗 In the U.K. **Automobile Association (AA)** ☎ 0870/600-0371 ⊕ www.theaa.com. **Royal Automobile Club (RAC)** ☎ 0800/731-7090 for membership, 0845/300-0755 for insurance ⊕ www.rac.co.uk.
🚗 In the U.S. **American Automobile Association** ☎ 800/564-6222 ⊕ www.aaa.com.

EMERGENCY SERVICES

Norsk Automobil-Forbund (NAF) offers roadside assistance. They patrol major roads and mountain passes from mid-June to mid-August. Another roadside assistance agency is Falken.

🚗 **Norsk Automobil-Forbund (NAF)** (Norwegian Automobile Association) ✉ Storgt. 2, Box 494, Sentrum, 0155 Oslo ☎ 22-34-14-00, 810-00-505 for 24-hr service ⊕ www.naf.no. **Falken** ✉ Maridalsv.

300, 0872 Oslo ☎ 02468, 02222 for 24-hr service ⊕ www.falken.no.

GASOLINE

Gas stations are plentiful, and *blyfri bensin* (unleaded gasoline) and diesel fuel are sold everywhere from self-service pumps. Those marked *kort* are 24-hour pumps, which take oil-company credit cards or bank cards, either of which is inserted directly into the pump. Gas costs approximately NKr 11.08 per liter (that's around US$4.50 per gallon). Don't wait until your tank is empty before looking for a gas station; hours vary greatly, especially outside the major cities.

INSURANCE

All vehicles registered abroad are required to carry international liability insurance and an international accident report form, which can be obtained from automobile clubs. Collision insurance is recommended.

ROAD CONDITIONS

Four-lane highways are the exception and are found only around major cities. Outside main routes, roads tend to be narrow and twisting, with only token guardrails. In summer, roads are always crowded. Along the west coast, waits for ferries and passage through tunnels can be significant. Don't expect to cover more than 240 km (150 mi) in a day, especially in fjord country.

Norwegian roads are well marked with directional, distance, and informational signs. Some roads, particularly those over mountains, can close for all or part of the winter. If you drive anywhere but on major roads in winter, make sure the car is equipped with proper snow tires. Roads are generally not salted but are left with a hard-packed layer of snow on top of the asphalt. If you're renting, choose a small car with front-wheel drive. Bring an ice scraper, snow brush, small shovel, and heavy clothes for emergencies. In remote areas, or when roads are icy or steep, consider bringing along a set of tire chains. Although the weather along the coast is sunny, a few hours inland temperatures may be about -9°C (15°F) colder, and snowfall is the rule rather than the exception.

RULES OF THE ROAD

Driving is on the right. Yield to vehicles approaching from the right. Make sure you have an up-to-date map before you venture out, because some highway numbers have changed in the past few years, particularly routes beginning with "E."

The maximum speed limit is 90 kph (55 mph) on major highways. On other highways the limit is 80 kph (50 mph) or 70 kph (43 mph). The speed limit in cities and towns is 50 kph (30 mph), and 30 kph (18 mph) in residential areas.

Keep your headlights on at all times; this is required by law. By Norwegian law, everyone, including infants, must **wear seat belts.** Children under four years of age must ride in a car seat, and children over four years must ride in the back. All cars must carry red reflective warning triangles, to be placed a safe distance from a disabled vehicle.

Norway has strict drinking-and-driving laws, and there are routine roadside checks. The legal limit is a blood-alcohol level of 0.02%, which effectively means that you should not drink any amount of alcohol before driving. If you are stopped, you may be required to take a breath test. If it is positive, you must submit to a blood test. No exceptions are made for foreigners, who can lose their licenses on the spot. Other penalties include fines and imprisonment. An accident involving a driver with an illegal blood-alcohol level usually voids all insurance agreements, so the driver becomes responsible for his own medical bills and damage to the cars.

Speeding is also punished severely. Most roads are monitored by radar and cameras in gray metal boxes. Signs warning of *Automatisk Trafikkontroll* (Automatic Traffic Monitoring) are posted periodically along many roads.

CHILDREN IN NORWAY

In Norway children are to be seen *and* heard and are genuinely welcome in most public places.

If you are renting a car, don't forget to arrange for a car seat when you reserve. For general advice about traveling with children, consult *Fodor's FYI: Travel with Your Baby* (available in bookstores everywhere).

DISCOUNTS

Children are entitled to discount tickets (often as much as 50% off) on buses, trains, and ferries throughout Norway, as well as reductions on Oslo and Bergen City Cards, which offer unlimited free travel on all kinds of public transportation and free admission to most museums. Children under age 12 pay 75% of the adult fare and children under age 2 pay 10% on SAS round-trips. There are no restrictions on children's fares when booked in economy class. "Family fares," only available in business class, are also worth looking into (⇨ Cutting Costs *in* Air Travel).

With the ScanRail Pass (⇨ Train Travel)— good for rail journeys throughout Scandinavia—children under age 4 (on lap) travel free; those ages 4 to 11 pay half fare and those ages 12 to 25 can get a ScanRail Youth Pass, providing a 25% discount off the adult fare.

FLYING

If your children are two or older, ask about children's airfares. As a general rule, infants under two not occupying a seat fly at greatly reduced fares or even for free. But if you want to guarantee a seat for an infant, you have to pay full fare. Consider flying during off-peak days and times; most airlines will grant an infant a seat without a ticket if there are available seats. When booking, confirm carry-on allowances if you're traveling with infants. In general, for babies charged 10% to 50% of the adult fare you are allowed one carry-on bag and a collapsible stroller; if the flight is full, the stroller may have to be checked or you may be limited to less.

Experts agree that it's a good idea to use safety seats aloft for children weighing less than 40 pounds. Airlines set their own policies: if you use a safety seat, U.S. carriers usually require that the child be ticketed, even if he or she is young enough to ride free, because the seats must be strapped into regular seats. And even if you pay the full adult fare for the seat, it may be worth it, especially on longer trips. Do **check your airline's policy about using safety seats during takeoff and landing.** Safety seats are not allowed everywhere in the plane, so get your seat assignments as early as possible.

When reserving, request children's meals or a freestanding bassinet (not available at all airlines) if you need them. But note that bulkhead seats, where you must sit to use the bassinet, may lack an overhead bin or storage space on the floor.

For all airlines servicing Norway, it is necessary to reserve children's and baby meals at least 24 hours in advance; travel of an unaccompanied minor should be confirmed at least three days prior to the flight.

LODGING

Most hotels in Norway allow children under a certain age to stay in their parents' room at no extra charge, but others charge for them as extra adults; be sure to find out the cutoff age for children's discounts.

SIGHTS & ATTRACTIONS

Places that are especially appealing to children are indicated by a rubber-duckie icon (🐤) in the margin.

CONSUMER PROTECTION

Whether you're shopping for gifts or purchasing travel services, **pay with a major credit card** whenever possible, so you can cancel payment or get reimbursed if there's a problem (and you can provide documentation). If you're doing business with a particular company for the first time, contact your local Better Business Bureau and the attorney general's offices in your state and (for U.S. businesses) the company's home state as well. Have any complaints been filed? Finally, if you're buying a package or tour, always consider travel insurance that includes default coverage (⇨ Insurance).

🛈 **BBBs Council of Better Business Bureaus** ✉ 4200 Wilson Blvd., Suite 800, Arlington, VA 22203 ☎ 703/276-0100 🖷 703/525-8277 ⊕ www. bbb.org.

CRUISE TRAVEL

Norway's most renowned boat is *Hurtigruten,* which literally means "Rapid Route." Also known as the Coastal Steamer, the boat departs from Bergen and stops at 36 ports along the coast in six days, ending with Kirkenes, near the Russian border, before turning back. Tickets, which can be purchased for the entire journey or for individual legs, are available through Norwegian Coastal Voyage and Hurtigruten Coastal Express Bookings. Special discounts are available for AARP members. Alternatively, you can contact one of the companies that run the service: FFR in Hammerfest, OVDS in Narvik, Hurtigruten in Bergen, and TFDS in Tromsø.

To learn how to plan, choose, and book a cruise-ship voyage, consult *Fodor's FYI: Plan & Enjoy Your Cruise* (available in bookstores everywhere).

🛈 **Cruise Lines Bentours-For Australia and NZ** ✉ Level 7, 189 Kent St., Sydney, NSW 2000 Australia ☎ 612/9247-3381 ⊕ www.bentours.com.au. **FFR** ✉ Box 308, 9615 Hammerfest ☎ 78-40-70-51 ⊕ www.ffr.no. **Hurtigruten** ✉ Coastal Express, Veiten 2B, 5012 Bergen ☎ 810-30-300. **Hurtigruten Coastal Express Bookings** ☎ 810-30-000, 78-54-17-41 timetables ⊕ www. hurtigruten.no. **Norwegian Coastal Voyage Inc.** ✉ 405 Park Ave., New York, NY 10022 ☎ 212/319-1300 ⊕ www.norwegiancoastalvoyage.us. **Norwegian Coastal Voyage Ltd.** ✉ 3 Shortlands., London, U.K. W68NE ☎ 020/8846-2600 ⊕ www. norwegiancoastalvoyage.com. **OVDS** ✉ Box 43, 8501 Narvik ☎ 76-96-76-76 ⊕ www.ovds.no. **TFDS** ✉ 9291 Tromsø ☎ 77-64-82-00 ⊕ www.tfds.no.

CUSTOMS & DUTIES

When shopping abroad, keep receipts for all purchases. Upon reentering the country, **be ready to show customs officials what you've bought.** Pack purchases together in an easily accessible place. If you think a duty is incorrect, appeal the assessment. If you object to the way your clearance was handled, note the inspector's badge number. In either case, first ask to see a supervisor. If the problem isn't resolved, write to the appropriate authorities, beginning with the port director at your point of entry.

IN AUSTRALIA

Australian residents who are 18 or older may bring home A$900 worth of souvenirs and gifts (including jewelry), 250 cigarettes or 250 grams of cigars or other tobacco products, and 2.25 liters of alcohol (including wine, beer, and spirits). Residents under 18 may bring back A$450 worth of goods. If any of these individual allowances are exceeded, you must pay duty for the entire amount (of the group of products in which the allowance was exceeded). Members of the same family traveling together may pool their allowances. Prohibited items include meat products. Seeds, plants, and fruits need to be declared upon arrival.

Australian Customs Service Customs House, 10 Cooks River Dr., Sydney International Airport, Sydney, NSW 2020 02/6275-6666 or 1300/363-263, 02/8334-7444 or 1800/020-504 quarantine-inquiry line 02/8339-6714 www.customs.gov.au.

IN CANADA

Canadian residents who have been out of Canada for at least seven days may bring in C$750 worth of goods duty-free. If you've been away fewer than seven days but more than 48 hours, the duty-free allowance drops to C$200. If your trip lasts 24 to 48 hours, the allowance is C$50; if the goods are worth more than C$50, you must pay full duty on all of the goods. You may not pool allowances with family members. Goods claimed under the C$750 exemption may follow you by mail; those claimed under the lesser exemptions must accompany you. Alcohol and tobacco products may be included in the seven-day and 48-hour exemptions but not in the 24-hour exemption. If you meet the age requirements of the province or territory through which you reenter Canada, you may bring in, duty-free, 1.5 liters of wine *or* 1.14 liters (40 imperial ounces) of liquor *or* 24 12-ounce cans or bottles of beer or ale. Also, if you meet the local age requirement for tobacco products, you may bring in, duty-free, 200 cigarettes, 50 cigars or cigarillos, and 200 grams of tobacco. You may have to pay a minimum duty on tobacco products, regardless of whether or not you exceed your personal exemption. Check ahead of time with the Canada Border Services Agency or the Department of Agriculture for policies regarding meat products, seeds, plants, and fruits.

You may send an unlimited number of gifts (only one gift per recipient, however) worth up to C$60 each duty-free to Canada. Label the package UNSOLICITED GIFT—VALUE UNDER $60. Alcohol and tobacco are excluded.

Canada Border Services Agency Customs Information Services, 191 Laurier Ave. W, 15th fl., Ottawa, Ontario K1A 0L5 800/461-9999 in Canada, 204/983-3500, 506/636-5064 www.cbsa.gc.ca.

IN NEW ZEALAND

All homeward-bound residents may bring back NZ$700 worth of souvenirs and gifts; passengers may not pool their allowances, and children can claim only the concession on goods intended for their own use. For those 17 or older, the duty-free allowance also includes 4.5 liters of wine or beer; one 1,125-ml bottle of spirits; and either 200 cigarettes, 250 grams of tobacco, 50 cigars, *or* a combination of the three up to 250 grams. Meat products, seeds, plants, and fruits must be declared upon arrival to the Agricultural Services Department.

New Zealand Customs Head office: The Customhouse, 17-21 Whitmore St., Box 2218, Wellington 09/300-5399 or 0800/428-786 www.customs.govt.nz.

IN NORWAY

Customs regulations have the following duty-free limits: 2 liters of beer, 1 liter of liquor (up to 60% alcohol), 1 liter of wine (up to 22%) or 2 liters of wine or 2 liters of beer if no liquor, 200 cigarettes or 250 grams of tobacco and 200 cigarette papers. You must be over 20 to take in liquor and over 18 years for wine, beer, and tobacco products. You may not bring any vegetables, fruits, dairy products, or other uncooked foods into Norway. Dried and canned foodstuffs are allowed.

IN THE U.K.

If you are a U.K. resident and your journey was wholly within the European Union, you probably won't have to pass through customs when you return to the United Kingdom. If you plan to bring back large quantities of alcohol or tobacco, check EU limits beforehand. In most cases, if you bring back more than 200 cigars, 3,200 cigarettes, 400 cigarillos, 3 kilograms of tobacco, 10 liters of spirits, 110 liters of beer, 20 liters of fortified wine, and/or 90 liters of wine, you have to declare the goods upon return.

From countries outside the European Union, including Iceland and Norway, you may bring home, duty-free, 200 cigarettes, 50 cigars, 100 cigarillos, or 250 grams of tobacco; 1 liter of spirits or 2 liters of fortified or sparkling wine or liqueurs; 2 liters of still table wine; 60 ml of perfume; 250 ml of toilet water; plus £145 worth of other goods, including gifts and souvenirs. Prohibited items include meat and dairy products, seeds, plants, and fruits.

🔳 **HM Customs and Excise** ✉ Portcullis House, 21 Cowbridge Rd. E, Cardiff CF11 9SS ☎ 0845/010-9000 or 0208/929-0152 advice service, 0208/929-6731 or 0208/910-3602 complaints ⊕ www.hmce.gov.uk.

IN THE U.S.

U.S. residents who have been out of the country for at least 48 hours may bring home, for personal use, $800 worth of foreign goods duty-free, as long as they haven't used the $800 allowance or any part of it in the past 30 days. This exemption may include 1 liter of alcohol (for travelers 21 and older), 200 cigarettes, and 100 non-Cuban cigars. Family members from the same household who are traveling together may pool their $800 personal exemptions. For fewer than 48 hours, the duty-free allowance drops to $200, which may include 50 cigarettes, 10 non-Cuban cigars, and 150 ml of alcohol (or 150 ml of perfume containing alcohol). The $200 allowance cannot be combined with other individuals' exemptions, and if you exceed it, the full value of all the goods will be taxed. Antiques, which U.S. Customs and Border Protection defines as objects more than 100 years old, enter duty-free, as do original works of art done entirely by hand, including paintings, drawings, and sculptures. This doesn't apply to folk art or handicrafts, which are in general dutiable.

You may also send packages home duty-free, with a limit of one parcel per addressee per day (except alcohol or tobacco products or perfume worth more than $5). You can mail up to $200 worth of goods for personal use; label the package PERSONAL USE and attach a list of its contents and their retail value. If the package contains your used personal belongings, mark it AMERICAN GOODS RETURNED to avoid paying duties. You may send up to $100 worth of goods as a gift; mark the package UNSOLICITED GIFT. Mailed items do not affect your duty-free allowance on your return.

To avoid paying duty on foreign-made high-ticket items you already own and will take on your trip, register them with a local customs office before you leave the country. Consider filing a Certificate of Registration for laptops, cameras, watches, and other digital devices identified with serial numbers or other permanent markings; you can keep the certificate for other trips. Otherwise, bring a sales receipt or insurance form to show that you owned the item before you left the United States.

For more about duties, restricted items, and other information about international travel, check out U.S. Customs and Border Protection's online brochure, *Know Before You Go*. You can also file complaints on the U.S. Customs and Border Protection Web site, listed below.

🔳 **U.S. Customs and Border Protection** ✉ For inquiries and complaints, 1300 Pennsylvania Ave. NW, Washington, DC 20229 ⊕ www.cbp.gov ☎ 877/227-5551, 202/354-1000.

DISABILITIES & ACCESSIBILITY

Facilities for travelers with disabilities are generally good, and most major tourist offices offer booklets and brochures on travel and accommodations. The Norwegian Association of the Disabled (NHF) gives advice on public transportation, sights and museums, hotels, and special-interest tours. You should get public transportation passes and make hotel reservations in advance of your visit to ensure a smooth trip.

🔳 **Local Resources Norwegian Association of the Disabled** (NHF) ✉ Schweigaardsgt. 12, Box 9217 Gronland, N-0134 Oslo ☎ 24-10-24-00 📠 24-10-24-99 ⊕ www.nhf.no.

LODGING
Best Western has properties with wheel-chair-accessible rooms in Oslo. If wheelchair-accessible rooms on other floors are not available, ground-floor rooms are provided.

🔲 **Wheelchair-Accessible Chain** Best Western ☎ 800/528-1234.

RESERVATIONS
When discussing accessibility with an operator or reservations agent, ask hard questions. Are there any stairs, inside *or* out? Are there grab bars next to the toilet *and* in the shower/tub? How wide is the doorway to the room? To the bathroom? For the most extensive facilities meeting the latest legal specifications, opt for newer accommodations. If you reserve through a toll-free number, consider also calling the hotel's local number to confirm the information from the central reservations office. Get confirmation in writing when you can.

SIGHTS & ATTRACTIONS
Although most major attractions in Oslo present no problems, areas in the older sections of the city may be challenging for travelers with disabilities.

TRANSPORTATION
The U.S. Department of Transportation Aviation Consumer Protection Division's online publication *New Horizons: Information for the Air Traveler with a Disability* offers advice for travelers with a disability, and outlines basic rights. Visit DisabilityInfo.gov for general information.

With advance notice, most airlines, buses, and trains can arrange assistance for those requiring extra help with boarding. Contact each company at least one week in advance, or discuss this at the time of booking. Call Oslo Taxi or Taxi 2 for vans and taxis equipped for wheelchairs.

Confirming ahead is especially important when planning travel to less-populated regions. The smaller planes and ferries often used in such areas are not all wheelchair accessible.

🔲 **Resources** Oslo Taxi ☎ 02323. Taxi 2 ☎ 02202.
🔲 **Information & Complaints** Aviation Consumer Protection Division (⇨ Air Travel) for airline-related

problems; ⊕ airconsumer.ost.dot.gov/publications/horizons.htm for airline travel advice and rights. **Departmental Office of Civil Rights** ✉ For general inquiries, U.S. Dept. of Transportation, S-30, 400 7th St. SW, Room 10215, Washington, DC 20590 ☎ 202/366-4648, 202/366-8538 TTY 🖷 202/366-9371 ⊕ www.dotcr.ost.dot.gov. **Disability Rights Section** ✉ NYAV, U.S. Dept. of Justice, Civil Rights Division, 950 Pennsylvania Ave. NW, Washington, DC 20530 ☎ 202/514-0301 ADA information line, 800/514-0301, 202/514-0383 TTY, 800/514-0383 TTY ⊕ www.ada.gov. **U.S. Department of Transportation Hotline** ☎ 800/778-4838 for disability-related air-travel problems, 800/455-9880 TTY.

TRAVEL AGENCIES
In the United States, the Americans with Disabilities Act requires that travel firms serve the needs of all travelers. Some agencies specialize in working with people with disabilities.

🔲 **Travelers with Mobility Problems** Access Adventures/B. Roberts Travel ✉ 1876 East Ave., Rochester, NY 14610 ☎ 800/444-6540 ⊕ www.brobertstravel.com, run by a former physical-rehabilitation counselor. **CareVacations** ✉ No. 5, 5110-50 Ave., Leduc, Alberta, Canada, T9E 6V4 ☎ 877/478-7827, 780/986-6404 🖷 780/986-8332 ⊕ www.carevacations.com, for group tours and cruise vacations. **Flying Wheels Travel** ✉ 143 W. Bridge St., Box 382, Owatonna, MN 55060 ☎ 507/451-5005 🖷 507/451-1685 ⊕ www.flyingwheelstravel.com.

DISCOUNTS & DEALS
Be a smart shopper and compare all your options before making decisions. A plane ticket bought with a promotional coupon from travel clubs, coupon books, and direct-mail offers or purchased on the Internet may not be cheaper than the least-expensive fare from a discount ticket agency. And always keep in mind that what you get is just as important as what you save.

DISCOUNT RESERVATIONS
To save money, look into discount reservations services with Web sites and toll-free numbers, which use their buying power to get a better price on hotels, airline tickets (⇨ Air Travel), even car rentals. When booking a room, always **call the hotel's local toll-free number** (if one is available) rather than the central

reservations number—you'll often get a better price. Always ask about special packages or corporate rates.

When shopping for the best deal on hotels and car rentals, look for guaranteed exchange rates, which protect you against a falling dollar. With your rate locked in, you won't pay more, even if the price goes up in the local currency.

⁊ Hotel Rooms Accommodations Express
☎ 800/444-7666 or 800/277-1064. **Hotels.com**
☎ 800/246-8357 ⊕ www.hotels.com. **Steigenberger Reservation Service** ☎ 800/223-5652
⊕ www.srs-worldhotels.com. **Turbotrip.com**
☎ 800/473-7829 ⊕ www.turbotrip.com.

PACKAGE DEALS

Don't confuse packages and guided tours. When you buy a package, you travel on your own, just as though you had planned the trip yourself. Fly/drive packages, which combine airfare and car rental, are often a good deal. In cities, ask the local visitor's bureau about hotel and local transportation packages that include tickets to major museum exhibits or other special events. If you **buy a rail/drive pass,** you may save on train tickets and car rentals. All EurailPass holders get a discount on Eurostar fares through the Channel Tunnel and often receive reduced rates for buses, hotels, ferries, sightseeing cruises, and car rentals.

Also check rates for ScanRail Passes (⇨ Train Travel).

EATING & DRINKING

Major cities offer a full range of dining choices, from traditional to international restaurants. The restaurants we list (all of which are indicated by a ✕) are the cream of the crop in each price category. Properties indicated by a ✕▥ are lodging establishments whose restaurants warrant a special trip. Price categories are as follows:

CATEGORY	OSLO & BERGEN	ELSEWHERE
$$$$	over 270	over 230
$$$	230–270	190–230
$$	180–230	150–190
$	110–180	90–150
¢	under 110	under 90

Prices are for a main course at dinner, including tax and a service charge.

CUTTING COSTS

Restaurant meals are a big-ticket item in Norway, but there are ways to keep the cost of eating down. Take full advantage of the large buffet breakfast often included in the cost of a hotel room. The traditional Norwegian lunch is sandwiches prepared at home—don't be surprised if you see Norwegians preparing their lunch from the breakfast buffet, especially in the mountains or other remote areas. At lunch, look for the menu that offers a set two- or three-course meal for a set price, or limit yourself to a hearty appetizer. Some restaurants now include a trip to the salad bar in the dinner price. A word to look out for in particular, whether at lunch or dinner, is "Dagens"—the daily special, usually a good-value meal. At dinner, pay careful attention to the price of wine and drinks, since the high tax on alcohol raises these costs considerably.

Ethnic restaurants, especially in the larger cities, can provide great value. The area east of Youngstorget in Oslo, for instance, is a haven for inexpensive Indian, Bangladeshi, Lebanese, and Vietnamese cuisine. Kebab shops, pizza places, and cheap Chinese restaurants are also ubiquitous, but tend to be on the bland side.

Norwegians on the road pack their own lunches or stop by gas stations for a quick, high-calorie fix: most offer a hot dog and soft drink deal for around NKr 30, and some serve sandwiches made to order, or even bake their own pastries. This isn't exactly health food, but it's usually better value than the average *veikro* (roadside cafeteria).

Some hotels and most campgrounds and hostels offer cooking facilities. If you want to prepare your own meals, consider bringing your favorite dried spices and condiments, as good replacements can be hard to come by. Supermarkets are plentiful: the chain Rema 1000 traditionally offers the best value for money, while upmarket chains such as Meny and Mega often have deli counters. For fresh produce, fish, or meats, speciality stores are always better and cheaper than supermarkets.

For more information on affordable eating, *see* Money Matters.

MEALS & SPECIALTIES
The surrounding oceans and plentiful inland lakes and streams provide Norway with an abundance of fresh fish and seafood: salmon, herring, trout, and seafood delicacies are mainstays, and are prepared in countless ways. Elk, deer, reindeer, and lamb feed in relatively unspoiled areas and have the succulent taste of wild game. Berries and mushrooms are still harvested from the forests; sausage appears in a thousand forms, as do potatoes and other root vegetables such as turnips, radishes, rutabaga, and carrots. Some northern tastes can seem unusual, such as the fondness for pickled and fermented fish—to be sampled carefully at first—but are coupled with an almost universal obsession with sweet pastries, ice cream, and chocolate.

Other novelties for the visitor might be the use of fruit in main dishes and soups, or sour milk on breakfast cereal, or preserved fish paste as a spread for crackers, or the prevalence of tasty, whole-grain crisp breads and hearty rye breads. The smörgåsbord, or, in Norwegian, *koldtbord,* a buffet meal, is less common these days, but is still the traveling diner's best bet for breakfast. A koldtbord usually comes with a wide range of cheeses, fresh fish, and vegetables alongside meat and breads and other starches.

MEALTIMES
Unless otherwise noted, the restaurants listed in this guide are open daily for lunch and dinner.

RESERVATIONS & DRESS
Reservations are always a good idea; we mention them only when they're essential or not accepted. Book as far ahead as you can, and reconfirm as soon as you arrive. (Large parties should always call ahead to check the reservations policy.) We mention dress only when men are required to wear a jacket or a jacket and tie.

WINE, BEER & SPIRITS
Restaurants' markup on alcoholic beverages is often very high in Norway: as much as four times that of a standard retail price.

ELECTRICITY
To use electric-powered equipment purchased in the United States or Canada, **bring a converter and adapter.** The electrical current in Norway is 220 volts, 50 cycles alternating current (AC); wall outlets take Continental-type plugs, with two round prongs.

If your appliances are dual-voltage, you'll need only an adapter. Don't use 110-volt outlets marked FOR SHAVERS ONLY for high-wattage appliances such as blow-dryers. Most laptops operate equally well on 110 and 220 volts and so require only an adapter.

EMBASSIES
◪ Australia ✉ Jerbanetorget 2, Oslo ☎ 22-47-91-70.
◪ Canada ✉ Wergelandsveien. 7, Oslo ☎ 22-99-53-00.
◪ New Zealand ✉ Billengstadsletta 19B, Oslo ☎ 66-77-53-30.
◪ U.K. ✉ Thomas Heftyes gt. 8, Oslo ☎ 23-13-27-00.
◪ U.S. ✉ Drammensveien. 18, Oslo ☎ 22-44-85-50.

EMERGENCIES
Ambulance, fire, and police assistance is available 24 hours.
◪ Ambulance ☎ 113. **Fire** ☎ 110. **Police** ☎ 112.

GAY & LESBIAN TRAVEL
Scandinavian countries were at the forefront of women's rights at the turn of the 20th century, and Scandinavia has also had a liberal attitude toward gays and lesbians. The government of Norway grants to same-sex couples the same or nearly the same rights as those who are married.
◪ Gay- & Lesbian-Friendly Travel Agencies Different Roads Travel ✉ 1017 N. LaCienega Blvd., Suite 308, West Hollywood, CA 90069 ☎ 800/429-8747 or 310/289-6000 (Ext. 14 for both) 🖷 310/855-0323 ✎ lgernert@tzell.com. **Kennedy Travel** ✉ 130 W. 42nd St., Suite 401, New York, NY 10036 ☎ 800/237-7433 or 212/840-8659 🖷 212/730-2269 ⊕ www.kennedytravel.com. **Now, Voyager** ✉ 4406 18th St., San Francisco, CA 94114 ☎ 800/255-6951 or 415/626-1169 🖷 415/626-8626 ⊕ www.nowvoyager.com. **Skylink Travel and Tour/Flying Dutchmen Travel** ✉ 1455 N. Dutton Ave., Suite A, Santa Rosa, CA 95401 ☎ 800/225-5759 or 707/546-9888 🖷 707/636-0951; serving lesbian travelers.

HEALTH

High-quality health care is widely available in Norway, even in relatively remote areas. Nearly all health care personnel speak English fluently. In case of a medical emergency, dial 113.

MEDICATIONS

You are permitted to take medicines for your own use into the country. To avoid problems with customs, bring a letter from your doctor stating your medical needs. Some medicines bought in Norway are marked with a red triangle, and should not be taken before operating a motorized vehicle.

HOLIDAYS

Major national holidays include: New Year's Eve (December 31); New Year's Day (January 1); Easter Week; May Day (May 1); Constitution Day (May 17); Ascenscion Day; Pentecost; Midsummer Eve and Midsummer Night (June 23 and 24); St. Olav's Day (July 29); Christmas Eve and Christmas Day (December 24 and 25); Boxing Day (December 26).

On major holidays such as Christmas, most shops close or operate on a Sunday schedule. On the eves of such holidays, many shops are also closed all day or are open with reduced hours.

On May Day the city centers are usually full of people, celebrations, and parades. In midsummer, locals flock to the lakes and countryside to celebrate the beginning of long summer days with bonfires and other festivities.

INSURANCE

The most useful travel-insurance plan is a comprehensive policy that includes coverage for trip cancellation and interruption, default, trip delay, and medical expenses (with a waiver for preexisting conditions).

Without insurance you'll lose all or most of your money if you cancel your trip, regardless of the reason. Default insurance covers you if your tour operator, airline, or cruise line goes out of business—the chances of which have been increasing. Trip-delay covers expenses that arise because of bad weather or mechanical delays. Study the fine print when comparing policies.

If you're traveling internationally, a key component of travel insurance is coverage for medical bills incurred if you get sick on the road. Such expenses aren't generally covered by Medicare or private policies. U.K. residents can buy a travel-insurance policy valid for most vacations taken during the year in which it's purchased (but check preexisting-condition coverage). British and Australian citizens need extra medical coverage when traveling overseas.

Always **buy travel policies directly from the insurance company**; if you buy them from a cruise line, airline, or tour operator that goes out of business you probably won't be covered for the agency or operator's default, a major risk. Before making any purchase, review your existing health and home-owner's policies to find what they cover away from home.

🔁 Travel Insurers In the United States: **Access America** ✉ 2805 N. Parham Rd., Richmond, VA 23294 ☎ 800/284-8300 🖷 804/673-1469 or 800/346-9265 ⊕ www.accessamerica.com. **Travel Guard International** ✉ 1145 Clark St., Stevens Point, WI 54481 ☎ 800/826-1300 or 715/345-1041 🖷 800/955-8785 or 715/345-1990 ⊕ www.travelguard.com. 🔁 In Australia: **Insurance Council of Australia** ✉ Level 3, 56 Pitt St., Sydney, NSW 2000 ☎ 02/9253-5100 🖷 02/9253-5111 ⊕ www.ica.com.au. In Canada: **RBC Insurance** ✉ 6880 Financial Dr., Mississauga, Ontario L5N 7Y5 ☎ 800/387-4357 or 905/816-2559 🖷 888/298-6458 ⊕ www.rbcinsurance.com. In New Zealand: **Insurance Council of New Zealand** ✉ Level 7, 111–115 Customhouse Quay, Box 474, Wellington ☎ 04/472-5230 🖷 04/473-3011 ⊕ www.icnz.org.nz. In the United Kingdom: **Association of British Insurers** ✉ 51 Gresham St., London EC2V 7HQ ☎ 020/7600-3333 🖷 020/7696-8999 ⊕ www.abi.org.uk.

LANGUAGE

Despite the fact that Norwegian is in the Germanic family of languages, it is a myth that someone who speaks German can understand it. Fortunately, English is widely spoken. German is the most common third language. English becomes rarer outside major cities, and it's a good idea to **take along a dictionary or phrase book.** Even here, however, anyone under the age of 50 is likely to have studied English in school. Fluent Swedish speakers can generally understand Norwegian.

Norwegian has three additional vowels: æ, ø, and å. Æ is pronounced as a short "a." The ø, sometimes printed as oe, is the same as ö in German and Swedish, pronounced very much like a short "u." The å is a contraction of the archaic "aa" and sounds like long "o." These three letters appear at the end of alphabetical listings, such as those in the phone book.

There are two officially sanctioned Norwegian languages, Bokmål and Nynorsk. Bokmål is used by 84% of the population and is the main written form of Norwegian and the language of books, as the first half of its name indicates. Nynorsk, which translates as "new Norwegian," is actually a compilation of older dialect forms from rural Norway. Every Norwegian also receives at least seven years of English instruction, starting in the second grade. The Sami (or Lapps), who inhabit the northernmost parts of Norway, have their own language, which is distantly related to Finnish.

LODGING

The lodgings we list are the cream of the crop in each price category. We always list all the facilities that are available—but we don't specify whether they cost extra. When pricing accommodations, always ask what's included.

CATEGORY	OSLO & BERGEN	ELSEWHERE
$$$$	over 2,000	over 1,500
$$$	1,600–2,000	1,000–1,500
$$	1,200–1,600	800–1,000
$	800–1,200	400–800
¢	under 800	under 400

Prices are for two people sharing a double room, including tax and a service charge.

Norwegian hotels have high standards in cleanliness and comfort and prices to match. Even the simplest youth hostels provide good mattresses with fluffy down comforters and clean showers or baths. Assume that hotels operate on the European Plan (EP, with no meals) unless we specify that they use the Continental Plan (CP, with a Continental breakfast), Modified American Plan (MAP, with breakfast and dinner), or the Full American Plan (FAP, with all meals).

Several hotel chains operate in Norway, including Radisson SAS, Scandic, Best Western, Choice, and Quality hotels. In recent years, Rica Hotels (⊕ www.rica.no) has been the most interesting chain, with newer designs like Rica Seilet in Molde (which resembles Dubai's Burj Al Arab) and Stavanger's elliptical Rica Forum. The chain Det virkelig gode liv (⊕ www.dvgl.no) has a few properties known for first-class service, fine food and wine, and traditional style.

The Farmer's Association operates simple hotels in most towns and cities. These reasonably priced accommodations usually have heimen as part of the name, such as Bondeheimen in Oslo. The same organization also runs cafeterias serving traditional Norwegian food, usually called Kaffistova. All of these hotels and restaurants are alcohol-free. Rustic cabins and campsites are also available all over the countryside, as are independent hotels.

In the Lofoten and Vesterålen islands, rorbuer, (fishermen's cabins) are the most popular form of accommodation. These rustic quayside cabins, with mini-kitchens, bunk beds, living rooms, and showers, are reasonably priced and listed through the local tourist office.

Norway has more than 100 youth hostels, part of **Hostelling International Norway/Norske Vandrerhjem** (⊕ www.vandrerhjem.no). Norwegian hostels are considered among the best in the world; they are squeaky clean and have excellent facilities. Most rooms sleep two to four, but there are also family rooms and dormitories. You don't have to be a member, but members get discounts, so it's worth joining. Membership can be arranged at any vandrerhjem (youth hostel) and after six Norwegian youth hostel stamps, nonmembers can become international members. Duvets and pillows are always provided, but linens are usually rented by the night. You're welcome to bring your own—if you haven't, you can buy a lakenpose (sheet sleeping bag) at many department stores and at most youth hostels as well. Advanced booking is recommended, especially in summer. No two Norwegian hostels are alike; they range from modern buildings to old wooden houses and fisherman's cabins. Prices per night range NKr 80–NKr 225 in dormitories, NKr 195–NKr 740 in double rooms, and NKr 300–NKr 600 for family rooms. Guests ages 3 to 15 in the same room as adults are eligible for 50% discounts, and children under 3 not sleeping in beds stay for free. The largest Norwegian hostels are open year-round; smaller ones are often open only for the summer season.

Norway has more than 500 inspected and classified campsites, many with showers, bathrooms, and hookups for electricity. Most also have cabins or chalets to rent by the night or longer.

Make reservations whenever possible.
Even countryside inns, which usually have space, are sometimes packed with vacationing Europeans. When making reservations, **ask about high and low seasons.** Some hotels lower prices during what they determine to be "tourist season," whereas others raise them during the same period.

APARTMENT & VILLA (OR HOUSE) RENTALS
If you want a home base that's roomy enough for a family and comes with cooking facilities, consider a furnished rental. These can save you money, especially if you're traveling with a group. Home-exchange directories sometimes list rentals as well as exchanges.

🚩 **International Agents Hideaways International** ✉ 767 Islington St., Portsmouth, NH 03801 ☎ 800/843-4433 or 603/430-4433 🖷 603/430-4444 ⊕ www.hideaways.com, annual membership $185.

CABINS & CAMPING
Norway has more than 1,000 campsites, all of which are given anywhere from one to five stars based on the standard facilities and activities available. Fees vary but generally each site costs NKr 80–NKr 160 per day. For camping information and a list of sites, contact local tourist offices. Open fires are illegal in forests or open land between April 15 and September 15.

Many of Norway's campsites also have cabins available. These are also rated on a five-star system. Most have electricity and heat, but you may have to bring your own bedding. Cost per night is around NKr 250–NKr 750. The DNT hiking organization runs hundreds of cabins and lodges, especially in the south.

The Norsk Campingkort (Norwegian Camping Card) entitles you to faster check-in service and discounts on cabins and campsites. The card costs NKr 60 for a year and can be ordered before traveling through the Reiselivsbedriftenes Landsforening (RBL).

🚩 **Den Norske Turistforening (DNT)** (The Norwegian Mountain Touring Association) ✉ Box 7, Sentrum, 0101 Oslo 1 ☎ 22-82-28-00 🖷 22-82-28-01 ⊕ www.turistforeningen.no. **Reiselivsbedriftenes Landsforening (RBL)** (Norwegian Hospitality Association) 🖈 Essendrpsgt. 6, 0305 Oslo ☎ 23-08-86-20 🖷 23-08-86-21 ⊕ www.camping.no.

FARM & COTTAGE HOLIDAYS
The old-fashioned farm or countryside holiday, long a staple for Norwegian city dwellers, is becoming increasingly available to tourists. In most cases you can choose to stay on the farm itself, and even participate in daily activities, or you can opt to rent a private cottage, which can include housekeeping. Seaside fisherman's cabins (or *rorbuer*) are also available, particularly in the Lofoten Islands. Contact local tourist boards for details.

HOME EXCHANGES
If you would like to exchange your home for someone else's, join a home-exchange organization, which will send you its updated listings of available exchanges for a year and will include your own listing in at least one of them. It's up to you to make specific arrangements.

🚩 **Exchange Clubs HomeLink USA** ✉ 2937 N.W. 9th Terr., Wilton Manors, FL 33311 ☎ 800/638-3841 or 954/566-2687 🖷 954/566-2783 ⊕ www. homelink.org; $75 yearly for a listing and online access; $45 additional to receive directories. **Intervac U.S.** ✉ 30 Corte San Fernando, Tiburon, CA 94920 ☎ 800/756-4663 🖷 415/435-7440 ⊕ www. intervacus.com; $128 yearly for a listing, online access, and a catalog; $68 without catalog.

HOSTELS

No matter what your age, you can save on lodging costs by staying at hostels.In some 4,500 locations in more than 70 countries around the world, Hostelling International (HI), the umbrella group for a number of national youth-hostel associations, offers single-sex, dorm-style beds and, at many hostels, rooms for couples and family accommodations. Membership in any HI national hostel association, open to travelers of all ages, allows you to stay in HI-affiliated hostels at member rates; a one-year membership is about $28 for adults (C$35 for a two-year minimum membership in Canada, £15 in the United Kingdom, A$52 in Australia, and NZ$40 in New Zealand); hostels charge about $10–$30 per night. Members have priority if the hostel is full; they're also eligible for discounts around the world, even on rail and bus travel in some countries.

The Norwegian branch, Norske Vandrerhjem, maintains a list of Norwegian hostels.

Organizations Hostelling International–Canada ⊠ 205 Catherine St., Suite 400, Ottawa, Ontario, K2P 1C3 ☎ 800/663–5777 or 613/237–7884 🖷 613/237–7868 ⊕ www.hihostels.ca. Hostelling International–USA ⊠ 8401 Colesville Rd., Suite 600, Silver Spring, MD 20910 ☎ 301/495–1240 🖷 301/495–6697 ⊕ www.hiusa.org. Norske Vandrerhjem (Hostelling International Norway) ⊠ Torggata 1, 0181 Oslo ☎ 23–13–93–00 🖷 23–13–93–50 ⊕ www.vandrerhjem.no. YHA Australia ⊠ 422 Kent St., Sydney, NSW 2001 ☎ 02/9261–1111 🖷 02/9261–1969 ⊕ www.yha.com.au. YHA England and Wales ⊠ Trevelyan House, Dimple Rd., Matlock, Derbyshire DE4 3YH, U.K. ☎ 0870/870–8808, 0870/770–8868, or 0162/959–2600 🖷 0870/770–6127 ⊕ www.yha.org.uk. YHA New Zealand ⊠ Level 1, Moorhouse City, 166 Moorhouse Ave., Box 436, Christchurch ☎ 0800/278–299 or 03/379–9970 🖷 03/365–4476 ⊕ www.yha.org.nz.

HOTELS

All hotels listed have private bath unless otherwise noted.

Inn Checks—prepaid hotel vouchers—offer discounts of up to 50% for accommodations ranging from first-class hotels to country cottages. The vouchers must be purchased from travel agents or from the Scandinavian Tourist Board (⇨ Visitor Information) before departure, and are sold individually and in packets for as many nights as needed. Winter bargains are often better than those in summer.

A Fjord Pass, which costs NKr 100, is valid for two adults and any number of children under the age of 15. Valid May through September, the discount card can make it possible to stay at a hotel for NKr 290 per person per day at more than 200 hotels, guesthouses, apartments, and holiday cottages. You can get the pass from travel agents and at tourist information offices, Fjord Pass hotels, some post offices, and railway stations.

ProSkandinavia checks can be used in 400 hotels across Scandinavia for savings up to 50%, for reservations made usually no earlier than 24 hours before arrival, although some hotels allow earlier bookings. One check costs about $35. Two checks will pay for a double room at a hotel, one check for a room in a cottage. The checks can be bought at many travel agencies in Scandinavia or ordered directly from ProSkandinavia.

Note that Norwegian bed dimensions are smaller than those in the United States. Double beds are often about 60 inches wide or slightly less. King-size beds (72 inches wide) are difficult to find and, if available, require special reservations.

Best Western Hotels Norway ☎ 800–11–624 ⊕ www.bestwestern.no. Norway Fjord Pass ☎ 55–55–76–60 ⊕ www.fjordpass.com. Nordic Hotel Pass ☎ 22–40–13–00 ⊕ www.choice.no. ProSkandinavia ⊠ Akersgt. 11, N-0158 Oslo ☎ 22–41–13–12 ⊕ www.proskandinavia. no. Scan+ Hotel Pass ☎ 23–08–02–80 ⊕ www.norlandia.no. Scandic Club Card ☎ 85–17–51–700 ⊕ www. scandic.hotels.com.

CUTTING COSTS

There's little doubt that accommodation will be a major expense on any trip to Norway, but there are budget alternatives. Before you leave home, **ask your travel agent about discounts,** including a summer Fjord Pass; summer hotel checks for Best Western and Scandic hotels; and enormous year-round rebates at SAS hotels for travelers over 65. All EuroClass (business class) passengers can get discounts of at least 10% at SAS hotels when they book through SAS.

Youth hostels in Norway are among the cleanest and most comfortable you'll run into anywhere, where large, dorm-style rooms are increasingly being replaced with smaller, four- to six–bed rooms. Be advised that alcohol consumption is usually not permitted on the premises, and some hostels still keep strict curfews. Bringing your own sheets can help keep costs to a minimum since these will sometimes cost you around an additional NKr 50.

For a surcharge of around NKr 40, the local tourist information office can book a room for you in a private home. Expect to pay around NKr 300 for a double room in the cities, and you might need to book for a minimum of two nights.

Camping grounds often rent cabins, from simple bunk bed huts to heated, deluxe-style cabins with shower and kitchen. Again, bring your own sheets or a sleeping bag, to keep additional costs down. Camping in the rough is a tradition enshrined in law, as long as you're at least 500 feet from the nearest building. It's considered good form to ask for permission from the landowner in advance, and keep in mind that there are restrictions on use of open fire. A good, waterproof tent and a warm sleeping bag are essentials—even summer nights can be chilly and wet in Norway.

RESERVING A ROOM

🚩 **Toll-Free Numbers Best Western** ☎ 800/528-1234 ⊕ www.bestwestern.com. **Choice** ☎ 800/424-6423 ⊕ www.choicehotels.com. **Clarion** ☎ 800/424-6423 ⊕ www.choicehotels.com. **Comfort Inn** ☎ 800/424-6423 ⊕ www.choicehotels.com. **Hilton** ☎ 800/445-8667 ⊕ www.hilton.com. **Quality Inn** ☎ 800/424-6423 ⊕ www.choicehotels.com. **Radisson** ☎ 800/333-3333 ⊕ www.radisson.com.

MAIL & SHIPPING

Most post offices are open weekdays 8 to 4 or 5, Saturday 9 to 1. In small towns, post offices are often closed Saturday. In recent years supermarkets and convenience stores have replaced post offices in certain rural areas.

POSTAL RATES

The rate for postcards and letters weighing up to 20 grams (¾ ounce) is NKr 10.50 for outside Europe.

MONEY MATTERS

Prices throughout this guide are given for adults. Substantially reduced fees are almost always available for children, students, and senior citizens. For information on taxes, see Taxes.

Costs are high in Norway. Here are some sample prices: cup of coffee, from NKr 14 in a cafeteria to NKr 25 or more in a restaurant; a 20-pack of cigarettes, NKr 60; a half liter of beer, NKr 40–NKr 50; the smallest hot dog (with bun plus *lompe*—a flat Norwegian potato bread—mustard, ketchup, and fried onions) at a convenience store, NKr 20; cheapest bottle of wine from a government store, NKr 60; the same bottle at a restaurant, NKr 120–NKr 200; urban transit fare in Oslo, NKr 20; soft drink, from NKr 20 in a cafeteria to NKr 35 in a better restaurant; sandwich at a cafeteria, NKr 40–NKr 50; 1½-km (1-mi) taxi ride, NKr 40–NKr 60 depending on time of day.

Be aware that sales taxes can be very high, but foreigners can get some refunds by shopping at tax-free stores (⇨ Taxes). City Cards can save you transportation and entrance fees in larger cities.

You can **reduce the cost of food by planning.** Breakfast is often included in your hotel bill; if not, you may wish to buy fruit, sweet rolls, and a beverage for a picnic breakfast. Electrical devices for hot coffee or tea should be bought abroad, though, to conform to the local current.

Opt for a restaurant lunch instead of dinner, since the latter tends to be significantly more expensive. Instead of beer or wine, **drink tap water**—liquor can cost four times the price of the same brand in a store—but do specify tap water, as the term "water" can refer to soft drinks and bottled water, which are also expensive. The tip is included in the cost of your meal.

Liquor and strong beer (over 3% alcohol) can be purchased only in state-owned shops, at very high prices, during weekday business hours, usually 9:30 to 6 and in some areas on Saturday until mid-afternoon. (When you visit friends or relatives in Norway, a bottle of liquor or fine wine bought duty-free on the trip over is often much appreciated.) Weaker beers and ciders are usually available in grocery stores, except in certain rural areas, especially along the coast of western Norway.

CREDIT CARDS

Throughout this guide, the following abbreviations are used: **AE,** American Express; **DC,** Diners Club; **MC,** MasterCard; and **V,** Visa.

CURRENCY

Norway is a non-EU country, and has opted to keep its currency while its neighbors convert to the euro. The Norwegian *krone* (plural: *kroner*) translates as "crown," written officially as NOK. Price tags are seldom marked this way, but instead read "Kr" followed by the amount, such as Kr 10. (In this book, the Norwegian krone is abbreviated NKr.) One krone is divided into 100 *øre,* and coins of 50 øre and 1, 5, 10, and 20 kroner are in circulation. Bills are issued in denominations of 50, 100, 200, 500, and 1,000 kroner.

CURRENCY EXCHANGE

At this writing, the rate of exchange was NKr 6 to the U.S. dollar, NKr 8 to the euro, NKr 5 to the Canadian dollar, NKr 11 to the pound sterling, NKr 5 to the Australian dollar, NKr 4 to the New Zealand dollar, and NKr 1 to the South African rand. Exchange rates fluctuate, so be sure to check them when planning a trip.

No limitations apply to the import and export of currency.

For the most favorable rates, **change money through banks.** Although ATM transaction fees may be higher abroad than at home, ATM rates are excellent because they're based on wholesale rates offered only by major banks. You won't do as well at exchange booths in airports or rail and bus stations, in hotels, in restaurants, or in stores. To avoid lines at airport exchange booths, get a bit of local currency before you leave home.

🇫 Exchange Services International Currency Express ✉ 427 N. Camden Dr., Suite F, Beverly Hills, CA 90210 ☎ 888/278-6628 orders 🖷 310/278-6410 ⊕ www.foreignmoney.com. **Travel Ex Currency Services** ☎ 800/287-7362 orders and retail locations ⊕ www.travelex.com.

TRAVELER'S CHECKS

Do you need traveler's checks? It depends on where you're headed. If you're going to rural areas and small towns, go with cash; traveler's checks are best used in cities. Lost or stolen checks can usually be replaced within 24 hours. To ensure a speedy refund, buy your own traveler's checks—don't let someone else pay for them: irregularities like this can cause delays. The person who bought the checks should make the call to request a refund.

PACKING

Bring a folding umbrella and a lightweight raincoat, as it is common for the sky to be clear at 9 AM, rainy at 11 AM, and clear again in time for lunch. **Pack casual clothes,** as Norwegians tend to dress more casually than their Continental brethren. If you have trouble sleeping when it is light or are sensitive to strong sun, **bring an eye mask and dark sunglasses;** the sun rises as early as 4 AM in some areas, and the far-northern latitude causes it to slant at angles unseen elsewhere on the globe. **Bring bug repellent** if you plan to venture away from the cities; large mosquitoes can be a real nuisance on summer evenings. If you plan on spending time by the sea or in the mountains, **bring a windbreaker and a warm sweater**—even in the middle of summer, weather can be treacherous and suddenly turn icy cold.

In your carry-on luggage, pack an extra pair of eyeglasses or contact lenses and enough of any medication you take to last a few days longer than the entire trip. You may also ask your doctor to write a spare prescription using the drug's generic name, as brand names may vary from country to country. In luggage to be checked, **never pack prescription drugs, valuables, or undeveloped film.** And don't forget to carry with you the addresses of offices that handle refunds of lost traveler's checks. Check *Fodor's How to Pack* (available at online retailers and bookstores everywhere) for more tips.

To avoid customs and security delays, carry medications in their original packaging. Don't pack any sharp objects in your carry-on luggage, including knives of any size or material, scissors, nail clippers, and corkscrews, or anything else that might arouse suspicion.

To avoid having your checked luggage chosen for hand inspection, don't cram bags full. The U.S. Transportation Security Administration suggests packing shoes on top and placing personal items you don't want touched in clear plastic bags.

CHECKING LUGGAGE

You're allowed to carry aboard one bag and one personal article, such as a purse or a laptop computer. Make sure what you carry on fits under your seat or in the overhead bin. Get to the gate early, so you can board as soon as possible, before the overhead bins fill up.

Baggage allowances vary by carrier, destination, and ticket class. On international flights, you're usually allowed to check two bags weighing up to 70 pounds (32 kilograms) each, although a few airlines allow checked bags of up to 88 pounds (40 kilograms) in first class. Some international carriers don't allow more than 66 pounds (30 kilograms) per bag in business class and 44 pounds (20 kilograms) in economy. If you're flying to or through the United Kingdom, your luggage cannot exceed 70 pounds (32 kilograms) per bag. On domestic flights, the limit is usually 50 to 70 pounds (23 to 32 kilograms) per bag. In general, carry-on bags shouldn't exceed 40 pounds (18 kilograms). Most airlines won't accept bags that weigh more than 100 pounds (45 kilograms) on domestic or international flights. Expect to pay a fee for baggage that exceeds weight limits. Check baggage restrictions with your carrier before you pack.

Airline liability for baggage is limited to $2,500 per person on flights within the United States. On international flights it amounts to $9.07 per pound or $20 per kilogram for checked baggage (roughly $640 per 70-pound bag), with a maximum of $634.90 per piece, and $400 per passenger for unchecked baggage. You can buy additional coverage at check-in for about $10 per $1,000 of coverage, but it often excludes a rather extensive list of items, shown on your airline ticket.

Before departure, itemize your bags' contents and their worth, and label the bags with your name, address, and phone number. (If you use your home address, cover it so potential thieves can't see it readily.) Include a label inside each bag and **pack a copy of your itinerary.** At check-in, make sure each bag is correctly tagged with the destination airport's three-letter code. Because some checked bags will be opened for hand inspection, the U.S. Transportation Security Administration recommends that you leave luggage unlocked or use the plastic locks offered at check-in. TSA screeners place an inspection notice inside searched bags, which are resealed with a special lock.

If your bag has been searched and contents are missing or damaged, file a claim with the TSA Consumer Response Center as soon as possible. If your bags arrive damaged or fail to arrive at all, file a written report with the airline before leaving the airport.

⑦ Complaints U.S. Transportation Security Administration Contact Center ☎ 866/289–9673 ⊕ www.tsa.gov.

PASSPORTS & VISAS

Make two photocopies of the data page of your passport—one for someone at home and another for you, carried separately from your passport. If you lose your passport, promptly call the nearest embassy or consulate and the local police.

U.S. passport applications for children under age 14 require consent from both parents or legal guardians; both parents must appear together to sign the application. If only one parent appears, he or she must submit a written statement from the other parent authorizing passport issuance for the child. A parent with sole authority must present evidence of it when applying; acceptable documentation includes the child's certified birth certificate listing only the applying parent, a court order specifically permitting this parent's travel with the child, or a death certificate for the nonapplying parent. Application forms and instructions are available on the Web site of the U.S. State Department's Bureau of Consular Affairs (⊕ travel.state.gov).

ENTERING NORWAY

All U.S. citizens, even infants, need only a valid passport to enter the country for stays of up to three months.

PASSPORT OFFICES

The best time to apply for a passport or to renew is in fall and winter. Before any trip, check your passport's expiration date, and, if necessary, renew it as soon as possible.

⚑ Australian Citizens Passports Australia Australian Department of Foreign Affairs and Trade ☎ 131-232 ⊕ www.passports.gov.au.
⚑ Canadian Citizens Passport Office ⊠ To mail in applications: 70 Cremazie St., Gatineau, Québec J8Y 3P2 ☎ 800/567-6868 or 819/994-3500 ⊕ www. ppt.gc.ca.
⚑ New Zealand Citizens New Zealand Passports Office ☎ 0800/225-050 or 04/474-8100 ⊕ www. passports.govt.nz.
⚑ U.K. Citizens U.K. Passport Service ☎ 0870/ 521-0410 ⊕ www.passport.gov.uk.
⚑ U.S. Citizens National Passport Information Center ☎ 877/487-2778, 888/874-7793 TDD/TTY ⊕ travel.state.gov.

SAFETY

Don't wear a money belt or a waist pack, both of which peg you as a tourist. Distribute your cash and any valuables (including your credit cards and passport) between a deep front pocket, an inside jacket or vest pocket, and a hidden money pouch. Do not reach for the money pouch once you're in public.

SENIOR-CITIZEN TRAVEL

To qualify for age-related discounts, mention your senior-citizen status up front when booking hotel reservations (not when checking out) and before you're seated in restaurants (not when paying the

bill). Be sure to have identification on hand. When renting a car, ask about promotional car-rental discounts, which can be cheaper than senior-citizen rates.

TRAIN TRAVEL

Seniors over 60 are entitled to discount tickets (often as much as 50% off) on buses, trains, and ferries in Norway, as well as reductions on City Cards. Eurail offers discounts on ScanRail and Eurail train passes (⇨ Train Travel).

⚑ Educational Programs Elderhostel ⊠ 11 Ave. de Lafayette, Boston, MA 02111 ☎ 877/426-8056, 978/323-4141 international callers, 877/426-2167 TTY ☎ 877/426-2166 ⊕ www.elderhostel.org. **Interhostel** ⊠ University of New Hampshire, 6 Garrison Ave., Durham, NH 03824 ☎ 800/733-9753 or 603/ 862-1147 ☎ 603/862-1113 ⊕ www.learn.unh.edu.

SIGHTSEEING GUIDES

Most tourist information offices can recommend local or regional tours, and have brochures for companies in the area. The Norwegian Tourist Board has lists of tours arranged by region.

SPORTS & OUTDOORS

BIKING

Norway has many cycling paths, some of them old roads that are in the mountains and along the western fjords. The Rallarvegen, from Haugastøl in the Hardangervidda National Park to Flåm, is very popular among cyclists. The southern counties of Vestfold and Rogaland have a well-developed network of cycling paths.

Most routes outside large cities are hilly and can be physically demanding. **Wear a protective helmet and use lights at night.**

Many counties have produced brochures that have touring suggestions and maps. Syklistenes Landsforening has maps and general information, as well as the latest weather conditions. Several companies, including Lillehammer's Trollcycling, organize cycling tours. Den Norske Turistforening (DNT; ⇨ Lodging) provides inexpensive lodging for cyclists planning overnight trips.

If you want to travel with your bike on an NSB long-distance train, you must make a reservation and pay an additional NKr 90. On local or InterCity trains, bikes are transported if space is available.

Resources Syklistenes Landsforening ⊠ Storgt. 23C, 0028 Oslo ☎ 22-47-30-30 🖷 22-47-30-31 ⊕ www.slf.no.

Cycling Tour Companies Cycle Tourism ⊠ Fylkeshuset, 3706 Skien ☎ 35-52-99-55 ⊕ www.bike-norway.com. **erik & reidar** ⊠ Kirkegt. 34A, 0153 Oslo ☎ 22-41-23-80 🖷 22-41-23-90. **PedalNor** ⊠ Kløvervn. 10, 4326 Sandnes ☎ 51-66-40-60 or 51-66-48-70. **Trollcycling** ⊠ Box 373, 2601 Lillehammer ☎ 61-28-99-70 🖷 61-26-92-50.

BIRD-WATCHING

Northern Norway has some of northern Europe's largest bird sanctuaries. The area teems with fantastic numbers of seabirds. Another popular spot is the island of Runde, just off Ålesund on the west coast. A half million birds nest there. Værøy, one of the Lofoten Islands in the Arctic Circle, is also a famous bird sanctuary, and the magnificent sea eagles are particularly impressive.

Resources Birding Norway ⊠ Vaagsgaten 6, 5161 Laksevaag ☎ 55-94-76-03 ⊕ www. birdingnorway.no. **Norwegian Wildlife and Rafting** ⊠ 2680 Våg ☎ 61-23-87-27 ⊕ www.nwr.no. **Runde Camping** ⊠ 6096 Runde ☎ 70-08-59-16 ⊕ www.runde.no.

CANOEING & RAFTING

There are plenty of lakes and streams for canoeing and kayaking in Norway. Popular spots include Aust-Agder, in the Sørlandet; Telemark; and suburban Oslo. Norges Padlerforbund (Norwegian Canoe Association) maintains a list of rental companies and regional canoeing centers.

Rafting excursions are offered throughout Norway. For more information, contact Norwegian Wildlife and Rafting, which operates guided two-day expeditions with accommodation and transport provided. The minimum age for white-water rafting is 18 (15 with parental guidance).

Resources Norges Padlerforbund ⊠ Service Boks 1, Ullevål Stadion, 0840 Oslo ☎ 21-02-98-35 ⊕ www.padling.no. **Norwegian Wildlife and Rafting** ⊠ 2680 Våg ☎ 61-23-87-27 ⊕ www.nwr.no.

DIVING

The Norwegian coast has many diving opportunities. There are centers with excellent facilities on the west coast, particularly in Møre og Romsdal county.

There are a few restrictions regarding sites. Special permission is required to dive in a harbor, and diving near army installations is restricted. Contact Norges Dykkeforbund or the local tourist office for a list of diving centers and clubs.

Norges Dykkeforbund ⊠ Service Boks 1, Ullevål Stadion, 0840 Oslo ☎ 21-02-97-42 ⊕ www.ndf.no.

FISHING

Norway's fjords, lakes, and rivers make it a fisherman's paradise. Check with fly shops or the local tourist office to see what licenses you may need.

Using live fish as bait is prohibited, and imported tackle must be disinfected before use. Infectious parasites that are harmless to humans have decimated salmon populations in certain rivers in Norway. To avoid spreading parasites, make sure you dry and clean your gear before moving to another river.

GLACIER WALKING

Glacier walking is an exhilarating way to experience the mountains of Norway. This sport requires the right equipment and training: only try it when accompanied by an experienced local guide. Since glaciers are always moving over new land, the ice and snow may just be a thin covering for a deep crevice. Glacier centers or local tourist offices can recommend guides and tours.

Resources Breheimsenteret ⊠ Jostedalen National Park Visitor's Center, Rte. 604, 6871 Breheimsenteret ☎ 57-68-32-50 ⊕ www.jostedal.com. **Jostedalsbreen Nasjonalparksenter** ⊠ Rte. 15, 6799 Oppstryn ☎ 57-87-72-00 ⊕ www. jostedalsbre.no. **Norsk Bremuseum** (Norwegian Glacier Museum) ⊠ Rte. 5, 6848 Fjærland ☎ 57-69-32-88 ⊕ www.bre.museum.no.

GOLF

The many golf courses spread out across the country welcome nonmember guests for fees ranging from NKr 150 to NKr 350. Local tourist offices and the

Norges Golfforbund can provide a list of golf clubs.

Resources Norges Golfforbund (Norwegian Golf Association) ✉ Box 163, Lilleaker, 0216 Oslo ☎ 22-73-66-20 ⊕ ngf.golf.no.

HANG GLIDING

The mountains and hills of Norway provide excellent take-off spots. However, winds and weather conspire to make conditions unpredictable. For details on local clubs, regulations, and equipment rental, contact Norsk Aeroklubb.

Resources Norsk Aeroklubb ✉ Rådhusgt. 5B, 0162 Oslo ☎ 23-01-04-50 ⊕ www.nak.no.

HIKING & MOUNTAINEERING

Naturally, hiking and mountaineering are popular pastimes in a land of mountain ranges and high plains. Well-known hiking areas include the Jotunheim Mountain Range; the Rondane and Dovrefjell mountains; the Hardangervidda (Hardanger plateau); the Trollheimen District; and Finnmarksvidda. On multiday hikes you can stay in hostels, camp out in your own tent, or head to one the DNT's cabins. Throughout the country, DNT organizes guided hiking tours as well as mountaineering courses year-round.

Resources Den Norske Turistforening (DNT; The Norwegian Mountain Touring Association) ✉ Box 7, Sentrum, 0101 Oslo 1 ☎ 22-82-28-22 ⊟ 22-82-28-23.

SAILING

Norway's rugged coastline can make for an ideal sailing vacation. Be sure to sail with up-to-date sea charts, since the water around Norway is filled with skerries and underwater rocks. Contact Norges Seilforbund about facilities around the country.

Resources Norges Seilforbund (Norwegian Sailing Association) ✉ Box Ullevål Stadion, 0840 Oslo ☎ 21-02-90-00 ⊕ www.seiling.no.

SNOW SPORTS

The Skiforeningen provides national snow-condition reports; tips on trails; and information on courses for cross-country and downhill skiing, telemarking, and snowboarding. If you can't make it to Norway in winter, Stryn Sommerskisenter, in the west, has a summer ski season that runs June–September.

Resources Skiforeningen ✉ Kongevn. 5, 0390 Oslo 3 ☎ 22-92-32-00 ⊕ www.skiforeningen.no. Stryn Sommerskisenter ✉ 6782 Stryn ☎ 57-87-40-40.

SPORTS FOR PEOPLE WITH DISABILITIES

Norway encouraged active participation in sports for people with disabilities long before it became common elsewhere, and has many Special Olympics medal winners. Beitostølen Helsesportsenter has sports facilities for people with disabilities as well as training programs for instructors. Sports offered include skiing, hiking, running, and horseback riding. For more information call Norges Funksjonshemmede Idrettsforbund.

Resources Beitostølen Helsesportsenter ✉ 2953 Beitostølen ☎ 61-34-11-07 ⊕ www.bhss. no. Norges Funksjonshemmede Idrettsforbund (Norwegian Sports Organization for the Disabled) ✉ Ullevål Stadion ☎ 21-02-90-00 ⊕ www.nfif.no.

SWIMMING

Swimming in the Norwegian outdoors is most enjoyable along the southern coast, where air temperatures can reach 20°C (68°F). In northern Norway inland temperatures are generally cooler.

STUDENTS IN NORWAY

IDs & Services STA Travel ✉ 10 Downing St., New York, NY 10014 ☎ 800/777-0112 24-hr service center, 212/627-3111 ⊟ 212/627-3387 ⊕ www.sta. com. **Travel Cuts** ✉ 187 College St., Toronto, Ontario M5T 1P7, Canada ☎ 800/592-2887 in the U.S., 416/979-2406 or 866/246-9762 in Canada, and 23-10-23-10 in Oslo [for KILROY Travels, the Norway Travel Cuts affiliate] ⊕ www.travelcuts.com.

TAXES

VALUE-ADDED TAX

Value-added tax, V.A.T. for short but called *moms* all over Scandinavia, is a hefty 25% on all purchases except books; it is included in the prices of goods. All purchases of consumer goods totaling more than NKr 308 for export by nonresidents are eligible for V.A.T. refunds. Carry your passport when shopping to prove you are a nonresident.

Global Refund is a Europe-wide V.A.T. refund processing service with 210,000 affiliated stores (some 3,000 shops subscribe to the service in Norway, where it is called "Norway Tax-Free Shopping"). In participating stores, **ask for the Global Refund form** (called a Shopping Cheque). Have it stamped like any customs form by customs officials when you leave the country (be ready to show customs officials what you've bought). Then take the form to one of the more than 700 Global Refund counters—conveniently located at every major airport and border crossing—and 11%–18% of the tax will be refunded on the spot in the form of cash, check, or a refund to your credit-card account (minus a small percentage for processing).

Shops that do not subscribe to this program have slightly more detailed forms, which must be presented to the Norwegian Customs Office along with the goods to obtain a refund by mail. This refund is closer to the actual amount of the tax.

One way to beat high prices is to **take advantage of tax-free shopping.** You can make major purchases free of tax if you have a foreign passport. Ask about tax-free shopping when you make a purchase for $50 (about NKr 320) or more. When your purchases exceed a specified limit (which varies from country to country), you receive a special export receipt. Keep the parcels intact and take them out of the country within 30 days of purchase.

⑦ Directorate of Customs and Excise
✉ Schweigaards gt. 15, Box 8122, 0032 Oslo
☎ 22-86-03-00 ⊕ www.toll.no. **Global Refund Canada** ⓐ Box 2020, Station Main, Brampton, Ontario L6T 3S3 ☎ 800/993-4313 🖶 905/791-9078 ⊕ www.globalrefund.com. **Global Refund Norge** ☎ 67/15-60-10.

TAXIS

Even the smallest villages have some form of taxi service. Towns on the railroad normally have taxi stands just outside the station. All city taxis are connected with a central dispatching office, so there is only one main telephone number for calling a cab. Look in the telephone book under "Taxi" or "Drosje."

Never use an unmarked, or pirate, taxi, since their drivers are unlicensed and in some cases may be dangerous.

TELEPHONES

The telephone system in Norway is modern and efficient; international direct service is available throughout the country. Phone numbers consist of eight digits.

AREA & COUNTRY CODES

The country code for Norway is 47. There are no area codes—you must dial all eight digits of any phone number wherever you are. Telephone numbers that start with a 9 or 4 are usually mobile phones, and are considerably more expensive to call. Telephone numbers starting with the prefix 82 cost extra. Toll-free numbers begin with 800 or 810. Numbers beginning with 815 cost NKr 1 per call. In this book, area codes precede telephone numbers.

DIRECTORY & OPERATOR ASSISTANCE

Dial 1881 for information in Norway, 1882 for international telephone numbers. To place a collect or an operator-assisted call to a number in Norway, dial 115. Dial 117 for collect or operator-assisted calls outside of Norway.

INTERNATIONAL CALLS

If you are able to dial directly, dial the international access code, 00, then the country code and the number. All telephone books list country code numbers, including those for the United States and Canada (1), Great Britain (44), Australia (61), and New Zealand (64). All international operators speak English.

⑦ Access Codes AT&T Direct ☎ 800/CALL-ATT. **MCI WorldPhone** ☎ 800/19912. **Sprint International Access** ☎ 800/19877.

LONG-DISTANCE SERVICES

AT&T, MCI, and Sprint access codes make calling long-distance relatively convenient, but you may find the local access number blocked in many hotel rooms. First ask the hotel operator to connect you. If the hotel operator balks, ask for an international operator, or dial the international operator yourself. One way to improve your odds of getting connected to your long-distance carrier is to travel with more than one company's calling card (a hotel may block Sprint, for example, but not MCI). If all else fails, call from a pay phone. If you are traveling for a longer period of time, consider renting a cell-phone from a local company.

Access Codes AT&T Direct ☎ 800/19011. **MCI WorldPhone** ☎ 800/19912. **Sprint International Access** ☎ 800/19877.

MOBILE PHONES
Scandinavia has been one of the world leaders in mobile phone development; almost 90% of the population owns a mobile phone. Although standard North American cellular phones will not work in Norway, some companies rent cellular phones to visitors. Contact the Norwegian Tourist Office for details.

PHONE CARDS
You can purchase Tellerskritt (phone cards) at Narvesen and Norsk Tipping shops and kiosks. Cards cost NKr 40 to NKr 140 and can be used in the 8,000 green-card telephones. About half of these public phones also take major credit cards.

PUBLIC PHONES
Public telephones are of two types. Pushbutton phones—which accept NKr 1, 5, and 10 coins (some also accept NKr 20 coins)—are easy to use: lift the receiver, listen for the dial tone, insert the coins, dial the number, and wait for a connection. The digital screen at the top of the box indicates the amount of money in your "account." Green-card telephones only accept phone cards or credit cards.

Local calls cost NKr 3 or NKr 5 from a pay phone. If you hear a short tone, it means that your purchased time is almost up.

TIME
Norway is one hour ahead of Greenwich Mean Time (GMT) and six hours ahead of Eastern Standard Time (EST).

TIPPING
Tipping is kept to a minimum in Norway because service charges are added to most bills. It is, however, handy to have a supply of NKr 5 or NKr 10 coins for less formal service. Tip only in local currency.

Room service usually includes a service charge in the bill, so tipping is discretionary. Round up a taxi fare to the next round digit, or tip anywhere from NKr 5 to NKr 10, a little more if the driver has been helpful. All restaurants include a service charge, ranging from 12% to 15%, in the bill. It is customary to add up to 10% for exceptional service, but it is not obligatory. Maître d's are not tipped, and coat checks have flat rates, usually NKr 10 per person.

TOURS & PACKAGES
Because everything is prearranged on a prepackaged tour or independent vacation, you spend less time planning—and often get it all at a good price.

BOOKING WITH AN AGENT
Travel agents are excellent resources. But it's a good idea to collect brochures from several agencies, as some agents' suggestions may be influenced by relationships with tour and package firms that reward them for volume sales. If you have a special interest, find an agent with expertise in that area. The American Society of Travel Agents (ASTA) has a database of specialists worldwide; you can log on to the group's Web site to find one near you.

Make sure your travel agent knows the accommodations and other services of the place being recommended. Ask about the hotel's location, room size, beds, and whether it has a pool, room service, or programs for children, if you care about these. Has your agent been there in person or sent others whom you can contact?

Do some homework on your own, too: local tourism boards can provide information about lesser-known and small-niche operators, some of which may sell only direct.

BUYER BEWARE
Each year consumers are stranded or lose their money when tour operators—even large ones with excellent reputations—go out of business. So check out the operator. Ask several travel agents about its reputation, and try to **book with a company that has a consumer-protection program.** (Look for information in the company's

brochure.) In the United States, members of the United States Tour Operators Association are required to set aside funds (up to $1 million) to help eligible customers cover payments and travel arrangements in the event that the company defaults. It's also a good idea to choose a company that participates in the American Society of Travel Agents' Tour Operator Program; ASTA will act as mediator in any disputes between you and your tour operator.

Remember that the more your package or tour includes, the better you can predict the ultimate cost of your vacation. Make sure you know exactly what is covered, and beware of hidden costs. Are taxes, tips, and transfers included? Entertainment and excursions? These can add up.

⑦ Tour-Operator Recommendations American Society of Travel Agents (⇨ Travel Agencies). **CrossSphere–The Global Association for Packaged Travel** ✉ 546 E. Main St., Lexington, KY 40508 ☎ 800/682-8886 or 859/226-4444 📠 859/226-4414 ⊕ www.CrossSphere.com. **United States Tour Operators Association** (USTOA) ✉ 275 Madison Ave., Suite 2014, New York, NY 10016 ☎ 212/599-6599 📠 212/599-6744 ⊕ www.ustoa.com.

TRAIN TRAVEL

NSB, the Norwegian State Railway System, has five main lines originating from the Oslo S Station. Its 4,000 km (2,500 mi) of track connect all main cities. Train tickets can be purchased in railway stations or from travel agencies. NSB has its own travel agency in Oslo.

Norway's longest rail route runs north to Trondheim, then extends onward as far as Fauske and Bodø. The southern line hugs the coast to Stavanger, while the stunning western line crosses Hardangervidda, the scenic plateau that lies between Oslo and Bergen. An eastern line to Stockholm links Norway with Sweden, while another southern line through Göteborg, Sweden, is the main connection with Continental Europe. Narvik, north of Bodø, is the last stop on Sweden's Ofot line, the world's northernmost rail system, which runs from Stockholm via Kiruna.

If you are traveling from south to north in Norway, flying is often a necessity:

Stavanger is as close to Rome as it is to the northern tip of Norway.

NSB trains are clean, comfortable, and punctual. Most have special compartments for travelers with disabilities and for families with children younger than age two. First- and second-class tickets are available.

Seat reservations are required on some European trains, particularly high-speed trains, and are a good idea on trains that may be crowded. In summer reserve your seats at least five days ahead; during major holidays, reserve several weeks or a month ahead for Friday and Sunday travel. You will also need a reservation if you purchase sleeping accommodations.

Many travelers assume that rail passes guarantee them seats on the trains they wish to ride. Not so. You need to book seats ahead even if you are using a rail pass.

FROM BRITAIN

Traveling from Britain to Norway by train is not difficult and takes 20 to 24 hours. The best connection leaves London's Victoria Station and connects at Dover with a boat to Oostende, Belgium. From Oostende there are overnight connections to Copenhagen, where there are express and overnight connections to Oslo. Call Rail Europe for further information.

⑦ NSB ✉ Skolen Tomtekaia 21, 0048 Oslo ☎ 81-50-08-88. **ScanAm World Tours** ✉ N. Main St. 108, Cranberry, NJ 08512 ☎ 800/545-2204. **Victoria Station** ✉ Terminus Pl., London ☎ 0845/748-4950 in the U.K.

CUTTING COSTS

To save money, **look into rail passes.** But be aware that if you don't plan to cover many miles, you may come out ahead by buying individual tickets.

A number of special discount passes are available, including the InterRail Pass, which is available for European residents of all ages, and the EurailPass, sold in the United States only. Norway participates in the following rail programs: EurailPass (and its FlexiPass variations), ScanRail Pass, ScanRail 'n Drive, InterRail, and Nordturist Card. A Norway Rail Pass is available for three, four, and five days of unlimited rail travel for nonresidents within Norway. The ticket is sold in the United States through ScanAm. First-class rail passes are about 30% higher.

Low-season prices are offered from October through April. Discounted fares also include family, student, senior-citizen (including their not-yet-senior spouses), and off-peak "mini" fares, which must be purchased a day in advance. NSB gives student discounts only to foreigners studying at Norwegian institutions.

Consider a ScanRail Pass, available for travel in Denmark, Sweden, Norway, and Finland for second-class train travel: you may have 5 days of unlimited travel in any two-month period ($291); 10 days of unlimited travel in two months ($390); or 21 consecutive days of unlimited train travel ($453). With the ScanRail Pass you also enjoy travel bonuses, including free or discounted ferry, boat, and bus travel and a Hotel Discount Card that allows 10% to 30% off rates for select hotels June through August.

Passengers ages 12 to 25 can buy ScanRail Youth Passes ($203 second class, 5 travel days in two months; $273 for 10 travel days in two months; $316 for 21 days of unlimited travel).

Those over age 60 can take advantage of the ScanRail Senior Pass, which offers the travel bonuses of the ScanRail Pass and discounted travel ($258 second class, 5 days in two months; $348, 10 days in two months; $400, for 21 consecutive days). Buy ScanRail passes through Rail Europe and travel agents.

For car and train travel, price the ScanRail 'n Drive Pass: in two months you can get five days of unlimited train travel and two days of car rental (choice of three car categories) with unlimited mileage in Denmark, Norway, and Sweden. You can purchase extra car-rental days. Individual rates for two adults traveling together (economy car $399; compact car: $439; intermediate car: $449; all with second-class train travel) are considerably lower (about 25%) than those for single adults; the third or fourth person sharing the car needs to purchase only a ScanRail pass.

In Scandinavia you can use EurailPasses, which provide unlimited first-class rail travel in all of the participating countries for the duration of the pass. If you plan to rack up the miles, get a standard pass. These are available for 15 days ($588), 21 days ($762), one month ($946), two months ($1,338), and three months ($1,654). Eurail- and EuroPasses are available through travel agents and Rail Europe.

If you are an adult traveling with a youth under age 26 and/or a senior, consider buying a EurailSaver Pass; this entitles you to second-class train travel at the discount youth or senior fare, provided that you are traveling with the youth or senior at all times. A Saver pass is available for $498 (15 days), $648 (21 days), $804 (one month), $1,138 (two months), and $1,408 (three months).

In addition to standard EurailPasses, ask about special rail-pass plans. Among these are the Eurail YouthPass (for those under age 26), the Eurail FlexiPass (which allows a certain number of travel days within a set period), the EurailDrive Pass, and the EuroPass Drive (which combines travel by train and rental car).

Whichever pass you choose, remember that you must **purchase your pass before you leave** for Europe.

RESERVATIONS
🚅 **Where to Buy Rail Passes Rail Europe** ☎ 877/257-2887 in the U.S., 800/361-RAIL in Canada ⊕ www.raileurope.com ☎ 0870/837-1371 in the U.K. ⊕ www.raileurope.co.uk.

TRAVEL AGENCIES
A good travel agent puts your needs first. Look for an agency that has been in business at least five years, emphasizes customer service, and has someone on staff who specializes in your destination. In addition, **make sure the agency belongs to a professional trade organization.** The American Society of Travel Agents (ASTA) has more than 10,000 members in some 140 countries, enforces a strict code of ethics, and will step in to mediate agent-client disputes involving ASTA members. ASTA also maintains a directory of agents on its Web site; ASTA's TravelSense.org, a

trip-planning and travel-advice site, can also help to locate a travel agent who caters to your needs. (If a travel agency is also acting as your tour operator, *see* Buyer Beware *in* Tours & Packages.)

🗷 **Local Agent Referrals American Society of Travel Agents (ASTA)** ✉ 1101 King St., Suite 200, Alexandria, VA 22314 ☎ 800/965-2782 24-hr hotline, 703/739-2782 🖶 703/684-8319 ⊕ www. astanet.com and www.travelsense.org. **Association of British Travel Agents** ✉ 68-71 Newman St., London W1T 3AH ☎ 020/7637-2444 🖶 020/7637-0713 ⊕ www.abta.com. **Association of Canadian Travel Agencies** ✉ 130 Albert St., Suite 1705, Ottawa, Ontario K1P 5G4 ☎ 613/237-3657 🖶 613/237-7052 ⊕ www.acta.ca. **Australian Federation of Travel Agents** ✉ Level 3, 309 Pitt St., Sydney, NSW 2000 ☎ 02/9264-3299 or 1300/363-416 🖶 02/9264-1085 ⊕ www.afta.com.au. **Travel Agents' Association of New Zealand** ✉ Level 5, Tourism and Travel House, 79 Boulcott St., Box 1888, Wellington 6001 ☎ 04/499-0104 🖶 04/499-0786 ⊕ www. taanz.org.nz.

VISITOR INFORMATION

Learn more about foreign destinations by checking government-issued travel advisories and country information. For a broader picture, consider information from more than one country.

For U.S. Government travel advisories by mail, send a request letter to the U.S. Department of State that includes a self-addressed, stamped, business-size envelope.

🗷 **Tourist Information Norwegian Tourist Board** ✉ Charles House, 5 Lower Regent St., London SW1Y 4LR, U.K. ☎ 44/207-839-6255 🖶 44/207-839-6014 ✉ Stortorvet 10, 0105 Oslo, Norway ☎ 47/2414-4600 🖶 47/2414-4601 ⊕ www.norway.com. **Scandinavian Tourist Board** ✉ 655 3rd Ave., New York, NY 10017

☎ 212/885-9700 🖶 212/855-9710 ⊕ www. goscandinavia.com. **U.S. Department of State** ✉ Overseas Citizens Services Office, Room 4811 N.S., 2201 C St. NW, Washington, DC 20520 ☎ 202/647-5225 ⊕ travel.state.gov/travel/html.

🗷 **Government Advisories Australian Department of Foreign Affairs and Trade** ☎ 300/139-281 travel advisories, 02/6261-1299 Consular Travel Advice ⊕ www.smartraveller.gov.au or www.dfat.gov.au. **Consular Affairs Bureau of Canada** ☎ 800/267-6788 or 613/944-6788 ⊕ www.voyage.gc.ca. **New Zealand Ministry of Foreign Affairs and Trade** ☎ 04/439-8000 ⊕ www.mft.govt.nz. **U.K. Foreign and Commonwealth Office** ✉ Travel Advice Unit, Consular Directorate, Old Admiralty Bldg., London SW1A 2PA ☎ 0870/606-0290 or 020/7008-1500 ⊕ www.fco.gov.uk/travel. **U.S. Department of State** ✉ Bureau of Consular Affairs, Overseas Citizens Services Office, 2201 C St. NW, Washington, DC 20520 ☎ 888/407-4747 or 317/472-2328 for interactive hotline, 202/647-5225 ⊕ www.travel.state.gov.

WEB SITES

Do check out the World Wide Web when planning your trip. You'll find everything from weather forecasts to virtual tours of famous cities. Be sure to visit Fodors.com (⊕ www.fodors.com), a complete travel-planning site. You can research prices and book plane tickets, hotel rooms, rental cars, vacation packages, and more. In addition, you can post your pressing questions in the Travel Talk section. Other planning tools include a currency converter and weather reports, and there are loads of links to travel resources.

🗷 **Resources Norwegian Tourist Board** ⊕ www. visitnorway.com. **Oslo Visitors and Convention Bureau** ⊕ www.oslopro.no. **Royal Norwegian Embassy in the United States** ⊕ www.norway.org.

Oslo

1

WHAT SETS OSLO APART from other European cities is not so much its cultural traditions or its internationally renowned museums as its simply stunning natural beauty. How many world capitals have subway service to the forest, or lakes and hiking trails within city limits? But Norwegians will be quick to remind you that Oslo is a cosmopolitan metropolis with prosperous businesses and a thriving nightlife.

Once overlooked by travelers to Scandinavia, Oslo is now a major tourist destination and the gateway to what many believe is Scandinavia's most scenic country. That's just one more change for this town of 500,000—a place that has become good at survival and rebirth throughout its nearly 1,000-year history. In 1348 a plague wiped out half the city's population. In 1624 a fire burned almost the whole of Oslo to the ground. It was redesigned and renamed Christiania by Denmark's royal builder, King Christian IV. After that it slowly gained prominence as the largest and most economically significant city in Norway.

During the mid-19th century, Norway and Sweden were ruled as one kingdom, under Karl Johan. It was then that the grand main street that's his namesake was built, and Karl Johans Gate has been at the center of city life ever since. In 1905 the country separated from Sweden, and in 1925 an act of Parliament finally changed the city's name back to Oslo. Today, Oslo is Norway's political, economic, industrial, and cultural capital. The Norwegian royal family lives in Oslo, and it's where the Nobel peace prize is awarded.

Open-minded and outgoing, Oslo has increasingly embraced global and European trends. For urban souls there are cultural attractions, nightclubs, cafés, and trendy boutiques, and for outdoors enthusiasts there is hiking, sailing, golfing, and skiing within the vast expanse of parks, forests, and fjords that make up greater Oslo.

EXPLORING OSLO

Karl Johans Gate, starting at Oslo Sentralstasjon (Oslo Central Station, also called Oslo S Station and simply *Jernbanetorget,* or "railway station" in Norwegian) and ending at the Royal Palace, forms the backbone of downtown Oslo. Many of Oslo's major museums and historic buildings lie between the parallel streets of Grensen and Rådhusgata. To the southeast of the center of town is **Gamlebyen,** a historic district with a medieval church. West of downtown are **Frogner** and **Majorstuen,** residential areas known for their fine restaurants, shopping, cafés, galleries, and the Vigeland sculpture park. Southwest is the **Bygdøy Peninsula,** with a castle and five interesting museums that honor aspects of Norway's taste for exploration. Northwest of town is **Holmenkollen,** with its stunning bird's-eye view of the city and the surrounding fjords, a world-famous ski jump and museum, and three historic restaurants. On the more multicultural east side, where a diverse immigrant population lives alongside native Norwegians, are the Munch Museum and the Botanisk Hage og Museum (Botanical Gardens and Museum). The trendy neighborhood of **Grünerløkka,** with lots of cafés and shops, is northeast of the center.

Numbers in the text correspond to numbers in the margin and on the Oslo map.

If you have
1 day

Begin your day walking down Karl Johans Gate, Oslo's main prome- nade and a hive of activity in summer. Start from the **Royal Palace (Kon- gelig Slottet) ❶** ☞ and continue along until you reach Oslo S Station on the east end. In between these two points, take in **Oslo Univer- sity (Universitet) ❷** and **Stortinget ❻**, the Parliament building. In between these two attractions, you can turn south down Roald Amundsens Gate and pass the **Nationaltheatret (National Theater) ❺**, the spiritual home of Norwegian playwright Henrik Ibsen, to see murals inside the **Rådhuset ❼**. In the afternoon, walk to the rear of the town hall to view the magnificent Oslo fjord from one of the docked Viking ships at Aker Brygge, a disused shipyard area rebuilt into a shopping and commercial center.

If you have
2 days

Follow the itinerary above on Day 1, and on the second day take in the mu- seums at Bygdøy, farther west along the Oslo fjord. Catch Ferry 91 from Pier 3 at the rear of the Rådhuset beside Aker Brygge. Start with the open-air **Norsk Folkemuseum ㉚**, where you can wander among more than 170 examples of traditional wooden housing from as far back as the 14th century. Next visit the **Vikingskiphuset ㉛**, which has the best-preserved Viking ships in existence. Continue along to either the **Kon-Tiki Museum ㉝** to learn about the travels of famous Norwegian explorer Thor Heyerdahl, or the **Fram-Museet ㉜** to board the legendary polar vessel, *Fram*.

If you have
3 days

Follow the itineraries for Days 1 and 2 above. On Day 3 visit the **Vigelandsparken ㉔** sculpture park. Norwegian artist Gustav Vigeland (1869–1943) spent a life- time creating his masterwork—a glorious park with more than 200 bronze, granite, and steel sculptures. Afterward, take the T-bane line 1 to Oslo's ski fields at **Holmenkollen,** no matter what the season. Experience the **Hol- menkollbakken ㉖** ski museum, then head to the historic Frognerseteren restau- rant to sample Norwegian specialties like reindeer and salmon.

Downtown: The Royal Palace to City Hall

Although the city region is huge (454 square km [175 square mi]), downtown Oslo is compact, with shops, museums, historic buildings, restaurants, and clubs concentrated in a small, walkable center that's brightly illuminated at night.

a good
walk

From the **Royal Palace (Kongelige Slottet) ❶** ☞, walk east along Karl Jo- hans Gate, Oslo's main promenade. To your right is a large courtyard and three yellow buildings, which were part of the old **Universitet ❷**— today they are used only by the law school. Murals painted by Munch decorate the interior walls of these buildings. Around the corner from the university on Universitetsgata is the **Nasjonalgalleriet ❸**. You can enter to see a few of the hundreds of Norwegian, Scandinavian, and other Eu-

Oslo

KEY

🛈 Tourist information

▶ Start of walk

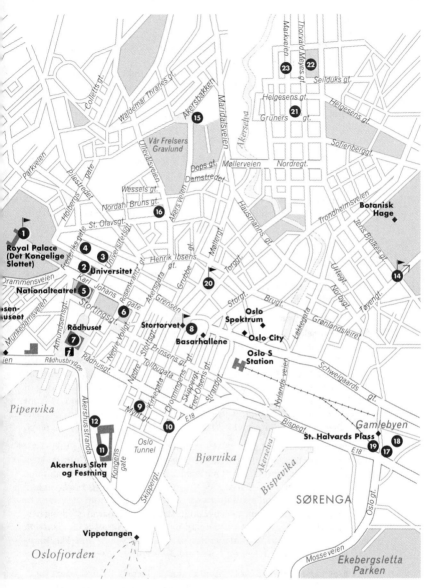

ropean works. To the rear of the National Gallery, across a parking lot, is a big cream-brick art nouveau–style building housing the **Historisk Museum ④**. Take an hour or so to view the impressive collection of Viking artifacts on display. Afterward, continue along Frederiksgate back to the university courtyard and cross Karl Johans Gate to Studenterlunden Park and the **Nationaltheatret ⑤**. This impressive building is not only the national theater, but a popular meeting place—many buses stop out front, and the suburban train line and T-bane (short for *tunnelbane*, which is an underground railway, or subway) is right beside it.

Walk farther down Karl Johans Gate to see **Stortinget ⑥**, the Norwegian Parliament, facing the castle. Then go back to Stortingsgata, the parallel street to Karl Johan on the other side of Stortinget. Head back in the direction of the Nationaltheatret and then turn left on Universitetsgata. Walk just a block to reach the redbrick **Rådhuset ⑦**, its two block towers a familiar landmark. After visiting Rådhuset, end your tour with an *øl* (beer) at one of the many outdoor cafés at Aker Brygge on the waterfront.

TIMING The walk alone should take no more than two hours. If you happen to be at the Royal Palace at midday, you might catch the changing of the guard, which happens every day at 1:30. Note that many museums are closed Monday.

What to See

▶ **❶ Det Kongelige Slottet** (The Royal Palace). At one end of Karl Johans Gate, the vanilla-and cream-color neoclassical palace was completed in 1848. Although generally closed to the public, the palace is open for guided tours in summer at 2 and 2:20 PM. The rest of the time, you can simply admire it from the outside. An equestrian statue of Karl Johan, King of Sweden and Norway from 1818 to 1844, stands in the square in front of the palace. ⊠ *Drammensvn. 1, Sentrum* ☎ *22–04–89–52* ⊕ *www. kongehuset.no* 🎫 *Tour NKr 90* ☉ *Mid-June–mid-Aug. (guided tours only).*

❹ Historisk Museum (Historical Museum). In partnership with the Vikingskiphuset (in Bygdøy), this forms the University Museum of Cultural Heritage, which concentrates on national antiquities as well as ethnographic and numismatic collections. See the intricately carved *stavkirke* (wood church) portals and exhibitions on subjects ranging from the Arctic to Asia. You can also gain a deeper understanding of Norway's Viking heritage through artifacts on display here. ⊠ *Frederiksgt. 2, Sentrum* ☎ *22–85–99–00* ⊕ *www.ukm.uio.no* 🎫 *NKr 40* ☉ *Mid-May–mid-Sept., Tues.–Sun. 10–4; mid-Sept.–mid-May, Tues.–Sun. 11–4.*

Ibsen-museet. Famed Norwegian dramatist Henrik Ibsen, known for *A Doll's House, Ghosts,* and *Peer Gynt,* among other classic plays, spent his final years here, in the apartment on the second floor, until his death in 1906. Every morning, Ibsen's wife, Suzannah, would encourage the literary legend to write before allowing him to head off to the Grand Café for his brandy and foreign newspapers. His study gives striking glimpses into his psyche. Huge, intense portraits of Ibsen and his Swedish archrival, August Strindberg, face each other. On his desk still sits his "devil's orchestra," a playful collection of frog and troll-like figurines that inspired him. Take a guided tour by well-versed and entertaining Ibsen scholars. Afterward, visit the museum's exhibition of Ibsen's drawings and paintings and first magazine writings. ⊠ *Arbiensgt. 1, Sentrum, across Drammensvn. from Royal Palace* ☎ *22–12–35–50* ⊕ *www.ibsenmuseet.no* 🖃 *NKr 50* ⊗ *Tues.–Sun., guided tours at noon, 1, and 2; June–Aug., additional guided tours at 11 and 3.*

★ ❸ **Nasjonalgalleriet** (National Gallery.) The gallery was recently amalgamated with the former National Museum of Art, Architecture, and Design. It houses Norway's largest collection of art created before 1945. The deep-red Edvard Munch room holds such major paintings as *The Dance of Life, Scream,* and several self-portraits. Classic fjord and country landscapes by Hans Gude and Adolph Tidemand—including *Bridal Voyage on the Hardangerfjord*—share space in galleries with other works by major Norwegian artists. The museum also has works by Monet, Renoir, Van Gogh, and Gauguin. ⊠ *Universitetsgt. 13, Sentrum* ☎ *22–20–04–04* ⊕ *www.nasjonalgalleriet.no* 🖃 *Free* ⊗ *Tues., Wed., and Fri. 10–6; Thurs. 10–8; weekends 10–5.*

❺ **Nationaltheatret** (National Theater). In front of this neoclassical theater, built in 1899, are statues of Norway's great playwrights, Bjørnstjerne Bjørnson, who also composed the national anthem, and Henrik Ibsen. Most performances are in Norwegian, so you may just want to take a guided tour of the interior, which can be arranged by appointment. Some summer performances are in English. ⊠ *Stortingsgt. 15, Sentrum* ☎ *22–00–14–00* ⊕ *www.nationaltheatret.no.*

❼ **Rådhuset** (City Hall). This redbrick building is best known today for the
FodorśChoice awarding of the Nobel peace prize, which takes place here every December.
★ In 1915, the mayor of Oslo made plans for a new City Hall, and ordered the clearing of slums that stood on the site. The building was finally completed in 1950. Inside, many museum-quality masterpieces are on the walls. After viewing the frescoes in the Main Hall, walk upstairs to the Banquet Hall to see the royal portraits. In the East Gallery, Per Krogh's mosaic of a pastoral scene covers all four walls, making you feel like you're part of the painting. On festive occasions, the Central Hall is illuminated from outside by 60 large spotlights that simulate daylight. ⊠ *Rådhuspl., Sentrum* ☎ *23–46–16–00* ⊕ *www.rft.oslo.kommune.no* 🖃 *NKr 40* ⊗ *May–Aug., daily 9–5; Sept.–Apr., daily 9–4.*

Stenersen-museet. Named for art collector Rolf E. Stenersen, this city-owned museum opened in 1994 displays highly regarded and sometimes provocative temporary exhibitions. It also houses three private art collections—including works by Edvard Munch—donated to the city at various times by Rolf E. Stenersen, Amaldus Nielsen, and Ludvig Ravensberg. ⊠ *Munkedamsvn. 15, Sentrum* ☎ *23–49–36–00* ⊕ *www.stenersen.museum.no* 🖃 *NKr 45* ⊗ *Tues. and Thurs. 11–7; Wed., Fri., and weekends 11–5.*

❻ **Stortinget** (Norwegian Parliament). Informative guided tours of this classic 1866 building are conducted daily in summer, and on Saturday the rest of the year. In front of the Parliament building, the park benches of Eidsvolls plass are a popular meeting and gathering place.

⊠ Munkedamsvn. 15, Sentrum ☎ 23–49–36–00 ⊕ www.stortinget. no ⊠ Free ⊙ Guided tours July–mid-Aug., weekdays at 10, 11:30, and 1; mid-Aug.–June, Sat. at 10, 11:30, and 1.

❷ Universitet (The University). The great hall in the middle building (there are three in all) is decorated with murals by Edvard Munch. Look for *The Sun,* which shows penetrating rays falling over a fjord. This building was the site of the Nobel peace prize award ceremony until 1989, when it was moved to the City Hall. *⊠ Aulaen, Karl Johans gt. 47, Sentrum ☎ 22–85–97–11 ⊠ Free ⊙ July, weekdays 10–2.*

Kvadraturen, Akershus Castle & Aker Brygge

The Kvadraturen is the oldest part of Oslo still standing. In 1624, after the town burned down for the 14th time, King Christian IV renamed the city Christiania and moved it from the area that is southeast of Oslo S Station, called Gamlebyen, rebuilding it adjacent to the Akershus fortress. In order to prevent future fires, the king decreed that houses were to be built of stone or brick instead of wood. He also built a stone wall around the rebuilt city to protect it from his enemies, the Swedes.

The Kvadraturen area, which includes Akershus Slott, is bound on the east side of the fortress by Skippergata and on the north side by Karl Johans Gate between Oslo Domkirke and Stortorvet. The boundary follows Øvre Vollgata around to the other side of the fortress. Kvadraturen translates roughly as "square township," which refers to the area's geometrically ordered streets. Be aware that the streets around Skippergata and Myntgata are a bit seedy and known as a mini red-light district at night.

Start at Stortorvet, the small market square outside the store GlasMagasinet. To the east of the square is **Oslo Domkirke ❽**, the city's landmark cathedral. Artists have been contributing to the cathedral's richly decorated interior since the 18th century.

From the cathedral, follow Kirkegata left past Karl Johans Gate to the **Museet for Samtidskunst ❾**, inside the 1906 Bank of Norway building. Spend time wandering through the museum's halls to admire both its art nouveau architecture and contemporary art. From the museum, take the side street Revierstredet to Dronningensgate, where there's a building that does not seem to fit in with its 17th-century neighbors. Designed and built in the early 1990s, this brick-and-steel office building houses the **Astrup Fearnley Museet for Moderne Kunst ❿**. The museum's permanent and temporary exhibitions emphasize modern art. Make a left into Dronningensgate and head up to Rådhusgata. Take a left and walk down the street. Keep an eye out for the 17th-century building at Rådhusgata 11. It houses the Statholdergaarden restaurant, in a building that was once the home of the *statholder,* the official representative from Copenhagen when Norway was under Danish rule.

Continue on Rådhusgata until you reach the corner of Nedre Slottsgate. The yellow building you see was originally the City Hall (1641), but since the 1800s has been Det Gamle Rådhus restaurant. Diagonally across Rådhusgata in two 17th-century buildings are an art gallery and a trendy, artsy café. The building that houses Kafé Celsius was one of the first buildings erected in Christian IV's town. Directly ahead is Christiana Torv—a re-creation of Christian IV's finger as he points to where the "new Oslo" was be built.

Turn left on Akersgata and walk alongside the grassy hill to the entrance of **Akershus Slott og Festning** ⑪, the center of Christian IV's Kvadraturen. It's a worthwhile stroll to the top for its incredible Oslo harbor-front and fjord views, especially at sunset. The castle became the German headquarters during the occupation of Norway in World War II, and many members of the Resistance were executed on the castle grounds. In a building next to the castle, at the top of the hill, is the **Norges Hjemmefront Museum** ⑫, which tells the gripping story of German occupation and Norwegian resistance.

For a break from history and architecture, walk over to **Aker Brygge** ⑬, the harbor in front of Akershus Castle. Aker Brygge is probably the most popular place in Oslo to enjoy a refreshing beer and a snack of shrimp during the long daylight hours of summer. You can sit at tables on the deck of one of the ships permanently docked in the bay, and window-shop in the boutiques surrounding the harbor.

TIMING   The walk alone will take at least three hours. Combined with museum visits and breaks, the itinerary could take the better part of a day. Akershus Slott will take at least half an hour. Try to do this tour during daylight hours, catching late-afternoon sun from atop the Akershus grounds. Finish the tour with a late lunch or early dinner at Aker Brygge.

What to See

⑬   **Aker Brygge.** This area was the site of a disused shipbuilding yard until
Fodor'sChoice   redevelopment saw the addition of residential town houses and a com-
★   mercial sector. Postmodern steel and glass buildings dominate the skyline now. The area has more than 40 restaurants and 60 shops, including upmarket fashion boutiques, as well as pubs, cinemas, theaters, and an indoor shopping mall. There is outdoor dining capacity of 2,500 as well as an open boulevard for strolling. Service facilities include banks, drugstores, and a parking lot for 1,600. ⊠ *Aker Brygge* ☎ *22–83–26–80* ⌨ *Free* ☉ *Shopping hrs weekdays 10–8, Sat. 10–6.*

⑪   **Akershus Slott og Festning** (Akershus Castle and Fortress). Dating to 1299, this stone medieval castle and royal residence was developed into a fortress armed with cannons by 1592. After that time, it withstood a number of sieges and then fell into decay. It was finally restored in 1899. Summer tours take you through its magnificent halls, the castle church, the royal mausoleum, reception rooms, and banqueting halls. ⊠ *Akershus Slott, Festningspl., Sentrum* ☎ *22–41–25–21* ⌨ *Grounds and concerts free, castle NKr 40* ☉ *Grounds: daily 6 AM–9 PM. Castle: May–mid-Sept., Mon.–Sat. 10–6, Sun. 12:30–4; mid-Sept.–Apr., Thurs. tours at 1. Guided tours: May–mid-Sept., daily at 11, 1, and 3; mid-Sept.–Apr., Thurs. at 1.*

⑩   **Astrup Fearnley Museet for Moderne Kunst** (Astrup Fearnley Museum for Modern Art). This privately funded museum opened in 1993 and earned an international reputation for its collections of postwar Norwegian and international art. In its smaller gallery, British artist Damien Hirst's controversial installation *Mother and Child Divided* is on display. The museum's permanent collection includes works by international artists, such as Yoko Ono and Jeff Koons, as well as Norwegians like Odd Nerdrum and Olav Christopher Jenssen. There's also a glassed-in sculpture garden with Niki de St. Phalle's sparrow and several other oversize 20th-century figures. ⊠ *Dronningensgt. 4, Sentrum* 🕾 *22–93–60–60* ⊕ *www. af-moma.no* 🕾 *Free* ☉ *Tues., Wed., and Fri. 11–5; Thurs. 11–7; weekends noon–5. Guided tours weekends at 1.*

off the beaten path

EMANUEL VIGELANDS MUSEET – Although he never gained the fame of his older brother Gustav, the creator of Vigeland Park, Emanuel is an artist of some notoriety. His alternately saucy, natural, and downright erotic frescoes make even the sexually liberated Norwegians blush. To get here, take the T-bane line 1 from Nationaltheatret Station toward Frognerseteren, and get off a Slemdal, one of Oslo's hillside residential neighborhoods. ⊠ *Grimelundsvn. 8, Slemdal, 20 mins north of city center via T-bane* 🕾 *22–14–57–88* ⊕ *www. emanuelvigeland.museum.no* 🕾 *NKr 30* ☉ *Sun. noon–4.*

❾ Museet for Samtidskunst (National Museum of Contemporary Art). A stunning granite-and-marble example of art nouveau architecture, this 1906 former bank building is the largest museum of postwar Norwegian and international art. Its ornate gilded interior contrasts with the modern and contemporary art shown in its permanent and temporary exhibitions. The permanent collection of 4,700 works spans the genres of graphic art, drawing, photography, sculpture, decorative arts, installations, and video. Take time to ponder the two fascinating permanent installations: Ilya Kabakov's *The Garbage Man* and Per Inge Bjøørlo's *Inner Room V.* ⊠ *Bankpl. 4, Sentrum* 🕾 *22–86–22–10* ⊕ *www.museumsnett.no/ mfs* 🕾 *Free* ☉ *Tues., Wed., and Fri. 10–5; Thurs. 10–8; Sat. 11–4; Sun. 11–5. Guided tours by appointment only.*

⓬ Norges Hjemmefront Museum (Norwegian Resistance Museum). Striped prison uniforms, underground news sheets, and homemade weapons tell the history of the resistance movement that arose before and during Norway's occupation by Nazi Germany. A gray, winding path leads to two underground stone vaults in which models, pictures, writings, and recordings trace the times between Germany's first attack in 1940 to Norway's liberation on May 8, 1945. Every year, on the anniversaries of these dates, Norwegian resistance veterans gather here to commemorate Norway's dark days and honor those who lost their lives. The former ammunitions depot and the memorial lie at the exact spot where Norwegian patriots were executed by the Germans. ⊠ *Akershus Slott, Sentrum* 🕾 *23–09–31–38* ⊕ *www.nhm.mil.no* 🕾 *NKr 30* ☉ *Mid-Apr.–mid-June, Mon.–Sat. 10–4, Sun. 11–4; mid-June–Aug., Mon., Wed., Fri., and Sat. 10–5, Tues. and Thurs. 10–6, Sun. 11–5; Sept., Mon.–Sat. 10–4, Sun. 11–4; Oct.–mid-Apr., weekdays 10–3, weekends 11–4.*

❽ Oslo Domkirke (Oslo Cathedral). Consecrated in 1697 as Oslo's third cathedral, this dark-brown brick structure has been Oslo's main church ever since. The original pulpit, altarpiece, and organ front with acanthus carvings still stand. Take a look at the endless ceiling murals made between 1936 to 1950 and stained-glass windows by Emanuel Vigeland. In the 19th century the fire department operated a lookout from the bell tower, which you can visit. ⊠ *Stortorvet 1, Sentrum* ☎ *23–31–46–00* 🖂 *Free* ⊙ *Daily 10–4.*

need a break? **Pascal Konditori** (⊠ Tollbugt. 11, Sentrum ☎ 22–42–11–19), a trendy, Parisian-style patisserie inside an old-fashioned Norwegian *konditori* (café), is known for its French coffee, homemade pastries, and ice cream. It's a place to see and be seen.

Munch Museum & Damstredet

The Munch Museum is east of the city center in Tøyen, an area in which Edvard Munch spent many of his years in Oslo. The Tøyen district has a much different feel than Oslo's cushy west side—it's ethnic and more industrial.

West of Tøyen, north of the city center near Vår Frelsers Gravlund, is the quiet, old-fashioned district of Damstredet, one of the few areas with original, 18th-century wooden houses.

a good walk Start by taking any T-bane from the city center (Sentrum) to Tøyen, where **Munchmuseet** ⑭ ► sits on a hill near the Botanisk Hage, a quiet oasis of plants and flowers. After visiting the museum, head back to town center. Take the T-bane and get off at Stortinget.

Head down Karl Johans Gate and take a right onto Akersgata. Follow it past the offices of *Aftenposten,* Norway's leading daily paper. As you head up the hill, you can see a huge rotund building, Deichmanske Bibliotek, the city's library, to your right. Continue along Akersveien and veer to your right as you pass Saint Olav's Church. Next head down Dops Gate and Damstredet—they are some of the city's oldest streets, with well-preserved houses dating from the 18th century when this area was a shantytown. Today the neighborhood has developed into an artist community. On your left is Vår Frelsers Gravlund (Our Savior's Graveyard), where you can seek out the gravestones of many famous Norwegians, including Ibsen and Munch. At the graveyard's northeastern corner is **Gamle Aker Kirke** ⑮, the city's only remaining medieval church.

After visiting the church, walk along the north side of the cemetery and then take a left onto Ullevålsveien. Take the road down the hill to the corner of St. Olavs Gate and Akersgata, where you'll find the **Kunstindustrimuseet** ⑯, one of Europe's oldest museums of decorative arts and design.

TIMING The Munch Museum will take up most of the morning, especially if you take a guided tour. The second half of the tour, through Damstredet, is a perfect way to spend a summer Sunday afternoon. Things are quiet, and locals tend to stroll around this area when the weather is nice. You can see the rest of the sights in a couple of hours.

What to See

★ ⑮ **Gamle Aker Kirke** (Old Aker Church). Dating to 1100, this medieval stone basilica is Oslo's oldest church—it's still in use as a parish church. Inside, the acoustics are outstanding, so inquire about upcoming concerts. ⊠ *Akersbakken 26, Bislett* ☎ *22–69–35–82* ⊕ *www.orgnett.no/kor/gak* ☞ *Free* ⊙ *Mon.–Sat. noon–2, Sun. 9* AM–11 AM.

⑯ **Kunstindustrimuseet** (Museum of Decorative Arts and Design). Rich Baldishol tapestries from 1100, Norwegian dragon-style furniture, and royal apparel (including Queen Sonja's wedding gown from 1968) make this a must-see museum. Founded in 1876, it also has exquisite collections of Norwegian 18th-century silver, glass, and faience. A contemporary Scandinavian section follows the history of design and crafts in the region. ⊠ *St. Olavs gt. 1, Sentrum* ☎ *22–03–65–40* ☞ *NKr 25, special exhibits NKr 65* ⊙ *Tues., Wed., and Fri. 11–4; Thurs. 11–7; weekends 11–4.*

▶ ⑭ **Munchmuseet** (Munch Museum). Edvard Munch, Norway's most famous
Fodor'sChoice artist, bequeathed his enormous collection of works (about 1,100 paint-
★ ings, 3,000 drawings, and 18,000 graphic works) to the city when he died in 1944. The museum is a monument to his artistic genius, housing the largest collection of his works and changing exhibitions. Munch actually painted several different versions of *The Scream,* the image for which he known best. An important one of his Scream paintings, as well as another painting, *The Madonna,* were stolen from the Munch Museum in an armed robbery in 2004 and have yet to be recovered. While most of the Munch legend focuses on the artist as a troubled, angst-ridden man, he moved away from that pessimistic and dark approach to more optimistic themes later in his career. ⊠ *Tøyengt. 53, Tøyen* ☎ *23–49–35–00* ⊕ *www.munch.museum.no* ☞ *NKr 60* ⊙ *June–mid-Sept., daily 10–6; mid-Sept.–May, weekdays 10–6, weekends 11–5.*

Gamlebyen & Grønland

If you've got a yen for history and archaeology, visit Gamlebyen (the Old Town), to the southeast of the center. Sometimes referred to as the "Pompeii of Scandinavia," Gamlebyen contains the last remains of medieval Oslo. Self-guided tour brochures for Gamlebyen can be picked up at the tourist office in Sentrum. North of Gamlebyen is the hip and multicultural neighborhood of Grønland. If Oslo has broken your budget, you may be glad to discover Grønland—it has the cheapest dining, drinking, and shopping in the city. If your time is limited, however, you need not plan to spend much time in either neighborhood. Gamlebyen is somewhat off the beaten track, and some of the ruins are barely discernible. Grønland can be sampled at night with dinner at an ethnic restaurant preceded or followed by a drink in a pub.

a good walk

To get to Gamlebyen, you can take trikk (cable car) 18 or 19 from beside Oslo S Station and get off at St. Halvard's plass, or walk for about 40 minutes through Grønland. To walk, head down Storgata, just north of Oslo S Station, and take a right down Brugata. Walk east down Brugata to find Vietnamese grocers alongside Middle-Eastern take-out stores and African silk and textile traders. Grønland has a number of

STEALING MUNCH

ON AUGUST 22, 2004, *Norway lost a national icon when armed robbers stole Edvard Munch's painting, The Scream from the Munch Museum in the Tøyen neighborhood of Oslo. Two masked thieves entered the museum in broad daylight, pulled the work and another painting, The Madonna, off the wall as guards and visitors watched, and sped away in a waiting vehicle. The car was later recovered outside some nearby tennis courts, along with the gun that was used to threaten museum staff during the robbery. Neither the paintings nor the thieves have been found, however, and the crime has left Norway and the art world wondering how security at a major museum could have failed to protect some of Norway's most important national treasures. Museum security has since been beefed up, but is it enough? Norwegian paintings have been the target of art thieves in the past.*

On the opening day of the 1994 Winter Olympic Games in Lillehammer, another Scream painting—Munch painted four versions altogether—was stolen from the Norwegian National Gallery. The painting was later discovered undamaged in a hotel room, and three suspects were arrested.

In an incident in 1988, The Vampire was stolen from the Munch Museum but was later recovered. And most recently, in March 2005 three Munch paintings were taken from a hotel in Moss, in southern Norway. These were also recovered, three days after the theft.

Despite this series of thefts, Norway is known for being a very safe country where people often leave their doors unlocked and where public parks and monuments, such as the Royal Palace, don't have gates. Until the late 1990s

Norway continually recorded insignificant crime rates. Police numbers, even in the capital of Oslo, were considered low compared to other European cities, and armed robbery continues to be rare. As the country moves toward modernization, however, one side effect has been an increase in unemployment, inner-city drug problems and crime.

While officials in Oslo work toward keeping the general crime rate low, investigators are still looking for The Scream and The Madonna, which are worth an estimated $19 million together. In April 2005, three men were arrested for the crime but the paintings are still missing.

As was expected, the Munch Museum revealed that the stolen paintings were not insured against theft. Indeed, many international galleries and collectors do not insure their art, either because they cannot afford to pay for insurance or they don't think they will need it. Theft continues to plague the art world, however, at least in galleries where security is minimal. Thousands of famous paintings and works of art are displayed uninsured across galleries worldwide, and an estimated $8 billion worth of art is stolen each year.

A year after The Scream disappeared, the Munch Museum announced the completion of a $6 million security upgrade that took 10 months to put into place. Visitors to the museum can expect to find metal detectors and bulletproof glass in front of some much safer paintings.

what Norwegians call *brun* (brown) pubs. These small, often dingy establishments serve the cheapest beer in town and are popular with local students. (*See* Nightlife.)

Brugata becomes Grønlandsleiret. Next, go over Schweigaards Gate to St. Halvards plass. During the 13th century, this area was the city's ecclesiastical center. Also here are the intact foundations of **St. Halvards Kirke** ╠, which dates from the early 12th century. Other ruins, including Korskirke and Olavs Kloster, lie in **Minneparken** ⑱. Nearby on Bispegata is **Oslo Ladegård** ⑲, a restored baroque-style mansion that sits on foundations of a 13th-century bishop's palace.

If you continue south, you'll find the oldest traces of human habitation in Oslo: the 5,000-year-old carvings on the runic stones near Ekebergsletta Park. They are across the road from the park on Karlsborgveien and are marked by a sign reading FORTIDSMINNE. To reach the park, walk south on Oslogate until it becomes Mosseveien. The stones will be on your right. The park is a good spot to rest your feet and end your tour.

TIMING You can walk through Grønland in 40 minutes and see the Gamlebyen sights in an hour. It's a 20- to 25-minute walk from Gamlebyen to the runic stones at Ekebergslettaparken. You can also take Tram 19 from St. Halvards plass for 10 stops to Ljabrua.

What to See

⑱ **Minneparken.** Oslo was founded by Harald Hardråde ("Hard Ruler") in 1048, and the earliest settlements were near what is now Bispegata, a few blocks behind Oslo S Station. Ruins are all that's left of the city's former religious center: the **Korskirke** (Cross Church; ✉ Egedesgt. 2), a small stone church dating from the end of the 13th century; **Olavs Kloster** (Olav's Cloister; ✉ St. Halvards pl. 3), built around 1240 by Dominican monks; and **Olavskirken** (Olav's Church; ✉ Egedesgt. 4), remnants of a 13th-century stone church. ✉ *Entrance at Oslogt. and Bispegt, Gamlebyen* 🎟 *Free* ⊙ *Sun. noon–2.*

⑲ **Oslo Ladegård.** The original building, the 13th-century Bispegård (Bishop's Palace), burned down in the famous 1624 fire, but its vaulted cellar survived. The present mansion was restored and rebuilt in 1725; it now belongs to the city council and contains scale models of 16th- to 18th-century Oslo. ✉ *St. Halvards pl., Oslogt. 13, Gamlebyen* ☎ *22–19–44–68* 🎟 *NKr 40* ⊙ *Late May–mid-Sept., Tues., Thurs., and Fri. 2–4; Wed. 2–6; guided tours Sun. at 4.*

⑰ **St. Halvards Kirke** (St. Halvard's Church). This medieval church, named for the patron saint of Oslo, remained the city's cathedral until 1660. ✉ *Minneparken, entrance at Oslogt. and Bispegt, Gamlebyen.*

Grünerløkka

Once a simple working-class neighborhood north of the center, Grünerløkka has undergone a revival since the '90s and now hosts a number of trendy bars, cafés, eateries, eclectic galleries, and gift stores. Popular with young people, the area is now known as Oslo's little

Greenwich Village. Take a shopping tour here during the day or come for dinner and a drink at night.

A Good Walk

Begin your tour just north of the city center at **Youngstorget** ㉒ ▶, the market square on Torggata, just north of Karl Johans Gate. The headquarters of Oslo's main political parties, as well as national union and employee organizations, surround this square.

Walk north along Torggata past Henrik Ibsen's Gate and note Rockefeller Music Hall on your left. Oslo's best medium-size live-music venue also hosts film and quiz nights midweek. Continue for three blocks to cross Akerbrua (Aker Bridge), where artist Dyre Vaa's bronze figures bring to life traditional Norwegian fairy tales, such as *Peer Gynt*. Across the bridge, veer to your right past a restaurant called Delicatessen. In summer you'll find its wall of windows open to the sidewalk. This is a great place to stop for a tapas lunch.

Turn left at Thorvald Meyers Gate and continue for three blocks. This street has several popular bars and is quite busy at night. You'll see a grassy square called Olaf Ryes plass on your left, and near that, on Gruners Gate, the **Parkteatret** ㉑, an old movie house converted into a hip café/bar. Back on Thorvald Meyers Gate, continue north to explore the shops, such as Boa, at No. 50, Probat at No. 24, and Rebella at No. 52.

Farther on to your right, stop for lunch at Fru Hagen Café and admire its classical-looking chandeliers and elegant velvet sofas. Alternatively, try the Mexican eatery Mucho Mas next door, or Hotel Havana, a Cuban-inspired delicatessen that also sells Norwegian fish products. Rest your feet at **Birkelundenparken** ㉒ at the next block. In summer, hundreds of locals sit in the park grilling Norwegian hot dogs on portable barbecues. Oslo council even has special garbage bins designed to hold the smoldering remains of *en-gang griller* (single-use grills).

At the top of the park, turn left down Schleppegrells Gate, then left again down **Markveien** ㉓ to begin the return leg of your journey. The Markveien strip of Grünerløkka hosts fewer restaurants but more galleries and gift stores.

TIMING The walking tour around Grünerløkka will take around two hours, not including shopping time. To skip the 15-minute walk from the center to Grünerløkka, catch Tram 12 from Oslo S Station for six stops and get off at Olav Ryes plass.

What to See

㉒ **Birkelundenparken.** This green lung and center of Grünerløkka features concerts, fairs, weekend markets, and political rallies in summer, as well as the usual host of stripped-down sun worshippers. The square and fountain were built in the late 19th century by merchant Thorvald Meyer and city planner G. A. Bull. ✉ *Off Thorvald Meyers gt., Grünerløkka.*

㉓ **Markveien.** This street hosts fewer restaurants but more galleries and gift stores than Thorvald Meyers Gate. **Galleri Markveien,** at No. 26, displays the work of the commercially successful artist Tone Granberg, who uses the same abstract motif in every one of her paintings. Visit **Lene Middelthon** next door, a glassblower with a distinctively Scandinavian style. Farther along Markveien, other shopping highlights include **Panda** for Asian pottery, silks, and furniture; and the **Ceramo Sculpture Gallery,** which sells African artifacts that are functional as well as aesthetically pleasing. **Den Kule Mage** (The Round Stomach) at No. 55 has every maternal item a mother could need and features Norway's only baby café, smartly decorated as a nursery. **Markveien Mat og Vinhus** is a highly recommended restaurant where you can sample delicacies such as giant Russian crab or Norwegian quail. ⊠ *Off Schleppegrells gt., Grünerløkka.*

㉑ Parkteatret. This atmospheric art deco–style movie house (built in 1907) has been converted into a funky bar, café, restaurant, and venue. Live music gigs, literary evenings, films, and theater are held in the converted cinema room inside, which has seating for 250. To get a sense of the laid-back Grünerløkka lifestyle, chill out here with a cocktail. Free jazz is held on weekends in the front bar. ⊠ *Olaf Reyes pl. 11, Grünerløkka* ☎ *22–35–63–00* ⊕ *www.parkteatret.no* ▧ *Free* ☉ *Daily, noon until performances end (around 1* AM*).*

㉒ Youngstorget. Cafés, eateries, and shops line the bazaar at the rear of this square, which has been used as an active marketplace on weekends to sell food and other wares since 1850. Large-scale exhibitions showcasing art, sport, fashion, and street culture are held here in summer and autumn. The square is also a starting point for political demonstrations. ⊠ *Torggata, Sentrum* ☎ *23–48–33–10* ⊕ *www.youngstorget.com.*

Frogner, Majorstuen & Holmenkollen

Among the city's most stylish neighborhoods, Frogner and Majorstuen combine classic Scandinavian elegance with contemporary European chic. Hip boutiques and galleries coexist with embassies and ambassadors' residences on the streets near and around Bygdøy Allé. Holmenkollen, the hill past Frogner Park, has the famous ski jump and miles of ski trails.

Catch the No. 15 Majorstuen *trikk* (cable car) from Nationaltheatret on the Drammensveien side of the Royal Palace grounds. You can also take the No. 15 from Aker Brygge.

Opposite the southwest end of the palace grounds is the triangular U.S. Embassy, designed by Finnish-American architect Eero Saarinen and built in 1959. Look to the right at the corner of Drammensveien and Parkveien for a glimpse of the venerable Nobel Institute. Since 1905 these stately yellow buildings have been the secluded setting where the five-member Norwegian Nobel Committee decides who will win the Nobel peace prize. The library is open to the public.

To walk from the southwest end of the palace grounds to Frognerparken, head east away from the city to the roundabout intersecting four roads and turn right down Frognerveien. This road winds through the pleasant, leafy district of Frogner, passing cafés, a bar, a cinema, and some impressive houses. After a 30-minute walk, or about 12 blocks, you will reach the corner of Frognerparken, also called **Vigelandsparken** ㉔ ▶, with the Oslo Bymuseum directly ahead of you.

TOURS IN & AROUND OSLO

ICKETS FOR ALL TOURS are available at both **Oslo tourist offices** (☎ 24–14–77–00), in Oslo S Station and in Sentrum. All tours, except HMK's Oslo Highlights tour, operate in summer only.

Starting at noon and continuing at 45-minute intervals until 10 PM, the **Oslo Train,** which looks like a chain of dune buggies, leaves Aker Brygge for a 30-minute ride around the town center. The train runs daily in summer. Contact a tourist center for departure times.

Boat Tours

Taking a boat tour in and around the Oslo fjords is a memorable way to see the capital. **Cruise-Båtene** (✉ Rosenkrantz gt. 22, Sentrum ☎ 22–42–36–98) organizes fjord excursions for all occasions on modern luxury or older restored vessels. The **Norway Yacht Charter** (✉ Rådhusbrygge 3, Sentrum ☎ 23–35–68–90) arranges lunch or evening tours or dinner cruises for anywhere from 12 to 600 passengers. **Viking Cruise** (✉ Skogfaret 20 B, Ullern ☎ 22–73–31–21) offers chartered tours on sailing yachts or replica Viking ships that serve traditional viking fare.

Bus Tours

Båtservice Sightseeing (✉ Rådhusbryggen 3, Sentrum ☎ 23–35–68–90) has a bus tour, five cruises, and one combination tour. Tickets for bus tours can be purchased on the buses. **HMK Sightseeing** (✉ Hegdehaugsvn. 4, Majorstuen ☎ 23–15–73–00) offers several bus tours in and around Oslo. Tours leave from the Tourist Information Center at Vestbanen; combination boat-bus tours depart from Rådhusbrygge 3, the wharf in front of City Hall.

Helicopter Tours

For a bird's-eye view of Oslo, take a helicopter tour with **Pegasus** (✉ Gardermoen Vest ☎ 64–81–92–00).

Private Guides

Guideservice (✉ Akershusstranda 35, Sentrum ☎ 22–42–70–20) caters to large groups in and around Oslo, and prices start at NKr 1,150 for a two-hour tour. **Oslo Guidebureau** (✉ Nedre Slottsgt. 13, Sentrum ☎ 22–42–28–18) specializes in guiding VIP clients and business delegations, and prices start at NKr 1,050 for two hours. **OsloTaxi** (☎ 02323) gives private car tours from NKr 250 per hour.

Special-Interest Tours

For an exhilarating experience, tour the forests surrounding Oslo (the marka) by dogsled. Both lunch and evening winter tours are available through **Norske Sledehundturer** (✉ Einar Kristen Aas, 1514 Moss ☎ 69–27–56–40 🖷 69–27–37–86). The tourist information center can arrange four- to eight-hour motor safaris through the marka, and in winter **Vangen Skistue** (✉ Laila and Jon Hamre, Fjell, 1404 Siggerud ☎ 64–86–54–81) can arrange an old-fashioned sleigh ride (in summer, they switch to carriages).

Walking Tours

Organized walking tours are available through **Oslo City and Nature Walks** (✉ Elgefaret 70B, 1362 Hosle ☎ 41–31–87–40 ⊕ www.oslowalks.no). Authorized city guides with acting experience lead you on themed walks, including a ghost walk through the old Kvadraturen area, exploring the creepier parts of Oslo's history. Contact **Oslo Byantikvar** (☎ 23–46–02–50), at the Antiquities Department of Oslo, for information on guided tours of Gamlebyen.

Walk through the front gates of the park and continue about 100 yards toward the monolith ahead. You'll find yourself in a stunning sculpture garden designed by one of Norway's greatest artists, Gustav Vigeland. You can study the method to Vigeland's madness at **Vigelandsmuseet** ㉕. Cross the street to the **Oslo Bymuseum** ㉖ for a cultural and historical look at the city and its development. After you leave the museum, take a left on Kirkeveien and continue past Frogner Park to the Majorstuen underground station, near the intersection of Bogstadveien. Here you have two options: you can walk down Bogstadveien, look at the shops, explore the Majorstuen area, and then take the Holmenkollen line of the T-bane to Frognerseteren; or you can skip the stroll down Bogstadveien and head right up to Holmenkollen. The train ride up the mountain passes some stunning scenery. If you have children, you may want to make a detour at the first T-bane stop, Frøen, and visit the **Internasjonale Barnekunstmuseet** ㉗.

Continue on the T-bane to the end of the line. This is Frognerseteren—a popular skiing destination on winter weekends. The Tryvann ski center is another kilometer farther up the mountain. The view of the city here is spectacular. The restaurant Frognerseteren also has a great view of Oslo. Downhill is **Holmenkollbakken** ㉘, where Norway's most intrepid skiers prove themselves every March during the Holmenkollen Ski Festival.

TIMING This is a good tour for Monday, since the museums mentioned are open, unlike most others in Oslo. You will need a whole day for Frogner and Majorstuen since there is some travel time involved. The trikk ride from the city center to Frogner Park takes about 15 minutes; the T-bane to Frognerseteren takes about 20 minutes. You're no longer in the compact city center, so distances between sights are greater. The walk from Frognerseteren to Holmenkollbakken is about 15 minutes and is indicated with signposts. Try to save Holmenkollen, with its magnificent views, for a clear day.

What to See

㉘ **Holmenkollbakken** (Holmenkollen Ski Museum and Ski Jump). A distinctive **Fodor'sChoice** part of the city's skyline, Oslo's ski jump holds a special place in the hearts ★ of Norwegians. Originally built in 1892, it was reconstructed for the 1952 Winter Olympics, and is still a popular site for international competitions; it also attracts a million visitors every year. Take the elevator and walk to the top for the view that skiers have in the moment before they take off. Back down at the base of the jump, turn right, past the statue of King Olav V on skis, to enter the oldest ski museum in the world. A hands-on exhibition awaits you, with alpine and cross-country skis, poles, and bindings that have been used through the ages. See the earliest skis, from AD 600; explorer Fridtjof Nansen's wooden skis from his 1888 Greenland crossing; and the autographed specimens used by retired champion Bjørn Daehlie. Then, head to the ski simulator outside for the thrilling sensation of a ski jump. ✉ *Kongevn. 5, Holmenkollen* ☎ *22–92–32–00* ⊕ *www.skiforeningen.no* 🎫 *NKr 50* ⊗ *Jan.–Apr. and Oct.–Dec., daily 10–4; May and Sept., daily 10–5; June–Aug., daily 9–8.*

🌙 **27** **Internasjonale Barnekunstmuseet** (International Museum of Children's Art). A brainchild of Rafael Goldin, a Russian immigrant, the museum showcases her collection of children's drawings from more than 150 countries. You can see the world though the eyes of a child in its exhibitions of textiles; drawings; paintings; sculptures; and children's music, dancing, and other activities. ⊠ *Lille Frøens vei 4, Blindern* ☎ *22–46–85–73* ⊕ *www.childrensart.com* 🎫 *NKr 50* ⊙ *Late June–early Aug., Tues.–Thurs. and Sun. 11–4; mid-Sept.–mid-Dec. and late Jan.–late June, Tues.–Thurs. 9:30–2, Sun. 11–4.*

26 **Oslo Bymuseum** (Oslo City Museum). One of the world's largest cities, Oslo has changed and evolved greatly over its thousand years. A two-floor, meandering exhibition covers Oslo's prominence in 1050, the Black Death that came in 1348, the great fire of 1624 and subsequent rebuilding, and the urban development of the 20th century. Among the more interesting relics are the red coats that the first Oslo police, the watchmen, wore in 1700, and the first fire wagon in town, which appeared in 1765. Plan to visit the museum near the beginning of your stay for a more informed understanding of the Norwegian capital. ⊠ *Frognervn. 67, Frogner* ☎ *23–28–41–70* ⊕ *www.oslobymuseum.no* 🎫 *NKr 50* ⊙ *Wed.–Sun. noon–4, Tues. 10–7.*

Skøytemuseet (Ice Skating Museum). Tucked away in Frogner Stadium, this is Norway's only museum devoted to ice skates and ice-skaters. Gleaming trophies, Olympic medals, and skates, skates, and more skates serve to celebrate the sport. Photographs of skating legends such as Johan Olav Koss, Hjalmar Andersen, and Oscar Mathisen line the walls. Take a look at ways that skates have evolved—compare the bone skates from 2000 BC to the wooden skates that came later. ⊠ *Frogner Park, Middelthunsgt. 26, Majorstuen* ☎ *22–43–49–20* ⊕ *www.oslosk.no/museet.htm* 🎫 *NKr 20* ⊙ *Tues. and Thurs. 10–2:30, Sun. 11–2.*

need a break?

Generations of families have warmed themselves by the open fires of **21 Frognerseteren** (⊠ Holmenkollen 200 ☎ 22–92–40–40) with a cup of hot chocolate after a long day skiing on the slopes. This restaurant and lookout occupies a special place in the hearts of Norwegians. The two-story log cabin has earthy wooden tables decked with iron candelabras, and traditional rosemaling and taxidermied animals adorning the walls. Try to get a seat on the upper floor to enjoy the view over the Oslo fjord, or use the telescopes on the terrace.

25 **Vigelandsmuseet.** "I am anchored to my work so that I cannot move. If I walk down the street one day a thousand hands from work hold on to me. I am tied to the studio and the road is never long," said Gustav Vigeland in 1912. This museum was the Norwegian sculptor's studio and residence. It houses models of almost all his works as well as sculptures, drawings, woodcuts, and the original molds and plans for Vigeland Park. Wander through this intense world of enormous, snowy-white plaster, clustered nudes, and busts of such famous Norwegians as Henrik Ibsen and Edvard Grieg. ⊠ *Nobelsgt. 32, Frogner* ☎ *23–49–37–00* ⊕ *www.vigeland.museum.no* ✉ *NKr 45* ⊙ *Sept.–May, Tues.–Sun. noon–4; June–Aug., Tues.–Sun. 11–5.*

㉔ **Vigelandsparken** (Vigeland's Park). Also known as Frogner Park, Vige-

Fodor'sChoice landsparken has 212 bronze, granite, and wrought-iron sculptures by
★ Gustav Vigeland (1869–1943). Most of the stunning park sculptures are placed on a nearly 1-km-long (½ mi-long) axis and depict the stages of life: birth to death, one generation to the next. See the park's 56-foot-high granite *Monolith Plateau,* a column of 121 upward-striving nude figures surrounded by 36 groups on circular stairs. The most beloved sculpture is a bronze of an enraged baby boy stamping his foot and scrunching his face in fury. Known as *Sinnataggen* (*The Angry Boy*), this famous statue has been filmed, parodied, painted red, and even stolen from the park. It is based on a 1901 sketch Vigeland made of a little boy in London. ⊠ *Kirkevn., Frogner* ☎ *23–49–37–00* ⊕ *www.vigeland. museum.no* ✉ *Free* ⊙ *Daily.*

Bygdøy

Several of Oslo's best-known historic sights are concentrated on the Bygdøy Peninsula (west of the city center), as are several beaches, jogging paths, and the royal family's summer residence.

a good walk

The most pleasant way to get to Bygdøy—available from May to September—is to catch Ferry 91 from the rear of the Rådhuset on Pier 3. Times vary, so check with Trafikanten (☎ 177) for schedules. Another alternative is to take Bus 30, marked "Bygdøy," from Stortingsgata at Nationaltheatret along Drammensveien to Bygdøy Allé, a wide avenue lined with chestnut trees. The bus passes Frogner Church and several embassies on its way to Olav Kyrres plass, where it turns left, and soon left again, onto the peninsula. The royal family's summer residence, actually just a big white frame house, is on the right. Get off at the next stop, Norsk Folkemuseum. The pink castle nestled in the trees is **Oscarshall Slott** ㉙ ►, once a royal summer palace.

The **Norsk Folkemuseum** ㉚ consists of an open-air museum as well as some indoor exhibits of folk art. Around the corner from the museum, to the right, is the **Vikingskiphuset** ㉛, one of Norway's most popular attractions; it houses some of the best-preserved Viking-era remains yet discovered.

Follow signs on the road to the **Fram-Museet** ㉜, a pyramid-shape structure resembling a Viking boathouse. After viewing the exhibitions, you can watch a panoramic movie about Norway's maritime past at the Norsk Sjøfartsmuseum. Across the parking lot is the older **Kon-Tiki Museum** ㉝, with Thor Heyerdahl's famous raft, along with the papyrus boat *Ra II.* You can get a ferry back to the City Hall docks from the dock in front of the Fram-Museet. If your children are squirming to break out of the museum circuit, entertain the thought of a trip to Tusenfryd, an amusement park packed with rides.

TIMING   Block out a day for Bygdøy. You could spend at least half a day at the Folkemuseum alone. Note that the museums on Bygdøy tend to be open daily, but close early. The tour bus company HMK conducts an afternoon trip to Tusenfryd, so count on spending half a day. It takes between 10 and 20 minutes to reach the park from downtown Oslo by bus. If you decide to go on your own from Oslo S Station, you might want to spend a leisurely day in the area by touring the surrounding beaches and grounds.

What to See

★ ⓒ ㉜ **Fram-Museet.** Once known as the strongest vessel in the world, the enormous, legendary Norwegian polar ship *Fram* has advanced farther north and south than any other surface vessel. Built in 1892, it made three arctic voyages conducted by Fridtjof Nansen (1893–96), Otto Sverdrup (1898–1902), and Roald Amundsen (1910–12). Climb on board and peer inside the captain's quarters, which has explorers' sealskin jackets and other relics on display. Surrounding the ship are many expedition artifacts. ⊠ *Bygdøynes, Bygdøy* ☎ *23–28–29–50* ⊕ *www.fram. museum.no* ⌧ *NKr 40* ☉ *Jan.–Apr., daily 10–3:45; May–mid-June, daily 10–5:45; mid-June–Aug., daily 9–6:45; Sept., daily 10–4:45; Oct.–Dec, daily 10–3:45.*

★ ⓒ ㉝ **Kon-Tiki Museum.** The museum celebrates Norway's most famous 20th-century explorer. Thor Heyerdahl made a voyage in 1947 from Peru to Polynesia on the *Kon-Tiki*, a balsa raft, to lend weight to his theory that the first Polynesians came from the Americas. His second craft, the *Ra II*, was used to test his theory that this sort of boat could have reached the West Indies before Columbus. The museum also has a film room and artifacts from Peru, Polynesia, and the Easter Islands. ⊠ *Bygdøynesvn. 36, Bygdøy* ☎ *23–08–67–67* ⊕ *www.kon-tiki.no* ⌧ *NKr 45* ☉ *Apr., May, and Sept., daily 10:30–5; June–Aug., daily 9:30–5:45; Oct.–Mar., daily 10:30–4.*

ⓒ ㉚ **Norsk Folkemuseum** (Norwegian Folk Museum). This is one of the largest open-air museums in Europe, and a perfect way to see Norway in a day. From the stoic stave church to farmers' houses made of sod, the old buildings here span Norway's regions and history as far back as the 14th century. Indoors, there's a fascinating display of folk costumes. The displays of richly embroidered, colorful *bunader* (national costumes) from every region includes one set at a Telemark country wedding. The museum also has stunning dragon-style wood carvings from 1550 and some beautiful rosemaling. The traditional costumes of the Sámi (Lapp) people of northern Norway are exhibited around one of their tents. If you're visiting in summer, inquire about Norwegian Evening, a summer program of folk dancing, guided tours, and food tastings. On Sundays in December, the museum holds Oslo's largest Christmas market. ⊠ *Museumsvn. 10, Bygdøy* ☎ *22–12–37–00* ⊕ *www.norskfolke.museum. no* ⌧ *NKr 90* ☉ *Mid-Sept.–mid–May, weekdays 11–3, weekends 11–4; mid-May–mid-Sept., daily 10–6.*

ⓒ **Norsk Sjøfartsmuseum** (Norwegian Maritime Museum). Norwegian fishing boats, paintings of fishermen braving rough seas, and intricate ship models are all on display here. The arctic vessel *Gjøa* is docked outside. The breathtaking, panoramic movie *The Ocean: A Way of Life* delves into Norway's unique coastal and maritime past. Also on display is the model of the Kvaldor boat (AD 600), a 19th-century armed wooden warship (*Kong Sverre*), and a modern-day tanker. ⊠ *Bygdøynesvn. 37, Bygdøy* ☎ *22–43–82–40* ⊕ *www.norsk-sjofartsmuseum.no* 🖃 *NKr 40* ⊙ *Mid-May–Aug., daily 10–6; Sept.–mid-May, Mon–Wed. and Fri.–Sun. 10:30–4, Thurs. 10:30–6.*

㉙ **Oscarshall Slott.** This small country palace was built (1847–52) in eccentric English Gothic style for King Oscar I. There's a park, pavilion, fountain, and stage on the grounds. The original interior has works by the Norwegian artists Adolph Tidemand and Hans Gude. ⊠ *Oscarshallvn., Bygdøy* ☎ *22–56–15–39* 🖃 *NKr 20* ⊙ *Late May–mid-Sept., Tues., Thurs., and Sun. noon–4.*

off the beaten path

TUSENFRYD – At Norway's foremost amusement park, the thrills are many. In May 2001 ThunderCoaster, a huge wooden roller coaster with the steepest drop in Europe, opened here. The tour bus company H. M. Kristiansen Automobilbyrå (HMK) provides an afternoon bus excursion from the Tourist Information Center. There's also a shuttle bus that departs from Oslo Bussterminalen Galleriet, the city's main bus station, which is right by Oslo S Station. ⊠ *Vinterbro* ☎ *64–97–64–00* ⊕ *www.tusenfryd.no* 🖃 *NKr 185* ⊙ *Early June–mid-Aug., daily 10:30–7; May and late Aug., weekends 10:30–7; Sept., weekends 11–5; Oct. 1–9, daily 11–5.*

㉛ **Vikingskiphuset** (Viking Ship Museum). The Viking legacy in all its glory lives on at this classic Oslo museum. Chances are you'll come away fascinated by the three blackened wooden Viking ships *Gokstad, Oseberg,* and *Tune,* which date to AD 800. Discovered in Viking tombs around the Oslo fjords between 1860 and 1904, the boats are the best-preserved Viking ships ever found and have been exhibited since the museum's 1957 opening. In Viking times, it was customary to bury the dead with food, drink, useful and decorative objects, and even their horses and dogs. Many of the well-preserved tapestries, household utensils, dragon-style wood carvings, and sledges were found aboard ships. The museum's rounded white walls give the feeling of a burial mound. Avoid summertime crowds by visiting at lunchtime. ⊠ *Huk Aveny 35, Bygdøy* ☎ *22–13–52–80* ⊕ *www.ukm.uio.no* 🖃 *NKr 40* ⊙ *May–Sept., daily 9–6; Oct.–Apr., daily 11–4.*

WHERE TO EAT

You can find nearly every type of cuisine in Oslo, from traditional Norwegian to sushi and Mexican. Many Oslo chefs have developed menus based on classic Norwegian recipes but with exciting variations, like Asian or Mediterranean cooking styles and ingredients. You may read about "New Scandinavian" cuisine on some menus—a culinary style that combines seafood and game from Scandinavia with spices and sauces from any other country. Fusion and crossover cooking have come to stay, even in fast-food restaurants.

Spend at least one sunny summer afternoon harborside at Aker Brygge eating shrimp and watching the world go by. Floating restaurants serve shrimp in bowls with baguettes and mayonnaise. Or better still, buy steamed shrimp off the nearby docked fishing boats and plan a picnic in the Oslo fjords or Vigeland or another of the city's parks. Note that some restaurants close for a week around Easter, in July, and during the Christmas holiday season.

Prices

WHAT IT COSTS In Norwegian Kroner					
	$$$$	$$$	$$	$	¢
AT DINNER	over 270	230–270	180–230	110–180	under 110

Prices are for a main course at dinner including tax and a service charge.

Downtown: Royal Palace to the Parliament

Restaurants downtown along Karl Johans Gate cater to tourists and offer a range of cuisines, including Indian, Chinese, and traditional Norwegian. Many are high-quality restaurants, and prices are generally steep.

$$$$ ✕ **Restaurant Eik.** This is Norway's first smoke-free restaurant, although cigar smoke would not be out of place here, among the plush chairs, deep-red sofa, somber artwork, and soft music. The food, in contrast, is thoroughly up-to-date. Three- and five-course prix-fixe menus change daily but might include lightly smoked wild salmon served with pasta and asparagus or chicken served with tarragon and corn puree. ⊠ *Hotel Savoy, Universitetsgt. 11, Sentrum* ☎ *23–33–54–50* ▤ *AE, DC, MC, V* ☉ *Closed Sun., Mon., and July.*

$$$–$$$$ ✕ **Babette's Gjestehus.** Near City Hall, this restaurant's dark-blue walls and lace curtains make it resemble an old-fashioned Norwegian living room. French chef Dominique Choquet serves Scandinavian and international dishes with flair. Try the reindeer fillet in port sauce, lamb with apricots, or monkfish. The staff is friendly and welcoming. ⊠ *Rådhuspassasjen, Fridtjof Nansens pl. 2, Sentrum* ☎ *22–41–64–64* ▤ *AE, DC, MC, V* ☉ *Closed Sun. and July. No lunch.*

$$–$$$ ✕ **Oro.** One of the city's hottest restaurants, Oro ("gold" in Spanish)
Fodor'sChoice was opened by celebrity chef Terje Ness in 2000. Ness has since resigned
★ following a fallout with the restaurant's investors, but Oro's unique Mediterranean menu and cool airy design remains. Large chandeliers hang over tables surrounded by slip-covered chairs. Contemporary art hangs on the walls and a fireplace burns at eye level. You can order à la carte or try the Taste of Oro prix-fixe menu (a 7- or 12-course dinner). Specialties include steak, game, and fowl. For dessert, savor the delicious Chocolate Oro—chocolate mousse with passion fruit, topped with gold leaf. ⊠ *Tordenskjolds gt. 6, Sentrum* ☎ *23–01–02–40* ⌕ *Reservations essential* ▤ *AE, DC, MC, V* ☉ *Closed Sun. No lunch.*

$$–$$$ ✕ **A Touch of France.** As its name suggests, this wine bar near the Parliament building is straight out of Paris. The waiters' long, white aprons; the art nouveau interior; old French posters; and closely packed tables all add to the illusion. The tempting menu includes a delicious, steaming-hot bouillabaisse and duck confit. ☒ *Øvre Slottsgt. 16, Sentrum* ☎ *23–10–01–65* ☐ *AE, DC, MC, V.*

$–$$$ ✕ **Terra Bar & Restaurant.** Spanish pottery and earth tones hint at the Mediterranean-inspired dishes served here. Across the street from the Parliament building, it attracts its share of politicians. Half the menu is fish, such as oven-baked salmon stuffed with sea scallops and baked cod with lobster sauce. A special treat is the Tired of Everything dessert: homemade vanilla ice cream topped with warm espresso syrup. ☒ *Stortingsgt. 2, Sentrum* ☎ *22–40–55–20* ☐ *AE, DC, MC, V* ☺ *No lunch July–mid-Aug.*

$–$$ ✕ **Dinner.** The simple name belies the fact that this is one of the best places
Fodor'sChoice in Oslo for Chinese food, as well as dishes that combine Norwegian and
★ Cantonese styles. Peking duck is a speciality here, or, for a lighter meal, try the delectable platter of seafood in chili-pepper sauce. ☒ *Stortingsgt. 22, Sentrum* ☎ *23–10–04–66* ☐ *AE, DC, MC, V* ☺ *No lunch.*

¢–$ ✕ **Vegeta Vertshus.** This innovative buffet-style vegetarian restaurant opposite the national theater was established in 1938. Vegeta Vertshus is a godsend for vegetarians in a town with meat- and fish-centric menus. A wide variety of meals are on offer here, including vegetarian pasta dishes, pizza, curries, and quiches. ☒ *Munkedamsvn. 3B, Sentrum* ☎ *22–83–42–32* ☐ *AE, DC, MC, V.*

¢ ✕ **Kaffistova.** Norwegian home cooking is served cafeteria-style at this downtown restaurant on the first floor of the Hotell Bondeheimen. Daily specials come in generous portions and include soup and a selection of entrées. There is always at least one vegetarian dish, as well as fish and, usually, homemade meatballs. ☒ *Hotell Bondeheimen, Rosenkrantz gt. 8, Sentrum* ☎ *23–21–42–10* ☐ *AE, DC, MC, V.*

Kvadraturen & Aker Brygge

If you're after typical Norwegian dining, try the restaurants around Kvadraturen in Sentrum (the center), which offer very traditional meals in typical Norwegian settings. The patrons are mostly locals and the food is usually quite simple, based on seasonal fish and game. Aker Brygge caters to tourists and young professionals with pricier restaurants that have a more international flavor, without being too daring or trendy.

$$$$ ✕ **Statholdergaarden.** Onetime Bocuse d'Or champion Bent Stiansen's Asian-inspired French dishes have long been popular with locals. The six-course gastronomic menu changes daily; you can also order from the à la carte menu. Try his sesame-roasted duck breast with ginger sauce or the panfried perch with tomato cannelloni. More than 400 years old, the rococo dining room is one of Norway's largest and seats 75 people. ☒ *Rådhusgt. 11, Sentrum* ☎ *22–41–88–00* ⌂ *Reservations essential* ⋔ *Jacket and tie* ☐ *AE, DC, MC, V* ☺ *Closed Sun. and 3 wks in July.*

★ $$$–$$$$ ✕ **Lofoten Fiskerestaurant.** Named for the Lofoten Islands off the northwest coast, this Aker Brygge restaurant is considered one of Oslo's best for fish, from salmon to cod to monkfish. It has a bright, fresh, minimalistic interior with harbor views and a summertime patio. From January through March, try the cod served with its own liver and roe; April through September, the shellfish; and from October through December, the lutefisk. Call ahead, since sometimes only large groups are served. ⊠ *Stranden 75, Aker Brygge* ☎ *22–83–08–08* ▭ *AE, DC, MC, V.*

$$$–$$$$ ✕ **Solsiden.** Meaning "sunny side," Solsiden's main claim to fame is that it receives more hours of daylight than restaurants on the opposite side of the wharf at Aker Brygge. With live lobster tanks and an open-air setting, Solsiden is a great place to go for alfresco seafood. There's a magnificent seafood platter for NKr 560. The restaurant is only open in spring and summer. ⊠ *Søndre Akershuskai 34, Aker Brygge* ☎ *22–33–36–30* ▭ *AE, DC, MC, V* ☺ *Closed Oct.–Mar.*

$$–$$$$ ✕ **Engebret Café.** This somber old-fashioned restaurant at Bankplassen was a haunt for bohemian literati at the turn of the 20th century and the building itself dates from the 17th century. The formal, French-tinged Norwegian dinner menu includes traditional seasonal fare around *Juletide* (Christmastime), including lutefisk and *pinnekjøtt* (sticks of meat), which is lamb steamed over branches of birch. For a real taste of Norway, try the *smalahove* (a whole sheep's head). Many Norwegian families consider it a treat to visit the restaurant around Christmas, so book early if that's your plan, too. During the rest of the year, try the reindeer in cream sauce or the poached catfish. ⊠ *Bankpl. 1, Sentrum* ☎ *22–82–25–25* ▭ *AE, DC, MC, V.*

$–$$$ ✕ **Det Gamle Rådhus.** Inside Oslo's City Hall, built in 1641, this is the city's oldest restaurant. Its reputation is based mostly on traditional fish and game dishes. An absolute must, if you're lucky enough to be visiting at the right time, is the house specialty, the pre-Christmas lutefisk platter. The backyard has a charming outdoor area for dining in summer. ⊠ *Nedre Slottsgt. 1, Sentrum* ☎ *22–42–01–07* ▭ *AE, DC, MC, V* ☺ *Closed Sun.*

¢–$$ ✕ **Sushi & Wok.** The sushi bar trend took a while to get to Oslo, but it's now firmly entrenched. This minimalist restaurant is one of a chain. Traditional nigiri-sushi and maki rolls garner rave reviews from aficionados. Try the Sushi Moriawase, which includes 10 assorted sushi and six maki rolls. You can drop by for "Sushi Happy Hour" between 3 and 7 for three specially priced meals. ⊠ *Bryggetorget 7, Aker Brygge* ☎ *22–83–63–51* ▭ *AE, DC, MC, V.*

Tøyen & Grønland

The most internationally diverse group of restaurants can be found east of downtown, particularly in multicultural Tøyen and Grønland. This area also has the most reasonable dining prices in Oslo.

$$$–$$$$ ✕ **Klosteret.** The name of this popular east-side restaurant means "the cloisters." Its not-very-medieval, informal dining room is in a spacious, candlelit, rounded brick cellar. Pictures of saints and other religious figures adorn the walls, and Gregorian chants play in the background. The handwoven menus, bound to look like hymnals, contain a list of appealing meat and fish dishes, plus a daily vegetarian option. Consider the baked cod with puree of Jerusalem artichoke and marinated beet. Three-course dinners cost NKr 425. ⊠ *Fredensborgvn. 13, Sentrum* ☎ *23–35–49–00* ▭ *AE, DC, MC, V* ☺ *Closed Sun. and July.*

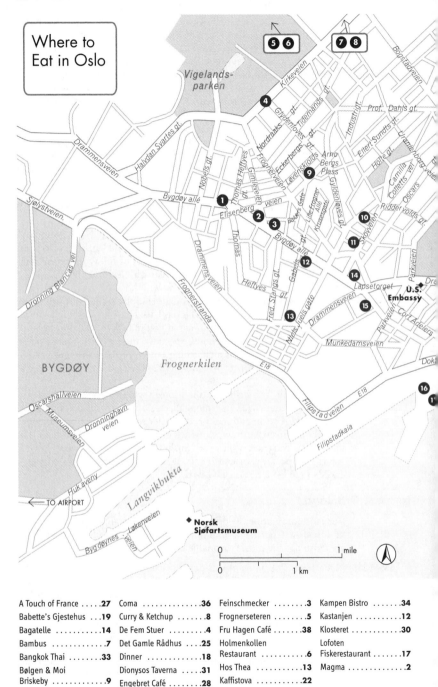

Where to
Eat in Oslo

Vigelands-
parken

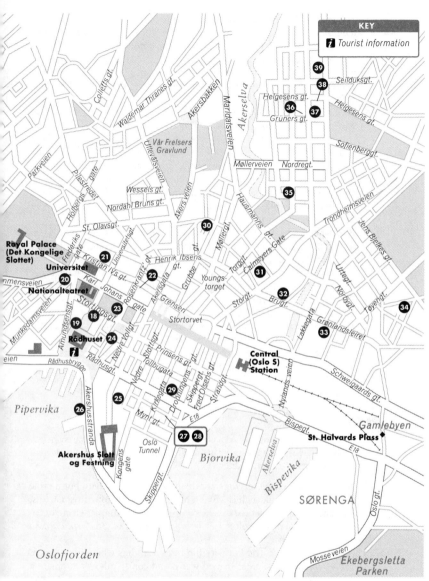

KEY

Tourist information

$ ✕ **Bangkok Thai.** Some of the best Thai food in Oslo can be had here, including *tom yum*, a hot-and-sour seafood-based soup; Thai beef salads; and all varieties of curry. Spacious and carefully decorated with Thai paintings and artifacts, this restaurant is a bit more upmarket than other eateries in this neighborhood. Sharp service here makes for pleasant dining. ✉ *Grønlandsleiret 27, Grønland* ☎ *22–17–70–03* ▭ *MC, V* ⊙ *Closed Mon.*

★ **$** ✕ **Dionysos Taverna.** Owner Charalambos Eracleous imports fresh fish, wine, and ouzo from Greece to serve at his cobalt-blue-and-white-washed restaurant. The *tzatziki* (yogurt and cucumber salad), souvlaki, and moussaka are authentically prepared, as are the more unusual casseroles, such as *exohiko* (lamb baked with red wine, tomatoes, and onions). For a taste of everything, order *mezes*, Greek-style tapas. A bouzouki trio accompanies your dining experience on Thursday, Friday, and Saturday nights. ✉ *Calmeyersgt. 11, Sentrum* ☎ *22–60–78–64* ▭ *MC, V* ⊙ *No lunch.*

$ ✕ **Kampen Bistro.** On the first floor of the community house in this traditionally working-class area, Kampen Bistro offers simple but tasty Mediterranean-inspired dishes in an unpretentious and cozy setting. The friendly staff, reasonable prices, and slightly corny interior have made this neighborhood café a hit with locals. Menus change daily, but the three-course special is always a feast. ✉ *Bøgata 21, Kampen* ☎ *22–19–77–08* ▭ *MC, V.*

¢ ✕ **Punjab Tandoori.** Plastic tables, a kitschy decor, and a refrigerator that hums will not suit picky diners. However, the homemade tandoori is a treat here, and prices go as low as NKr 60 for a main course. You may have to wait for a table as local Indians also recognize the value of Punjab Tandoori—always a good sign. ✉ *Grønland 24, Grønland* ☎ *22–17–20–86* ▭ *MC, V.*

Grünerløkka

Grünerløkka, just north of the center, is Oslo's up-and-coming artsy neighborhood. Most of its restaurants serve modern versions of Norwegian fare and international dishes.

$$ ✕ **Mucho Mas.** Large servings are the order of the day here but a table may be hard to find, such is Mucho Mas's popularity. Burritos, nachos, and quesadillas are served as spicy as you like in a simple setting decorated with cool pastel colors. ✉ *Thorvald Meyers gt. 36, Grünerløkka* ☎ *22–37–16–09* ▭ *AE, DC, MC, V.*

$–$$ ✕ **Coma.** This eccentric but very hip restaurant has white, blue, green, and purple ceiling lights, striped walls, and comfy pillows to create a dreamy mood. Tongue-in-cheek signs over the door are there to let you know when you are entering and when you are leaving the coma. Try one of the fish dishes on the French-inspired menu. ✉ *Helgesensgt. 16, Grünerløkka* ☎ *22–35–32–22* ▭ *AE, DC, MC, V.*

$–$$ ✕ **Markveien Mat og Vinhus.** This restaurant in the heart of the Grünerløkka district serves fresh French-inspired cuisine. It's a relaxed, artsy place with a bohemian clientele. Paintings cover the yellow walls, and the tables are laid with white linen. The menu lists delicacies such as giant Russian crab and Norwegian quail. For a special treat, try the home-made cheesecake. ✉ *Torvbakkgt. 12, entrance on Markvn. 57, Grün-erløkka* ☎ *22–37–22–97* ⊟ *AE, DC, MC, V* ☾ *Closed Sun.*

$–$$ ✕ **Sult.** Trendy, Norwegian, bohemian informality is the essence of this small restaurant, whose name means "hunger." Large windows, small square tables, and a simple homemade look attract students and writers. Try one of the fish or pasta specials. Next door, the bar-lounge, appropriately named *Tørst* (thirst), has it own unique blended drinks, including Raspberry Parade, a blend of raspberry juice, champagne, and vodka. ✉ *Thorvald Meyers gt. 26, Grünerløkka* ☎ *22–87–04–67* ⊟ *AE, DC, MC, V.*

$ ✕ **Fru Hagen Café.** Classic chandeliers and elegant velvet sofas decorate this old-fashioned café and restaurant. The fare is light and inexpensive—American-style hamburgers, pastas, and spicy chicken salads, for example. At night, Fru Hagen doubles as a bar with a DJ. ✉ *Thorvald Meyers gt. 40, Grünerløkka* ☎ *22–35–67–87* ⊟ *AE, DC, MC, V.*

Frogner & Majorstuen

Some of Oslo's best restaurants are here in the wealthier western side of the city. The upmarket international dining scene includes many French-inspired kitchens.

$$$$ ✕ **Bagatelle.** Chef and owner Eyvind Hellstrøm has established an in-
FodorsChoice   ternational reputation for his modern Norwegian cuisine and superb ser-
★   vice. Bagatelle attracts the who's who of Oslo society, and is widely recognized as one of the city's best restaurants. Paintings by contemporary Norwegian artists accent the understated, elegant dining room. The three-, five-, and seven-course menus change daily. The lobster is always a standout. ✉ *Bygdøy Allé 3, Frogner* ☎ *22–12–14–40* ⊟ *AE, DC, MC, V* ☾ *Closed Sun. mid-July–mid-Aug. No lunch.*

$$$$ ✕ **Feinschmecker.** The name is German, but the food is international and Scandinavian. Modern and stylish, the dining room's warm, earthy tones give it a cozy look. Owners Lars Erik Underthun, one of Oslo's foremost chefs, and Bengt Wilson, a leading food stylist, make sure the food looks as good as it tastes. Feinschmecker is a haven for vegetarians with a three-course menu of local produce that changes according to the season. ✉ *Balchensgt. 5, Frogner* ☎ *22–12–93–80* ⌂ *Reservations essential* ⊟ *AE, DC, MC, V* ☾ *Closed Sun. and last 3 wks July. No lunch.*

$$$$ ✕ **Restaurant Le Canard.** Behind the Royal Castle, this elegant restaurant is in what looks like a brick manor house. Inside are such antique furnishings as a stained-glass window by Maria Vigeland, the wife of Emanuel. Chef Trond Andresen shows off his simple, French-inspired compositions in a menu that changes weekly. The wine cellar of 30,000 bottles includes rare champagne from 1928. In summer you can dine in special style on Le Canard's stunning garden terrace. ✉ *Pres. Harbitz gt. 4, Frogner* ☎ *22–54–34–00* ⌂ *Reservations essential* ⊟ *AE, DC, MC, V* ☾ *Closed Sun. No lunch.*

$$–$$$ ✕ **Bølgen & Moi Briskeby.** Restaurateurs Toralf Bølgen and Trond Moi
FodorsChoice   have a winner in this minimalistic restaurant. If you're tired of eating
★   breakfast in your hotel, rise and shine here instead. Housed in a former

power station, the restaurant incorporates the past with a long, eye-catching cement dining table and open fires. Well-known Norwegian artists such as photographer Knut Bry showcase their work in the restaurant's bar, brasserie, and formal dining room. Try the oversize Thorenfeldt burger, or the three-course set menu, which changes daily. Most dishes are cooked in the wood-burning oven in the corner. ⊠ *Løvenskioldsgt. 26, Frogner* ☎ *24–11–53–53* ▤ *AE, DC, MC, V* ☺ *Closed Sun. and Mon.*

★ **$$–$$$** ✕ **Hos Thea.** An intimate yet lively dining experience awaits in this white-and-blue restaurant with a fleur-de-lis motif. From the open kitchen, owner Sergio Barcilon and the other chefs often serve the French and Spanish food themselves. The small menu lists four or five choices for each course, but every dish is superbly prepared. Noise and smoke levels can be high at night. ⊠ *Gabelsgt. 11, entrance on Drammensvn., Skillebekk* ☎ *22–44–68–74* ⌂ *Reservations essential* ▤ *AE, DC, MC, V* ☺ *No lunch.*

$$–$$$
Fodor'sChoice
★
✕ **Magma.** Vibrant, warm, and intense, the orange- and yellow-splashed interior captures the character of this Mediterranean restaurant-bar and its celebrity chef, Sonja Lee. Fresh from successes in London and Provence, Lee and partner Laurent Surville (also a chef) opened Magma in April 2000. It has become one of the city's hottest restaurants, attracting everyone from businesspeople to artists. The changing menu is based on seasonal ingredients and follows the owners' philosophy of rough-hewn simplicity. Consider the ricotta ravioli and the spit-roasted veal with macaroni gratin. There is also live jazz on Sunday starting at 11 AM. ⊠ *Bygdøy Allé 53, Frogner* ☎ *23–08–58–10* ▤ *AE, DC, MC, V.*

$$–$$$ ✕ **Palace Grill & Palace Reserva.** A tiny, eight-table restaurant near the Royal Palace, the Palace Grill is one of the most fashionable spots on the Oslo dining scene. Don't let the "grill" part fool you: it may be relaxed, but its French-inspired cuisine is certainly not fast food. The original Palace Grill doesn't take reservations and is usually full, so try to get here before 5 PM for a table. Alternatively, reserve a table at its new sister restaurant, the more spacious and slightly less expensive Palace Reserva. ⊠ *Solligt. 2, off Drammensvn., Frogner* ☎ *22–56–14–02* ▤ *AE, DC, MC, V* ☺ *Closed Sun. and Mon.*

★ **$$** ✕ **Kastanjen.** This rustic, laid-back Frogner bistro, named after the chestnut trees that line the street, is the kind every neighborhood needs. Try the Norwegian white fish *kveite* with bacon as a main course and the homemade sorbet for dessert. The warmly lighted downstairs lounge serves drinks and light snacks. ⊠ *Bygdøy Allé 18, Frogner* ☎ *22–43–44–67* ▤ *AE, DC, MC, V* ☺ *Closed Sun. and July.*

$ ✕ **Bambus.** Vietnamese owner Heidi NGuyen and her friendly staff have all lived and cooked throughout Asia, and "Bamboo" reflects this: the menu has delicious and authentic Thai, Japanese, Vietnamese, and Chinese dishes. Try the tom yum soup for a starter and the teppanyaki for a main course. The *banh tom ho tay* (Vietnamese shrimp and sweet-potato pancakes) and *kaeng phets* (duck, shrimp, or lamb in coconut milk and vegetables) are both good. The yellow, orange, and pink interior has a bamboo floor and Andy Warhol–type prints in an Asian theme. ⊠*Kirkevn. 57, Majorstuen* ☎ *22–85–07–00* ▤ *AE, DC, MC, V* ☺ *No lunch.*

$ ✕ **Village Tandoori.** Walking through this restaurant feels like a night-time wander through an Indian or Pakistani village, about a hundred years ago. Pakistani owner Mobashar Hussain has collected antique rugs, including vibrant silk ones with embroidery and beadwork. The chicken and lamb curries and tandooris are delicious. ✉ *Bygdøy Allé 65, Frogner* ☎ *22–56–10–25* ▤ *AE, DC, MC, V* ⊘ *No lunch.*

¢–$ ✕ **Curry & Ketchup.** Just down the road from the elegant, pan-Asian Bambus, this popular, boisterous Indian restaurant is cozy and homely, with tiny tables that seem almost stacked on top of each other, and plates, glasses, and cutlery that rarely match. The menu holds few surprises, but the basic north-Indian fare, from *rogan josh* (Kashmiri lamb curry) to *palak paneer* (spinach-and-cheese curry), comes in generous portions, and is reasonably priced. That's probably why the clientele is generally more cheerful than the notoriously grumpy but efficient staff. The lamb curry and chicken *tikka masala* (marinated in a tomato, coconut milk, and curry sauce) are also delicious. ✉ *Kirkevn. 51, Majorstuen* ☎ *22–69–05–22* ▤ *MC, V.*

¢–$ ✕ **Pizza da Mimmo.** Named for owner Domenico Giardina, aka Mimmo,
Fodor'sChoice this is Oslo's best pizzeria. In 1993, Mimmo, who's originally from Calabria, was the first to bring thin-crust Italian pizza to the city. Taste his perennially popular panna and prosciutto pizza, and the Pizza Calabrigella. The casual restaurant is on the basement level in a white-brick building; earthy colors, hanging rugs, and small cellar windows give it a cavelike appearance. ✉ *Behrensgt. 2, Frogner* ☎ *22–44–40–20* ⤷ *Reservations essential* ▤ *AE, DC, MC, V.*

Holmenkollen

This small wealthy neighborhood is a 15-minute drive northwest of the center, halfway into the forest. It's a popular place for downhill and Nordic skiing, and the few restaurants here are popular in winter and serve hearty, traditional Norwegian meals.

$$$–$$$$ ✕ **De Fem Stuer.** Near the famous Holmenkollen ski jump, in the his-
Fodor'sChoice toric Holmenkollen Park Hotel, this restaurant has first-rate views and food. Chef Jørn Dahl's modern Norwegian dishes have strong classic roots. The fish dishes, particularly those made with salmon, cod, and wolffish, are his specialty. Try the four-course menu called A Taste of Norway to get exactly that. ✉ *Holmenkollen Park Hotel, Kongevn. 26, Holmenkollen* ☎ *22–92–27–34* ⤷ *Jacket and tie* ▤ *AE, DC, MC, V.*

$$–$$$$ ✕ **Holmenkollen Restaurant.** An old-fashioned, luxury mountain cabin café, restaurant, and banquet hall, this Oslo institution dates to 1892. The spacious café is perfect for an afternoon coffee and cake after walking or skiing. In the smaller, formal restaurant, dishes come from the hands of well-known chef Harald Osa. The menu focuses on Norwegian fish and game dishes served with innovative sauces. ✉ *Holmenkollvn. 119, Holmenkollen* ☎ *22–13–92–00* ▤ *AE, DC, MC, V.*

$–$$ ✕ **Frognerseteren.** Just above the Holmenkollen ski jump and therefore with sweeping mountain views, this is possibly Oslo's most famous restaurant. Popular with locals and travelers, it specializes in fish and game. The scrumptious apple cake is legendary, and perfect for dessert or for an afternoon treat with coffee. Eating reindeer in brown sauce with local *tittebær* (red berries) at Frognerseteren would have to be the ultimate Norwegian experience. Take the Holmenkollbanen to the end station and then follow the signs downhill to the restaurant. ⊠ *Holmenkollvn. 200, Holmenkollen* ☎ *22–92–40–40* ⊟ *DC, MC, V.*

WHERE TO STAY

"Comfort and convenience at a cost" is a perfect characterization of Oslo hotels. Most lodgings, from the elegant Radisson SAS classics to the no-frills Rainbows, are central, just a short walk from Karl Johans Gate. Many are between the Royal Palace and Oslo S Station, with the newer ones closer to the station. For a quiet stay, choose a hotel in either Frogner or Majorstuen, elegant residential neighborhoods behind the Royal Palace and within walking distance of downtown.

Television and phones can be expected in most Oslo hotel rooms. Typical Oslo hotels operate on the European Plan, that is, rates are for a double room without breakfast.

Prices
Special summer and weekend rates may save you money. Consider cutting costs by buying an Oslo Card, which entitles you to discounts and free public transportation throughout the city. Inquire at hotel chains about their discount programs. Through the Rainbow and Norlandia hotels, you can purchase the money-saving Scan+ Hotel Pass. The pass entitles you to receive up to a 50% discount and a fifth night free at 200 of their hotels in Scandinavia.

WHAT IT COSTS In Norwegian Kroner				
$$$$	**$$$**	**$$**	**$**	**¢**
FOR 2 PEOPLE over 2,000	1,600–2,000	1,200–1,600	800–1,200	under 800

Prices are for two people in a standard double room in high season.

Downtown: Royal Palace to the Parliament
Downtown has many traditional Norwegian hotels dating from the 19th and early-20th centuries. These establishments are pricey, but they cater to travelers with the best service and amenities.

$$–$$$$ 🏨 **Grand Hotel.** In the center of town on Karl Johans Gate, the Grand opened in 1874. The hotel is the choice of visiting heads of state, and there is even a Nobel suite. Ibsen used to drink brandy at the Grand Café in the company of journalists. Munch was also a regular guest; you can see him with his contemporaries in Per Krohg's painting on the café's far wall. Norwegians book several years in advance for National Day, May 17, in order to have a room overlooking the parades below. ⊠ *Karl Johans gt. 31, Sentrum, 0101* ☎ *23–21–20–00* 🖷 *23–21–21–00* ⊕ *www. grand.no* 🛏 *288 rooms, 51 suites* ⅙ *2 restaurants, indoor pool, health club, sauna, bar, meeting room* ⊟ *AE, DC, MC, V.*

★ **$$–$$$$** 🏨 **Hotel Continental.** With its elegant early 20th century facade, the Continental is an Oslo landmark that continues to attract with gracious service and wonderful restaurants. Near Nationaltheatret, and close to many cafés, clubs, and movie theaters, the hotel is ideal for leisure as well as business travelers. The hotel's Theatercafeen restaurant is an Oslo landmark, and the nightspot Lipp is a trendy hangout for the well-to-do. Dagligstuen (The Sitting Room) is a popular meeting place for drinks and quiet conversation. ⊠ *Stortingsgt. 24–26, Sentrum, 0161* ☎ *22–82–40–00* 🖷 *22–42–96–89* ⊕ *www.hotel-continental.no* 🖙 *159 rooms, 23 suites* ᗷ *3 restaurants, cable TV, in-room data ports, 2 bars* ▤ *AE, DC, MC, V.*

$$$ 🏨 **Hotel Bristol.** With its interior design inspired by Edwardian England, the Bristol has a dignity and class all its own. Rooms are elegant and understated. The lounge and bar were decorated in the 1920s with an intricate Moorish theme and recall Fez more than Scandinavia. Josephine Baker performed in the piano bar in the 1920s. Today, the library and bar, with their red, burnished leather sofas, are among Oslo's places to see and be seen. ⊠ *Kristian IVs gt. 7, Sentrum, 0130* ☎ *22–82–60–00* 🖷 *22–82–60–01* ⊕ *www.bristol.no* 🖙 *252 rooms, 10 suites* ᗷ *3 restaurants, health club, sauna, 3 bars, nightclub, convention center* ▤ *AE, DC, MC, V.*

$–$$$ 🏨 **Radisson SAS Scandinavia Hotel.** Popular with business travelers, this 1974 hotel has a winning combination of service and classic style. Simple, elegant rooms come in different designs: art deco, Italian, Asian, Continental, Scandinavian, and—predictably, for a hotel run by an airline—69 high-tech business-class rooms. The Summit 21 Bar has a stunning, panoramic view of Oslo—it's a great place for an evening cocktail. ⊠ *Holbergsgt. 30, Sentrum, 0166* ☎ *23–29–30–00* 🖷 *23–29–30–01* ⊕ *www.radissonsas.com* 🖙 *488 rooms, 4 suites* ᗷ *Restaurant, cable TV, pool, health club, 2 bars, business services* ▤ *AE, DC, MC, V.*

$$ 🏨 **Rainbow Hotel Stefan.** A home away from home, this hotel tries hard to make guests feel well looked after. Hot drinks are served to late arrivals, and breakfast tables come with juice boxes and plastic bags for packing a lunch (request this service in advance). The top-floor lounge has magazines in English, and the restaurant serves one of the best buffet lunches in town. Reflecting its name, the hotel's facade, reception, dining hall, and café/bar are filled with bright colors. ⊠ *Rosenkrantz gt. 1, Sentrum, 0159* ☎ *23–31–55–00* 🖷 *23–31–55–55* ⊕ *www.rainbow-hotels.no/stefan* 🖙 *150 rooms, 11 suites* ᗷ *Restaurant, cable TV, in-room broadband, lounge, library, meeting room* ▤ *AE, DC, MC, V.*

$$ 🏨 **Rica Victoria.** This modern business hotel occupies one of the city center's taller buildings, giving some top-floor rooms views of Oslo's rooftops. The rooms, built around a center atrium, are elegant and stylish: they're furnished with Biedermeier reproductions, brass lamps, and paisley fabrics in bold reds and dark blues. ⊠ *Rosenkrantz gt. 13, Sentrum, 0121* ☎ *24–14–70–00* 🖷 *24–14–70–01* ⊕ *www.rica.no* 🖙 *199 rooms, 5 suites* ᗷ *Restaurant, cable TV, in-room data ports, bar, convention center, meeting rooms, no-smoking rooms* ▤ *AE, DC, MC, V.*

$–$$ 🏨 **Norlandia Karl Johan Hotel.** The late-19th-century Karl Johan Hotel, once known as the Nobel, is elegant, with stained-glass windows that line the circular staircase, bringing to mind 19th-century Paris. During a renovation in 2004, rooms were painted and given new carpets

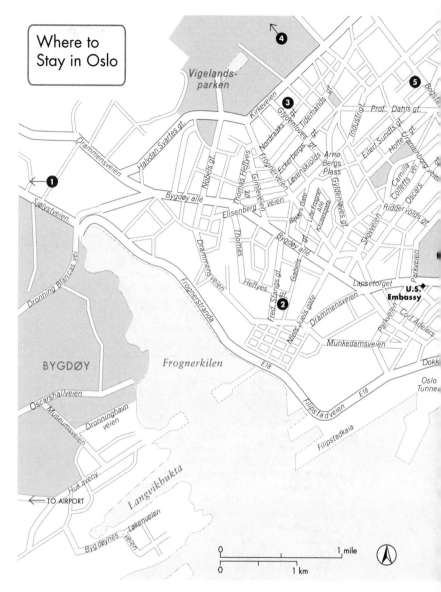

Where to
Stay in Oslo

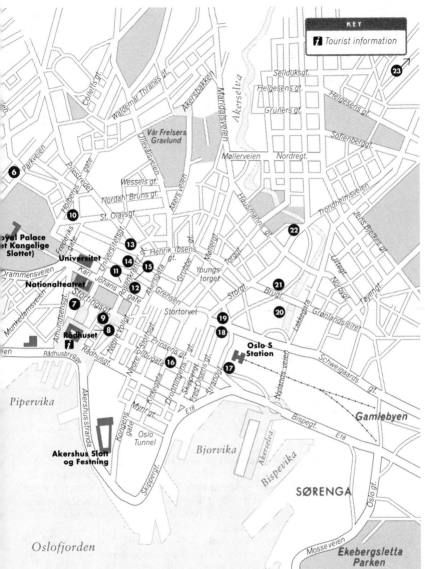

and furnishings. Most rooms also have Norwegian antique pieces, giving the place an air of sophisticated luxury. ⊠ *Karl Johans gt. 33, Sentrum, 0162* ☎ *23–16–17–00* 🖷 *22–42–05–19* ⊕ *www.norlandia.no* ⇥ *112 rooms, 1 suite* ♨ *Restaurant, bar, meeting room, business services* ⊟ *AE, DC, MC, V.*

$ 🏨 **Anker Hotel Best Western.** Just north of the center, the Anker is the closest hotel to the trendy shopping and nightlife neighborhood of Grünerløkka. There are neat, smart rooms with hardwood furniture and yellow walls. A Scandinavian-style hot-and-cold buffet is served for breakfast. ⊠ *Storgata 55, Sentrum, 0182* ☎ *22–99–75–00* 🖷 *22–99–75–20* ⊕ *www.anker-hotel.no* ⇥ *137 rooms* ♨ *Dining room, cable TV, bar, meeting room* ⊟ *AE, DC, MC, V* ⊙| *BP.*

$ 🏨 **Best Western Hotell Bondeheimen.** Founded in 1913 for country folk visiting the city, Bondeheimen, which means "farmers' home," still gives discounts to members of Norwegian agricultural associations. Rooms have a minimalistic look, in dark greens and earthy reds. This is a good choice for families, but if you are looking for quiet, ask for a room in back. The Kaffistova restaurant is in the same building. ⊠ *Rosenkrantz gt. 8, entrance on Kristian IVs gt., Sentrum, 0159* ☎ *23–21–41–00* 🖷 *23–21–41–01* ⊕ *www.bondeheimen.com* ⇥ *127 rooms, 5 suites* ♨ *Cafeteria, in-room broadband, shop, meeting rooms* ⊟ *AE, DC, MC, V.*

$ 🏨 **Rainbow Cecil.** A short walk from Parliament, this modern hotel is a
Fodor'sChoice relatively inexpensive option in the center of town. Although the rooms
★ are basic, they are perfectly suited to the active, on-the-go traveler. The second floor opens onto a plant-filled atrium, the hotel's "activity center." In the morning it's a breakfast room, but in the afternoon it becomes a lounge, serving coffee, juice, and fresh fruit. ⊠ *Stortingsgt. 8, Sentrum, 0130* ☎ *23–31–48–00* 🖷 *23–31–48–50* ⊕ *www.rainbow-hotels.no* ⇥ *111 rooms, 2 suites* ♨ *Lounge, cable TV, in-room data ports, no-smoking rooms* ⊟ *AE, DC, MC, V.*

Grønland

¢ 🏨 **Rainbow Hotel Spectrum.** This hotel has a central, quiet location on a pedestrian street east of downtown Oslo. Rooms are spacious and light, with large windows, bordered by heavy drapes, overlooking the street or the rear courtyard. Polished floorboards match the tan, dark-green, and slate-blue furnishings. The clean lines and simple forms are characteristic of Scandinavian interior design. Free newspapers, coffee, and fruit are provided. ⊠ *Brugata 7, Grønland 0105* ☎ *23–36–27–00* 🖷 *23–36–27–50* ⊕ *www.rainbow-hotels.no/spectrum* ⇥ *151 rooms* ♨ *Dining room, cable TV, meeting rooms* ⊟ *AE, DC, MC, V.*

Sinsen

Sinsen is about 4 km (2½ mi) from downtown Oslo.

¢ 🏨 **Vandrerhjem Haraldsheim.** Named for King Harald, Oslo's hilltop hostel is Europe's largest. It opened in 1954 and has maintained an old-fashioned Scandinavian style. Most of the large rooms have four beds and full bathrooms. You can bring your own sheets or rent them here.

A supermarket is close by and local public transport is easily accessible. To get here, catch cable car 17 to Sinsenkrysset and look for the signs ahead at the freeway underpass. ⊠ *Haraldsheimvn. 4, Sinsen, 0409* ☎ *22–22–29–65* 🖷 *22–22–10–25* ⊕ *www.haraldsheim.oslo.no* 🖙 *71 rooms, 40 with bath* ⚑ *Cafeteria, meeting room* ▤ *MC, V.*

Frogner, Majorstuen & Holmenkollen

These leafy suburbs west of the center are known for large beautiful homes inhabited by prosperous Norwegians. The hotels are mainly from the 19th century and range from upmarket boutique properties to affordable bed-and-breakfasts.

$$–$$$ 🏨 **Holmenkollen Park Hotel Rica.** Dating to 1894, this stunning and distinguished hotel has a peaceful mountaintop setting with unparalleled views of the city below. Guest rooms have earth tones and dark-wood furniture. Next to the Holmenkollen Ski Arena, the property provides the perfect base for outdoor pursuits such as cycling, skiing, and running. It's worth a visit even if you don't stay here, perhaps to dine at De Fem Stuer, the wonderful restaurant. ⊠ *Kongevn. 26, Holmenkollen, 0787* ☎ *22–92–20–00* 🖷 *22–14–61–92* ⊕ *www.holmenkollenparkhotel. no* 🖙 *220 rooms* ⚑ *2 restaurants, cable TV, in-room broadband, pool, gym, sauna, spa, cross-country skiing, bar, cinema, convention center, meeting rooms* ▤ *AE, DC, MC, V.*

$$ 🏨 **Clarion Collection Hotel Gabelshus.** In a blending of old and new styles, the Gabelshus became part of the Choice Hotels Scandinavia Group in 2005 when it literally joined together with a neighboring hotel, formerly the Oslo Ritz. The original building of the Gabelshus retains its Old English charm, while its newer counterpart offers rooms with a modern, minimalistic, Scandinavian style. ⊠ *Gabelsgt. 16, Frogner, 0272* ☎ *22–55–22–60* 🖷 *23–27–65–60* ⊕ *www.gabelshus.no* 🖙 *114 rooms* ⚑ *In-room broadband, sauna, steam room, lounge, meeting rooms* ▤ *AE, DC, MC, V.*

★ ¢ 🏨 **Villa Frogner.** In a white 19th-century villa close to Vigelandparken, this elegant bed-and-breakfast will appeal to anyone who appreciates charming individually decorated rooms and homemade breakfasts. With hardwood floors, Persian rugs, antique furniture, and long drapes, the rooms are cozy and inviting, but the proximity of the park and Bogstadveien, a major shopping street, will make you want to explore. The villa was first owned by Norwegian shipowners and in the late 1980s became the Indonesian embassy for a brief period. ⊠ *Nordraaks gt. 26, Frogner 0260* ☎ *22–56–19–60* 🖷 *22–56–07–42* ⊕ *www.bedandbreakfast.no* 🖙 *7 rooms, 7 apartments* ⚑ *Some kitchens, sauna, lounge* ▤ *AE, DC, MC, V* ¶⊙¶ *CP.*

¢–$ 🏨 **Rainbow Hotel Gyldenløve.** Nestled among the many shops and cafés on Bogstadveien, this hotel is a very good value for its location. Rooms are light and airy and have stylish Scandinavian furniture. It is within walking distance of Vigelandparken, and the trikk stops just outside the door. ⊠ *Bogstadvn. 20, Majorstuen, 0355* ☎ *23–33–23–00* 🖷 *22–60–33–90* ⊕ *www.rainbow-hotels.no* 🖙 *168 rooms* ⚑ *Coffee shop, cable TV with movies, some in-room data ports* ▤ *AE, DC, MC, V.*

¢ ▥ **Cochs Pensjonat.** A stone's throw from the Royal Palace, this no-frills guesthouse has reasonably priced, comfortable, but rather spartan rooms. Some have TVs, but there are no phones. Most of the 88 rooms have private bathrooms, but check when you make your reservation; some also have kitchenettes. ⊠ *Parkvn. 25, Majorstuen, 0350* ☎ *23–33–24–00* ᐯ *23–33–24–10* ⊕ *www.virtualoslo.com/cochs_pensjonat/* ⇨ *88 rooms* ☖ *No room phones, no TV in some rooms* ⊟ *MC, V.*

Near Oslo Airport & Oslo S Station

The hotels near Oslo Airport have all been built since the late 1990s, like the airport itself, and offer modern facilities. Most are part of a large chain and cater to business travelers. The hotels near Oslo S Station vary more in age and style and are closer to the center, but they're also more expensive than hotels near the airport. A taxi ride from the airport to Karl Johans Gate will cost you around NKr 500.

★ **$–$$$** ▥ **Clarion Royal Christiania Hotel.** What was once bare-bones housing for 1952 Olympians is now a luxury hotel. Although the original plain exterior remains, the interior is more recent, designed using feng shui principles. Rooms have white walls and mahogany furniture. ⊠ *Biskop Gunnerus gt. 3, 0106* ☎ *23–10–80–00* ᐯ *23–10–80–80* ⊕ *www. royalchristiania.no* ⇨ *412 rooms, 91 suites* ☖ *Restaurant, indoor pool, health club, sauna, bar, business services, convention center* ⊟ *AE, DC, MC, V.*

$$$ ▥ **Radisson SAS Airport Hotel.** Steps away from Oslo Airport, this is a real beauty of a business hotel. The interiors make use of stone and metal and have a color scheme that emphasizes burnt orange and deep purple. There are three room styles: Asian, Scandinavian, and maritime. Both the restaurant, Toot's International Bar and Grill, and the lobby bar are relaxing and inviting. The spacious sports center is larger than most. There are spinning classes, a trainer on call, and massage services. ⊠ *Hotellvegen, Box 163, 2061 Gardermoen* ☎ *63/93–30–00* ᐯ *63/93–30–30* ⊕ *www.radissonsas.com* ⇨ *306 rooms, 37 suites* ☖ *Restaurants, cable TV, in-room data ports, health club, massage, sauna, bar, business services, meeting room* ⊟ *AE, DC, MC, V* ⋈ *CP.*

$$$ ▥ **Rainbow Hotel Opera.** Named after the Opera building under construction next door that is scheduled to open in 2007, this is arguably Oslo's most conveniently located hotel. It's just 110 yards from Karl Johans Gate, and a stone's throw from the Oslo S railway station. Rooms are elegant and well equipped, although slightly plain. Views from most of the rooms aren't special, but the two grand suites, the gym, and the Scala restaurant offer sweeping views of the Oslo fjord. ⊠ *Christian Frederiks pl. 5, 0103* ☎ *24–10–30–00* ᐯ *24–10–30–10* ⊕ *www. rainbow-hotels.no* ⇨ *434 rooms, 2 suites* ☖ *Restaurant, in-room broadband, gym, sauna, bar, convention center* ⊟ *AE, DC, MC, V.*

★ **$–$$$** ▥ **Radisson SAS Plaza Hotel.** Standing out from other buildings on the city's skyline, northern Europe's largest hotel is the jewel of the Radisson SAS chain. The understated, elegant rooms have gilded fixtures and marble, and many have spectacular views. The Plaza SkyBar on the top floor, the fit-for-a-king breakfast buffets, and luxuriously grand bathtubs all make a stay in this 37-floor glass extravaganza memorable. Since it's next to Oslo S Station, buses and other local transit are convenient. ☒ *Sonja Henies pl. 3, 0134* ☎ *22–05–80–00* 🖷 *22–05–80–10* ⊕ *www. radissonsas.com* ⇗ *673 rooms, 20 suites* ⚐ *2 restaurants, in-room data ports, indoor pool, health club, sauna, 2 bars, convention center* ▭ *AE, DC, MC, V* ⦿⧳ *CP.*

$–$$ 🏨 **Rica Oslo Hotel.** Close to Oslo S Station, this former office building calls itself an art hotel. There are paintings by Norwegian artists throughout, and many prints of works that are in the National Gallery. Rooms are painted cream and have red-painted wood furnishings. The Rica is popular with business travelers because it's central and has a convention center on the premises. ☒ *Europarådetspl. 1, 0105* ☎ *23–10–42–00* 🖷 *23–10–42–10* ⊕ *www.rica.no* ⇗ *174 rooms, 2 suites* ⚐ *Restaurant, cable TV, in-room data ports, gym, sauna, bar, convention center* ▭ *AE, DC, MC, V.*

$ 🏨 **First Hotel Millennium.** This boutique hotel is comfortable, with an understated, downtown chic. Guest rooms are simple, with a dark-blue, green, and yellow color theme; all have bathtubs. Several rooms are geared toward women and come with a bathrobe, skin products, and women's magazines. The main-floor lounge has games, a music room, Internet access, and a library. The restaurant-bar, Primo, serves an impressive international menu, which includes quail and swordfish. ☒ *Tollbugt. 25, 0157* ☎ *21/02–28–00* 🖷 *21/02–28–30* ⊕ *www.firsthotels.com* ⇗ *112 rooms, 10 suites* ⚐ *Restaurant, cable TV, in-room data ports, bar, lounge, meeting rooms* ▭ *AE, DC, MC, V.*

NIGHTLIFE & THE ARTS

Nightlife

More than ever, the Oslo nightlife scene is vibrant and varied. Cafés, restaurant-bars, and jazz clubs are laid-back and mellow. But if you're ready to party, there are many pulsating, live-rock and dance clubs to choose from. Day or night, people are usually out on Karl Johans Gate, and many clubs and restaurants in the central area stay open until the early hours. Aker Brygge, the wharf area, has many bars and some nightclubs, attracting mostly tourists, couples on first dates, and other people willing to spend extra for the waterfront location. Grünerløkka and Grønland have even more bars, pubs, and cafés catering to a younger crowd. A more mature upmarket crowd ventures out to the less busy west side of Oslo, to Frogner and Bygdøy.

Drinking out is very expensive in Oslo, starting at around NKr 50 for a beer or a mixed drink. Many Norwegians save money by having drinks at friends' houses—called a *forschpiel*—before heading out on the town. Some bars in town remain quiet until 11 PM or midnight when the first groups of forschpiel partyers arrive.

For nightlife listings, pick up a copy of the free monthly paper *Natt og Dag* or Friday's edition of *Avis 1.*

Bars & Lounges

With its 1970s theme, **Café Con Bar** (✉ Brugt. 11, Grønland
☎ 22–05–02–00), is one of Oslo's trendy crowd pleasers. The kitchen
closes at 10 and guest DJs spin on weekends. For cheap beer and an in-
formal crowd, visit the popular student hangout **Stargate Pub** (✉ Grønlandsleiret 33, Grønland ☎ 22–04–13–77) at Brugata, just alongside
the bridge. **Choice Bar** (✉ Grønlandsleiret 38, Grønland ☎ 22–12–23–00)
opposite Stargate Pub, is another low-key dive bar. Down the street from
Choice and Stargate, try **Olympen,** (✉ Grønlandsleiret 15, Grønland
☎ 22–17–28–08) to experience 1950s deco and Bulgarian folk bands
in a large barnlike setting. The clientele is friendly and the atmosphere
always relaxed.

Bar Boca (✉ Thorvald Meyers gt. 30, Grünerløkka ☎ 22–04–13–77) is
an intimate '50s-inspired bar in an American diner. **Kaos** (✉ Thorvald
Meyers gt. 56, Grünerløkka ☎ 22–04–69–90), near Olav Ryes plass,
showcases DJs playing funk and soul. The young and hip should take
a drink at the retro-style **Memphis** (✉ Thorvald Meyers gt. 63, Grünerløkka ☎ 22–04–12–75). **Parkteatret** (✉ Olaf Ryes pl. 11, Grünerløkka
☎ 22–35–63–00), set in a converted art deco theater, has either theater,
film, live music, or DJs every night of the week.

The trendiest of the postcollegiate crowd drink the night away at **Beach
Club** (✉ Aker Brygge ☎ 22–83–83–82), a kitschy hamburger joint with
tables and booths that wouldn't look out of place in an American diner.

If you're more partial to lounging than drinking, try the English-style
pub **Bristol** (✉ Kristian IVs gt. 7, Sentrum ☎ 22–82–60–00). **Onkel Don-
ald** (✉ Universitetsgt. 26, Sentrum ☎ 23–35–63–10) is the trendiest meeting place in the center and has a capacity for hundreds. For a change of
pace, try **Lorrys** (✉ Parkvn. 12, Sentrum ☎ 22–69–69–04), behind the
Royal Palace grounds. It has stuffed wildlife and early-20th-century
sketches of famous Norwegians adorning the walls. It also advertises
180 different types of beer, but don't be surprised if not all of them are
in stock.

Serious beer drinkers may find **Oslo Mikrobryggeriet** (✉ Bogstadvn. 6,
Majorstuen ☎ 22–56–97–76) worth a stop. Eight different beers are
brewed on the premises, including the increasingly popular Oslo Pils.
The **Underwater Bar** (✉ Dalsbergstein 4, St. Hans Haugen
☎ 22–46–05–26) is a pub with an undersea theme, complete with fish
tanks and scuba gear, and live opera on Tuesday and Thursday at 9 PM.

Cafés

As a mark of Oslo's growing cosmopolitanism, the city now has a Continental café culture, with bohemian coffeehouses and chic cafés dot-
ting the sidewalks. Grünerløkka especially has lots of cafés to suit every
taste; they're great for people-watching and whiling away warm summer afternoons.

Café Bacchus (✉ Dronningensgt. 27, Sentrum ☎ 22–33–34–30), in the
old Basarhall at the rear of Oslo Domkirke, is tiny but serves a mean
brownie. Background music is classical during the day, jazz at night.

With its mulitcolor furniture, oversize coffee mugs, and children's play area, **Clodion Art Café** (⊠ Bygdøy Allé 63, Frogner ☎ 22–44–97–26) is popular with families. **Glazed & Amused** (⊠ Vestheimgt. 4B, Frogner ☎ 22–56–25–18) offers a twist on a normal coffee shop, since you can paint your own ceramic mug here. A cup of coffee to go takes on new meaning.

For a slightly bohemian experience, head to **Fru Hagen** (⊠ Thorvald Meyers gt. 40, Grünerløkka ☎ 22–35–68–71), with its classical-looking chandeliers and elegant velvet sofas. Aim for a window seat to check out the passing traffic. **Kaffebrenneriet** (⊠ Storgt. 2, Sentrum) is Oslo's answer to Starbucks, with good coffee and shops throughout town. Head to the **Tea Lounge** (⊠ Thorvald Meyers gt. 33B, Grünerløkka ☎ 22–37–07–07) for alcoholic and nonalcoholic tea drinks. It's very stylish, with mellow music, a mosaic tile bar, picture windows, and high-backed plush red sofas, and it attracts a trendy crowd.

Festivals

The popular outdoor music festival **Norwegian Wood** (☎ 67/10–34–50 ⊕ www.norwegianwood.no) is held at the Frognerbadet (Frogner Swimming Pool) in June. Begun in the early '90s, the festival hosts performers such as Iggy Pop and Bob Dylan as well as fledgling Norwegian bands. The large **Øya Music Festival** (⊕ www.oyafestivalen.com) is held at Middelalderparken in Gamlebyen August 10–13 and features well-known bands such as Franz Ferdinand and Sissy Wish.

Gay Bars

For information about gay and lesbian clubs and bars in Oslo, you can read *Blikk*, the gay newsletter; check out www.gaysir.no; or call **LLH** (Landsforening for Lesbisk og Homofil Frigjøring; ☎ 22–41–11–33), the national gay and lesbian liberation association. A fixture on Oslo's gay scene since the 1970s, **London Pub** (⊠ C. J. Hambros pl. 5, Sentrum ☎ 22–70–87–00) has a piano bar on the top floor and Sunday theme parties. A younger breed frequents the bar **Chairs** on the ground floor. **Potpurriet** (⊠ Øvre Vollgt. 13, Sentrum ☎ 22–41–14–40) organizes well-attended women's dance nights on the last Friday of each month. A popular spot is **Soho** (⊠ Kirkegt. 34, Sentrum ☎ 22–42–91–00), a large venue with nightclub, lounge, and bar areas, and a separate stage with live shows or DJs spinning the decks.

Jazz Clubs

Norwegians take their jazz seriously. Every August, the **Oslo Jazz Festival** (⊠ Tollbugt. 28, Sentrum ☎ 22–42–91–20) brings in major international artists and attracts big crowds. **Blå** (⊠ Brennerivn. 9C, Grünerløkka ☎ 22–20–91–81), on the Akers River, is considered the leading club for jazz and related sounds in the Nordic countries. The riverside patio is popular in summer. At **Herr Nilsen** (⊠ C. J. Hambros pl. 5, Sentrum ☎ 22–33–54–05), some of Norway's most celebrated jazz artists perform in a stylish space. There's live music three nights a week and jazz on Saturday and Sunday afternoon. **Stortorvets Gjæstgiveri** (⊠ Grensen 1, Sentrum ☎ 23–35–63–60) often presents New Orleans–style jazz on Thursday and Saturday afternoon from 1:30 to 5 PM.

Music Clubs

At Oslo's numerous rock clubs, the cover charges are low, the crowds young and boisterous, and the music loud. **Oslo Spektrum** (⊠ Sonia Henies pl. 2, Sentrum ☎ 22–05–29–00), one of Norway's largest live-music venues, is just behind the Oslo City shopping center. Past acts have included big names such as Radiohead and Britney Spears. The lineup at **Rockefeller/John Dee** (⊠ Torggt. 16, Sentrum ☎ 22–20–32–32) features everything from hard-rock to alternative and hip-hop acts, including Nick Cave, Blondie, and Ashe.

Nightclubs

Most dance clubs open late, so the beat doesn't really start until midnight. Many establishments have a minimum age for entry, which can be as high as 25. There's also usually a cover of around NKr 50–NKr 100. **Cosmopolite** (⊠ Møllergt. 26, Sentrum ☎ 22–20–78–76) has a big dance floor and plays music from all over the world, especially Latin America. **Galleriet** (⊠ Kristian IVs gt. 12, Sentrum ☎ 22–42–29–46), a hot spot in town, has a live jazz club, a disco, and a bar spread over its four art-bedecked floors. Oslo's beautiful people congregate at **Lille** (⊠ Bygdøy allé 5, Bygdøy ☎ 22–44–80–44) on the west side of Oslo. **Lipp** (⊠ Olav Vs gt. 2, Sentrum ☎ 22–82–40–60) is an upscale nightclub, bar, and restaurant. Serious clubbers should try **Skansen** (⊠ Rådhusgt. 25, Sentrum ☎ 22–42–28–88) for house and techno music. It has a good dance floor and DJs on weekends.

Most of the big hotels have discos that appeal to the over-30 crowd. **Smuget** (⊠ Rosenkrantz gt. 22, Sentrum ☎ 22–42–52–62) is an institution: it hosts live rock and blues bands every night except Sunday, when crowds flock to the in-house discotheque.

The Arts

The monthly tourist information brochure *What's on in Oslo* lists cultural events in Norwegian, as does *Aftenposten,* Oslo's (and Norway's) leading newspaper, in its evening OsloPuls section and the Friday edition of *Avis 1* newspaper. The Friday edition of *Dagbladet,* Oslo's daily liberal tabloid, also gives an exhaustive preview of the week's events. Tickets to virtually all performances in Norway, from classical or rock concerts to hockey games, can be purchased at any post office.

Film

Movie going is a favorite pastime for many Norwegians. A number of festivals, including the Oslo Internasjonale Filmfestival, usually held in November, celebrate the medium. Films are usually subtitled in Norwegian and shown in their original language, though children's films are dubbed. Tickets cost NKr 60 or more and are discounted on some days in summer. **Filmweb.no** is the Web site used nationally for ordering tickets. Oslo has a gay-and-lesbian film festival called **Skeive Filmer** (☎ 98/28–00–66) in mid-June. Tickets cost NKr 75.

Near the Studenterlunden park, there is a six-screen cinema called **Saga** (⊠ Stortingsgt. 28, Sentrum ☎ 82/03–00–01). Across the street from Saga, the four-screen **Klingenberg** (⊠ Olav Vs gt. 4, Sentrum ☎ 82/

03–00–01) plays the latest box office hits. If you like alternative or classic films and film festivals, try **Cinemateket** (✉ Dronningensgt. 16, Sentrum ☎ 22–47–45–05), the city's only independent cinema. **Eldorado Kino** (✉ Torggata 9, Sentrum ☎ 82/03–00–01) is a cinema close to Youngstorget market square, 220 yards north of Karl Johans Gate. **Felix Kino** (✉ Akker Brygge ☎ 82/03–00–01) has two large screens. **Vika Kino** (✉ Ruseløkkvn 14, Vika ☎ 82/03–00–01) has four separate screens and is located behind the Saga cinema near the center.

Music

The **Oslo Philharmonic Orchestra** is one of Europe's leading ensembles. Its home, **Konserthuset** (✉ Munkedamsvn. 14, Sentrum ☎ 23–11–31–00), was built in 1977 of marble, metal, and rosewood. In summer folk dancing is performed here twice a week. **Den Norske Opera** (✉ Storgt. 23, Sentrum ☎ 23–31–50–00 information, 815/44–488 tickets) and the ballet perform at the Opera House alongside Youngstorget. The opulent **Gamle Logen** (✉ Grev Wedels pl. 2, Sentrum ☎ 22–33–44–70), Norway's oldest concert hall, often sponsors classical music series, especially piano music.

Theater

Det Norske Teatret (✉ Kristian IVs gt. 8, Sentrum ☎ 22–42–43–44) is a showcase for pieces in Nynorsk (a language compiled from rural Norwegian dialects) as well as regular Norwegian theater productions, such as *Piaf* and *Peer Gynt.*

Nationaltheatret (✉ Stortingsgt. 15, Sentrum ☎ 22–00–14–00) performances are in Norwegian: bring along a copy of the play in translation, and you're all set. The biennial Ibsen Festival, during which plays by the great dramatist are performed in both Norwegian and English, takes place in the summer of even-numbered years.

SPORTS & THE OUTDOORS

Oslo's natural surroundings and climate make it ideally suited to outdoor pursuits. The Oslo fjord and its islands, the forested woodlands called the *marka,* and as many as 18 hours of daylight in summer all make the Norwegian capital an irresistible place for outdoor activities. Just 15 minutes north of the city center by tram is the **Oslomarka**, where locals ski in winter and swim in the lakes or hike in summer. The area contains 27 small *hytter* (cabins), which are often available free of charge for backpackers on foot or on skis. These can be reserved through **Den Norske Turistforening** (✉ Storgt. 3, Sentrum ☎ 22–82–28–00), which has maps of the marka surrounding Oslo as well as equipment for rent, and other information; it also organizes events. The **Villmarkshuset** (✉ Christian Krohgs gt. 16, Sentrum ☎ 22–05–05–22) is an equipment, activities, and excursion center specializing in hiking, climbing, hunting, fishing, cycling, and canoeing. You can rent a canoe from here, drop it into the Akers River at the rear of the store, and paddle out into the Oslo fjord. There's also an indoor climbing wall, a pistol range, and a diving center and swimming pool. Books and maps are also available. The **Oslo Archipelago** is a favorite destination for sunbathing urbanites, who hop ferries to their favorite isles.

Beaches

Beaches are scattered throughout the archipelago. Sun-loving Scandinavians pack every patch of sand during the long summer days to make up for lack of light in winter. The most popular beach is at Huk (on the Bygdøy peninsula), one portion of which is for nude bathing. A family beach is located nearby at Paradisbukta. To get to the beach, follow signs along Huk Aveny from the Folk and Viking Ship museums. You can also take Bus 30A, marked "Bygdøy," to its final stop. To get to the archipelago of island beaches on the Oslo fjord alongside Aker Brygge, take a ferry leaving from the southern pier of Vippetangen in summer. To get to Vippetangen, take Bus 60 from town or walk to the Forsvarsmuseet (Armed Forces Museum) on Akershusstranda and look for the signs. These islands are great for bathing and relaxing, and one of them, Hovedøya, has monastery ruins dating from 1100.

Biking

Oslo is a great biking city. One scenic ride starts at Aker Brygge and takes you along the harbor to the Bygdøy peninsula, where you can visit the museums or cut across the fields next to the royal family's summer house. **Syklistenes Landsforening** (National Organization of Cyclists; ⊠ Storgata 23D, Sentrum ☎ 22–47–30–30) sells books and maps for cycling holidays in Norway and abroad and gives friendly, free advice.

Glåmdal Cycledepot (⊠ Waldemar Thranes gt. 51, Grünerløkka ☎ 22–83–52–08), rents bikes and equipment, including helmets. The store also offers five different sightseeing tours and has maps of the area for those braving it on their own. If you feel like roughing the terrain of the Holmenkollen marka, you can rent mountain bikes from **Tomm Murstad** (⊠ Tryvannsvn. 2, Holmenkollen ☎ 22–13–95–00) in summer. Just take T-bane line 1 to Frognerseteren and get off at Voksenkollen Station.

Fishing

A national fishing license and a local fee are required to fish in the Oslo fjord and the surrounding lakes. For information on fishing areas and on where to buy a license, contact **Oslomarkas Fiskeadministrasjon** (⊠ Sørkedalen 914, Holmenkollen ☎ 40/00–67–68). You can also fish throughout the Nordmarka woods area in a canoe rented from **Tomm Murstad** (⊠ Tryvannsvn. 2, Holmenkollen ☎ 22–13–95–00). Ice fishing is popular in winter, but finding an ice drill could prove difficult—you may want to bring one from home.

Golf

More and more Norwegians are taking up golf. Oslo's international-level golf course, **Oslo Golfklubb** (⊠ Bogstad, 0740 ☎ 22–51–05–60) is private and heavily booked. However, it admits members of other golf clubs weekdays before 2 and weekends after 2 if space is available. Visitors must have a handicap certificate of 20 or lower for men, 28 or lower for women. Fees range from NKr 250 to NKr 500. **Golfsenteret** (✉ Sandakerveien 24C, Torshov ☎ 23–22–65–65), just five minutes outside the center, has a driving range, putting green, simulator, and pro shop. A driving range is available at **Groruddalen Golfklubb** (✉ Tokeruddalen 22, Stovner ☎ 22–79–05–60).

Health Clubs

If you need a fitness fix, whether aerobics, weight training, spinning, or climbing, try one of the health clubs that use the "klippekort" system. In this method, you pay a charge that entitles you to a certain number of workout sessions, which are marked as "klips" on your card. **Friskis & Svettis** (✉ Munkedamsvn. 19, Sentrum ☎ 22–83–94–40) offers free aerobics classes on the green of Frogner Park from mid-May to mid-August. Class types and times vary, so call for the summer schedule. **SATS** (✉ Filipstadbrygge 2, Sentrum ☎ 22–04–80–80) has some of the better-equipped and more attractive clubs around the city and throughout Norway.

Hiking & Running

Head for the woods surrounding Oslo, the marka, for jogging or walking; there's an abundance of trails, and many are lighted. Frogner Park has many paths, and you can jog or hike along the Aker River, but take extra care late at night or early in the morning. Or you can take the Sognsvann trikk to the end of the line and walk or jog along Sognsvann Lake.

Grete Waitz and Ingrid Kristiansen put Norway on marathon runners' maps two decades ago. Every May, a women's minimarathon is held in Grete Waitz's name; hundreds of women flock to Oslo to enjoy a nice day—and usually night—out. In September, the Oslo Marathon attracts runners from around the world. The popular Holmenkollen Marathon is held in early May. **Norges Friidretts Forbund** (✉ Sognsvn. 75, 0855 ☎ 21/02–90–00) has information about local clubs and competitions.

Sailing

Spend a sunny summer afternoon at Oslo's harbor, Aker Brygge, admiring the docked boats; or venture out into the fjords on a charter or tour. Sky-high masts and billowing white sails give the *Christian Radich* (☎ 22–47–82–70) a majestic, old-fashioned style. This tall ship makes nine different sailing trips, varying from a three-day voyage to an autumn sail across the Atlantic. Although you aren't required to have prior sailing experience, do expect rough seas, high waves, lots of rain, and being asked to participate in crew-members' tasks. For general information on boating, call, the Royal Norwegian Sailing Association, **Kongelig Norsk Seilforening** (☎ 23–27–56–00).

Skiing

Cross-country, downhill, telemarking, and snowboarding—whatever your snow-sport pleasure, Oslo has miles of easily accessible outdoor areas minutes from the center of town. Nine alpine ski areas have activities until late at night. More than 2,600 km (1,600 mi) of prepared cross-country ski trails run deep into the forest, of which 90 km (50 mi) are lighted for special evening tours.

The **Skiforeningen** (✉ Kongevn. 5, 0787 ☎ 22–92–32–00) provides national snow-condition reports and can give tips on cross-country trails. They also offer cross-country classes for young children (3- to 7-year-olds), downhill classes for older children (7- to 12-year-olds), and both kinds of classes, as well as instruction in telemark-style racing and snowboarding techniques, for adults.

Among the **floodlit trails in the Oslomarka** are the **Bogstad** (3½ km [2 mi]), marked for the disabled and blind; the **Lillomarka** (25 km [15½ mi]); and the **Østmarka** (33 km [20½ mi]).

The downhill skiing season usually lasts from mid-December to March. There are 15 city slopes, or you can take organized trips to several outside slopes, including **Norefjell** (☎ 32/15–01–00), 100 km (66 mi) north of the city.

You can rent downhill and cross-country skis from **Tomm Murstad Skiservice** (✉ Tryvannsvn. 2, Holmenkollen ☎ 22–13–95–00) at the Tryvann T-bane station. This is a good starting point for skiing; although there are few downhill slopes in this area, a plethora of cross-country trails meet every skill level. Oslo's most accessible ski center is the **Tryvann Winter Park** (✉ Tryvannsveien 64, Holmenkollen ☎ 40/46–27–00 ⊕ www.tryvann.no). It has 11 downhill slopes, six lifts, and a terrain park with a half-pipe for snowboarders. It's open weekdays until 10 PM.

Swimming

If you don't want to head to the beach, there are several public swimming pools in the city. All pools cost NKr 40 but are free with the Oslo Card. **Besserudtjernet** (✉ Holmenkollen) is a small summer lake at the foot of the Holmenkollen ski jump. The south-facing terraces are ideal for sunbathing. Swimming here is a novelty, with fantastic views of Oslo spread out before you. Lifeguards aren't posted, so swim here at your own risk. **Frognerbadet** (Frogner Swimming Pool; ✉ Vigeland Park, Majorstuen ☎ 23–27–54–50) has four large outdoor swimming pools for all ages and a waterslide. The pools are open from mid-May through late August, depending on the weather (weekdays 7 AM–7:30 PM, weekends 10–5:30). In June, you can hear performances from the nearby Norwegian Wood music festival. **Tøyenbadet** (Tøyen Swimming Pool; ✉ Helgesensgt. 90, Tøyen ☎ 23–30–44–70) is across the road from the Munch Museum and Botanical Gardens. The facilities include one indoor and three outdoor swimming pools for all ages, a sauna, a solarium, a waterslide, and an exercise area.

Tennis

There are several tennis clubs throughout the city to consider for a game, set, or match. **Frognerpark** has municipal tennis courts, open in summer. Reserve courts on arrival. **Holmenkollen Tennisklubb** (✉ Bjørnvn. 74, Holmenkollen ☎ 22–13–60–00) has 11 outdoor courts, a minicourt, and 4 winter courts inside bubbles that protect them from the elements. **Oslo Tennisklubb** (✉ Hyllvn. 5, Frogner ☎ 22–55–69–81) is the biggest outdoor tennis club in Norway. It has 10 clay courts, 2 hard courts, and 4 indoor courts for winter play. Near Vigelandsparken, the easily accessible club has a casual dress code, rents rackets, and charges roughly NKr 150 per hour for court time.

SHOPPING

Oslo is the best place in the country for buying anything Norwegian. Popular souvenirs include knitwear, wood and ceramic trolls, wood spoons, boxes with rosemaling, gold and silver jewelry, pewter, smoked salmon, caviar, *akvavit* (a schnapps), chocolate, and goat cheese.

Established Norwegian brands include Porsgrund porcelain, Hadeland and Magnor glass, David Andersen jewelry, and Husfliden handicrafts. You may also want to look for popular, classical, or folk music CDs; English translations of Norwegian books; or clothing by a Norwegian designer.

Prices in Norway, as in all of Scandinavia, are generally much higher than in other European countries. Prices of handmade articles such as knitwear, are controlled making comparison shopping useless. Otherwise, shops have both sales and specials—look for the words *salg* and *tilbud*. In addition, if you are a resident of a country other than Norway, Sweden, Finland, or Denmark, you can have the Norwegian Value Added Tax (*moms*) refunded at the airport when you leave the country. When you make a purchase, you must clearly state your country of residence in order to have the necessary export document filled in by store staff.

Department Stores

GlasMagasinet (✉ Stortorvet 8, Sentrum ☎ 22–90–87–00), opposite Oslo Domkirke, is more accurately an amalgam of shops under one roof rather than a true department store. Many of its stores sell handcrafted glass, silver, and pewter. Traditionally, families visit GlasMagasinet at Christmastime, so the store is usually open on Sunday in December. **Steen & Strøm** (✉ Kongensgt. 23, Sentrum ☎ 22–00–40–45), one of Oslo's first department stores, sells the usual: cosmetics, clothing, books, and accessories. It also has a well-stocked floor of accoutrements for outdoor activities.

Shopping Centers

Aker Brygge, Norway's first major shopping center, is right on the water across from the Tourist Information Center at Vestbanen. Shops are open until 8 most days, and some open on Sunday. **ByPorten** (⊠ Jernbanetorget 6, Sentrum ☎ 23–36–21–60) is a shopping center with about 30 fashion, food, and gift stores next to Oslo S Station. **Gunerius Shopping Center** (⊠ Storgata 32, Grønland ☎ 22–17–10–97) is set on three levels and caters to the more price-conscious shopper with budget stores for shoes, clothing, and books as well as a large supermarket. **Oslo City** (⊠ Stenersgt. 1, Sentrum ☎ 815/44–033), at the other end of downtown, with access to the street from Oslo S Station, is the city's largest indoor mall, but the shops are run-of-the-mill, and the restaurants mostly serve fast food. The elegant **Paleet** (⊠ Karl Johans gt. 39–41, between Universitetsgt. and Rosenkrantz gt., Sentrum ☎ 22–03–38–88) opens up into a grand, marbled atrium and has many clothing, accessories, and food stores, including a basement food court.

Shopping Neighborhoods

Basarhallene, the arcade behind the cathedral, is worth a browse for glass and crystal and handicrafts made in Norway. Walk 15 minutes west of the city center and you can wander up the tree-lined Bygdøy Allé and browse the fashionable **Frogner** and **Bygdøy** areas, which are brimming with modern and antique-furniture stores, interior design shops, food shops, art galleries, haute couture, and Oslo's beautiful people. The streets downtown around **Karl Johans Gate** draw many of Oslo's shoppers. The concentration of department stores is especially high in this part of town. **Majorstuen** starts at the T-bane station with the same name and proceeds down Bogstadveien to the Royal Palace. There's a flower market on Stortorget in front of the Oslo Cathedral, and a fruit-and-vegetable market at Youngstorget. Every Saturday, a flea market is open at **Vestkanttorget,** at Amaldus Nilsens plass near Frognerparken. **Grünerløkka,** a 15-minute north of the center, is blooming with trendy new and bohemian fashion boutiques.

Specialty Stores

Antiques

Norwegian rustic antiques (those objects considered of high artistic and historic value) cannot be taken out of the country, but just about anything else can with no problem. The Frogner district has many antiques shops, especially on Skovveien and Thomas Heftyes Gate between Bygdøy Allé and Frogner plass. Deeper in the heart of Majorstuen, Industrigate is famous for its good selection of shops. **Blomqvist Kunsthandel** (⊠ Tordenskjolds gt. 5, Sentrum ☎ 22–70–87–70) has a good selection of small items and paintings, with auctions six times a year, and has been in business for more than 130 years. The rare volumes at **Damms Antiqvariat** (⊠ Tollbugt. 25, Sentrum ☎ 22–41–04–02) will catch the eye of any antiquarian book buff, with volumes in English as well as Norwegian. **Esaias Solberg** (⊠ Kirkeristen, Sentrum ☎ 22–86–24–80), behind Oslo Cathedral, has exceptional small antiques. **Kaare Berntsen** (⊠ Universitetsgt. 12, Sentrum ☎ 22–99–10–10) sells paintings, furniture, and small antique items. **Marsjandisen** (⊠ Fridtjof Nansens pl. 2, Sentrum ☎ 22–42–71–68), specializes in Hadeland glass, silver, cups, and mugs. **West Sølv og Mynt** (⊠ Niels Juels gt. 27, Frogner ☎ 22–55–75–83) has the largest selection of antique silver in town.

Art Galleries

The **Ceramo Sculpture Gallery** (⊠ Olaf Ryes pl. 3, Grünerløkka ☎ 22–38–14–26) sells African artifacts that are functional as well as aesthetically pleasing. **Galleri Elenor** (⊠ Kirkevn. 50, Frogner ☎ 22–46–16–90), near Frognerparken west of the center, displays modern Norwegian and international art. **Galleri Markveien** (⊠ Markveien 30, Grünerløkka ☎ 93/42–10–65) displays the work of the commercially successful artist Tone Granberg, who uses the same abstract motif in every one of her paintings. **Kunstnernes Hus** (The Artists' House; ⊠ Wergelandsvn. 17, Sentrum ☎ 22–85–34–10 ☐ 22–85–34–11 ⊕ www.kunstnerneshus.no) exhibits contemporary art, and hosts an art show every fall. The gallery also has a bar/restaurant that is a weekend hot spot for artists and local celebrities.

Books

In Oslo bookshops, you can always find some English-language books. You may want to pick up some classic works by Henrik Ibsen and Knut Hamsun in translation, as well as some by contemporary writers such as Jostein Gaarder, Linn Ullmann, and Nikolaj Frobenius.

ARK Qvist (⊠ Drammensvn. 16, Sentrum ☎ 22–54–26–00), considered Oslo's "English bookshop," specializes in fiction, crime, and Norwegian-Scandinavian translations. **Avalon** (⊠ Paleet, Karl Johans gt. 39–41, Sentrum ☎ 22–33–33–08) has Norway's largest selection of science fiction and fantasy (all in English) as well as comics and board, computer, and card games. **Bjørn Ringstrøms Antikvariat** (⊠ Ullevålsvn. 1, Sentrum ☎ 22–20–78–05), carries a wide selection of used books and records.

Bokkilden Interbok (⊠ Akersgt. 34, Sentrum ☎ 23–31–77–00) stocks an amazing 6,000 maps as well as two walls of travel books. Head to **Nomaden** (⊠ Uranienborgvn. 4, Frogner ☎ 22–56–25–30), behind the Royal Palace, for travel-related books and guidebooks as well as photography books and equipment. **Norli** (⊠ Universitetsgt. 24, Sentrum ☎ 22–00–43–00) is a bookstore chain that has the largest number of titles in Norway. This store keep a substantial number of Scandinavian-language fiction and travel books on hand. **Tanum** (⊠ Karl Johans gt. 43, Sentrum ☎ 22–41–11–00) is strong in the arts, health and healing, and travel. **Tronsmo** (⊠ Kristian Augusts gt. 19, Sentrum ☎ 22–99–03–99) carries books on such topics as politics, feminism, gay and lesbian interests, and movies, as well as mainstream fiction and nonfiction. There are English-language books, plus a comic-book section in the basement.

Clothing

Norway is famous for its hand-knit, colorful wool sweaters, and even mass-produced (machine-knit) models are of top quality. Prices are regulated and they are always lower than prices for Norwegian sweaters abroad.

Stylish men's, women's, and children's fashions are available at several chains. For designer clothing, Oslo has an increasing number of exclusive boutiques carrying Norwegian and international labels. Look out for clothes designed by established Norwegian design stars such as Pia Myrvold.

KNITWEAR **Boa** (⊠ Thorvald Meyers gt. 50, Grünerløkka ☎ 22–38–04–91) produces innovative and modern knitwear designs. **Maurtua Husflid** (⊠ Akershusstranda, Sentrum ☎ 22–41–31–64), on the waterfront beneath Akershus Castle, has a large selection of sweaters and blanket coats. The designer at **Oleana** (⊠ Stortingsgt. 8, Sentrum ☎ 22–33–31–63), Solveig Hisdahl, takes traditional women's sweater patterns and updates them in elegant ways. **Oslo Sweater Shop** (⊠ SAS Scandinavia Hotel, Tullinsgt. 5, Sentrum ☎ 22–11–29–22) is known for having one of the widest selections in the city. **Rein og Rose** (⊠ Ruseløkkvn. 3, Sentrum ☎ 22–83–21–39), in the Vika shopping district, has friendly salespeople and a good selection of knitwear, yarn, and textiles. **William Schmidt** (⊠ Fridtjof Nansens pl. 9, Sentrum ☎ 22–42–02–88), founded in 1853, is Oslo's oldest shop. The firm specializes in sweaters and souvenirs.

EMBROIDERY **Husfliden** (⊠ Møllergt. 4, Sentrum ☎ 24–14–12–80) sells embroidery kits, including do-it-yourself bunader, the national costumes of Norway.

FASHION & SPORTSWEAR **H & M** (Hennes & Mauritz; ⊠ Oslo City and other locations, Sentrum ☎ 22–17–13–90) carries fresh, up-to-date looks at reasonable prices. **Kamikaze** (⊠ Hegdehaugsvn. 24, Majorstuen ☎ 22–60–20–25) and the nearby **Kamikaze Donna** (⊠ Hegdehaugsvn. 27, Majorstuen ☎ 22–59–38–45) specialize in men's and women's designer fashions, mainly from France and Italy. **Soul** (⊠ Vognhallene, Karenlyst Allé 18, Skøyen ☎ 22–55–00–13) carries Norwegian and international labels from major London, Milan, and Paris fashion houses; shoes and accessories; and home products.

Grünerløkka, north of the city center, is becoming a major shopping district filled with hip little boutiques. **Den Kule Mage** (The Round Stomach ⊠ Markveien 55, Grünerløkka ☎ 22–35–76–90) has every maternal item a mother could need and features Norway's only baby café, smartly decorated as a nursery. **Probat** (⊠ Thorvald Meyers gt. 54, Grünerløkka ☎ 22–35–20–70) sells just hip T-shirts from all around the world. **Rebella** (⊠ Thorvald Meyers gt. 52, Grünerløkka ☎ 22–37–94–22), next door to Probat, showcases edgier clothes by young Norwegian fashion designers.

Norwegian sportswear chain stores are easy to spot in the city's malls and on Karl Johans Gate, but also consider checking out some specialty shops. **Peak Performance** (⊠ Bogstadvn. 13, Majorstuen ☎ 22–96–00–91) is a top choice for fashionable sportswear. **Skandinavisk Høyfjellutstyr** (⊠ Bogstadvn. 1, Majorstuen ☎ 23–33–43–80) has a great selection of traditional mountain sportswear.

FUR **HanssonPels** (⊠ Kirkevn. 54, Majorstuen ☎ 22–69–64–20), near Majorstuen, has an excellent selection of furs. **Studio H. Olesen** (⊠ Karl Johans gt. 31, enter at Rosenkrantz gt., Sentrum ☎ 22–33–37–50) stocks exclusive furs.

Food

Throughout Oslo, there are bakeries, delis, fishmongers, and gourmet food shops to tempt all tastes. **Åpent Bakeri** (⊠Inkognito Terrasse 1, Frogner ☎ 22–44–94–70) bakes the city's best-tasting bread for devoted locals and top restaurants. **Fjelberg Fisk og Vilt** (⊠ Bygdøy Allé 56, Frogner ☎ 22–44–60–41) has a reputation for its high-quality fish and seafood, including salmon (smoked, tartar, fresh, and cured), lobster, shrimp, and fish soup. A good restaurant is also on the premises. **Hotel Havana** (⊠ Thorvald Meyers gt. 36, Grünerløkka ☎ 23–23–03–23) is a hip delicatessen with cheeses, Cuban coffee and cigars, tapas plates, and fresh fish. **Skafferiet** (⊠ Elisenbergvn. 7, Frogner ☎ 22–44–52–96), open daily from 10 to 10, is popular with sophisticated Oslo residents for its gourmet foods and fresh flowers. **Vinderen Spesial** (⊠ Holmenveien 1, Holmenkollen ☎ 22–14–90–70) has a good selection of cheeses and fine foods.

Furniture

Several Oslo furniture shops highlight Scandinavian and international designers. **Expo Nova Møbelgalleri** (⊠ Bygdøy Allé 58B, Frogner ☎ 23–13–13–40) is an established outlet with a large showroom including separate departments for furniture, kitchen, and lighting. **Rom for Idé** (⊠ Jacob Aalls gt. 54, Majorstuen ☎ 22–59–81–17) stocks international and Norwegian designs by established and up-and-coming names. **Tannum** (⊠ Stortingsgt. 28, Sentrum ☎ 23–11–53–90), located across the road from the Nationaltheatret Station, is a perfect starting point for classic and contemporary designs.

Glass, China, Ceramics & Pewter

The shops at **Basarhallene,** behind the cathedral, sell glass and ceramics. **Gastronaut** (⊠ Bygdøy Allé 56, Frogner ☎ 22–44–60–90) sells top-quality china, cutlery, linen, and glass, as well as spices and condiments from Spain and Italy.

If there's no time to visit a glass factory outside of town, department stores are the best option: **GlasMagasinet** (⊠ Stortorvet 8, Sentrum ☎ 22–90–87–00) stocks both European and Norwegian designs in glass, pewter, and silver. **Lenes Glass** (⊠ Markveien 30, Grünerløkka ☎ 22–35–47–15) is a glassblower producing modern vases, glasses, and gifts with distinctive blue and gray tones. **Norway Designs** (⊠ Stortingsgt. 28, Sentrum ☎ 23–11–45–10) showcases Scandinavian art glass, kitchenware, ceramics, silver, and other household items.

Handicrafts

Basarhallene, the arcade behind the cathedral, is worth a browse for handicrafts made in Norway. **Heimen Husflid A/S** (⊠ Rosenkrantz gt. 8, enter at Kristian IVs gt., Sentrum ☎ 23–21–42–00) has small souvenir items and a department dedicated to traditional Norwegian costumes. **Husfliden** (⊠ Møllergt. 4, Sentrum ☎ 22–14–12–80), one of the finest stores for handmade goods in the country, has an even larger selection than that at Heimen Husflid. You can find pewter, ceramics, knits, and Norwegian handmade textiles, furniture, felt boots and slippers, loafers, sweaters, traditional costumes, wrought-iron accessories, Christmas ornaments, and wooden kitchen accessories. **Norsk Kunsthandverkeri** (⊠ Munkedamsvn. 57, Sentrum ☎ 22–94–40–80) has beautiful, colorful pieces.

Jewelry

Gold and precious stones are no bargain, but silver and enamel jewelry and Viking-period productions can be. Some silver pieces are made with Norwegian stones, particularly pink thulite. **David-Andersen** (⊠ Karl Johans gt. 20, Sentrum ☎ 24–14–88–00 ⊠ Bogstadvn. 23, Majorstuen ☎ 22–59–50–00) is Norway's best-known goldsmith. He makes stunning silver and gold designs. The **ExpoArte** (⊠ Drammensvn. 40, Frogner ☎ 22–55–93–90) gallery specializes in custom pieces and displays the work of avant-garde Scandinavian jewelers. **Heyerdahl** (⊠ Roald Amundsensgt. 6, Sentrum ☎ 22–41–59–18), near City Hall, is a good dependable jeweler.

Music

More and more Norwegian artists are making names for themselves internationally, often crossing over to singing in English. Some of the bigger Norwegian music names include Sissel and Lene Marlin for pop music, Leif Ove Andsnes for classical music, Silje Nergaard for jazz, Sissel Kyrkjebo for classical music, and Kari Bremnes for folk singing. Ask informed record store staff to recommend other Norwegian-Scandinavian artists. Run by one of Norway's most celebrated jazz sax players, Bodil Niska, **Barejazz** (⊠ Grensen 8, Sentrum ☎ 22–33–20–80) is a specialist store for jazz lovers. Eccentric, eclectic **Los Lobos** (⊠ Thorvald Meyers gt. 30, Grünerløkka ☎ 22–38–24–40) carries rockabilly, surf-guitar, salsa and mambo, and blues music. They also sell vintage Hawaiian shirts and leather jackets from the '50s. **Musikk-huset** (⊠ Storgaten 3, Sentrum ☎ 22–82–59–00) is the last store in Norway dedicated to classical music. **Platekompaniet** (⊠ Oslo City, Sentrum ☎ 22–42–77–35) has the most reasonable prices and best overall selection of mainstream music as well as alternative rock, house, and techno.

Perfume

Gimle Parfymeri (⊠ Bygdøy Allé 39, Frogner ☎ 22–44–61–42) is a tiny, traditional Oslo perfume institution. **Parfymeriet Kilden Lisbet Willoch** (⊠ Klingenberggata 5, Sentrum ☎ 22–83–21–07) carries the latest in fragrances and skin care.

Watches

Swiss watches are much cheaper in Norway than in many other countries. **Thune Gullsmed & Urmaker** (⊠ Rådhuspassasjen, Olav Vs gt. 6, Sentrum ☎ 22–42–99–66) has a good selection of watches by the top Swiss manufacturers. **Urmaker Bjerke** (⊠ Karl Johans gt. 31, Sentrum ☎ 23–01–02–10 ⊠ Prinsensgt. 21, Sentrum ☎ 22–42–60–50) has established a reputation for quality and selection.

OSLO A TO Z

To research prices, get advice from other travelers, and book travel arrangements, visit www.fodors.com

AIR TRAVEL TO & FROM OSLO

CARRIERS SAS Scandinavian Airlines is the main carrier, with both international and domestic flights. Norwegian Air Shuttle operates from eight cities in Norway and has flights from southern Europe and London. Other major airlines serving Oslo Airport include British Airways, Air France, Aeroflot, Finnair, KLM, and Lufthansa.

Aeroflot ☎ 64-81-04-14. **Air France** ☎ 23-50-20-01. **Braathens** ☎ 815/20-000. **British Airways** ☎ 800/33-142. **Crossair** ☎ 810/00-021. **Finnair** ☎ 810/01-100. **KLM Royal Dutch Airlines and Northwest Airlines** ☎ 820/02-002. **LOT Polish Airlines** ☎ 810/00-023. **Lufthansa** ☎ 23-35-54-00. **Norwegian Air Shuttle** ☎ 815/21-815. **Sabena** ☎ 23-16-25-68. **SAS** ☎ 815/20-400. **Swissair** ☎ 810/00-012. **Tap Air Portugal** ☎ 810/00-015. **Widerøe** ☎ 810/01-200.

AIRPORTS & TRANSFERS

Oslo Airport is 45 km (28 mi) north of the city. The spacious airport has huge windows that give excellent views of the landscape and the Nordic light. State-of-the-art weather systems have decreased the number of delayed flights, but always check with your airline regarding the status of your flight.

Oslo Airport ☎ 64-81-20-00, 815/50-250 flight information ⊕ www.osl.no.

AIRPORT TRANSFERS Oslo Airport is a 50-minute car ride via the E6 from Oslo's city center. From Oslo S Station, it's a 19-minute ride by Flytoget (express train, NKr 150 one-way), with trains scheduled every 10 minutes (4:40 AM–1:16 AM).

Flybussen buses depart from Oslo Bussterminalen Galleriet every 20 minutes and reach Oslo Airport approximately 45 minutes later (NKr 100 one-way, NKr 150 round-trip). Going to the airport, they operate daily from 6 AM to 9:40 PM (7:40 on Saturay night). Going from the airport to Oslo, the buses operate daily from 7:30 AM to 11:30 PM (11 on Saturday night).

Flybussekspressen can be picked up at any one of 114 stops, including Oslo S Station, Stortinget, Nationaltheatret, and Aker Brygge on its way to the airport. There are two bus lines following two different routes to the airport. One traverses the inner city, while the other follows the ring roads. Passengers simply hail the bus from bus stops on the street. Buses leave twice per hour and the trip costs NKr 100–NKr 140 depending on where you get on. Call the information number for details of the routes.

There is a taxi line at the front of the airport. By taxi the trip into town takes about 50 minutes and is extremely expensive—upward of NKr 600—so try to catch the Flytoget. All taxi reservations should be made through the Oslo Airport Taxi no later than 20 minutes before pickup time.

For Ryan Air flights from Oslo's second airport, Torp at Sandefjord, take the Torp Express Buss from the main bus terminal at the rear of Galleri Oslo. Buses depart every hour and the journey takes two hours.

Taxis, Shuttles & Trains Flybussekspressen ☎ 820/21-300 departure information, 820/54-301 recorded information. **Flybussen** ☎ 22-80-49-71. **Flytoget** ☎ 815/00-777. **Oslo Airport Taxi** ☎ 23-23-23-23 dial 1 for direct reservation. **Torp Express Buss** ☎ 23-00-24-00.

BOAT & FERRY TRAVEL

Several ferry lines connect Oslo with the United Kingdom, Denmark, Sweden, and Germany. Color Line sails to Kiel, Germany, and to Hirtshals, Denmark; DFDS Scandinavian Seaways to Copenhagen via Helsingborg, Sweden; and Stena Line to Frederikshavn, Denmark.

A ferry to Hovedøya and other islands in the harbor basin leaves from Aker Brygge (take Bus 60 from Jernbanetorget). These are great spots for picnics and short hikes. From April through September, ferries run between Rådhusbrygge 3, in front of City Hall, and Bygdøy, the western peninsula, where many of Oslo's major museums are located. There is also ferry service from Aker Brygge to the town of Nesodden, as well as to popular summer beach towns along the fjord's coast, including Drøbak.

FARES & SCHEDULES ⛴ **Bygdøfergene Skibs A/S** ☎ 23–35–68–90. **Color Line** ☎ 810/00–811. **DFDS Scandinavian Seaways** ☎23–10–68–00 ⊕ www.dfds.no. **Nesodden Bunnefjord Dampskibsselskap** ☎ 23–11–52–20. **Stena Line** ☎ 23–17–91–00.

BUS TRAVEL TO & FROM OSLO

The main bus station, Oslo Bussterminalen Galleriet, is across from the Oslo S Station. You can buy local bus tickets at the terminal or on the bus. Tickets for long-distance routes on Nor-Way Bussekspress can be purchased here or at travel agencies. Trafikanten provides transit information.

⛴ **Nor-Way Bussekspress** ✉ Oslo Bussterminalen Galleriet, Sentrum ☎ 820/21–300, 177 within Oslo 🖶 22–17–59–22 ⊕ www.nor-way.no. **Oslo Bussterminalen** ☎ 23–00–24–00. **Trafikanten** ☎ 815/00–176, 177 within Oslo ⊕ www.trafikanten.no.

BUS TRAVEL WITHIN OSLO

About 50 bus lines, including 16 night buses on weekends, serve the city. Most stop at Jernbanetorget opposite Oslo S Station. Tickets can be purchased from the driver.

CAR RENTAL

⛴ **Major Agencies in Oslo Avis** ☎ 64–81–06–60 at Oslo Airport, 815/33–044 downtown. **Europcar** ☎ 64–81–05–60 Oslo Airport, 22–83–12–42 downtown. **Hertz** ☎ 67/16–80–00 at Oslo Airport, 22–21–00–00 downtown.

CAR TRAVEL

The E18 connects Oslo with Göteborg, Sweden (by ferry between Sandefjord and Strömstad, Sweden); Copenhagen, Denmark (by ferry between Kristiansand and Hirtshals, Denmark); and Stockholm directly overland. The land route from Oslo to Göteborg is the E6. All streets and roads leading into Oslo have tollbooths a certain distance from the city center, forming an "electronic ring." The toll is NKr 20 and was implemented to finance road development in and around Oslo. If you have the correct amount in change, drive through one of the lanes marked "Mynt." If you don't, or if you need a receipt, use the "Manuell" lane. Car rentals can be made directly at Oslo Airport or downtown.

If you plan to do any amount of driving in Oslo, buy a copy of the *Stor Oslo* map, available at bookstores and gasoline stations. It may be a small city, but one-way streets and few exit ramps on the expressway make it very easy to get lost.

EMERGENCY **⚠ Falken** ☎ 02468. **NAF Car Rescue** (Norwegian Automobile Association) ☎ 810/
SERVICES 00-505.

PARKING Oslo Card holders can park for free in city-run street spots or at reduced
rates in lots run by the city (P-lots), but pay careful attention to time
limits and be sure to ask at the information office exactly where the card
is valid. Parking is very difficult in the city—many spaces have one-hour
limits and can cost more than NKr 25 per hour. Instead of individual
parking meters in P-lots, a machine dispenses validated parking tickets
to display in your car windshield. Travelers with disabilities who have
valid parking permits from their home country are allowed to park free
and with no time limit in specially reserved spaces.

EMBASSIES & CONSULATES

⚠ Canada ✉ Wergelandsvn. 7, Sentrum ☎ 22-99-53-00.
⚠ New Zealand ✉ Billengstadsletta 19, Billingstad ☎ 66/77-53-30.
⚠ United Kingdom ✉ Thomas Heftyes gt. 8, Frogner ☎ 23-13-27-00 ⊕ www.
britain.no.
⚠ United States ✉ Drammensvn. 18, Sentrum ☎ 22-44-85-50 ⊕ www.usa.no.

EMERGENCIES

Norway's largest private clinic, Volvat Medisinske Senter, is near the Bor-
gen and Majorstuen T-bane stations, not far from Frogner Park. It is
open weekdays from 8 AM to 10 PM, weekends from 10 to 10. Oslo Akutten is an emergency clinic downtown, near Stortinget. Centrum Legesenter is a small, friendly clinic across from City Hall.

For dental emergencies, Oslo Kommunale Tannlegevakt at Tøyen Senter is open evenings and weekends. Oslo Private Tannlegevakt, near the
American Embassy, is a private dental clinic open seven days a week.

Oslo Kommunale Legevakt, the city's public and thus less expensive,
but slower, hospital, is on Storgata 2 km (1 mi) west of the center, near
Grünerløkka and is open 24 hours. Volvat Medisinske Senter operates
an emergency clinic from 8 AM to 10 PM weekdays and 10 to 10 on
weekends. Jernbanetorgets Apotek, across from Oslo S Station, is open
24 hours. Sfinxen Apotek, near Frogner Park, is open weekdays from
8:30 AM to 9 PM, Saturday from 8:30 AM to 8 PM, and Sunday from 5
PM to 8 PM.
⚠ Doctors & Dentists Oslo Akutten ✉ Nedre Vollgt. 8, Sentrum ☎ 22-00-81-60. **Oslo
Kommunale Tannlegevakt** ✉ Kolstadgt. 18, Tøyen ☎ 22-67-30-00. **Oslo Private
Tannlegevakt** ✉ Hansteensgt. 3, Frogner ☎ 815/00-345. **Volvat Medisinske Senter**
✉ Borgenvn. 2A, Majorstuen ☎ 22-95-75-00.
⚠ Emergency Services Ambulance ☎ 113. **Fire** ☎ 110. **Police** ☎ 112.
⚠ Hospitals Centrum Legesenter ✉ Fritjof Nansens pl., Sentrum ☎ 22-41-41-20. **Oslo
Kommunale Legevakt** ✉ Storgt. 40, Sentrum ☎ 22-93-22-93.
⚠ Late-Night Pharmacies Jernbanetorgets Apotek ✉ Jernbanetorget 4B, Sentrum
☎ 22-41-24-82. **Sfinxen Apotek** ✉ Bogstadvn. 51, Majorstuen ☎ 22-46-34-44.
⚠ Lost & Found Police ☎ 22-66-98-65. **NSB (Norwegian State Railway)** ✉ Oslo
S Station, Sentrum ☎ 23-15-40-47. **Oslo Sporveier (trams, buses, subway)**
☎ 22-08-53-61.

INTERNET SERVICE

🔌 **Arctic Internet** ✉ Oslo S Station, Sentrum ☎ 22-17-19-40. **Studenten Nett-Café** ✉ Karl Johans gt. 45, Sentrum ☎ 22-42-56-80.

LAUNDRY

Self-service laundry facilities are available in several Oslo neighborhoods.

🔌 **A-Vask Selvbetjening** ✉ Thorvald Meyers gt. 18, Grünerløkka ☎ 22-37-57-70 ⊘ Daily 10-8. **Majorstua Myntvaskeri** ✉ Vibesgt. 15, Majorstuen ☎ 22-69-43-17 ⊘ Weekdays 8-8, weekends 8-5.

LODGING

The tourist office at Oslo S Station can book you in anything from a luxury hotel to a room in a private home for a fee of NKr 45. Usually there are last-minute discount rooms.

If you want to rent an apartment, contact Oslo Apartments, open weekdays 8–4. Most of their 90 apartments are reasonably close to downtown Oslo, but there are also a few in Majorstuen, 5 minutes away. There are also some in Skøyen, a grassy suburban area that's closer to both the airport and city center. All are within a 10-minute walk from public transport.

🔌 **Oslo Apartments** ✉ St. Edmundsv. 37, Skøyen ☎ 22-51-02-50 🖨 22-51-02-59.

MONEY MATTERS

CURRENCY EXCHANGE Foreign currencies can be exchanged at a variety of places throughout the city. At most post offices, hours are limited to weekdays from 9 to 5 and Saturday from 9 to 1. The Tourist Information Center at Vestbanen also exchanges currency.

At most banks, the hours are weekdays from 8:30 to 3:30, with many open until 5 on Thursday. The express Flytoget terminal at Oslo S Station has automatic currency exchange machines available 24 hours. The K Bank Bureau de Change at Oslo S Station is open weekdays from 7 to 7, weekends 8 to 5. At Oslo Airport, there are 16 automatic currency machines as well as a Bureau de Change in the Departure and the Arrival Halls.

🔌 **American Express** ✉ Fr. Nansens pl. 6, Sentrum ☎ 22-98-37-35. **Oslo Central Post Office** ✉ Dronningensgt. 15, Sentrum ☎ 23-14-90-00.

SUBWAY TRAVEL

Oslo has seven T-bane (subway) lines, which converge at Stortinget Station. The four eastern lines all stop at Tøyen before branching off, whereas the four western lines run through Majorstuen before emerging aboveground for the rest of their routes to the northwestern suburbs. Tickets can be purchased at the stations.

🔌 **Trafikanten** (public transportation information) ✉ Jernbanetorget, Sentrum ☎ 815/00-176, 177 within Oslo ⊕ www.trafikanten.no ⊘ Weekdays 7 AM-8 PM, weekends 8-6.

TAXIS

Taxis are radio dispatched from a central office, and it can take up to 30 minutes to get one during peak hours. Cabs can be ordered from 20 minutes to 24 hours in advance. (If you leave a cab waiting after you've sent for one, there is an additional fee added to your fare.) Special transport, including vans and cabs equipped for people with disabilities, can be ordered. Taxi stands are located all over town, usually near Narvesen newsstands and kiosks. In the center, there are taxi stands at Stortinget in Karl Johans Gate, at Stortorget by the cathedral, at Youngstorget, and at Oslo Central Station. If there are no available taxis after midnight, take a night bus leaving from outside Oslo S Station.

It is possible to hail a cab on the street, but cabs are not allowed to pick up passengers within 100 yards of a stand. It is not unheard of to wait for more than an hour at a taxi stand in the wee hours of the morning, after everyone has left the bars. Never take pirate taxis; all registered taxis should have their roof lights on when they're available. Rates start at NKr 30 for hailed or rank cabs, and NKr 49 for ordered taxis, depending on the time of day.

🚖 **Norgestaxi** ☎ 08000. **Oslo Taxi** ☎ 02323. **Taxi 2** ☎ 02202.

TELEPHONES
Public telephones take NKr 1, 5, 10, and 20 coins, and you need NKr 5 to get through. Most phone booths in Oslo accept both credit cards and cash. International phone cards are the best value for long-distance calls. These are available at newsstands across town. The international prefix for dialing out of Norway is 00.

TRAIN TRAVEL
Norway's state railway, NSB (Norges Statsbaner), has two train stations downtown—Oslo Sentralstasjon (Oslo S), and a station at Nationaltheatret. Long-distance domestic and international trains arrive at and leave from Oslo S Station. Suburban commuter trains use one or the other station. Commuter cars reserved for monthly-pass holders are marked with a large black "M" on a yellow circle. Trains marked "C," or InterCity, offer such upgraded services as breakfast and office cars—with phones and power outlets—for an added fee.

🚆 **NSB Customer Service** ☎ 815/00-888.

TRANSPORTATION AROUND OSLO
The subways and most buses and trikken start running at 5:30 AM, with the last run after midnight. On weekends, there's night service on certain routes. Trips on all public transportation within Oslo cost NKr 30, with a one-hour free transfer; tickets that cross municipal boundaries have different rates. It often pays to buy a pass or multiple-travel card, which includes transfers. A day card *(dagskort)* costs NKr 55 and a seven-day pass costs NKr 190. Tickets can be used on subway, bus, or trikk.

A *flexikort* for NKr 150 is available at Narvesen newsstands, 7-Eleven stores, tourist information offices, T-bane stations, and on some routes; it is valid for eight trips by subway, bus, or trikk. The **Oslo Card** offers unlimited travel on all public transport in greater Oslo. A one-day Oslo Card costs NKr 190, a two-day card NKr 285, and a three-day card NKr 375. Children's cards cost NKr 75, NKr 95, and NKr 125 and a family card costs NKr 395. The cards can be purchased at tourist information offices and hotels. The Oslo Card also includes free admission to museums and sightseeing attractions; free parking in certain public spaces; a miniboat cruise; admission to public swimming pools; discounts on car, ski, and skate rentals; and discounts at specified restaurants and theaters.

TRAVEL AGENCIES

The city's travel agencies cater to different markets and different age groups. Ving is a popular overall choice among Norwegians because of the package tours they offer. Bennett BTI Nordic is an international, business travel agency. Kilroy Travels Norway and STA Travel cater to the youth and university market, distributing ISIC cards for students and GO cards for people younger than 25.

Local Agent Referrals American Express ⊠ Mariboesgt. 13, Sentrum ☎22-98-37-00. **Bennett BTI Nordic** ⊠ Christian Krohgs gt. 32, Sentrum ☎ 22-59-78-00. **Kilroy Travels Norway** ⊠ Universitetssenteret, Blindern ☎ 02633 ⊠ Nedre Slottsgt. 23, Sentrum ☎ 02633. **Scantours UK** ☎ 0207/839-2927 in London ☎ 0207/839-5891. **STA Travel** ⊠ Karl Johans gt. 8, Sentrum ☎ 815/59-905. **Ving** ⊠ Christian Fredriks pl. 4, Sentrum ☎ 08888.

VISITOR INFORMATION

The tourist information office in Sentrum is open weekdays 9 to 7 in July, 9 to 5 the rest of the year.

In Oslo Oslo Sentralstasjonen (Oslo S Station) ⊠ Jernbanetorget, Sentrum ☎ No phone ⊙ Daily 8 AM–11 PM. **Tourist Information Center in Oslo** ⊠ Fridtjof Nansens pl. 5, entrance from Roald Amundsens gt., Sentrum ☎ 24-14-77-00 ☎ 22-42-92-22 ⊕ www.visitoslo.com.

Side Trips from Oslo

WORD OF MOUTH

"My top pick [for a side trip from Oslo] would be a cruise to Drøbak, a very charming white-wooden-house village located where the Oslo Fjord is slimmest."

—Bjorn

"Check out the old town and fortress in Fredrikstad, about an hour from Oslo on Rte. 110."

—Morten

NORTH OF THE OSLO FJORD

The lush, green, and hilly suburbs and towns northwest of Oslo are a pleasure to visit in themselves, but they also contain many historic monuments, museums, and manor houses that give you a glimpse into the region's past. Day trips to this area are easily manageable from the capital, by bus or train, and are great for catching a glimpse of the countryside even if you're on a purely urban trip.

Bærum

One of Oslo's fashionable suburbs, Bærum is about 20 minutes from the city. The area is mostly residential, but along the banks of the ❶ Lomma River is the charming **Bærums Verk.** In the 1960s the owners of the Bærums Verk iron foundry fixed up their old industrial town and made it into a historical site. Today the stores, workshops, and exhibitions among the idyllic surroundings attract many visitors to its grounds. As you explore the beautifully restored village, notice the cramped wooden cottages lining **Verksgata,** where the workers once lived. Notice that the doors are in the back of the buildings; this was in case a fire from the works spread through the main street. The Museum Bærums Verk has an extensive collection of iron ovens, temporary exhibitions, and restaurants. Take Bus 143 or 753 from Grønland or Universitetsplassen to Triangelen. ✉ *Bærums Verk* ☎ *67–13–00–18* ⊕ *www.baerumsverk.no* ⊠ *Museum NKr 20* ⊙ *Museum: mid-June–mid-Aug., daily noon–4; mid-Aug.–mid-June, weekends noon–4; Verksgata: Tues.–Fri. 10–5, Sat. 10–4, Sun. noon–4.*

Where to Eat

$$$
Fodor'sChoice
★
✕ **Værtshuset Bærums Verk.** Norway's oldest restaurant, this spot is a must on any itinerary that includes the neighboring ironworks. The inn opened in 1640 and was a frequent stop on the King's Road road from Oslo to Bergen. It is now one of the country's finest restaurants, specializing in Norwegian cuisine. Low ceilings, pastel-painted wood floors, and shiny pewter tableware make you feel as though you've stepped into 19th-century Norway. The fresh salmon and the venison in brown sauce are particularly good. ✉ *Vertshusvn. 10, Bærums Verk* ☎ *67–80–02–00* ▭ *AE, DC, MC, V.*

Høvikodden

🌿 ❷ The **Henie-Onstad Kunstsenter** (Henie-Onstad Art Center) is just outside Oslo, about 12 km (7 mi) southwest on E18. It houses Norway's largest collection of international modern art. After skater Sonja Henie married shipping magnate Niels Onstad, they began to put together a fine collection of early-20th-century art, with important works by Munch, Picasso, Bonnard, and Matisse. Henie died in 1969, but she still skates her way through many a late-night movie. The ultramodern, minimalist building, designed by Norwegian architects Jon Eikvar and Sven Erik Engebretsen, stands out impressively by the scenic Oslo fjord. There are also a library, children's work space, and sculpture park. Restaurateurs

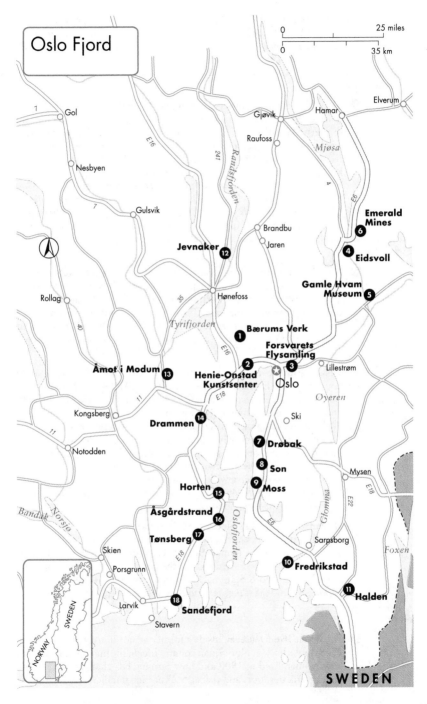

Oslo Fjord

0 ————— 25 miles

0 ————— 3.5 km

Elverum

1

Gol

Gjøvik   Hamar

Raufoss   *Mjøsa*

Nesbyen

E16

Gulsvik

7

Randsfjorden

241

Brandbu

Jevnaker 12   Jaren

Emerald Mines 6

Eidsvoll 4

Rollag

40

35

Hønefoss

Gamle Hvam Museum 5

Tyrifjorden

Bærums Verk 1

Åmot i Modum 13

E16

2

Forsvarets Flysamling 3

Lillestrøm

Henie-Onstad Kunstsenter

Oslo

Øyeren

11

Kongsberg

Drammen 14

E18

Ski

11

Notodden

Drøbak 7

Son 8

Mysen

Moss 9

E18

Bandak   *Norsjø*

Horten 15

Åsgårdstrand 16

Oslofjorden

Glomma

E22

Tønsberg 17

Sarpsborg

Foxen

Skien

E18

Porsgrunn

Fredrikstad 10

Larvik

18

Halden 11

Stavern

Sandefjord

NORWAY   SWEDEN

SWEDEN

Toralf Bølgen and Trond Moi run the restaurant on the premises. Buses 151, 161, 252, and 261 from Oslo S Station stop near the grounds. ⊠ *1311 Høvikodden* ☎ *67–80–48–80* ⊕ *www.henieonstad.no* ✉ *NKr 80* ☉ *Tues.–Thurs. 11–7, Fri.–Sun. 11–6.*

Gardermoen

❸ The Military Plane Collection, **Forsvarets Flysamling,** at the Sør-Gardermoen Culture and Business Center at Oslo Airport, contains aircraft from the early days of flying, rare World War II planes, and all of the Norwegian Air Force jets from the Cold War era. By car, take E6 in the direction of Rte. 174 to Nannestad. Turn onto Road 4 and go about 3 km (1½ mi) before turning right and heading toward the airplane collection. ⊠ *Sør-Gardermoen culture and business center* ☎ *63–92–86–60* ✉ *NKr 60* ☉ *Dec.–Feb., weekends noon–4; Mar.–mid-June, Tues., Thurs., and weekends noon–4; mid-June–mid-Aug., Tues.–Thurs. and weekends 11–5; mid-Aug.–Nov., Tues., Thurs., and weekends noon–4.*

Eidsvoll

❹ Norway's constitution was written and passed in 1814 at **Eidsvoll,** a manor house about 60 km (38 mi) north of Oslo. May 17, National Day, commemorates that occasion. Portraits of all the members of the 1814 Norwegian parliament hang here. Trains for Eidsvoll depart from Oslo S Station. ⊠ *Carsten Ankers v., Eidsvoll Verk* ☎ *63–92–22–10* ⊕ *www. eidsvoll1814.museum.no* ✉ *NKr 50* ☉ *Mid-May–mid-Aug., daily 10–5; Sept.–Dec., Tues.–Fri. 10–2, weekends noon–5.*

Galleri Festiviteten. Festiviteten is a gallery and café in a handsome 1909 house opposite Eidsvoll and beside the scenic And River. The changing exhibitions of paintings, ceramics, sculptures, and graphics are by well-known and up-and-coming Norwegian artists, such as the painter Arne Ekeland and sculptor Nils Aasland. The atmospheric entry hall is decorated with black-and-white photos of the construction workers who built the house. The café serves tea, coffee, and pastries, and you can take your tea into the adjacent garden overlooking the river. On weekends there are concerts with jazz and classical music. ⊠ *Festiviteten Sagveien 2, Eidsvoll Verk* ☎ *63–95–76–00* ⊕ *www.festiviteten.com* ✉ *Free* ☉ *Wed.–Sun. noon–5.*

Skibladner, the world's oldest paddle steamer, makes a stop at Eidsvoll, as well as at Hamar, Gjøvik, Lillehammer, and elsewhere. While aboard, dine in the first-class lounge on boiled salmon and fresh strawberries. Schedules for the steamer (and for the corresponding train stops) are available at Oslo S Station. ⊠ *Torggt. 1* ☎ *61–14–40–80* ✉ *NKr 120–NKr 320* ☉ *Sailings late June–mid-Aug., Wed., Fri., and Sun.*

Årnes

❺ The **Gamle Hvam Museum,** inside a former manor house that dates from 1728, looks back at Norwegian country life. In the main building, learn how women lived in 1900 and how farming has changed since 1950. Take a walk outdoors and visit agriculture and handicraft exhibits, rose gardens, and beds of other flowers. To get here, take the train to Årnes. On weekdays you can also take Bus 835. ⊠ *Hvam* ☎ *63–90–96–09* ⊕ *www.gamlehvam.museum.no* ⊠ *NKr 50* ⊙ *Late May–Aug., weekdays 11–4, weekends noon–5.*

Byrud Gård

❻ This town at the southern end of Lake Mjøsa is best known for its **Emerald Mines** (Smaragdgruvene) at Minnesund, the only such mines in northern Europe. Ask for a guided tour or go on a treasure hunt: in one section, emerald finders are emerald keepers. Handmade emerald and stone items are available at the gift shop. ⊠ *Rte. 33 off E6* ☎ *63–96–86–11* ⊠ *NKr 80* ⊙ *Mid-Apr.–Oct., daily 8–6.*

EAST OF THE OSLO FJORD

The eastern side of the Oslo Fjord is summer-vacation country for many Norwegians, who retreat to cabins by the water in July. Many towns along the fjord offer history and culture as well as a place to swim. Viking ruins and inscriptions, fortified towns, and bohemian 19th-century artists' colonies provide a glimpse into the region's rich heritage.

Some of the towns mentioned can easily be visited as day trips from Oslo. Roads can be winding, though, adding to the driving time, so you might want to devote several days to exploring the area. Note that ferries shuttle cars and people back and forth between the archipelago islands and across the fjord, so it is possible to combine this tour with a trip to the west side of the Oslo Fjord and make a complete circle without backtracking. Trains from Oslo S Station stop at Fredrikstad and Halden.

Drøbak

❼ *35 km (21 mi) south of Oslo.*

Drøbak's pretty collection of white wooden houses and small winding streets gives the impression of a typical Sørlander (southern) town, yet it is only one hour's drive from the capital. Oslovians often take day trips to Drøbak to sit by the beach and eat fresh shrimp. During World War II Norwegian forces sunk the German cruiser *Blucher* here. From May to September you can take the scenic one-hour ferry ride from Oslo's Aker Brygge to Drøbak on the **M/S Prinsessen** (☎ 23/11–52–20).

More than 1,000 species of fish and marine life from the Oslo Fjord are exhibited in the **Drøbak Akvarium** (aquarium). There's a children's area where kids can handle a variety of shellfish, and a special exhibit explains how you can make lutefisk, the Norwegian fish delicacy popular at Christmastime. ⊠ *Havnegata* ☎ *64–98–87–80* ⊕ *www.akvarium. net* ⊠ *NKr 30* ⊙ *May–Aug., daily 11–5; Sept.–Apr., daily 11–4.*

| need a break? | On the main square, stop in **Det Gamle Bageri Ost & Vinstue** (The Old Bakery Wine and Cheese Room; ☎ 64–93–21–05) for salads, pies, and hearty fare such as salmon in a mouthwatering sweet-mustard sauce. The wood interior dates from 1740, and classical music soirees are held on weekends. |

🕐 **Jegstad Gård farm,** a traditional Norwegian dairy, has animals to visit and horse carriages to ride. Wander along the nature trail or visit the stable, farm museum, and Viking burial mounds. You can play sports or relax on the large lawn. The farm is between Drøbak and Vestby, to the south. ⊠ *Rte. E6, Vestby* ☎ *64–95–00–58* ✉ *NKr 50* ⊙ *Apr.–Aug., Sun. noon–4 (July, daily); by special arrangement rest of yr.*

🕐 The inviting **Tregaardens Julehus** (Christmas House) dominates the town's central square. Just around the corner from the post office, this 1876 building was once a mission for seafarers unable to reach Oslo because the fjord was frozen over. Now it's a retail store that sells Christmas wares and gifts such as wooden dolls and mice made of cloth—all handmade by Eva Johansen, the store's creator and owner. Many Norwegian children believe Father Christmas resides in Drøbak because there's a Santa's post office in this store. ⊠ *Main Sq.* ☎ *64–93–41–78.*

Shopping

Take time to stroll downtown and browse through the charming small shops. **Galleri Finsrud** (⊠ Torrkildes stranda ☎ 64–93–23–99) sells paintings, drawings, and bronze sculptures produced by local artists. Artists and craftspeople also exhibit and sell their work at **Galleri Havstad** (⊠ Storgt. 15 ☎ 64–93–46–55).

Where to Stay

$ 🏨 **Reenskaug Hotel.** Old-fashioned, wooden, and whitewashed, this early-20th-century hotel is on Drøbak's main road. With its traditional Norwegian country-style interior, it is a very Scandinavian place to stay. Ask for Room 213; in 1904 Norway's Nobel Prize for Literature winner Knut Hamsun wrote here. ⊠ *Storgt. 32, 1440* ☎ *64–93–33–60* 🖷 *64–93–36–66* ⊕ *www.reenskaug.no* ⇥ *30 rooms* ⚐ *Restaurant, in-room data ports, bar, meeting rooms* ⊟ *AE, DC MC, V.*

Son

❽ *25 km (15 mi) south of Drøbak.*

You can swim, sail, or sun on the banks of Son (pronounced *soon*), just south of Drøbak. An old fishing and boating village, this resort town has traditionally attracted artists and writers. Artists still flock here, as do city folk in summer.

In summer you can count on **Klubben Soon** (☎ 64–95–70–42) for a good mix of disco, jazz, and other concerts.

Moss

❾ *10 km (6 mi) south of Son.*

Although the area has been inhabited since Viking times, Moss gained borough status in 1720 and is one of the area's main commercial and shipping centers, with around 30,000 inhabitants.

off the beaten path

GALLERI F15 – A 5-km (3-mi) ride from Moss, on the island of Jeløy, is an art center set on an old farm. Exhibits displayed here range from photography to large art installations and Scandinavian crafts. ⊠ *Alby Gård* ☎ *69–27–10–33* ✉ *NKr 40* ☉ *June–Aug., Tues.–Sun. 11–7; Sept.–May, Tues.–Sun. 11–5.*

Where to Stay & Eat

★ **$–$$** ✕🖼 **Refsnes Gods.** This historic hotel has one of Norway's best kitchens and a fine wine cellar. The French-Norwegian food is especially good; ask about the Grand Menu consisting of seven courses of meat and local game. While dining, take a look at one of the seven Munch paintings in the dining room, including *Blue Lady.* The main building dates from 1767, and used to be part of a family estate. The Victorian-style, blue-and-beige rooms are airy and pretty, while the suites contain paintings by famous artists Frans Widerberg and Jacob Weidemann, whose works also hang in the National Gallery. ⊠ *Godset 5, 1502* ☎ *69–27–83–00* 🖨 *69–27–83–01* ⊕ *www.refsnesgods.no* ⇗ *57 rooms, 4 suites* ⚴ *Restaurant, pool, gym, sauna, beach, boating, meeting room* ☰ *AE, DC, MC, V.*

Fredrikstad

🔟 *34 km (20 mi) south of Moss.*

Norway's oldest fortified city lies peacefully at the mouth of the Glomma, the country's longest river. Its bastions and moat date from the 1600s. After spending time in town browsing the shops and museum, take the ferry to the little island of Hvaler, a popular vacation spot.

★ In the center of town is **Fredrikstad Domkirke** (Fredrikstad Cathedral). Built in 1860 in a flamboyant neo-Gothic style, it contains stained-glass decorations by Emanuel Vigeland, whose work also adorns Oslo Cathedral. ☎ *69–30–02–80* ✉ *Free* ☉ *Tues.–Fri. 11–3.* •

The **Fredrikstad Museum** documents the town's history in two separate exhibitions and locations. The first focuses on the town's maritime and shipping heritage and has period commercial vessels and sailing boats. The second tells the story of the development of the town and city from 1860 to 1960 through objects related to its industrial, commercial, hospital, and day-to-day life. ☎ *69–95–85–00* ✉ *NKr 40* ☉ *June–Sept., weekdays 9–4.30, weekends noon–5.*

Fodor'sChoice **Gamlebyen** (Old Town) has been preserved and has museums, art galleries, cafés, artisans' workshops, antiques shops, and old bookstores.

Where to Stay

$–$$ 🖼 **Hotel City.** This comfortable, stylish hotel is in the center of downtown, but is still quiet and peaceful. The restaurant serves a mixture of Norwegian and Italian dishes. ⊠ *Nygaardsgt. 44–46, 1607* ☎ *69–38–56–00* 🖨 *69–38–56–01* ⇗ *110 rooms* ⚴ *Restaurant, cable TV, sauna, bar, nightclub, convention center, meeting rooms* ☰ *MC, V.*

Shopping

Glashytte (✉ Torsnesvn. 1 ☎ 69–32–28–12) is a well-known glass-blowing studio and shop; its glassware is exhibited and sold in galleries throughout Norway. You can watch glassblowers perform their magic, creating everything from schnapps glasses to vases in primary colors. If you're in the area, you can place a special order and go see your glass object blown. You can pick it up a few days later after it's been cooled slowly in a kiln, which makes it less fragile.

Halden

⓫ *30 km (18 mi) south of Fredrikstad.*

This idyllic little town has several historic attractions well worth a visit. Since it's close to the Swedish border, it once needed fortifications in order to fend off attacks—Norwegians and Swedes had ongoing border disputes. The most famous skirmish at Fredriksten fortress resulted in the death of King Karl XII in 1718.

★ ⛰ Built in the late 1600s in the shape of a star to keep out Swedish invaders, the complex of buildings that make up the **Fredriksten Festning** (Fredriksten Fortress) are at the city's highest point. The exhibit in the former prison describes Halden war history from the 17th century to World War II. An old pharmacy in the residence illustrates the history of pharmacology, including the use of bird claws in folk medicine. At the far end of the inner courtyard the bakery and brewery could bake enough bread to feed 5,000 men and brew 3,000 liters of beer. The exhibition "Byen brenner," which means "the city is burning," documents the many fires suffered by Halden's primarily wood buildings. Inside the fort itself is **Fredriksten Kro,** an old-fashioned pub with outdoor seating. ☎ *69–19–09–80 or 69–18–54–11* 🎟 *NKr 40* ☉ *Mid-May–Aug., daily 10–5.*

Fodor'sChoice **Rød Herregård** is one of the finest and best-preserved 18th-century
★ manors in Norway. A restored building houses period furniture, artwork, and an amazing display of stuffed-animal hunting trophies. An impressive baroque garden and an English garden surround the manor on the edge of the fjord. The house, open only for tours, has a unique weapons collection, a café, and a gallery. ✉ *1771 Halden* ☎ *69–18–54–11* 🎟 *NKr 40* ☉ *Tours: July–mid-Aug., Tues.–Sun. at noon, 1, and 2.*

Where to Eat

$-$$ ✕ **Rekekafeen.** Near dockside sheds on a floating pier in the marina, Rekekafeen has a reputation for fresh fish and seafood. Taste their smoked fish and shrimp. You can also have eel, choosing yours from those swimming in a nearby tank. At a separate fish counter, fishing equipment and bait are sold, and there are changing exhibitions of local arts and crafts. On weekends musicians perform. ✉ *Waterfront* ☎ *69–18–29–06* ▭ *AE, DC, MC, V.*

East of the Oslo Fjord A to Z

To research prices, get advice from other travelers, and book travel arrangements, visit www.fodors.com.

BOAT & FERRY TRAVEL

An underground tunnel links Drøbak, on the east side of the fjord, with Hurum, on the west side, just north of Horten. The tunnel toll is NKr 55. Contact Drøbak Turistinformasjon for schedule information. You can also take a ferry, the M/S *Prinsessen,* from Aker Brygge in Oslo to Drøbak for NKr 50.

🚢 **M/S *Prinsessen*** ⊠ Stranden 1 ☎ 23/11-52-20 ⊕ www.nbds.no.

BUS TRAVEL

The trip on Bus 541 or 542 from Strandgata at the corner of Prinsensgata in Oslo to Drøbak affords great glimpses of the fjord (and bathers in summer). The trip takes an hour, and buses depart hourly at 15 minutes to and 15 minutes past the hour during the week, with reduced service on weekends. Bus 100 (E6 Ekspress) departs during the day at 7:15 AM, 12:15 PM, and 3:15 PM, stopping at Svindsen, where you can catch a local bus to Halden.

🚌 **Bus Information Nor-Way Bussekspress** ☎ 815/44-444 ⊕ www.nor-way.no.

CAR TRAVEL

Follow Route E18 southeast from Oslo to Route E6. Follow signs to Drøbak and Son. Continue through Moss, following signs to Halden, farther south on E6. The road then takes you north to Sarpsborg, where you can turn left to Fredrikstad.

TRAIN TRAVEL

Trains for Halden leave from Oslo S Station and take two hours to make the 136-km (85-mi) trip, with stops in Moss, Fredrikstad, and Sarpsborg.

VISITOR INFORMATION

🚩 **Tourist Information Drøbak** Drøbak Turistinformasjon ☎ 64-93-50-87 ⊕ www. drobakguiden.no. **Fredrikstad** Fredrikstad Turistkontor ⊠ Turistsentret vøstre Brohode ⊠ 1632 Gamle Fredrikstad ☎ 69-30-60-00 ⊕ www.fredrikstad.kommune.no. **Halden** Halden Turist Kontor ⊠ Storgt. 6, Box 167, 1751 Halden ☎ 69-19-09-80 ⊕ www.haldentourist.no. **Moss** Moss Turistkontor ⊠ Fleischersgt. 17, 1531 Moss ☎ 69-24-15-20 ⊕ www.moss.kommune.no. **Son** Son Kystkultursenter ⊠ 1555 Son ☎ 64-95-82-13.

WEST OF THE OSLO FJORD

Towns lining the western side of the fjord are more industrial on the whole than their neighbors on the eastern side. Still, the western towns have traditionally been some of Norway's oldest and wealthiest, their fortunes derived from whaling and lumbering. Populations in the western towns are also more multicultural.

Jevnaker

⑫ *Follow E16 toward Hønefoss, then follow Rte. 241 to Jevnaker, which is about 70 km (42 mi) northwest of Oslo; it's about a 2-hr drive.*

A day trip to Jevnaker combines a drive along the Tyrifjord, where you can see some of the best fjord views in eastern Norway, with a visit to Norway's oldest glassworks, in operation since 1762.

Ⓒ   At **Hadeland Glassverk** you can watch artisans blowing glass, or, if you get there early enough, you can blow your own for NKr 75. Both practical table crystal and one-of-a-kind art glass are produced here, and you can buy first-quality pieces as well as seconds in the gift shop. Learn the history of glass at the Glass Museum. For children, there's a Honey House of bees and a Children's House that celebrates Christmas every weekend from April through December. There is also a bakery and a restaurant, Kokkestua, which serves traditional Norwegian meals. ⌂ *Rte. 241, Postboks 85* ☎ *61–31–66–00* ⊕ *www.hadeland-glassverk.no* ✉ *Glass museum NKr 30* ⊙ *Weekdays 10–5, Sat. 10–4, Sun. 11–5.*

Åmot i Modum

⑬ *If you're coming from Jevnaker, take Rte. 35 south, along the Tyrifjord. If you're coming from the E18, take Rte. 11 west to Hokksund, and Rte. 35 to Åmot. Then turn onto Rte. 287 to Sigdal. Åmot i Modum is 70 km (42 mi) west of Oslo.*

The small village of Åmot is famous for its cobalt mines. The blue mineral was used to make dyes for glass and porcelain industries around the world.

★ Ⓒ   The **Blaafarveværket** (Cobalt Works) was founded in 1773 to extract cobalt from the Modum mines. Today the complex is a museum and a national park. A permanent collection displays old cobalt-blue glass and porcelain. Sign up for a guided tour in English. **Nymoen,** the on-site museum of social history, has exhibits with letters and photographs that depict how the cobalt workers lived and spent their leisure time. Official documents demonstrate the Blaafarveværket's humane compensation policies, including sick pay, pension program, and a poverty-relief fund. Elsewhere in the park you'll find a petting farm for children, and a café that serves Norwegian country fare. ✉ *Rte. 507* ☎ *32–78–67–00* ⊕ *www.blaa.no* ✉ *Special exhibitions NKr 60; cobalt works free* ⊙ *Mid-May–mid-June, daily 10–4; mid-June–mid-Aug., daily 10–6; mid-Aug.–mid-Sept., Tues.–Sun. 11–6.*

A 10-minute walk up the hill from Blaafarveværket is **Haugfoss,** the highest waterfall in eastern Norway. Besides pausing for the beautiful view, you can also visit the nearby **general store,** which dates from the early 18th century. The store offers fresh-ground coffee, old-fashioned sweets, and gifts such as wooden ladles and leather bags. There is also a jewelry shop selling original handmade pieces, wrought-iron gifts, and baskets. ✉ *Rte. 507* ☎ *32–78–67–00* ⊕ *www.blaa.no* ⊙ *Store: Mid-May–mid-June, daily 10–4; mid-June–mid-Aug., daily 10–6; mid-Aug.–mid-Sept., Tues.–Sun. 11–6.*

The **Theodore Kittelsen Museet** has Norway's largest collection of the haunting and mysterious works of this artist, whose paintings depict trolls, fairies, and other fantastic creatures in Norwegian landscapes. Many of the paintings were inspired by Norwegian folk tales. The museum is on the Skuterudhøyden ridge, a five-minute drive from the Cobalt Mines. ⌧ *Rte. 507* ☎ *32–78–67–00* ⊕ *www.blaa.no* ⌧ *NKr 40* ☉ *Mid-May–mid-June, daily 10–4; mid-June–mid-Aug., daily 10–6; mid-Aug.–mid-Sept., Tues.–Sun. 11–6.*

Drammen

⑭ *40 km (25 mi) from Oslo, 45 km (27 mi) south of Åmot i Modum.*

Drammen, a timber town and port for 500 years, is an industrial city of 55,000 on the Drammen River. Called the River City, it was the harbor for exported silver from the Kongsberg mines. These days many cars are imported into Norway here. A number of unattractive industrial sites along the river make Drammen the butt of jokes among other townspeople, but Drammen actually has a pretty town square (the oldest in Scandinavia), an impressive Gothic church, and outlying hills that are perfect for hiking, skiing, and other outdoor activities. The river divides the city into two: Bragernes (historically more prosperous) and Strømsø.

The **Drammen Museum of Art and Cultural History** actually comprises several smaller museums scattered around the city. Marienlyst Manor (built in 1770) has Nøstetangen glass and rustic folk and church art. The Art Department's permanent gallery has many great works of 19th- and 20th-century Norwegian masters, including Hans Heyerdahl's *The Champagne Girl*. At Spiraltoppen, the Open Air Museum chronicles 300 years of area architecture. Gulskogen Gård and Boathouse is an elegant manor estate dating from 1804, with a shrubbery maze, canals, and a variety of birdlife. ⌧ *Konnerudgt. 7* ☎ *32–20–09–30* ⌧ *NKr 30* ☉ *Tues.–Sat. 11–3 (Thurs. 11–8), Sun. 11–5.*

Spiralen is the name of the spiraled, more than 1¼-mi-long tunnel cut through Bragernesåsen (Bragernes Hill). **Spiraltoppen,** the area around the tunnel entrance, has a marvelous view of Drammen, the river, and the fjord. In summer, Drammens Museum runs a small, open-air heritage museum here that's free of charge. Spiraltoppen is also the starting point for many downhill and cross-country skiing trails. Several footpaths make up a 2-km (1-mi) nature trail. ⌧ *Spiraltoppen* ☎ *32–20–09–30.*

Where to Stay & Eat

$$–$$$ ✕ **Skutebrygga.** Right on the riverbank and just off the square, this popular meeting place has a strong nautical theme, with miniature boats, anchors, and old maps. A patio overlooking the river is perfect for outdoor dining in summer. Inside, stained Norwegian pine and a modern circular fireplace make the restaurant cozy in any season. The seafood dishes, such as creole-style fish and gratinéed lobster, are delicious. ⌧ *Nedre Strandgt. 2* ☎ *32–83–33–30* ▭ *AE, DC, MC, V.*

$–$$ ✕ **Åspavilongen.** This hillside restaurant and bar is known for its panoramic view of the entire valley and fjord. Dating back to the turn of the 20th century, its walls are covered with historic photographs. Try the *kjøttballer* (Norwegian meatballs). ✉ *Bragernesåsen* ☎ *32–83–37–47* ☰ *AE, DC, MC, V* ⊘ *Closed early Sept. and Nov.–Apr.*

$–$$ ✕ **Glass.** True to its name, this upscale brasserie and bar appears as a
Fodor'sChoice large glass box at the bank of the Drammen River. The owners wanted
★ to create a transparent building through which patrons could admire the flow of the river. If you dine on the outdoor terrace, you'll feel as though you're almost on the water. The stylish bar inside has light-blue walls and leather sofas. Try the wok-fried chicken or the panfried fresh salmon. ✉ *Nedre Strandgt. 4* ☎ *32–82–00–70* ☰ *AE, DC, MC, V.*

$$ ▦ **Rica Park.** As with all Rica hotels, the Park is relaxed. The rooms are comfortable, light, and airy. Faux ancient Greek statues in the lobby and an abundance of mirrors in the glass-walled restaurant contribute to a gaudy interior that has probably been untouched since the 1980s. Take a walk in the nearby woods, and then have coffee and cake at the Spiraltoppen Café, which has great views. ✉ *Gamle Kirkepl. 3, 3019* ☎ *32–26–36–00* 🖶 *32–26–37–77* ⊕ *www.rica.no* ➷ *100 rooms, 2 suites* 🗝 *Restaurant, cable TV, in-room broadband, bar, nightclub* ☰ *AE, DC, MC, V.*

$–$$ ▦ **First Hotel Ambassadeur.** One of the better places to stay in Drammen, this hotel is especially popular with business travelers who like its stylish, comfortable guest rooms. Its elegant pink facade makes it easily recognizable, and it lies close to both the railway station and the bus terminal. ✉ *Strømsø Torg 7, 3044* ☎ *31/01–21–00* 🖶 *31/01–21–11* ⊕ *www.first-hotels.no* ➷ *230 rooms, 12 suites* 🗝 *Restaurant, cable TV, gym, sauna, bar, convention center, meeting rooms* ☰ *AE, DC, MC, V.*

Shopping

Nedre Storgata is a good street for a variety of shopping. The city's main shopping mall, **Steen & Strom Magasinet** (✉Nedre Storgt. 6 ☎32–21–39–90) has 65 shops and restaurants.

About 8 km (5 mi) from Drammen, on Route 135 toward Hokksund, is **Buskerud Storsenter** (☎ 32–23–15–45), the region's largest shopping mall, with more than 80 shops and restaurants.

Sports & the Outdoors

Drammen is known throughout Norway for its wealth of outdoor activities, which include fishing, skiing, cycling, boating, and hiking. Four cycling trails are outlined on maps available from the tourist office. Wherever you are, you are never more than a few minutes from footpaths, nature trails, miles of forest land, lakes, grassy hills, and scenic countryside.

BOATING **M/S *Drammen* Charter and Turistbåt** (✉Bragernes Torg 13 ☎32–83–50–45) organizes river excursions and fjord tours from May to September. A boat with catering and crew is available for hire.

FISHING The fjord and the Drammen River have great fishing, particularly at Hokksund and Hellefossen. Salmon and trout are most prized; it's not uncommon to catch salmon weighing 22–44 pounds. Forty other kinds of fish can also be caught in the river. The fishing season runs from mid-May through September. Contact the **Drammens Sportfiskere**

(☎ 32–88–66–73) for information on national and local fishing licenses as well as regulations and events.

HORSE RACING The **Drammen Racecourse** is one of 10 permanent betting courses in Norway. Tuesday is racing day, beginning at 6 PM; there are also five special Saturday races. The horses can be seen at close range, making the race that much more immediate and exciting. ⊠ *Buskerudvn. 200* ☎ *32–21–87–00.*

SKIING Cross-country skiers have 100 km (60 mi) of trails available outside the city, including 45 km (28 mi) of well-maintained tracks that are lit up at night. Downhill skiers can head to Haukåsløypa on the Strømsø side or Aronsløypa on the Bragernes side.

SWIMMING Make a splash poolside at one of Drammen's indoor and outdoor swimming complexes. **Marienlystbadet** (☎ 32–83–34–05 ⊙ Late June–mid-Aug.) has an Olympic-size pool, diving pool, and children's pool all heated to nearly 80° F (26° C). The complex also has a waterslide, water toys, beach-volleyball courts, a sauna, and places to sunbathe. **Sentralbadet** (☎ 32–83–65–86 ⊙ Mid-Aug.–May) has an indoor 25-meter swimming pool and a warm pool that's heated to 93°F (34 °C). There's also a Jacuzzi, waterslide, solarium, sauna, Nautilus exercise room, and a lounge.

Nightlife

If you want to have a drink, hear live music, or go dancing, try the city's hotels, or head downtown to check out Drammen's bars, pubs, and clubs. **Pavarotti** (⊠ Nedre Torggt. 9 ☎ 32–83–55–74) is known for its live jazz on Wednesday night and on Saturday starting at 3 PM. The **Riggen Pub** (⊠ Amtmann Blomsgt. ☎ 32–83–67–00) has blues performances on Wednesday, Friday, and Saturday nights. **Rock på Union Scene** (⊠ Gronland 68 ☎32–83–77–88) books new bands for concerts every Friday night.

Horten

❶⑤ *35 km (17 mi) south of Drammen.*

Off the main route, E18, going south, the coastal village of Horten has several distinctive museums worth an afternoon's visit. The town was once an important Norwegian Royal Navy station and still retains the cadet school. A car ferry travels across the fjord to Moss every 30 minutes.

The **Horten Bil Museum** traces the development of motor vehicles from 1900 to 1970 through exhibits of 35 cars and motorcycles. Everything from the earliest autos to modern Porsches is on view. ⊠ *Sollistrandvn. 12* ☎ *33–02–08–50* 🎫 *NKr 35* ⊙ *Mid-June–mid-Aug., daily noon–3; mid-Aug.–mid-June, Sun. noon–3.*

The **Marinemuseet** (Royal Norwegian Navy Museum), built in 1853 as a munitions warehouse, displays 16th- and 17th-century Danish and Norwegian naval relics. Outside is the world's first torpedo boat, from 1853, and some one-person submarines. ⊠ *Karl Johans Vern* ☎ *33–03–35–46* 🎫 *Free* ⊙ *May–Sept., daily noon–4; Oct.–Apr., Sun. noon–4.*

The **Norsk Museum for Fotografi: Preus Fotomuseum** (Norwegian Museum for Photography: Preus Photography Museum) houses the fascinating private collection of Leif Preus. Opened in 1994, it was later sold, and reopened in May 2001 on the fourth and fifth floors of the huge naval warehouse. The extensive collection has between 4,500 and 5,000 cameras, including a rare 1840s camera obscura. All kinds of photographs—documentary, press, portraits, scientific, fine art—are here, including the work of August Sander and Tom Sandberg. The museum has one of the world's largest libraries of photography books. Look for the photographer's studio of a hundred years ago, as well as the tiny camera used for early aerial photographs: it was strapped to a pigeon. A bookstore is also on site. ⊠ *Karl Johans Vern* ☎ *33–03–16–30* ⊕ *www.foto.museum.no* 🖃 *NKr 35* ☉ *Tues.–Sun. noon–5.*

Åsgårdstrand

⑯ *10 km (6 mi) south of Horten.*

Since 1920 the coastal town of Åsgårdstrand has been a popular vacation and bathing spot. A couple of decades before that, it was known as an artists' colony for outdoor painting, attracting Edvard Munch, Fritz Thaulow, and others. In summer the local tourist office can arrange guided history tours of the area, led by well-versed guides.

FodorsChoice
★ **Munchs lille hus** (Munch's little house) was the summer house and studio in which the artist spent seven summers. Now a museum, it was here that he painted *Girls on the Bridge* and earned a reputation as a ladies' man. ⊠ *Munchsgt.* ☎ *33–08–21–31* 🖃 *NKr 40* ☉ *May and Sept., weekends 11–7; June–Aug., Tues.–Sun. 11–7.*

Where to Stay

$ 🏨 **Åsgårdstrand Hotell.** Steps away from the harbor, the Åsgårdstrand has large, airy rooms, some with spectacular ocean views. Perfect for those who want to be part of the town's active sailing culture, it even has a harbor that guests can use. ⊠ *Havnegt. 6, 3167* ☎ *33–08–10–40* 🖶 *33–08–10–77* ⊕ *www.asgardstrand-hotell.no* 🛏 *73 rooms, 5 suites* ⚐ *Restaurant, cable TV, bar, sauna* ☰ *AE, DC, MC, V.*

en route | Travel south from Åsgårdstrand toward **Tønsberg** and you'll pass **Slagen,** where the *Oseberg* Viking ship, dating from around 800, was found. (It's now on display at Vikingskiphuset in Oslo.) Look for the mound where it was buried as you pass Slagen's church.

Tønsberg

⑰ *11 km (6½ mi) south of Åsgårdstrand.*

According to the Sagas, Tønsberg is Norway's oldest non-Sámi settlement, founded in 871. Little remains of Tønsberg's early structures, although the ruins at **Slottsfjellet** (Castle Hill), by the train station, include parts of the city wall, the remains of a church built around 1150, and a 13th-century brick citadel, the **Tønsberghus.** Other medieval remains are below the cathedral and near Storgata 17. Today Tønsberg is a popular summer retreat with scenic fishing and swimming spots.

The intriguing art in **Haugar Vestfold Kunstmuseum** is mostly done by regional and other Norwegian artists. The building was erected in 1922 as a school for sailors, and soon after received architectural awards. The impressive facade was codesigned by sculptor Wilhelm Rasmussen, who embellished it with 12 caryatids in local granite. ✉ *Gråbrødragt. 17* ☎ *33–30–76–70* ⊕ *www.haugar.com* ✎ *NKr 45* ⊙ *Sept.–May, Tues.–Fri. 11–4, weekends noon–5; June–Aug., weekdays 11–5, weekends noon–5.*

North of the railroad station, the **Vestfold Fylkesmuseum** (Vestfold County Museum) houses a small Viking ship, several whale skeletons, and some inventions. See the whale-factory ships where whales were processed on board. The open-air museum focuses on farming life. ✉ *Farmannsvn. 30* ☎ *33–31–24–18* ✎ *NKr 40* ⊙ *Mid-May–mid-Sept., Mon.–Sat. 10–5, Sun. noon–5; mid-Sept.–mid-May, weekdays 10–2.*

off the beaten path

VERDENS ENDE – The "end of the world" is a scenic camping, swimming, and fishing retreat on the southernmost point of the island of Tjøme, 30 minutes' drive from Tønsberg. Standing on the rocky shoreline you get a near-180-degree view of the ocean, and you will literally feel like you are at the end of the world. Cabins dot the area and can be rented for NKr 450 for a weekend. ✉ *Verdens Ende, Tjøme* ☎ *33–39–10–10 campground.*

Where to Stay

$–$$ 🏨 **Best Western Grand Hotel.** This art deco hotel first opened its doors in 1931. The rooms are simple but modern and comfortable. One- to three-room luxury apartments have attractive Chesterfield furniture and Italian-style kitchens. ✉ *Øvre Langgt. 5, 3126* ☎ *33–35–35–00* 📠 *33–35–35–01* ⊕ *www.grandhotel-toensberg.no* ⬎ *64 rooms, 3 suites, 12 apartments* ⚐ *Restaurant, some kitchens, cable TV, in-room data ports, bar, meeting rooms* ☰ *AE, DC, MC, V.*

Sandefjord

⑱ *125 km (78 mi) south of Oslo, 25 km (15 mi) south of Tønsberg.*

Back in 1400 the Vikings had settlements and grave sites in Sandefjord. A natural harbor, the city was once the whaling capital of the world. Around 1900 it was possibly Norway's wealthiest city. Now that the whales are gone, all that remains of its commercial importance is a monument to it. With many beaches, 116 islands, and an archipelago, Sandefjord earns its nickname of "Badebyen," or "Bathing City." In summer, boating and tourism thrive. From the Sandefjord Gjestehavn (guest, or public, harbor), take a short walk to the city's restaurants, shopping, and attractions. The town also has Oslo's second airport, Torp, which offers flights to Norwegian cities as well as to Frankfurt, Glasgow, and Stansted.

Kommandør Christensens Hvalfangstmuseum (Commander Christensen's Whaling Museum) is perhaps best known for the suspended life-size model of a blue whale. The museum traces the development of the industry from small, primitive boats to huge floating factories. An especially intriguing display chronicles whaling in the Antarctic. ⊠ *Museumsgt. 39* ☎ *33–48–46–50* 🖃 *NKr 25* ⊙ *Daily 11–5.*

Take a break from the beach to see the fascinating **Sandefjords Sjøfartsmuseum** (Sandefjord's Maritime Museum), which chronicles man's life at sea. Discover maritime history at exhibits about the sailing ships of the 19th century as well as more modern vessels. ⊠ *Prinsensgt. 18* ☎ *33–48–46–50* 🖃 *NKr 25* ⊙ *Early May–late June and mid-Aug.–late Sept., Sun. noon–4; late June–mid-Aug., daily noon–4.*

Where to Stay & Eat

★ **$$$** ✕ **Ludls Gourmet Odd Ivar Solvold.** Celebrity chef Odd Ivar Solvold works his culinary magic here. In a place famous for its seafood, Solvold's grilled crayfish, turbot, catfish, scallops, and mussels are all highly recommended. For dessert, there's a wonderfully decadent chocolate truffle cake as well as a caramelized hazelnut-and-pistachio custard. ⊠ *Rådhusgt. 7* ☎ *33–46–27–41* ▤ *AE, DC, MC, V.*

$$ 🏨 **Comfort Home Hotel Atlantic.** The Atlantic Home was built in 1914, when Sandefjord was a whaling center. The history of whaling is traced in exhibits in glass cases and in pictures throughout the hotel. There's no restaurant, but the room rate includes an evening buffet of cold cuts, hot soup, pasta, and meat dishes served near the reception area. ⊠ *Jernbanealleen 33, 3201* ☎ *33–42–80–00* 🖷 *33–42–80–20* ⊕ *www.choicehotels.no* 🛏 *109 rooms* ௹ *Cable TV, sauna, lobby lounge, library, meeting rooms* ▤ *AE, DC, MC, V.*

$$ 🏨 **Rica Park Hotel.** The interior looks much the same as it did when the hotel was built in 1959. Ask for one of the 50 redecorated rooms, which are more spacious than the standard rooms. ⊠ *Strandpromenaden 9, 3200* ☎ *33–44–74–00* 🖷 *33–44–75–00* ⊕ *www.rica.no* 🛏 *233 rooms, 8 suites* ௹ *2 restaurants, in-room data ports, indoor pool, health club, sauna, spa, bar, nightclub, convention center* ▤ *AE, DC, MC, V.*

Cafés

Like many other Norwegian cities, Sandefjord has several trendy little spots that serve a great cup of coffee. If you need to go online, head to **cafe 4u.no** (⊠ Storgt. 14 ☎ 33–42–94–98), an Internet café that serves coffees and breakfast, lunch, and dinner. The name's a play on Norway's top-level domain name, "no." The popular café and bar **første etage** (⊠ Torvet 5 ☎ 33–46–27–80) also serves lunch and dinner. **Fru Wold** (⊠ Kongensgt. 5 ☎ 33–46–42–71) serves espresso drinks and light lunches.

Sports & the Outdoors

Sandefjord is probably best known for its beaches and bathing. The tourist office has information on the multitude of sports played by locals, including soccer, handball, badminton, and tennis.

SWIMMING & DIVING Sandefjord has a beautiful 146-km (90-mi) coastline brimming with wonderful beaches, especially those at the following islands and locations, all of which are accessible by car. Langeby is probably the nicest beach and is accessible by bus from the town center (7 km [4½ mi]):

Vesterøya: Asnes, Sjøbakken, Langeby, Grubesand, Vøra og Fruvika. Østerøya: Flautangen, Skjellvika, Truber, and Yxnøy. **Along Highway 303 toward Larvik:** Granholmen. **Along Highway 303 toward Tønsberg:** Solløkka.

Neptun Dykkersenter (✉ Bjerggt. 7 ☎ 33–46–14–90) is a diving center that teaches classes and sells and rents diving and water-sports equipment.

West of the Oslo Fjord A to Z

To research prices, get advice from other travelers, and book travel arrangements, visit www.fodors.com.

BOAT & FERRY TRAVEL
The most luxurious and scenic way to see the region is by boat. There are guest marinas at just about every port. The Drammen tourist office can provide information on boat rentals.

BUS TRAVEL
Because train service to towns south of Drammen is infrequent, bus travel is the best alternative to cars. Check with Nor-Way Bussekspress for schedules. Torpekspressen coaches from the Oslo bus terminal connect with Ryan Air flights at Sandefjord Torp Airport, stopping at Asker and Drammen along the way.

🚌 Bus Information **Nor-Way Bussekspress** ☎ 815/44–444 ⊕ www.nor-way.no. **Torpekspressen** ☎ 67–11–69–90 ⊕ www.torpekspressen.no.

CAR TRAVEL
Route E18 south from Oslo follows the coast to this region's towns.

TRAIN TRAVEL
Take a suburban train from Nationaltheatret or trains from Oslo S Station to reach Horten, Tønsberg, and Sandefjord.

VISITOR INFORMATION
🚩 Tourist Information **Blaafarveværket** ☎ 32–78–67–00. **Drammen** Drammen Kommunale Turistinformasjonskontor ✉ Engene 1, 3008 Drammen ☎ 32–80–62–10 ⊕ www.drammen.kommune.no. **Hadeland** ☎ 61–31–66–00. **Horten and Åsgårdstrand** Horten Turist Kontor ✉ Tollbugt. 1A, 3187 Horten ☎ 33–03–17–08. **Sandefjord** Sandefjord Reiselivsforening ✉ Torvet, 3201 Sandefjord ☎ 33–46–05–90 ⊕ www.visitsandefjord.com/eng. **Tønsberg** Tønsberg og Omland Reiselivslag ✉ Nedre Langgt. 36B, 3110 Tønsberg ☎ 33–31–02–20 ⊕ www.visitvestfold.com/en.

Southern Norway

3

WORD OF MOUTH

"The absolute best part of the trip was our hike up Pulpit Rock [Preikestolen in Norwegian]. It was a solid two-hour hike, hard in parts, but our 5- and 7-year-old boys did it fairly easily. The reward was definitely worth the hard work we put in to get to the top. The view was spectacular!"
—Molly Donnelly

"Stavanger is one of my favorite towns."
—Helen

IN SUMMER, MANY OF OSLO'S RESIDENTS MIGRATE to the forests of Telemark and the sunny southern coast. Southern Norway is an ideal area for those who want to get close to nature, with a mild summer climate and terrain varying from inland mountains and forests to coastal flatland.

Southwest of Oslo lies a landscape of wide-open vistas and deep forests: Telemark and the Setesdal Valley. The region is veined with swift-flowing streams and scattered with peaceful lakes. Forested hills and deeply etched valleys stretch across the serene countryside. Here are natural surroundings so powerful and silent that, a few generations ago, trolls were the only reasonable explanation for what lurked in, or plodded through, the shadows. Telemark was the birthplace of skiing as well as the birthplace of many Norwegian-Americans: the poor farmers of the region were among the first Norwegians to emigrate to the United States in the 19th century.

Continuing south from Telemark, you reach the famed beaches and fjords of the coast. Many splendid points mark the route of the North Sea Road. Beginning in the relaxed resort town of Kristiansand, the road winds west along the major section of Norway's southern coast, Sørlandet. Wide, sun-kissed, inviting beaches have their blue waters warmed by the Gulf Stream. Sandy terrain turns to coastal flatlands, inland mountain peaks and green forests ideal for cycling, hiking, and mountaineering. Freshwater lakes and rivers, and this section of the ocean, are some of the best places to go salmon fishing—they're also superb for canoeing, kayaking, and rafting. The region is the perfect habitat for such wildlife as beavers, deer, foxes, and many birds.

When the North Sea Road reaches its final destination, it's in a landscape of fjords, islands, mountains, and valleys. Stavanger, Norway's oil capital, is here; a cosmopolitan city yet with small-town charm, it has some of the country's best restaurants, hotels, and cultural life.

Numbers in the margin correspond to points of interest on the Southern Norway map

Exploring Southern Norway

Situated right in the middle of southern Norway, surrounded by the beaches and fjords of the south coast, Telemark is often described as a miniature of the whole Norwegian landscape. In the north and west of the region is the Hardangervidda high mountain plateau, and the Telemark countryside has lowland forests and river valleys. Telemark and the Setesdal Valley are best explored by car from Oslo, although be warned that some of the roads are mountainous. There is regular but sometimes infrequent bus service from Oslo to the towns and villages in Telemark. Summer is the best time to visit Telemark, when you can enjoy the bucolic countryside at its most picturesque.

Nicknamed Norway's Rivieria, Sørlandet and the coast stretching to Stavanger in the west is marked by fjords, fjord arms, islands, skerries and beaches, and coastal resort towns such as Kristiansand. During your time in southern Norway, look out for the picturesque, colorful, 18th- and

19th-century wooden houses that dot the countryside. The drive along the North Sea Road is a real pleasure, and along the way you can take in wonderful views and explore the picturesque coastal villages, with their colorful boats and busy waterfronts.

About the Hotels & Restaurants

The hotels and restaurants we list are the cream of the crop in each price category. Those properties indicated by an ✕🍴 are lodging establishments whose restaurant warrants a special trip.

WHAT IT COSTS In Norwegian Kroner				
$$$$	**$$$**	**$$**	**$**	**¢**
RESTAURANTS over 230	190–230	150–190	90–150	under 90
HOTELS over 1,500	1,000–1,500	800–1,000	400–800	under 400

Restaurant prices are for a main course at dinner. Hotel prices are for two people in a standard double room in high season, including tax and a service charge.

TELEMARK & THE SETESDAL VALLEY

Kongsberg

❶ *84 km (52 mi) southwest of Oslo.*

Kongsberg, with 23,000 people today, was Norway's silver town for about 200 years. In 1623 two local children discovered a large ox butting a cliff in the area with his horns, revealing a silver vein in the hillside. News of the silver find reached King Christian IV in Copenhagen. He sent experts to investigate the area's mining potential. A year later, the king himself came and founded the mining town of "Konningsberg." Norway's first industrial town was prominent until about 1805, when other industries became more important. The mine was finally closed in 1957.

Kongsberg Kirke (Kongsberg Church), finished in 1761, was built during the heyday of the silver mines. Along one wall is an impressive gilded baroque altar, organ, and pulpit. The famous large glass chandeliers were made at **Nøstetangen glassworks** (☎ 32–73–19–02), which now produces less extravagant glass items for the consumer.

The Arts

In the first week of July music fans descend on Kongsberg for its annual **jazz festival** (☎ 32–73–31–66 ⊕ www.kongsberg-jazzfestival.no).

Where to Stay & Eat

$$ ✕ **Gamle Kongsberg Kro.** This café, next to the waterfall at Nybrofossen, has a reputation for traditional, hearty Norwegian dishes at reasonable prices. Try the broiled salmon with horseradish sauce or the pepper steak. ⊠ *Thornesvn. 4* ☎ *41/63–14–51* ➠ *DC, MC, V.*

$$–$$$ 🍴 **Quality Grand Hotel.** A statue of Kongsberg's favorite son, Olympic ski jumper Birger Ruud, stands in the park in front of this modern, centrally located hotel. The rooms are in a minimalist style of white walls contrasting with dark furniture. ⊠ *Christian Augusts gt. 2, 3600*

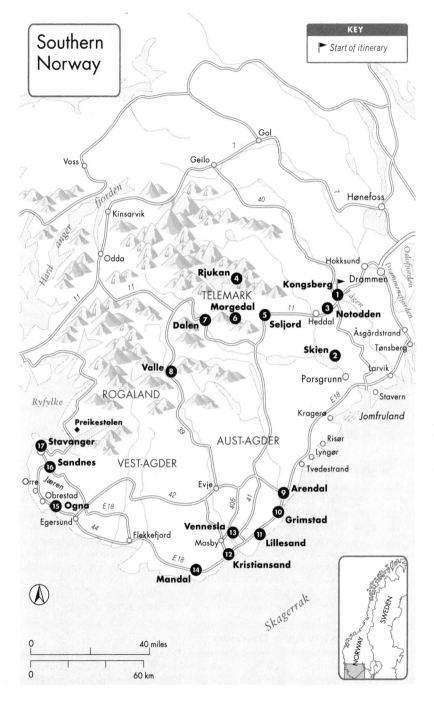

Southern Norway

☏ 32–77–28–00 🖷 32–73–41–29 ⊕ *www.quality-grand.no* ➷ *175 rooms, 12 suites ᕲ 2 restaurants, cable TV, in-room data ports, indoor pool, spa, 2 bars, nightclub, meeting room* ▭ *AE, DC, MC, V.*

Skien

➋ *88 km (55 mi) south of Kongsberg on Rtes. 32 and 36.*

Best known as the birthplace of playwright Henrik Ibsen, Skien, with a population of 50,000, is the capital of the Telemark region. Skien celebrates its favorite son every summer with the **Ibsen-Kultur-festival** (☏ 35–90–55–20), which includes concerts as well as plays.

The **Telemark Museum at Brekkeparken,** housed in a 1780 manor house, displays folk art from the 18th and 19th centuries. Brekkeparken is one of northern Europe's largest tulip parks, with more than 25,000 tulips. The exhibit "90 Years of Scouting" chronicles the activities of Norwegian boy scouts in the Skien area. ✉ *Øvregt. 41* ☏ *35–54–45–00* ⊕ *www. telemark.museum.no* 🎫 *NKr 50* ☉ *Mid-May–Aug., daily 10–6.*

Now the Henrik Ibsen Museum, **Venstøp** looks just as it did when the Ibsen family lived here from 1835 to 1843. The dark attic was the inspiration for the *Wild Duck.* This house, part of Skien's County Museum, is 5 km (3 mi) northwest of the city. ✉ *Venstøphøgda 74* ☏ *35–52–57–49* 🎫 *NKr 50* ☉ *Mid-May–Aug., daily 10–6; otherwise by appointment.*

> **off the beaten path**

BØ SOMMARLAND – Norway's largest water park has wave pools, one of the steepest waterslides in Europe, and Las Bøgas, a *tivoli* (amusement park). Always a surefire hit with families, it hosts more than 100 activities, including live concerts, each year on land and water. The park is 50 km (30 mi) from Skien and 25 km (15 mi) from Notodden. ✉ *3800 Bø* ☏ *35–06–16–00* ⊕ *www.sommarland.no* 🎫 *NKr 245* ☉ *Mid-June–mid-Aug., daily 10 AM–8 PM.*

Where to Stay & Eat

★ **$$$$** ✕ **Boden Spiseri.** The consistently excellent kitchen here serves French-influenced Norwegian dishes. The fillet of reindeer is rich and delicious. For dessert, try the strawberry ice cream or the passion-fruit cake. ✉ *Landbrygga 5* ☏ *35–52–61–70* ▭ *AE, DC, MC, V* ☉ *No lunch.*

$$ 🏨 **Rainbow Høyers Hotell.** This venerable hotel in the center of town has style and sophistication. The exterior, with its cornices and pedimented windows, is reflected in the hotel's lobby, in an incongruous mixture of old and new. The large rooms are bright, thanks to big windows, and have modern furnishings. ✉ *Kongensgt. 6, 3700* ☏ *35–90–58–00* 🖷 *35–90–58–05* ⊕ *www.rainbow-hotels.no/hoyers* ➷ *73 rooms, 8 suites ᕲ Restaurant, in-room data ports, bar, meeting rooms* ▭ *AE, DC, MC, V.*

Sports & the Outdoors

BIKING The Coastal Route goes along the Telemark coastline and is part of the North Sea Cycle Route, which passes through six other countries. There's also a 115-km (71-mi) path along the Telemark Canal from Ulefoss to Dalen. **Telemark Reiser** (☎ 35–90–00–30) has cycling maps, and bicycle package trips that include accommodation and transport.

GOLF   About 7 km (4½ mi) north of Skien is **Jønnevald** (☎ 35–59–07–03), an 18-hole championship golf course. It costs NKr 400 to play.

en route   Running 105 km (65 mi) from Skien to Dalen with a detour to Notodden, **Telemarkskanalen** (Telemark Canal; ☎ 35–90–00–30 ⊕ www.telemarkskanalen.com) was carved into the mountains more than 100 years ago. It took 500 men 5 years to blast through the mountains to create 28 locks. The canal became "the fast route" between east and west Norway and upper and lower Telemark. Telemarkskanalen still has its original stone walls, locks, and closing mechanism.

Notodden

❸ *68 km (42 mi) northwest of Skien, 35 km (21 mi) west of Kongsberg.*

Notodden today is not much more than a small industrial town. It's believed that the area was prosperous in the Middle Ages, though, because of the size of the town's *stavkirke* (stave church), which is 85 feet high and 65 feet long. Notodden is known for its **summer blues festival** (⊕ www.bluesfest.no), which lasts four days in August; past acts have included the Robert Cray Band.

★ **Heddal Stave Church** is Norway's largest stave church still in use. Dating back to the 12th century, the structure is resplendent with rosemaling (decorative flower painting from the 17th century), a bishop's chair, and incense vessels from the Middle Ages. Look out for the stylized animal ornamentation and the grotesque human heads on the portals. ☎ 35–02–04–00 🖾 NKr 35 ⊙ Mid-May–mid-June and mid-Aug.–mid-Sept., daily 10–5; mid-June–mid-Aug., daily 9–7.

Rjukan

❹ *96 km (59 mi) northwest of Notodden.*

The town of Rjukan may not ring a bell, but mention "heavy water," and those who lived through World War II or saw the film the *Heroes of Telemark* with Kirk Douglas, will recall the sabotage of the heavy water factory here, which thwarted German efforts to develop an atomic bomb. Rjukan became a town in the decade between 1907 and 1916, when its population grew from a few hundred to 10,000 because of a different kind of water: hydroelectric power.

Heavy water (used in nuclear reactors) was produced as a by-product in the manufacture of fertilizer at Vemork, where a museum, **Industriarbeidermuseet Vemork** (Norwegian Industrial Workers Museum) has been built. Vemork was the world's largest power station in 1911. In the machine hall you can see a demonstration of a miniature power plant. Exhibitions document the development of hydroelectric power and the events that took place in Rjukan during World War II. ⊹ *6 km (4 mi) west of*

*Rjukan along Rte. 37 ☎35–09–90–00 ⊕www.visitvemork.com ✆NKr
60 ⊙ Mid-June–mid-Aug., daily 10–6; mid-Aug.–Sept., daily 10–4;
Oct., weekends 11–4; Apr., Sat. 11–4; May–mid-June, daily 10–4.*

Rjukan is the site of northern Europe's first cable car, **Krossobanen**
(Krosso Cable Car), built in 1928 by Hydro (the hydroelectric company)
as a gift to the Rjukan inhabitants, so they could escape the shadowed
valley and see Hardanger Mountain Plateau and Mt. Gausta.
☎35–09–12–90 ✆NKr 35 ⊙ Times vary.

Where to Stay

$–$$ 🏨 **Gaustablikk Høyfjellshotell.** At the foot of Mt. Gausta, the highest moun-
tain in southern Norway, this wooden cabin is a popular ski resort. There
are nine downhill slopes and 80 km (50 mi) of cross-country trails. In
summer these marked trails are ideal for walks and hikes. ☒ 3660
☎35–09–14–22 🖷35–09–19–75 ⊕www.gaustablikk.no ✍98 rooms,
6 suites △ Restaurant, indoor pool, meeting rooms, sauna, bar ⊟ AE,
DC, MC, V.

$–$$ 🏨 **Park Hotell.** This small tourist hotel in the center of town has a tra-
ditional Scandinavian look, and is family-friendly. Rooms are cheerful
and painted with light colors. The restaurant is named Ammonia for
the Norwegian ship of that name that sank during World War II. The
menu is typically Norwegian—try the delicious pepper steak. ☒ Sam
Eydes gt. 67, 3660 ☎35–08–21–88 🖷35–08–21–89 ⊕www.parkhotell-
rjukan.no ✍39 rooms △ Restaurant, bar, pub, nightclub, meeting
rooms ⊟ AE, DC, MC, V.

Sports & the Outdoors

CYCLING Rjukan's local tourist office rents bikes weekdays 9–7 and weekends 10–6.

FISHING Telemark has more than 1,000 good fishing lakes. Contact the tourist
office to find out about maps, licenses, and guides.

HORSEBACK Take the reins of an Icelandic horse on a riding trip organized by **Kalhovd**
RIDING **Turisthytte** (☒ Atrå ☎ 35–09–05–10 ⊕ www.kalhovd.com) on Hardangervidda. Contact the tourist office for more information.

MOUNTAINEERING Whether you're an experienced mountain climber or a beginner, **Telemark Opplevelser** (☎ 99–51–31–40) can show you the ropes. They teach
all levels of climbing courses and organize wilderness climbing and
camping trips.

Seljord

❺ *50 km (30 mi) south of Rjukan.*

A serpent adorns the coat of arms of this otherwise peaceful town. The
reason for its inclusion in the town's crest can be found in the depths
of the nearby lake, Seljordsvatnet, where a giant sea serpent, reminiscent of the Loch Ness monster, and known affectionately by the locals
as Selma, is supposed to live. She's thought to have occasionally broken through the lake's surface on warm summer days, or even to have
crawled ashore. The serpent is quite an obsession for the people of Seljord
(even the mayor claims to have proof of her existence), and serpent sou-

venirs aren't hard to come by. If scanning the lake for monsters gets tedious, you could always have a look at the beautiful 12th-century stone church, or stroll through the town and have a bite to eat.

In the center of town, **Dyrskuplassen** (☎ 35–06–52–40) is a modern marketplace and fairground hosting a variety of events throughout the year, including an agricultural show, a country festival, and a Christmas market.

Morgedal

6 *77 km (46 mi) southwest of Rjukan via Åmot.*

In the heart of Telemark is Morgedal, the birthplace of modern skiing, thanks to the persistent Sondre Norheim, who in the 19th century perfected his skis and bindings and practiced jumping from his roof. His innovations included bindings that close behind the heel and skis that narrow in the middle to facilitate turning. In 1868, he took off for a 185-km (115-mi) trek to Oslo just to prove it could be done. A hundred years ago skiers used one long pole, held diagonally, much like highwire artists. Eventually the use of two short poles became widespread, although purists still feel that the one-pole method is the "authentic" way to ski.

★ ♺ The **Norsk Skieventyr** (Norwegian Skiing Adventure Center) in Morgedal guides you through the 4,000-year history of the winter sport with life-size exhibits of typical ski cottages and authentic skis and costumes. Displays include the inside of Norway's original and last ski-wax factory, where specialists melted a variety of secret ingredients, including cheese, to make uphill and downhill slides smoother. Visit Norheim's cottage, Øvrebø, above the edge of the forest, where the Olympic flame was lighted. Several action-packed skiing films can be seen here. ⊠ *Rte. 11 between Brunkeberg and Høydalsmo* ☎ *35–05–42–50* ≅ *NKr 55* ☉ *Late May–mid-June, daily 11–5; mid-June–mid-Aug., daily 9–7; mid-Aug.–late Aug., daily 11–5; Sept.–mid-Dec. and mid-Jan–late May, Sat. 11–4.*

Dalen

7 *60 km (37 mi) southwest of Morgedal.*

The area around Dalen is the place to hike, bike, and be outdoors. From Skien you can take boat tours on the Telemark waterways, a combination of canals and natural lakes between Skien, Dalen, and Notodden.

The trip to Dalen takes you through Ulefoss, where you can visit the neoclassical **Ulefoss Manor** (⊠ Hovedgård ☎ 35–94–56–10), which dates from 1807. It's open weekdays June through September from noon to 5 and Sunday from noon to 3.

The historic **Dalen Hotel** is worth a peek, whether or not you stay there. A number of royal families have been guests, and locals are said to think ghosts haunt its creaky wooden halls. For trips to Dalen, contact the **Telemarkreiser tourist organization** (☎ 35–90–00–20 ⊕ www.telemarkreiser.no).

At Eidsborg, just north of Dalen, **Vest-Telemark museum Eidsborg** (☎ 35–07–73–31 ⌨ NKr 30 ✪ June–Aug., daily 11–6) is an open-air museum consisting of more than 30 sod buildings set in lush green surroundings. The centerpiece is the small but beautiful **Eidsborg Stavkirke** (⌨ NKr 30; NKr 50 includes admission to rest of museum), known for its prime examples of rosemaling.

Where to Stay

$–$$ ⌨ **Dalen Hotel.** At one end of the Telemark Canal, this opulent, Victorian, Swiss-style hotel has retained its original decorations. Look for the dragonhead carvings and stained-glass windows on the balcony overlooking the stunning entrance hall. When the weather's fine, you can go rowing, or play croquet in the garden. ⌨ *3880* ☎ *35–07–70–00* 🖷 *35–07–70–11* ⊕ *www.dalenhotel.no* ↩ *38 rooms* ⌂ *Restaurant, in-room data ports, bar, lobby lounge, meeting room; no a/c, no room TVs* 🗖 *AE, V* ✪ *Closed Christmas–Easter.*

Valle

❽   *The Setesdal road, Rte. 9, follows the Otra River downstream and then runs alongside the Byglandsfjord; Valle is 56 km (35 mi) southwest of Dalen.*

Near Valle sits **Sylvartun,** a clump of grass-roof cottages that house a silversmith's workshop, a jewelry shop, and an art gallery. It's also a cultural center that hosts concerts and displays local crafts, including many Hardanger fiddles. Every summer during the "Setesdal Evenings," professional musicians and folk dancers perform while a traditional Norwegian dinner is served. ⌨ *Rte. 19 near Valle, Nomeland* ☎ *37–93–63–06* ✪ *Silversmith's shop: May–Oct., Mon.–Sat. 10–6, Sun. 11–6. Call for program schedules.*

> **off the beaten path**

SETESDAL MINERAL PARK – About 97 km (57 mi) south of Valle, just south of Evje, in Hornnes, is an interesting park where rock formations from Norway and elsewhere are displayed inside a mountain. ⌨ *Rte. 39, 4737 Evje* ☎ *38–00–30–70* ⌨ *NKr 60* ✪ *Mid-June–Aug., daily 10–5.*

Telemark & the Setesdal Valley A to Z

BUS TRAVEL

The many bus lines that serve the region are coordinated through Nor-Way Bussekspress in Oslo. Buses in the region rarely run more than twice a day, so get a comprehensive schedule from the tourist office or the bus company's office in Oslo.

🚩 Bus Information **Nor-Way Bussekspress** ⌨ Oslo Bussterminalen Galleriet ☎ 815–44–444 🖷 22/17–59–22.

CAR TRAVEL

On Route E18 from Oslo, the drive southwest to Kongsberg takes a little more than an hour. If you arrive by way of the Kristiansand ferry, the drive up Route 9 to Evje takes about the same time.

Roads in the southern part of the interior region are open and flat, but others are curvy and mountainous. Route E134 passes through Heddal and Morgedal, and connects with Routes 37 and 38, which go north to Rjukan and south toward Dalen. E134 also connects with Route 9, the main Setesdal road, which goes through Valle and Evje, proceeding all the way to Kristiansand.

TRAIN TRAVEL

The Norwegian State Railways (NSB) local train from Oslo S Station to Kongsberg takes 1 hour and 25 minutes; bus connections to Telemark are available. The only train service in the southern part of the region is the Oslo–Stavanger line (via Kristiansand).

VISITOR INFORMATION

🚩 Tourist Information **Kongsberg** ✉ Karschesgt. 3 ☎ 32-29-90-50. **Notodden** ✉ Teatergt. 3 ☎ 35-01-50-00. **Rjukan** ✉ Torget 2 ☎ 35-09-12-90 ⊕ www.rjukan-turistkontor.no. **Setesdal** ✉ 4735 Evje ☎ 37-93-14-00. **Skien** ✉ Reiselivets Hus, N. Hjel-legt. 18 ☎ 35-90-55-20. **Telemarkreiser** (Telemark Canal tourist organization) ✉ Nedre Hjellegt. 18, 3702 Skien ☎ 35-90-00-20 🖷 35-90-00-21 ⊕ www.telemarkreiser.no.

SØRLANDET TO STAVANGER: THE NORTH SEA ROAD

Arendal

❾ *260 km (418 mi) south of Oslo.*

In Arendal's Tyholmen, the old town, there are many painted houses bearing window boxes filled with pink-and-red flowers. The town hall (built 1815) is Norway's tallest timber structure and has more than 300 antique portraits, most of them painted in the 19th century by local artists.

Established in 1832, the **Aust-Agder Museet** displays fascinating coastal artifacts and relics, from toys to farm tools. Find out about the 1767 slave ship *Fredensborg*, and learn more about the region's folk art and geology. ✉ *Langsæ gård, Arendal* ☎ *37–07–35–00* ⊕ *www.aust-agder. museum.no* 🎟 *NKr 20* ◷ *Mid-June–mid-Aug., weekdays 9–5, Sun. noon–5; mid-Aug.–mid-June, weekdays 9–3, Sun. noon–5.*

An unusual gallery space, the restored **Bomuldsfabriken** (Cotton Factory) operated from 1898 to 1960, producing jeans, shirts, and cotton flannel clothing. Today, it has changing art exhibitions and a permanent collection of 35 works by some of Norway's foremost painters. ✉ *Oddenvn. 5* ☎ *37–02–65–19* ⊕ *www.bomuldsfabriken.com* 🎟 *NKr 20* ◷ *Tues.–Sun. noon–4.*

off the beaten path

MERDØGAARD MUSEUM – On the island of Merdøy, a 30-minute boat ride from Arendal's Langbrygga (long wharf), is an early-18th-century sea captain's home, now a museum exploring life in the region. After visiting, enjoy a swim on the beach or a walk around the island. ✉ *Merdøy* ☎ *37–07–35–00* 🎟 *NKr 20* ◷ *Late June–mid-Aug., daily noon–5.*

Where to Stay

$$–$$$ 🏨 **Clarion Tyholmen Hotel.** This maritime hotel has the sea at close quarters and a magnificent view of the fjord. A blue-painted interior and wood furniture make the hotel cheerful and bright. The hotel's outdoor restaurant, Bryggekanten, serves fish and steak dishes. It's a popular summer spot. ⊠ *Teaterpl. 2, Tyholmen, 4801* 🕾 *37–07–68–00* 🖷 *37–02–68–01* ⊕ *www.choicehotels.no* ⟲ *60 rooms* ♨ *2 restaurants, sauna, bar, Internet room* ⊟ *AE, DC, MC, V.*

Grimstad

❿ *15 km (9 mi) south of Arendal.*

Grimstad is a pretty coastal town with a charming wharf. In the mid to late 19th century, the town was famous as a shipbuilding center, and from 1844 to 1850 the teenage Henrik Ibsen worked as an apprentice at the local apothecary shop. Later, in the early 20th century, author Knut Hamsun, winner of the Nobel Prize for Literature yet infamous for his support of Nazi Germany, lived here. Today Grimstad is called the "Town of Poets," and is still home to many artists. A popular Norwegian short-film festival is held here in early summer.

★ Grimstad Apotek is now a part of **Ibsenhuset–Grimstad Bymuseum** (the Ibsen House) and has been preserved with its 1837 interior intact. Ibsen wrote his first play, *Catlina*, here. Every summer Grimstad holds an Ibsen festival celebrating the famous playwright. The museum also has a maritime department and a section honoring Terje Vigen, a folk hero who was the subject of a poem by Ibsen. He is credited with riding to Denmark to bring back food for the starving Norwegians. ⊠ *Henrik Ibsens gt. 14, 4890* 🕾 *37–04–04–90* ⊕ *www.ibsen.net* 🖭 *NKr 35* ☉ *May–Sept. 11–5.*

Lillesand

⓫ *20 km (12 mi) south of Grimstad.*

An idyllic summer vacation town, Lillesand has one of Norway's best guest (public) harbors, which is usually bustling. In town you will see many of the white wooden houses typical of the region.

Dating from AD 1000, the 33-foot-long stone **Høvåg Kirke** was lengthened and restored in 1768 and 1828. Construction wasn't completed until 1966. 🕾 *91/72–93–52* ☉ *May–Sept., daily 9–4.*

In an 1827 Empire-style building, the **Lillesand By og Sjøfartsmuseum** (Lillesand City and Maritime Museum) reconstructs maritime-related workplaces. You can see how sailmakers worked and also see the city's first fire pump. ⊠ *Carl Knudsen gården* 🕾 *37–27–04–30* 🖭 *NKr 15* ☉ *Mid-June–Aug., weekdays 11–3, Sat. 11–2.*

Where to Stay

$$–$$$ 🏨 **Lillesand Hotel Norge.** Right on the harbor, this old hotel certainly has rooms with views. The sea-inspired guest rooms are classic yet modern. The restaurant serves delicious seafood dishes. ⊠ *Strandgt. 3, 4790* 🕾 *37–27–01–44* 🖷 *37–27–30–70* ⊕ *www.hotelnorge.no* ⟲ *25 rooms* ♨ *Restaurant, bar; no a/c in some rooms* ⊟ *AE, DC, MC, V.*

Kristiansand

⑫ *55 km (34 mi) south of Grimstad on E18.*

Nicknamed "Sommerbyen" ("Summer City"), Norway's fifth-largest city has 75,000 inhabitants. Norwegians come here for its sun-soaked beaches and beautiful harbor. Kristiansand has also become known internationally for the outdoor **Quart Festival** (☎ 38–14–69–69 ⊕ www. quart.no), which hosts local and international rock bands every July.

According to legend, in 1641 King Christian IV marked the four corners of Kristiansand with his walking stick, and within that framework the grid of wide streets was laid down. The center of town, called the **Kvadraturen**, still retains the grid, even after numerous fires. In the northeast corner is **Posebyen**, one of northern Europe's largest collections of low, connected wooden house settlements, and there's a market here every Saturday in summer. Kristiansand's **Fisketorvet** (fish market) is near the south corner of the town's grid, right on the sea. **Christiansholm Festning** (⊘ Mid-May–Aug., daily 9–9) is a fortress on a promontory opposite Festningsgata. Completed in 1674, the circular building with 16-foot-thick walls has played more a decorative role than a defensive one; it was used once, in 1807 during the Napoleonic Wars, to defend the city against British invasion. Now it contains art exhibits.

The **Agder naturmuseum og botaniske hage** (Agder Nature Museum and Botanical Gardens) takes on Sørlandet's natural history from the Ice Age to the present, examining the coast and moving on to the high mountains. There's a rainbow of minerals on display, as well as a rose garden with varieties from 1850. There's even the country's largest collection of cacti. ⊠ *Gimlevn. 23, 4630* ☎ *38–09–23–88* ⊕ *www.museumsnett. no/naturmuseum* 🕿 *NKr 45* ⊘ *Mid-June–mid-Aug., Tues.–Fri. 10–6, Sat.–Mon. noon–6; mid-Aug.–mid-June, Tues.–Fri. 10–3, Sun. noon–5.*

A wealthy merchant-shipowner built **Gimle Gård** (Gimle Manor) around 1800 in the Empire style. Inside are furnishings from that period, including paintings, silver, and hand-printed wallpaper. To get there from the city center, head north across the Otra River on Bus 22 or drive to Route E18 and cross the bridge over the Otra to Parkveien. Turn left onto Ryttergangen and drive to Gimleveien; take a right. ⊠ *Gimlevn. 23, 4630* ☎ *38–09–02–28* 🕿 *NKr 45* ⊘ *Mid-June–mid-Aug., weekdays noon–4, Sun. noon–6; May–mid-June and mid-Aug.–early Jan., Sun. noon–5.*

The Gothic Revival **Kristiansand Domkirke** (Kristiansand Cathedral) from 1885 is the third-largest church in Norway. It often hosts summer concerts in addition to the weeklong **International Church Music Festival** (☎ 38–12–09–40) in mid-May. Organ, chamber, and gospel music are on the bill. ⊠ *Kirkegt., 4610* ☎ *38–10–77–50* 🕿 *Free* ⊘ *June–Aug., daily 9–2.*

★ ☺ One of Norway's most popular attractions, **Kristiansand Dyreparken** is actually five separate parks, including a water park (bring bathing suits and towels); a forested park; an entertainment park; a theme park; and a zoo, which contains an enclosure for Scandinavian animals such as wolves and elk, and a large breeding ground for Bactrian camels. The theme park, **Kardemomme By** (Cardamom Town), is named for a book by Norwegian illustrator and writer Thorbjørn Egner. In the zoo the "My Africa" exhibition allows you to move along a bridge observing native savanna animals such as giraffes and zebras. The park is 11 km (6 mi) east of town. ⊠ *Kristiansand Dyreparken, Kardemomme By* ☎ *38–04–97–25* ⊕ *www.dyreparken.no* ⊠ *NKr 225, includes admission to all parks and rides; discounts offered off-season* ⊙ *June–Aug., daily 10–7; Sept.–May, weekdays 10–3, weekends 10–5.*

At the **Kristiansand Kanonmuseum** (Cannon Museum) you can see the cannon that the occupying Germans rigged up during World War II. With calibers of 15 inches, the cannon was said to be capable of shooting a projectile halfway to Denmark. In the bunkers, related military materials are on display. ⊠ *Møvik* ☎ *38–08–50–90* ⊠ *NKr 50* ⊙ *May–Sept., daily 11–6; prebooked tours available all yr.*

The striking rune stone in the cemetery of **Oddernes Kirke** (Oddernes Church) tells that Øyvind, godson of Saint Olav, built this church in 1040 on property he inherited from his father. One of the oldest churches in Norway, it has a baroque pulpit from 1704 and is dedicated to Saint Ola. ⊠ *Oddernesvn., 6430* ☎ *38–09–01–87* ⊠ *Free* ⊙ *May–Aug., Sun.–Fri. 9–2.*

Fodor$**Choice** A favorite with hikers and strolling nannies, **Ravnedalen** (Raven Valley)
★ is a lush park that's filled with flowers in springtime. Wear comfortable shoes to hike the narrow, winding paths up the hills and climb the 200 steps up to a 304-foot lookout. ⊠ *Northwest of Kristiansand.*

☺ **Vest-Agder Fylkesmuseum** (County Museum), the region's largest cultural museum, has more than 40 old buildings on display. The structures, transported from other locations in the area, include two *tun*—farm buildings traditionally set in clusters around a common area—which suited the extended families. If you have children with you, check out the old-fashioned toys, which can still be played with. The museum is 4 km (2½ mi) east of Kristiansand on Route E18. ⊠ *Kongsgård* ☎ *38–09–02–28* ⊕ *www.museumsnett.no/vafymuseum* ⊠ *NKr 30* ⊙ *Mid-June–mid-Aug., Tues.–Fri. 10–6, Sat.–Mon. noon–6; mid-Aug.–mid-June, Sun. noon–5.*

Where to Stay & Eat

$$$–$$$$ ✕ **Luihn.** In the center of town, Luihn is an elegant, intimate restaurant, perfect for a quiet dinner. Fish dishes are a specialty, and the menu varies according to season. Don't hesitate to call in advance if you have any special cravings—providing they can get hold of it, the chefs can prepare just about anything for you. The wine selection is impressive. ⊠ *Rådhusgt. 15* ☎ *38–10–66–50* ⊟ *AE, DC, MC, V.*

★ **$$$–$$$$** ✕ **Sjøhuset Restaurant.** Considered one of the city's best restaurants, Sjøhuset was built in 1892 as a salt warehouse—a white-trimmed red building. The specialty is seafood. Take a seat on the sunny patio and dine on fresh lobster, or try the baked fillet of monkfish with pancetta, served with artichoke risotto. ⊠ *Østre Strandgt. 12A* ☎ *38–02–62–60* ⊟ *AE, DC, MC, V.*

$$–$$$$ ✕ **Bølgen & Moi.** Toralf Bølgen and Trond Moi, Norway's most celebrated restaurateurs, opened this southernmost addition to their chain of high-profile restaurants. Near the old fishing pier, the scene is more chic than rustic, with artwork and even dinnerware designed by local artist Kjell Nupen. Norwegian game and fish are cooked in an international style. ⊠ *Sjølystvn. 1A* ☎ *38–17–83–00* ⊟ *AE, DC, MC, V.*

$$–$$$ ▦ **Clarion Ernst Park Hotel.** Convenience is the main reason to stay at this rather traditional city hotel. It is central, and close to the city beach and main shopping street, Markens. The staff at the reception desk will gladly tell you about local attractions and help you purchase tickets to Dyreparken. You can get connected online at a nearby Internet café. ⊠ *Rådhusgt. 2, 4601* ☎ *38–12–86–00* 🖷 *38–02–03–07* ⊕ *www.ernst. no* ⟿ *136 rooms, 5 suites* ⌂ *Restaurant, 2 bars, meeting rooms; no a/c in some rooms* ⊟ *AE, DC, MC, V.*

$$$ ▦ **Quality Hotel Kristiansand.** Nicknamed "the children's hotel," this chain hotel is perfect for young families on the go. Inside, there are a huge playroom, activity leaders, child care, and a children's buffet. Even more toys are outdoors. Rooms are comfortable, with cheerful pastel walls and wood furniture. ⊠ *Sørlandsparken, 4696* ☎ *38–17–77–77* 🖷 *38–17–77–80* ⊕ *www.quality-kristiansand.no* ⟿ *210 rooms* ⌂ *Restaurant, pool, babysitting, children's programs (ages 3–12), playground, Internet room; no a/c in some rooms* ⊟ *AE, DC, MC, V.*

$$–$$$ ▦ **Rica Dyreparken Hotel.** Built like Noah's Ark, this modern hotel is designed to appeal to children of all ages. Inspired by the Kristiansand Dyreparken, many of the rooms go a little wild, with tiger-stripe chairs and paw prints on walls. Children have their own playroom and cinema on board this ark. ⊠ *Dyreparken, 4609* ☎ *38–14–64–00* 🖷 *38–14–64–01* ⊕ *www.rica.no* ⟿ *160 rooms* ⌂ *Restaurant, bar, children's programs (ages 3–12)* ⊟ *AE, DC, MC, V.*

Nightlife & the Arts

Markens gate, the city's main street, is the place for clubbing, pubbing, and live music.

Dr. Fjeld (⊠ Rådhusgt. 2 ☎ 38–12–86–00) at Clarion Ernst Park Hotel is a popular place to dance the night away. Party types in their late twenties and thirties head to **Lobbybaren** (⊠ Vestre Strandgt. 7 ☎ 38–11–21–00) at Radisson SAS Caledonien Hotel. A younger crowd flocks to **Club Etcetera** (⊠ Vestre Strandgt. 23 ☎ 38–02–96–66) for up-to-date beats.

Every summer, **Agder Teater** (⊠ Kongensgt. 2A ☎ 38–02–43–00) moves its performances outdoors to Fjøreheia near Grimstad. The **Kristiansand Symfoniorkester** (Kristiansand Symphony Orchestra; ⊠ Marviksveien. 140 ☎ 38–07–70–00) performs year-round. **Musikkens Hus** (⊠ Kongensgt. 54 ☎ 38–14–87–30) schedules concerts throughout the year.

Sports & the Outdoors

Troll Mountain (⊠ Setesdal Rafting og Aktivitetssenter, Rte. 9, Evje ☎ 37–93–11–77), about one hour's drive from Kristiansand, organizes many activities. Be it mountain climbing, sailing, biking, rafting, paintball, or even beaver or deer safaris, this is the place for outdoorsy types.

BIKING Kristiansand has 70 km (42 mi) of bike trails around the city. The tourist office can recommend routes and rentals. **Kristiansand Sykkelsenter** (✉ Grim Torv ☎ 38–02–68–35) rents bicycles and off-road vehicles.

CLIMBING Whether you're an experienced pro or just a gung-ho beginner, you can rent climbing equipment or learn more about the sport from **Samsen Kulturhus** (✉ Vestervn. 2 ☎ 38–00–64–00).

FISHING Just north of Kristiansand there's excellent trout, perch, and eel fishing at Lillesand's **Vestre Grimevann** lake. You can get a permit at any sports store or at the **Lillesand Tourist Office** (☎ 37–40–19–10).

GOLF Enjoy Kristiansand's sunny weather and a round of golf at **Kristiansand Golfklubb** (☎ 38–14–85–60), which has a 9-hole course, equipment rentals, instruction, and a café. On rainy days there's always **Kristiansand Golfsenter** (✉ Barstølv 28B ☎ 38–01–40–55), which has a modern simulator, courses, driving range, and billiards.

HIKING In addition to the gardens and steep hills of Ravnedalen, the **Baneheia Skog** (Baneheia Forest) is full of evergreens, small lakes, and paths that are ideal for a lazy walk or a challenging run. It's just a 15-minute walk north from the city center.

RIDING If you're at home in the saddle, then head to **Islandshestsenteret** (The Icelandic Horse Center; ✉ Søgne ☎ 38–16–98–82). Specializing in the Icelandic horse breed, this center offers courses, trips, and camping for children and adults.

WATER SPORTS **Dykkeren** (✉ Kongsgårds Allé 53 ☎ 38–05–86–20) has everything related to diving, including organized trips, classes, and equipment. **Kuholmen Marina** (✉ Roligheden Camping ☎ 38–09–33–50) rents boats, water skis, and water scooters.

Combining history with sailing, the magnificent square-rigger *Sørlandet* (✉ Gravene 2 ☎ 38–02–98–90), built in 1927, takes passengers for two weeks trips, usually stopping for several days in a northern European port. The price is about NKr 750 per day.

Shopping

There are many shops next to Dyreparken in Kristiansand. **Kvadraturen** (☎ 38–02–44–11) has 300 stores and eating spots. **Sørlands Senteret Steen and Strom** (☎ 38–04–91–00) is one of the region's larger shopping centers, with 100 stores, a pharmacy, and a post office.

Vennesla

⓭ *15 km (9 mi) north of Kristiansand. Follow Rte. 39 from Kristiansand to Mosby, veer right onto Rte. 405, and continue to Grovane.*

Untouched forests and excellent salmon fishing in the Otra River have made Vennesla a popular outdoor destination.

Setesdalsbanen (Setesdal Railway), a 7-km-long (4½-mi-long) stretch of narrow-gauge track, has a steam locomotive from 1896 and carriages from the early 1900s that are available for round-trip rides. The railway remained in normal use until 1962. An exhibition at Grovane Station explains the history of the locomotive. ✉ *Vennesla Stasjon*

☎ *38–15–64–82* ⊕ *www.setesdalsbanen.no* ✉ *NKr 100 round-trip* ⊗ *Mid-June–Aug., Sun. 11:30, 1, and 2:30; additional departures in July: Tues.–Fri. 6, Thurs. noon.*

Mandal

⑭ *42 km (28 mi) southwest of Kristiansand and 82 km (51 mi) from Evje.*

Mandal is Norway's southernmost town. Once a Dutch port, it is now famous for its historic core of well-preserved wooden houses and its long, sandy beach, Sjøsanden.

Lindesnes Fyr, Norway's first lighthouse, was lighted in the Lindesnes municipality in February 1656, at the southernmost point in Norway. It was closed the same year by the Danish king because its light was considered not strong enough, and it didn't reopen for 69 years. Many lighting methods have been used since, including coal in the early 1800s. An exhibition in the museum traces the changing methods. ✉ *Mandal* ☎ *97/54–08–15* ⊕ *www.lindesnesfyr.no* ✉ *NKr 40* ⊗ *Daylight hrs.*

Mandal Kirke, built in 1821, is Norway's largest Empire-style wooden church. ☎ *38–27–28–70* ⊗ *Tues.–Thurs. 11–2.*

Ogna

⑮ *93 km (57 mi) northwest of Flekkefjord on Rte. 42.*

Ogna has a stretch of sandy beach that inspired many Norwegian artists, among them Kitty Kielland (1843–1914), who was best known for her impressionist landscape paintings.

The complex making up **Hå Gamle Prestegaard** (Old Parsonage) was built in 1637 to face the ocean. It now houses a gallery of changing art and cultural exhibitions that are often worth visiting. The archaeological finds from an 8,200-year-old settlement in the area are also on display. ✉ *Ogna* ☎ *51–79–16–60* ✉ *NKr 40* ⊗ *Mid-May–mid-Sept., Tues.–Fri. 11–5, weekends noon–5; mid-Sept.–mid-Apr., weekends noon–5.*

The ancient **Hå grave site** lies below the Hå parsonage near the Obrestad lighthouse. The roughly 60 mounds, including two shaped like stars and one shaped like a boat, date from around AD 500. To get here take coastal Route 44.

The Outdoors

FISHING Three of the 10 best fishing rivers in Norway, the Ognaelva, Håelva, and Figgjo, are in Jæren, just south of Stavanger. Fishing licenses, sold in grocery stores and gas stations, are required at all of them.

Sandnes

⑯ *25 km (16 mi) south of Stavanger, 52 km (32 mi) north of Orre.*

For good reason, this city of 53,000 is called Bicycle Town. Local company Øglænd DBS, founded in 1898, has manufactured nearly 2 million bicycles here. Sandnes has 200 free city bicycles, miles of bicycle paths, a bicycle museum, the Bicycle Blues Festival, a bicycle library, and an active racing club. Besides bicycles, brickworks, pottery, and textiles have been the traditional industries. Eleven factory outlets and art galleries sell historic and modern Sandnes crafts and products at reduced prices.

The Sandnes, Øglænd, and Krossens Havremølle (Krossen's Oatmeal) museums have been combined as part of the larger Jærmuseet to form the **Sandnes Museum**. The museum documents the town's development, with special attention to the oat-milling and bicycle-manufacturing industries. Photographs, and cultural and industrial artifacts, including a working model of an oat mill, are on display. ⊠ *St. Olavs gt. 26* ☎ *51–97–25–40* ⊕ *www.museumsnett.no/jaermuseet/avd_sandn.htm* 🖾 *NKr 40* ☉ *Mid-June–mid-Aug., weekdays noon–5, weekends noon–4; mid-Aug–mid-Dec. and mid-Mar.–mid-June, Sun noon–3.*

Where to Stay & Eat

$$–$$$ ✕⌂ **Hotel GamlaVærket Gjæstgiveri og Tracteringsted.** A former brick-and-pottery works, this intimate hotel has a warm, old-fashioned charm. Simple white-wall rooms have slanted ceilings and dark-wood furniture. The well-regarded restaurant has a menu that ranges from sandwiches to delicious seven-course meals. ⊠ *St. Olavs gt. 38, 4306* ☎ *51–68–51–70* 🖶 *51–68–51–71* ⊕ *www.gamlavaerket.no* 🛏 *26 rooms* ⌂ *Restaurant, bar, meeting rooms; no a/c in some rooms* ⊟ *AE, DC, MC, V.*

Sports & the Outdoors

BICYCLING Can you actually visit Norway's bicycle town and not spin a few wheels yourself? If the cycling mood strikes, borrow one of the 200 that are available for free downtown. The tourist office has bicycle maps of the area. **Scan One Tours** (☎ 51–89–39–00) organizes and sells packaged bicycle trips. You can rent a bike at **Spinn Sykkelshop** (☎ 51–68–62–65) or **Naboen** (☎ 51–57–07–10).

WATER SPORTS One of Scandinavia's largest indoor swimming facilities, **Havanna Badeland** holds a total of 264,000 gallons of water. A 300-foot waterslide, playhouse, reading corner, whirlpool baths, saunas, and a Turkish bath entertain children and adults. The Havanna Lekeland next door has a pool, play equipment, climbing labyrinths, and five slides. ⊠ *Hanavn. 17* ☎ *51–61–92–00* ⊕ *www.havanna.no* 🖾 *NKr 120* ☉ *Daily 10–8.*

Shopping

OUTLET STORES Sandnes has a tempting selection of factory outlets offering as much as 70% off regular prices. Several times a year in summer, the local tourist board organizes free bus trips to them. The region's most visited factory outlet, **Byrkjedalstunet** (⊠ Rte. 45, Dirdal ☎ 51–61–29–00) has a candle maker, children's activities, and a mountain farm as well as stores selling handicrafts and souvenirs. For fine porcelain, go to **Figgjo** (☎51–68–35–70), in the nearby town of the same name. It's the largest supplier to professional kitchens in Norway. **Skjæveland** (⊠ Ålgård ☎ 51–61–24–19) carries high-quality knit sweaters and jackets for men and women.

Stavanger

❶ *256 km (123 mi) northwest of Kristiansand, 4½ hrs southeast of Bergen by car and ferry, 8–9 hrs southwest of Oslo by car.*

Stavanger has always prospered from the riches of the sea. During the 19th century huge harvests of brisling and herring established it as the sardine capital of the world. Some people claim the locals are called Siddis, from S (tavanger) plus *iddis,* which means "sardine label," although linguists argue it's actually a mispronunciation of the English word "citizen."

During the past three decades a different product from the sea has been Stavanger's lifeblood—oil. Since its discovery in the late 1960s, North Sea oil hasn't just transformed the economy, Stavanger has emerged as cosmopolitan and vibrant, more bustling than other cities with a population of only 110,000. Norway's most international city, it has attracted residents from more than 90 nations. Roam its cobblestone streets or wander the harborfront and you're likely to see many cafés, fine restaurants, and lively pubs. For many visitors, Stavanger is a place to be entertained. As you tour the city, keep an eye out for 23 rusty figures, sculptures created by British artist Antony Gormley.

Designed to help children learn about the prehistoric past, the **Arkeologisk Museum** (Museum of Archaeology) has changing exhibitions, instructive models, open archives, and movies designed to make learning history fun. Children can research their ancestors in computer games, treasure hunts, and other activities. In summer children can look through stones in search of fossils and other signs of life. There are also old-fashioned games and toys, which have become popular attractions. ⊠ *Peder Klowsgt. 30A* ☎ *51–84–60–00* ✉ *NKr 20* ⊙ *June–Aug., Tues.–Sun. 11–5; Sept.–May, Tues. 11–8, Wed.–Sat. 11–3, Sun. 11–4.*

Take a scented stroll in Stavanger's wild rose garden. At the **Botanisk Hage** (Botanical Gardens), you can find some 2,000 varieties of herbs and perennials. ⊠ *Rektor Natvig Pedersensv. 40* ☎ *51–50–78–61* ✉ *Free* ⊙ *Apr.–Sept., weekdays 7 AM–8 PM, weekends 10–8; Oct.–Mar., weekdays 7–5, weekends 10–5.*

★ **Breidablikk** manor house has a perfectly preserved interior and exterior and feels as if the owner has only momentarily slipped away. The building is an outstanding example of what the Norwegians call "Swiss-style" architecture, and also has some elements of the Norwegian National Romantic style. It was built in 1882 by the Norwegian merchant and shipowner Lars Berentsen. ⊠ *Eiganesvn. 40A* ☎ *51–84–27–00* ⊕ *www. stavanger.museum.no* ✉ *NKr 50* ⊙ *Mid-June–mid-Aug., daily 11–4; mid-Aug.–mid-June, Sun. 11–4 or by appointment.*

If you have a Norwegian branch on your family tree, trace your roots at **Det Norske Utvandresenteret,** in a harborside wharf house from the early 1700s. The Norwegian Emigration Center has passenger lists, parish registers, census records, and a comprehensive collection of books on Norway's rural past. Bring along any information you have, especially the dates and places from which your ancestors left Norway. The center organizes the annual Norwegian Emigration Festival in October, with exhibitions, concerts, and excursions to historical sites. ⊠ *Strandkaien 31* ☎ *51–53–88–60* 🖷 *51–53–88–63* ⊕ *www.emigrationcenter.com* ✉ *NKr 35* ⊙ *Mon. and Wed.–Fri. 9–3, Tues. 9–7.*

More than 35 military and civilian planes make up the collection at the **Flyhistorisk Museum Sola** (History of Flying Museum, Sola municipality), which emphasizes aviation history from World War II on. Besides checking out changing exhibitions, you can sit in a passenger seat of a 1950s Metropolitan plane and see the changing designs through the years of the Norwegian Air Force's jet fighters. ⊠ *Sjøflyhaven, Stavanger Lufthavn* ☎ *51–65–56–57* ⊠ *NKr 40* ☉ *Late June–mid-Aug., daily noon–4; May–late June and mid-Aug.–Nov., Sun. noon–4.*

Although it's a reconstruction, the **Jernaldergarden** late Iron Age farm complex from the Migration Period (AD 350–550) feels like the real thing. The reconstructed historical buildings have been positioned on original foundations. Relics such as a Bronze Age gravestone have been discovered here. Research is still underway. Taste some mead, the Vikings' favorite drink, or have breakfast or lunch on wooden benches before fireplaces. ⊠ *Ullandhaugvn. 165* ☎ *51–84–60–00* ⊠ *NKr 40* ☉ *Mid-June–mid-Aug., daily 11–4; mid-Aug.–mid-June, by appointment.*

☾ **Kongeparken** amusement park has go-carts, radio cars, bumper boats, Norway's longest bobsled run, and its largest merry-go-round. In the Chocolate Factory children can make their own Freia-brand milk chocolate. ⊠ *4330 Ålgård* ☎ *51–61–26–66* ⊕ *www.kongeparken.no* ⊠ *NKr 140* ☉ *May–Aug., daily 10–6; Sept., weekends 10–6; mid-Nov.–mid-Dec., daily 10–6.*

Ledaal, the royal family's Stavanger residence, is a mansion museum and is used for receptions by the Stavanger Council. It was built for shipping magnate Gabriel Schanche Kielland, and completed in 1803. The building is a prime example of the Norwegian neoclassical style, and it's decorated with rococo furnishings and details, as well as pieces in the Empire, and Biedermeier styles. The second-floor library is dedicated to writer Alexander Kielland, a social critic and satirist. ⊠ *Eiganesvn. 45* ☎ *51–84–27–00* ⊕ *www.stavanger.museum.no* ⊠ *NKr 50* ☉ *Mid-June–mid-Aug., daily 11–4; mid-Aug.–mid-June, Sun. 11–4 or by appointment.*

Lysefjordsenteret. Lysefjord Center has a slanting roof that mimics the mountains. An exhibition shows how a trickling brook created this sliver of a fjord. You'll also learn about the geology and culture of Lysefjord. A ferry to the bottom of Pulpit Rock drops off passengers midway. For more information, call **Rogaland Traffik** (☎ 51–86–87–00) or **Clipper Fjord Sightseeing** (☎ 51–89–52–70). The center has a café and can help with finding accommodations. ⊠ *Oanes, Forsand* ☎ *51–70–31–23* ☉ *May–Aug., weekdays 11–6, Sat. 11–6, Sun. noon–8.*

☾ The **Norsk Barnemuseum** (Norwegian Children's Museum) has Norway's largest collection of children's toys. Storytelling, dramatic performances, and other activities focus on the country's culture and history. ⊠ *Sølvberget (Stavanger Culture Center)* ☎ *51–91–23–93* ⊕ *www.norskbarne.museum.no* ⊠ *NKr 65* ☉ *Wed.–Fri. 1–7, Sat. noon–5, Sun. 1–5.*

The fascinating **Norsk Hermetikkmuseum** (Norwegian Canning Museum) is in a former canning factory. From the 1890s to the 1960s, canning fish products like brisling, fish balls, and sardines was Stavanger's main industry. On special activity days the public can take part in the production process, sometimes tasting newly smoked brisling—on the first Sunday of every month and Tuesday and Thursday in summer, the ovens used for smoking fish are stoked up once again. ⊠ *Øvre Strandgt. 88A* ☎ *51–84–27–00* ⊕ *www.stavanger.museum.no* ☒ *NKr 50* ☉ *Mid-June–mid-Aug., daily 11–4; early June and late Aug., Mon.–Thurs. 11–3, Sun. 11–4; Sept.–May, Sun. 11–4 or by appointment.*

Fodor'sChoice Resembling a shiny offshore oil platform, the dynamic **Norsk Oljemu-**
★ **seum** (Norwegian Petroleum Museum) is an absolute must-see. In 1969 oil was discovered off the coast of Norway. The museum explains how oil forms, how it's found and produced, its many uses, and its impact on Norway. Interactive multimedia exhibits accompany original artifacts, models, and films. A reconstructed offshore platform includes oil workers' living quarters—as well as the sound of drilling and the smell of oil. The highly recommended museum café, by restaurateurs Bølgen & Moi, serves dinners as well as lighter fare. ⊠ *Kjeringholmen, Stavanger Havn* ☎ *51–93–93–00* ⊕ *www.norskolje.museum.no* ☒ *NKr 80* ☉ *Sept.–May, Mon.–Sat. 10–4, Sun. 10–6; June–Aug., daily 10–7.*

Fodor'sChoice The charm of the city's past is on view in **Old Stavanger,** Northern Eu-
★ rope's largest and best-preserved wooden house settlement. The 150 houses here were built in the late 1700s and early 1800s. Wind down the narrow, cobblestone streets past small, white houses and craft shops with many-paned windows and terra-cotta roof tiles.

★ **Preikestolen** (Pulpit Rock). A huge cube with a vertical drop of 2,000 feet, the Pulpit Rock is not a good destination if you suffer from vertigo—it has a heart-stopping view. The clifflike rock sits on the banks of the finger-shape Lysefjord. You can join a tour to get to the region's best-known attraction, or you can do it on your own from early June to early September by taking the bus—it costs NKr 50 one-way from the town of Tau to the Pulpit Rock. The buses are paired with morning ferry departures from Stavanger at 8:20 and 9:15. Then you can hike the two-hour walk on a marked trail. (The ferry and bus take a total of about 40 minutes from Stavanger.)

Rogaland Kunstmuseum (Rogaland Museum of Fine Arts) has the country's largest collection of works by Lars Hertervig (1830–1902), the greatest Romantic painter of Norwegian landscapes. With Norwegian paintings, drawings, and sculptures, the museum's permanent collection covers the early 19th century to the present. The Halvdan Haftsten Collection has paintings and drawings done between the world wars. There's also a collection of works by Kitty Kielland. The museum is near Mosvannet (Mos Lake), which is just off highway E18 at the northern end of downtown. ⊠ *Tjensvoll 6, Mosvannsparken* ☎ *51–53–09–00* ☒ *NKr 50* ☉ *Tues.–Sun. 11–4.*

Along Strandkaien, warehouses face the wharf; the shops, offices, and apartments face the street on the other side. Housed in the only two shipping merchants' houses that remain completely intact is the **Sjøfartsmuseet** (Stavanger Maritime Museum). Built between 1770 and 1840, the restored buildings trace the past 200 years of trade, sea-traffic, and ship-building. Visit a turn-of-the-20th-century general store, an early-1900s merchant's apartment, and a sailmaker's loft. A reconstruction of a shipowner's office and a memorial are here, as are two 19th-century ships, *Anna af Sand* and *Wyvern,* moored at the pier. ⊠ *Nedre Strandgt. 17–19* ☏ *51–84–27–00* ⊕ *www.stavanger.museum.no* ⊠ *NKr 50* ☉ *Early–mid June and mid–late Aug., Mon.–Thurs. 11–3, Sun. 11–4; mid-June–mid-Aug., daily 11–4; Sept.–Nov. and Jan.–May, Sun. 11–4 or by appointment.*

Legend has it that Bishop Reinald of Winchester ordered the construction of **Stavanger Domkirke** (Stavanger Cathedral) in 1125, so that the king could marry his third wife there, after his divorce from Queen Malmfrid. The church was built in Anglo-Norman style, probably with the aid of English craftsmen. Patron saint St. Svithun's arm is believed to be among the original relics. Largely destroyed by fire in 1272, the church was rebuilt to include a Gothic chancel. The result: its once elegant lines are now festooned with macabre death symbols and airborne putti. Next to the cathedral is **Kongsgård,** formerly a residence of bishops and kings but now a school and not open to visitors. ⊠ *Near Torget* ☏ *Free* ☉ *Mid-May–mid-Sept., Mon. and Tues. 11–6, Wed.–Sat. 10–6, Sun. 11–6; mid-Sept.–mid-May, Wed.–Sat. 10–3.*

The **Stavanger Museum** is made up of five smaller museums, including a former smaller version of the Stavanger Museum, Stavanger Sjøfartsmuseum, Norsk Hermetikkmuseum, Ledaal, and Breidablikk. In the zoological department you'll find a collection of preserved birds and animals from around the world. In the Department of Cultural History there are reenactments of church and school life and artisans at work. It traces Stavanger's growth from its 12th-century beginnings to the oil city it is today. Buy a ticket to one of the museums and you get free admission to the other four on the same day. ⊠ *Muségt. 16* ☏ *51–84–27–00* ⊕ *www.stavanger.museum.no* ⊠ *NKr 50* ☉ *Mid-June–mid-Aug., daily 11–4; early June and late Aug., Mon.–Thurs. 11–3, Sun. 11–4; Sept.–Nov. and Jan.–May, Sun. 11–4 or by appointment.*

The site where Norway was founded has been memorialized by the **Sverd i fjell** (Swords in the Mountain). The three huge bronze swords were unveiled by King Olav in 1983 and done by artist Fritz Røed. The memorial is dedicated to King Harald Hårfagre (Harald the Fairhaired), who through an 872 battle at Hafrsfjord managed to unite Norway into one kingdom. The Viking swords' sheaths were modeled on ones found throughout the country; the crowns atop the swords represent the different Norwegian districts that took part in the battle. ⊠ *Hafrsfjord, on Grannesveien to Sola, 6 km (4 mi) south of Stavanger.*

off the beaten path

UTSTEIN KLOSTER – Originally the palace of Norway's first king, Harald Hårfagre, and later the residence of King Magnus VI, Utstein was used as a monastery from 1265 until 1537, when it reverted to the royal family. Just one bus departs for Utstein from Stavanger weekdays at 9 AM, and it doesn't return from the monastery until 4:05 PM, so its best to hire a car. By bus or car it's about a half-hour trip to the palace, north of Stavanger on coastal Highway 1, through the world's second-longest undersea car tunnel. If you rent a car to get to Utstein Kloster, you can also take in the medieval ruins nearby on **Åmøy Island** as well as the lighthouse, **Fjøløy Fyr.** Turn left after the tunnel and look for the tourist information sign before the bridge. ☎ *51–72–47–05.*

As Stavanger grew into an important town in the Middle Ages, watchmen were hired to look out for fires, crime, and anything else out of the ordinary. The **Vektermuseet i Valbergtårnet** (Watchman's Museum in the Valberg Tower) examines the role the watchmen played in keeping the town safe. The Valbergtårnet was built in the 1850s to give a panoramic view of the town below. With so many wooden houses, an early warning was essential. The view remains as incredible as ever. ⊠ *Valbergtårnet* ☎*90/ 72–63–94* ⌨*NKr 10* ☉ *Mon.–Wed. and Fri. 10–4, Thurs. 10–6, Sat. 10–2.*

Where to Eat

Stavanger has established a reputation for culinary excellence. In fact, the city has the distinction of having the most bars and restaurants per capita in Norway. Many restaurant menus burst with sumptuous international dishes. The city is home to the Culinary Institute of Norway, and hosts many food and wine festivals every year, including the Gladmat Festival, Garlic Week, Stavanger Wine Festival, Chili Festival, and Creole Week.

$$$$ ✕ **Cartellet Restaurant.** The elegant dining room reflects the timelessness of this classic restaurant that was founded in 1890 in Stavanger's first hotel. It has gold accents, stone walls hung with richly colored paintings, a dark-wood interior, and leather furniture. Based on fresh, seasonal ingredients from Norway's fjords and mountains, the menu changes every day. ⊠ *Øvre Holmegt. 8* ☎ *51–89–60–22* ⌨ *Reservations essential* ▭ *AE, DC, MC, V.*

$$$$ ✕ **Straen Fiskerestaurant.** Right on the quay, this esteemed fish restaurant claims it's "world famous throughout Norway." The nostalgic interior filled with memorabilia and the white-clothed tables make the restaurant comforting and homey. If you're traveling with a group, reserve the bookshelf-lined library dining room. Try the famous fish soup of salmon and cream of shellfish, or the grilled monkfish, or lutefisk. The three-course meal of the day is always the best value. The aquavit bar carries more than 30 varieties. ⊠ *Nedre Strandgt. 15* ☎ *51–84–37–00* ▭ *AE, DC, MC, V.*

$$$–$$$$ ✕ **Craigs Kjøkken & Bar.** Oklahoman Craig Whitson's café-restaurant is a great place for wining as well as dining. Stylish glass cabinets house the collection of more than 600 bottles of wine, with a focus on Italy and the Rhone and Alsace regions of France. The food is seasonal, experimental, and eclectic, its influences ranging from Mediterranean to Asian. Try the popular spring lamb burger or the huge, juicy Babe burger. The café hosts annual events such as chili and wine festivals. Whitson's offbeat sense of humor comes through in the "12 disciples" that sit against one wall—a dozen smoked, salted, and dried pigs' heads. ⊠ *Breitorget* ☎ *51–93–95–90* ▭ *AE, DC, MC, V.*

$$$–$$$$ ✕ **Gaffel & Karaffel.** Framed shiny forks playfully line the red walls of this hip restaurant, whose name means "fork and carafe." Called a tapas restaurant, its international menu delights with items such as cheese-filled salmon rolls, beefsteak sukiyaki, and herb-marinated catfish. ⊠ *Øvre Holmegt. 20* ☎ *51–86–41–58* ⊟ *AE, DC, MC, V.*

$$$–$$$$ ✕ **Timbuktu Bar and Restaurant.** This is one of the Stavanger's trendiest restaurants. Within its airy interior of blond wood and yellow and black accessories, enthusiastic chefs serve Asian-inspired cuisine with African ingredients such as tuna fish from Madagascar. Known for its NKr 350 three-course dinners and its sushi, the restaurant often has visiting celebrity chefs, and hosts special events such as salsa parties and nights of Spanish tapas. ⊠ *Nedre Strandgt. 15* ☎ *51–84–37–40* ⊟ *AE, DC, MC, V.*

$$$–$$$$ ✕ **Vertshuset Mat & Vin.** The style of this restaurant matches the traditional Norwegian dishes served up by the kitchen. Amid wood walls, white lace curtains, and traditional paintings, you can enjoy popular dishes such as monkfish with saffron and *komler* (dumplings) with salted meats. ⊠ *Skagen 10* ☎ *51–89–51–12* ⊟ *AE, DC, MC, V.*

$$–$$$$ ✕ **Saken er Biff.** A Norwegian country-style steak house, this restaurant has a whole lot more than beef on its menu. Be daring and try venison, reindeer, or moose, prepared rare, medium, or well done. ⊠ *Skagenkaien 28* ☎ *51–89–60–80* ⊟ *AE, DC, MC, V.*

$$–$$$$ ✕ **Sjøhuset Skagen.** A sort of museum, this 18th-century former boathouse is filled with wooden beams, ship models, lobster traps, and other sea relics. The Norwegian and international menu has such dishes as halibut, monkfish, and grilled medallions of reindeer, plus potatoes and vegetables. ⊠ *Skagenkaien 16* ☎ *51–89–51–80* ⊟ *AE, DC, MC, V.*

$–$$$$ ✕ **N. B. Sørensen's Dampskibsexpedition.** Norwegian emigrants waited
Fodor'sChoice here before boarding steamships crossing the Atlantic to North America 150 years ago. Restored in 1990, the historic wharf house is now a
★ popular waterfront restaurant and bar. Emigrants' tickets, weathered wood, nautical ropes, old maps, photographs, and gaslights set the scene. At street level is an informal brasserie where you can get barbecued spareribs. Upstairs is an elegant and more expensive dining room with prix-fixe menus including such entrées as a delicious grilled entrecôte with garlic. ⊠ *Skagen 26* ☎ *51–84–38–20* ⊟ *AE, DC, MC, V.*

$$–$$$ ✕ **Harry Pepper.** Norway's first Tex-Mex restaurant is still considered one of the country's best. Earth tones, cacti, and tacky souvenirs combine to make the joint lighthearted and playful. Try the sizzling fajitas or the lime-grilled fish kebab served with triple pesto. Have a tequila shot or two at the lively bar. ⊠ *Øvre Holmegt. 15* ☎ *51–56–79–67* ⊟ *AE, DC, V.*

Where to Stay

$$–$$$$ 🏨 **Radisson SAS Atlantic Hotel Stavanger.** In the heart of downtown, the Atlantic overlooks Breiavatnet pond. All rooms are elegantly decorated in understated yellows, beiges, and reds, with plush furniture. The King Oscar lobby bar, Alexander Pub, and Café Ajax are popular with Stavanger's residents. ⊠ *Olav Vs gt. 3, 4001* ☎ *51–76–10–00* 🖷 *51–53–48–69* ⊕ *www.radisson.com* ⤴ *350 rooms, 4 suites* ⚐ *Restaurant, café, cable TV with movies, in-room data ports, sauna, bar, lounge, pub, dance club, nightclub, meeting rooms* ⊟ *AE, DC, MC, V.*

$$–$$$$ ☒ **Victoria Hotel.** Stavanger's oldest hotel was built at the turn of the 20th century and retains a clubby Victorian style, with elegant carved furniture and floral patterns. Ask for a room overlooking the harbor. Stavanger's museums, Gamle Stavanger, and shopping are all within short walking distances. ✉ *Skansegt. 1, Postboks 279, 4001* ☎ *51–86–70–00* 🖷 *51–86–70–10* ⊕ *www.victoria-hotel.no* ⇘ *107 rooms, 3 suites* ⚒ *Restaurant, bar, meeting rooms* ⊟ *AE, DC, MC, V* ⊙⎮ *BP.*

$$–$$$ ☒ **Rica Park Hotel.** Understandably popular among business travelers, this hotel was designed for people who need space and facilities to work. All rooms have wireless Internet access and one room is wheelchair accessible. Stylish and comfortable, the rooms have subtle colors and patterns, dark-wood furniture, and sea-theme paintings. ✉ *Kannikgt. 7, 4000* ☎ *51–50–05–00* 🖷 *51–50–04–00* ⊕ *www.rica.no* ⇘ *59 rooms* ⚒ *Restaurant, cable TV with movies, in-room data ports, sauna, bar, meeting rooms* ⊟ *AE, DC, MC, V.*

★ $$–$$$ ☒ **Skagen Brygge Hotell.** A symbol of Stavanger, this classic hotel's white wooden wharf houses are common subjects for city postcards and photographs. It has a well-deserved reputation for superb service. The blue-accented, wood-beam rooms tend to have somewhat irregular shapes. Half the rooms face the harbor, and half face the street. Have a coffee anytime at the fourth floor's relaxing Kaffekroken lounge. On weekends Hovemesteren Bar is a popular nightspot. The hotel has an arrangement with 14 area restaurants whereby when you dine at any of them, you can arrange for the tab to be added to your hotel bill. ✉ *Skagenkaien 30, Postboks 793, 4004* ☎ *51–85–00–00* 🖷 *51–85–00–01* ⊕ *www.skagenbryggehotell.no* ⇘ *110 rooms, 2 suites* ⚒ *Restaurant, minibars, in-room data ports, sauna, steam room, bar, convention center* ⊟ *AE, DC, MC, V.*

$$–$$$ ☒ **Clarion Hotel Stavanger.** This downtown business hotel has an up-to-the-minute design. Famed local artist Kjell Pahr Iversen's vibrant paintings hang on the hotel's walls. The light, simple interior is punctuated by the clean lines of Phillipe Starck lamps and Erik Jørgensen chairs. The rooms are also bright and simply furnished. ✉ *Ny Olavskleiv 8, 4008* ☎ *51–91–00–00* 🖷 *51–91–00–10* ⊕ *www.clhs.no* ⇘ *250 rooms, 23 suites* ⚒ *Restaurant, café, cable TV, in-room data ports, gym, hot tub, sauna, bar, meeting rooms* ⊟ *AE, DC, MC, V.*

Festivals

Stavanger has earned the title "Festivalbyen" (festival city) for its year-round celebrations. More than 20 official festivals are held throughout the year—comedy, garlic, chili, food, chamber music, jazz, literature, beach volleyball, wine, belly dancing, vintage boats, emigrants, immigrants. There are probably just as many unofficial events, since locals love any reason to have a party. Contact **Destination Stavanger** (☎ 51–85–92–00 ⊕ www.visitstavanger.com) for a listing.

Nightlife & the Arts

CAFÉS Stavanger has its share of cozy and hip locations to have a drink, read the papers, listen to live music, or just hang out. **Amys Coffeebar** (✉ Salvågergt. 7 ☎ 51–86–07–65) is a sweet little spot for an afternoon coffee or take-away lunch. **Café Sting** (✉ Valberget 3 ☎ 51–89–38–78), a combination restaurant, nightclub, art gallery, and performance venue, is an institution. At **Café Italia** (⊠ Skagen 8 ☏ 51–56–33–88), there's an Italian coffee bar, a restaurant, and even a boutique selling Italy's top fashion names. News junkies head to Norway's first news café, **Newsman** (⊠ Skagen 14 ☏ 51–84–38–80), for CNN on the TV and for Norwegian and foreign periodicals. For a quick snack or a glass of freshly squeezed fruit juice, stop by **Sitrus Sandwichbar** (⊠ Bakkegt. 7, entrance from Salvågergt. ☏ 51–89–15–90); the smoothies are delicious. **Stavanger Sportscafé** (⊠ Skagenkaien 14A ☏ 51–89–17–41) is a big hit with sports fans.

CLUBS & PUBS   Stavanger clubs and pubs can show you a good time year-round. Walk along **Skagenkaien** and **Strandkaien** streets for a choice of pubs and nightclubs. In summer, harborside places with patios don't usually close until dawn. **Checkpoint Charlie** (⊠ Lars Hertevig gt. 5 ☏ 51–53–22–45) is popular with the twentysomethings, and sometimes doubles as a concert venue. Step into the stylish wine cellar **Flaskehalsen** (⊠ Øvre Holmegt. 20 ☏ 51–86–41–58) if you're seeking quiet, romantic moments. College kids hang out at **Folken** (⊠ Ny Olavskleiv 16 ☏ 51–56–44–44), an independent student club that frequently holds rock concerts. Sun-kissed **Hansen Hjørnet** (⊠ Skagenkaien 18 ☏ 51–89–52–80 ☉ Mid-May–mid-Sept.) is a bar and restaurant that always attracts a crowd. With its open fireplace and stone walls, **Nåloyet** (⊠ Nedre Strandgt. 13 ☏ 51–84–37–60) is Stavanger's answer to the London pub. Dance the night away to pulsating sounds at the lively **Taket Nattklubb** (⊠ Nedre Strandgt. 15 ☏ 51–84–37–20), popular with those in their twenties and thirties.

THE ARTS   If chamber music's more your style, attend the **International Chamber Music Festival** (☏51–84–66–70), held every August. **Litteraturuken** (Literature Week; ☏ 51–89–32–84) takes place during the last week in October, with readings, lectures, and discussions at Café Sting. Every May, Norwegian and international jazz artists play at the **MaiJazz** (☏ 51–84–66–67) festival.

Rogaland Kunstsenter (Rogaland Art Center; ⊠ Nytorget ☏ 51–59–97–60) has a respected gallery and art shop. **Rogaland Theatre** (☏ 51–91–90–90 ⊕ www.rogaland-teater.no) performs plays throughout the region. In the heart of the city, **Sølvberget** (Stavanger Culture House; ⊠ Sølvberggt. 2 ☏ 51–50–71–70) has exhibitions, cultural events, a library, Internet access, and movie theaters. **Stavanger Konserthus** (⊠ Concert Hall, Bjergsted ☏ 51–53–70–00) often hosts local artists, and there are free summertime concerts in the foyer. **Stavangeren Kultur & Revyscene** (⊠ Vaisenhusgt. 37 ☏ 51–84–38–50) is a popular meeting place and venue for readings, one-act plays, live music, and art exhibitions. **Stavanger Symphony Orchestra** (☏ 51–50–88–30) performs throughout the year except in July.

Built on an island in the archipelago in the Middle Ages and once a palace as well as a monastery, **Utstein Kloster** (⊠ Mosterøy ☏ 51–72–47–05 ⊕ www.herlige-stavanger.no) has superior acoustics—classical and jazz music concerts are performed here from June to August.

Sports & the Outdoors

FISHING   Angling for saltwater fish doesn't require a license or a fee of any kind. The local tourist office can help you get the permits required for other types of fishing.

North of Stavanger is the longest salmon river in western Norway, the Suldalslågen, made popular 100 years ago by a Scottish aristocrat who built a fishing lodge there. **Lakseslottet Lindum** (✉ 4240 Suldalsosen ☎ 52/79–91–61) still has rooms, cabins, and camping facilities, as well as an upscale restaurant. The main salmon season is July through September. Wear diving gear and you can go on a **Salmon Safari** (✉ Mo Laksegard ☎ 52/79–76–90), floating in the river 2 km (1 mi) to study wild salmon in their natural environment.

On the island of Kvitsøy, in the archipelago just west of Stavanger, you can rent an apartment, complete with fish-smoking and -freezing facilities, and arrange to use a small sailboat or motorboat. **Kvitsøy Kurs & Konferanse** (✉ Box 35, 4090 Kvitsøy ☎ 51–73–51–88) can help with arrangements.

GOLF Golf enthusiasts can work on their game at several local courses. The **Sola Golf Klubb** (✉ Åsenveien, Sola ☎ 51–70–91–70) has an 18-hole course set amid a forest. If you'd like to golf next to the sea, head to **Sandnes og Sola Golfklubb** (✉ Solastranden Golfbane ☎ 51–69–68–90) 20 km (12 mi) from Stavanger. The **Stavanger Golf Klubb** (✉ Longebakken 45, Hafrsfjord ☎ 51–55–50–06) has a lush park and forest near its 18-hole, international-championship course.

HIKING Specialized books and maps are available through **Stavanger Turistforening** (✉ Postboks 239, 4001 ☎ 51–84–02–00 ⊕ www.stavangerturistforening.no). The office can help you plan a hike through the area, particularly in the rolling Setesdalsheiene and the thousands of islands and skerries of the Ryfylke Archipelago. The tourist board oversees 33 cabins for members (you can join on the spot) for overnighting along the way.

HORSEBACK **Fossanmoen** (☎ 51–70–37–61 ⊕ www.fossanmoen.no) organizes riding
RIDING camps and trips on Iceland ponies that go through scenic surroundings. They can last anywhere from an hour to all day.

ICE-SKATING From November through March you can skate outdoors at **Kunstisbanen** (✉ Åsen, Sørmarka ☎ 51–58–06–44). **Stavanger Ishall** (✉ Siddishallen ☎ 51–53–74–50) has ice skating from mid-September to mid-April.

SKIING Skiing in the Sirdal area, 2½ hours from Stavanger, is possible from January to April. Special ski buses leave Stavanger on weekends at 8:30 AM during the season. Especially recommended is **Sinnes** (☎ 38–37–12–02) for its non-hair-raising cross-country terrain. Downhill skiing is available at **Ålsheia**, which is on the same bus route. Other places to ski include **Gullingen skisenter, Suldal** (☎ 52/79–99–01), **Sandalen skisenter, Sauda** (☎ 52/78–56–56), and **Stavtjørn alpinsenter** (☎ 51–45–17–17). Contact **Connex Vest** (✉ Treskevn. 5, Hafrsfjord, Stavanger ☎ 51–59–90–00) for transportation information.

WATER SPORTS Diving is excellent all along the coast—although Norwegian law requires all foreigners to dive with a Norwegian as a way of ensuring that wrecks are left undisturbed. If you just want to take a swim, plan a trip to **local beaches** such as **Møllebukta** and **Madia,** which are both deep inside the

Hafrsfjord. **Solastranden** has 2⅓ km (1½ mi) of sandy beach ideal for windsurfing and beach volleyball. Other prime beach spots are Vaulen badeplass, Godalen badeplass, Viste Stranden, and Sande Stranden. The World Tour Beach Volleyball tournament is held downtown on a temporary beach volleyball court at the end of June.

The local swimming pool is **Stavanger Svømmehall** (☎ 51–50–74–51). **Gamlingen Friluftsbad** (✉ Tjodolfsgt. 53 ☎ 51–52–74–49) is an outdoor heated swimming pool that's open year-round.

Shopping

Kvadrat Steen & Strøm (✉ Forus between Stavanger and Sandnes ☎ 51–96–00–00) is Norway's biggest shopping center, with 160 shops, restaurants, a pharmacy, post office, a state wine store, and a tourist information office. Bookworms might find literary treasures in the aptly titled **Odd Book Shop** (✉ Kirkegt. 30 ☎ 51–89–47–66). Reindeer hides, sheepskin, and other souvenirs are sold at **Olaf Pettersen & Co.** (✉ Kirkegt. 31 ☎ 51–89–48–04). If jewelry's your passion, head to the city's best shop: **Sølvsmeden på Sølvberget** (✉ Sølvberggt. 5 ☎ 51–89–42–24). **Stavanger Storsenter Steen & Strøm** (✉ Klubbgt. 5 ☎ 51–93–80–00) is a centrally located shopping center.

In an early-17th-century wharf house, **Straen Handel** (✉ Strandkaien 31 ☎ 51–52–52–02) has an impressive collection of knitted items, rosemaling, Norwegian dolls, trolls, books, and postcards.

Sørlandet to Stavanger A to Z

To research prices, get advice from other travelers, and book travel arrangements, visit www.fodors.com.

AIR TRAVEL

Kristiansand and Stavanger are served by SAS Braathens, with nonstop flights from Oslo, Bergen, Trondheim, and Newcastle, as well as Copenhagen, Aberdeen, Göteborg, and London. MUK Air serves Aalborg, Denmark; Agder Fly serves Göteborg, Sweden, and Billund, Denmark. Tickets on the last two airlines can be booked through SAS Braathens. The low-cost Norwegian Air Shuttle has flights from Oslo to Stavanger. Widerøe flyveselskap specializes in flights within Norway.

🛪 **Airlines & Contacts SAS Braathens** ☎ 05400. **Norwegian Air Shuttle** ☎ 815–21–815. **Widerøe** ☎ 810–01–200.

AIRPORTS

Kristiansand's Kjevik Airport is about 16 km (10 mi) outside town. The airport bus departs from the Braathens office approximately one hour before every departure and proceeds to Kjevik, stopping at downtown hotels along the way. A similar bus makes the return trip from the airport.

In Stavanger, Sola Airport is 14 km (11 mi) south of downtown. The Flybussen (airport bus) leaves the airport every 20 minutes. It stops at hotels and outside the railroad station in Stavanger. It then heads back to the airport.

🛪 **Flybussen** ☎ 51–52–26–00.

BOAT & FERRY TRAVEL

Color Line has four ships weekly on the Stavanger–Newcastle route. High-speed boats to Bergen are operated by Flaggruten. Fjord Line offers car ferries that go from Stavanger to Newcastle, England, and from Egersund to Hanstholm, in northern Denmark. Another line connects Larvik to Frederikshavn, on Denmark's west coast. For information about this crossing, contact DSB in Denmark, or Color Line or DFDS Scandinavian Seaways in Norway.

Color Line A/S ✉ Nygt. 13, 4006 Stavanger ☎ 810-00-811 ⊕ www.colorline.no. **DFDS Scandinavian Seaways** ☎ 38-17-17-60 ⊕ www.seaeurope.com. **DSB** ☎ 33-14-17-01, 42-52-92-22 in Denmark ⊕ www.dsb.dk. **Fjord Line** ☎ 815-33-500 ⊕ www.fjordline.com. **Flaggruten** ☎ 51-86-87-80.

BUS TRAVEL

Aust-Agder Trafikkselskap, based in Arendal, has one departure daily in each direction for the 5½- to 6-hour journey between Oslo and Kristiansand. Nor-Way Bussekspress runs between Oslo and Stavanger, which is about a 10-hour trip. Sørlandsruta, based in Mandal, has two departures in each direction for the 4½-hour trip from Kristiansand bus terminal to Stavanger. The main bus terminal is outside the train station.

Bus connections in Sørlandet are infrequent; the tourist office can provide a comprehensive schedule. HAGA Reiser operates buses between Stavanger and Hamburg.

Aust-Agder Trafikkselskap ☎ 37-02-65-00. **HAGA Reiser** ☎ 51-67-65-00 or 38-12-33-12. **Kristiansand Bus Information** ✉ Strandgt. 33 ☎ 38-00-28-00. **Ruteservice Stavanger, Nor-Way Bussekspress** ☎ 820/53-300. **Sørlandsruta** ☎ 38-03-83-00.

CAR TRAVEL

From Oslo it is 320 km (199 mi) to Kristiansand and 452 km (281 mi) to Stavanger. Route E18 parallels the coastline but stays slightly inland on the eastern side of the country and farther inland in the western part. Although seldom wider than two lanes, it is easy driving because it is so flat. Driving from Bergen to Stavanger along the jagged western coastline is difficult and requires a detour of 150 km (93 mi).

Sørlandet is also flat, so it's easy driving throughout. The area around the Kulturhus in the Stavanger city center is closed to car traffic, and one-way traffic is the norm in the rest of the downtown area.

CAR RENTALS **Major Agencies** Avis Bilutleie ☎ 815–33–044. **Budget** ☎ 815–60–600. Hertz Bilutleie ☎ 67/16–80–00.

EMERGENCIES

For emergency medical care in Kristiansand, go to Kristiansand Legevekt, open daily from 4 PM to 8 AM. For an emergency in Stavanger, you can call Rogaland Sentralsykehusgo or go to Forus Akutten medical center, open 8 AM–8 PM weekdays.

In Kristiansand, Elefantapoteket (Elefant Pharmacy) is open weekdays from 8:30 to 8, Saturday from 8:30 to 6, and Sunday from 3 to 6. In

Stavanger, Løveapoteket is open daily from 9 AM to 11 PM except for Christmas, New Year's Day, and Easter Sunday, when it closes at 8 PM.

🚑 **Ambulance** ☎ 113. **Egil Undem, Stavanger dentist** ✉ Kannikbakken 6 ☎ 51-52-84-52. **Elefantapoteket** (Elefant Pharmacy) ✉ Gyldenløvesgt. 13, 4611 Kristiansand ☎ 38-12-58-80. **Emergency Doctor, Stavanger** ☎ 51-51-02-02. **Fire** ☎ 110. **Forus Akutten medical center, Stavanger** ☎ 51-70-94-94. **Kristiansand Legevekt** ✉ Egsvn. 102 ☎ 38-07-69-00. **Løveapoteket** (Løve Pharmacy) ✉ Olav Vs gt. 11, 4005 Stavanger ☎ 51-91-08-80. **Police** ☎ 112. **Rogaland Sentralsykehus** ☎ 51-51-80-00.

TAXIS

All Kristiansand and Stavanger taxis are connected with a central dispatching office. Journeys within Stavanger are charged by the meter, elsewhere strictly by distance.

🚕 **Taxi Information Norgestaxi Stavanger** ☎ 08000. **Stavanger Taxisentral** ☎ 51-90-90-90. **Taxi Sør** ☎ 38-02-80-00 Kristiansand.

TOURS

Tours of Kristiansand are offered only in summer. The City Train is a 15-minute tour of the center part of town. The MS *Maarten* gives two-hour tours of the eastern archipelago and a three-hour tour of the western archipelago daily at 10 AM, from early June until August 8.

In Stavanger a two-hour bus tour leaves from the marina at Vågen daily at 1 between June and August. Rødne Clipper Fjord Sightseeing offers three different tours. FjordTours operates sightseeing and charter tours by boat.

🚌 **Fees & Schedules City Train** ✉ Nedre Torv ☎ 38-03-05-24. **FjordTours** ☎ 51-53-73-40. **MS *Maarten*** ✉ Pier 6 by Fiskebrygga ☎ 38-10-83-84. **Rødne Clipper Fjord Sightseeing** ✉ Skagenkaien 18, 4006 ☎ 51-89-52-70.

TRAIN TRAVEL

The Sørlandsbanen leaves Oslo S Station four times daily for the 5-hour journey to Kristiansand and five times daily for the 8½- to 9-hour journey to Stavanger. Two more trains travel the 3½-hour Kristiansand–Stavanger route. Kristiansand's train station is at Vestre Strandgata. For information on trains from Stavanger, call Stavanger Jernbanestasjon.

🚆 **Train Information Kristiansand Train Station** ☎ 38-07-75-32. **NSB** (Norwegian State Railways) ☎ 815-00-888. **Stavanger Jernbanestasjon** (Stavanger Train Station) ☎ 51-56-96-10.

VISITOR INFORMATION

ℹ️ **Tourist Information Arendal SørlandsInfo** ✉ Arendal Næringsråd, Friholmsgt. 1, 4800 ☎ 37-00-55-44. **Destinasjon Sørlandet: Kristiansand** ✉ Vestre Torv, Vestre Strandgt. 32, Box 592, 4665 ☎ 38-12-13-14 🌐 www.sorlandet.com. **Destinasjon Sørlandet: Lillesand** ✉ Strandgt. 14, 4790 ☎ 37-26-16-80. **Destinasjon Sørlandet: Vennesla** ✉ Vennesla stasjon, 4700 ☎ 38-13-72-00. **Destinasjon Stavanger** ✉ Rosenkildetorget ☎ 51-85-92-00 🌐 www.regionstavanger.com. **Hå Tourist Information** ✉ Hå Folkebiblioteket ☎ 51-43-40-11. **Mandal** Mandal og Lindesnes Turistkontor ✉ Bryggegt., 4500 ☎ 38-27-83-00. **Sandnes Tourist Board** ✉ Våsgt. 22 ☎ 51-97-55-55.

Bergen

WORD OF MOUTH

"Bergen is fantastic. You can see it in two days, but if you like an unhurried pace, stopping to read every sign and post as we do, take three days. Hanging around the market at the marina is great fun."

—joegri

"Bergen is a walking town, except for the wonderful funicular ride to the top of the mountain."

—USNR

MANY FALL IN LOVE at first sight with Bergen, Norway's second-largest city. Seven rounded lush mountains, pastel-color wooden houses, historic Bryggen, winding cobblestone streets, and Hanseatic relics all make it a place of enchantment. Its many epithets include "Trebyen" (Wooden City; it has many wooden houses), "Regnbyen" (Rainy City, due to its 200 days of rain a year), and "Fjordbyen" (Gateway to the Fjords). Surrounded by forested mountains and fjords, it's only natural that most Bergensers feel at home either on the mountains (skiing, hiking, walking, or at their cabins) or at sea (fishing and boating). As for the rainy weather, most visitors quickly learn the necessity of rain jackets and umbrellas. Bergen is even the site of the world's first umbrella vending machine.

Residents take legendary pride in their city and its luminaries. The composer Edvard Grieg, the violinist Ole Bull, and Ludvig Holberg, Scandinavia's answer to Molière, all made great contributions to Norwegian culture. Today their legacy lives on in nationally acclaimed theater, music, film, dance, and art. The singer Sondre Lerche, pianist Leif Ove Andsnes, choreographer Jo Strømgren, and author Gunnar Staalesen all live in Bergen. Every year a host of lively festivals attracts national and international artists.

This harbor city has played a vital role in the Norwegian economy. Before the discovery of North Sea oil and Bergen's subsequent rise as the capital of Norway's oil industry, the city was long a major center of fishing and shipping. In fact, Bergen was founded in 1070 by Olav Kyrre as a commercial center. In the 14th century, Hanseatic merchants settled in Bergen and made it one of their four major overseas trading centers. The surviving Hanseatic wooden buildings on Bryggen (the quay) are topped with triangular cookie-cutter roofs and painted in red, blue, yellow, and green. Monuments in themselves (they are on the UNESCO World Heritage List), the buildings tempt travelers and locals to the shops, restaurants, and museums inside. In the evening, when the Bryggen is illuminated, these modest buildings, together with the stocky Rosenkrantz Tower, the Fløyen, and the yachts lining the pier, are reflected in the waters of the harbor—and provide one of the loveliest cityscapes in northern Europe.

EXPLORING BERGEN

The heart of Bergen is Torgallmenningen, the city's central square, which runs from Ole Bulls plass to Fisketorget on the harbor, facing Bryggen. From here, the rest of Bergen spreads up the sides of the seven mountains that surround it, with some sights concentrated near the university and others near a small lake called Lille Lungegårdsvann. Fløyen, the mountain to the east of the harbor, is the most accessible for daytrippers. Before you begin your walking tour, you can take the funicular (cable car) up to the top of it for a particularly fabulous overview of the city.

Numbers in the text correspond to numbers in the margin and on the Bergen map.

Historic Bergen: Bryggen to Fløyen

a good walk

Start your tour in the center of town at Torget, also called **Fisketorget ❶** ➤ or the fish market, where fishermen and farmers sell their goods. Next, walk over to **Bryggen ❷**, the wharf on the northeast side of Bergen's harbor. The gabled wood warehouses lining the docks mark the site of the city's original settlement. Take time to walk the narrow passageways between buildings; shops and galleries are hidden among the wooden facades. Follow the pier to the **Hanseatisk Museum ❸** at Finnegårdsgaten and have a look inside. Afterward, continue your walk down the wharf, past the historic buildings, to the end of the Holmen promontory and to **Bergenhus Festning ❹** (Bergenhus Fort), which dates from the 13th century; the nearby Rosenkrantztårnet is a 16th-century tower residence. After you've spent some time out here, retrace your steps back to the Radisson SAS Royal Hotel. Beside the hotel is **Bryggens Museum ❺**, which houses magnificent archaeological finds. Just behind the museum is the 12th-century church called **Mariakirken ❻**. Around the back of the church up the small hill is Øvregaten, a street that's the back boundary of Bryggen. Walk down Øvregaten four blocks to **Fløibanen ❼**, the funicular that runs up and down Fløyen, one of the city's most popular hiking mountains. Don't miss a trip to the top, whether you hike or take the funicular—the view is like no other. When you've returned, walk south on Øvregaten to the **Domkirke ❽** (Bergen Cathedral). It's on your left, at the intersection with Kong Oscars Gate. Finally, head back to Torgallmenningen in the center of town for a late-afternoon snack at one of the nearby cafés.

TIMING This tour will take a good portion of a day. Be sure to get to the Fisketorget early in the morning, since many days it may close as early as 1 or 2. Also, try to plan your trip up Fløyen for a sunny day. It may be difficult, as Bergen is renowned for rain, but you may want to wait a day or two and see if the skies clear up.

What to See

 Akvariet. Here you will see one of the largest collections of North Sea fish and invertebrates in Europe, as well as tropical saltwater and freshwater fish. The aquarium has 60 tanks and three outdoor pools of seals, carp, and penguins. On a realistic nesting cliff, adorable penguins rest, waddle by, and stare back curiously at onlookers. Watch the seals, Kobbe-Lars, Amalie, and their companions, as they zoom by like swimming torpedoes. Tanks inside are filled with schools of brilliantly colored tropical fish as well as Norwegian salmon and common eels, which tend to wrap around each other. *The Aquarium: Bergen and the Local Coastline*—a 360-degree video directed by one of Norway's most beloved animators, the late Ivo Caprino—is shown every hour, as is *SOS Planet*, a 3-D film that you watch with special glasses. The aquarium is on Nordnes Peninsula, a 20-minute walk from the fish market. You can also get to it by taking Bus 11 or the ferry from the fish market. ⊠ *Nordnesbakken 4, Nordnes* ☎ *55–55–71–71* ⊕ *www.akvariet.com* ☜ *NKr 100* ⊙ *May–Aug., daily 9–8; Sept.–Apr., daily 10–6. Feeding times: May–Aug., daily noon, 3, and 6; Sept.–Apr., daily noon and 3.*

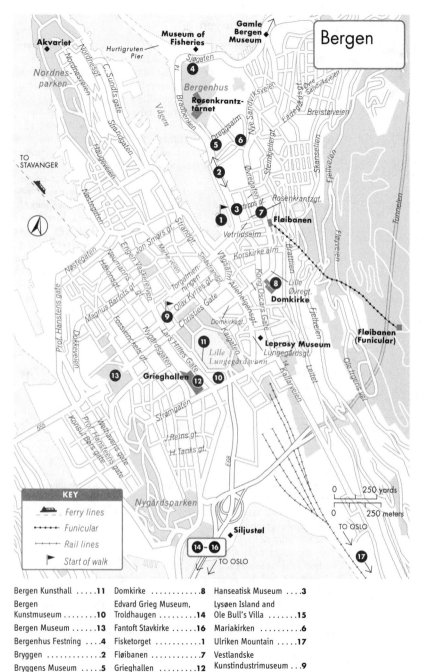

Bergen

Akvariet

Nordnes-parken

Hurtigruten Pier

Museum of Fisheries

Gamle Bergen Museum

Nordnesvn.

Nordnesgt.

C. Sundts gate

Sjøgaten

4

Bergenhus

Rosenkrantz-tårnet

Dreggsalm.

Nye Sandviksveien

Ladegårdsgt.

Øvre Sandvikveien

Breistølveien

Bradbenken

Vågen

5

6

TO STAVANGER

Strandgaten

Haugeveien

Nøstegaten

Øvregaten

Stølen

2

Steinkjellegt.

Skanseveien

Fjellveien

Lepps gt.

1

3

Rosenkrantzgt.

7

Fløibanen

Vetrlidsalm.

Fløyveien

Tunnelen

Korskirke alm.

Vetrlidsalm.

Vågsalm.

Allehelgensgt.

Brattlien

Marken

Kong Oscars Gate

8

Lille Øvregt.

Domkirke

Prof. Hansteins gate

Dokkeveien

Magnus Barfots gt.

Fosswinckels gt.

Neumanns gt.

Jon Smørs gt.

Engen Teatergaten

Torgalmenningen

Olav Kyrres Gate

Christies Gate

Torgalmenningen

Markeveien

Småstrandgt.

9

Domkirkegt.

Kaigaten

Fjellveien

Kalfarveien

Fløibanen (Funicular)

Lars Hilles Gate

Nygårdsgaten

11

Leprosy Museum

Lungegårdsgt.

Lille Lungegårdsvann

13

Grieghallen

12

10

Prof. Hansteens gate

Konsul Børs gate

Strømgaten

Veltbauens gate

Prof. Hansteens gate

Reins gt.

H. Tanks gt.

E68

666

TO OSLO

0 ———— 250 yards
0 ———— 250 meters

Nygårdsparken

Siljustøl

14 - 16

TO OSLO

17

TO OSLO

❹ Bergenhus Festning (Bergenhus Fortress). The buildings here date from the mid-13th century. **Håkonshallen,** a royal ceremonial hall erected during the reign of Håkon Håkonsson between 1247 and 1261, was badly damaged by the explosion of a German ammunition ship in 1944, but was restored by 1961. Erected in the 1560s by the governor of Bergen Castle (Bergenhus), Erik Rosenkrantz, **Rosenkrantztårnet** (Rosenkrantz Tower) served as a combined residence and fortified tower. ⊠ *Bergenhus, Bryggen* ☎ *55–58–80–10* ◻ *NKr 25* ⊗ *Mid-May–mid-Aug., daily 10–4; mid-Aug.–mid-May, Sun. noon–3. Closed during Bergen International Music Festival.*

❷ Bryggen (The Wharf). A trip to Bergen is incomplete without a trip to Fodor'sChoice Bryggen. A row of mostly reconstructed 14th-century wooden buildings ★ that face the harbor makes this one of the most charming walkways in Europe, especially on a sunny day. The originals were built by Hansa merchants, while the oldest reconstruction dates from 1702. Several fires, the latest in 1955, destroyed the original structures.

❺ Bryggens Museum. This museum contains archaeological finds from the Middle Ages. An exhibit on Bergen circa 1300 shows the town at the zenith of its importance, and has reconstructed living quarters as well as artifacts such as old tools and shoes. Back then, Bergen was the largest town in Norway, a cosmopolitan trading center and the national capital. ⊠ *Dreggsalmenning 3* ☎ *55–58–80–10* ⊕ *www.uib.no/bmu* ◻ *NKr 40* ⊗ *May–Aug., daily 10–5; Sept.–Apr., weekdays 11–3, Sat. noon–3, Sun. noon–4.*

❽ Domkirke (Bergen Cathedral). The cathedral's long, turbulent history has shaped the eclectic architecture of the current structure. The Gothic-style choir and the lower towers are the oldest, dating from the 13th century. Note the cannonball lodged in the tower wall—it dates from a battle between English and Dutch ships in Bergen harbor in 1665. From June through August, a Sunday service is held in English at 9:30 AM in the Chapter House, an organ recital is held Thursday at noon, and there is a concert in the church every Sunday at 7:30 PM. September through May the Sunday concerts are held at 6 PM. ⊠*Kong Oscars gt. and Domkirke gt.* ☎*55–59–32–73* ⊗ *June–Aug., Mon.–Sat. 11–4; Sept.–May, Tues.–Fri. 11–12:30.*

▶ **❶ Fisketorget** (Fish Market). Turn-of-the-20th-century photographs of this pungent square show fishermen in Wellington boots and raincoats and women in long aprons. Now the fishmongers wear bright-orange rubber overalls as they look over the catches of the day. In summer the selection is mostly limited to shrimp, salmon, and monkfish. There is much greater variety and more locals shop here the rest of the year. There are also fruit, vegetable, and flower stalls, and some handicrafts and souvenir vendors at this lively market. You'll also find the world's first umbrella vending machine. Have a classic lunch of smoked shrimp or salmon on a baguette with mayonnaise and cucumber. ⊠ *Zachariasbryggen* ☎ *55–31–56–17* ⊕ *www.torgetibergen.no* ⊗ *June–Aug., daily 7–7; Sept.–May, Mon.–Sat. 7–4.*

★ **❼ Fløibanen** (Fløyen Funicular). A magnificent view of Bergen and its suburbs can be taken in from the top of **Mt. Fløyen,** the most popular of the city's seven mountains. The eight-minute ride on the funicular takes you to the top, 1,050 feet above the sea. A car departs every half hour. Take a break at the restaurant and café (open daily in summer and weekends the rest of the year), the gift shop, or the children's playground. Stroll down the walking path back to downtown or explore the mountains that lead to Ulriken, the highest of the mountains surrounding Bergen. ⊠ *Vetrlidsalmenning 21, Bryggen* ☎ *55–33–68–00* ⊕ *www.floibanen. no* 🎫 *NKr 60* ۩ *Sept.–Apr., Mon.–Thurs. 7:30 AM–11 PM, Fri. 7:30 AM–11:30 PM, Sat. 8 AM–11:30 PM, Sun. 9 AM–11 PM; May–Aug., same start times, runs until midnight.*

★ ❸ **Hanseatisk Museum.** One of the best-preserved buildings in Bergen, the Hanseatic Museum was the 16th-century office and home of an affluent German merchant. The apprentices lived upstairs, in boxed-in beds with windows cut into the wall. Although claustrophobic, the snug rooms had the benefit of being relatively warm—a blessing in the unheated building. ⊠ *Finnegårdsgaten 1A* ☎ *55–54–46-90* ⊕ *www. hanseatisk.museum.no* 🎫 *NKr 45, off-season NKr 25* ۩ *May, daily 11–2; June–Aug., daily 9–5; early–mid Sept., daily 10–3; late Sept. daily 11–2; Oct.–Apr., Tues.–Sat. 11–2, Sun. noon–5.*

❻ **Mariakirken** (St. Mary's Church). Considered one of the most out-
Fodor'sChoice standing Romanesque churches in Norway, this is the oldest building
★ in Bergen used for its original purpose. It began as a church in the 12th century but gained a Gothic choir, richly decorated portals, and a splendid baroque pulpit, much of it added by the Hanseatic merchants who owned it from 1408 to 1766. See the gilded triptych at the high altar that dates from the late Middle Ages. Organ recitals are held every Tuesday at 7:30 PM from late June through August. ⊠ *Dreggen, Bryggen* ☎ *55–59–32–73* 🎫 *NKr 20* ۩ *Late June–Aug., weekdays 9:30–11:30 and 1–4; Sept.–early June, Tues.–Fri. 11–12:30.*

Rasmus Meyers Allé & Grieghallen

a good walk

From Torgallmenningen, walk to Nordahl Bruns Gate and turn left for the **Vestlandske Kunstindustrimuseum ❾** ☞, the West Norway Museum of Decorative Art. After you've had your fill of the museum's elaborately crafted works, head out for Christies Gate. Follow it along the park and turn left on Rasmus Meyers Allé, which runs along the small lake, Lille Lungegårdsvann, to reach the **Bergen Kunstmuseum ❿** (Bergen Art Museum), which encompasses the **City Art Collection**, the **Stenersen Collection**, and the **Rasmus Meyer Collection**, all housed next to each other. Nudged in between is the bright green building housing the **Bergen Kunsthall ⓫** (Bergen Art Hall), a gallery featuring contemporary art. Near these galleries, right on Lars Hilles Gate, is **Grieghallen ⓬**, Bergen's famous music hall.

Behind the hall, on Nygårdsgaten, walk up Herman Foss Gate to Muséplass to the **Bergen Museum ⓭**. Heading back into the center of the city, walk down Nygårdsgaten to Strømgaten to Kong Oscars Gate to the **Leprosy Museum.**

TOURS IN & AROUND BERGEN

BERGEN IS THE GUIDED-TOUR *capital of Norway because it is the starting point for most fjord tours. Tickets for all tours are available from the* **tourist office** *(✉ Vågsalmenningen 1 ☎ 55-55-20-00 ⊕ www.visitbergen.com).*

The ambitious all-day Norway-in-a-Nutshell bus-train-boat tour (you can book through the tourist office) goes through Voss, Flåm, Myrdal, and Gudvangen—truly a breathtaking trip—and is the best way to see a lot of the area in a short amount of time. The ticket is valid for weeks, so it is possible to break the trip up into more manageable chunks and stay a night or two at hotels along the way. If you choose to do that, the tourist office can assist with bookings.

Boat Tours
Traveling by boat is an advantage because the contrasts between the fjords and mountains are greatest at water level. The vessels are comfortable and stable (the water is practically still), so seasickness is rare. Stops are frequent, and all sights are explained. **Bergen Fjord Sightseeing** *(☎ 55-25-90-00) offers several local fjord tours.* **Fjord1 Fylkesbaatane** *(☎ 55-90-70-70 ⊕ www.fjord1.no) has several combination tours. Tickets are sold at the tourist office and at the quay.*

Norway's largest and oldest tall sailing ship, **Statsraad Lehmkuhl,** *(☎ 55-30-17-00 ⊕ www.lehmkuhl.no) is the pride of Bergen. Sailing cruises, short skerry cruises, and charters are available. The* **TMSY Weller** *(☎ 55-19-13-03 or 40-82-58-28 ⊕ www.weller.no) can be booked for charter and fishing tours.*

Bus & Walking Tours
Bergens-Expressen *(☎ 55-53-11-50), a "train on tires," leaves from Torgallmenningen for a one-hour ride around the center of town (summer only).*

Bergen Guide Service *(☎ 55-30-10-60 ⊕ www.bergenguideservice.no) has about 100 authorized guides who give different city walking tours such as Unknown Bergen and Bergen Past and Present.*

TIMING   The museums on this tour are quite small and very near each other, so
          you will be able to view most of them on a single outing if you want to,
          and you probably won't need more than half a day to go around them.

What to See

⓫ Bergen Kunsthall (Bergen Art Hall). Nestled snuggly between its more
established cousins, this small museum focuses solely on contemporary
art, usually Norwegian. It features two art galleries and a café, **Landmark,** which is popular among local art students and sometimes also
doubles as an extra showroom, theater, or concert hall. ⊠ *Rasmus
Meyers Allé 5, City Center* ☎ *55–55–93–10* ⊕ *www.kunsthall.no*
⌦ *NKr 50* ☉ *Tues.–Sun. noon–5.*

⓾ Bergen Kunstmuseum (Bergen Art Museum). This important Bergen institution, one of the largest museums in Norway, is made up of the Lysverket, Rasmus Meyer, and Stenersen collections. They are housed in
buildings along the Lille Lungegårdsvann lake. The large, neoclassicist
Lysverket building used to house the municipal power company, but was
bought by the city council and reopened as an art museum in 2003. The
permanent exhibit showcases both medieval icons and Dutch Renais-
sance masters, but there's also a large collection of classic and contemporary Norwegian art on display. The changing exhibits usually feature
contemporary art. ⊠ *Bergen Art Museum, Rasmus Meyers Allé 3 and
7, Lars Hilles gt. 10, City Center* ☎ *55–56–80–00* ⊕ *www.
bergenartmuseum.no* ⌦ *NKr 50* ☉ *Daily 11–5.*

⓭ Bergen Museum. Part of the University of Bergen, this museum has two
collections. The **Cultural History Department** has a fascinating collec-
tion of archaeological artifacts and furniture and folk art from western
Norway. Some of the titles of the displays are "Inherited from Europe,"
"Viking Times," "Village Life in the Solomon Islands," and "Ibsen in
Bergen"; the latter focuses on the famous playwright's six years in
Bergen working with the local theater. The **Natural History Department**
is perfect for lovers of the outdoors, since it includes botanical gardens.
Exhibits include "The Ice Age," "Oil Geology," "Fossils," "Mineral Col-
lections," and "The Evolution of Man." ⊠ *Haakon Sheteligs pl. 10 and
Musépl. 3, City Center* ☎ *55–58–81–72 or 55–58–29–05* ⊕ *www.
museum.uib.no* ⌦ *NKr 40* ☉ *June–Aug., Tues.–Fri. 10–4, weekends
11–4; Sept.–May, Tues.–Fri. 10–2, weekends 11–3.*

---

off the
beaten
path

GAMLE BERGEN MUSEUM (Old Bergen Museum) – This family-
friendly open-air museum transports you to 18th- and 19th-century
Bergen. Streets and narrow alleys with 40 period wooden houses
show town life as it used to be. A baker, dentist, photographer,
 jeweler, shopkeeper, and sailor are represented. Local artists often
hold exhibitions here. The grounds and park are open free of charge
year-round. ⊠ *Nyhavnsveien 4, Sandviken* ☎ *55–39–43–00*
⊕ *www.gamlebergen.museum.no* ⌦ *NKr 60* ☉ *May 8–Sept. 4;
guided tours every hr 10–5.*

⓬ Grieghallen. Home of the Bergen Philharmonic Orchestra and stage for
the annual International Festival, this music hall is a conspicuous slab

of glass and concrete. The acoustics are marvelous. Built in 1978, the hall was named for the city's famous son, composer Edvard Grieg (1843–1907). From September to May, every Thursday and some Fridays and Saturdays at 7:30 PM, the orchestra gives concerts. Throughout the year, the hall is a popular venue for cultural events. ⊠ *Edvard Griegs pl. 1* ☎ *55–21–61–00* ⊕ *www.grieghallen.no.*

Leprosy Museum. St. George's Hospital houses the Bergen Collection of the History of Medicine, which includes this museum. Although the current buildings date from the early 1700s, St. George's was a hospital for lepers for more than 500 years. This unusual museum profiles Norway's contribution to leprosy research. Many Norwegian doctors have been recognized for their efforts against leprosy, particularly Armauer Hansen, after whom "Hansen's disease" is named. ⊠ *St. George's Hospital, Kong Oscars gt. 59* ☎ *55–96–11–55* ⊕ *www.lepra.no* ⊠ *NKr 30* ⊗ *Mid-May–Aug., daily 11–3.*

off the beaten path

NORWEGIAN MUSEUM OF FISHERIES – The sea and its resources, territorial waters, management and research, boats and equipment, whaling and sealing, and fish farming are all covered in the exhibits here. There are also substantial book, video, and photography collections. ⊠ *Bontelabo 2* ☎ *55–32–27–10* ⊕ *www.fiskerimuseum. no* ⊠ *NKr 30* ⊗ *June–Aug., daily 10–6; Sept.–May, Sun.–Fri. 11–4.*

Fodor'sChoice ★ **Rasmus Meyer Collection.** When the businessman Rasmus Meyer (1858–1916) was assembling his superb collection of works by what would become world-famous artists, most of them were unknowns. On display are the best Edvard Munch paintings outside Oslo, as well as major works by J. C. Dahl, Adolph Tidemand, Hans Gude, Harriet Backer, and Per Krogh. Head to the Blumenthal Room to see a fine 18th-century interior and some incredible frescoes. ⊠ *Bergen Art Museum, Rasmus Meyers Allé 3 and 7, Lars Hilles gt. 10, City Center* ☎ *55–56–80–00* ⊕ *www.bergenartmuseum.no* ⊠ *NKr 50* ⊗ *Mid-May–mid-Sept., daily 11–5; mid-Sept.–mid-May, Tues.–Sun. 11–5.*

★ **Stenersen Collection.** This is an extremely impressive collection of modern art for a town the size of Bergen. Modern artists represented include Max Ernst, Paul Klee, Vassily Kandinsky, Pablo Picasso, and Joan Miró, as well as Edvard Munch. There's also a large focus here on Norwegian art since the mid-18th century. ⊠ *Bergen Art Museum, Rasmus Meyers Allé 3 and 7, Lars Hilles gt. 10, City Center* ☎ *55–56–80–00* ⊕ *www.bergenartmuseum.no* ⊠ *NKr 50* ⊗ *Mid-May–mid-Sept., daily 11–5; mid-Sept.–mid-May, Tues.–Sun. 11–5.*

▶ ❾ **Vestlandske Kunstindustrimuseum** (West Norway Museum of Decorative Art). One of Norway's best museums, this eclectic collection contains many exquisite art and design pieces. Its permanent "People and Possessions" exhibit spans 500 years and has everything from Bergen silverware to Ole Bull's violin, which was made in 1562 by the Italian master Saló. Bull's violin has a head of an angel on it, carved by Benvenuto Cellini. A fine collection traces the history of chair design. "The Art of China," the other permanent exhibition, presents one of Europe's largest collections of Buddhist marble sculptures alongside porcelain, jade, bronzes, textiles, and paintings. The silk robes embroidered with dragons and other ceremonial garments are stunning. Changing exhibitions focus on painting, decorative art, and design. ⊠ *Permanenten, Nordahl Bruns gt. 9, City Center* ☎ *55–33–66–33* ⊕ *www.vk.museum.no* ⊠ *NKr 50* ⊙ *Mid-May–mid-Sept., daily 11–5; mid-Sept.–mid-May, Tues.–Sun. noon–4.*

Troldhaugen, Fantoft, Lysøen & Ulriken

a good drive

Once you've gotten your fill of Bergen's city life, you can head out to the countryside to tour some of the area's interesting, and lesser-known, low-key attractions. Follow Route 580 or the E39 (toward Stavanger) out of town about 6 km (4 mi) to **Edvard Grieg Museum, Troldhaugen** ⑭, the villa where Grieg lived for 22 years. After you've wandered the grounds, head for **Lysøen Island and Ole Bull's Villa** ⑮, the Victorian dream castle of Norwegian violinist Ole Bull. Getting here is a 30-minute trek by car and ferry, but it's well worth the effort. From Troldhaugen, get back on Route 580 and drive south toward the airport. At Rådal make a left onto Route 546 (toward Fana). When you reach Fana Kirke, a beautiful 12th-century stone church, Route 546 branches off to the right. Continue straight ahead, leaving Route 546, and drive over Fanafjell to Sørestraumen. Follow signs to Buena Kai. From here, take the ferry to Lysøen. On your way back to Bergen, you can see the **Fantoft Stavkirke** ⑯, which was badly damaged in a fire in 1992 but has been completely rebuilt. End your day with a hike up **Ulriken Mountain** ⑰, the tallest of Bergen's seven mountains. If you're worn out from your sightseeing, but still want take in the view from the top, you can take the Ulriken cable car up the mountain.

About 12 km (7 mi) from Bergen city center, following Route 580 to the airport, is **Siljustøl**, the former home of composer Harald Sæverud. His home is now a music school and museum.

TIMING   Driving and visiting time (or bus time) will consume at least a day or several days, depending on your pace and interest. Visiting these sights is a pleasant way to explore Bergen's environs.

What to See
⑭ **Edvard Grieg Museum, Troldhaugen** (Hill of the Trolls). Built in 1885, this was the home of Norway's most famous composer, Edvard Grieg. In the little garden hut by the shore of Lake Nordås, he composed many of his best-known works. In 1867 he married his cousin Nina, a Danish soprano. They lived in the white clapboard house with green gingerbread trim for 22 years beginning in about 1885. A salon and gathering place for many Scandinavian artists then, it now houses mementos—a piano, paintings, prints—of the composer's life. Its 1907 interior shows it the way that Grieg knew it. At Troldsalen, a concert hall seating 200, chamber music is performed. Summer concerts are held on Wednesday and weekends, and daily during the Bergen International Festival. To get here, catch a bus from Platform 19, 20, or 21 at the bus station, and get off at Hopsbroen. Turn right, walk 200 yards, turn left

on Troldhaugsveien, and follow the signs for roughly 2 km (1 mi). ☒ *Troldhaugv. 65* ☎ *55–92–29–92* ⊕ *www.troldhaugen.com* ☒ *NKr 60* ☉ *May–Sept., daily 9–6; Oct., Nov., and Apr., weekdays 10–2, weekends noon–6; mid-Jan.–Mar., weekdays 10–2.*

⑯ Fantoft Stavkirke (Fantoft Stave Church). During the Middle Ages, when FodorśChoice European cathedrals were built in stone, Norway used wood to create ★ unique stave churches. These cultural symbols stand out for their dragon heads, carved doorways, and walls of staves (vertical planks). Though as many as 750 stave churches may have once existed, only 30 remain standing. The original stave church here, built in Fortun in Sogn in 1150 and moved to Fantoft in 1883, burned down in 1992. Since then, the church has been reconstructed to resemble the original structure. From the main bus station next to the railway station, take any bus leaving from Platform 19, 20, or 21. ☒ *Paradis* ☎ *55–28–07–10* ☒ *NKr 30* ☉ *Mid-May–mid-Sept., daily 10:30–2 and 2:30–6.*

⑮ Lysøen Island and Ole Bull's Villa. The beautiful villa of Norwegian violin virtuoso Ole Bull (1810–80) is on Lysøen, which means "island of light." Bull was a musician and patron of great vision. In 1850, after failing to establish a "New Norwegian Theater" in America, he founded the National Theater in Norway. He then chose the young playwright Henrik Ibsen to write full time for the theater, and later encouraged and promoted another neophyte—15-year-old Edvard Grieg.

Built in 1873, this villa, with an onion dome, gingerbread gables, curved staircase, and cutwork trim just about everywhere, has to be seen to be believed. Stroll along the 13 km (8 mi) of pathways Bull created, picnic or swim in secluded spots, or rent a rowboat. In summer (the only season that Bull lived here), concerts are performed in the villa.

To get here by bus (Monday–Saturday), take the Lysefjordruta bus from Platform 19 or 20 at the main bus station to Buena Kai, where the *Ole Bull* ferry will take you across the fjord to the island. By car, it's a 25-km (15-mi) trip from Bergen to the ferry. Take road E39 south out of the city. Fork left onto Route 546, signposted FANA; continue straight over Fanafjell Mountain to Sørestraumen and follow signs to Buena Kai from there. ☎ *56–30–90–77* ⊕ *www.lysoen.no* ☒ *NKr 25* ☉ *May 18–Aug., Mon.–Sat. noon–4, Sun. 11–5; Sept., Sun. noon–4.*

off the
beaten
path

SILJUSTØL – Norway's most important composer of the 20th century, Harald Sæverud (1897–1992), called this unusual house home. He built it in 1939 of wood and stone and followed old Norwegian construction methods. Concerts are occasionally held here on Sunday at 3 PM (admission NKr 150). Take Bus 23 from the Bergen bus station, Platform 19. By car, drive 12 km (7 mi) from Bergen center to Route 580 heading toward the airport. ☒ *Siljustølsvegen 50* ☎ *55–92–29–92* ⊕ *www.siljustol.no* ☒ *NKr 50* ☉ *Mid-June–mid-Oct., Sun. noon–4.*

⑰ Ulriken Mountain. There are great views of the city, fjords, islands, and coast from the top of the highest of the seven Bergen mountains. The famous Ulriken cable car, running every seven minutes, transports you here. Bring a lunch and hike on well-marked trails in unspoiled mountain wilderness. Or take a break at Ulriken Restaurant and Bar. To get here from downtown, take the Bergen in a Nutshell sightseeing bus along the harbor and Bryggen, through the town center. The same bus returns you to town afterward. ☒ *Ulriken 1, 5009* ⊕ *www.ulriken.no* ☎ *55–20–20–20* ☒ *Round-trip, including bus and cable car, NKr 130* ☉ *June–Aug., daily 9 AM–10 PM; May and Sept., daily 9 AM–7 PM; Oct.–Apr., sunny days only 10 AM–5 PM.*

WHERE TO EAT

"Bergen is the city with the ocean and sea completely in its stomach," someone once said. Bergensers love their seafood dishes: *Fiskepudding* (fish pudding), *fiskekaker* (fish cakes), *fiskeboller* (fish balls), and *Bergensk fiskesuppe* (Bergen fish soup)—delicious renditions of such classic dishes show up on local menus with great regularity.

Any Bergen dining experience should start at *Fisketorget*, the fish market. Rain or shine, fresh catches go on sale here in shiny, stainless-steel stalls. The fishmongers dole out shrimp, salmon, monkfish, and friendly advice. Usually, they have steamed *reker* (shrimp), or smoked *laks* (salmon), served on a baguette with mayonnaise and cucumber—a perfect quick lunch. As for desserts, *skillingsbolle*, a big cinnamon roll, or *sommerbolle*, the same with a custard center, are both popular. *Lefse* is a round flat cake of oatmeal or barley that has a sugar or cream filling. Like other major Norwegian cities, Bergen has international cuisines from Tex-Mex, tapas, and Mediterranean to Japanese sushi restaurants. Some Oslo celebrity chefs—for example Bølgen & Moi—have also opened restaurants here.

WHAT IT COSTS In Norwegian Kroner					
	$$$$	**$$$**	**$$**	**$**	**¢**
AT DINNER	over 270	230–270	180–230	110–180	under 110

Prices are for a main course at dinner, including tax and a service charge.

$$$$ ✕ **Lucullus.** Although the eclectic interior—modern art matched with lace doilies and boardroom chairs—seems a bit out of kilter with the classic French menu here, don't be alarmed; the food is consistently good. The trout with savoy cabbage is excellent. For a meatier treat, try the duck breast with pistachios and orange. The five-course meal is particularly indulgent. ☒ *Hotel Neptun, Walckendorfsgt. 8* ☎ *55–30–68–20* ᵐ *Jacket and tie* ▱ *DC, MC, V* ☉ *Closed Sun. No lunch.*

★ **$$$$** ✕ **To Kokker.** Ranked among Bergen's best restaurants by many, To Kokker is on Bryggen wharf. The 300-year-old building has crooked floors and slanted moldings. The seafood and game are excellent. Try the Jerusalem artichoke soup with smoked reindeer heart—a great starter that combines two traditional Norwegian staples. The halibut au gratin with Parmesan sits in a delicate beetroot sauce, a very tasty combination. ☒ *Bryggen 29* ☎ *55–30–69–55* ⟟ *Reservations essential* ▱ *AE, DC, MC, V* ☉ *Closed Sun. No lunch.*

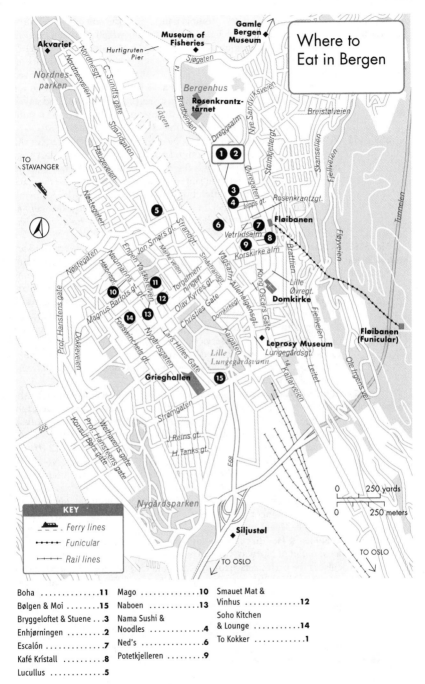

Where to
Eat in Bergen

$$$–$$$$
Fodor'sChoice
★
✕ **Enhjørningen.** This restaurant is named after the unicorn that adorns the doorway of the old wooden building in which it is housed. Enhjørningen has traditions dating back to the Middle Ages, but there's nothing medieval about the menu—it's contemporary Norwegian and it changes according to the day's catch. Try the herb-fried anglerfish served with morel mushroom sauce. If you have trouble deciding, just go for the classic fish platter: salmon, anglerfish, and catfish, steamed and served with two sauces. Enhjørningen is in the running for best seafood restaurant in Bergen. ⊠ *Bryggen 29* ☎ *55–32–79–19* ▭ *AE, DC, MC, V.*

$$$–$$$$
✕ **Ned's.** Right at the fish market, Ned's, formerly Fiskekrogen (or the Fishhook), is a quintessential seafood restaurant. The market's last original fish tank from 1888 holds the fresh lobster, codfish, and crab on offer here. The blue-and-white interior and open kitchen make the place feel rustic, as does the stuffed brown bear that still growls. Although Ned's also serves game, stick to seafood dishes such as the grilled salmon with caviar buerre blanc. ⊠ *Zachariasbryggen* ☎ *55–55–96–60* 🍴 *Reservations essential* ▭ *AE, DC, MC, V.*

$$$–$$$$
Fodor'sChoice
★
✕ **Potetkjelleren.** A popular contemporary restaurant in very old surroundings, Potetkjelleren literally means "potato cellar," and the restaurant's two main dining rooms are in fact old brick-walled storage rooms in the basement. Everything but the menu seems slightly off balance here: the chairs and tables have a rickety feel, mostly due to the uneven stone-tile floor. What the restaurant lacks in comfort it more than makes up for in quality and atmosphere. The cozy cellar is perfect for a romantic candlelight dinner, the service is friendly and efficient, and the kitchen turns out such dishes as grilled halibut with seafood paella. It's no wonder Potetkjelleren gets rave reviews from local media. ⊠ *Kong Oscars gt. 1 A* ☎ *55–32–00–70* ▭ *AE, DC, MC, V.*

$$$
Fodor'sChoice
★
✕ **Kafé Krystall.** This small, intimate restaurant is one of the most fashionable in town. The chef combines his own eclectic contemporary style with traditional Norwegian ingredients in lavish set menus. Try the duck breast with Gorgonzola polenta and foie gras or the three kinds of fish soup with clear mussel sauce. ⊠ *Kong Oscars gt. 16* ☎ *55–32–10–84* 🍴 *Reservations essential* ▭ *AE, DC, MC, V* 🕐 *Closed Sat. No lunch.*

$$–$$$
✕ **Boha.** This modern Italian-inspired restaurant is popular both for business dinners and romantic candlelight suppers. The chef does a particularly good job with seafood. Try the fresh trout with creamy mussels, or the red snapper with pureed celery and garlic. ⊠ *Vaskerelven 6* ☎ *55–31–31–60* ▭ *AE, DC, MC, V.*

★ **$$–$$$**
✕ **Bølgen & Moi.** In the same building as the Bergen Art Museum, this local outlet of Norway's fast-expanding Bølgen & Moi restaurant franchise is the perfect place for a break from the galleries. The lunch menu offers excellent value for money, but the brasserie is well worth a visit later in the evening. Try the fried mackerel with creamed summer cabbage, a modern take on a Norwegian classic. For a hearty lunch, try one of the burgers, such as the Gorgonzola burger with chili mayonnaise. The well-stocked bar is a trendy meeting place for local businesspeople. ⊠ *Rasmus Meyers Allé 9* ☎ *55–59–77–00* ▭ *AE, DC, MC, V.*

$$–$$$
✕ **Bryggeloftet & Stuene.** Dining here on lutefisk in fall and at Christmastime is a time-honored tradition for many Bergensers. Also consider

the *pinnekjøtt* (lumpfish) or the reindeer fillets. The hearty Norwegian country fare suits the somber, wooden dining room, with its fireplace and old oil paintings on the walls. ✉ *Bryggen 11* ☎ *55–31–06–30* ▭ *AE, DC, MC, V.*

$$–$$$ ✕ **Smauet Mat & Vinhus.** Inside a cozy blue cottage is one of Bergen's least-expensive fine restaurants. Hidden away in a small alley near Ole Bulls plass, this cozy restaurant has a reputation for being innovative with Mediterranean and Norwegian cuisine. Try the glazed guinea hen or one of the seafood dishes. ✉ *Vaskerelvssmauet 1* ☎ *55–21–07–10* ⌂ *Reservations essential* ▭ *AE, DC, MC, V.*

$$ ✕ **Mago.** The menu here offers modern Mediterranean takes on classic Norwegian ingredients, such as scallops with pureed cauliflower and beetroot. For a main course, try the chicken stuffed with foie gras. Mago used to be a health-food restaurant, and appliances once used to make fiber-laced fruit shakes have now come to better use, for making homemade ice cream. Mago (which means "magician" in Norwegian) also has one of Bergen's best selections of wine by the glass. If you find one you like, you can take your glass downstairs to get cozy in front of a huge fireplace in the wine bar. ✉ *Neumanns Gate 5* ☎ *55–96–29–80* ▭ *AE, DC, MC, V.*

$$ ✕ **Nama Sushi & Noodles.** The city's most popular sushi bar ("nama" means "fresh and raw" in Japanese) has garnered good reviews for its minimalist, aquatic-inspired interior, and half-sushi, half-noodles menu. Their fish comes fresh from the market nearby, and there are daily happy hour sushi specials. The sashimi *moriawase* (assortment), the breast of duck, and the banana mousse dessert are delicious. The café/bar is perfect for an afternoon coffee break. ✉ *Lodin Lepps gt. 2 B* ☎ *55–32–20–10* ▭ *AE, DC, MC, V.*

$$ ✕ **Soho Kitchen & Lounge.** Perhaps the owners of Soho couldn't decide whether to start a sushi bar or a modern Mediterranean-inspired place, as this restaurant has elements of both. It's an eclectic, interesting restaurant in a suitably schizoid environment that's either minimalist or excessive and flashy, depending on which way you're facing. The bento box is a pricey but tasty lunch deal with miso soup, sushi, and the dessert of the day. If you're hungry for more European flavors, try the succulent roasted chicken breast stuffed with Brie and spinach. ✉ *Håkonsgt. 27* ☎ *55–90–19–60* ▭ *AE, DC, MC, V.*

¢–$$ ✕ **Naboen.** Although many Norwegian restaurants specialize in more traditional dishes, this Swedish restaurant offers delicious, modern variations on Scandinavian classics. Naboen has two menus, an à la carte menu with contemporary styled Swedish and Norwegian specialties, and a moderately priced Swedish menu. Try the popular *Køttbullar* (Swedish meatballs) from the Swedish menu, or if you are feeling more adventurous, the tasty *ristet gravlaks* (roasted cured salmon) from the à la carte menu. ✉ *Neumanns gt. 20* ☎ *55–90–02–90* ▭ *AE, DC, MC, V.*

¢ ✕ **Escalón.** Near the Fløibanen, this tiny tapas restaurant and bar is a trendy place to go for a bite or a drink. Taste the *gambas al ajillo* (scampi in wine and garlic) or the *albódigas en salsa de tomate* (meatballs in tomato sauce). ✉ *Vetrlidsalmenningen 21* ☎ *55–32–90–99* ▭ *AE, DC, MC, V.*

WHERE TO STAY

From the elegance of the Radisson SAS hotels to the no-frills Crowded House, Bergen has a good selection of accommodation options for every traveler's budget and style. Most Bergen hotels are within walking distance of the city's shopping, restaurants, entertainment, and other attractions. Many hotels offer favorable summer and weekend rates depending on vacancies. Last-minute summer rates may be booked 48 hours prior to arrival June 16–August 31. Off-season (September–May) there are often weekend specials. Bergen Tourist Information Office will assist you in booking your accommodations for a fee of NKr 30, make a reservation for NKr 50, and process a cancellation for NKr 50.

WHAT IT COSTS In Norwegian Kroner					
	$$$$	**$$$**	**$$**	**$**	**¢**
FOR 2 PEOPLE	over 2,000	1,600–2,000	1,200–1,600	800–1,200	under 800

Prices are for a standard double room in high season, including tax and a service charge.

★ **$$$** ▦ **First Hotel Marin.** On the harborside near Bryggen, in an elegant brick building that once housed one of Bergen's largest print shops, this business hotel is within walking distance of the city's buses, ferries, and trains. Every room has a bathtub and is decorated in yellows and blues, with oak furniture and hardwood floors. Some rooms feature original artwork from local artists. The penthouse suites have magnificent views of Bergen. ⊠ *Rosenkrantzgt. 8, 5003* ☎ *53–05–15–00* 🖷 *53–05–15–01* ⊕ *www.firsthotels.com* 🛏 *122 rooms, 28 suites* ♿ *2 restaurants, café, cable TV, gym, sauna, Turkish bath, meeting rooms, no-smoking rooms* ▤ *AE, DC, MC, V.*

$$–$$$ ▦ **Radisson SAS Hotel Norge.** A Bergen classic, this hotel attracts important people, from prime ministers to musicians. The architecture is modern, with large salmon-color, dark-wood rooms that blend contemporary Scandinavian comfort with traditional warmth. The restaurant T. G. I. Fridays has American-style fare, and the Contra Bar and Library Bar are popular with locals and visitors alike. The Metro nightclub is packed on weekends. The hotel's fresh smörgåsbord breakfast is the perfect way to start your day. Ask for a room facing Lille Lungegårdsvann for a scenic view. Rooms facing Ole Bulls plass can be noisy at night. ⊠ *Ole Bulls pl. 4, 5012* ☎ *55–57–30–00* 🖷 *55–57–30–01* ⊕ *www.radissonsas.com* 🛏 *347 rooms, 12 suites* ♿ *Restaurant, cable TV, indoor pool, health club, 2 bars, nightclub, meeting room* ▤ *AE, DC, MC, V.*

$$–$$$ ▦ **Radisson SAS Royal Hotel.** Behind Bryggen, this hotel stands where old warehouses used to be. Ravaged by nine fires since 1170, the warehouses were repeatedly rebuilt in the same style, which has been carried over into the Radisson's facade. The small but comfortable rooms have light gold walls and wood accents. Under a glass ceiling, the Café Royal Restaurant serves Scandinavian and international dishes as well as light snacks. The Madam Felle pub and bar on the waterfront is known for its live jazz and rock music, as well as its whiskeys. Engelen nightclub keeps

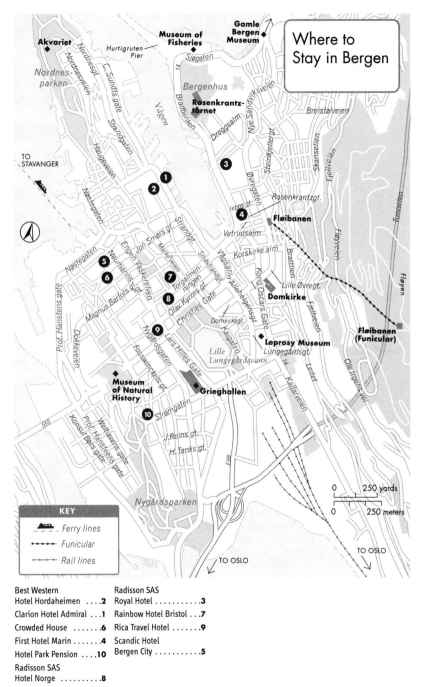

Where to
Stay in Bergen

Best Western
Hotel Hordaheimen 2

Clarion Hotel Admiral ...1

Crowded House 6

First Hotel Marin 4

Hotel Park Pension 10

Radisson SAS
Hotel Norge 8

Radisson SAS
Royal Hotel 3

Rainbow Hotel Bristol ...7

Rica Travel Hotel 9

Scandic Hotel
Bergen City 5

people dancing until the early hours. ✉ *Bryggen, 5003* ☎ *55–54–30–00* 🖷 *55–32–48–08* ⊕ *www.radissonsas.com* 🛏 *273 rooms, 10 suites* ⚐ *2 restaurants, cable TV, indoor pool, health club, sauna, bar, pub, dance club, nightclub, convention center* ⊟ *AE, DC, MC, V.*

$$$ 🏨 **Clarion Hotel Admiral.** Known as "the hotel with the sea on three sides," the Clarion has stunning views of the wharf, the fish market, and Mt. Fløien. Book well in advance for the rooms with the best harbor views. Most rooms have upscale chain-hotel-style furnishings. Some of the suites, however, are decorated with hardwood antique reproductions. Sjøtonnen, the à la carte restaurant, specializes in seafood. After dinner, have a nightcap in the hotel's cognac-and-cigar lounge, which has burnished red-leather sofas. ✉ *C. Sundtsgt. 9–13 5004* ☎ *55–23–64–00* 🖷 *55–23–64–64* ⊕ *www.admiral.no* 🛏 *210 rooms, 2 suites* ⚐ *Restaurant, cable TV, bar, lounge, business services, meeting rooms, no-smoking rooms* ⊟ *AE, DC, MC, V.*

$$ 🏨 **Best Western Hotel Hordaheimen.** Dating from1913, one of the city's oldest and most distinctive hotels is on a quiet, central street. The lobby has a memorable collection of painted Norwegian furniture by Lars Kinsarvik. The hotel's café-restaurant, Hordastova, is well known for its traditional fare, especially *klippfisk* (salted and sun-dried cod), fried mackerel, and smoked cod. Rooms are small but nicely decorated with simple Scandinavian-style furniture in solid colors like beige and plum. ✉ *C. Sundtsgt. 18, 5004* ☎ *55–33–50–00* 🖷 *55–23–49–50* ⊕ *www.hordaheimen.no* 🛏 *64 rooms, 8 suites* ⚐ *Restaurant* ⊟ *AE, DC, MC, V.*

$–$$ 🏨 **Rainbow Hotel Bristol.** The Bristol is within walking distance of many
Fodor'sChoice popular attractions. Built in the 1930s but redecorated in 2001, its
★ rooms are small but comfortable, with cheerful yellow and maroon furnishings. They offer excellent value for money, and several are wheelchair-accessible. ✉ *Torgallmenningen 11, 5014* ☎ *55–55–10–00* 🖷 *55–23–23–19* ⊕ *www.rainbow-hotels.no* 🛏 *134 rooms, 1 suite* ⚐ *Restaurant, cable TV, bar* ⊟ *AE, DC, MC, V.*

$–$$ 🏨 **Rica Travel Hotel.** Popular with business travelers, this hotel is steps away from Torgallmenningen. The rooms are stylish and the location is ideal, but there are few facilities. A public swimming pool and a popular fitness center are nearby. ✉ *Christiesgt. 5–7, 5808* ☎ *55–36–29–00* 🖷 *55–31–32–50* ⊕ *www.rica.no* 🛏 *144 rooms* ⚐ *Restaurant, cable TV, bar, meeting rooms, parking (fee)* ⊟ *AE, DC, MC, V.*

★ $ 🏨 **Hotel Park Pension.** Near the university, this intimate family-run hotel, one of Norway's historic hotels, is in a well-kept Victorian structure built in the 1890s. Both the public rooms and the guest rooms are furnished with antiques. It's a short distance to Grieghallen, downtown, and the bus and railway stations. ✉ *Harald Hårfagres gt. 35, 5007* ☎ *55–54–44–00* 🖷 *55–54–44–44* ⊕ *www.parkhotel.no* 🛏 *21 rooms* ⚐ *Dining room, cable TV* ⊟ *AE, DC, MC, V.*

$ 🏨 **Scandic Hotel Bergen City.** This business hotel runs Bergen Congress Center, the city's largest convention center, and has warm, stylish, comfortable rooms. Take a seat in a wicker chair in the spacious lobby bar to meet people or relax. The hotel is right between Bergen Kino, two cinema multiplexes, and it's a short walk to Den Nationale Scene theater, Grieghallen, and restaurants. ✉ *Håkonsgt. 2–7, 5015*

☎ *55–30–90–80* 🖷 *55–23–49–20* ⊕ *www.scandic-hotels.com* ⬂ *171 rooms, 4 suites ◊ Restaurant, cable TV, bar, business services, convention center* ⊟ *AE, DC, MC, V.*

¢ 🎔 **Crowded House.** Named after an Australian band that was popular in the 1980s, this no-frills lodge is perfect for students and budget travelers. It's a short walk from shopping, restaurants, entertainment, and other attractions, as well as train, bus, and ferry connections. Most of the spartan rooms have good beds, telephones, and washbasins. Showers and toilets are in the corridor. ⊠ *Håkonsgt. 27, 5015* ☎ *55–90–72–00* 🖷 *55–23–13–30* ⊕ *www.crowded-house.com* ⬂ *34 rooms without bath ◊ Café* ⊟ *AE, DC, MC, V.*

NIGHTLIFE & THE ARTS

Nightlife

Bars & Clubs

Bergen is a university town, and the thousands of students who live and study here all year round contribute to making the city's nightlife livelier than you might expect of a small town. Most nightspots center around Ole Bulls plass, the plaza at one end of Torgallmenningen. Within a stone's throw of the plaza you can find dozens of relaxing bars, lively pubs, dancing, live music, and trendy cafés.

If you prefer a quiet glass of wine in peaceful historic surroundings, try **Altona** (⊠ Strandgaten 81 ☎ 55–30–40–72), a bar in a 400-year-old wine cellar neighboring the Augustin Hotel. **Kamelon** (⊠ Vågsalmenning 16 ☎ 91–87–07–23), next door to the nightclub Mood, caters to a more relaxed crowd. Here you will often find live music, ranging from contemporary pop to folk, mostly by local artists. If you prefer conversation over dancing, try **Logen Bar** (⊠ Øvre Ole Bulls pl. 6 ☎ 55–23–20–15), a popular meeting place with live acoustic music every Sunday. **Metro** (⊠ Nedre Ole Bulls pl. 4 ☎ 55–96–02–92) is right in front of the Ole Bull statue, and is a nightclub popular among local twentysomethings. It features pulsating dance music, minimalist decor, and serious crowds on weekends. **Mood** (⊠ Vågsalmenning 16 ☎ 55–55–96–55) is one of Bergen's largest nightclubs, but is still usually packed weekends with local clubbers in their twenties and thirties.

Gay Bars

Bergen has an active gay community. Call Wednesday from 7 to 9 PM or check the Web site of **Landsforeningen for Lesbisk og Homofil Frigjøring** (⊠ Nygårdsgt. 2A ☎ 55–31–21–39), the National Association for Lesbian and Gay Liberation, to ask about events in the city. In the same building as the Landsforeningen, there's the popular gay bar **Fincken** (⊠ Nygårdsgt. 2A ☎ 55–32–13–16), which is open daily until 1 AM.

Cafés

Café Opera (⊠ Engen 18 ☎ 55–23–03–15) is a classic, both sumptuous and stylish. It's often crowded on Friday and Saturday nights. **Jonsvoll** (⊠ Engen 10 ☎ 55–90–03–84), just across the street from Café Opera, is another popular hangout, both for the sensible food served during the day and for the hip crowd sipping cocktails and beer at night. **Kafe Kippers** (✉ Georgernes Verft 12 ☎ 55–31–00–60), Bergen's largest outdoor café, has cozy wool blankets and a spectacular view of the water at sunset. **Vågen Fetevare** (✉ Kong Oscars gt. 10 ☎ 55–31–65–13) is a homey and bohemian coffeehouse. Books are sold and readings are held here.

Pygmalion (✉ Nedre Korskirke Allmenning 4 ☎ 55–32–33–60) serves tasty organic food and has contemporary art on the walls. Just up the road from Pygmalion is **Godt Brød** (✉ Nedre Korskirke Allmenning 12 ☎ 55–32–80–00), a popular organic bakery that makes scrumptious cinnamon rolls and delicious open-faced sandwiches and subs to order. A second location near the theater has more seating space and is often even busier.

Live Music

Bergensers love jazz. The **Bergen Jazz Forum** (✉ Kulturhuset USF, Georgernes Verft 3 ☎ 55–30–72–50 ⊕ www.usf.no) is *the* place to find it—there are concerts every Friday from September to May. The international **Nattjazz** festival offers more than 60 concerts in late May and early June. Since the mid-'90s, Bergen has become a haven for up-and-coming pop and rock bands. A lot of them have their concert debut at **Garage** (✉ Christies gt. 14 ☎ 55–32–19–80), a hangout popular with local musicians.

Bergenfest (☎ 55–21–50–60 ⊕ www.bergenfest.no), formerly known as Ole Blues, runs from late April to early May and features several internationally known rock and blues artists. **Det Akademiske Kvarter** (✉ Olav Kyrres gt. 49–53 ☎ 55–30–28–00) is run by students from Bergen University, and there are pop, rock, and jazz concerts here on a weekly basis most of the year. During the university semester, the rock club **Hulen** (✉ Olaf Ryes vei 48 ☎ 55–33–38–38) attracts college students and other music enthusiasts to weekly rock concerts in a rebuilt air-raid shelter.

The Arts

Bergen is known for its **Festspillene** (International Music Festival), held each year during the last week of May and the beginning of June. Famous names in classical music, jazz, ballet, the arts, and theater perform. Tickets are available at Grieghallen from the **festival office** (✉ Lars Hilles gt. 3, 5015 ☎ 55–21–61–50 ⊕ www.fib.no). Tickets can also be ordered from **Billettservice** (☎ 815–33–133 ⊕ www.ticketmaster.no).

Classical Music

Recitals are held at **Troldhaugen** (☎ 55–92–29–92 ⊕ www.troldhaugen. com), home of composer Edvard Grieg, all summer. Tickets are sold at the tourist office and at the door. Performances are given from late June through August, Wednesday and Sunday at 7:30 and Saturday at 2; and from September through November, Sunday at 2.

The **Bergen Filharmonsike Orkester** (Bergen Philharmonic Orchestra; ✉ Grieghallen, Lars Hilles gt. 3, 5015 ☎ 55–21–61–50) performs from September to May. The **Bergen International Chamber Music Festival** (✉ Gamle Norges Bank, Vågsalmenning ☎ 55–31–04–45) takes place every autumn.

A special concert series, **Grieg in Bergen** (✉Gamle Norges Bank, Vågsalmenning ☎ 55–31–04–45 ⊕www.musicanord.no), is held every evening from mid-June to late August. The venue is easy to find, in the old bank building at Vågsalmenning, across the plaza from the tourist office.

Film

If you're in the mood for a movie, all foreign films are shown in their original languages, with subtitles in Norwegian. Only children's films are dubbed in Norwegian. **Konsertpaleet** (✉ Bergen Kino, Neumannsgt. 3 ☎ 55–56–90–50) is a complex of several theaters. Just down the road, **Magnus Barfot** (✉ Magnus Barfots gt. 12 ☎ 55–56–90–50) is a more modern complex with five theaters.

Folk Music

Twice a week in summer the **Bergen Folklore Dance Group** performs a one-hour program of traditional dances and music from rural Norway at the Bryggens Museum. Tickets are sold by the tourist office and at the door. ✉ *Dreggsalmenning 3* ☎ *55–55–20–06* 🎫 *NKr 95*.

The extensive **Fana Folklore** program is an evening of traditional wedding food, dances, and folk music, plus a concert—at the 800-year-old Fana Church. Tickets are also available from the tourist office. ✉ *Flø`lo, Torgalmenning 9* ☎ *55–91–52–40* 🎫 *NKr 300, includes dinner and return bus transportation* ☉ *June–Sept., Thurs. and Fri. at 7 PM. Catch the bus from Festplassen in the center of Bergen and return by 10:30 PM.*

Revues & Cabarets

There are a number of locations that host revues and cabaret shows in the city center, including **Logen Teater** (✉ Ole Bulls pl. ☎ 55–23–20–15 ⊕www.logen-teater.no) and **Rick's** (✉Veiten 3 ☎55–55–31–31 ⊕www. ricks.no). **Radisson SAS Hotel Norge** (✉ Ole Bulls pl. 4 ☎ 55–57–30–00), stages performances in July and August.

Theater

Although theater is generally performed in Norwegian, check listings for occasional English performances in the city center. **Bergen International Theater (BIT)** (✉ Nøstegt. 54 ☎ 55–23–22–35 ⊕ www.bit-teatergarasjen.no) has Norwegian and international theatrical and modern dance performances. **Den Nationale Scene** (✉ Engen ☎55–54–97–00 ⊕ www.dns.no) has performances on three stages. It's closed in July and most of August.

SPORTS & THE OUTDOORS

Bergen is literally wedged between the mountains and the sea, and there are plenty of opportunities to enjoy the outdoors. Bergensers are quick to do so on sunny days. In summer, don't be surprised to see many Bergensers leaving work early to enjoy sports and activities outdoors, or just relax in the parks.

Fishing

With so much water around, it's no wonder sport fishing is a popular pastime in Bergen. Angling along the coast around Bergen is possible all year, although it is unquestionably more pleasant in summer. In late summer many prefer to move up the area rivers to catch spawning salmon and trout. Whether you prefer fishing in streams, fjords, or the open sea, there are several charter services and fishing tours available. Most can also provide all the fishing gear you need, but be sure to bring warm and waterproof clothes, even in summer.

The **Bergen Angling Association** (⊠ Fosswinckelsgt. 37 ☎ 55–32–11–64 ⊕ www.bergen.sportsfiskere.no) has information and fishing permits. A local fishing supply store, **Campelen** (⊠ Strandgt. 17 ☎ 93–41–29–58 ⊕ www.campelen.no) also arranges fjord fishing, deep-sea fishing, and charter tours, all departing from central Bergen. **Norwegian Sportsfishing Adventures** (☎ 91–10–72–48) specializes in guided tours for small groups. **Sotra Rorbusenter** (⊠ Spildepollen ☎ 56–31–79–76 ⊕ www.rorbusenter.com) offers boat rental, guided tours, and chartered tours from Sotra outside Bergen.

Golf

Near the Flesland airport and Siljustøl, **Fana Golf Club** (⊠ Rådal ☎ 55–29–41–40 ⊕ www.melandgolf.no) is an 18-hole course that opened in the summer of 2004. North of Bergen at Fløksand, the **Meland Golf Club** (⊠ Frekhaug ☎ 56–17–46–00 ⊕ www.melandgolf.no) has an 18-hole championship course with high-quality golf clubs and carts for rent.

Hiking

Like most Norwegians, Bergensers love to go hiking, especially on one or more of the seven mountains that surround the city. **Bergen Turlag** (Bergen Hiking Association; ⊠ Tverrgt. 4–6, 5017 ☎ 55–33–58–10 ⊕ www.bergen-turlag.no) is a touring club that arranges hikes and maintains cabins for hikers. You can pick up maps of many self-guided walking tours around Bergen from the office, as well as from bookstores around Bergen. Bergen Turlag stages the **7-fjellsturen,** or Seven-Mountain Hike, an event that attracts thousands of hikers for the one-day trek across seven nearby mountains.

Take the funicular up **Mt. Fløyen** (⊠ Vetrlidsallmenningen 21, 5014 ☎ 55–33–68–00 ⊕ www.floibanen.no), and minutes later you'll be in the midst of a forest. From the nearby gift shop and restaurant, well-marked paths fan out over the mountains. Follow Fløysvingene Road down for an easy stroll with great views of the city and harbor.

Mt. Ulriken (⊠ Ulriken 1 5009 ☎ 55–20–20–20 ⊕ www.ulriken.no) is popular with walkers and hikers of all levels. The easiest way to reach the summit is via the cable car from Haukeland University Hospital. (To get there, take the double-decker bus that leaves from Torget.) Once you get off the cable car, you'll find trails leading across the mountain plateau, **Vidden,** which is above the tree line. The plateau connects the Fløyen and Ulriken mountains, and you can hike between them in 4 to 6 hours. Views from the alpine trail are spectacular. Be advised that foggy and rainy weather, even in the summer months, can make hiking here dangerous. Consult the tourist information center or Bergen Turlag for maps and general advice.

Racket Sports

Take your favorite racket and head to a couple of sports facilities outside downtown Bergen. **Bergen Racquet Center** (⊠ Fjellsdalen 9, Bønes ☎ 55–12–32–30) has tennis, badminton, squash, soccer, and handball. The well-equipped **Paradis Sports Senter** (☎ 55–91–26–00) has five indoor tennis courts, four squash courts, and badminton courts. There's also spinning, aerobics, and sun beds.

Swimming

☺ The most exciting place to swim in Bergen is **Vannkanten** (⊠ Off Rte. 555 ☎ 55–50–77–99 ⊕ www.vannkanten.no), a water complex of several pools, which also has a coffee bar and restaurants. To get there, take buses 411 or 439 from the main bus station. **Nordnes sjøbad** (⊠ near Akvariet aquarium) is a popular recreational facility that has a heated outdoor swimming pool. **Sentralbadet** (⊠ Teatergt. ☎ 55–56–95–70) is the city's main swimming pool, in the center of town.

SHOPPING

Shopping Centers

Bergen has several cobblestoned pedestrian shopping streets, including Gamle Strandgaten, (Gågaten), Torgallmenningen, Hollendergaten, and Marken. Stores selling Norwegian handicrafts are concentrated along the Bryggen boardwalk. Near the cathedral, the tiny Skostredet has become popular with young shoppers. The small, independent speciality stores here sell everything from army surplus gear to tailored suits and designer trinkets. Most Bergen shops are open Monday–Wednesday and Friday from 9 to 5; Thursday from 9 to 7; and Saturday from 10 to 3. Bergen's shopping centers—Galleriet, Kløverhuset, and Bergen Storsenter—are open weekdays from 9 to 8 and Saturday from 9 to 6.

Sundt (⊠ Torgallmenningen 14) is the closest thing Norway has to a traditional department store, with everything from fashion to interior furnishings. But you can get better value for your kroner if you shop around for souvenirs and sweaters. **Kløverhuset** (⊠ Strandkaien 10), between Strandgaten and the fish market, has 40 shops under one roof, including outlets for the ever-so-popular Dale knitwear, souvenirs, leathers, and fur. **Galleriet**, on Torgallmenningen, is the best of the downtown shopping malls. Here you will find **GlasMagasinet** and more exclusive small shops along with all the chains, including **H & M (Hennes & Mauritz)**. **Bergen Storsenter,** by the bus terminal near the train station, is a newer shopping center.

Specialty Stores

Antiques

There are many antiques shops on **Øvregaten,** especially around Fløibanen.

Books

Melvær (⊠ Galleriet and other locations downtown ☎ 55–96–28–10) has a wide selection of maps, postcards, books about Norway, dictionaries, travel guides, novels, children's books, and books in English.

Clothing
Oleana (✉ Strandkaien 2A, Bryggen ☎ 55–31–05–20) sells Norwegian wool sweaters, silk scarves from Tyrihans, and Norwegian silver.

Fishing Supplies
Campelen (✉ Strandkaien 2A and 18 ☎ 55–32–34–72 or 55–23–07–30 ⊕ www.campelen.no) has fishing equipment. Its staff also arranges fishing trips that leave from Bergen Harbor. **Finn de Lange** (✉ Marken 32 ☎ 55–32–34–44) sells fishing gear as well as outdoor clothing.

Food
Kjøttbasaren (✉ Vetrlidsalmenning 2 ☎ 55–55–22–23) is in a restored 1877 meat market. The Meat Bazaar sells everything from venison to sweets. **Kvamme kolonial og fetevarer** (✉ Strandkaien 18 ☎ 55–23–14–25) is a fine-foods store, selling rare Norwegian products like cured leg of indigenous wild mutton, as well as the usual dairy products and smoked and cured meats. Famous all over Norway, **Søstrene Hagelin** (✉ Olav Kyrres gt. 33 ☎ 55–32–69–49) is a Bergen institution, a delicatessen that sells traditional fish balls, fish pudding, and other seafood products made following its secret recipes.

Glass, Ceramics, Pewter
Hjertholm (✉ Olav Kyrres gt. 7 ☎ 55–31–70–27) is the ideal shop for gifts; most everything is of Scandinavian design. The pottery and glassware are of the highest quality—much of it made by local artisans. **Tilbords, Bergens Glasmagasin** (✉ Olav Kyrres gt. 9 ☎ 55–31–69–67) claims to have the town's largest selection of glass and china, in both Scandinavian and European designs.

Handicrafts
Amerie (✉ Finnegårdsgt. 6 ☎ 55–31–18–20) has traditional and modern knitwear, jewelry, souvenirs, leather goods, china, and crystal. **Berle Bryggen** (✉ Bryggen 5 ☎ 55–10–95–00) has the complete Dale of Norway collection in stock and other traditional knitwear and souvenir items—don't miss the troll cave. **Husfliden** (✉ Vågsalmenning 3 ☎ 55–54–47–70) caters to all your handicrafts needs, including a department for Norwegian national costumes. This is one of the best places to pick up handmade Norwegian goods, especially handwoven textiles and hand-carved wood items.

Interior Design
Norwegian designers recommend the **Black & White Studio** (✉ Kong Oscars gt. 4 ☎ 55–90–35–40) for Scandinavian furniture and lamps. **Inside Design** (✉ Veiten 1 ☎ 55–55–33–66) has a wide variety of Scandinavian furniture in stock.

Jewelry
Juhls' Silver Gallery (✉ Bryggen 39 ☎ 55–32–47–40) has its own exclusive jewelry called "Tundra," which is inspired by the Norwegian north. **Theodor Olsens** (✉ Torgallmenningen 15 ☎ 55–55–14–80) stocks silver jewelry of distinctive Norwegian and Scandinavian design.

Toys

Take a stroll through **Troll** (⌧ Bryggen ☎ 55–21–51–00) for adorable, mean-looking trolls of all shapes and sizes. The same complex that holds Troll also has an all-year **Julehuset** (⌧ Bryggen ☎ 55–21–51–00 ⊕ www.goshopNorway.com), or Christmas House, full of cheery Norwegian *Nisser* (gnomes).

BERGEN A TO Z

To research prices, get advice from other travelers, and book travel arrangements, visit www.fodors.com.

AIR TRAVEL TO & FROM BERGEN

CARRIERS SAS Braathens, KLM, Norwegian, Widerøe and Sterling are the major airlines flying into Bergen.

🔢 **KLM** ☎ 22–64–37–52 ⊕ www. klm.com. **Norwegian** ☎ 815–21–815 ⊕ www. norwegian.no. **SAS Braathens** ☎05400 ⊕www.sasbraathens.no. **Sterling** ☎815–58–810 ⊕ www.sterlingticket.com. **Widerøe** ☎ 810–01–200 ⊕ www.wideroe.no.

AIRPORT TRANSFERS Flesland is a 30-minute bus ride from the center of Bergen at off-peak hours. The Flybussen (Airport Bus) departs every 15 minutes (less frequently on weekends) from the SAS Royal Hotel, the Radisson SAS Hotel Norge, and the bus station.

Driving from Flesland to Bergen is simple, and the road is well marked. Bergen has an electronic toll ring surrounding it, so any vehicle entering the city weekdays between 6 AM and 10 PM has to pay NKr 15. There is no toll in the other direction.

A taxi stand is outside the Arrivals exit. The trip into the city costs about NKr 250.

🔢 **Taxis & Shuttles Bergen Taxi** ☎ 07000. **Norgestaxi** ☎ 08000.

BOAT & FERRY TRAVEL

Boats have always been Bergen's lifeline to the world.

Fjord Line serves North Norway, Stavanger and Haugesund, and Hardangerfjord and Sunnhordland. There's also service to Sognefjord, Nordfjord, and Sunnfjord.

The Smyril Line has a ferry that departs once a week in summer to the Shetland Islands, the Faroe Islands, and Iceland. Smyril also has service between Bergen and Scotland.

Hurtigruten (the Coastal Steamer) departs daily from Frielenes Quay, Dock H, for the 11-day round-trip to Kirkenes in the far north.

HSD express boats (to Hardangerfjord, Sunnhordland, Stavanger, and Haugesund) and Fylkesbaatane express boats (to Sognefjord, Nordfjord, and Sunnfjord) depart from Strandkai Terminalen.

International ferries depart from Skoltegrunnskaien.

🔢 **Boat & Ferry Information Fjord Line** ☎ 815-33-500 ⊕ www.fjordline.com. **Fjord1 Fylkesbaatane** ☎ 55-90-70-70 ⊕ www.fjord1.no. **HSD** ☎ 55-23-87-80 ⊕ www.

hsd.no. *Hurtigruten* ☎ 810-30-000 ⊕ www.hurtigruten.com. **Smyril Line** ☎ 55-59-65-20 ⊕ www.smyril-line.com. **Strandkai Terminalen** ☎ 55-90-70-70.

BUS TRAVEL TO & FROM BERGEN

The summer-only bus from Oslo to Bergen, Geiteryggekspressen (literally, "Goat-Back Express," referring to the tunnel through Geiteryggen Mountain, which looks like a goat's back, between Hol and Aurland) leaves the Nor-Way bus terminal at 8 AM and arrives in Bergen 12½ hours later. Buses also connect Bergen with Trondheim and Ålesund. Western Norway is served by several bus companies, which use the station at Strømgaten 8.

🛈 **Bus Information Central Bus Station** ⊠ Strømgt. 8 ☎ 177.

CAR TRAVEL

Bergen is 478 km (290 mi) from Oslo. Route 7 is good most of the way, at least until the ferry crossing at Hardangerfjord. The ferry, from Brimnes to Bruravik, runs from 5 AM to midnight and takes 10 minutes. From Granvin, 12 km (7 mi) farther north, to Bergen, Route 7 hugs the fjord part of the way, making for spectacular scenery, but the quality of the road deteriorates considerably. A quicker, better but less scenic drive is to follow Route 13 from Granvin to Voss, and take E16, an alternative route to Oslo, from Voss to Bergen. In winter, several mountain passes are prone to closing at short notice. The Public Roads Administration's **road information line** can give you the status of most roads.

Driving from Stavanger to Bergen involves two to four ferries and a long journey packed with stunning scenery. The Stavanger tourist information office can help plan the trip and reserve ferry space.

Downtown Bergen is enclosed by an inner ring road. The area within is divided into three zones, which are separated by ONE WAY and DO NOT ENTER signs. To get from one zone to another, return to the ring road and drive to an entry point for the desired zone. It's best to leave your car at a parking garage (the cheapest and most accessible is the ByGarasjen near the train station) and walk. You pay a NKr 15 toll every time you drive into the city—but driving out is free.

🛈 **Car Emergencies Norsk Automobil Forbund (NAF)** ☎ 810-00-505 operates 24 hours a day.

🛈 **Road Information Public Roads Administration** ☎ 175 ⊕ www.vegvesen.no.

🛈 **Car Rental Agencies Avis** ⊠ Lars Hilles gt. 20B ☎ 815-33-044. **Budget** ⊠ Lars Hilles gt. 120A ☎ 815-60-600. **Europcar** ☎ 55-36-70-00. **Hertz** ⊠ Nygårdsgt. 89 ☎ 55-96-40-70. **National** ⊠ Minde Allé 30 ☎ 55-59-97-15.

EMERGENCIES

The dental emergency center at Vestre Strømkai 19 is open weekdays from 6 PM to 8:30 PM and weekends from 3:30 PM to 8:30 PM. An emergency room at the outpatient center at the same location is open 24 hours. Apoteket Nordstjernen, Bergen Storsenter (55–21–83–84), is open Monday through Saturday from 8 AM to 11 PM, and Sunday from 10 AM to 11 PM.

🛈 **Doctors & Dentists Emergency Dental Care** ⊠ Vestre Strømkai 19 ☎ 55-56-87-17.

🛈 **Hospital Emergency Room** ⊠ Vestre Strømkai 19 ☎ 55-56-87-00.

🔢 **Late-Night Pharmacy Vitus Apoteket Nordstjernen** ✉ Bergen Storsenter, Strømgt. 8 ☎ 55-21-83-84.

INTERNET SERVICE
🔢 **Accezzo** ✉ Galleriet, Torgallm. 8 ☎ 55-31-11-60. **Cyberhouse** ✉ Hollendergt. 3 ☎ No phone.

LAUNDRY
🔢 **Jarlens Vaskoteque** ✉ Lille Øvregt. 17 ☎ 55-32-55-04.

MONEY MATTERS
Most Bergen banks in downtown are open Monday, Tuesday, Wednesday, and Friday from 8:15 to 3:30, and Thursday from 8:15 to 6. Some are open on Saturday from 10 to 1. From mid-May through September, most close a half hour earlier. The 24-hour **Bergen Card,** which costs NKr 165 (NKr 245 for 48 hours), gives admission to most museums, as well as Fantoft Stave Church, St. Mary's Church, Banco Rotto, and Bergen Trotting Park; unlimited bus travel in central Bergen; parking at public meters and outdoor automatic ticket machines; unlimited funicular rides; and discounts at Akvariet aquarium, Troldhaugen, Vannkanten, and selected restaurants, and on car rentals, concerts, theater, and selected souvenirs. The card is available at the tourist office and in most hotels. The Fjord Pass gives considerable discounts on hotel rooms, and can be purchased at the railway station.
🔢 **Fjord Pass** ☎ 55-55-76-60 ⊕ www.fjordpass.no.

CURRENCY EXCHANGE The Tourist Information Office in Bergen exchanges money outside banking hours.

TAXIS
Taxi stands are in strategic locations downtown. Taxis are dispatched by the Bergen Taxi central office and can be booked in advance. Bergen Taxi runs the largest and most reliable service.
🔢 **Taxi Companies Bergen Taxi** ☎ 07000 ⊕ www.bergentaxi.no. **Norgestaxi** ☎ 08000. **Taxi1** ☎ 55-50-00-37.

TRAIN TRAVEL
The Bergensbanen has several departures daily in both directions on the Oslo–Bergen route; it's widely acknowledged to be one of the most beautiful train rides in the world. Trains leave from Oslo S Station for the 7½- to 8½-hour journey.
🔢 **Train Information NSB** (Norwegian state railways) ☎ 55-96-69-00 or 815-00-888.

VISITOR INFORMATION
Bergen's Tourist Information Office is in the Fresco Hall in Vågsalmenning Square opposite the fish market. The office's staff sells the Bergen Card, brochures, and maps, arranges accommodations and sightseeing, and exchanges currency.
🔢 **Tourist Information Tourist Information Office** ✉ Vågsalmenningen 1 ☎ 55-55-20-00 ⊕ www.visitbergen.com.

The West Coast: Fjord Country

5

THE INTRICATE OUTLINE OF THE FJORDS makes Norway's coastline of 21,347 km (13,264 mi) longer than the distance between the north and south poles. Majestic and magical, the fjords can take any traveler's breath away in a moment. Among the world's most spectacular geological formations, a typical fjord consists of a long, narrow, and deep inlet of the sea, with steep mountainsides stretching into mountain massifs. Fjords were created by glacier erosion during the ice ages. In spectacular inlets like Sognefjord and Geirangerfjord, walls of water shoot up the mountainsides, jagged snowcapped peaks blot out the sky, and water tumbles down the mountains in an endless variety of colors. Lush green farmlands edge up the rounded mountainsides and the chiseled, cragged, steep peaks of the Jotunheimen mountains, Norway's tallest, seem to touch the blue skies.

The farther north you travel, the more rugged and wild the landscape. The still, peaceful Sognefjord is the longest inlet, snaking 190 km (110 mi) inland. At the top of Sogn og Fjordane county is a group of fjords referred to as Nordfjord, with the massive Jostedalsbreen, mainland Europe's largest glacier, to the south. In the county of Møre og Romsdal, you'll see mountains that would seem more natural on the moon—all gray rock—as well as cliffs hanging over the water below. Geirangerfjord is Norway's best-known fjord. In the south, the Hardangerfjord, Norway's fruit basket, is best seen in early summer when it's in full blossom.

Numbers in the margin correspond to points of interest on the West Coast map.

Exploring Fjord Country

Western Norway is one of the country's most-visited regions. Although the Hardanger, Sogn, and Geiranger fjords are best known, other fjords, such as Nordfjord, are worth exploring. The Atlantic Ocean is the region's wild, western border. Along the coastline, flat beaches, friendly coasts, steep mountains, and islands abound. Amid this dramatic setting some of Norway's most vibrant cities thrive: Bergen, the gateway to the fjords, is here, as is Ålesund, the art nouveau city.

Boat cruises are the classic way of exploring this region, but there's much to be gained by more up-close-and-personal experiences. You can walk or climb on one of Norway's 1,630 glaciers, remnants of the 30 ice ages that carved the fjords. Head to Eid and ride one of the ponylike Fjord horses, originally bred for farmwork. In Selje, visit the ruins of a 10th-century cloister. You can also fish for freshwater trout or go rafting in the fjord waters.

About the Hotels & Restaurants

WHAT IT COSTS In Norwegian Kroner				
	$$$$	$$$	$$	$	¢
RESTAURANTS	over 230	190–230	150–190	90–150	under 90
HOTELS	over 1,500	1,000–1,500	800–1,000	400–800	under 400

Restaurant prices are for a main course at dinner. Hotel prices are for two people in a standard double room in high season.

Timing

In spring and summer, from mid-May to August, the weather is usually best for traveling to the west coast of Norway. Throughout the year the region often has the country's highest rainfall. Summer is high tourist season, so the attractions and hotels are often crowded—try to book accommodations as early as possible. Early spring or late fall are better choices if you want to avoid the crowds, but can have unpredictable weather, and many attractions have shortened opening hours during these seasons.

NORDVESTLANDET

The coastal fjord country that extends from Kristiansund to Selje is called Nordvestlandet, or "Northwest Land," by Norwegians, even though it's located toward the middle of the western coastline. Small weather-beaten islands dot the coastline, and if you follow the fjords as they wend their way inland, you quickly come to steep, jagged, beautiful mountains. This region is traditionally where some of Norway's most successful fishing companies were based—halfway between the rich waters of the north and the important commercial center of Bergen. It's also where some of Norway's most spectacular scenery is most accessible. Ålesund is a good base and starting point from which Geirangerfjord and Nordfjord are both just a couple of hours' drive away.

Åndalsnes

❶ *495 km (307 mi) north of Bergen, 354 km (219 mi) south of Trondheim.*

Åndalsnes is an industrial alpine village of 3,000 people that is best known for three things: its position as the last stop on the railway, making it a gateway to fjord country; the Trollstigveien (Troll Path); and the Trollveggen (Troll Wall). The tourist office has special maps and guides outlining the popular trails and paths. The tourist office can also make arrangements for you to join a fishing trip to the fjords. Trips last four hours, and leave three times a day; the cost is NKr 250. Six or seven species of mostly white fish, such as cod, live in the waters.

★ From **Horgheimseidet,** which used to have a hotel for elegant tourists—often European royalty—you can view **Trollveggen** (Troll Wall), Europe's highest vertical rock face at 3,300 feet. The birthplace of mountain-climbing sports in Scandinavia, this rock face draws elite climbers from all over.

Fodor's Choice **Trollstigveien,** Norway's most popular tourist road, starts in Åndalsnes.
★ The road took 100 men 20 summers (1916–36) to build, in a constant struggle against the forces of rock and water. Often described as a masterpiece of construction, the road snakes its way through 11 hairpin bends up the mountain to the peaks named **Bispen** (the Bishop), **Kongen** (the King), and **Dronningen** (the Queen), which are 2,800 feet above sea level. The roads Trollstigveien and Ørneveien (at the Geiranger end) zigzag over the mountains separating two fjords. Roads are open only in summer. Halfway up, the road crosses a bridge over the waterfall **Stigfos-**

5

If you have 3 days

Western Norway's coastal cities are small enough to explore if you have only a few days. Spend your first night in ⊡ **Ålesund,** which is easily accessible from Oslo by airplane or bus. The city is set on three islands and between two fjords. You can visit the Atlantic Sea Park on your first morning, and take a bus up to the top of Aksla Mountain for a splendid view of the city and the surrounding area. On your second day, drive or take a catamaran up to ⊡ **Molde,** about 64 km (40 mi) north of Ålesund, where you can visit the Romsdal Open-Air Museum. If you have another day to spend in the area, take the ferry or bus still farther north, on your third morning, to ⊡ **Kristiansund.** Spend a leisurely day visiting the city's lively harbor, with its many seafood restaurants and shops selling local handicrafts. Return to Ålesund the next morning, and then back to Oslo.

If you have 1 week

The best way to see Fjord Country is to make an almost circular tour. From Oslo or Bergen, travel by plane to ⊡ **Ålesund,** ⊡ **Åndalsnes,** out to the coastal towns of ⊡ **Molde,** and ⊡ **Kristiansund,** then over Trollstigveien (the "Troll Path" tourist road) to ⊡ **Geiranger.** From there, take a ferry to Hellesylt, down to ⊡ **Stryn, Loen & Olden,** and through the subglacial tunnel to ⊡ **Fjærland,** and go by ferry to Balestrand, connecting with another ferry down to ⊡ **Flåm.** In Flåm the railroad connects with Myrdal on the Bergen line. Then you can either continue on to Bergen or return to Oslo.

If you have 10 days

You can complete a good tour around the fjords of Norway's west coast if you have a week to spend in the area. Aside from this itinerary, a good planning tool is the Web site **Fjord Norway** (⊕ www.fjordnorway.com). Western Norway offers so many opportunities for fjord-hopping. Choose three different fjords and discover each on its own. An excellent combination for scenery and activities is Hardanger, Sogn, and Nordfjord.

Here you will experience Norway's most spectacular natural settings—Sogn Fjord is widely considered Norway's most stunning fjord, and Jotunheimen has Norway's wildest, highest mountains. For the first day or two, take a leisurely pace and discover Sogn Fjord, by car, bus, or fjord boat. You can make stops at popular spots like Balestrand and Fjærland, the Book Town. During the rest of your stay, venture into Jotunheimen National Park and wander around its well-marked trails.

---

sen (Path Falls), which has a vertical fall of nearly 600 feet. Walk to the lookout point, Stigrøra, by taking the 15-minute return path to the plateau. Signs show the way.

One of Norway's most famous mountaineers, Arne Randers Heen (1905–91), and his wife, Bodil Roland, founded the **Norsk Tindemuseum** (Norwegian Mountain Museum), which is dedicated to mountain climbing. Displays of Heen's equipment and photography follow the development of the sport and Heen's many feats. The mountain nearest to

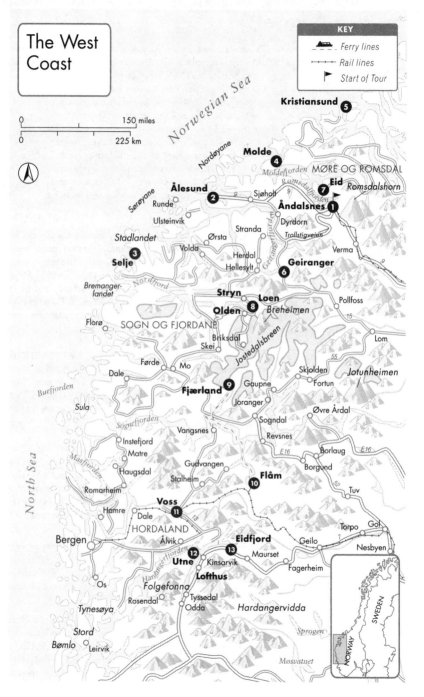

The West Coast

KEY

🚢 Ferry lines

┣━━━┫ Rail lines

🚩 Start of Tour

0 _____ 150 miles

0 _____ 225 km

Norwegian Sea

Kristiansund **5**

Molde **4**

Nordøyane

Moldefjorden

Romsdalsfjorden

MØRE OG ROMSDAL

Ålesund **2**

Sjøholt

Eid **7**

Romsdalshorn

Sørøyane

Runde

Åndalsnes **1**

Ulsteinvik

Dyrdorn

Stranda

Stadlandet

Ørsta

Herdal

Trollstigveien

Verma

Volda

Selje **3**

Hellesylt

Geiranger **6**

Bremanger-landet

Nordfjord

Stryn

Loen

Breheimen

Pollfoss

Olden **8**

Florø

SOGN OG FJORDANE

Briksdal

Jostedalsbreen

15

Skei

Lom

Førde

Mo

Skjolden

55

Jotunheimen

Dale

Fortun

Buefjorden

Fjærland **9**

Gaupne

Sula

Joranger

Øvre Årdal

Sognefjorden

Vangsnes

Sogndal

Instefjord

Matre

Revsnes

Masfjorden

E16

Borlaug

E16

Haugsdal

Gudvangen

Borgund

North Sea

Romarheim

Stalheim

Flåm **10**

52

Tuv

Hamre

Dale

Voss **11**

18

Torpo

Gol

HORDALAND

Ålvik

Geilo

7

Nesbyen

Bergen

Eidfjord **13**

Utne **12**

Kinsarvik

Maurset

Os

Lofthus

Fagerheim

Hardangerfjorden

Folgefonna

Tyssedal

Hardangervidda

Rosendal

Odda

Tynesøya

Sprogen

Stord

Bømlo Leirvik

Møsvatnet

NORWAY

SWEDEN

his heart was Romsdalshorn, 5,101 feet high. He climbed that mountain 233 times, the last time when he was 85. He was the first to climb several mountains, especially in northern Norway. ⊠ *2 km (1 mi) south of Åndalsnes center, along E139* ☎ *71–22–36–08* 🗌 *NKr 30* ☉ *Mid-June–mid-Aug., Tues.–Sun. 1–5.*

Where to Stay

$$ 🎬 **Grand Hotel Bellevue.** Travelers often begin their exploration of the region at this hotel. All the rooms are done in bright yellow, with old prints of the fjord on the walls. The hotel's restaurant, Trollstua, has delicious seafood dishes, based on fresh, local catches. ⊠ *Åndalsgt. 5, 6301* ☎ *71–22–75–00* 🗌 *71–22–60–38* ⊕ *www.grandhotel.no* 📞 *86 rooms* ⚲ *Restaurant, bar, meeting room* ⊟ *AE, DC, MC, V.*

Ålesund

❷ *240 km (150 mi) west of Åndalsnes.*

On three islands and between two bright-blue fjords is Ålesund, home to 38,000 inhabitants and one of Norway's largest harbors for exporting dried and fresh fish. About two-thirds of its 1,040 wooden houses were destroyed by a fire in 1904. In the rush to shelter the 10,000 homeless victims, Germany's Kaiser Wilhelm II, who often vacationed here, led a swift rebuilding that married German art nouveau (*Jugendstil*) with Viking flourishes. Winding streets are crammed with buildings topped with turrets, spires, gables, dragon heads, and curlicues. Today, it's considered one of the few art nouveau cities in the world. Inquire at the tourism office for one of the insightful walking tours.

FodorsChoice A little gem, the **Ålesunds Museum** highlights the city's past, including ★ the escape route that the Norwegian Resistance established in World War II—its goal was the Shetland Islands. Handicrafts on display are done in the folk-art style of the area. You can also see the art nouveau room and learn more about the town's unique architecture. ⊠ *Rasmus Rønnebergsgt. 16* ☎ *70–12–31–70* 🗌 *NKr 30* ☉ *July and Aug., Mon.–Sat. 11–4, Sun. noon–4; Sept., Oct., Jan., and Apr.–June, Mon.–Sat. 11–3, Sun. noon–3; Nov., Dec., Feb., and Mar., weekdays 11–3.*

You can drive or take a bus up nearby Aksla Mountain to a vantage point, **Kniven** (the knife), for a splendid view of the city—which absolutely glitters at night. ☎ *70–13–68–00 for bus information.*

☪ **Ålesund Akvarium, Atlanterhavsparken** (Atlantic Sea Park). Teeming with aquatic life, this is one of Scandinavia's largest aquariums. Right on the ocean, 3 km (2 mi) west of town, the park emphasizes aquatic animals of the North Atlantic, including anglers, octopus, and lobster. Nemo, the park's adorable seal mascot, waddles freely throughout the complex. See the daily diving show at which the fish are fed. The divers actually enter a feeding frenzy of huge, and sometimes aggressive, halibut and wolffish. After your visit, have a picnic, hike, or take a refreshing swim at the adjoining Tueneset Park. Bus 18, which leaves from St. Olavs Plass, makes the 15-minute journey to the park once every hour during the day, Monday through Saturday. ⊠ *Tueneset* ☎ *70–10–70–60* ⊕ *www.*

atlanterhavsparken.no ✉ *NKr 90* ☉ *June–Aug., Sun.–Fri. 10–7, Sat. 10–4; Sept.–May, daily 11–4.*

> off the
> beaten
> path

RUNDE – Norway's southernmost major bird rock—one of the largest in Europe—is the breeding ground for some 240 species, including puffins, gannets, and cormorants. The region's wildlife managers maintain many observation posts here. In summer, straying into the bird's nesting areas is strictly forbidden. A catamaran leaves from Skateflua quay in Ålesund for the 25-minute trip to Hareid, where it connects with a bus for the 50-km (31-mi) trip to Runde. A path leads from the bus stop to the nature reserve. Call the Runde tourist office for more information.

Where to Stay & Eat

$-$$ ✕ **Fjellstua.** This mountaintop restaurant has tremendous views over the surrounding peaks, islands, and fjords. The old-fashioned brick building has a stone and marine-blue interior, with picture windows. On the menu, try the Norwegian bacalao, salmon, and lamb. ✉ *Top of Aksla Mountain* ☎ *70–10–74–00* ▭ *AE, DC, MC, V* ☉ *Closed Jan.*

★ $$ ▥ **Quality Hotel Scandinavia.** Part of the Quality chain, this hotel has impressive towers and arches and dates back to 1905. The modern rooms are beautifully decorated, especially those done in an art nouveau style. ✉ *Løvenvoldgt. 8, 6002* ☎ *70–15–78–00* ☎ *70–15–78–05* ⊕ *www. choicehotels.no* ⇔ *65 rooms* ☧ *Restaurant, pizzeria, bar, meeting room* ▭ *AE, DC, MC, V.*

Selje

➌ *135 km (85 mi) southwest of Ålesund.*

From the town of the same name, the ruins of the **Selje Cloister,** on Selje Island, are a 15-minute boat ride away. Dedicated to St. Sunniva, western Norway's patron saint, the cloister was built by the Benedictine order in the 10th century. Legend has it that on this island St. Sunniva was martyred after fleeing her native Ireland when it was overrun by heathens. She died in St. Sunniva Cave, a large mountainside cavern. The island also has ruins of the first parish church, St. Sunniva Church; and St. Albanus Church, dedicated to the English saint. On the south side of the island several Viking graves and remains of an Iron Age longhouse have been found. In summer a boat departs three times daily from Selje Harbor for two-hour guided tours of the island. During the rest of the year, tours of the island are available by appointment only. The boat has limited capacity, so it's always a good idea to book the tour in advance. ☎ *57–85–66–06* ⊕ *www.seljekloster.no* ✉ *NKr 140* ☉ *Late June–Aug., daily 10–3.*

Where to Stay

$-$$ ▥ **Selje Hotel.** Set on an idyllic coastal beach, this is one of Norway's most popular spa hotels. The modern spa is based on thalassotherapy, focused on massage, and has skin, and body treatments. Rooms are comfortable, although some of the furnishings are a bit dated. Book well in advance for a room with an ocean view—they are slightly more expensive

TOURS AROUND THE WEST COAST

A 1½-HOUR GUIDED STROLL through Ålesund, concentrating mostly on the art nouveau buildings, departs from the tourist information center (Rådhuset) Saturday, Tuesday, and Thursday at 1 PM from mid-June to mid-August. **Aak Fjellsportsenter** (☎ 71–22–71–00 ⊕ www.aak.no) in Åndalsnes specializes in walking tours of the area.

From Easter through September, **Jostedalen Breførlag** (✉ 5828 Gjerde ☎ 57–68–31–11 ⊕ www.jostedalen-breforarlag.no) conducts glacier tours, from an easy 1½-hour family trip on the Nigard branch (equipment is provided) to advanced glacier courses with rock and ice climbing. Besides ice climbing, **Olden Aktiv Briksdalsbreen** (✉ Briksdalsbre ☎ 57–87–38–88 ⊕ www.oldenaktiv.no) offers a Blue Ice Excursion of 3–4 hours, and an easier glacier walk. **Briksdal Breføring** (Glacier Guiding Association; ✉ 6792 Briksdalsbre ☎ 57–87–68–00

⊕ www.briksdalsbre.no) leads glacier walks, ice climbing, and other excursions on and around Briksdalsbreen from May to September.

From June through August, the **MS Geirangerfjord** (✉ Geiranger ☎ 70–26–30–07 ⊕ www.geirangerfjord.no) offers 90-minute guided cruises on the Geirangerfjord. Tickets are sold at the dock in Geiranger.

"Norway in a Nutshell," Sognefjord & Flåmsbanen railway, and other package tours are available through **Fjord Tours AS** (☎ 55–55–20–00 ⊕ www.fjord-tours.com). **Kystopplevelser AS** (☎ 55–31–59–10) operates several Fjord Explorer tours.

---

than those without, but well worth it. ✉ *Seljesanden, 6740 Selje* ☎ *57–85–88–80* 🖨 *57–85–88–81* ⊕ *www.seljehotel.no* 🛏 *49 rooms* 🍽 *Restaurant, indoor pool, hot tub, spa, bar, lounge, dance club, meeting rooms* ▤ *AE, DC, MC, V.*

Molde

4 *69 km (43 mi) north of Ålesund on Rte. 668.*

Known as the "City of Roses," Molde has kept its 19th-century nickname even though the only reminder today is the city hall rooftop rose garden that blooms in July and August. Molde is best known for its annual jazz festival, which includes art exhibitions, street festivals, and jazz films as well as performances by international and Norwegian artists.

If you like to walk, take the footpath that leads uphill to the charming **Romsdalsmuseet** (Romsdal Open-Air Museum). On the way, stop at Reknes Park for a view of the 222 mountain peaks on the other side of the Romdalsfjord. Costumed tour guides lead you through the museum's 40 sod farmhouses and churches dating back to the 14th century. See the collection of children's toys. During the jazz festival, the museum is a venue for the larger concerts. Inquire about the museum's other attraction, Hjertøya, a fish museum 3 km (2 mi) from the city. ⊠ *Per Amdams veg 4* ☎ *71–20–24–60* ⊕ *www.romsdalsmuseet.no* 🎫 *NKr 45* ⊙ *July, weekdays 11–6, Sun., noon–6; late-June and early Aug., weekdays 11–3, Sun. noon–3.*

Where to Stay

★ **$$–$$$**   🏨 **Rica Seilet Hotel.** Shaped like its namesake, the 15-floor "Sail" is the western coast's high-design hotel, by Norwegian architect Kjell Mosberg. The hotel has its own seaside wharves and terraces. A sky bar, traditional Norwegian restaurant, and sauna and fitness club round out the features. Ask for a front room so you'll have a fantastic view of the mountains between Molde and Ålesund. ⊠ *Gideonvegen 2, 6412* ☎ *71–11–40–00* 🖨 *71–11–40–01* ⊕ *www.rica.no* 🛏 *169 rooms* ⚒ *Restaurant, gym, sauna, 2 bars, meeting rooms* ⊟ *AE, DC, MC, V.*

Kristiansund

❺   *68 km (42 mi) north of Molde on Rte. 64.*

By the 19th century, timber and *klippfisk* (fish salted and sun dried on slabs of rock) had made Kristiansund one of Norway's biggest export ports. Today Kristiansund is the offshore petroleum capital of central Norway: the Draugen and Åsgad oil fields are nearby. The city's lively harbor, Vågen, has the world's oldest collection of small boats. During World War II almost everything in town was destroyed except for Vågen, where some well-preserved buildings remain.

The **Nordmøre Museum** is actually comprised of several old warehouses and exhibits, some right on the harbor. **Milnbrygga**, the Klippfisk Museum, pays tribute to the process and the history of the town's klippfisk industry—fishy smells and all. Also worth a visit is **Woldbrygga** (☎ 71–58–70–00), a cooper's workshop in use from 1875 to 1965. The equipment is still in working order. At the **Handelshuset Patrick Volkmar** you can have a cup of coffee as well as browse through the wooden handicrafts, metal toys, and offbeat gifts available for sale. Every other Saturday in summer there's an open market held here. ⊠ *Harbor* ☎ *71–58–70–00* 🎫 *NKr 30* ⊙ *Mid-June–mid-Aug., Mon.–Sat. noon–5, Sun. 1–4.*

off the beaten path

GRIP – This group of 80 islands lies 15 km (9 mi) out in the open sea, a 2½-hour boat ride away. See the little stave church that was built around 1400 on the Grip's highest point, just 25 feet above sea level. Few people live year-round on the historic islands now, and most of those who come stay in summer houses. ☎ *71–58–54–54* ⊙ *Mid-May–Aug., daily boats at 10:30 AM, 12:30 PM, and 2 PM.*

Where to Stay & Eat

$–$$$ ✕ **Smia Fiskerestaurant.** The antiques, exposed brick, and fireplace inside this 1787 house are in keeping with the food served. The dishes are based on *nordmørske mattradisjoner,* local food traditions that emphasize fish. Try the famous fish soup; fish balls; or *bacalao*, the popular Mediterranean salt cod that's also a part of local culture. ⊠ *Fosnagt. 30B* ☎ *71–67–11–70* ⊟ *AE, DC, MC, V.*

$$–$$$ 🏨 **Rica Hotel Kristiansund.** This popular business hotel opened a conference center in 2001. The art-filled rooms are calm and fairly standard. The Sky Bar, on the 10th floor, has a wonderful view of the harbor. ⊠ *Storgt. 41, 6508* ☎ *71–57–12–00* 🖹 *71–57–12–01* ⊕ *www.rica.no* 🛏 *102 rooms* ⚒ *Restaurant, minibars, gym, sauna, 2 bars, nightclub, convention center, meeting rooms* 🖃 *AE, DC, MC, V.*

Geirangerfjord

★ ❻ *85 km (52½ mi) southwest of Åndalsnes, 413 km (256 mi) from Bergen.*

Geirangerfjord, which made the UNESCO World Heritage List in 2005, is Norway's most spectacular and perhaps best-known fjord. The 16-km-long (10-mi-long), 960-foot-deep Geirangerfjord's most stunning attractions are its roaring waterfalls—the Seven Sisters, the Bridal Veil, and the Suitor. Perched on mountain ledges along the fjord, deserted farms at Skageflå and Knivsflå are being restored and maintained by local enthusiasts.

The village of Geiranger, at the end of the fjord, is home to only 300 year-round residents, but in spring and summer its population swells to 5,000 due to visitors traveling from Hellesylt to the east. In winter, snow on the mountain roads means that the village is often isolated.

The most scenic route to Geiranger is the two-hour drive along Route 63 over Trollstigveien from Åndalsnes. Once you are here, the Ørneveien (Eagles' Road) road to Geiranger, which has 11 hairpin turns and was completed in 1952, leads directly to the fjord.

Where to Stay

$$$ 🏨 **Union Hotel.** One of the biggest hotels in the region, the Union is famous for its location near the fjords. Decked out in rosemaling-decorated wood furniture, the lobby has a country feel, although the rooms are modern. Ask for one of the rooms with good fjord views. ⊠ *Off Rte. 63, 6216 Geiranger* ☎ *70–26–30–00* 🖹 *70–26–31–61* ⊕ *www.union-hotel.no* 🛏 *168 rooms, 13 suites* ⚒ *Restaurant, miniature golf, 2 pools, sauna, Turkish bath, bar, nightclub, playground* 🖃 *AE, DC, MC, V* ☉ *Closed Jan. and Feb.*

Hiking

Trekking through fjord country can occupy a few hours or several days. Trails and paths are marked by signs or cairns with a red T on them. Area tourist offices and bookshops have maps, and of course you can always ask residents for directions or destinations.

Eid

❼ *Along E39, near Hornindalsvatnet Lake.*

A small agricultural community of about 6,000, Eid offers such fjord-village attractions as mountain walks, dairy and farm visits, and skiing. It is also near Hornindalsvatnet, northern Europe's deepest lake. The town is best known for the **fjordhest** (fjord horse), which even appears on the official town shield. This historic Norwegian horse was bred for farmwork and played a big role in helping western Norway develop. Every May the community hosts the **Hingsteutstillinga** (State Stallion Show), which attracts horse enthusiasts from Norway and beyond.

The **Norsk Fjordhestsenter** is the official center for the breeding and use of the fjord horse. Open year-round, the center's summer tourist program includes riding camps, riding and horse-drawn carriage trips, cabin rentals, and mountain horseback riding trips. ⊠ *Myroldhaug* ☎ *57–86–48–00* ⊕ *www.norsk-fjordhestsenter.no.*

Stryn, Loen & Olden

❽ *From Geiranger to Stryn, take the ferry across the Geiranger Fjord to Hellesylt, a 55-min ride. It's about 50 km (30 mi) from Hellesylt to Stryn on Rte. 60.*

Stryn, Loen, and Olden, at the eastern end of Nordfjord, were among the first tourist destinations in the region. English salmon fishermen became the first tourists in the 1860s. By the end of the 19th century more hotels had been built, and cruise ships added the area to their routes. Tourism grew into an important industry. The most famous attraction in Stryn is the Briksdal Glacier, which lies between cascading waterfalls and high mountaintops. It's one arm of the Jostedal Glacier.

Covering the mountains between the Sognefjord and Nordfjord, **Jostedalsbreen Glacier** is the largest in Europe. Nearly ¾ km (⅓ mi) wide in parts, it has grown in recent years due to increased snowfall. There are about a hundred known routes for crossing Jostedal Glacier: if you want to hike it, you must have a qualified guide. Contact the Jostedalsbreen Glacier National Park Center or another tourist office. Such hikes should only be attempted in summer; mountain boots and windproof clothing are both essential.

Many of Jostedalsbreen's arms are tourist attractions in their own right. The best-known arm, **Briksdal Glacier,** lies at the end of Oldedal Valley, about 20 km (12 mi) south of Olden. It can be visited by bicycle, by car, or on foot from April to October.

Right outside Stryn, **Jostedalsbreen Nasjonalparksenter** (Jostedalsbreen Glacier National Park Center; ☎ 57–87–72–00 ⊕ www.jostedalsbre. no) covers the glacier and the surrounding region in detail. Landscape models, mineral and photograph collections, films and dioramas describe the region's unique geography, flora, and fauna. There's also a garden of 325 types of wildflowers.

Where to Stay & Eat

$–$$$ ✕ **Kjenndalstova Kafé and Restaurant.** Perhaps western Norway's best-kept secret, this café and restaurant serves up delicious traditional dishes. Close to Kjendal's glacier, towering mountains, cascading waterfalls, and a pristine lake, the scenery from the restaurant alone is well worth a visit. Try the fried fresh trout, the fish stew, and the dessert cakes. ⊠ *Prestestegen 15, Loen* ☎ *94–53–83–85* ▭ *AE, DC, MC, V* ☉ *Closed Oct.–Apr.*

¢–$ ✕ **Briksdalsbre Fjellstove** (Briksdal Glacier Mountain Lodge). The cafeteria at this lodge has a no-frills menu of fresh, hearty country fare. The trout, the fillet of reindeer, and the deep-fried cod's jaws are all worth a try. Accommodation is also available, and as you'd expect from its location, a large gift shop is nearby. ⊠ *Briksdalsbre* ☎ *57–87–68–00* ▤ *AE, DC, MC, V.*

$$$ ✕▦ **Olden Fjordhotel.** Close to the fjord and cruise terminal, this modern hotel has simple, comfortable rooms with standard, chain-hotel-style furniture and balconies overlooking the fjord. Glossy hardwood floors in most common areas and some rooms lend the hotel a degree of sophistication. An extremely helpful and friendly staff will ensure a pleasant stay. Allergen-free rooms and larger rooms for families are also available. ⊠ *6788 Olden* ☎ *57–87–04–00* 🖶 *57–87–04–01* ⊕ *www. olden-hotel.no* ➷ *60 rooms* ⚐ *Restaurant, cable TV, bar, library, nightclub* ▤ *AE, DC, MC, V.*

$$–$$$ ✕▦ **Visnes Hotel.** Dating from 1850, this small hotel has lovely individually decorated rooms filled with pretty antiques. The walls are lined with old-fashioned wallpaper, and most rooms have balconies overlooking the fjord. The hotel is five minutes from Stryn's center. Specialities in the restaurant include smoked salmon and venison. The nearby **Villa Visnes,** a restored 1898 home with classic Norwegian carved-wood dragons arching out from the eaves, now houses an apartment and conference center. ⊠ *Prestestegen 1, 6781 Stryn* ☎ *57–87–10–87* 🖶 *57–87–20–75* ⊕ *www.visnes.no* ➷ *14 rooms, 1 suite* ⚐ *Restaurant, convention center* ▤ *AE, DC, MC, V.*

★ $$–$$$ ▦ **Alexandra.** This hotel was built in 1884, but has been entirely refurbished with stone and oak in a modern style. It remains one of the most luxurious hotels in the region. The rooms are spacious and decorated in cheerful, light colors. Many offer a spectacular view of either the fjord or the entrance to Lodalen valley. The hotel also has a popular spa, and the friendly staff, some clad in traditional folk costumes, can assist in arranging various outdoor activities in the Nordfjord area. ⊠ *6789 Loen* ☎ *57–87–50–00* 🖶 *57–87–50–51* ⊕ *www.alexandra.no* ➷ *191 rooms, 9 suites* ⚐ *2 restaurants, tennis court, indoor pool, gym, 3 bars, nightclub, convention center* ▤ *AE, DC, MC, V.*

Sports

In addition to taking a guided walk on the glaciers, you can follow the many other trails in this area. Ask at the Stryn tourist office for a walking map and hiking suggestions.

SKIING The **Stryn Sommerskisenter** (Summer Ski Center) has earned a reputation as northern Europe's best summer-skiing resort. Its seasons last from May through September, depending on the weather. The trails run over Tystig Glacier. The center has a ski school, a snowboard park, and a children's tow in June and July. Skis and snowboards are available for rent. ⊠ *Rte. 258 near Videseter* ☎ *57–87–54–74* ⊕ *www.stryn-sommerski.no* ☉ *May–Aug., daily 10–4.*

SOGNEFJORDEN

Sognefjorden, Europe's longest fjord, stretches 200 km (124 mi) into the country and meets Jotunheimen National Park, with some of the country's highest and wildest mountains, and Jostedalsbreen Glacier National Park with Europe's largest glacier at 500 square km (310 square mi). Along the fjord's wide banks are some of Norway's best fruit farms, with fertile soil and lush vegetation (the blossoms in May are spectacular). In summer this area draws mountain sports enthusiasts, who climb, hike, and glacier-walk. Ferries are the lifeline of the region.

Fjærland

9 *From Olden it's 62 km (37 mi) south to Skei, at the base of Lake Jølster, where Rte. 5 goes under the glacier for more than 6 km (4 mi) of the journey to Fjærland.*

Breheimsenteret is Jostedalsbreen National Park's visitor center, with fascinating exhibitions on, for instance, glacier-walking on Nigardsbreen, one of the arms of the glacier. Getting there is easiest by car: from Fjærland, take Route 5 to Sogndal, then Route 55 to Gaupne, and finally Route 604 to Jostedal. If you don't have a car, **Fjord 1** operates a special Glacier Bus that runs from Fjærland, Flåm and several other towns in Sogn to Jostedal. ✉ *Jostedal* ☎ *57–68–32–50* ⊕ *www.jostedal.com* ☽ *Late June–late Aug., daily 9–7; May–late June and late Aug.–Sept., daily 10–5.*

At **Norsk Bremuseum** (Norwegian Glacier Museum), one of Norway's most innovative museums, you can study glaciers up close by conducting experiments with thousand-year-old glacial ice. Exhibitions show glacier finds. Take time to watch Ivo Caprino's unforgettable panoramic film of Jostedal Glacier. The museum is in the center of town. ✉ *6848 Fjærland* ☎ *57–69–32–88* ⊕ *www.bre.museum.no* ✎ *NKr 80* ☽ *June–Aug., daily 9–7; Apr., May, Sept., andOct., daily 10–4.*

off the beaten path

ASTRUPTUNET – Halfway across the southern shore of Lake Jølster (about a 10-minute detour from the road to Fjærland) is Astruptunet, the farm of one of Norway's best-known artists, Nicolai Astrup (1880–1928). Astrup is known for his landscape paintings of western Norway. Set on a steep hill, this cluster of small sod houses was Astrup's home and studio until he died. His paintings and sketches are on view. The entertaining guides explain much about him and his family. The cozy café serves waffles and *rømmegrot* (sour-cream porridge). ✉ *Sandal i Jølster* ☎ *57–72–67–82 or 57–72–67–67* ⊕ *www.astruptunet.com* ✎ *NKr 50* ☽ *July, daily 10–6; late May–June and early Aug., daily 10–5; mid-Aug.–early Sept., weekends 11–5.*

Where to Stay & Eat

$$–$$$ ✕🏨 **Hotel Mundal.** Artists, mountaineers, and tourists first began coming to the Mundal in the late 1800s, via boat. This wooden yellow-and-white hotel has an eclectic style, mixing antiques from Norwegian *bonderomantikk* (country romantic) with contemporary furnishings. Descendants of the original owners run the hotel and have retained its country look. The small restaurant serves sumptuous traditional Norwegian fare. The café is popular in the evening among locals and guests. ✉ *Town Center, 6848* ☎ *57–69–31–01* 🖷 *57–69–31–79* ⊕ *www.fjordinfo.no/*

mundal 🛏 *35 rooms* 🛎 *Restaurant, café, billiards, bar, lounge, library, meeting rooms* ⊟ *DC, MC, V* ⊗ *Closed mid-Sept.–mid-May.*

★ **$$$–$$$$** 🏨 **Kvikne's Hotel.** This 1913 hotel is best known for its unforgettable views of Sognefjord. Kings, presidents, famous artists, and movie stars have stayed here. While the inside of the Swiss chalet–style hotel has been modernized, old-fashioned touches like a veranda and dragon-style furniture have been retained. The area is ideal if you're interested in swimming, hiking, rowing, and fishing. The rooms in the old, main building offer by far the best views. ⊠ *Balholm, 6898 Balestrand* ☎ *57–69–42–00* 🖷 *57–69–42–01* ⊕ *www.kviknes.no* 🛏 *210 rooms* 🛎 *2 restaurants, gym, fishing, bar* ⊟ *AE, DC, MC, V.*

★ **¢–$$$** 🏨 **Turtagrø Hotel.** Turtagrø is called the cradle of mountain sports in Norway. This legendary hotel originally opened in 1888, burned down in 2001, and was rebuilt in the shape of a mountain, with brick, stone, and wood. Its interior is a blend of Scandinavian and Zen design in white and heavy oak furniture. Historic photographs show early-20th-century mountain sports, and rooms have very comfortable beds for you to sink into after a hiking trip. The hotel hosts the Nordic Mountain Film and Mountain Book festivals. The original Swiss villa section of the hotel has simpler rooms with bunk beds. ⊠ *6877 Fortun* ☎ *57–68–08–00* 🖷 *57–68–08–01* ⊕ *www.turtagro.no* 🛏 *74 rooms* 🛎 *Restaurant, lounge, library* ⊟ *AE, DC, MC, V.*

Shopping

Even if you can't read Norwegian, you may still be fascinated by Hotel Mundal's **Den norske bokbyen** (⊠ Town Center ☎ 57–69–31–01 ⊕ www. bokbyen.no). From June through August, the "Norwegian Book Town" has 150,000 used books, cartoons, magazines, and records for sale in buildings around town.

Flåm

🔟 *66 km (41 mi) northeast of Voss.*

One of the most scenic train routes in Europe zooms from Myrdal, high into the mountains and down to the town of Flåm. After the day-trippers have departed, it's a wonderful place to extend your tour and spend the night.

Fodor'sChoice
★ The **Flåmsbana** (Flåm Railway) is only 20 km (12 mi) long, but it takes 40 to 55 minutes (one way) to travel the 2,850 feet up the steep mountain gorge. The line includes 20 tunnels. From Flåm it's also an easy drive back to Oslo on E16 along the Lærdal River, one of Norway's most famous salmon streams—it was King Harald's favorite. ⊠ *Flåm train station* ☎ *57–63–21–00* ⊕ *www.flaamsbana.no.*

If you have time to kill before the train departs, make sure you visit the **Flåmsbana Museet** (Flåm Railway Museum). Building the Flåm Railway was a remarkable feat in engineering, and this museum illustrates the challenges the builders faced in detail. You'll find it in the old station building, just 300 feet from the present one. ⊠ *Flåm train station* ☎ *57–63–23–10* 💰 *NKr 30, free with ticket to the railway* ⊗ *May–Sept., daily 9–5; Oct.–Apr., daily 12–3.*

Shopping

Saga Souvenirs (✉ Flåm train station ☎ 57–63–19–00 ⊕ www. sagasouvenir.no) is one of the largest gift shops in Norway. The selection of traditional items includes knitwear, wood and ceramic trolls, and jewelry.

Where to Stay

$ 🏨 **Fretheim Hotell.** One of western Norway's most beautiful hotels, the Fretheim has a classic, timeless look. Staying true to the Fretheim's 1866 roots, the rooms are furnished simply. Book in advance for a room with a fjord view. Rooms in the new northern wing of the hotel are slightly higher in standard than the older ones, although the price is exactly the same. If you can spring for a suite, you'll have more space and nicer furnishings. There's a spectacular view of the fjord from the restaurant and bar. ✉ *Flåm Harbor, 5742 Flåm* ☎ *57–63–63–00* 🖷 *57–63–64–00* ⊕ *www.fretheim-hotel.no* 🛏 *111 rooms, 7 suites* ♨ *Restaurant, bar, business services, convention center* ▭ *AE, MC, V.*

Voss

⑪ *120 km (75 mi) south of Fjærland, 80 km (50 mi) south of Vangsnes, 80 km (50 mi) north (1 hr by train) from Bergen.*

Set between the Hardanger and Sogne fjords, Voss is in a handy place to begin an exploration of Fjord Norway. Once considered a stopover, Voss now attracts visitors drawn by its concerts, festivals, farms, and other attractions. Norwegians know Voss best for its skiing and Vossajazz, its annual jazz festival. People come from all over Norway for the Sheep's Heads Festival, a celebration of the culinary delicacy of this area.

Galleri Voss shows the works of Norwegian artists in a bright, airy space. ✉*Stallgt. 6–8* ☎*56–51–90–18* ⊙ *Wed., Fri., and Sat. 10–4, Thurs. 10–6, Sun. noon–3.*

Dating from 1277, the enchanting **Voss Kyrkje–Vangskyrkja** (Voss Church) holds services every Sunday. Take a walk through to see the stained glass within. Concerts are occasionally held here. Guided tours are available. ✉ *Vangsgt. 3* ☎ *56–51–22–78* ⊕ *voss.kyrkjer.net* 🖼 *Nkr 15* ⊙ *June–Aug., weekdays 10–4, Sat. 10–1, Sun. 2–4.*

Perched on the hillside overlooking Voss, **Mølstertunet** is an open-air museum. The 16 farm buildings here were built between 1600 and 1870. Along with handcrafted tools and other items, they reveal much about area farmers' lives and struggles. ✉ *Mølstervn. 143* ☎ *56–51–15–11* 🖼*NKr 35* ⊙ *Mid-May–mid-Sept., daily 10–5; mid-Sept.–mid-May, weekdays 10–3, Sun. noon–3.*

Where to Stay & Eat

★ $$$ ✕🏨 **Fleischer's Hotel.** One of Norway's historic wooden hotels, the beautiful, gabled Fleischer looks like a manor from a fairy tale. Its carved wood dragons are fine examples of stave church-style architecture, developed in Hardanger in the late 19th century. First seen in churches, the style became fashionable and eventually was used all over southern Norway to decorate everything from silverware and furniture to prominent buildings like this luxurious hotel. Rooms in the old wing still have some flavor from that era. The restaurant Magdalene serves traditional renditions of sheep's head, grilled venison, fresh mountain trout, and salmon dishes. The hotel is steps away from the railway tracks leading to Bergen. ⊠ *Evangervegen 13, 5700* ☎ *56–52–05–05* 🖷 *56–52–05–01* ⊕ *www.fleischers.no* ↪ *90 rooms* ♨ *Restaurant, pool, sauna, bar, nightclub, laundry facilities, meeting rooms* ⊟ *AE, DC, MC, V.*

★ **$$$** ✕🖸 **Stalheim Hotel.** Originally a coach station on the old postal route from Oslo to Bergen, this hotel is perched high over the 13 hairpin turns of the dramatic Stalheimskleiva road, halfway between Voss and Flåm. The rooms are comfortable, and an interesting folk museum is on the premises, but it's the view that really makes the Stalheim Hotel worth a visit. To get there by car, follow Route E16. If you're on the Norway in a Nutshell tour, one of the regular stops is just outside the hotel. You can hop off the bus there and pick up the tour again the next day. ⊠ *5715 Stalheim, 32 km (22 mi) north of Voss* ☎ *56–52–01–22* 🖷 *56–52–00–56* ⊕ *www.stalheim.com* ↪ *124 rooms* ♨ *Restaurant, bar, lounge, shop; no room TVs* ⊟ *AE, DC, MC, V.*

Sports & the Outdoors

FISHING The tourist information office in Voss sells fishing licenses and has a Voss fishing guide to the nearly 500 lakes and rivers in the area where fishing is allowed. Fishing licenses (one-day for NKr 50) are also sold at campsites and the post office.

HIKING Walks and hikes are especially rewarding in this region, with spectacular mountain and water views everywhere. Be prepared for abrupt weather changes in spring and fall. Voss is a starting point for mountain hikes in Slølsheimen, Vikafjell, and the surrounding mountains. Contact the **Voss Tourist Board** (☎ 56–52–08–00 ⊕ www.voss-promotion.no) for tips. **Hangursheisen** (☎ 56–51–12–12 ⊕ www.voss-fjellheisar.no) is a cable car that runs from the center of Voss to Hanguren mountain. The summit is a good starting point for skiing in winter, and hiking and mountain biking in summer.

PARACHUTING At **Bømoen Airstrip** (☎ 56–51–10–00 ⊕ www.skydivevoss.no), 5 km (3 mi) from downtown, there's an active parachuting club. Jumps can be booked daily from mid-June to late August.

PARAGLIDING One of the best places to paraglide in Norway, Voss has easily accessed starting points and constant thermals. The tandem season runs roughly from June to August. To take a tandem paraglider flight (in which an instructor goes with you), you must weigh between 70 and 240 pounds. The flight lasts an hour and costs NKr 1,000. Contact the **Voss Adventure Senter** (☎ 90–68–62–19).

RIVER SPORTS Rivers around Voss are ideal for river paddling, kayaking, and other water sports. **Nordic Ventures** (☎ 56–51–00–17 ⊕ www.nordicventures.com) runs guided sea-kayak tours past the waterfalls and mountains of Sognefjord from April to October; prices start at NKr 400. **Voss Rafting Senter** (☎ 56–51–05–25) offers rafting, river-boarding, and canyoneering at prices beginning around NKr 500. **Voss Ski & Surf** (☎ 56–51–30–43) offers one- to three-day courses in river kayaking for both beginners and experienced kayakers. They also book tandem kayak trips with instructors.

SKIING   Voss and its varied mountain terrains are ideal for winter sports. An important alpine skiing center in Norway, **Voss Fjellheisar** (☎ 56–51–12–12 ⊕ www.voss-fjellheisar.no) has 40 km (25 mi) of alpine slopes, one cable car, eight ski lifts, eight illuminated and two marked cross-country trails, a snowboard park, and the Voss School of Skiing.

HARDANGERFJORD

Hardangerfjord, known as the "Garden of Fjord Norway," is a place that Norwegians identify with blossoms and fruit. The mild climate and clear, light summer nights are ideal for fruits like apples and cherries. Composer Edvard Grieg got inspiration for some of his masterpieces here. Springtime is the most enchanting season to visit the fjord: fruit trees bloom against the backdrop of the blue fjord, snow-topped mountains, and foaming waterfalls. Beginning in early May, the cherry and plum blossoms can be seen, and later in the month, pink apple blossoms. Cherries ripen in July and early August, followed by plums, pears, and apples from mid-August to late October. Farmers sell fresh fruit at farm shops and storehouses, and many open their farms for sightseeing and refreshments.

Utne, Lofthus & Folgefonna

❷ *65 km (41 mi) south of Voss via Rtes. 13 and 7, and the Utne ferry*

In the very heart of Hardanger lies **Utne**, a tiny village that rests at the tip of the peninsula dividing the inlet of Hardangerfjord from the arm that stretches south towards Odda, the Sørfjord. It's an excellent starting point for exploring the area. Going south on both sides of the fjord, you can explore farming communities with traditions dating back to the Middle Ages, or go hiking in the steep mountainsides and the plateaus or glaciers beyond. To get to Utne from Voss, take Route 13 to Granvin, and then Route 7 to Kvanndal where you catch the ferry to Utne. Buses are available from both Bergen (platform 4 on the main bus station) and Voss to Kvanndal several times daily.

Hardanger Folkemuseum is within walking distance of the ferry landing at Utne. Focusing primarily on local heritage, it's one of the largest and best museums of its kind in western Norway. The exhibit on folk costumes is particularly good, and several of the oldest surviving *Hardingfele* (Hardanger fiddles) are on display here. The ornate, usually eight-stringed fiddle was developed in Hardanger and produces a unique sound that inspired great Norwegian composers like Ole Bull and Edvard Grieg. On a little hill overlooking the main building you can sample fresh-baked local delicacies every Tuesday in July. ✉ *Utne* ☎ *53–67–00–40* 🖷 *53–67–00–41* ⊕ *www.hardanger.museum.no* 🎫 *NKr 50* ⏱ *May, daily 10–4; June–Aug., daily 10–5; Sept.–Apr., weekdays 10–3.*

Agatunet is an open-air museum composed of a cluster of old farmhouses—the oldest dating back to the 13th century. Serfdom was not practiced widely in western Norway. In some communities independent farmers clustered their houses together, and divided the pastures and orchards evenly. Although this led to some bizarre situations, like two farmers owning one half of the same apple tree, this semi-communal farming system was practiced until the 19th century. Very few clustered villages remain today, however, and even fewer are in as pristine condition as the Agatunet. The admission covers guided tours and indoor exhibits. Wandering the idyllic grounds is free. ⊠ *Aga, 17 km (11 mi) south of Utne* ☏ *53/66–22–14 or 53–67–00–40* 🖷 *53–66–30–90* 🖾 *NKr 50* 🕘 *Early May–mid Aug., daily 10–5.*

On the eastern side of the Sørfjord is the village of **Lofthus,** one of the oldest fruit-farming communities in the area, and a spectacular sight in early summer, when its 450,000 fruit trees are in bloom. The last week in July, **Morellfestivalen** (the Morello Festival) celebrates the sweet cherry of the same name, brought here in 1146 by traveling Yorkshire monks. The main event is the Norwegian Championship in Morello Pit Spitting. To get to Lofthus, take the ferry from Utne to Kinsarvik, and follow Route 13 towards Odda, approximately 10 km (6 mi).

The **Folgefonna** glacier straddles the mountain ridge between Rosendal and Sørfjorden. Folgefonna is actually a set of three glaciers, Nordfonna, Midtfonna, and Sørfonna. The latter is the third-largest glacier in Norway. Several hiking paths lead up to the glacier, but you should only attempt to hike on the glacier itself accompanied by a guide. Good footwear and wind- and waterproof clothing are essential, even on sunny days. The easiest way to get up close to the glacier is to drive up to the **Folgefonna Sommarskisenter** (Summer Ski Center) from Jondal, 31 km (19 mi) south of Utne. The drive from Jondal up to the glacier itself is spectacular though bumpy.

off the beaten path

BARONIET ROSENDAL – In 1658 a wealthy Norwegian heiress, Karen Mowat, wed a Danish nobleman, Ludvig Rosenkrantz, and the two were given a farm at Hattberg, tucked away in a valley west of Folgefonna, as their wedding present. They built a castle on the land, and a few years later the king of Denmark and Norway at the time, Christian V, gave the estate status as a barony, the only one of its kind in Norway. The estate was bequeathed to the University of Oslo in 1927, and today the barony is a combined museum, theater, and gallery with its own bed-and-breakfast on the premises. The castle is in fact a small-ish mansion, decorated in a variety of styles spanning the barony's history over 250 years and surrounded by a rose garden and stunning scenery. In summer there are concerts, lectures, and performances in the mansion or the courtyard. In mid-July the **Theatre Set-Up** company from London performs Shakespeare plays in English. ⊠ *Rosendal, From Utne, follow Rte. 550 south toward Odda, then take the Folgefonn tunnel west and follow Rte. 48 to Rosendal* ☏ *53–48–29–99* 🖷 *53–48–29–98* ⊕ *www.baroniet.no* 🖾 *NKr 75, concerts NKr 150–NKr 250* 🕘 *Late June–mid-Aug., weekdays 10–7, weekends 10–5; May–late June and mid -Aug.–early Sept., weekdays 11–3, weekends 11–5; mid-late Sept., Sun. noon–2.*

Where to Stay

$$$ 🏨 **Hotel Ullensvang.** This large hotel by the fjord in Lofthus offers comfortable, modern rooms. The restaurant, Zanoni, has a great view of both the fjord and the Folgefonna glacier. Rooms with a fjord and glacier view are about NKr 100 more expensive than those without the views. ✉ *5787 Lofthus* ☎ *53–67–00–00, 53–67–01–00 booking* 🖶 *53–67–00–01* ⊕ *www.hotel-ullensvang.no* 🛏 *157 rooms* ♦ *Restaurant, cable TV, pool, gym, massage, sauna, pub, meeting rooms* ▭ *AE, DC, MC, V.*

$$$
Fodor'sChoice
★
🏨 **Utne Hotel.** This small, cozy hotel was built in 1722, and has been operating continuously since, making it Norway's oldest. The white, wooden main building has a wood-paneled, hand-painted dining room decorated with copper pans, old china, and paintings. The hotel was completely renovated and partly modernized in 2003, but still retains much of its original charm. All 26 rooms have their own distinctive flavor, and several are furnished with unique antiques and artwork from the area. The rooms can be on the chilly side in winter, but the friendly staff makes up for that with exceptionally warm service, and extra wool blankets. Utne Hotel fills up fast in the high season, so book well in advance. ✉ *5797 Utne* ☎ *53–66–64–00* 🖶 *53–66–69–50* ⊕ *www.dehistoriske.no/utne_hotel* 🛏 *26 rooms* ♦ *Restaurant, pub, meeting rooms* ▭ *AE, DC, MC, V.*

Sports

HIKING Steep paths that offer quite literally breathtaking scenery lead from Lofthus up to the westernmost part of the Hardangervidda plateau. Contact the local tourist office for tips and hiking suggestions. **Folgefonni Breførarlag** (☎ 55–29–89–21 or 951–17–792 ⊕ www.folgefonni-breforarlag.no) offers guided tours on the Folgefonna glacier.

SKIING The **Folgefonn Sommarskisenter** (Summer Ski Center) is not as well known as the center in Stryn, but is quickly gaining popularity for its proximity to Bergen, the spectacular scenery, and good snow conditions. The season usually starts in May and lasts through August. The Folgefonn Ski Center also runs an annual **Snowboard Camp** that attracts teenagers and young adults. To get there, follow Route 550 from Utne to Jondal, where you turn left onto the paved but bumpy and narrow road to the ski center. From Bergen it takes around 2½ hours by car. Follow the E16 (toward Voss) out of town, and at Trengereid take Route 7 to Norheimsund. From there, follow signs toward Tørvikbygd and the ferry to Jondal. After the ferry crossing, follow signs to Folgefonna. There are also regular buses from Bergen to Jondal, and a bus runs from Jondal to the ski center daily at 10:35. ✉ *Jondal* ☎ *57–87–54–74* ⊕ *www.folgefonn.no* ⊙ *May–Aug., daily 9–4.*

Eidfjord

⓭ *40 km (25 mi) northeast of Lofthus via Rtes. 7 and 13*

Eidfjord sits at the very eastern edge of the Hardangerfjord and is a gateway to the fjords as well as the Hardangervidda plateau. Eidfjord's sister village, Øvre Eidfjord, some 6 km (4 mi) southeast, is home to the **Hardangervidda Natursenter** (⇨ Chapter 6). Since 2000 Eidfjord has been working hard to fulfill its ambitions to become a major tourist destination. The small village opened a cruise port in 2005.

For thousands of years, the 600-foot waterfall **Vøringfossen** has cut like a knife through the Hardangervidda plateau, every year adding another minute fraction of an inch to the ravinelike Måbødalen Valley. Vøring-fossen is part of a river system that is regulated for hydroelectric power, but during the tourist season the power company keeps the faucet open, and for a few weeks every summer this provides one of the most dramatic vistas in Norway. There are a number of ways to take in the Vøring-fossen waterfall and the valley beneath it. The most accessible cliff-top lookout points are off Route 7, just past the last of the many tunnels between Eidfjord and Fossli. Another good viewing point is from the rather unassuming Fossli Hotel, a large, wooden building most notable for its close proximity to the waterfall. For a dazzling and damp view from beneath, you can go for a half-hour hike from the road to the bottom of the waterfall. The trail is slippery even in dry weather, and hard to find, but well worth it. The **Eidfjord tourist office** (☎ 53–66–59–00) can help plan your trip.

Served by the Vøringfossen waterfall, **Sima Kraftverk,** or the Sima power station, is the largest in Norway open to the public. The huge production hall is an impressive sight, located 2,300 feet inside the mountain, 7 km (4 mi) from Eidfjord. Inside it, you can see the large, solid metal turbines that generate huge amounts of electricity daily. The magnetic field surrounding the turbines is so intense that people with surgically implanted metal can sometimes feel discomfort near them. Follow signs towards Simadalen from Eidfjord. Guided tours are available in summer and by special appointment the rest of the year. ✉ *Simadalen* ☎ *53–67–34–00* ✉ *Free* ☉ *Mid-May–mid-Aug., guided tours at 10, 2, and 4; mid-Aug.–mid-May, by appointment.*

Dotted around the steep hillsides that flank the fjords are a number of small, seemingly inaccessible farms perched atop sheer cliffs. The farmers who settled there would literally climb up and down the cliffs to their farms, using an ingenious system of ropes and pulleys to bring supplies up. One of these farms, **Kjeåsen,** suddenly became accessible when contractors working on the Sima power station built a narrow switchback road to the top of the cliff. Because the road snaking upward from the fjord is single-lane, the following restrictions apply: during the first 30 minutes of every hour, traffic is allowed up to the farm, and during the last 30 minutes of every hour, traffic is allowed back down. A more strenuous but rewarding way to visit Kjeåsen is via the footpath the inhabitants used to take. The path starts at the parking lot near the Sima power station—expect to walk about 1½ hours each way. You need to be in good physical condition and fairly comfortable with heights. Ropes and ladders provide hand grips on the more difficult portions of the trail. The view from the top of the cliff alone is worth the trek, but if you're lucky the proprietor at the farm will offer to give you a tour. ✉ *Simadalen.*

Where to Stay

$$–$$$ 🏨 **Quality Hotel Vøringfoss.** This hotel was constructed in 2001 and stands a stone's throw away from the Eidfjord cruise port. You have a choice between a spectacular view of the Hardangerfjord or a less-spectacular view of the valley. The rooms are comfortable and furnished in a modern style, and service is friendly and efficient. The hotel offers special weekend half-board deals, which includes admission to local attractions. ✉ *5786 Eidfjord* ☎ *53–67–41–00* 🖷 *53–67–41–11* ⊕ *www. choicehotels.no/hotels/no087* ↩ *81 rooms* ♿ *Restaurant, cable TV, pub, meeting rooms* 🖃 *AE, DC, MC, V.*

The West Coast A to Z

To research prices, get advice from other travelers, and book travel arrangements, visit www.fodors.com.

AIR TRAVEL

CARRIERS SAS Braathens has nonstop flights to Ålesund from Oslo, Bergen, Trondheim, and Stavanger.

🛂 **SAS Braathens** ☎ 05400.

AIRPORTS

Ålesund's Vigra Airport is 15 km (9 mi) from the center of town. It's a 25-minute ride from Vigra to town via Flybussen. Tickets cost NKr 50. Buses are scheduled according to flights—they leave the airport about 10 minutes after all arrivals and leave town about 60 or 70 minutes before each departure.

🛂 **Flybussen** ☎ 70-13-68-00 ⊕ www.flybussen.no. **Taxi** ☎ 70-10-30-00. **Vigra Airport information** ☎ 70-11-48-00.

BOAT & FERRY TRAVEL

Car ferries are a way of life in western Norway, but they are often crowded and don't run as frequently as they should in summer, which causes delays. Considerable hassle can be eliminated by reserving ahead, as cars with reservations board first. Call the tourist office of the area to which you're heading for ferry information. Hardanger Sunnhordalandske Dampskipselskap (HSD) operates fjord express boats from Bergen to Hardangerfjord and Sunnhordland, and most ferries south and east of Bergen, including all ferries across Hardangerfjord. Fjord1 express boats operate on routes between Bergen and Sognefjord, Nordfjord and Sunnfjord.

The *Hurtigruten* (coastal steamer) stops at Skansekaia in Ålesund, at noon. It then heads northward at 3. It returns at midnight and heads southward at 1 AM.

A catamaran runs between Ålesund and Molde at least twice daily. In addition to regular ferries to nearby islands, boats connect Ålesund with other points along the coast. Excursions by boat can be booked through the tourist office.

🛂 **Fjord1** ☎ 57-75-70-00 ⊕ www.fjord1.no. **Hardanger Sunnhordalandske Dampskipselskap (HSD)** ☎ 55-23-87-00 ⊕ www.hsd.no. **Hurtigruten** ☎ 810-30-000 ⊕ www.hurtigruten.com.

BUS TRAVEL

In western Norway the bus routes are fairly extensive: there are north–south express routes, like Bergen to Ålesund, and east–west routes like Trondheim to Oslo, all operated by Nor-Way. HSD Bus operates routes in the Bergen–Hardangerfjord region. Fjord1 operates routes in the Sognefjord and Northwest regions, and has glacier buses that run between Stryn and Briksdal.

🚌 **Fjord1** ☎ 57-75-70-50 ⊕ www.fjord1.no. **HSD Buss** ☎ 815-33-103 ⊕ www.hsd. no. **Nor-Way Bussekspress** ☎ 815-44-444 ⊕ www.nor-way.no.

CAR TRAVEL

Traveling around western Norway by car can be both spectacular and frustrating. A good rule of thumb is to stick as much as possible to the routes that qualify as Europavei, the ones that have a capital E in front of the route code, such as Route E16 that runs across the mountains from Oslo to Bergen, or Route E39 that runs along the coastline from Trondheim through Ålesund and Bergen to Stavanger. The road network in Norway is very much a work in progress, however, and not all E-coded routes are up to standard yet. Ask around at your hotel or the nearest tourist office if you're in doubt which route to take.

From Oslo to Ålesund it's 450 km (295 mi) on Route E6 to Dombås and then E136 through Åndalsnes to Ålesund.

From Ålesund to Bergen the E39 is a 381-km (237-mi) drive. It's reasonably well maintained and open most of the year. It involves several ferry crossings and a few tollbooths.

Voss is easily accessible from Bergen via the E16. The 102-km (63-mi) drive takes around 90 minutes. The E16 runs all the way to Oslo. In summer an alternate route is via Route 13 from Voss to Granvin, and from there pick up Route 7, across the Hardangervidda plateau to Oslo.

Route 7 from Oslo to Bergen passes through Eidfjord, and runs to Brimnes, where there's a ferry crossing to Bruravik. The road continues via Granvin to Bergen. At Brimnes Route 13 branches off to the south, past Kinsarvik, where there's a ferry to Utne, and then further south to Lofthus. Both Route 7 and Route 13 can be very narrow and windy, and especially tricky to negotiate in winter.

Route 5 connects E16 and E39. It branches off E16 at Lærdal, passes through Fjærland through a tunnel beneath the Jostedalsbreen glacier, and joins E39 at Skei, a couple of hours' drive from Stryn. Route 5 has a fairly high standard.

🚗 **Car-Rental Agencies Avis** ✉ Ålesund Vigra Airport ☎ 70-18-34-60. **Budget** ✉ Ålesund Vigra Airport ☎ 70-18-33-07. **Europcar** ✉ Ålesund Vigra Airport ☎ 70-18-23-00. **Hertz** ✉ Ålesund Vigra Airport ☎ 70-18-36-50.

EMERGENCY SERVICES 🚗 **Car Emergencies Norsk Automobil Forbund (NAF)** ☎ 810-00-505 operates 24 hours a day.

ROAD CONDITIONS The roads mentioned in this chapter cover some of the most breathtaking scenery in the world. They are narrow two-lane ventures much of the time; passing is difficult, and in summer, traffic can be heavy. Some roads, especially mountain passes, may close at short notice in winter and early spring.

🚗 **Road Information Statens vegvesen** (Public Roads Administration) ☎ 175 ⊕ www. vegvesen.no.

DISCOUNTS & DEALS

Fjord Pass, which costs NKr 100 for two adults and children under 15, is one of Norway's best hotel discount cards. The pass offers substantial discounts on accommodation at approximately 200 hotels, inns, cottages, and apartments all over Norway. Prices can be as low as NKr 225 per person per night.

🎫 **Fjord Pass** ☎ 55-55-76-60 ⊕ www.fjordpass.no.

EMERGENCIES

Apotek1 Nordstjernen, a pharmacy in Ålesund, is open weekdays and Saturday 9–5, and Sunday 6 PM–8 PM. Most other pharmacies follow normal business hours.

🎫 **Ålesund Hospital** ☎ 70-10-50-00. **Ålesund Emergency Room** ☎ 70-14-31-13. **Apotek1 Nordstjernen, Ålesund** ✉ Korsegt. 8, Ålesund ☎ 70-12-59-45. **Førde Central Hospital** ☎ 57-83-90-00. **Førde Pharmacy** ☎ 57-83-98-50. **Lærdal Hospital** ☎ 57-64-00-00. **Voss Hospital** ☎ 56-53-35-00. **Voss Pharmacy Apotek1** ✉ Vangsgt. 42, Voss ☎ 56-53-04-40.

TRAIN TRAVEL

The *Dovrebanen* and *Raumabanen* between Oslo S Station and Åndalsnes via Dombås run three times daily in each direction. It's a 6½-hour ride. At Åndalsnes, buses wait outside the station to pick up passengers heading to points not served by the train. The 124-km (76-mi) trip to Ålesund takes close to 2 hours.

Voss is accessible via the *Bergensbanen* between Oslo and Bergen. Express trains run several times daily from Oslo and Bergen, all stop at both Voss station and Myrdal. There are also local trains from Bergen that run to Voss. The steep *Flåmsbanen* railway, featured in the "Norway in a Nutshell" tour, runs from Myrdal to Flåm.

🎫 **Train Information Flåmsbana train station** ✉ Flåm train station ☎ 57-63-21-00 ⊕ www.flaamsbana.no. **NSB** (Norwegian state railways) ☎ 815-00-888 ⊕ www.nsb.no.

VISITOR INFORMATION

Fjord Norway in Bergen is a clearinghouse for information on western Norway. Its Web site and holiday guide are excellent resources for fjord travel planning.

🎫 **Tourist Information Ålesund** ✉ Keiser Wilhelms gt. 11 ☎ 70-15-76-00. **Åndalsnes & Romsdal** ✉ Jernbanegt. 1 ☎ 71-22-16-22. **Eidfjord** ☎ 53-66-59-00. **Fjord Norway** ☎ 815-33-500 ⊕ www.fjordnorway.no. **Flåm** ✉ Railroad station ☎ 57-63-21-06 ⊕ www.visitflam.com. **Geiranger** ✉ Dockside ☎ 70-26-30-99. **Hardangerfjord** ☎ 56-55-38-70 ⊕ www.hardangerfjord.com. **Lofthus** ☎ 53-66-11-90. **Molde** ✉ Torget 4 ☎ 71-20-10-00. **Sognefjorden** ☎ 57-67-23-00 ⊕ www.sfr.no. **Stryn & Nordfjord** ✉ Stryn ☎ 57-87-40-40 ⊕ www.nordfjord.no. **Utne** ☎ 53-66-18-22. **Voss** ☎ 56-52-08-00 ⊕ www.voss-promotion.no.

Central Norway

6

THE MOUNTAIN COUNTRY between Hallingdal Valley and Hardanger-fjord is a feast for the eyes—here are some of Europe's tallest peaks and the continent's largest plateau, the Hardangervidda, which also serves as Norway's largest national park. In summer the landscape provides a spectacular backdrop for hikers and for bikers on the Eventyrvegen (Adventure Road): crystal-clear streams ramble down mountainsides, sheep graze in pastures, and snowcapped summits glisten in the distance. In winter this area—especially Geilo, Gol, and Hemsedal—teems with skiers, both cross-country and downhill. Rest your muscles between activities at a mountain farm where you can milk goats, or explore medieval stave churches or relics-filled folk museums.

As you travel northward in Norway's inner midsection, the land turns to rolling hills and green forests. The town of Lillehammer draws skiers from around the world to its slopes and trails. As you travel north, you'll enter Gubrandsdalen (*dal* means valley), one of the longest and most beautiful valleys in the country. Gudbrandsdalen extends from Lake Mjøsa, north of Oslo, diagonally across the country to Åndalsnes. At the base of the lake is Eidsvoll, where Norway's constitution was signed on May 17, 1814.

Venture still farther north to reach the copper-mining town of Røros, which is listed on UNESCO's World Heritage List. This bucolic little town seems to have stood still for the past 100 years. The triangle between Oppland and Hedmark counties, heading south to Lillehammer, is called Troll Park.

Numbers in the margin correspond to points of interest on the Central Norway map.

Exploring Central Norway

Central Norway is dominated by Hardangervidda, one of Europe's largest mountain plateaus. Several mountain areas and valleys—Hallingdal, Numedal, and Hemsedal—surround the plateau. North of Oslo are the famous valleys of Gudbrandsdalen and Valdres, and the mountain regions of Rondane, Dovrefjell, and Jotunheimen. Route 7 crosses Hardangervidda, and the Oslo-to-Bergen railway serves many towns in the region, including some in remote mountain areas that are hard to reach, such as Finse. Traveling by car involves lots of mountain driving, and may be impeded by the occasional avalanche or bad winter weather.

About the Hotels & Restaurants

The hotels of the interior run the gamut from international chains and resort hotels in Lillehammer to traditional country hotels and mountain cabins with few frills in more remote areas. Restaurants tend to concentrate on the region's fish and game, served with typically Norwegian sauces made with berries and mushrooms. The mountain lamb here is delicious, as is the reindeer.

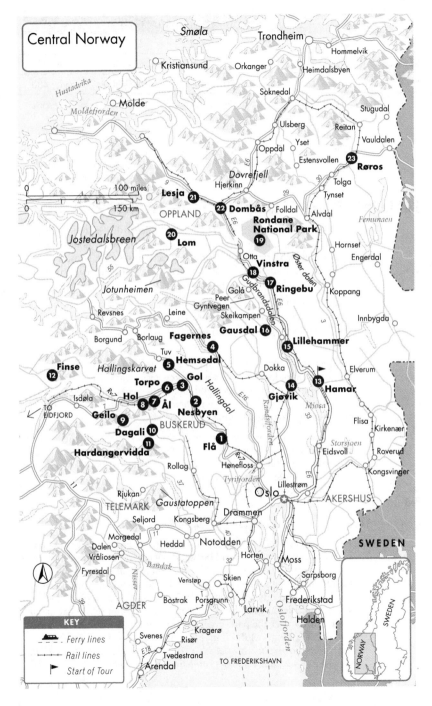

Central Norway

KEY

🚢 Ferry lines

┼─┼ Rail lines

▶ Start of Tour

WHAT IT COSTS In Norwegian Kroner					
	$$$$	**$$$**	**$$**	**$**	**¢**
RESTAURANTS	over 230	190–230	150–190	90–150	under 90
HOTELS	over 1,500	1,000–1,500	800–1,000	400–800	under 400

Restaurant prices are for a main course at dinner. Hotel prices are for two people in a standard double room in high season.

Timing

With a temperate inland climate, the hills and valleys of Norway's interior are excellent for travel year-round. You can ski in stable weather conditions here in winter, go on rambles and hike in the summer months.

HALLINGDAL VALLEY TO HARDANGERFJORD

This section begins with the Hallingdal Valley at Flå and moves on to the heart of the valley at Nesbyen, then follows the towns along the Hemsil River, which branches west in the direction of Geilo. Most towns in this region are small places which often have only one main road, the highway running through them.

Route 7 and the Bromma River wind through the historic Hallingdal Valley, which begins in the port town of Drammen. The valley is lined with small fishing villages and ski-resort towns and is known for its log buildings.

Between the Hallingdal and Valdres valleys lies Vassfaret, a forested, 30-km-long (18-mi-long) valley of large lakes, rivers and streams, steep rocky areas, mountain farms, and abandoned settlements. Many brown bears and *elg* (moose) make their homes here. The elg, often 6 feet in height, is known in Norway as "king of the forest."

After the Black Death swept through the valley in the Middle Ages, it remained uninhabited until the 1740s. Land was cleared and permanent settlements established, which lasted until 1921. In 1985 Vassfaret was declared a preserved nature area.

Flå

❶ *87 km (54 mi) northwest of Oslo, on Rte. 7.*

Five brown bears (Rugg, Berte, Birgjit, Frigg, and Frøya) make their home within the 10-acre **Vassfaret Bjørnepark** (Vassfaret Bear Park). There's also a separate moose enclosure for an adult male and female and a calf. Children can visit rabbits and chickens in the hen village and pet lambs, goats, pigs, and other farm animals. Take a seat in a Sámi tent, where you can picnic on grilled meats. The store Seterbua sells local handicrafts. In summer the park organizes special events, such as tours and horseback riding. ⊠ *Rt. 7 at Flå, 3539* ☎ *32–05–35–10* ⊕ *www. vassfaret-bjornepark.no* 🕮 *NKr 100* ☉ *Mid-Mar.–mid-June and Sept.–mid-Oct., daily noon–4; mid-June–Aug., daily 11–6.*

Nesbyen

❷ *33 km (20 mi) northwest of Flå.*

This small town in the heart of Hallingdal Valley has some memorable attractions. Overlooking the mountains and fjords between Hallingdal and Numedal is the family-owned **E.K.T. Langedrag Villmarkspark/Fjellgård og Leirskole** (Langedrag Wildlife Park and Mountain Farm). Caretakers of more than 250 animals representing 25 species, the Thorson family is well known in Scandinavia thanks to a nature series on television. Mountain farm life is emphasized—you can milk one of the farm's 40 goats or just learn about the making of goat cheese. Ponylike fjord horses are available for rides, riding lessons, and carriage trips. In the surrounding countryside, moose, deer, wild reindeer, wolves, cougars, polar foxes, and wild pigs can be spotted. Fishing and theme activities are organized year-round. ✉ *Tunhovd, 3540* ☎ *32–74–25–50* ⊕ *www.langedrag.no* 🎟 *NKr 110* ⊙ *Daily 10–6.*

One of the oldest open-air museums in Norway, **Hallingdal Folkemuseum** was founded in 1899 next to Rukkedøla River. Several 19th-century timber-and-sod houses have an extensive collection of regional clothes, weapons, and art. In summer, handicrafts are demonstrated every Wednesday. An emigrant center shows changing exhibitions and has a genealogical archive. Between 1839 and 1915, 750,000 Norwegians—many of them born in this valley—emigrated to America. The museum maintains close ties with the Hallingdal League of America. The paths and waterfalls nearby were traversed by famous Norwegian painter and farmer Hans Gude (1825–1903). ✉ *Møllevn. 18* ☎ *32–07–14–85* ⊕ *www.museumsnett.no/hallingdal* 🎟 *NKr 60* ⊙ *Early June and late Aug., daily 11–3; mid-June–mid-Aug., daily 10–5; Sept.–May, Sat. 11–3.*

Gol

❸ *21 km (13 mi) northwest of Nesbyen.*

This small town is popular with summer campers and winter skiers, who throng the mountains north and east. The original 12th-century **Gol stavkyrkje** (Gol Stave Church) still stands, but nowadays in Oslo's Norsk Folkemuseum. This replica has an exhibition highlighting the principles of stave church architecture. A service is held every Wednesday at 9 PM in summer. ✉ *Storeøyni* ☎ *32–07–54–11* 🎟 *NKr 70* ⊙ *Daily 9–4.*

You can try your hand at blowing crystal glass every weekday from 10:30 to 3 for NKr 135 at **Halling Glass.** The store also sells the beautiful objects made here by its artisans. ✉ *Sentrumsvn. 18* ☎ *32–07–53–11* ⊕ *www.hallingglass.no* ⊙ *Demonstrations weekdays 9–3; store weekdays 9–4, Sat. 10–2.*

off the beaten path

EVENTYRGÅRDEN HUSO – This is a popular *støl*, or summer mountain farm. To get here, take Route 52 north from Gol to Robru; then take Øvrevegen to Huso. A country courtyard has 12 log houses from the 17th century and several exhibition halls and presentations on the area's culture and business life. Don't miss the re-created house of a Viking chief and the Iron Age assembly hall. Sheep, goats, rabbits, chickens, and ducks inhabit the pasture. You can venture into the valley on a horseback tour, and go canoeing or fishing in the river. ☒ *Huso* ☎ *32–07–54–11* ⊕ *www.pers.no* ☜ *NKr 70* ☽ *Mid-June–mid-Aug., daily 11–6; Sept., weekends 11–6.*

Sports
Fjell og Fjord Ferie A/S (☒ Gamlevegen 6 ☎ 32–02–99–26 ⊕ www. eventyrveien.no) offers fishing, hiking, horseback riding, and bike tours. They also rent bikes.

Fagernes

❹ *25 km (15 mi) south of Lom, via E16.*

Surrounded by fjords and mountains, Fagernes, on Strandefjorden, is the capital of Valdres. Many travelers hiking in Jotunheimen National Park come to Fagernes for its shopping, cafés, pubs, and restaurants. Fagernes also has an airport, opened in 1987, while the Valdres Alpine Ski Center is located nearby.

On Storøya, a beautiful peninsula on the Strandefjord, the open-air **Valdres Folkemuseum** covers 30 acres with 95 houses and buildings dating from 1200 to 1950. Some 20,000 artifacts, a natural park, changing exhibitions, a playground, and an arts and crafts shop round out the attractions. See the permanent exhibition on *bunader,* Norwegian traditional costumes. If you have Norwegian ancestry, the museum may allow you to research in its archives. ☒ *Tyinvegen 27* ☎ *61–35–99–00* ⊕ *www. valdres.museum.no* ☜ *NKr 60* ☽ *June 10–30 and Aug. 5–18, daily 10–4; July–Aug. 4, daily 10–5; Aug. 19–June 9, weekdays 9–3.*

Where to Stay & Eat
★ **$$$** ✕⊞ **Quality Hotel and Resort Fagernes.** This cosmopolitan hotel's stained glass and butterscotch-leather couches welcome international travelers to the Norwegian mountains. Classic and elegant, the light, airy, yellow rooms are spacious and well equipped. Take a seat at either the Klokkerstua Spiseri or Stor Stua restaurant and try any of their international dishes, like oven-baked *ørret* (trout) or Thai noodles. The hotel is located 10 minutes from Valdres Alpine Ski Center and bus connections. ☒ *Jerbaneveien, 2900* ☎ *61–36–11–00* 🖷 *61–36–14–20* ⊕ *www. fagernes-hotel.no* ⇌ *139 rooms, 12 suites* ♢ *2 restaurants, bar, dance club, meeting rooms* ▤ *AE, DC, MC, V.*

★ **$–$$$** ✕⊞ **Nythun Høyfjellstue.** Husband and wife Jørn and Marit run this family hotel in the mountains, 14 km (9 mi) from Fagernes. In peaceful, forested surroundings, you can stay in the country-style hotel rooms or one of the self-service mountain cabins. Jørn's French-inspired dishes have earned the restaurant a No. 3 ranking in a guide to Norway's best restaurants. Sample the reindeer fillet with mushroom, or treat yourself to a seven-course dinner. ☒ *2900 Fagernes, Take the Leira turn off from Rte. E16 and follow the signs towards Etnedal and Nythun Høyfjell-*

stue ☎ *61–35–79–30* 🖷 *61–35–79–40* ⊕ *www.nythun.com* 🛏 *60 beds* ♿ *Restaurant, bar* ▭ *AE, DC, MC, V.*

Hemsedal

❺ *35 km (21½ mi) from Gol.*

The mountains in the area are nicknamed the Scandinavian Alps, and Hemsedal has some of Norway's most stunning high-mountain scenery: you can see mountains and glaciers, numerous lakes, four rivers, as well as fjords and cascading waterfalls. It's the country's most popular skiing town, where Norway's top skiers and snowboarders live and train. The Maifestivalen (May Festival), which takes place on the first weekend of May, marks the end of the ski season; it's a well-attended event. In the summer months you can hike, play golf, and go fishing.

Where to Stay & Eat

★ $ ✕ **Hemsedal Café.** This hip café is a place to see and be seen, or you can just come for the simple dishes like burgers, Thai chicken, or the filling skier's breakfast. Internet usage at the several computers is free. ⊠ *Brustabygge* ☎ *32–05–54–10* ▭ *MC, V.*

★ $$$–$$$$ ✕▦ **Harahorn.** On a mountaintop 3,280 feet above Hemsedal's center, Harahorn is comprised of 11 mountain cabins clustered around the main house. Decorated in deep blues and earthy shades, the luxurious *bonderomantikk*, or "country romantic," pine cabins are filled with antiques and art. You can visit the hotel just to dine at the main house's restaurant, or opt to stay here. There are many outdoor sports and activities available, such as skiing, dogsledding, mountain climbing, and moose safaris. ⊠ *3580 Hemsedal* ☎ *32–06–23–80* 🖷 *32–06–23–81* ⊕ *www. harahorn.no* 🛏 *22 rooms, 11 cabins* ♿ *Restaurant, café, lounge, meeting room* ▭ *AE, DC, MC, V.*

$$$–$$$$ ✕▦ **Skarsnuten Hotell.** Perched like an eagle's nest, this mountainside
Fodor's Choice hotel overlooks the village of Skarsnuten Landsby. In 2003 the inn was
★ sold to the Good Life hotel chain. The minimalist interior is dominated by *skifer* (Norwegian stone), gray brushed wool, and wood. Framed mountain-sports photographs line the white walls. Rooms have spectacular views and names like Little Matterhorn. Kids are thoroughly entertained at their own disco and an Internet café. Take the hotel's ski lift down to its resort, Hemsedal Skisenteret. The hotel's restaurant is well regarded for its French-inspired menu based on seasonal Norwegian ingredients. ⊠ *Skarsnuten Landsby, 3560* ☎ *32–06–17–10* 🖷 *32–06–17–11* ⊕ *www. skarsnuten.no* 🛏 *35 rooms, 2 suites* ♿ *Restaurant, bar, lounge, laundry facilities, business services, meeting rooms, no-smoking rooms* ▭ *AE, DC, MC, V.*

Sports & the Outdoors

GOLF **Golf Hemsedal** (☎ *32–06–23–77* ⊕ www.golfhemsedal.com) is really a country club of sorts with a 9-hole driving range and putting green. You can also play tennis and go horseback riding here.

HIKING & Experienced guides at **HeimVegen** (⊠ Aalstveit ☎ *32–06–06–20* or
CLIMBING *90–65–64–07* ⊕ www.heimvegen.no) offer mountain touring courses year-round.

HORSEBACK RIDING	**Elvestad Fjellridning** (☎ 90–88–45–45 ⊕ www.hemsedal.com) offers half-day riding trips in the forest and mountains for all levels of riders. From late June through August every Tuesday, rides start at 9:30, last 3 to 3½ hours, and cost NKr 380.
PARAGLIDING	Paraglide in tandem with an experienced instructor. **Oslo Paragliding Klubb** (☎ 22–15–08–18 ⊕ www.opk.no) has its main base in Hemsedal.
SKIING	**Hemsedal Skisenteret** (☎ 32–05–53–90 ⊕ www.hemsedal.no) has 34 km (21 mi) of alpine slopes, 175 km (108 mi) of cross-country trails, and 17 ski lifts. The Ski School has superbly run courses for novices from children to adults.

Torpo

❻ *52 km (32 mi) from Hemsedal.*

Although there are seven stave churches in the valley, this tiny village's medieval church is the oldest and best preserved. **Torpo stave church** is the only 12th-century church left in Hallingdal. Its decorative ceiling, which depicts the legend of Saint Margaret, dates back 700 years. ☎ *32–08–31–37* 🖃 *NKr 30* ⊘ *June–Aug., daily 8:30–6.*

Ål

❼ *5 km (3 mi) west of Torpo.*

The small mountain town of Ål is best known for the **Ål Stavkyrkjemuseum** (Ål Stave Church Museum). Richly decorated, the museum highlights and explains stave church history and architecture. See the museum's copy of the famous west portal, which no longer exists. ✉ *Prestegårdslåven* ☎ *32–08–50–04* ⊘ *Year-round by appointment.*

Some Norwegian farmers send their cattle and sheep to graze at the traditional **summer farms.** Many of these farms welcome visitors between early July and mid-August to sample their dairy products such as cheese, sour cream, and *rømmegrøt* (sour-cream rice pudding). Local summer farms, open to the public, include **Fagerdalen** (✉ Mountain road between Ål on Rte. 7 and Hovet on Rte. 50 ☎ 32–08–98–06 or 91–10–97–79 ⊕ www.fagerdalen.no) and **Tormodset** (✉ off Rte. 7, about a mile past Ål ☎ 32–08–42–30 or 91–58–86–02). You should telephone in advance for an appointment to visit.

Kite-Skiing

Kite-skiing or ski-sailing (skiing with a large kite or parachute to harness the wind), is one of the newest innovations in skiing and extreme sports. Norwegian kite-skiing enthusiasts have established a base at **Bergsjøstølen Mountain Lodge** (✉ 3570 Ål ☎ 32–08–46–18 🖷 32–08–46–72 ⊕ www.bergsjostolen.no). To get there from Ål, take Route 7 west for about 3 km (1.8 miles) and turn off at Vats. Then follow the signs to Bergsjøstølen Fjellstue. At **Rødungst øl Høyfjellshotell** (✉ 3570 Ål ☎ 32–08–46–22 ⊕ www.rodungstol.no) you can take a course on ski-sailing and rent equipment. To get there from Route 7, take the turn off for Vats (3 km/1.8 miles east of Ål) and follow the signs.

Hol

8 *5 km (3 mi) west of Ål.*

Hol is best known in the valley for its **Holsdagen** (☎ 32–09–59–00) festival, held annually on the last Saturday in July. Back in 1957, the festival began as a way of keeping local traditions and customs alive. During the festival, a traditional wedding ceremony is performed in the 11th-century Hol Gamle Kyrkje. Then the bridal pair rides in a lively procession to Hol Bygdemuseum, where folk music, dance, performances, and traditional Hallingdal dishes await them.

You can see reconstructed buildings from the 1700s at the **Hol Bygdemuseum** (Village Museum). Costumed museum staff reenact early Norwegian farm life in its 17 sod houses, which include a tenant farmer's house, a barn, stables, and a smithy. Rosemaling, the late-18th-century folk art of decorative painting on furniture, and local costumes from the region are on view. ⊠ *Hagafoss* ☎ *32–08–81–40* ⊠ *NKr 30* ☉ *Late June–mid-Aug., Wed.–Sun. noon–4.*

Geilo

9 *35 km (21 mi) west of Torpo.*

More than a million visitors a year head to the slopes and cross-country trails of this *alpeby* (Alpine town) halfway between Oslo and Bergen. Many people ski directly from their hotel or cabin doors. Plan ahead if you want to visit at Easter, since Norwegians flock here for a final ski weekend. The summer season, beginning in June, has such activities as guided mountain walks, horseback riding, and fishing.

In the center of Geilo, the 17th-century farm of **Geilojordet** is a part of Hol Bygdemuseum. The cattle house, storage house, farmer's living quarters, and other buildings were brought here from the surrounding area and then restored. Cultural activities and events, such as rosemaling, wood carving, and folk-music performances, take place here. A café serves coffee, waffles, *rømmebrød* (sour-cream loaf), *lefse* (potato pancakes filled with sugar or cream), and other traditional sweets. ⊠ *Hagafoss* ☎ *32–07–14–85* ⊠ *Free* ☉ *Late June–mid-Aug., daily 11–5.*

Where to Stay & Eat

Norway's most popular resort town has many hotels, mountain lodges, traditional cabins, apartments, and camping sites. Rooms are booked early for high season: you can contact **Geilo Booking** (☎ 32–09–59–40 ⊕ www.geilo.no) for advice on accommodations.

$$$–$$$$ ✕ **Halling-stuene.** The region's best-known chef, Frode Aga, has become a celebrity through his cookbooks and television appearances. His downtown restaurant has an elegant *bonderomantikk* style. His modern Norwegian cuisine features fish and game with an international influence. Try classic Aga dishes like reindeer fillet with fresh vegetables and mushrooms, or the *bacalao tomat* (dried salt cod with tomato, onion, and paprika). ⊠ *Geilovn. 56* ☎ *32–09–12–50* ⊟ *AE, DC, MC, V* ☉ *Closed May.*

★ **$$$–$$$$** ✕🖼 **Dr. Holms Hotel.** Built in 1909 as a sanitorium for asthma sufferers, the building is now a well-established resort hotel. Resembling a luxury mountain cabin, the hotel has elegantly decorated rooms and panoramic views of the surrounding mountains. Its Galleriet restaurant serves Continental-Norwegian dishes. Have drinks by the fire in the classy Ski bar, one of Norway's most popular après-ski bars. You can read in the peaceful library, which has 2,000 volumes, or watch stand-up comedy at the Recepten pub. Be pampered in the Japanese-style Dr. Holms Spa Klinikk. Make reservations well in advance. ✉ *Timrehaugvn. 2, 3580* ☎ *32–09–57–00* 🖶 *32–09–16–20* ⊕ *www.drholms.com* ⇥ *124 rooms, 3 suites* ⟁ *Restaurant, cable TV, 2 indoor pools, gym, spa, 3 bars, lounge, pub, library, business services, meeting rooms, no-smoking rooms* ▭ *AE, DC, MC, V.*

Sports & the Outdoors

BIKING Ask for bike maps at the Geilo tourist information office. Besides Rallarvegen, the Adventure Road, and Numedalsruta, there's excellent cycling in the countryside around Geilo on mountain roads. Bike rentals are available through **Intersport Geilo** (☎ 32–09–55–80 ⊕ www.intersport-geilo.no) for NKr 180 per bike per day.

FISHING Geilo's 90 mountain lakes and river stretches are open to the public from June to September and most are well stocked with trout. Inquire about recreation maps for Geilo and Hallingskarvet at the tourist office. Fishing licenses, which are mandatory, cost NKr 30 for a day and can be purchased at any post office or tourist office. Fishing permits, needed for fishing in certain areas, are available at local shops and the Geilo tourist office for NKr 40 per day. Fishing tackle and boat rentals can be organized through **Geilo Camping** (☎ 32–09–07–33) for NKr 120 a day, while rowboats cost NKr 90 for three hours.

HORSEBACK RIDING Many Geilo businesses offer horseback riding and riding lessons and lead mountain trips, which can last from several hours to a week. **Eivindsplass Fjellgard** (☎ 32–09–48–45) offers trips only in July. **Geilo Hestesenter** (☎ 32–09–01–81) operates June through October. **Hakkesetstølen** (☎32–09–09–20) operates mid-June through late September. **Hallingskarvet Høgfjellshotell** (☎ 32–08–85–25) operates June through August. **Prestholtseter** (☎ 92–03–75–14) operates in July and August. **Ustaoset Hesteridning** (☎ 91–64–82–88) operates July through mid-August.

MOUNTAIN HIKES & WALKS For independent walking, **Den Norske Turistforening (DNT)** (Norwegian Mountain Touring Association) has marked trails across the Hardangervidda plain and in the countryside around Hallingskarvet. Inquire at the tourist office about DNT routes and the use of their cabins.

Experienced guide Turid Linseth of **Hardangervidda Mountain Guiding** (☎ 97–54–18–60 ⊕ www.fjellguiding.no) has designed guided mountain walks and ski trips for all levels and interests.

SKIING Geilo has 38 pistes, three snowboard parks, 20 lifts, and plenty of slopes for children on both sides of the valley. You can purchase a downhill ski pass that allows you to use all the lifts. A free shuttle bus goes between the five ski centers. For cross-country skiers, there are 220

SKI TOWNS OF CENTRAL NORWAY

NORWAY IS A LAND OF
MOUNTAINS, *and as such has
long been traversed on skis.
There are innumerable ski
resorts across the country, and the
landscape is crisscrossed with cross-country
trails. Norwegians are justifiably proud of
their great skiing tradition, and some might
even go so far as to say that they are
obsessed with the sport. If you like to ski,
Norway is your country, and within it
central Norway contains some of the best
ski resorts and trails for both downhill,
cross-country, and snowboarding. This is
where members of the Norwegian royal
family learned to ski, and where famous
arctic explorers trained and tested their
equipment. You can customize your skiing
holiday to suit your taste, perhaps
combining cross-country and downhill.*

*First, you can head to **Gudbrandsdalen**
or **Rondane** and spend several days
traversing the pristine cross-country trails.*

*Then travel south to the **Lillehammer** area
and its popular ski resorts for some
wonderful downhill skiing. **Geilo,** with its
alpine slopes and cross-country trails,
draws over a million visitors a year for
the ski season, which begins in late
November and ends at Easter or late
April. Rentals are readily available in most
towns, and with such convenient access
there's nothing stopping you from
exploring Norway on skies.*

km (137 mi) of groomed and marked cross-country trails through woodland, Hardangervidda's hills and moors, and around Hallingskarvet, which is 6,341 feet above sea level. Snow rafting is the latest winter thrill: participants slide down snowy slopes on rubber rafts.

Geilo Skiheiser (☎ 32–09–59–20) has 24 km (15 mi) of Alpine slopes, 130 km (81 mi) of cross-country trails, 18 lifts, and a ski-board tunnel. **Halstensgård** (☎ 32–09–10–20) and **Slaatta** (☎ 32–09–03–70) have a range of Alpine and cross-country trails. **Havsdalsenteret** (☎ 32–09–17–77) attracts a young crowd to its long alpine slopes. **Vestlia** (☎ 32–09–55–10), west of the Ustedalsfjord, has easier slopes so it's a good choice for families.

Dagali

❿ *25 km (15 mi) southeast of Geilo, off Rte. 40, on the border of Numedal and Hallingdal.*

The small village of Dagali borders the Hardangervidda National Park and makes a good launching point for mountain hiking, skiing, fishing, and white-water rafting. To replenish expended calories, savor the traditional Norwegian dishes at Dagali Hotell.

The **Dagali Museum** is in the heart of town, in the birch wood below the Fagerlund farm. Teacher Gunnar Stensen lived at Fagerlund from 1870 to 1970. He dedicated his life to the preservation of Norwegian and local culture. The museum houses his collections of agricultural equipment, furniture, and curiosities in 10 houses, an old schoolhouse, and an exhibition hall dating from the 1700s. ⊠ *Dagali center* ☎ *32–09–37–93* 🖼 *NKr 50* ⊙ *Mid-June–mid-Aug., daily 10–5.*

Where to Stay & Eat

$–$$$
Fodor'sChoice
★

✕🖼 **Dagali Hotel.** Ole and Kirsten Halland will make you feel at home in their charming chalet-style hotel 2,870 feet above sea level and overlooking Dagali. The hotel was originally on one of the oldest farms in Dagali—it dates from the 1700s. Rooms are decorated in keeping with the Norwegian *bonderomantikk* style of this period. The restaurant is popular with locals for its traditional and seasonal Norwegian dishes. Try Kirsten's mountain trout, which she catches herself in the local lake in September. During the Christmas season, sample *rakfisk*, a salt-cured fish dish, and *lefse* (traditional Norwegian pastry). A short distance away the Dagali ski center offers downhill skiing and snowboarding, and on the property are 2½ km (1½ mi) of well-lighted cross country ski trails. In summer Kirsten or Ole will give you a tour of the family's private village museum. ⊠ *Off Rte. 40, 3580 Dagali* ☎ *32–09–37–00* 🖨 *32–09–38–10* ⊕ *www.dagalihotel.no* 🛏 *43 rooms* ⚐ *Restaurant, cross-country skiing, bar, lounge, library; no TVs in some rooms* ⊟ *AE, DC, MC, V.*

Rafting

Eivind Erik Scharffenberg and his international guides at **Dagali Rafting** (☎ 32–09–38–20 or 90–94–36–12 ⊕ www.dagalirafting.no) lead white-water trips on the Numedal River.

Hardangervidda

⓫ *90 km (56 mi) from Geilo to Eidfjord on Rte. 7, the main road that crosses Hardangervidda.*

Norwegians take great pride in their largest national park, which is also Europe's largest mountain plateau—10,000 square km (3,861 square mi). Hardangervidda is home to the largest wild reindeer herds in Europe and is the southernmost outpost of the arctic fox, snowy owl, and other arctic animals and plants. A plateau with a thousand lakes, it has gently rolling hills and wide stretches of level ground. In the west the mountains become more dramatic, the plant life richer, the climate wetter, and temperatures more moderate. In the east the small amount of snow means that it's an almost barren, windswept moorland.

Some 250 Stone Age sites have been found in Hardangervidda. The earliest date from 6,300 BC, which proves that man reached the plateau at the same time as the reindeer. When touring the plateau, either on horseback or on foot, you can find a trail for any level of ability. Den Norske Turistforening (DNT; The Norwegian Mountain Touring Association) has built cabins along the trails. The association organizes tours and activities. All plant and animal life is protected by law. Respect the area to make sure it remains a thing of beauty.

At the foot of Vøringfossen waterfall and Måbødalen valley, the **Hardan-gervidda Natursenter Eidfjord** (Hardangervidda Nature Center at Eid-fjord) focuses on the area's geology, biology, and archaeology. Over half a billion years ago Norway was south of the equator. Twenty-five mil-lion years ago glaciers began their descent over Norway. An interac-tive program explains how glaciers form, grow, and recede. ☒ *Øvre Eidfjord* ☎ *53–66–59–00* ⊕ *www.hardangervidda.org* ▨ *NKr 80* ☉ *June–Aug., daily 9–8; Sept., Oct., Apr,. and May, daily 10–6; Nov.–Mar., by arrangement.*

About an hour's drive north of Geilo is Hardangervidda's highest peak, **Hardangerjøkulen** (Hardanger Glacier), at 6,200 feet. In summer you can join guided glacier walks led by **Jøklagutane** (☎ 95–90–53–53 ⊕ www.finsehytta.no). Near Hardangerjøkulen you can take a guided hike to the archaeological digs of 8,000-year-old Stone Age settlements. Turid Linseth at **Hardangervidda Mountain Guiding** (☎97–54–18–60 ⊕www.fjellguiding.no) leads guided walks explaining Hardangervidda's history, flora, and fauna.

Finse

⓬ *On the railway line from Oslo to Bergen, in the Hardangervidda plateau.*

The only way to get to car-free Finse is by train, cycling, hiking, or skiing, making a visit there a unique and very remote Norwegian mountain experience, 4,008 feet above sea level. On the Oslo-to-Bergen line, the railway station here is northern Europe's highest. Glistening glaciers, white plateaus, and extreme temperatures and conditions have made Finse a legendary place of pilgrimage for ad-venturers and outdoors lovers. Some of the oldest traces of Norwe-gian civilization were found here: the remains of reindeer-hunting settlements dating back 7,000 years. Finse is not a town; its year-round population is fewer than 10 people, and besides the train station there are only a hotel and a few other buildings.

In the 1870s and 1880s, urban-dwelling Norwegian artists and univer-sity professors began to hike in the mountains here, and foreign tourists, particularly from Great Britain, started to visit the near-arctic clime. By the early 1900s polar explorers Fridtjof Nansen, Robert F. Scott, and Sir Ernest Shackleton tested their equipment here before setting off on their respective expeditions. In 1979, battle scenes of the second Star Wars film *The Empire Strikes Back* were filmed here.

Long cross-country ski trips, telemarking, ski-sailing, glacier walking on Hardangerjøkulen, dogsledding, hiking, and cycling are still common pastimes. On the last Saturday in April, the traditional end to the ski season, Norwegian skiers gather here for the Skarverennet race.

Every first weekend in February the **Finse Jazz festival** (⊕ www.bergenjazzforum.no) is arranged by Bergen Jazzforum, presenting mu-sicians from all over the world.

Galleri Finse is a small gallery run by Norwegian artist Rannveig Barstad in cooperation with the Bryggen Kunstskole (art school). Changing exhibitions feature Barstad's and regional artists' works. ☎ *56–52–63–57 or 97–56–47–97* ☒ *NKr 20* ⊙ *Jan.–Sept., daily 9 AM–9 PM.*

Rallarmuseet Finse (Railroaders Museum Finse) recalls the legendary turn-of-the-20th-century construction of the Bergen Railway. One exhibition shows how the railway's high mountain section was built, between 1871 and 1909. Another exhibition, "Kampen mot snøen" ("The Fight Against the Snow"), chronicles man's struggle against fierce winter forces. ☒ *Østre lokomotivstall, Finse stasjon* ☎ *56–52–69–66* ⊕ *www.rallarmuseet.no* ☒ *NKr 30* ⊙ *Mid-Jan.–Sept., daily 10 AM–10 PM.*

Where to Stay & Eat

$$$$ ✕🏠 **Finse 1222.** Named for Finse's position 1,222 meters (4,008 feet) above sea level, this 1909 hotel originally served travelers on the Bergen Railway who became snowed in. Despite its remote location, this *villmarkshotell* (wilderness hotel) quickly became a gathering place for Europe's rich and famous. Murals and photographs throughout depict ski scenes and past guests. Guest rooms are spartan, with no televisions, radios, or telephones. The kitchen serves first-class Norwegian fare ($$), including warm smoked salmon and leg of wild lamb. The pub and disco Boggin has authentic railway seating. Summer and winter activities, tours, courses, and ski and bike rentals are available. Make reservations as early as possible, especially for weekends. ☒ *Next to Finse train station, 5719* ☎ *56–52–71–00* 🖨 *56–52–67–17* ⊕ *www.finse1222.no* ➟ *44 rooms* ⌂ *Restaurant, bar, pub, dance club, library, meeting room; no room TVs, no room phones* ▱ *AE, DC, MC, V* ⊙ *Closed late Oct.–mid-Jan. and June.*

Sports & the Outdoors

BIKING   In summer, cycling enthusiasts flock to **Rallarvegen,** widely considered to be one of the best mountain-biking routes in the world. The ride is on a gentle incline from Haugastøl, at 2,950 feet above sea level, to Finse, at 4,010 feet above sea level. Bike rental is available through **Haugastøl Tourist Center** (☎ 32–08–75–64) or at the Finse 1222 hotel.

HIKING, GLACIER   Finse is an important connection for mountain trips, whether in sum-
WALKING   mer or winter. Several hotels, including Finse 1222 and **Jøklagutane** (☎ 90–84–15–99) have programs and expert guides for mountain hikes and glacier walks.

DNT (☎ 56–52–67–32) arranges mountain trips; maintains well-marked trails south and north of Finse; and operates Finsehytta, a mountain cabin.

SKIING, SKI-   **Finse Skilag** (☎ 55–31–79–56) arranges skiing trips as well as summer
SAILING   mountain activities. **Parmann AS Skiseiling** (☎ 90–56–45–07) offers ski-sailing courses and sells sails.

BIKING THE RALLARVEGEN & EVENTYRVEGEN

THE MOST POPULAR BIKE TREK in Norway is the 80-km (50-mi) **Rallarvegen**, which follows the Bergen Railway, westbound over the Hardangervidda, from Haugastøl to Flå. The route was originally a construction and transportation track used during the building of the railway. (Rallar was the Norwegian name for the railway workmen.) The bikeway was established in 1974, and attracts 20,000 cyclists each year. You can rent a bicycle at Haugastøl, Finse, or nearly every town along the way.

Another popular cycling route is the **Eventyrvegen** (Adventure Trail), a network of bicycle routes that follow the Hallingdal and Hemsil rivers and pass near Krøderen Lake. Eventyrvegen's Route 52, for example, goes from Gol to Hemsedal following the Hemsil River, which is

popular with anglers. You can buy an Adventure Road cycling map at tourist offices or bookshops.

When looking for a place to stay, watch for SYKLIST VELKOMMEN signs. This means that the lodgings are bicycle friendly, welcoming cyclists with bike repair kits, safe parking, and laundry facilities. Not all the cyclists who follow these routes are experienced with mountainous terrain; you can try out some of the less-challenging trails even if you are only a recreational cyclist.

HAMAR TO RØROS

Hamar

13 *134 km (83 mi) north of Oslo, 66 km (41 mi) north of Eidsvoll.*

On a northeast fork of Lake Mjøsa, Hamar was the seat of a bishopric during the Middle Ages. Four Romanesque arches, which are part of the cathedral wall, remain; they are today the symbol of the city. Ruins of the 13th-century monastery now form the backbone of a glassed-in exhibition of regional artifacts, some of which are from the Iron Age.

The **Hamar Olympiahall** hosted the speed- and figure-skating events of the Lillehammer Winter Olympics in 1994, which helped rejuvenate the town's economy and gave it a new stadium. The multipurpose stadium is now used for exhibitions, conferences, fairs, concerts, and sports events. Shaped like an upside-down Viking ship, Olympiahall was voted most magnificent structure of the 20th century by the national Norwegian newspaper *Dagbladet.* ⊠ *Åkersvikaveien* ☎ *62–51–75–00* ⊕ *www.hoa.no.*

The four Romanesque arches that formed part of the wall of the medieval cathedral that stood here now form the centerpiece of the **Hedmarksmuseet and Domkirkeodden** (Hedmark Museum and Cathedral Point). The glass superstructure on the ruins of the previous Hamar cathedral is one of the most unusual museum buildings in Europe. Also on the grounds of the museum sit 50 or so idyllic grass-roof houses from the region that show the cultural and social life of Hamar when it was a flourishing town. There is an organic garden that has 350 different types of herbs. The museum is about a mile west of the city center. ⊠ *Strandveien 100* ☎ *62–54–27–00* ⊕ *www.hedmarksmuseet.museum. no* 🖃 *NKr 70* ☉ *Late-May–mid-June and mid-Aug.–Sept., daily 10–4; mid-June–mid-Aug., daily 10–6.*

One of Europe's first railway museums, opened in 1896, the **Jernbanemuseet** documents the development of Norway's railways. Exhibits with train memorabilia are inside, while locomotives and carriages are on narrow-gauge tracks outside and in sheds. You can take a short ride on Tertittoget, the last steam locomotive built by Norway's state railway, from mid-May to mid-August. ⊠ *Strandvn. 132* ☎ *62–51–31–60* ⊕ *www. jernbanemuseet.no* 🖃 *NKr 70* ☉ *Jan.–June and mid-Aug.–Dec., daily 10:30–3:30; July–mid-Aug., daily 10:30–5.*

The world's oldest paddle steamer still in operation, the **DS** *Skibladner,* also called the *White Swan of the Mjøsa,* was first launched in 1856. She departs daily from Hamar, connecting towns along the lake. The steamer creeps up to Lillehammer three days a week. The other days it stops at Eidsvoll. The Gentlemen's Saloon and Ladies Saloon have been restored. A traditional dinner, consisting of poached salmon and potatoes, with strawberries and cream for dessert, is available for an extra charge. ⊠ *Torggt. 1* ☎ *61–14–40–80* ⊕ *www.skibladner.no* 🖃 *NKr 220 one-way* ☉ *Mid-May–mid-Aug., Tues.–Sun. 9:30–7.*

Gjøvik

⑭ *45 km (27 mi) west of Hamar.*

The DS *Skibladner* stops several times a week at this quiet hillside town, which claims to be home to the world's largest underground auditorium. The **Gjøvik Olympiske Fjellhall** (Olympic Mountain Hall) is buried 400 feet below the mountain in the middle of town. The hall was built on the site of an underground swimming pool, which was expanded to accommodate ice-hockey matches for the 1994 Winter Olympics. ⊠ *Town Center* ☎ *61–13–82–11* 🖃 *NKr 15* ☉ *Weekdays 11–9, weekends 10–5.*

Lillehammer

⑮ *40 km (25 mi) from Gjøvik, 60 km (37 mi) from Hamar, 180 km (111 mi) from Oslo.*

Many Norwegians have great affection for Lillehammer, the winter-sports resort town that hosted the 1994 Winter Olympics. In preparation for the games, the small town built a ski-jumping arena, an ice-hockey arena, a cross-country skiing stadium, and a bobsled and luge track. Lillehammer is known for the slopes on the mountains Nordseter and Sjusjøen; Vinterspillene, its Winter Arts Festival, held in February; and its many old wooden buildings. Lillehammer is a cultural center as well. It hosts the Norwegian Literature Festival in May. Sigrid Undset, who won the Nobel Prize in literature in 1928, lived in the town for 30 years.

off the beaten path

HUNDERFOSSEN PARK – The world's biggest troll sits atop a cave in this tiny amusement park. The glittering gold Eventyrslottet, or fairy-tale castle, is a must-see. There's a petting zoo for small children; plenty of rides; plus an energy center, with Epcot-like exhibits about oil and gas; and a five-screen theater. The park is 13 km (8 mi) north of Lillehammer. ⊠ *Fåberg* ☎ *61–27–72–22* ⊕ *www.hunderfossen. no* 🖃 *NKr 240* ⊙ *Late May–late June, daily 10–5; late June–early-Aug., daily 10–8; early Aug.–late Aug., daily 10–5.*

Fodor'sChoice ★

One of the most important art collections in Norway is housed at the **Lillehammer Kunstmuseum** (Lillehammer Museum of Art), which opened in 1927. The 1,000 works include pieces by Edvard Munch and Adolph Tidemand. The original 1963 building has been remodeled and joined by a new building designed by Snøhetta. Sculptor Bård Breivik created a sculpture garden using stone and water between the two buildings. ⊠ *Stortorgt. 2* ☎ *61–05–44–60* ⊕ *www.lillehammerartmuseum.com* 🖃 *NKr 60* ⊙ *Late Aug.–June, Tues.–Sun. 11–4; July–late Aug., daily 11–5.*

★ ☉ Europe's largest open-air museum, **Maihaugen–Sandvigsche Sammlungen,** was founded in 1887. The massive collection of the artifacts of folk life was begun by Anders Sandvik, an itinerant dentist who accepted odds and ends—and eventually entire buildings—from the people of Gudbrandsdalen in exchange for his services. Eventually Sandvik turned the collection over to the city of Lillehammer, which provided land for the museum. The exhibit "We Won the Land" is an inventive meander through Norway's history. It begins in 10,000 BC. After walking past life-size, blue-hue mannequins representing periods like the Black Death and the 400 years of Danish rule, you reach unsettling exhibits about the 20th century. ⊠ *Maihaugvn. 1* ☎ *61–28–89–00* ⊕ *www.maihaugen. no* 🖃 *NKr 90, includes guided tour* ⊙ *Oct.–mid-May, daily 11–4; mid-May–Sept., daily 10–5.*

The **Norges Olympiske Museum** (Norwegian Olympic Museum) covers the history of the games from their start in ancient Greece in 776 BC. Multimedia presentations and artifacts like sailboats and skis illustrate Norwegian sporting history in the **Gallery of Honor.** Some of the exhibition captions are in English. ⊠ *Håkons Hall, Olympic Park* ☎ *61–25–21–00* ⊕ *www.ol.museum.no* 🖃 *NKr 60* ⊙ *June–Sept., Tues.–Sun. 10–6; Oct.–May, daily 11–4.*

The **Olympiaparken** has a range of winter as well as summer activities. You can visit the ski-jump tower, take the chairlift, or step inside the bobsled simulator at the **Lysgårdsbakkene Ski Jump Arena,** where the

Winter Olympics' opening and closing ceremonies were held. Also in the park are **Håkons Hall,** the main hockey arena, which now holds sporting events and includes simulated, indoor golf-course holes. The **Birkebeineren Ski Stadium** holds cross-country and biathlon events. You can go tobogganing at the **Kanthaugen Freestyle Arena.** And at the **Olympic Bobsleigh and Luge Track** you can bobsled on ice. This involves a rubber bobsled with wooden runners that seats five passengers and can travel as fast as 80 kph (50 mph). ⊠ *Elvegt. 19* ☎ *61–25–11–40* ⊕ *www. olympiaparken.no* ⊠ *Arena NKr 20; fee varies for athletic events* ☉ *June–Sept., daily 9–5; Oct.–May, daily 11–4.*

Right on the pedestrian street, the tiny café **One Hand Clapping** (⊠ Storgata) serves some of the best international coffees to be found between Oslo and Trondheim.

Where to Stay & Eat

$–$$$ ✕ **Blåmann Restaurant & Bar.** Named after a Norwegian folktale about a buck called Blueman, this popular restaurant has a completely blue interior. You'll also find an outdoor café, a bar on the second floor, and a nightclub next door. Try the Mexican tacos, or a reindeer or ostrich steak. ⊠ *Lilletorget 1* ☎ *61–26–22–03* ⊠ *Reservations essential* ☰ *AE, DC, MC, V.*

¢–$ ✕ **Nikkers, Svare & Berg.** Nikkers has a rustic, mountain-cabin style, with the predictable moose head. Svare & Berg has a roaring fireplace and caricatures of famous authors hanging on the walls. Next door to each other, these restaurant-bars share the same owner and international cuisine, ranging from nachos to pastas. ⊠ *Elvegt. 18* ☎ *61–24–74–30* ☰ *AE, DC, MC, V.*

$$$ ✕⊡ **Rica Victoria Hotel.** Red burnished leather chairs dot the English library–style lobby at this central hotel. Guest rooms are furnished in styles ranging from pure rural romanticism to more classic styles. The hotel has eight "ladies rooms," each with bed alcove and rocking chair. Victoria Stuene and Daily, the hotel's two restaurants, face a pedestrian street. ⊠ *Storgt. 84B, 2600* ☎ *61–25–00–49* ☐ *61–25–24–74* ⊕ *www.rica. no* ⊠ *109 rooms, 17 suites* ☒ *2 restaurants, cable TV, in-room data ports, bar, nightclub, meeting room* ☰ *AE, DC, MC, V.*

★ $$ ⊡ **Mølla Hotell.** In this converted 1863 mill the small reception area gives the feeling of a private home. The yellow rooms in the former grain silo have rustic pine furniture. At the top of the silo, the Toppen Bar gives you a panoramic view of the Olympic ski jump and Lake Mjøsa. The Egon Restaurant is a beautiful outdoor retreat along the Mesna River. ⊠ *Elvegt. 12, 2600* ☎ *61–26–92–94* ☐ *61–26–92–95* ⊕ *www. mollahotell.no* ⊠ *58 rooms* ☒ *Restaurant, cable TV, in-room data ports, sauna, bar* ☰ *AE, DC, MC, V.*

$–$$ ⊡ **Birkebeineren Hotel/Motel & Apartments.** Ski trails and hiking terrain are steps away from this hotel's doors. The cream-color rooms are understated and country-style. Black-and-white photographs of skiers decorate the walls. ⊠ *Birkebeineren 24, Olympiaparken, 2618* ☎ *61–26–47–00* ☐ *61–26–47–50* ⊕ *www.birkebeineren.no* ⊠ *75 rooms, 40 apartments* ☒ *Dining room, some in-room data ports, sauna, meeting rooms* ☰ *AE, DC, MC, V.*

Sports & the Outdoors

A highlight of Lillehammer's ski year is the **Birkebeineren cross-country ski race.** The Birkebeiners were a faction in Norway's 13th-century civil war, who got their name because they wrapped their legs in birchbark (hence *birkebeiner*—birch legs). Birch bark was commonly used as footwear by people who couldn't afford wool or leather leggings. The ski race commemorates the trek of two Birkebeiner warriors who carried the heir to the throne, Prince Haakon, to safety from the rival Bagler faction who were pursuing him. The backpack carried by participants during the race is meant to symbolize the young prince being brought to safety through harsh weather conditions.

FISHING Within Troll Park, the **Gudbrandsdalåen** is touted as one of the best-stocked rivers in the country, and the size and weight of Mjøsa trout (locals claim it's 25 pounds) is legendary. Contact the local tourist board for information about fishing seasons, how to get the required national and local licenses, and other useful tips.

HIKING & BICYCLING The Nordseter and Sjusjøen tourist centers are good starting points for mountain-biking and -hiking excursions. From **Nordseter Aktivitetssenter** (⊠ Off Rte. 6 ☎ 61–26–40–37), about 15 km (9 mi) from the city center, you can hike to Mt. Neverfjell, at 3,573 feet. There you can see the Jotunheimen and Rondane mountain ranges. The center rents mountain bikes, canoes, and other boats. Mt. Lunkefjell (3,320 feet) is a popular hiking destination accessible from **Sjusjøen Sport & Aktiviteter** (⊠ Sjøen ☎ 62–36–30–04). Regular bicycles and mountain bikes can be rented. The center also organizes walks, bicycle and fishing trips, and canoeing.

RAFTING & CANOEING The **Sjoa River,** close to Lillehammer, offers some of the most challenging rapids in the country. Contact **Heidal Rafting** (☎ 61–23–60–37).

SKIING Lillehammer–Sjusjøen and Nordseter and the four other nearby skiing destinations—Hafjell, Skeikampen, Kvitfjell, and Gålå—are collectively called **Lillehammer Ski Resorts** (⊕ www.lsr). Together, they have 35 lifts, 78 pistes, and more than 1,500 km (932 mi) of cross-country trails. Each destination has its particular charm. A Lillehammer Ski Resorts Pass admits you to all five.

With both high-mountain and forest terrain, **Hafjell** (⊠ 10 km [6 mi] north of Lillehammer ☎ 61–27–70–00) is the largest Alpine facility. Snow conditions are generally stable here. The Hunderfossen Familiepark with snowboarding is popular. There's also a child-care center, a ski school, and several after-ski entertainment spots.

Gålå (⊠ Near Vinstra, 89 km [40 mi] north from Lillehammer via the E6 ☎ 61–29–76–65) is an all-around ski facility, with spectacular high-mountain terrain and views of Jotunheimen and Rondane national parks. It has cross-country trails and organized activities that include ice fishing, snow rafting, sledding, winter riding, and sleigh riding.

Shopping

Most of Lillehammer's 250-odd shops are on or near Storgata Street. From Lilletorget you can walk to the old industrial area of Mesna Brug, where there's the Mesnasenter (Mesna Center) group of clothing and craft shops. **Husfliden** (⊠ Sigrid Undset pl. ☎ 61–26–70–70 ⊕ www.husfliden.no), one of the biggest and oldest home crafts stores in Europe, specializes in hand-knit sweaters and traditional and handmade goods from the Gudbrandsdalen area. Glassblowing is demonstrated at **Lillehammer Kunst Glass** (⊠ Elvegt. 17 ☎ 61–25–79–80); you can also buy special glass souvenirs here.

Gausdal

⑯ *18 km (11 mi) northwest of Lillehammer.*

The composer of Norway's national anthem and the 1903 Nobel Prize winner in literature, Bjørnstjerne Bjørnson, lived at **Aulestad,** in Gausdal, from 1875 until he died in 1910. After his wife died in 1934 their house was opened as a museum. ⊠ *Follebu, south of Gausdal off Rte. 255* ☎ *61–22–41–10* ☎ *NKr 50* ☉ *Mid-May and Sept., daily 11–2:30; June, daily 10–3:30; July, daily 10–5:30.*

The scenic, well-marked **Peer Gynt Vegen** (Peer Gynt Road) begins in Gausdal. It's named for the real-life man behind Ibsen's character. Just 3 km (2 mi) longer than the main route, the road gives you splendid views of the mountains of Rondane, Dovrefjell, and Jotunheimen as you travel past old farmhouses. It passes two major resorts, **Skeikampen/Gausdal** and **Gålå/Wadahl,** before rejoining E6 at Vinstra.

Ringebu

⑰ *50 km (31 mi) north of Lillehammer, 30 km (20 mi) northeast of Gausdal.*

Ringebu is home to former Winter Olympic site Kvitfjell, now one of the World Cup Alpine Skiing venues. Although it has the challenging downhill course used in the 1994 Olympic Games, **Kvitfjell** (☎ 61–28–36–30 ⊕ www.kvitfjell.no) also has easier courses, including a family-friendly 2-km (1-mi) slope with a drop of 1,150 feet. There's also a snowboard park and more than 600 km (124 mi) of prepared cross-country trails.

The stave church **Ringebu Stavkirke** (☎ 61–28–03–74) dates from the 13th century and is open for guided summer tours.

Weidemannsamlingen-Ringebu Prestegård shows paintings by late Norwegian painter Jacob Weidemann. ⊠ *Ringebu Prestegård* ☎ *61–28–27–00* ☎ *NKr 30* ☉ *June–mid Aug., Tues.–Sun. 10–5.*

Where to Stay & Eat

$–$$ ✕▤ **Venabu Fjellhotell.** The Tvete family has been welcoming regulars
Fodor'sChoice to its mountain retreat in the village of Venabygd for many years. Guests
★ can join their unforgettable guided ski and mountain trips. Horseback riding, sleigh and wagon rides, canoeing, mountain biking, and snowshoeing are among other activities. Although the guest rooms are basic, without televisions, most guests spend their time outdoors and socializing in the lounges. Every meal is served buffet style, and the Wednes-

day-night traditional Norwegian buffet is delicious, cooked with fresh local ingredients. ⊠ *2632 Venabygd, From Ringebu, take Rte. E6 north for 4 km (2.5 miles), then turn right on Rte. 27 toward Folldall for 15 km (9.3 miles)* 🕾 *61–29–32–00* 🖷 *61–29–32–50* ⊕ *www.venabu.no* 🛏 *56 rooms* ⚐ *Restaurant, hiking, cross-country skiing, Internet room; no room TVs* ⊟ *AE, DC, MC, V.*

Vinstra

⓲ *18 km (11 mi) north of Gausdal.*

Vinstra is the administrative, service, trade, and education center of the district. It is best known for the Peer Gynt Festival, named after the Ibsen play, which was based upon Per, a resident of Sødorp near Vinstra. The festival is held every summer for one week in July or August. A wooden 1743 farmhouse where the historical Per lived, the **Peer Gynt Stugu** (Peer Gynt's House), has an exhibition based on the play and the man who inspired it. Photographs, posters, programs, costumes, and books have been gathered from *Peer Gynt* theatrical productions around the world. ⊠ *Hågå, Sødorp* 🕾 *61–29–20–04* ☺ *Mid-June–mid-Aug., daily 10–5.*

> off the beaten path

SOLBRÅ MOUNTAIN FARM MUSEUM – In Gålå you'll find one of Norway's most famous mountain farms. Solbrå is where Gudbrandsdalen, the brown Norwegian cheese, was first made, in 1863. Dairymaid Anne Hov first used only cow milk in the cheese; later, goat milk was added. The old cheese house is now a museum. ⊠ *Gålå, 12 km (7.5 miles) south of Vinstra* 🕾 *61–29–70–48* 🎟 *Free* ☺ *Early July–late Aug., Wed. and Sat. 11–3.*

Where to Stay & Eat

★ **$$$–$$$$** ✕🖭 **Gålå Høgfjellshotell og Hytter.** North of Vinstra, this is one of Norway's finest high-mountain hotels, known for more than a century for its excellent service. Elegant navy-blue rooms are furnished in bonderomantikk style. In the intimate hotel restaurant Mor Aases, freshly caught trout from Gålå Lake, wild game, fresh berries, and herbs are prepared in traditional Norwegian style. Plan to dine here on Wednesday night for the superb fish buffet. Downstairs, in Anitras bar, you can have coffee or browse the library of best-sellers available in several languages. High-standard *hytter* (mountain cabins) are also available for rent. The hotel is close to the summer festival stage. ⊠ *2646 Gålå* 🕾 *61–29–81–09* 🖷 *61–29–85–40* ⊕ *www.gala-resort.com* 🛏 *42 rooms* ⚐ *Restaurant, pool, cross-country skiing, downhill skiing, library, children's programs (ages 5–10), meeting room* ⊟ *AE, DC, MC.*

★ **$$–$$$** ✕🖭 **Fefor Høifjellshotell og Hytter.** Norway's oldest winter sports hotel was built in 1891. The mountain lodge's lobby has an open fireplace, stuffed trophy heads, and rustic wooden furniture; black-and-white photographs recount the hotel's heyday, when the royal family and explorers Fridtjof Nansen and Sir Robert Scott numbered among the guests. Every room is simple yet comfortable, some affording stunning views. Nearby is the trail up to Fefor Kampen, from which you can see many of the country's highest mountains. Guests come to cross-country or downhill ski, or canoe and fish in peaceful surroundings. Traditional Norwegian dishes based on seasonal ingredients are served in the restaurant. ⊠ *13 km (8 mi) off Rte. E6 from Vinstra, 2640 Vinstra-Gudbrandsdalen* ☎ *61–29–00–99* 🖶 *61–29–17–60* ⊕ *www.fefor.com* ↩ *114 rooms, 6 suites, 20 cabins* ⚐ *Restaurant, indoor and outdoor pools, cross-country skiing, downhill skiing* ▭ *AE, DC, MC, V.*

The Arts

Norwegian violinist Øystein Rudi and his wife Nina live on a cozy 17th-century farm, **Rudi Gard** (⊠ East on Rte. E6 from Vinstra ☎ 61–29–86–60 or 91–38–53–88 ⊕ www.rudigard.no). They've renovated the barn into a theater venue, gallery, and café. In summer Rudi Gard has performances by some of Norway's top folk musicians and actors, plus a sheep-shearing competition and other events. Overnight accommodation is available.

Sports & the Outdoors

BOATING Guided canoe safaris or independent trips are possible on four mountain lakes along the Peer Gynt Road. Contact **Gålå Sommer Arena** (☎ 61–29–76–30 ⊕ www.gala.no) and **Fefor Høifjellshotell** (☎ 61–29–00–99 ⊕ www.fefor.com).

CYCLING Area hotels rent mountain bikes. Contact **Norske Bygdeopplevelser** (☎ 61–28–99–70 ⊕ www.norske-bygdeopplevelser.no) for cycling, trekking, and skiing tours, guided or independent, for four to seven days. Overnight accommodation will be arranged at hotels and mountain lodges.

HIKING A network of marked trails and footpaths such as those kept by the **DNT (Norwegian Mountain Touring Association)**, the **Peer Gynt Trail**, and the **Pilgrims' Track** offer varied challenges. You can pick up maps at **Vinstra Skysstasjon** (Vinstra Tourist and Transport Centre ⊠ Øvre Årdal ☎ 57–66–35–62).

HORSEBACK **Sulseter Rideleir** (☎ 61–29–13–21) offers weeklong and weekend treks
RIDING in Rondane National Park.

SKIING Considered one of the best resorts for cross-country skiing (there are 630 km [391 mi] of trails), the **Peer Gynt Ski Region** (⊕ www.peergyntskiregion.com) includes the destinations Espedalen, Fefor, and Gålå. For downhill skiers there are pistes for all levels in Snowboard, Telemark, and Alpine.

Rondane National Park

⑲ *19 km (12 mi) north of Vinstra off Rte. E6.*

Rounded, harmonious mountains distinguish Rondane National Park, as you travel north from Vinstra on Route E6. A good point of entry to the park is the resort of Høvringen, off Route E6. For thousands of years the area has given hunters their livelihood, and they've left their mark in the form of reindeer traps and burial mounds. Today Rondane is a popular recreation area, attracting hikers and skiers. Ten of the peaks rise more than 6,500 feet. Norwegian artist Harald Sohlberg (1869–1935) immortalized the Rondane mountains in his painting *Vinternatt,* which was declared Norway's national painting in 1995 and hangs in the National Gallery in Oslo.

Where to Stay & Eat

★ **$$$–$$$$** ✕🏨 **Rondablikk Hotell.** Nestled in the mountains, near Kvam, Rondablikk has spectacular views of Rondane National Park and several lakes. Rooms are simply furnished and comfortable. Many guests spend their days cross-country skiing or mountain hiking. You can opt to order *halvpensjon* (half board), which includes the traditional Norwegian buffets at breakfast, lunch, and dinner. Rondablikk shares a lunch exchange program with Rondane SPA Hotel and Rondeslottet Mountain Hotel. Every August, Norway's best musicians play on the hotel's outdoor stage as part of the Peer Gynt Festival. ⊠ *Rte. E6, 2642 Kvam* ☎ *61–29–49–40* 🖷 *61–29–49–50* ⊕ *www.rondablikk.com* ↪ *72 rooms* ⚭ *Restaurant, pool, exercise equipment, sauna, cross-country skiing, bar, lounge, meeting rooms* ☰ *AE, DC, MC, V.*

★ **$$$–$$$$** ✕🏨 **Rondane SPA Hotel.** This hotel is high in the mountains south of Otta. The bright, simply furnished rooms have a country charm. A full range of services, from massage to baths, is on offer at the spa. Chef Steinar Havnen changes the menu of international dishes based on Norwegian fish and game daily. To get to the hotel, turn right off Route E6 before the exit for Otto, and follow signs to Mysuseter and Rondane Spa. ⊠ *Mysuseter, 2670 Otta, Off Rte. E6, 20 km (12 miles) north of Vinstra* ☎ *61–23–39–33* 🖷 *61–23–39–52* ⊕ *www.spa.no* ↪ *52 rooms* ⚭ *Restaurant, pool, massage, sauna, spa* ☰ *AE, DC, MC, V.*

Lom

➋⓪ *62 km (38 mi) west of Otta, via Rte. 15.*

Torgeir Garmo shares his passion for geology in his geological museum and jewelry gallery in the **Fossheim Steinsenter** (Fossheim Stone Center). His collection is the largest private exhibition of Norwegian minerals and precious stones in the country. In the sales galleries you can buy jewelry, minerals, and fossils. The Collector Mania museum shows rare objects that people have collected through the ages. ⊠ *2686 Lom* ☎ *61–21–14–60* 🖃 *Free* ☉ *June–Aug., daily 9–9, otherwise by appointment.*

Glaciers, lakes, fertile valleys, and mountains make up **Jotunheimen National Park,** of which 90% lies in the municipality of Lom. One of the park's well-known landmarks is **Galdhøpiggen,** the country's highest mountain, at 8,098 feet. Established in 1980, the park covers an area of 1,150 square km (444 square mi), and contains 27 of Norway's highest peaks. The rural town of Lom is distinguished by its dark-brown painted log-cabins and a stave church from 1170.

At **Lom Bygdamuseum Presthaugen** (Lom Open Air Museum), a well-preserved 19th-century farm, you can see **Olavsstugu,** where Saint Olav is said to have spent the night; there are also exhibitions, including one about watering techniques and grain in Storstabburet. ⊠ *Town Center* ☎ *61–21–19–33* 🖃 *NKr 20* ☉ *July, daily 1–4; guided tours noon–4.*

CloseUp

BEST PLACES TO HIKE

THE EXTRAORDINARY MOUNTAINS *of central Norway draw hikers of every level of experience. The terrain varies from the relatively level Hardangervidda plateau to the rounded Rondane mountains to the jagged, tall peaks of the Jotunheimen range.*

Trails are usually well marked, and there are cabins owned by the Norwegian Mountain Touring Association (DNT), which are kept for hikers who require overnight accommodations during their outing. The DNT local offices throughout the region can help you plan a hike, or sign you up for scheduled mountain trips organized for hikers of all levels of fitness and ability. One of Norway's classic mountain trips is hytte til hytte (cabin to cabin) in Jotunheimen National Park. You have to contact the organization before your hike to gain access to the cabins near your trail.

The Hardangervidda plateau's gentle slopes are perfect for beginners and those who aren't sufficiently fit to attempt high-altitude climbing. Experienced hikers tend to head to the tougher, steeper, alpine trips in Hemsedal, Rondane, and Jotunheimen. Mountain guides based in towns throughout the region can design trips tailored to your level of fitness.

One of Norway's oldest and most beautiful stave churches, **Lom Stavkyrkje** (Lom Stave Church), dates to the 12th century and still is the principal church in Lom. Its oldest section is Romanesque; the church was enlarged in 1634. Wood-carver Jakop Sæterdalen created the choir stalls and the pulpit. The church's baroque painting collection is one of Norway's largest. ☎ *61–21–29–90* ⊠ *NKr 40* ☯ *Mid-May–mid-June and mid-Aug.–mid-Sept., daily 10–4; mid-June–mid-Aug., daily 9–9.*

A woolly mammoth looms at the entrance to **Norsk Fjellmuseum** (Norwegian Mountain Museum). The museum focuses on people's relationship with the Norwegian mountain landscape, from the primitive hunters and gatherers who lived here to modern Norwegian society, with its belief in leisure time and outdoor recreational activities. Among the most interesting of the exhibitions is one dealing with early mountaineering and mountain road building. You can read the late-19th-century journals of W. C. Slingsby, the British father of Norwegian mountaineering, and see a reconstructed campsite. ⊠ *Town Center* ☎ *61–21–16–00* ⊕ *www.fjell.museum.no* ⊠ *NKr 60* ☯ *May and mid-Sept., daily 9–4, weekends 10–5; early June and late Aug, weekdays 9–6,* *weekends 10–5; mid-June–mid-Aug., weekdays 9–9, weekends 10–8; late Sept.–Apr., weekdays 9–4, weekends by appointment.*

Where to Stay & Eat

$$$$ ✕▥ **Røisheim Hotel.** Formerly a farm and coaching inn, this beautiful
Fodor'sChoice property is made up of 12 well-preserved buildings, most from the 18th
★ century and one dating back to the 16th century. Rooms with hardwood floors and antique furniture retain the traditional look and feel of the original interior. The restaurant is renowned for its excellent cuisine, which revolves around local and seasonal ingredients, and vast wine cellar. But perhaps Røisheim's greatest asset is its location in a high-mountain pass near the road to Sognefjell, about 12 km (7.5 miles) outside of Lom. Walking trails in the area will leave you speechless at the beauty of the Jotunheimen range's peaks and glaciers. ✉ *2687 Bøverdalen* ☎ *47–61–21–20–31* 🖷 *47–61–21–21–51* ⊕ *www.roisheim.no* 🗪 *24 rooms* ♨ *Restaurant, bar, meeting rooms* 🖃 *AE, DC, MC, V.*

★ **$$$** ✕▥ **Fossheim Turisthotell.** Svein Garmo and his family have run this mountain hotel since it began as a staging post in 1897. Solid-timber walls and antique furnishings give it a cozy look. Chef Kristofer Hovland and his dishes based on local ingredients have made the restaurant popular. Among the best-known dishes is the succulent fillet of reindeer. In summer take a seat in the aromatic outdoor café Urtehagen, surrounded by herbs and flowers. ✉ *Off Rte. E6, 2686 Lom* ☎ *61–21–95–00* 🖷 *61–21–95–01* ⊕ *www.fossheimhotel.no* 🗪 *54 rooms, 4 apartments* ♨ *Restaurant, café, bar, meeting room* 🖃 *AE, DC, MC, V.*

Sports & the Outdoors

FISHING **Lom Fiskeguiding DA** (☎ 61–21–10–24) rents fishing boats and organizes fishing trips.

HIKING & GLACIER WALKING Go glacier walking and climb Galdhøpiggen or other mountains. Call **Juvasshytta** (☎ 61–21–15–50) or **Natur Opplevingar** (☎ 61–21–11–55 ⊕ www.naturopplevingar.no).

HORSEBACK RIDING **Jotunheimen Hestesenter** (Jotunheimen Equestrian Center; ✉ Raubergstulen ☎ 61–21–18–00) has mountain riding tours for all ages, beginner to advanced, on Icelandic horses.

RAFTING Several local outfitters cater to your Sjoa River rafting needs, including **Lom Rafting** (☎ 90–80–90–90 ⊕ www.lomrafting.no) and **Villmarken** (☎ 61–23–39–57 ⊕ www.villmarken.net).

SUMMER SKIING You can go summer skiing at **Galdhøpiggen Sommerskisenter** (✉ Lom ☎ 61–21–17–50) on a glacier 6,068 feet above sea level.

Lesja

㉑ *159 km (99 mi) north of Lom.*

As you follow Route E6 from Otta toward Lesja, the broad, fertile valleys and snowcapped mountains of the Upper Gudbrandsdal surround you. The area around Lesja is trout-fishing country; Lesjaskogvatnet, the lake, has a mouth at either end, so the current changes in the middle.

off the beaten path

JØRUNDGARD MIDDELALDER SENTER – Anyone who read Sigrid Undset's 1928 Nobel prize–winning trilogy, *Kristin Lavransdatter,* will remember that the tale's heroine grew up on a farm of the same name as this one. The medieval-style farm, built for the 1995 Liv Ullmann movie, now houses the Jorundgård Medieval Center, a historical and cultural museum. ⊠ *Sel* ☎ *61–23–37–00* ⊕ *www. jorundgard.no* 🔲 *NKr 50* ⊙ *June–mid-Sept., daily 10–6; guided tours every ½ hr.*

Dombås

❷ *80 km (50 mi) east of Lesja on Rte. E136.*

From Dombås you can follow Route E6 up to **Dovrefjell,** one of the last virtually intact high-mountain ecosystems in Europe. Wild reindeer, wolverines, wild musk ox, arctic fox, and rare plant species make their home here. Snøhetta, the highest peak in the park at 7,500 feet, is a popular hiking destination. There are many restrictions regarding hiking in the area, so contact the tourist office before setting out.

From 1932 to 1953, musk ox were transported from Greenland to the Dovrefjell, where about 60 still roam—bring binoculars to see them. For information on tours, call the **Dombås Tourist Office** (⊠ Frich-gården ☎ 61–24–14–44 ⊕ www.dovrenett.no). **Dovre Eventyr** (☎ 61–24–01–59) has guides that lead tours of the local flora and fauna. They also offer musk-ox safaris and mountain-climbing courses. **Dovrefjell Aktivitetssenter** (☎ 61–24–15–55) organizes family rafting, moose safaris, mountain trips, and climbing and overnight wilderness camps.

Where to Stay & Eat

★ $$$ ✕▦ **Norlandia Dovrefjell Hotell.** This quiet, peaceful mountain hotel is part of the Norlandia hotel chain, but it was built as a German hospital during World War II. Rustic Norwegian bonderomantikk style dominates the lounges and dining rooms. The guest rooms are plainer. Take time to enjoy the outdoors in Dovrefjell, whether on mountain hikes, fishing trips, or musk-ox safaris. ⊠ *2659 Dombås* ☎ *61–24–10–05* 🖶 *61–24–15–05* ⊕ *www.norlandia.no/dovrefjell* 🛏 *89 rooms* ⚐ *Restaurant, pool, sauna, bar* ▤ *AE, DC, MC, V.*

Røros

❸ *317 km (197 mi) east of Lesja, 157 km (97 mi) south of Trondheim.*

At the northern end of the Østerdal, the long valley to the east of Gudbrandsdalen, lies Røros, one of Norway's great mining towns. For more than 300 years practically everyone who lived in this one-company town was connected with the copper mines. In 1980 Røros was named a UNESCO World Heritage Site. Norwegian artist Harald Sohlberg's paintings of Røros made the town famous. His statue now stands in Harald Sohlberg's plass, looking down the stretch of road that he immortalized.

The **Bergstadens Ziir** (Røros Church) towers over the wooden houses of the town. The eight-sided stone structure dates from 1784. On the tower you can see the symbol of the mines. Called "the mountain's cathedral," it can seat 1,600, quite surprising in a town with a population of only about 3,500. The pulpit looms above the center of the altar, and seats encircle the top perimeter. ☎ 72–41–95–05 ᎒ NKr 25 ☉ Mid–late June, Mon.–Sat. 11–1; late June–late Aug., Mon.–Sat. 10–5, Sun. 2–4; late Aug.–mid-Sept, Mon.–Sat. 11–1; mid-Sept.–May, Sat. 11–1.

off the beaten path

OLAVSGRUVA MINE – This is the only Norwegian copper mine that was saved for posterity (in 1977 the copper works went bankrupt). Known as Olavsgruva, it consists of Nyberget (1650) and Crown Prince Olav's Mine (1936). A museum has been built over the mine shaft. Visitors can walk 164 feet underground and approximately 1,640 feet into the Miners' Hall, complete with sound and light effects. Bring warm clothing and good shoes, as the temperature below ground is about 5°C (41°F). ⊠ Near Rte. 31 ☎ 72–40–61–70 ᎒ NKr 60 ☉ Guided tours early June and late Aug.–early Sept., Mon.–Sat. at 1 and 3, Sun. at noon; late June–mid-Aug., daily at 10:30, noon, 1:30, 3, 4:30, and 6; early Sept.–May, Sat. at 3.

★ Røros's main attraction is the **Old Town,** with its 250-year-old workers' cottages, slag dumps, and managers' houses, one of which is now City Hall. Descendants of the man who discovered copper ore in Røros live in the oldest of the nearly 100 protected heritage buildings. A 75-minute tour starts at the information office and ends at the church. ⊠ Peder Hiorts gt. 2 ☎ 72–41–00–50 ᎒ NKr 50 ☉ Tours June and late Aug.–mid-Sept., Mon.–Sat. at 11; July–mid-Aug., Mon.–Sat. at 10, noon, 1, 2, and 3, Sun. at 1; mid-Sept.–May, Sat. at 11.

Røros Museum is in an old smelting plant, opened in 1646. In 1953 a fire destroyed the smelting works in Røros; the plant was closed and the machines were moved to Sweden. "Smelthytta," the smelting house, has been reconstructed using drawings of the workshop from 1888. Exhibitions show models of waterwheels, lift mechanisms, horse-driven capstans, mine galleries, and 19th-century clothing. ⊠ Off Rte. 30 ☎ 72–40–61–70 ᎒ NKr 65 ☉ Late July–mid-Aug., weekdays 10:30–6, weekends 10:30–4; mid-Aug.–late July, weekdays 11–3, weekends 11–2.

Where to Stay & Eat

If you want to explore the green, pastured mountains just south of Røros, more than a dozen farmhouses take overnight visitors. Some are hytter (cabins), but others, such as the **Vingelsgaard Gjestgiveri** (☎ 62–49–45–43), have entire wings devoted to guest rooms. Rates at Vingelsgaard are around 480 NKr per person. Contact **Vingelen Turistinformasjon** (☎ 62–49–46–65 or 62–49–46–83 ⊕ www.vingelen.com) for more information.

$$–$$$ ✕᎒ **Bergstadens Hotel.** An elegant, country-style hotel, this is a Røros landmark. The staff is warm and friendly, creating a personal and intimate mood. The restaurant has a changing menu of traditional Norwegian fare. ⊠ Oslovn. 2, 7361 ☎ 72–40–60–80 ᎒ 72–41–60–81

⊕ *www.bergstaden.no* ↪ *90 rooms, 4 suites* ♨ *2 restaurants, 2 bars, pub, nightclub, meeting room* ⊟ *AE, DC, MC, V.*

Sports & the Outdoors

BOATING   Femunden and Hodal lakes make great starting points for day trips or longer tours. A canoeing trip on your own or accompanied by a guide can be memorable. **Hodalen Fjellstue** (☎ 62–49–60–72) has boat and fishnet rentals and fishing permits.

CYCLING   Easy terrain in the Røros region makes it ideal for cyclists. The Røros tourist office offers bicycling package tours, which include maps and accommodation. Contact **Heimly Huskies Adventure** (☎ 72–41–47–93 ⊕ www.heimly-huskies.com) for mountain-bike tours of three to four hours (600 NKr) or seven to eight hours (980 NKr), or dogsled tours with authentic Siberian huskies lasting from one hour to one week.

FISHING   Fishing is possible in the Gaula, one of Norway's finest salmon rivers, or in the Glåma, Norway's longest river, recommended for grayling and trout. An angling guidebook and fishing licenses are sold at the tourist office, in shops and gas stations, and at the rangers' office in Holtålen. Skilled guides can show you the area and advise you on where and how to fish, preserving and cooking your catch. Contact **Ålen Fjellstyre** (☎ 72–41–55–77).

SKIING   At the northern end of the Gudbrandsdalen region, west of Røros, is **Oppdal** (45 km [28 mi] of Alpine pistes, 186 km [116 mi] of cross-country trails; 10 ski lifts), Norway's largest downhill skiing area and a World Cup venue. Like most other areas, it has lighted trails and snowmaking equipment.

Central Norway A to Z

To research prices, get advice from other travelers, and book travel arrangements, visit www.fodors.com.

AIR TRAVEL

Coast Air operates flight routes between Stavanger on the southern coast and Fagernes several times weekly.

🛈 **Coast Air** ✉ Haugesund Lufthavn, Postboks 163 ☎ 815-44-442 ⊕ www.coastair.no

BUS TRAVEL

Several bus companies operate in the region. Nor-Way Busekspress and Nettbuss both have services connecting most interior cities, including Geilo, Gol, Ål, and Hemsedal. Hallingdal Billag has service between Oslo and Geilo. Sogn Billag has service from Sogn to Hemsedal, Gol, Oslo, and Bergen. JVB TUR serves Serving Jotunheimen and Valdres. Contact the local tourist office regarding special seasonal ski buses

🛈 **Hallingdal Billag** ☎ 32-08-60-60 ⊕ www.hallingdalbillag.no. **JVB TUR** ☎ 61-36-59-00 ⊕ www.jvb.no. **Nettbuss** ☎ 815-00-184 or 177. **Nor-Way Busekspress** ☎ 815-44-444 ⊕ www.nor-way.no. **Sogn Billag** ☎ 177 or 57-65-95-12 ⊕ www.sognbillag.no.

CAR TRAVEL

The wide, two-lane Route E6 north from Oslo passes through Hamar and Lillehammer. Route 3 follows Østerdalen (the eastern valley) from Oslo. Route 30 at Tynset leads to Røros and E6 on to Trondheim, 156 km (97 mi) farther north.

Roads in the north become increasingly hilly and twisty as the terrain roughens into the central mountains. The northern end of the region is threaded by E16, E6, and Routes 51 and 3. High-tech markers at the roadside, particularly prevalent in the area of Vinstra and Otta, are cameras. Exceed the speed limit, and you may receive a ticket in the mail.

For the Hallindal Valley, follow Route 7 between Oslo–Hønefoss and Bergen. Your trip will probably involve some mountain driving. In summer, road conditions are good, but in winter there can be avalanches and other obstacles.

LODGING

For information on the region's top ski resorts, check out Scandinavia's online ski booking Web site, **Skistar** (⊕ www.skistar.com).

TOUR OPERATORS

🚹 **Fjell og Fjord Ferie AS** ✉ Gamlevegen 6, Gol ☎ 32-02-99-26 ⊕ www.eventyrveien. com.

TRAIN TRAVEL

This region is served by the Oslo–Bergen line of the Norwegian State Railway (the whole run takes nearly seven hours). Between late June and mid-September, a bicycle train, which stops at Finse, runs between Oslo and Voss.

🚹 **NSB (Norwegian State Railway)** ☎ 815-00-888 ⊕ www.nsb.no.

VISITOR INFORMATION

🚹 **Hallingdal Valley to Hardangerfjord Ål** ☎ 32-08-10-60 ⊕ www.aal.as. **Geilo** ☎ 32-09-59-00 ⊕ www.geilo.no. **Gol** ☎ 32-02-97-00 ⊕ www.golinfo.no. **Hallingdal (Nesbyen)** ☎ 32-07-01-70 ⊕ www.nesbyen.no. **Hemsedal** ☎ 32-05-50-30 ⊕ www.hemsedal.com.

🚹 **Lillehammer to Røros Dovre/Dovrefjell/Rondane Tourist Office** ☎ 61-24-14-44 ⊕ www.dovrenett.no. **Gjøvik** ✉ Jernbanegt. 2 ☎ 61-14-67-10 ⊕ www.visitgjovik-toten.com. **Hamar** ✉ Vikingskipet, Olympia Hall ☎ 62-52-12-17. **Lillehammer** ✉ Skysstasjon ☎ 61-28-98-00 ⊕ www.lillehammerturist.no. **Lom/Jotunheimen Reiseliv** ☎ 61-21-29-90 ⊕ www.visitlom.com. **Otta** ☎ 61-23-03-23. **Øyer-Hafjell/Hunderfossen** ☎ 61-27-70-00. **Røros** ☎ 72-41-00-00 ⊕ www.rorosinfo.com. **Vågå/Jotunheimen** ✉ Vågå 37 ☎ 61-23-78-80 ⊕ www.jotunheimen-turist.com. **Vinstra (Peer Gynts Rike)** ✉ Vinstra Skysstasjon ☎ 61-29-47-70 ⊕ www.peergynt.no.

Trondheim to the North Cape

7

A NARROW BUT IMMENSELY LONG strip of land stretches between Trondheim and Kirkenes in northern Norway. In this vast territory you'll encounter the sawtooth, glacier-carved peaks of the Lofoten Islands and the world's strongest tidal current, in Bodø. Thousands of islands and skerries hug the coast of northern Norway, and the provinces of Nordland, Troms, and Finnmark, up to the North Cape. Along this wild, unpredictable coast the weather is as dramatic as the scenery: in summer you can see the midnight sun, and in winter experience aurora borealis, the northern lights.

Northern Norwegians still make their living in the fishing villages of the Lofoten Islands, in small, provincial towns, and in modern cities like Tromsø. Tourism plays an important role in the region, especially with those seeking wild landscapes, outdoor activities, and adventure, whether it's mountaineering, dogsledding, skiing, caving, or wreck-diving. Basking in the midnight sun is one of Norway's most popular attractions; every year, thousands of people flock to Nordkapp (the North Cape) for it. To cater to the large number of visitors, northern Norway has well-run tourist offices which stock excellent maps and travel literature on the area.

Numbers in the margin correspond to points of interest on the Trondheim & the North map.

Exploring Trondheim & the North

Wild and beautiful, northern Norway is known for its fast-changing weather and vast distances, and is famous as the land of the northern lights, midnight sun, and polar night. It's a land marked by high mountains, glaciers, fjords, islands, and rocky shores. The Gulf Stream warms the coast, making it the longest ice-free coast in the polar regions.

The Arctic Circle region stretches along the coast of Helgeland, which has high mountains, the Svartisen glacier, and caves. Farther north, the Lofoten wall of mountains rises out of the ocean, on the remote Lofoten Islands. Even farther north, and seemingly forgotten by visitors, the Vesterålen Islands are covered in mountains that are ancient, rounded, and green. In the town of Tromsø, near the North Pole, the jagged Lyngen Alps attract the most experienced mountain climbers. The northernmost province of Norway, Finnmark, is on the same latitude as Siberia, Greenland, and Alaska.

About the Hotels & Restaurants

Traditional lodgings in the region, especially on the Lofoten Islands, are called *rorbuer*. A rorbu is traditionally a fisherman's cabin, and staying in one is an essential part of the Lofoten experience. Rorbuer vary greatly in standards and age but they tend to be basic, so bring your own provisions. Northern Norway's restaurants are famous for serving the fish that are abundant in the lakes and along the coast. A regional specialty is *surlaks* (marinated salmon served with sour cream). Other common ingredients found in the arctic region are game, reindeer, and fowl, accompanied with berries, potatoes, and vegetables.

WHAT IT COSTS In Norwegian Kroner				
	$$$$	**$$$**	**$$**	**$**	**¢**
RESTAURANTS	over 230	190–230	150–190	90–150	under 90
HOTELS	over 1,500	1,000–1,500	800–1,000	400–800	under 400

Restaurant prices are for a main course at dinner. Hotel prices are for two people in a standard double room in high season, including tax and a service charge.

Timing

Summer is the best season for visiting northern Norway. The weather is erratic, but northern summers can be warm and sunny, reaching temperatures of 25°C (77°F). If you like cold weather, northern winters offer snowmobiling, ice fishing, cross-country skiing, and other snowy activities. Above the Arctic Circle the midnight sun appears approximately between mid-May and late July. The dark period known as the polar night occurs between late November and late January. Many festivals are held to celebrate the seasons; among these are the Hammerfest Dark Season Festival in November, the Tromsø Northern Lights Festival in January, and the Alta Borealis Winter Festival in March.

Trondheim

❶ *494 km (307 mi) north of Oslo, 657 km (408 mi) northeast of Bergen.*

One of Scandinavia's oldest cities, Trondheim is Norway's third largest, with a population of 150,000. Founded in 997 by Viking king Olav Tryggvason, it was first named Nidaros (still the name of the cathedral), a composite word referring to the city's location at the mouth of the Nid River. The city was also the first capital of Norway, from AD 997 to 1380. Today Trondheim is a university town as well as a center for maritime and medical research, but the wide streets of the historic city center are still lined with brightly painted wood houses and striking warehouses.

King Olav formulated a Christian religious code for Norway in 1024, during his reign. It was on his grave that **Nidaros Domkirke** (Nidaros Cathedral) was built. The town became a pilgrimage site for the Christians of northern Europe, and Olav was canonized in 1164.

Although construction began in 1070, the oldest existing parts of the cathedral date from around 1150. It has been ravaged on several occasions by fire and rebuilt each time, generally in a Gothic style. Since the Middle Ages, Norway's kings have been crowned and blessed in the cathedral. The crown jewels are on display here. Forty-five minute guided tours are offered in English from mid-June to mid-August, weekdays at 11 and 4. ⊠ *Kongsgårdsgt. 2* ☎ *73–53–91–60* ⊕ *www. nidarosdomen.no* 🎫 *NKr 40. Ticket also permits entry to Erkebispegården* ☉ *Call for hrs.*

The **Erkebispegården** (Archbishop's Palace) is the oldest secular building in Scandinavia, dating from around 1160. It was the residence of

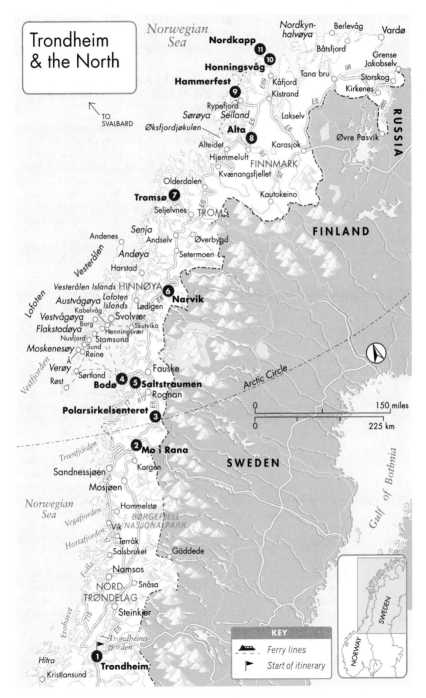

Trondheim & the North

Norwegian Sea

Nordkapp 11 10

Nordkyn-halvøya Berlevåg Vardø

Båtsfjord

Honningsvåg

Hammerfest 9

Grense Jakobselv

Tana bru 98 Storskog

Kåfjord Kirkenes

Rypefjord Kistrand

R U S S I A

TO SVALBARD

Sørøya Seiland Lakselv

Øksfjordjøkulen Alta 8

Karasjok Øvre Pasvik

Alteidet

Hjemmeluft

FINNMARK

Kvænangsfjellet

Olderdalen

Kautokeino

Tromsø 7

Seljelvnes **TROMS**

FINLAND

Andenes *Senja* Andselv Øverbygd

Vesterålen *Andøya* Setermoen

Harstad

Lofoten Vesterålen Islands HINNØYA 6

Austvågøya Lofoten Islands Lødigen **Narvik**

Vestvågøya Kabelvåg Svolvær

Flakstadøya Borg Skutvika

Nusfjord Henningsvær

Moskenesøy Stamsund

Å Sund Reine

Verøy Sørtland Fauske

Vestfjorden Røst **Bodø** 4 5 **Saltstraumen**

Rognan

Polarsirkelenteret 3

Arctic Circle

0 ——————— 150 miles

0 ——————— 225 km

2 **Mo i Rana**

Trænfjorden Korgen

Sandnessjøen **S W E D E N**

Mosjøen

Norwegian Sea Hommelstø

Vegafjorden Vik

BØRGEFJELL NASJONALPARK

Hortafjorden Terråk

Salsbruket Gäddede

Folla Namsos

NORD-TRØNDELAG Snåsa

Gulf of Bothnia

Steinkjer

Trondheims-fjorden

Frohavet

Hitra

Kristiansund 1 **Trondheim**

SWEDEN

NORWAY

KEY

Ferry lines

Start of itinerary

the archbishop until the Reformation in 1537; after that it was a residence for Danish governors, and later a military headquarters. The oldest parts of the palace, which face the cathedral, are used for government functions.

The **Archbishop's Palace Museum** (⊠ Kongsgårdsgt. ☎ 73–53–91–60 ☜ NKr 35) has original sculptures from Nidaros Cathedral and archaeological pieces from throughout its history.

Within the Erkebispegården's inner palace is the **Rustkammeret/Resistance Museum** (☎ 73–99–52–80), which traces the development of the army from Viking times to the present through displays of uniforms, swords, and daggers. The Resistance Museum deals with events in central Norway during World War II, and its memorial hall remembers those who lost their lives. ⊠ *Kongsgårdsgt.* ☎ *73–99–52–80* ⊕ *www.nidarosdomen. no* ☜ *NKr 40. Ticket also permits entry to Nidaros Cathedral* ☉ *Archbishop's Palace Museum: May–mid-June and mid-Aug.–mid-Sept., Mon.–Sat. 9–3, Sun. 1–4; mid-June–mid-Aug., weekdays 9–5, Sat. 9–2, Sun. 1–4; mid-Sept.–Apr., Mon.–Sat. 11–3, Sun. noon–4. Resistance Museum: June–Aug., weekdays 9–3, weekends 11–4; Mar.–May, Sept., and Oct., weekends 11–4; guided tours by appointment.*

Built after the great fire of 1681, the **Kristiansten Festning** (Kristiansten Fort) saved the city from conquest by Sweden in 1718. During Norway's occupation by Germany, from 1940 to 1945, members of the Norwegian Resistance were executed here; there's a plaque in their honor. The fort has a spectacular view of the city, the fjord, and the mountains. ☎ *73–99–52–80* ☜ *Free* ☉ *June–Aug., weekdays 10–3, weekends 11–4.*

★ The Tiffany windows are magnificent at the **Nordenfjeldske Kunstindustrimuseum** (National Museum of Decorative Arts), which houses an impressive collection of furniture, silver, and textiles. The Scandinavian Design section features a room interior designed by the Danish architect Finn Juhl in 1952. The 1690 bridal crown by Adrian Bogarth is also memorable. "Three Women–Three Artists" features tapestries by Hannah Ryggen and Synnøve Anker Aurdal, and glass creations by Benny Motzfeldt. ⊠ *Munkegt. 5* ☎ *73–80–89–50* ⊕ *www.nkim. museum.no* ☜ *NKr 50* ☉ *June–late Aug., Mon.–Sat. 10–5, Sun. noon–5; late Aug.–May, Tues., Wed., Fri., and Sat. 10–3, Thurs. 10–5, Sun. noon–4.*

Near Nidaros Cathedral, the **Trondheim Kunstmuseum** (Trondheim Art Gallery) houses more than 2,700 paintings dating from as early as 1800. Regional artists represented include Håkon Bleken, Jakob Weidemann, Adolph Tidemand, Christian Krohg, and Harald Solberg. There's a permanent exhibition of graphics by Edvard Munch. ⊠ *Bispegt. 7B* ☎ *73–53–81–80* ☜ *NKr 40* ☉ *June–Aug., daily 10–5; Sept.–May, Tues.–Sat. 11–4.*

Near the ruins of King Sverre's medieval castle is the **Sverresborg Trøndelag Folkemuseum,** which has re-creations of coastal, inland, and mountain-village buildings that depict life in Trøndelag during the 18th and

19th centuries. The Haltdalen stave church, built in 1170, is the northernmost preserved stave church in Norway. In the Old Town you can visit a 1900 dentist's office and an old-fashioned grocery that sells sweets. A special exhibit examines how the stages of life—childhood, youth, adulthood, and old age—have changed over the past 150 years. The audiovisual **Trønderbua** depicts traditional regional wedding ceremonies with artifacts and a 360-degree film. ⊠ *Sverresborg Allé* ☎ *73–89–01–00* ⊕ *www.sverresborg.no* ✉ *NKr 80* ☺ *June–Sept., daily 11–6; Oct.–May, weekdays 11–3, weekends noon–4.*

off the beaten path

MUNKHOLMEN (Monks' Island) – Now a swimming and recreation area, Monk's Island was Trondheim's execution grounds in ancient times. In the 11th century, Benedictine monks built a monastery on the island, likely one of the first monasteries in Scandinavia. In 1658 the monastery was converted into a prison and fort and, later, a customs house. There is a display of handicrafts in what was once the caretaker's house. Boats to the island depart from the fish market. ☎ *73–80–63–00* ⊕ *www.lilletorget.no* ✉ *NKr 50* ☺ *Mid-May–late Aug., boats depart daily on the hr 10–6.*

Norway's oldest institution of science, the **NTNU Vitenskapsmuseet** (NTNU Science Museum) covers flora and fauna, minerals and rocks, church history, southern Sami culture, and archaeological finds. The eclectic exhibits have relics from the Bronze Age as well as ecclesiastical articles from the 13th to 18th century. ⊠ *Erling Skakkes gt. 47* ☎ *73–59–21–45* ⊕ *www.ntnu.no/vmuseet* ✉ *Free* ☺ *May–mid-Sept., weekdays 9–4, weekends 11–4; mid-Sept.–Apr., Tues.–Fri. 9–2, weekends noon–4.*

Fodor'sChoice ★ Scandinavia's largest wooden palace, **Stiftsgården,** was built between 1774 and 1778 as the home of a prominent widow. Sold to the state in 1800, it's now the official royal residence in Trondheim. The architecture and interior are late baroque and highly representative of 18th-century high society's taste. Tours offer insight into the festivities marking the coronations of the kings in Nidaros Domkirke. ⊠ *Munkegt. 23* ☎ *73–80–89–50* ✉ *NKr 50* ☺ *June 1–19, Mon.–Sat. 10–3, Sun. noon–5; June 20–Aug. 20, Mon.–Sat. 10–5, Sun. noon–5. Tours on the hr.*

Off Munkegata near the water you can see an immense variety of seafood at **Ravnklohallen Fiskehall** (Fish Market; ☎73–52–55–21 ⊕www.ravnkloa.no). A former 1725 prison now houses the little **Trondhjems Sjøfartsmuseum** (Maritime Museum). Models of sailing ships, figureheads, marine instruments, and photographs of local ships make up the exhibits. Standouts include a harpoon gun from a whaler and recovered cargo from *The Pearl*, a frigate that was wrecked in 1781. ⊠ *Fjordgt. 6A* ☎ *73–89–01–00* ✉ *NKr 30* ☺ *June–Sept., daily 10–3.*

The **Modern Art Gallery** (⊠ Olav Tryggvasongt. 33 ☎ 73–87–36–80) shows contemporary art, including watercolors, lithographs, and art posters from Norway and abroad.

<table>
<tr><td>off the
beaten
path</td><td>**RINGVE MUSEUM** – Norway's national museum of music and musical instruments is on a country estate outside Trondheim. The **Museum in the Manor House,** the oldest section, focuses on instruments in the European musical tradition. Guides demonstrate their use. The **Museum in the Barn** features modern sound-and-light technology as well as Norwegian folk instruments. ⊠ *Lade Allé 60* ☎ *73–92–24–11* ⊕ *www.ringve.com* ✉ *NKr 70* ☉ *July–mid-Aug., daily 11–5; mid-Aug.–mid-Sept., daily 11–3; mid-Sept.–mid-Dec., Sun. 11–4.*</td></tr>
</table>

Where to Stay & Eat

Trondheim is known for the traditional dish *surlaks* (marinated salmon served with sour cream). A sweet specialty is *tekake* (tea cake), which looks like a thick-crust pizza topped with a lattice pattern of cinnamon and sugar. The city's restaurant scene is vibrant and evolving, with more and more international restaurants serving Continental food, and bars and cafés where the city's considerable student population gathers.

★ $$$–$$$$ ✕ **Bryggen Restaurant.** One of the city's most popular restaurants is on the bank of the Nid River. The 250-year-old warehouse exudes elegant country style, with blond woods and earthy tones. Most diners choose one of the prix-fixe menus, which are often based on traditional Norwegian ingredients such as fish and reindeer. The wine list is extensive, with many French and Italian choices. ⊠ *Øvre Bakklandet 66* ☎ *73–87–42–42* ⌕ *Reservations essential* ☰ *AE, DC, MC, V* ☉ *Closed Sun. No lunch.*

★ $$$–$$$$ ✕ **Havfruen Fiskerestaurant.** "The Mermaid" is Trondheim's foremost and most stylish fish restaurant. Taking its cues from France, the restaurant excels at bouillabaisse as well as many other fish dishes, which change seasonally. The warm decor uses orange, greens, and reds accented by wood. The wine list includes a wide range of whites, highlighting dry French varieties. ⊠ *Kjøpmannsgt. 7* ☎ *73–87–40–70* ☰ *AE, DC, MC, V* ☉ *Closed Sun. No lunch.*

$$–$$$$ ✕ **Vertshuset Tavern.** Housed in what was once a 1739 tavern in downtown Trondheim, this restaurant is now part of the Trøndelag Folk Museum. The traditional menu includes homemade fish cakes; *rømmegrøt* (sour-cream porridge); *spekemat* (cured meat); and *Trøndelag klubb,* the local variation on potato dumplings. ⊠ *Sverresborg Allé 7* ☎ *73–87–80–70* ☰ *AE, DC, MC, V.*

$$–$$$ ✕ **Grønn Pepper.** Tex-Mex is extremely popular throughout Norway, and this Trondheim restaurant serves a good rendition. Striped, vibrant Mexican blankets brighten up the hardwood floors and dark-wood furniture. Mexican beer and tequila go well with the fiery food on offer, which includes some Cajun and creole dishes. ⊠ *Søndregt. 17 and Fjordgt. 7* ☎ *73–53–26–30* ☰ *AE, DC, MC, V.*

$$–$$$ ✕ **Sushi Bar.** Trondheim's only sushi bar also serves other Japanese dishes in a bright and elegant space. Besides an excellent wine list, Japanese beer and sake are on the beverage menu. Come between 4 and 6 for early-dinner specials. ⊠ *Munkegt. 59* ☎ *73–52–10–20* ☰ *AE, DC, MC, V.*

$$$–$$$$ ✕⌂ **Britannia Hotel.** One of the Rica hotels, this classic in the heart of Trondheim opened in 1897. Luxurious rooms have regal yellow walls,

gold accents, and dark-wood furniture. The elegant Palmehaven Restaurant ($$) is popular for special occasions and serves breakfast, lunch, and dinner. You can dance here in the evening. The Jonathan Restaurant is more rustic and laid-back, and the Hjørnet Bar & Brasserie is ideal for steak tartare or a quick cup of coffee. ⊠ *Dronningensgt. 5, 7401* ☎ *73–800–800* 🖷 *73–800–801* ⊕ *www.britannia.no* ⤵ *247 rooms* ⚒ *3 restaurants, cable TV, in-room data ports, 2 bars, pub, meeting room* ☰ *AE, DC, MC, V.*

★ **$$$–$$$$** ✕🏨 **Radisson SAS Royal Garden Hotel.** This extravaganza of glass on the Nid River is Trondheim's largest hotel. Superb service and beautiful decor make a stay here memorable. The marble-accented atrium is full of thriving plants. Sun-kissed yellow rooms are subtly accented with deep blues and reds. Prins Olav Grill ($$$) is the hotel's main restaurant. The breakfast room Bakkus Mat & Vin is also ideal for lunch or a casual dinner overlooking the river. The Galleriet Bar is a popular meeting place for drinks. Musicians perform several nights a week in the Blue Garden bar. ⊠ *Kjøpmannsgt. 73, 7410* ☎ *73–80–30–00* 🖷 *73–80–30–50* ⊕ *www.radissonsas.com* ⤵ *298 rooms, 9 suites* ⚒ *Restaurant, café, cable TV, in-room data ports, indoor pool, gym, sauna, bar* ☰ *AE, DC, MC, V.*

$$–$$$$ 🏨 **Clarion Hotel Grand Olav.** This reasonably priced hotel is in the same building as Trondheim's large concert hall. The interior is decorated with vibrant paintings and rich, bold colors. ⊠ *Kjøpmannsgt. 48, 7010* ☎ *73–80–80–80* 🖷 *73–80–80–81* ⊕ *www.choicehotels.no* ⤵ *106 rooms* ⚒ *Cable TV, in-room data ports, bar, meeting rooms* ☰ *AE, DC, MC, V.*

Nightlife

Olavskvartalet is the center of much of the city's nightlife, with dance clubs, live music, bars, and cafés. The bustling **Mojo** (⊠ Nordregt. 24 ☎ 73–53–40–4–0) is a funky tapas restaurant and bar open until 3:30 AM on weekends. **Monte Cristo** (⊠ Prinsensgt. 38–40 ☎ 73–60–60–80) has a restaurant, bar, and dance club. Young people in search of cheap drinks, music, and dancing gravitate toward **Strossa** (⊠ Elgesetergt. 1 ☎ 73–89–95–10). **Café Remis** (⊠ Kjøpmannsgt. 12 ☎ 73–52–05–52) is one of the most popular gay clubs in Trondheim.

Downtown, in the area known as Solsiden (the Sunny Side), are several bars and clubs. **Blæst, Bar muda, and Luna Lounge** (⊠ TMV-Kaia 5, Nedre Elvehavn ☎ 73–60–06–10), are especially popular summer spots, partly because of their outdoor terraces. **Choco Boco** (⊠ Verfts gt. 2E ☎ 73–80–79–90) is a chocolate-obsessed café.

Arts

In late July and early August the annual **St. Olav Festival in Trondheim** (⊠ Dronningensgt. 1B ☎ 73–84–14–50 ⊕ www.olavsfestdagene.no) features a program of indoor and outdoor concerts, opera, and organ concerts at Nidaros Cathedral. Exhibits and children's activities are also staged. The **Trondheim Symphony Orchestra** (⊠ Olavskvartalet, Kjøpmannsgt. 46 ☎ 73–53–98–50 ⊕ www.tso.no) performs weekly concerts with internationally acclaimed soloists and conductors.

Sports & the Outdoors

CYCLING Some 300 **Trondheim Bysykkel City Bikes** can be borrowed in the city center. Parked in easy-to-see stands at central locations, the distinctive green bikes have shopping baskets. You'll need a 20-kroner piece to release the bike (your money's refunded when you return the bike to a parking rack).

The Trampe elevator ascends the steep Brubakken Hill near Gamle Bybro and takes cyclists nearly to Kristiansten Festning (Kristiansten Fort). Contact the tourist office to get the card you need in order to use the Trampe.

FISHING The Nid River is one of Norway's best salmon and trout rivers, famous for its large salmon (the record is 70 pounds). You can fish right in the city, but you need a license. For further information and fishing licenses, contact **TOFA (Trondheim og Omland Jakt- og Fiskeadministrasjon)** (⊠ Leirfossvn. 76 ☎ 73–96–55–80 ⊕ www.tofa.org).

HIKING & **Bymarka,** a wooded area on Trondheim's outskirts, has a varied and well-
WALKING developed network of trails—60 km (37 mi) of gravel paths, 80 km (50 mi) of ordinary paths, 250 km (155 mi) of ski tracks. The **Ladestien** (Lade Trail) is a 14-km (9-mi) trail that goes along the edge of the Lade Peninsula and offers great views of Trondheimsfjord. The **Nidelvstien Trail** runs along the river from Tempe to the Leirfossene waterfalls.

SKIING **Bymarka** and **Estenstadmarka,** wooded areas on the periphery of Trondheim, are popular with cross-country skiers. Bymarka's Skistua (ski lodge) also has downhill runs.

Vassfjellet Skisenter (☎ 72/83–02–00 ⊕ www.vassfjellet.com), 8 km (5 mi) south of Trondheim's city limits, has six tow lifts and 10 runs. There are facilities for downhill and telemark skiing as well as snowboarding and tobogganing. In season (roughly mid-October through Easter), the center is open daily, and ski buses run every evening and weekend.

SWIMMING The Trondheimsfjord and inland lakes are both options for swimming. **Trondheim Pirbadet** (⊠ Havnegt. 12 ☎ 73–83–18–00 ⊕ www.pirbadet. no) is Norway's largest indoor swimming center. There's a wave pool, a sauna, and a Jacuzzi as well as a gym here.

Shopping

Trondheim's **Mercur Centre** (⊠ Nordregt. ⊕ www.mercursenteret.no) and **Trondheim Torg** shopping centers have helpful staffs and interesting shops.

Arne Ronning (⊠ Nordregt. 10 ☎ 73–53–13–30) carries fine sweaters by Dale of Norway. Trondheim has a branch of the handicraft store **Husfliden** (⊠ Olav Tryggvasongt. 18 ☎ 73–83–32–30). For knitted sweaters by such makers as Oleana and Oda, try **Jens Hoff Garn & Ide** (⊠ Olav Tryggvasongt. 20 ☎ 73–53–15–27). Founded in 1770 and Norway's oldest extant goldsmith, **Møllers Gullsmedforretning** (⊠ Munkegt. 3) sells versions of the Trondheim Rose, the city symbol since the 1700s.

Mo i Rana

❷ *450 km (280 mi) north of Trondheim.*

Mo i Rana, meaning "Mo on the Ranafjord," is known as the "Arctic Circle City" because the Arctic Circle crosses the municipal area from east to west. The city has long been a center for iron and steel smelted from the ore supplied by nearby mines. Starting in Mo i Rana, in Helgeland—the Arctic Circle region—you can discover thrilling coastline, high mountains, and glaciers. Year-round activities include fishing, crabbing, mountain rambling, mountaineering, island-hopping, glacier-trekking, caving, canoeing, rowing, sailing, rafting, and skiing.

The **Grønligrotta** (Grønli Cave) is one of almost 200 caves 26 km (16 mi) northwest of Mo i Rana. With 7,920 feet of charted underground paths, many narrow passages, natural chimneys, and an underground river, it's the only illuminated Scandinavian show cave. For almost 100 years, tourists have been visiting the "grotta." A 40-minute tour takes you several hundred feet inside. There's an underground waterfall, naturally formed potholes, and a rock formation carved by glacial flow over thousands of years. ⊠ *Grønli* ☎ *75–13–25–86* 🖃 *NKr 80* ☉ *June 20–Aug. 30, daily 10–7.*

off the beaten path

SVARTISEN GLACIER – Glacier fans can hike on the Svartisen, which means "black ice." The second-largest glacier in Norway covers 370 square km (230 square mi); the Arctic Circle crosses the glacier inside the Saltfjellet–Svartisen Nasjonale Park. Several entrances to the park are accessible from Mo i Rana.

The easiest way to get to the glacier from Mo i Rana is to head north 32 km (20 mi) by car to Svartisvannet Lake. The boat *Svartisbåten* crosses the lake to within 2½ km (1½ mi) of the Østerdal arm of the glacier. From there it's a 3-km (2-mi) hike up to Austerdalsvatnet Lake and the glacier. Glacier walking is extremely hazardous and should never be attempted without a professional guide. Contact the **Svartisen Tourist Center** (⊠ Holandsfjord, Halsa ☎ 75–75–00–11) for referrals. Four-hour guided tours of the Engenbreen glacial arm are offered by **Svartisen bre-og turlag** (☎ 75–75–47–99 ⊕ www.svartisen.no). No previous experience is necessary.

Polarsirkelsenteret

❸ *80 km (50 mi) north of Mo i Rana.*

★ A bleak stretch of treeless countryside marks the beginning of the Arctic Crcle. The **Polarsirkelsenteret** (Arctic Circle Center) is right on the line in the Saltfjellet Mountains. Here you can build a small cairn as evidence you passed the circle. You can also get an Arctic Circle certificate to show the folks back home. ⊠ *Rte. E6, Rognan* ☎ *75–12–96–96 or 75–69–02–40* ⊕ *www.polarsirkelsenteret.no* 🖃 *NKr 50* ☉ *May and Sept., daily 9–6; June–Aug., daily 8 AM–10 PM.*

Bodø

❹ *174 km (108 mi) north of the Polarsirkelsenteret.*

Bodø, a modern city of about 43,000 just above the Arctic Circle, is best known as the terminus of the Nordlandsbanen railroad and the *Hurtigruten* (a coastal boat)—it's also the gateway to the Lofoten Islands and the north of Norway. The midnight sun is visible from June 2 to July 10, and the polar night descends from December 15 to December 29. Like many coastal towns, Bodø began as a small fishing community, but today it is a commercial and administrative center.

Bodø is the best base for boat excursions to the coastal bird colonies on the Væren Islands. Sea eagles soar high above town and perch on the rocks on nearby islands. The friendly city offers above-standard lodgings, entertainment, shopping, and outdoor activities. In August there's the **Nordland Festival of Music** (☎ 75–54–90–40 ⊕ www.nmfu.no).

The **Salten Museum,** in one of the city's oldest buildings (built in 1904), covers regional history, including the fishing industry and the changes that the 20th century brought about. An exhibit on Sámi culture features a 350-year-old wooden box with inscribed runes. There's also silver treasure that dates back 1,000 years to the Rønvik era: these English and Arabic coins and jewelry were discovered in 1919. The "Byen vårres" ("Our City") exhibition shows the history of Bodø. The museum's open-air section at Bodøsjøen has 14 historic buildings and a boat collection, which includes *Anna Karoline af Hopen,* the sole surviving Nordland cargo vessel, or *jekt.* ⊠ *Prinsensgt. 116* ☎ *75–52–16–40* ⊕ *www.museumsnett.no/nordlandsmuseet* ☒ *NKr 30* ⊙ *Mid-June–mid-Aug., daily 11–5; mid-Aug.–mid-Dec., weekdays 9–3.*

Down the road from Bodø's airport and 15 minutes from the town's center, the jumbo **Norwegian Aviation Museum** is housed in a building shaped like a propeller. The high-ceiling and spacious exhibition hall Rotunda illustrates "Man's Primeval Dream of Flight." On either side are exhibition halls, one for civilian aviation and the other for military aviation. Among the collection are a Junkers Ju-52, a U-2, and a Thunderwing Spitfire from 1993. Climb the control tower for an unforgettable view of the wild northern Norwegian landscape. Finally, take a turn on the flight simulators for a glimpse inside the controls of an F-16 or a Harrier. ⊠ *Olav V gt.* ☎ *75–50–78–50* ⊕ *www.aviationmuseum.no* ☒ *NKr 80* ⊙ *Mid-June–mid-Aug., Sun.–Fri. 10–7, Sat. 10–5; mid-Aug.–mid-June, weekdays 10–4, weekends 11–5.*

Set amid narrow fjords edging the peninsula, the **Old Kjerringøy Trading Post** has 15 well-preserved 19th-century buildings where Erasmus Zahl once made handsome profits buying and selling fish. Take a guided tour of the manor—many its original furnishings are intact. ⊠ *Rte. 834, 40 km (25 mi) north of Bodø, then 10-min ferry ride* ☎ *75–51–12–57* ⊕ *www.museumsnett.no/nordlandsmuseet* ☒ *NKr 45* ⊙ *Late May–mid-Aug, daily 10–5.*

Zahlfjøsen (Zahl's Farm). Author Knut Hamsun visited Kjerringøy in 1879 and found inspiration for his writing here. Several movies based on his novels were filmed here, including *Rosa and Benoni, The Telegraphist* (based on the book *Dreamers*), and *Pan*. An exhibition about the filming of Hamsun's literature includes clips from more than 20 films made since 1921. There is also locally produced art for sale here, and a boat-builder's workshop. For opening times, contact Destinasjon Bodø. ⊠ *Kjerringøy, Branch road RV 834, 40 km (25 mi) north of Bodø* ☎ *48–00–12–62* ✑ *NKr 30* ◷ *Late May–late-June, weekdays noon–3, Sat. noon–6, Sun. 1–6; late-June–Aug., Mon.–Sat. 11–6, Sun. 1–6.*

🕐 North Norway's major private collection of art and artifacts, **Atelier 88–Galleri Bodøgård** is known for its ethnographic collections. The history of Bodø and northern Norway is shown through exhibits on hunting and fishing, handicrafts, and agriculture, as well as the Russian prisoner-of-war camp Bodøgård. There are pictures and handicrafts for sale. ⊠ *Skeidalen 2, 2½ km (1½ mi) from Bodø city center* ☎ *75–56–32–41* ⊕ *www.bodogaard.no* ✑ *NKr 50* ◷ *May–Aug., daily 10–5; Sept.–Apr., weekdays 9–4.*

off the beaten path

ARTSCAPE NORDLAND – If you're an art lover, you can plan encounters with Artscape Nordland, an international art project involving artists from 18 countries. The Nordland county does not have an art museum and people have to travel long distances to study modern art in museums and galleries. The idea behind the project, begun in 1992 and completed in 1998, was to collect modern art and place one sculpture in every municipality, with the landscape as the backdrop to the art. Today sculptures like English artist Antony Gormley's *Havmann* (Ocean Man) are located in beautiful, varied, and often brutal landscapes along the coast of the Atlantic in 33 Nordland municipalities. ⊕ *www.skulpturlandskap.no.*

Where to Stay & Eat

$$–$$$ ✕⌂ **Landego Fyr.** Braving Vestfjord's pounding waves on Fyrholmen light-
Fodor$Choice house rock is this red-and-white cast-iron lighthouse that dates from 1902.
★ You can stay in the former lighthouse keepers' sky-blue and forest-green quarters, which maintain their original, wood-paneled, nautical style. Soak in the seawater-filled outdoor hot tub. Sea eagles, cormorants, and other sea birds keep you company, constantly circling overhead. Chef and manager Sindre Laksmark's fish dishes, especially the soups, are delicious. From the lighthouse's lookout, you can see as far as the Lofoten Islands on a clear day. Mainly available to groups, the lighthouse also accepts reservations from individuals, but only between July and early August. ⊠ *Eggsløysa, Bodø, 8005* ☎ *75–58–46–44 or 75–52–24–00* ⊕ *www.skagen-hotel.no* ⇆ *13 rooms* ⌂ *Restaurant, café, bar, meeting rooms* ☐ *AE, DC, MC, V.*

★ **$$–$$$** ⌂ **Skagen Hotel.** Skagen is a real gem of a hotel, known for its first-class, personal service. It has many regulars, so be sure to book early. The cherrywood rooms have different personalities, from artsy and crowded to elegant and understated. There are complimentary waffles and coffee in the afternoon, in the English-style Library Bar. A complimentary evening buffet is served between 7 and 10. ⊠ *Nyholmsgt. 11, 8005* ☎ *75-52-24-00* 📠 *75-52-59-30* ⊕ *www.skagen-hotel.no* 🛏 *72 rooms* ♨ *Restaurant, cable TV, in-room broadband, bar, library* ⊟ *AE, DC, MC, V.*

$$ 🏨 **Sulitjelma Hotel.** In remote former mining country, surrounded by northern Norway's highest mountains, the Sulitjelma Hotel, 100 km (62 mi) east of Bodø, is perfect for year-round wilderness adventures. In the Sulitjelma wilderness area you can ski, snowmobile, hike, fish, and more. The cozy rooms have modern furniture and are decorated in warm shades. The spa has massage, aromatherapy, and skin-care and other treatments. In late June the Mons Petter Festival celebrates the area's mining history with concerts, exhibitions, entertainment, athletic competitions, and mine tours. ⊠ *Nyholmsgt, 11, 8005 Bodø* ☎ *75-64-04-01* 📠 *75-64-06-54* ⊕ *www.skagen-hotel.no* 🛏 *58 rooms* ♨ *Restaurant, indoor pool, hot tub, sauna, spa, bar* ⊟ *AE, DC, MC, V.*

Cafés & Bars

Red leather sofas and a library theme set the scene at **Bonsak** (⊠ Sjøgt. 17 ☎ 75-52-29-90), a piano bar and nightclub named after former bishop Mathias Bonsak Krogh. Popular Italian restaurant **Da Carlo** (⊠ Glasshuset ☎ 75-50-46-12) also has an informal café and a terrace café and bar, TopHat. The café **En Kopp** (⊠ Storgt. 2, Radisson SAS Hotel ☎ 75-52-46-40) serves up freshly roasted coffee and light meals; lounge music plays in the background, and there are Internet terminals, board games, and regular cultural events. In summer you can sit outside. The **Kafé Kafka** (⊠ Sandgt. 5B ☎ 75-52-35-50) pays homage to its namesake author with a lovely painting of a Prague street scene. Come for the many desserts. Trendy **Metz** (⊠ Glasshuset ☎ 75-54-00-99) has an aquarium; it's a coffee bar by day and popular pub by night. The bohemian **Min Plass** (⊠ Sjøgt. 12 ☎ 75-52-26-88) is an easy place to lose an entire day, having a coffee or a cocktail, listening to live music, and dining on an international menu that offers everything from jambalaya to bruschettas. The American-style **Rock Café** (⊠ Tollbugt. 13b ☎ 75-50-46-30) attracts a younger crowd with its concerts, DJs, comedians, rock and pop, and big-screen TV showing sports events. If you're after a panoramic view of Bodø and the surrounding islands, head to **Top 13** (⊠ Storgt. 2, Radisson SAS Hotel ☎ 75-51-90-26).

Sports & the Outdoors

BIRD-WATCHING Bodø is known as the sea eagle capital, because nowhere else are there more of these majestic birds. In July and early August sea-eagle safaris are led by **Landego Lighthouse** (⊠ Eggsløysa ☎ 75-52-24-00 ⊕ www.skagen-hotel.no).

BOATING **Aurora Borealis** (☎ 75-52-17-75 ⊕ www.gox.no) offers sailing trips on S/Y *Goxsheim*, one of north Norway's biggest sailing vessels. Boats for fishing and other activities can be rented at several places in town. **Kjerringøy Rorbu Center** (☎ 75-58-50-07 ⊕ www.kjerringgoy-rorbusenter.no) has 14- to 17-foot boats with outboard motors and facilities for overnight accommodation. They also provide information on deep-sea fishing.

CYCLING Heading out on bicycle, especially on the Coastal Highway and Vest-fjord route, is an excellent way to explore Bodø and the surrounding countryside. **Destinasjon Bodø** rents bicycles; rates range from NKr 60 to NKr 150 per day; there are also special weekly rates. Contact the tourist office for more information.

DIVING **Polardykk** (☎ 75–52–52–93 or 91–64–23–30 ⊕ www.polardykk.no) offers diving excursions to shipwrecks and the world's strongest mael-strom. They conduct courses, and have equipment rental.

FISHING Local rivers and lakes are home to trout, char, and salmon. **Destinasjon Bodø** (✉ Sjøgt. 3 ☎ 75–54–80–00 ⊕ www.visitbodo.com) has a list of outfitters that sell fishing licenses. **Salmon Islands** (☎ 75–75–99–99 ⊕ www.salmon-islands.no) offers salmon fishing, deep-sea fishing, and rafting expeditions.

HIKING & **Bodø og Omegn Turistforening- BOT** (Bodø Mountain Touring Associa-
WALKING tion; ✉ Storgt. 17 ☎ 75–52–14–13), the local chapter of the Norwe-gian Mountain Touring Association, owns and operates 25 cabins at 15 sites. It also services the 600-km (373 mi) stretch from the Saltenfjord in the north to the Arctic Circle in the south. The association has youth, glacier, cave-exploring, and rock-climbing groups.

Saltstraumen

❺ *33 km (20 mi) southeast of Bodø on Rte. 80–17.*

Saltstraumen is a 3-km-long (2-mi-long) and 500-foot-wide section of water between the outer fjord, which joins with the sea, and the inner fjord basin. During high tide the volume of water rushing through the strait and into the basin is so great that whirlpools form. In fact, every six hours 500 million cubic yards of water rushes through the narrow sound. This is the legendary maelstrom (*malstrøm* in Norwegian)—and the strongest one in the world. The rush of water brings an abundance of fish, including cod, saithe, wolffish, and halibut, making the mael-strom a popular fishing spot.

On the shores of the maelstrom, you can visit **Saltstraumen Opplevelsesenter** (Saltstraumen Adventure Center). The center looks at 10,000 years of regional history, from the Ice Age, when humans first came here, through the Iron and Viking ages, and on to the present day. There's also an aquar-ium holding indigenous fish and an outdoor seal pond. ✉ *Saltstraumen, Hwy. RV 17 ☎ 75–51–91–11 ⊕ www.skagen-hotel.no 🎫 NKr 60 🕙 June–late Aug., daily 11–6.*

Every summer the **World Saithe Fishing Championships** (☎ 75–54–8000 ⊕ www.visitbodo.com) attract anglers from near and far to compete in catching saithe, also known as pollack or coalfish. There are different categories, such as fishing from land or from a boat, as well as overall awards for the largest saithe caught. The world record for saithe caught with a fishing pole was set here by a 22.7-kg (50-lb.) catch.

off the beaten path

BLODVEIMUSEET (Blood Road Museum) – Ninety minutes southeast of Bodø, in Rognan, the Blood Road Museum re-creates the sinister atmosphere of an icy northern Norway Nazi prison camp, where Russian, Serb, and Polish prisoners of war were incarcerated by the Germans between 1942 and 1945. **Saltdal Bygdetun,** a collection of historic houses, is a few yards away. The stretch of road between Saltnes and Saksenvik was called "Blood Road" by the prisoners of war who worked on it; this later became its official name, in 1995. War memorials can be seen at Stamnes, Sundby, Røkland, Storjord, and on the Arctic Circle. ⊠ *Bygetunet, Saltnes, Rognan* ☎ *75–68–22–90 or 75–68–23–00* ⊕ *www.museumsnett.no/ saltdalmuseum* ⊠ *NKr 30* ☉ *Mid-June–mid-Aug., weekdays 10–3:30, Sat. 1–4, Sun. 1–6.*

Where to Stay & Eat

$$ ✕⊞ **Saltstraumen Hotel.** Although it's rather plain, the hotel's position— it's practically on top of the maelstrom—makes it a memorable place to stay. The restaurant ($$) serves delicious steamed halibut in butter sauce. The Saltstraumen Gallery has regional paintings and other graphic art on display. ⊠ *8056 Saltstraumen* ☎ *75–50–65–60* ⊕ *www. saltstraumen-hotel.no* ⊠ *28 rooms, 4 suites, 12 cabins* ⌂ *Restaurant, meeting room* ⊟ *AE, DC, MC, V.*

Narvik

❻ *336 km (210 mi) north of Saltstraumen.*

Narvik was established as an ice-free port for exporting iron ore mined around the Swedish town of Kiruna.

From mid-June to September you can take a seven-minute trip on the **Narvik Mountain Lift,** a cable car that offers a view of the Ofotenfjord, the mountains, the midnight sun, and the city below. A restaurant is at the summit. Mount Fagernesfjellet and its marked trails are popular for hikes and hang gliding. A downhill mountain bike trail begins near the lift as well. ☎ *76–96–04–94* ⊠ *NKr 100 round-trip* ☉ *Mid-June–July, daily noon–1 AM; Aug., daily 1–9.*

In April and May 1940, the Battle of Narvik and the fight for ore left the city razed and began five years of Nazi occupation. The **Nordland Red Cross War Memorial Museum** recounts this dark period in Narvik's history through an exhibition of photographs, models, and World War II equipment. ⊠ *Torget–Narvik City Sq.* ☎ *76–94–44–26* ⊠ *NKr 40* ☉ *Mar.–June 2, daily 10–4; June 3–Aug. 19, daily 10–10; Aug. 20–Sept. 30, daily 10–4.*

Narvik has ancient rock carvings in the city center. At **Brennholtet** a rock carving estimated at 3,000 years old shows a Norwegian forefather's hope for good hunting. ⊠ *City center.*

At the turn of the 19th century this fishing- and agriculture-based community was transformed by the building of the Ofotbanen railway and the development of the ore shipment port. The **Ofoten Museum,** in the center of town, traces these developments through permanent and changing exhibitions. ⊠ *Administrasjonsveien 3* ☎ *76–96–00–50* ⊕ *www.ofoten.museum.no* ✉ *NKr 30* ☉ *Mid-June–mid-Aug., weekdays 10:30–3, weekends noon–3; mid-Aug.–mid-June, weekdays 10:30–3.*

off the beaten path

RALLARVEIEN – Here you can walk in the footsteps of the railway workers (navvies). This dirt track was vital to the building of Ofotbanen railway from Kiruna to Narvik. Some 5,000 men were employed in the construction of the ore shipment railway, which was completed in 1902. The road has been reopened as a site of cultural history and a cycling trail. It runs through a mountain realm between Sweden's Abisko and Rombaksbotn. Every summer, participants in the Svarta-Bjørn Walk (Black Bear Walk) take a train up to Katterat, wander down into Rombaksbotn, and take a boat back to Narvik. The lodge **Katterat Fjellstue** offers guided tours and gold panning. ⊠ *Navvies' Rd.* ☎ *90–85–45–84.*

Where to Stay & Eat

$$$ ✕⊞ **Radisson SAS Grand Royal Hotel.** Narvik's best hotel, this Radisson property has an elegant style and top-notch service. The Royal Blue restaurant ($$$) has a menu based on first-rate ingredients from the north of Norway. Both the fresh char and the meal of the day are highly recommended. The nightclub and traditional pub are popular with travelers and locals. ⊠ *Kongensgt. 64, 8501* ☎ *76–97–70–00* 📠 *76–97–70–07* ⊕ *www.grandroyal.no* ↪ *107 rooms* ⚪ *2 restaurants, sauna, 2 bars, convention center* ⊟ *AE, DC, MC, V.*

Sports & the Outdoors

CAVING Around Narvik there are innumerable caves to explore on guided tours or guided adventures. Contact the Narvik Tourist Information office for schedules.

DIVING During World War II about 50 planes were shot down and 46 ships sank in the Narvik area. Three of the 11 German battleships that were sunk are still under water. There are several licensed dive shops, with experienced instructors who specialize in wreck exploration. Contact **Narvik Wreck Diving** (☎ 90–72–11–05).

FISHING You can take fjord- and sea-fishing trips year-round on the *Delphin Senior,* a 46-foot fishing boat. Contact Narvik Tourist Information.

HIKING & WALKING In the area stretching from Troms in the north to Hellemofjorden/Tysfjord, **Narvik & Omegn Turistforening (NOT)** (☎ 76–94–37–90 ⊕ www.narvikfjell.no) owns and operates 22 mountain cabins at 11 sites. The mountainous terrain varies in height from 1,312 feet to 3,280 feet above sea level. NOT arranges various mountain hikes, some of which are designed for families. Contact the tourist information office for details.

MOUNTAINEERING **Nordland Adventures** (☎ 75–58–43–58 ⊕ www.nordlandturselskap.no) leads tours of the region's mountains, forests, and caves. Deep fjords and mountains up to 6,230 feet high make Narvik's landscape perfect for the walks and tours led by **North Norwegian School of Mountaineering** (☎ 76–07–49–11 ⊕ www.nord-norskklatreskole.no).

SKIING   Set amid fjords and mountains, the **Narvik Ski Center** (☎ 76–94–16–05 ⊕ www.narvikinfo.no ☼ Nov.–May) has challenging trails and off-piste skiing, making it an ideal stop for experienced skiers.

Lofoten & the Islands of the North

Extending out into the ocean north of Bodø are the Lofoten Islands, a 190-km (118-mi) chain of jagged peaks. In summer the farms, fjords, and fishing villages draw caravans of visitors, whereas in winter the coast facing the Arctic Ocean is one of Europe's stormiest. The midnight sun is visible here from late May to mid-July. If you are lucky enough to be visiting on a clear midnight, drive over to the western side, where the spear-shape mountains give way to flat, sandy beaches that look oddly fluorescent in the hush of night. It is a spectacular sight.

Until the 1950s, fishing was the area's only industry. As many as 6,000 boats with 30,000 anglers would mobilize between January and March for Lofotfisket, the world's largest cod-fishing event. They fished in open boats, and took shelter during stormy nights in *rorbuer,* simple cabins built right on the water. Today, income from tourism helps supplement that from the still-thriving fisheries, and many rorbuer have been converted into tourist lodgings. Lofotfisket, however, is still an annual tradition.

The principal islands of Lofoten are Austvågøy, Gimsøy, Vestvågøy, Flakstadøy, Moskenesøy, Værøy, and Røst. The best way to visit Lofoten is by car. On Austvågøy is **Svolvær,** the main town and administrative center for the villages on the islands. It's connected with the other islands by express boat and ferry, and with Bodø by coastal steamers and airplanes. The oldest part of Svolvær, about 1 km (½ mi) from the town center, is **Svinøya;** this is where, in 1828, the first fish-trading company in Lofoten was established. It faces Svolværgeita, the town's famous goat-shape mountain, and is an idyllic place full of fishermen's cabins and art galleries.

You can chat with artists at the **North Norwegian Artists' Center** and browse in the shop, which sells paintings, handicrafts, books, posters, and postcards. ⊠ *Svinøya, Svolvær* ☎ *76–06–67–70* ▣ *NKr 30* ☼ *Mid-June–Aug., daily 10–6; Sept.–mid-June, Mon. 11–3.*

Gunnar Berg (1863–93), Lofoten's most famous artist, was born and raised on Svinøya. The **Gunnar Berg Gallery** houses the largest collection of his works, including *The Battle of Trollfjord.* ⊠ *Gunnar Bergsvei 1, Svolvær* ☎ *76–06–99–30* ▣ *NKr 50* ☼ *June 15–Aug. 25, daily 10–6; Aug. 26–June 14, Tues.–Sun. 11–3.*

The **Lofoten War Memorial Museum** commemorates World War II events in Lofoten and northern Norway through an exhibition of uniforms and other objects. ⊠ *Svolvær town center, near Coastal Voyage docks* ☎ *91–73–03–28* ⊕ *www.lofotenkrigmus.no* ▣ *NKr 50* ☼ *June–mid-Sept., weekdays 10–4, rest of yr by appointment.*

The **Lofoten Temagalleri** (Lofoten Theme Gallery) focuses on whaling and Lofoten. See the short film *Islands in the Sea* by Bjørn Kenneth

Hansen. ⊠ *5-min walk from Svolvær town sq.* ☎ *76–07–03-36* ⊕ *www. lofoten-temagalleri.no* 🗐 *Free* ☉ *Daily 10–3:30; also open summer evenings 6–10.*

Just south of Svolvær, the hamlet of **Kabelvåg,** on the site of an old fishing settlement, provides the perfect introduction to the string of Lofoten Islands, their history, and their inhabitants. There is a cluster of museums less than a mile from the quiet village center.

The **Lofotmuseet** (Lofoten Museum; ☎ 76–07–82–23 ⊕ www. lofotmuseet.no 🗐 NKr 50), in an 1815 manor on the grassy edge of a fjord inlet, has exhibitions, including restored fishing cabins, that depict the rigorous life of a fishing community. It's open January through May, weekdays from 9 to 3 and weekends from 11 to 3; June through August, daily from 9 to 6; September, weekdays from 9 to 3 and Sunday from 11 to 3; and October through December, weekdays from 9 to 3.

Next door to Lofotmuseet, the **Galleri Espolin** (☎ 76–07–84–05 ⊕ www. galleri-espolin.no 🗐 NKr 50) exhibits dark, haunting paintings and lithographs depicting fishermen in stormy weather by nationally renowned artist Kaare Espolin Johnsen, who died in 1994. It's open in May, daily from 11 to 3; June through August, daily from 10 to 6; and September through April, Sunday to Friday, from 11 to 3.

☾ The **Lofot-Akvariet** (Lofoten Aquarium; ⊠ Storvågan ☎ 76–07–86–65 ⊕ www.lofotakvariet.no 🗐 NKr 70) includes a salmon farm exhibit, an aquarium, and seal and otter ponds.

Southwest of Kabelvåg is **Henningsvær.** This village is home to **Lofoten House Gallery,** which exhibits Lofoten-inspired paintings by well-known Norwegian artists, including Karl Erik Harr. You can also view a slide show by Frank A. Jenssen, and photos of white-tailed eagles. ⊠ *Henningsvær* ☎ *76–07–15–73* 🗐 *NKr 60* ☉ *Early Mar.–early Apr., daily noon–3; early Apr.–late May, by appointment; late May–late Aug., daily 10–7.*

Viking enthusiasts might want to veer northwest to Borg, where archaeologists unearthed a long, low chieftain's house—the largest Viking building ever discovered. For the Vikings, the banquet hall was a sacred place where religious and political rituals took place. Rebuilt exactly as it was, **Lofotr–The Viking Museum of Borg** houses the 1,000-year-old artifacts that were discovered here, including gold-foil fertility figures, Frankish pottery, and Rhineland glass. The objects document contact with Germany, France, and England. Reconstructed Viking ships and a boathouse are also on display. ⊠ *Prestergårdsvn. 59* ☎ *76–08–49–00* ⊕ *www.lofotr.no* 🗐 *NKr 90* ☉ *Mid-May–Aug., daily 10–7; Sept.–mid-May, Fri. 1–3 or by appointment.*

Other scenic stops include tucked-away **Nusfjord,** a 19th-century fishing village on an official European conservation list; **Sund,** with its smithy and small fisheries museum; and festive **Reine.**

The traditional **Gammelbua** (✉ On the harbor, Reine
☎ 76–09–22–22) serves excellent salmon mousse and chilled
Norwegian beer. Locals and tourists flock here to eat, drink, and
gossip.

A drive to the outer tip of Lofoten (130 km [80 mi] from Svolvær)—
gets you to a town with the enigmatic name of Å. Here you can visit
the **Norwegian Fishing Village Museum,** comprised of fishing houses dating back to the mid-19th century. Exhibitions include "Life in the Fishing Village," "the Lofoten Fishery," "Stockfish," and "Cod-Liver Oil."
You can take home a souvenir bottle of cod-liver oil or a cod-liver oil
lamp. ✉ *Å, Hwy. E10, 10 km (6 mi) from Reine* ☎ *76–09–14–88*
⊕ *www.lofoten-info.no/nfmuseum* 💰 *NKr 50* ⊙ *Mid-June–mid-Aug.,
daily 10:30–5:30; mid-Aug.–mid-June, weekdays 11–3:30.*

Off the tip of Moskenesøy, the last island on the Lofoten chain with a
bridge, is **Moskenesstraumen,** a maelstrom that's not as dramatic as Saltstraumen.

North of the Lofotens are the **Vesterålen Islands,** with similar, stunning
coastal landscapes, as well as fishing villages and rorbuer. There are fewer
tourists in Vesterålen than on the Lofoten Islands, which means lower
prices and more whale sightings.

Andenes island is the site of the islands' biggest attraction, Whale Safari. Andøya Island has many cultural monuments—medieval farms, Iron
Age remnants, and northern Norway's best preserved Iron Age farm.

Just off Nordmela, a nature reserve reachable by boat, is the largest colony
of common seals in Norway. The island of Bleiksøya is a haven for
seabirds, including 70,000 pairs of puffins. Sortland, the region's com-
munication and service center, is known as Blå Byen (Blue City) because
the city's artists have been painting the buildings blue. Stokmarknes,
known for its lively market place, is the home of the new Coastal
Steamer Museum.

East of the Vesterålen Islands, on Hinnøya, Norway's largest island, is
Harstad, where the year-round population of 23,000 swells to 42,000
during the annual June cultural festival (the lineup includes concerts,
theater, and dance) and the July deep-sea-fishing festival.

Where to Stay & Eat
Staying in a rorbu (fisherman's cabin) is essential to the Lofoten experience. Rorbu is a combination of the Norwegian words "bu" for
"dwelling" and "ro" for "rowing." The original, red-painted rorbuer
were usually comprised of two rooms, one for living quarters and the
other for the storage of nets, bait, and supplies. Rorbuer vary greatly
in standards; some date back to the 19th century, and others are brand
new. If you do stay in a rorbu, it is completely self-service, so expect to
shop for food to stock the refrigerator. Most villages have grocery
stores. You can bring linens, or rent them for about NKr 100.

$$$ ✕ **Fiskekrogen Restaurant.** This quayside restaurant in a former fish fac-
tory is family-run. Specialties of chef and owner Otto Asheim include

cod fish tongue, fried catfish, bacalao, "homemade" caviar directly from the sea, and the Krogen seafood plate—a selection of seasonal fare. ⊠ *Henningsvær* ☎ *76–07–46–52* ☰ *AE, DC, MC, V.*

$$$ ⌂ **Edvardas Hus.** Named after a character in Knut Hamsun's book, Edvardas Hus pays homage to Norway's famous author. Rooms are individually decorated with vintage furniture and antique reproductions. There's a fireplace in the dining room and a cozy library. On Tranøy, intimate Edvardas Hus is a favorite vacation spot for many Norwegians visiting Hamarøy island. ⊠ *8297 Tranøy* ☎ *75–77–21–82* ≞ *75–77–22–82* ⊕ *www.edvardashus.no* ⋧ *9 rooms* ⌂ *Dining room; no room TVs, no room phones, no smoking* ☰ *AE, DC, MC, V.*

★ **$$$** ⌂ **Henningsvær Bryggehotell.** Right on the quay of the island's largest fishing village, this member of Det Virkelig Gode Liv chain is one of Lofoten's finest hotels. Bright colors, stylish furniture, and modern art distinguish the hotel, which emphasizes high standards in facilities and service. ⊠ *8312 Henningsvær* ☎ *76–07–47–50* ≞ *76–07–47–30* ⊕ *www. dvgl.no* ⋧ *31 rooms, 1 suite* ⌂ *Restaurant, sauna, bar, lounge, meeting room* ☰ *V.*

$$$ ⌂ **Nyvågar Rorbuhotell.** Within the fishing village of Kabelvåg, Nyvågar is a rorbu and recreation complex, part of Det Virkelig Gode Liv hotel chain. Its red wooden rorbuer are well maintained and decorated in earthy colors. The Lorchstua restaurant serves seasonal, country-style dishes. Activities are well organized, with fishing-boat tours, eagle safaris, and deep-sea rafting, as well as evening entertainment. Nyvågar is a two-minute walk from Storvågan's museums. ⊠ *Storvåganveien 22, Kabelvåg, 8310* ☎ *76–06–97–00* ≞ *76–06–97–01* ⊕ *www.nyvaagar.no* ⋧ *30 rorbuer* ⌂ *Restaurant, meeting room* ☰ *AE, DC, MC, V.*

$$$ ⌂ **Rica Hotel Svolvær.** With red, rustic rorbu style, this hotel blends right into the Lofoten setting. The rooms are small yet comfortable. The lobby and Bauen restaurant are inside an unusual boat-shape building with panoramic harbor views. Try chef Karl Magnus's salmon or grilled dried fish. ⊠ *Lamholmen, 8301 Svolvær* ☎ *76–07–22–22* ≞ *76–07–20–01* ⊕ *www.rica.no* ⋧ *147 rooms* ⌂ *Restaurant, bar, convention center* ☰ *AE, DC, MC, V.*

$–$$$ ⌂ **Lofoten Rorbuferie.** In the quiet fishing village of Kabelvåg, these basic red rorbuer bear names like the Seagull and Sea Eagle. They are adequate, if basic, accommodations while you're on a fishing trip. Reserve far in advance, as the cabins get booked up quickly. ⊠ *8310 Kabelvåg* ☎ *76–07–84–44* ≞ *76–07–84–53* ⊕ *www.lofoten-rorbuferie.no* ⋧ *15 rorbuer* ☰ *AE, DC, MC, V.*

$$ ⌂ **Svinøya Rorbuer.** Svinøya is the oldest and most memorable part of Svolvær island. Many of the original wooden rorbuer here have been converted into tourist accommodations. Step outside and you'll see cod drying on fish racks and screaming seagulls. The reception area has a museum of curiosities like fishermen's wooden-soled rubber boots. The former fish landing station, built in 1828, is now Borsen Spiseri restaurant. It's known for fish dishes like *boknafisk* (half-dried cod). Explore the island's artistic side at the Northern Norwegian Artist Center, Studio Lofoten, and Gallery Gunnar Berg. ⊠ *Gunnar Bergsvei 2, Svinøya,*

8300 Svolvær ☎ *76–06–99–30* 🖳 *76–07–48–98* ⊕ *www.svinoya.no*
🛏 *30 rorbuer* ⚲ *Restaurant, bar* ▱ *AE, DC, MC, V.*

$–$$ 🖳 **Nusfjord Rorbuanlegg.** These secluded cabins are extremely attractive
for families—many stay for weeks. There's plenty to do—hiking, fishing, boating—in the surrounding area. For a glimpse at the midnight
sun, drive to Flakstad, at the other side of the island. Rowboats are included in the price of a rorbu, and you can rent fishing gear and mo-
torboats. ✉ *8380 Ramberg* ☎ *76–09–30–20* 🖳 *76–09–33–78* 🛏 *34*
1- or 2-bedroom rorbuer ⚲ *Restaurant, pub, laundry facilities* ▱ *AE,*
DC, MC, V.

Sports & the Outdoors

BIRD-WATCHING   A high-pitched hum emanates from some of northern Norway's arctic
island cliffs, which pulsate with thousands of birds. From Moskenes,
just north of Å, or from Bodø, you can take a ferry to the bird sanctuaries of **Værøy** and **Røst.** Many types of seabirds inhabit the cliffs, particularly *eider* (sea ducks). From Røst you can take boat trips to the
cliff-side seabird colonies and to Skomvær Lighthouse; from Reine,
boats visit the seabird colonies of rocky Værøy, where puffins and cormorants live. Contact **Eventyr Rafting** (☎ 76–09–20–00)

COASTAL CAVES   There are coastal caves, some 100 yards deep and 50 yards tall, at the
tip of Lofotodden headland. Red Stone Age cave drawings were found
in the caves. **Eventyr Rafting Lofoten** (☎ 76–09–20–00 ⊕ www.lofoten-
info.no/rafting) organizes daily guided tours to the Refsvikhula cave. They
depart from Reine on a giant rubber dinghy.

CYCLING   In Lofoten many accommodations have bicycles available for rent. Or
you can contact the tourist offices in Moskenes and Leknes for information about hiring bicycles.

DIVING &   Consider donning a wetsuit, diver's mask, and snorkel for an underwater
UNDERWATER   safari with **Lofoten Opplevelser** (☎ 99–23–11–00 ⊕ www.lofoten-
SAFARIS   opplevelser.no). **Lofotdykk** (☎ 99–63–91–66 ⊕ www.lofotdykk.no) organizes dives, overnight accommodation, tank refills, and equipment
rental.

FISHING   Book with the adventure-tour company **XXLofoten** (☎ 91–65–55–00
⊕ www.xxlofoten.no) to take a fishing trip on the *Symra*. The restaurant at the Henningsvær Bryggehotell will prepare your cod catch for
you. XXLofoten also organizes mountaineering, skiing, and hiking
trips.

MOUNTAINEERING   The **North Norwegian School of Mountaineering** (☎ 76–07–49–11 ⊕ www.
nordnorskklatreskole.no) is based in Henningsvær. The school offers week-
or day-long mountaineering courses and guided mountain tours, and
has a shop that sells mountaineering equipment. Climbs of famous
Svolværgeita Peak take place daily in summer. The school's café/pub,
Den Siste Viking (the Last Viking), is often described as a combination
of English pub, Nepalese tea house, and Everest base camp.

WATER SPORTS   **Coastal Odyssey** (☎ 76–07–52–64 ⊕ www.coastalodyssey.com) gives
guided tours, rents kayaks, and plans expeditions and tours. **Jann's Adventure Lofoten** (☎ 76–07–89–10 ⊕ www.lofoten-aktiv.no) offers lessons

in sea kayaking and rents kayaks. They also can arrange hiking, mountain walks, cycling, and fishing trips, and ski rentals.

WHALE-
WATCHING

The island of Andøya, part of the Vesterålen Islands, is the northernmost place in the world where sperm whales can be watched. The season runs from late May to mid-September. Brush up on your knowledge of the sea mammal at the island's **Whale Centre** (☎ 76–11–56–00), where you can see an exhibition on whales and whale research and a slide show. Since 1988 **Whale Safari** (☎ 76–11–56–00 ⊕ www.whalesafari. no) has organized whale watches. They have qualified researcher guides, and a whale-sighting guarantee. **Whale Tours A/S** (✉ Stø ☎ 76–13–44–99 ⊕ www.whaletours.no) scours the sea for minke, sperm, and killer whales, seals, and seabirds.

Tromsø

❼ *318 km (197 mi) northeast of Harstad.*

Tromsø surprised visitors in the 1800s: they thought it very sophisticated and cultured for being so close to the North Pole. It looks the way a polar town should—with ice-capped mountain ridges and jagged architecture that is an echo of the peaks. The midnight sun shines from May 21 to July 21, and it is said that the northern lights decorate the night skies over Tromsø more than over any other city in Norway. Tromsø is about the same size as Luxembourg, but home to only 58,000 people. The city's total area—2,558 square km (987 square mi)—is actually the most expansive in Norway. The downtown area is on a small, hilly island connected to the mainland by a slender bridge. The 13,000 students at the world's northernmost university are one reason the nightlife here is uncommonly lively for a northern city.

The **Ishavskatedralen** (Arctic Cathedral) is the city's signature structure. Designed by Jan Inge Hovig, it's meant to evoke the shape of a Sámi tent as well as the iciness of a glacier. Opened in 1964, it represents northern Norwegian nature, culture, and faith. The immense stained-glass window depicts the Second Coming. ✉ *Tromsdalen* ☎ *77–75–34–40* 🖬 *NKr 22* ⊗ *June–mid-Aug., Mon.–Sat. 9–7, Sun. 1–7; mid-Aug.–May, daily 4–6.*

The **Tromsø Museum, Universitetsmuseet,** northern Norway's largest museum, is dedicated to the nature and culture of the region. Learn about the northern lights, wildlife, fossils and dinosaurs, minerals and rocks, and church art from 1300 to 1800. Outdoors you can visit a Sámi *gamme* (turf hut), and a replica of a Viking longhouse. ✉ *Universitetet, Lars Thørings v. 10* ☎ *77–64–50–00* ⊕ *www.imv.uit.no* 🖬 *NKr 30* ⊗ *Mid-Sept.–mid-May, weekdays 9–3:30, weekends 11–5; mid-May–mid-June, daily 9–6; mid-June–mid-Aug., daily 9–8; mid-Aug.–mid-Sept., daily 9–6.*

In an 1830s former customs warehouse, the **Polarmuseet i Tromsø** (Polar Museum) documents the history of the polar region, focusing on Norway's explorers and hunters. ✉ *Søndre Tollbugt. 11B* ☎ *77–68–43–73* ⊕ *www.polarmuseum.no* 🖬 *NKr 43* ⊗ *Mar.–mid-June, daily 11–5; mid-*

June–mid-Aug., daily 10–7; mid-Aug.–Sept., daily 11–5; Oct.–Feb., daily 11–3.

Ludvik Mack founded **Macks Ølbryggeri** (Mack's Brewery) in 1877 and it is still family-owned. You can take a guided tour, at the end of which you're given a beer stein, pin, and a pint of your choice in the Ølhallen pub. Call ahead to reserve a place on the tour. ⊠ *Storgt. 5–13* ☎ *77–62–45–00* ⊕ *www.mack.no* ✉ *NKr 100* ☉ *Guided tours June–Aug., Mon.–Thurs. at 1 and 3:30; Sept.–May, Mon.–Thurs. at 1.*

🐧 The adventure center **Polaria** examines life in and around the polar and Barents regions with exhibits on polar travel and arctic research, and a panoramic film from Svalbard. The aquarium has sea mammals, including seals. ⊠ *Hjarmar Johansens gt. 12* ☎ *77–75–01–00* ⊕ *www.polaria. no* ✉ *NKr 80* ☉ *Mid-May–mid-Aug., daily 10–7; mid-Aug.–mid-May, daily noon–5.*

★ **Tromsø Botaniske Hage** (Tromsø Botanic Garden) has plants from the Antarctic and Arctic as well as mountain plants from all over the world. Encompassing 4 acres, the garden has been designed as a natural landscape, with terraces, slopes, a stream, and a pond. Guides are available by advance arrangement. ⊠ *Tromsø University, Breivika* ☎ *77–64–50–78* ⊕ *www.uit.no/botanisk* ✉ *Free* ☉ *Daily 24 hrs.*

🐧 To get a sense of Tromsø's immensity and solitude, take the **Fjellheisen** (cable car) from behind the cathedral up to the mountains, just a few minutes out of the city center. **Storsteinen** (Big Rock), 1,386 feet above sea level, has a great city view. In summer a restaurant is open at the top of the lift. ⊠ *Sollivn. 12* ☎ *77–63–87–37* ✉ *NKr 80* ☉ *Apr.–Aug., daily 10–5; Sept.–Mar., weekends 10–5.*

Where to Stay & Eat

$$ ✕ **Vertshuset Skarven.** Whitewashing recalls the Greek Islands at this landmark restaurant known for its fish. Sample the fish soup, beef stew, or seal lasagna. The lunch buffet for only NKr 85 is good value. The Skarvens Biffhus and Sjømatrestauranten Arctandria restaurants are in the same building. ⊠ *Strandtorget 1* ☎ *77–60–07–20* ⌕ *Reservations essential* ☰ *AE, DC, MC, V.*

★ **$$–$$$$** 🏨 **Rica Ishavshotel.** Shaped like a ship, Tromsø's snazziest hotel is right at the harbor and stretches over the sound toward Ishavskatedralen. Inside, polished wood furnishings with brass trim evoke the life of the sea. The breakfast buffet is one of the best in Norway, and even includes vitamins. Guests represent a mixture of business executives, tourists, and participants at scientific conferences. ⊠ *Fr. Langesgt. 2, Box 196, 9252* ☎ *77–66–64–00* 🖷 *77–66–64–44* ⊕ *www.rica.no* 🛏 *180 rooms* ⌕ *Restaurant, cable TV, in-room data ports, 2 bars, convention center, meeting rooms* ☰ *AE, DC, MC, V.*

$$$ 🏨 **Comfort Home Hotel With.** This comfortable hotel on the waterfront has a great location. Breakfast and dinner are included in the room price. The ever-popular top-floor lounge has skylights. ⊠ *Sjøgt. 35–37, 9257* ☎ *77–66–42–00* 🖷 *77–68–96–16* ⊕ *www.with.no* 🛏 *76 rooms* ⌕ *Dining room, cable TV, in-room data ports, sauna, Turkish bath, lounge, meeting room* ☰ *AE, DC, MC, V* ⏍ *MAP.*

$$–$$$ ☒ **Comfort Hotel Saga.** Centrally located on a pretty town square, this hotel has basic rooms that are loaded with blond wood and warm colors. The hotel serves a free buffet-style dinner for all guests. ⊠ *Richard Withs pl. 2, 9008* ☎ *77–68–11–80* 🖷 *77–60–70–00* ⊕ *www.sagahotel. no* ↘ *67 rooms* ♺ *Dining room, cable TV, in-room data ports* 🖃 *AE, DC, MC, V.*

$$–$$$ ☒ **Radisson SAS Hotel Tromsø.** You can see splendid views over the Tromsø shoreline at this modern hotel. Rooms are tiny but stylish, and the service is professional and efficient. ⊠ *Sjøgt. 7, 9008* ☎ *77–60–00–00* 🖷 *77–68–54–74* ⊕ *www.radissonsas.com* ↘ *195 rooms, 2 suites* ♺ *Restaurant, pizzeria, cable TV, in-room data ports, sauna, 2 bars* 🖃 *AE, DC, MC, V.*

Nightlife

Rock music and the city's largest selection of beer are at the **Blå Rock Café** (⊠ Strandgt. 14–16 ☎ 77–61–00–20), which has live concerts and DJs on weekends. The university's café and cultural center **DRIV** (⊠ Søndre Tollbod gt. 3 ☎ 77–60–07–76) is in a 1902 quayside building. Concerts, theater, and other cultural events are staged here. One of the city's largest cafés, **Meieriet Café & Storpub** (⊠ Grønnegt. 37/39 ☎ 77–61–36–39) has soups and wok dishes, billiards, backgammon, newspapers, and DJs on weekends. Since 1928, polar explorers, arctic skippers, hunters, whalers, and sealers have been meeting at Mack Brewery's **Ølhallen** (⊠ Storgt. 5 ☎ 77–62–45–80). At **Rica Ishavshotel** (⊠ Fr. Langesgt. 2 ☎ 77–66–64–00) you can see some of the best views in the city from the fifth-floor Skibsbroen Bar. **Victoria Fun Pub/Subsirkus/Amtmandens Datter** (⊠ Grønnegt. 81 ☎ 77–68–49–06), a lively evening entertainment complex, has something for everyone. Subsirkus has bands and attracts a young crowd, while a broader range of ages is found at the English-style Victoria. The smoky Amtmandens Datter is a mellow Continental café.

Sports & the Outdoors

DIVING **Dykkersenteret** (⊠ Stakkevollveien 72 ☎ 77–69–66–00 ⊕ www. dykkersenteret.no), the world's northernmost five-star PADI center, sells and rents equipment and gives guided diving tours.

DOGSLEDDING Some 20 km (12 mi) outside the city, **Tromsø Villmarkssenter** (☎ 77–69–60–02 ⊕ www.villmarkssenter.no) organizes winter dogsledding trips, glacier walking, kayaking, summit tours, and Sámi-style dinners, which take place around a campfire inside a *lavvu* (a Sámi tent).

HIKING & Tromsø has more than 100 km (62 mi) of walking and hiking trails in
WALKING the mountains above the city. They're reachable by funicular. Stay overnight in the middle of the Lyngen Alps, then set out for guided mountain and glacier walking with **Bo-med-oss** (☎ 77–71–06–92 ⊕ www.bo-med-oss.no). **Svensby Tursenter** (☎ 77–71–22–25) offers accommodation in small, self-serviced huts at the foot of the Lyngen Alps and arranges dogsledding, northern lights–viewing safaris, and fishing tours. **TROMSO Troms Turlag-DNT** (☎ 77–68–51–75 ⊕ www.turistforeningen.no) organizes tours and courses and has overnight cabins.

HORSEBACK RIDING **Holmeslet Gård** (☎ 77–61–9974) has horseback riding, carriage tours, northern lights–viewing adventures, and sleigh rides.

SKIING Eight minutes away by funicular, **Tromsø Alpine Ski Center** (☎ 77–60–66–80) is a convenient place for downhill skiing. There are also 71 km (43 mi) of cross-country trails, all of which are floodlighted.

en route
The drive from Tromsø to Alta is mostly along the coast. At one point you'll drive along the **Kvænangsfjellet Ridge,** where Kautokeino Sámi spend the summer in turf huts—you might see a few of their reindeer along the way. Thirteen kilometers (8 mi) west of Alteidet you'll pass by **Øksfjordjøkelen,** the only glacier in Norway that calves (separates or breaks) into the sea.

Alta

❽ *409 km (253 mi) northeast of Tromsø, 217 km (134 mi) from the North Cape.*

Alta, population 17,020, has three centers—Bossekop, which keeps old trading and market traditions; Elvebakken, in the east, with the airport and harbor; and the city center itself. The borough encompasses the mineral-rich island of Stjernøya, Langfjorden, and fishing villages on the banks of the Altafjord. Alta serves as the transportation, service, trade, research, and education center for the regions of West Finnmark and North Troms. Most travelers spend the night here before ascending to the North Cape.

Northern Europe's biggest canyon is the **Sautso–Alta Canyon,** on the Alta River, where you can go hiking and take riverboat trips and bus tours. At the **Alta Hydroelectric Power Station** you can view the reservoir and concrete dam through a panoramic window. Contact the **Destination Alta tourist office** (☎ 78–45–77–77) for information.

off the beaten path
ALTA MUSEUM – It's worth a trek to Hjemmeluft, southwest of the city, to see four groupings of 2,500- to 6,200-year-old prehistoric rock carvings encompassing 3,000 figures. These are the largest groupings of prehistoric rock carvings in Europe. The pictographs were discovered in 1972 and form part of the museum, which is a UNESCO's World Heritage Site. Exhibits cover prehistoric Finnmark and local history. The museum café has a stunning view of Altafjord, a souvenir shop, and playground. ✉ *Altaveien 19* ☎ *78–45–63–30* ⊕ *www.alta.museum.no* 🎫 *NKr 40* ⊙ *May and Sept., daily 9–6; June–Aug., daily 8–9; Oct.–Apr., weekdays 9–3, weekends 11–4.*

Where to Stay

$$–$$$ 🏨 **Rica Hotel Alta.** The decor here is light and airy, from the reflectors on the ceilings of public rooms to the white furniture in the guest rooms. ✉ *Lokkevn. 1, 9501* ☎ *78–48–27–00* 🖷 *78–48–27–77* ⊕ *www.rica.no* 🛏 *155 rooms* ⚐ *2 restaurants, cable TV, some in-room data ports, sauna, 2 bars, lobby lounge, nightclub, meeting rooms* ▭ *AE, DC, MC, V.*

★ **$$$** 🏨 **Alta Igloo Hotel.** Looking like a huge ice cube jutting out on the horizon, this amazing igloo hotel is completely made of snow and ice—the rooms, the beds, even the glasses in the bar. Besides the totally frozen bar, there's an ice gallery, an ice chapel, and several lounges. And the hotel is decorated throughout with spectacular ice sculptures. Although room temperature is a chilly -4°C (25°F), you'll sleep warmly in sleeping bags on reindeer-hide mattresses. ⊠ *Alta Friluftspark, Storelvdalen, 9501* 🕾 *78–43–33–78* 🖷 *78–43–34–65* ⊕ *www.alta-friluftspark.no* 🛏 *20 rooms, 2 suites* ⅛ *Bar, lounge* ▭ *AE, DC, MC, V.*

Sports & the Outdoors

On the banks of Alta River, **Alta Friluftspark AS Leisure Park** (🕾 78–43–33–78 ⊕ www.alta-friluftspark.no) has snowmobile safaris, riverboat trips, fishing, reindeer racing, dogsled rides, and Sámi lavvu for overnight stays. It also has a hotel, the Alta Igloo.

DOGSLEDDING Whether half-, full-day, or longer excursions, sled-dog tours are a classic winter activity on Finnmarksvidda. Contact **Canyon Huskies** (🕾 78–43–33–06 ⊕ www.canyonhuskies.no), **HolmenHundesenter** (🕾 78–43–66–45 ⊕ www.holmenhundesenter.no), or **Parken Gård Husky** (🕾 78–48–23–13 ⊕ www.parkengaard-husky.no).

FARM VISITS One of the first Finnmark farms, **Altafjord Camping** is now a regional farm museum that was occupied by German soldiers during World War II. The battleship *Sharnehorst* was anchored nearby. Sámi reindeer herders, who have their summer settlements in Langfjordbotn, have frequent contact with the farm. Accommodation facilities include 25 huts, camping spaces, and a big communal hot tub. ⊠ *Hwy. E6, 80 km (50 mi) west of Alta, 3 km (2 mi) from Troms county border* 🕾 *78–43–28–24* ⊕ *www.altafjord-camping.no* ☉ *June–Sept., daily. Call for hrs.*

FISHING **AKU Finnmark** (🕾 78–43–48–40 ⊕ www.aku-finnmark.no) leads deep-sea, salmon, and other types of fishing trips. You can go on a fishing trip on the famed river Bubbelen (The Bubble), which is actually an underground spring; contact **Altafjord Adventures and Camping** (🕾 78–43–28–24 ⊕ www.altafjord-camping.no) to organize an expedition. They also offer outings for deep-sea fishing below glaciers. You can also rent boats and fishing tackle here.

Hammerfest

❾ *145 km (90 mi) north of Alta.*

The world's northernmost town is one of the most widely visited and oldest places in northern Norway. "Hammerfest" means "mooring place" and refers to the natural harbor formed by the crags in the mountain. In 1891 the residents of Hammerfest, tired of the months-long night that winter always brought, decided to brighten the situation. They purchased a generator from Thomas Edison, and Hammerfest thus became the first city in Europe to have electric street lamps.

On Mount Salen, **Mikkelgammen** (🕾 78–48–62–04 ⊕ www.mikkelgammen.no) is a traditional turf hut where you can learn about

Sámi culture and traditions. Gather around a campfire for a meal of *bidos,* a Sámi reindeer dish. *Joik,* a kind of singing-chanting, is performed, and stories are told. You can also participate in reindeer herding in winter. Contact the tourist office for information on both programs.

Although it covers Finnmark's history since the Stone Age, the **Museum of Post-War Reconstruction** mainly focuses on World War II, when Finnmark's population was forced by the German army to evacuate, and the county was burnt to the ground as part of a "scorched earth" policy. Through photographs, videos, and sound effects, the museum recounts the residents' struggle to rebuild their lives. The exhibition includes authentic rooms that were built in caves after the evacuation, as well as huts and postwar homes. ✉ *Kirkegt. 21* ☎ *78–42–26–30* ⊕ *www. museumsnett.no/gjenreisningsmuseet* 💳 *NKr 40* ☉ *Jan.–mid-June, daily 11–2; mid-June–late Aug., daily 9–4; late Aug.–Dec., daily 11–2.*

The **Royal and Ancient Polar Bear Society** was founded by two businessmen whose goal was to share the town's history as a center for hunting and commerce. Exhibits depict aspects of arctic hunts, including preserved and stuffed polar bears, seals, lynx, puffins, and wolves. ✉ *Town Hall basement* ☎ *78–41–31–00* 💳 *NKr 20* ☉ *Call for hrs.*

Where to Stay & Eat

$$–$$$ ✕🍴 **Rica Hotel Hammerfest.** Guest rooms here are basic and small, but fairly comfortable. The restaurant serves hearty local dishes, and the hotel nightclub gets crowded on Saturday. ✉ *Sørøygt. 15, 9600* ☎ *78–41–13–33* 🖨 *78–41–13–11* ⊕ *www.rica.no* 🛏 *86 rooms* ♨ *Restaurant, cable TV, sauna, bar, nightclub, convention center* ☰ *AE, DC, MC, V.*

Honningsvåg

🔟 *130 km (80 mi) northeast of Hammerfest.*

Honningsvåg was completely destroyed at the end of World War II, when the Germans burned everything as they retreated. The town's northerly location and infrastructure have since made it one of the most important harbors in Norway.

Many people make an 18-km (11-mi) round-trip hike to **Knivskjelodden** (Crooked Knife), Europe's northernmost point. It has a spectacular view toward the North Cape Plateau. You can write your name in the hiking association's minute book and buy a diploma attesting to your visit.

The **Nordkappmuseet** (North Cape Museum), on the third floor of Nordkapphuset (North Cape House), documents the history of the fishing industry in the region as well as the history of tourism at the North Cape. You can learn how the trail of humanity stretches back 10,000 years and about the development of society and culture in this region. ✉ *Fiskerivn. 4* ☎ *78–47–28–33* ⊕ *www.museumsnett.no/ nordkappmuseet* 💳 *NKr 30* ☉ *June–mid-Aug., Mon.–Sat. 10–7, Sun. noon–7; mid-Aug.–May, weekdays noon–4.*

Where to Stay & Eat

$$ ✕⊠ **Rica Hotel Honningsvåg.** Right on the harbor, the town's best hotel has reasonably priced rooms. They're bright and cheerful, decorated in yellow and light woods. Bryggen Restaurant ($$) is a good choice for traditional food. The hotel is open only from May to August. ⊠ *Vågen 1, 9750* ☎ *78–47–23–33* 🖷 *78–47–33–79* ⊕ *www.rica.no* 📞 *174 rooms* ⚬ *Restaurant, bar, sauna, meeting room* ⊟ *AE, DC, MC, V* ⊘ *Closed Sept.–Apr.*

Nordkapp

⑪ *34 km (21 mi) north of Honningsvåg.*

On your journey to the Nordkapp (North Cape), you'll see an incredible treeless tundra, with crumbling mountains and sparse dwarf plants. The subarctic environment is very vulnerable, so don't disturb the plants. Walk only on marked trails and don't remove stones, leave car marks, or make campfires. Because the roads are closed in winter, the only access is from the tiny fishing village of Skarsvåg via Sno-Cat, a thump-and-bump ride that's as unforgettable as the desolate view.

The contrast between this near-barren territory and **Nordkapphallen** (North Cape Hall), the tourist center, is striking. Blasted into the interior of the plateau, the building is housed in a cave and includes an ecumenical chapel, a souvenir shop, and a post office. Exhibits trace the history of the cape, from Richard Chancellor, an Englishman who drifted around it and named it in 1533, to Oscar II, king of Norway and Sweden, who climbed to the top of the plateau in 1873. Celebrate your pilgrimage to the Nordkapp at Café Kompasset, Restaurant Kompasset, or at the Grotten Bar coffee shop. ⊠ *Nordkapplatået* ☎ *78–47–68–60* 🖷 *78–47–68–61* ⊕ *www.visitnorthcape.no* 🎫 *NKr 190* ⊘ *Call for hrs.*

Sports & the Outdoors

BIRD SAFARIS **Gjesvær Turistsenter** (☎ 78–47–57–73 ⊕ www.birdsafari.com) organizes bird safaris and deep-sea fishing. **Nordkapp Reiseliv** (☎ 78–47–70–30 ⊕ www.northcape.no) books adventures and activities including bird safaris, deep-sea fishing, boat excursions, and winter expeditions.

DIVING Scuba-dive at the top of Europe with **North Cape Adventures** (☎ 78–47–22–22 ⊕ www.northcapeadventures.com), which also provides deep-sea rafting, kayaking, ski and guided tours, and bike rentals.

RAFTING Deep-sea rafting is as exhilarating as it is beautiful. Among the tours offered is a three-hour trip to the North Cape. Call **Nordkapp Safari** (☎ 78–47–52–33).

Trondheim & the North Cape A to Z

To research prices, get advice from other travelers, and book travel arrangements, visit www.fodors.com.

AIR TRAVEL

CARRIERS SAS Braathens, Norwegian, Widerøe, and Arctic Air are the major carriers offering extensive connections throughout northern Norway.

Widerøe flies to 19 destinations in the region, including Honningsvåg, the airport closest to the North Cape.

☎ Airlines & Contacts Arctic Air ☎ 78-98-77-01 ⊕ www.arctic.no. **Finnair** ☎ 810-01-100 in Oslo ⊕ www.finnair.com. **Norwegian** ☎ 815-21-815⊕ www.norwegian.no. **SAS Braathens** ☎ 815-20-400⊕ www.sasbraathens.no. **Widerøe** ☎ 810-01-200.

AIRPORTS

Trondheim's Værnes Airport is 32 km (21 mi) northeast of the city. With the exception of Harstad, all other cities in northern Norway are served by airports less than 5 km (3 mi) from the center of town. Tromsø is a crossroads for air traffic between northern and southern Norway and is served by SAS Braathens and Widerøe. Honningsvåg is served by Widerøe.

☎ Airport Information Honningsvåg ☎78-47-29-92. **Tromsø Airport** ☎77-64-84-00. **Trondheim Værnes Airport** ☎ 74-84-33-00.

BOAT & FERRY TRAVEL

Hurtigruten (the coastal express boat, which goes to 35 ports from Bergen to Kirkenes) stops at Trondheim, southbound at St. Olav's Pier, Quay 16, northbound at Pier 1, Quay 7. Other stops between Trondheim and the North Cape include Bodø, Stamsund and Svolvær (Lofotens), Sortland (Vesterålen), Harstad, Tromsø, Hammerfest, and Honningsvåg.

For travel on the *Hurtigruten* between any harbors, it is possible to buy tickets on the boats. OVDS (Ofotens og Vesterålens Dampskibsselskap), in partnership with TFDS (Troms Fylkes Dampskibsselskap), operates the Coastal Express ferries and express boats that serve many towns in the region.

Getting to the Lofoten Islands is easiest and most enjoyable by taking the *Hurtigruten* from Bodø or another coastal port of call.

☎ Boat & Ferry Information Hurtigruten ☎ 810-30-000 ⊕ www.hurtigruten.com. **OVDS** ☎76-96-76-00. **TFDS** ✉Tromsø ☎77-64-81-00 ✉Trondheim ☎73-51-51-20.

BUS TRAVEL

Bus 135 (Østerdalsekspress) runs overnight from Oslo to Trondheim via Røros. Buses also connect Bergen, Molde, and Ålesund with Trondheim.

Nor-Way Bussekspress can help you put together a bus journey to destinations in the North. The Ekspress 2000 travels regularly between Oslo, Trondheim, Kautokeino, Alta, Nordkapp, and Hammerfest.

All local Trondheim buses stop at the Munkegata–Dronningens Gate intersection. Some routes end at the bus terminal at Trondheim Sentralstasjon.

North of Bodø and Narvik (a five-hour bus ride from Bodø), buses go virtually everywhere, but they don't go often. Get a comprehensive bus schedule from a tourist office or travel agent before making plans. Local bus companies include Saltens Bilruter, Ofotens Bilruter, Tromsbuss, Midttuns Busser, Finnmark Fylkesrederi og Ruteselskap, and Ekspress 2000.

☎ Bus Information Ekspress 2000 ✉ Alta ☎ 78-44-40-90. **Finnmark Fylkesrederi og Ruteselskap** ☎ 78-40-70-00 ⊕ www.ffr.no. **Lofoten (Connex)** ☎ 76-11-11-11.

Midttuns Busser ☎ 77-67-27-87 Tromsø. **Nor-Way Bussekspress** ☎ 815-44-444. Ofotens Bilruter ✉ Narvik ☎ 76-92-35-00. **Saltens Bilruter** ✉ Bodø ☎ 75-55-22-10 ⊕ www.saltensbil.no. **Tromsbuss** ☎ 77-67-75-00 Tromsø ⊕ www.tromsbuss.no. **Trondheim Sentralstasjon** ☎ 73-52-14-30.

CAR RENTALS

Book a rental car as far in advance as possible. There's no better way to see the Lofoten and Vesterålen Islands than by car. Nordkapp (take the plane to Honningsvåg) is another excursion best made by car. 🚗 **Local Agencies Avis Bilutleie** ☎ 77-61-58-50. **Budget Bilutleie** ☎ 73-94-10-25.

CAR TRAVEL

Trondheim is about 494 km (308 mi) from Oslo: a seven- to eight-hour drive. Speed limits are 80 kph (50 mph) or 100 kph (60 mph) much of the way. The two alternatives are the E6 through Gudbrandsdalen or Route 3 through Østerdalen. It's 723 km (448 mi) from Trondheim to Bodø on Route E6, which goes all the way to Kirkenes. There's an NKr 30 toll on E6 just east of Trondheim. The highway toll also covers the NKr 11 toll (6 AM–10 PM) for cars entering the downtown area. Anyone who makes it to the North Cape sans tour bus will be congratulated with a NKr 150 toll.

The best way to see the Lofoten Islands is by car, since bus service is often limited and there is much to see. The main tourist office in Svolvær can point you to local rental agencies, whose rates tend to be quite high. If you plan to stay in one village for a few days, you can rent a bicycle to visit the neighboring villages that are short distances from your base.

ROAD CONDITIONS Most roads in northern Norway are quite good, although there are always narrow and winding stretches, especially along fjords. Distances are formidable. Route 17—the **Kystriksvegen** (Coastal Highway) from Namsos to Bodø—is an excellent alternative to E6. Getting to Tromsø and the North Cape involves additional driving on narrower roads off E6. In winter, near-blizzard conditions and icy roads sometimes make it necessary to drive in a convoy. You must also drive with special studded winter tires.

EMERGENCIES

In Tromsø, Svaneapoteket pharmacy is open daily from 8:30 to 4:30 and 6 to 9. In Trondheim, Svaneapoteket pharmacy is open weekdays from 8:30 to 3 and Saturday from 9 to 3. 🚑 For medical emergencies, call 113. **St Olavs Hospital** ✉ Olav Kyrres gt. 17, Trondheim ☎ 73 86 80 00. **Svaneapoteket** ✉ Kongensgt. 14B, Tromsø ☎ 73-99-03-70 ✉ Fr. Langesgt. 9, Trondheim ☎ 73-99-03-70.

TAXIS

🚕 **Bodø Taxi** ☎ 075-500. **Nordland Taxi, Narvik** ☎ 075-500. **Tromsø** ☎ 77-60-30-00. **Trøndertaxi** ✉ Trondheim ☎ 73-92-49-04.

TRAIN TRAVEL

The Dovrebanen has frequent departures daily on the Oslo–Trondheim route. Trains leave from Oslo S Station for the 7- to 8-hour journey. Trondheim is the gateway to the north, and two trains run daily in each direction on the 11-hour Trondheim–Bodø route. The Nordlandsbanen has three departures daily in each direction on the Bodø–Trondheim route, an 11-hour journey. The *Ofotbanen* has two departures daily in each direction on the Stockholm–Narvik route, a 21-hour journey.

VISITOR INFORMATION
Bodø-based Nordland Reiseliv publishes a helpful holiday guide and a guide to interesting tours of the region. Their "Footprints in the North" pamphlet is a cultural history of northern Norway and Namdalen, listing 103 sites. Finnmark Reiseliv publishes a detailed annual guide to Finnmark.

🚩 Tourist Information **Alta (Destinasjon Alta)** ☎ 78-44-95-55 ⊕ www.destinasjonalta. no. **Bodø (Destinasjon Bodø)** ✉ Sjøgt. 3, 8001 ☎ 75-54-80-00 ⊕ www.visitbodo. com. **Finnmark Reiseliv** ☎ 78-44-00-20 ⊕ www.visitnorthcape.com. **Hamarøy (Kingdom of Hamsun)** ☎ 75-77-18-90 ⊕ www.hamsuns-rike.no. **Hammerfest** ✉ 9600 ☎ 78-40-62-37 ⊕ www.hammerfest-turist.no. **Harstad** ☎ 77-01-89-89 ⊕ www. destinasjonharstad.no. **Lofoten (Destination Lofoten)** ✉ 8301 Svolvær ☎ 76-06-98-00 ⊕ www.lofoten.info. **Mo i Rana (Polarsirkelen Reiseliv** ✉ 8601 Mo ☎ 75-13-92-00 ⊕ www.arctic-circle.no. **Narvik (Narvik Aktiv)** ☎ 76-96-56-00 ⊕ www.narvikinfo. no. **Nordkapp** ✉ Fiskerivn. 4, Honningsvåg ☎ 78-47-70-30 ⊕ www.northcape.no. **Nordland Reiseliv** ☎ 75-54-52-00 ⊕ www.visitnordland.no. **Tromsø** ✉ Storgt. 61-63, 9253 ☎ 77-61-00-00 ⊕ www.destinasjontromso.no. **Trondheim** ✉ Munkegt. 19, Torget, 7001 ☎ 73-80-76-60 ⊕ www.visit-trondheim.com. **Vesterålen** ✉ Kjøpmannsgt. 2, 8401 Sortland ☎ 76-11-14-80 ⊕ www.visitvesteralen.com.

Samiland
to Svalbard

WORD OF MOUTH

"I'd say [my strangest restaurant experience] would have to be at Karasjok, Norway. There was a sort of touristy reproduction of a Sami sod-covered hut buried in the ground with an open fire in the middle and the smoke going up through a hole in the roof. Everyone sat on rustic benches at rustic little tables. We ate reindeer tongue and heart as appetizers, then reindeer filet for the main course. We guessed that the red "wine" was really reindeer blood— only kidding."

—Patrick

EUROPE'S ONLY ANCIENT INDIGENOUS PEOPLE, the Sami, live on the rooftop of the Continent, atop the vast, windswept Finnmarksvidda. They recognize no national boundaries, and Samiland, formerly called Lapland, stretches from the Kola Peninsula in Russia through Finland, Sweden, and Norway. The majority of Sami, some 43,000, live in Norway. Norwegian Samiland is centered around the communities of Karasjok and Kautokeino, in the Finnmark region.

The traditional symbol of the Sami is the reindeer herder, but only about a fifth still live this way. Many also earn their living from fishing, farming, or selling Sami arts and crafts. Most Sami still live in traditional tents and dress in colorful costumes, although the most visible evidence of their lifestyle is roadside souvenir stands and tourist exhibits. As you'd expect, the Sami have their own language, music, art, and handicrafts. The desolate expanses and treeless tundra make an inspiring trekking destination—you're almost guaranteed an encounter with reindeer. Take time to experience this traditional culture, whether it's expressed through the Samis' *lavvu* (tents made of reindeer skin), *joik* (their distinctive songs), or their cuisine, rich in reindeer and wild salmon dishes.

Numbers in the margin correspond to points of interest on the Samiland to Svalbard map.

Exploring Samiland to Svalbard

Finnmark is Norway's northernmost region. It encompasses Samiland and the Finnmarksvidda mountain plateau. Numerous fjords, islands, and peninsulas distinguish the region. Svalbard, Norway's arctic archipelago, nicknamed "one big ice cube," is halfway between the Norwegian mainland and the north pole. Travel in this region is time-consuming, but roads are well maintained, and it's easiest to explore by car, although there is regular bus service to most towns.

About the Hotels & Restaurants

Traditional Sami cooking methods, with food prepared over an open fire with little seasoning, has had a strong influence on the culinary habits of northern Norway. Common ingredients include reindeer, whale, cod, arctic char, stockfish, cranberries, crowberries, and cloudberries. Northern specialty dishes are based on meat or seal, and are served with jams or sauces made with locally grown berries. At restaurants you will typically find young goat meat, homemade goat sausage, ham of seal marinated in home-brewed ale and then smoked and dried, as well as reindeer tongue and heart.

Traditional dwellings in Finnmark are *lavvu* (tents) and *gammes* (sod houses). Hotels are similar to what you'll find throughout the country, with a strong presence of chain hotels in the bigger towns. Some of the region's hotels make an effort to appear more "authentic" by adopting traditional Sami motifs in their design, and many serve regional cuisine in their restaurants.

Fishing   Throughout the region, in fresh or salt water, fishing is a year-round occupation and activity for locals and visitors from other parts of Norway. The region is dotted with fishing villages and the cooler waters in the area provide some of the best-tasting fish in the country. Finnmark's many rivers and lakes provide ample opportunities for anglers of all stripes. Note that a fishing license may be required; it's always best to check with the visitor information center in the area.

Snow Sports   Snowmobiling, often called scootering, is an extremely popular form of transportation as well as sport in northern Norway. Scooter owners have much more freedom to ride their vehicles in Finnmark than they do in southern Norway. Scooter driving is limited to the extensive network of prepared trails.

Water Sports   Considered a mecca for scuba diving, Finnmark attracts divers year-round. In summer, they dive by the light of the midnight sun and in winter beneath the northern lights. Water visibility is extremely high. Natural conditions for diving include forests of seaweed and sea tangle, vertical rock faces, deep fjords, and undulating isles and skerries. In the east, wreck diving is highly regarded.

WHAT IT COSTS In Norwegian Kroner				
	$$$$	$$$	$$	$	¢
RESTAURANTS	over 230	190–230	150–190	90–150	under 90
HOTELS	over 1,500	1,000–1,500	800–1,000	400–800	under 400

Restaurant prices are for a main course at dinner. Hotel prices are for two people in a standard double room in high season, including tax and a service charge.

Timing

The most memorable times of year to visit Finnmark are the winter polar night and summer midnight sun. The polar night occurs between late November and late January, while the midnight sun season lasts from the middle of May to late July. Keep in mind that the mosquito high season is late June to late July.

Kautokeino–Guovdageaidnu

❶ *129 km (80 mi) southeast of Alta.*

Kautokeino, with 3,000 inhabitants, is in the heart of Finnmarksvidda (the Finnmark mountain plateau). This is where most Sami come for supplies, and Kautokeino really looks more like a trading post than a town. Because of such institutions as the Nordic Sami Institute, Sami Theater, and Sami College, it has become the center for Sami culture, research, and education.

Samiland to Svalbard

KEY

Ferry lines

Start of itinerary

off the beaten path

MÁZE ZION – A mountain church stood here from 1721 to 1768, but only ruins remain. Headstones in the cemetery have names written in an old form of Sami, in which special characters are used for each name. ⊠ *Hwy. 93 en route to Alta from Kautokeino.*

PIKEFOSSEN FALLS – These beautiful falls on the Alta River between Kautokeino and Máze were named after a girl ("pike" means girl) who mysteriously drowned here. If you stay in the area overnight in a Sami tent, legend has it that you may hear the girl's screams in the falls.

Hiking & Fishing

The plains and forests around Kautokeino make it excellent terrain for hiking year-round. There is also an abundance of lakes excellent for fishing. This area actually has one of the largest areas of untouched nature in northern Europe. The **Nordkalott Route,** an 800-km (500-mi) trail with ends in Kvikkjokk, Sweden, and Sulitjelma, Norway, cuts through Kautokeino.

The **Suohpatjávri Nature and Cultural Trail,** 7 km (4½ mi) south of Kautokeino, is popular. Along the 4½-km (2¾-mi) marked trail, there's a picnic area, a *gamme* (earth-and-turf hut), and a *siedi* (sacrificial stone), which is a protected cultural monument.

Contact the **Kautokeino Tourist Office** (☎ 78–48–65–00) for more information on where to hike and fish.

Nightlife & the Arts

Traditional Sami culture is celebrated at Kautokeino's long-standing annual **Easter Festival** (☎ 95/07–86–29 ⊕ www.saami-easterfestival.org), which has craft exhibits as well as joik, a haunting kind of a cappella solo. Joik are usually songs of praise for nature. The festival also includes more recent cultural developments, including large Sami weddings, reindeer races, concerts, theatrical performances, skiing, fishing competitions, and snowmobile rallies.

Shopping

A number of jewelers line the main street of Kautokeino in summer selling their wares from stands.

Inside what was once a secret military facility, **Juhls' Silver Gallery** (☎ 78–48–43–30), home of Finnmark's first silversmith, carries the best selection of contemporary Sami art—everything from paintings and posters to sculpture. Part Frank Lloyd Wright and part Buddhist temple, the interiors have been designed and decorated by the Danish-German Frank and Regine Juhls. Don't miss the ornamental ceiling in the Afghan room. It was made to honor the Samis.

Where to Stay

$$ 🏨 **Norlandia Kautokeino Hotel.** This standard hotel has comfortable rooms. The restaurant serves Sami dishes, Norwegian home fare, and international dishes. ⊠ *9520 Kautokeino* ☎ *78–48–62–05* 🖶 *78–48–67–01* ⊕ *www.norlandia.no* 🛏 *50 rooms* 🍴 *Restaurant, sauna, bar, meeting room* ⊟ *AE, DC, MC, V* ☉ *Closed mid-Dec.–Mar.*

Karasjok–Kárásjoga

❷ *178 km (110 mi) northeast of Kautokeino.*

A Samiland crossroads as well as the Sami capital, Karasjok has 2,900 residents and is 18 km (11 mi) from the Finnish border. Many of the most significant Sami institutions are here, including Sámetinget, the Sami parliament; De Samiske Samlinger, the Sami Collections; and the Sami Kunstnersenter, Sami Artists' Center. If you're heading to the North Cape, Karasjok is a natural place to stop and take in the stunning scenery.

Karasjok Opplevelser A/S (☎ 78–46–88–10) organizes Samiland adventures. These may include dining in a lavvu, visiting a Sami camp, listening to Sami songs, and heading to Basevuovdi (Helligskogen, or the Sacred Forest) for gold panning. From late fall to early spring you can go **reindeer sledding.** A guide takes you out on a wooden sled tied to a couple of unwieldy reindeer, and you clop through the barren, snow-covered scenery of Finnmark.

Opened in 2000, the stunning **Sametinget** (Sami Parliament; ☎ 78–74–00–00) building blends ancient Sami forms with Scandinavian modernism. Inside, the walls are covered with Sami art.

The **Sami Artists' Center** holds 12 temporary exhibitions of contemporary and traditional Sami visual art per year. Guided tours must be arranged in advance. ✉ *Jeagilvármádii 54* ☎ *78–46–99–40* 🎫 *Free* ⏲ *Mid-June–mid-Aug., daily 10–5; mid-Aug.–mid-June, weekdays 10–3 (Thurs. 10–7), Sun. noon–5.*

★ The **Samiid Vuorká Dávvirat–De Samiske Saminger** (Sami Collections) is an indoor and open-air museum dedicated to Sami culture and history. It emphasizes the arts, reindeer herding, and the status of women in the Sami community. There are also examples of the hunting pits used to catch wild reindeer. ✉ *Museumsgt. 17* ☎ *78–46–99–50* 🎫 *NKr 50* ⏲ *Mar.–May, daily 9–3; June–mid-Aug., daily 9–9; mid-Aug.–Nov., daily 9–3.*

The **Sápmi** theme park is based on four elements of Sami culture. *Siida* is the traditional Sami settlements; Stalubakti is the realm of magical theater; *Duoddji* explores Sami handicrafts; and traditional Sami cuisine. ✉ *Porsangervn. 1* ☎ *78–46–88–00* 🌐 *www.sapmi.no* 🎫 *NKr 90* ⏲ *Mon.–Wed. and Fri. 10–6, Thurs. 10–8, Sat. noon–9, Sun. noon–5.*

Where to Stay & Eat

★ **$$–$$$** ✕🏨 **Rica Hotel Karasjok.** Looking like a cozy ski chalet, this hotel has bright, warm rooms accented with blond woods and blues and reds. The highly regarded Sami restaurant, Storgammen, is in a gamme. The kitchen produces centuries-old Sami dishes, including reindeer in lingonberry sauce, cooked over an open fire. ✉ *Porsangervn. 1, 9730 Karasjok* ☎ *78–46–74–00* 📠 *78–46–68–02* 🌐 *www.rica.no* *56 rooms* *2 restaurants, gym, sauna, bar, nightclub, meeting rooms* 💳 *AE, DC, MC, V.*

Sports & the Outdoors

DOGSLEDDING Sven Engholm leads dogsledding tours in winter. You can lead your own dogsled, accompany one on skis, or just go along for the ride. Engholm also organizes gold panning, fishing trips, and wilderness tours. Dine in a gamme, or rent a cabin. In summer you can hike with the huskies. Contact **Engholms Husky** (☎ 78–46–71–66 🌐 www.engholm.no) for information.

HIKING & FISHING **Finnmarksvidda,** the plateau between Alta and Karasjok, has marked trails with places to stay overnight in lodges, cabins, lavvu, and tents. Fishing and canoe trips can be organized with a guide in July and August. Rather than hike to the fishing lakes, you can take an airplane or a helicopter: contact **Nils Rolf Johnsen** (✉ Svenskebakken 35, 9730 Karasjok ☎ 78–46–63–02), who handles fishing trips and wilderness adventures on the Finnmarksvidda Plains. **Karasjok Opplevelser A/S** (☎ 78–46–88–10) offers guided hiking and fishing trips in Finnmark.

Shopping

Sami crafts, particularly handmade knives, are a specialty in this area. **Samelandssenteret** (☎ 78–46–71–55), a shopping center, has lots of stores selling northern crafts. See how an authentic Sami knife is made at Knivsmed Strømeng A/S (☎ 78–46–71–05).

Kirkenes

🟢 *320 km (200 mi) northeast of Karasjok.*

At its very top, Norway hooks over Finland and touches Russia for 122 km (75 mi). The towns in east Finnmark have a more heterogeneous population than those in the rest of the country. A century ago, during hard times in Finland, many industrious Finns settled in this region, and their descendants keep the language alive.

During World War II, Nazi-held Kirkenes was bombed more than 300 times by the allies. The entire region was held by the Nazis as a deployment area for the "Lapland Front," and convoys with soldiers and equipment traveled along the Norwegian coast. Only Malta was bombed more—and virtually all buildings had to be rebuilt. Many residents sought cover in subterranean tunnels dug for use as bomb shelters.

A good way to visit here is to fly to Kirkenes and then explore the region by car. Kirkenes itself has 7,000 residents. The town was built up around Sydvaranger, an iron ore mining company that operated until 1996. Today the town's industries include tourism and ship repair.

Dedicated to the works of the Sami artist John Andras Savio (1902–38), the **Savio Museum** showcases his woodcutting, watercolors, and oils. Savio is best known for depicting Sami life. The museum also has changing exhibits of contemporary Sami art. ✉ *Førstevannslia* ☎ *78–99–92–12.*

Wedged between Russia and Finland, **Pasvikdalen** is a valley known for its flora and fauna: Norway's largest bear population shares the valley with species of plants and birds that can't be found anywhere else in the country.

off the beaten path

ST. GEORGS KAPELL (St. Georg's Chapel) – The only Russian Orthodox chapel in Norway lies 45 km (28 mi) west of Kirkenes. This tiny building is where the Orthodox Skolt-Sami had their summer encampment. An annual outdoor mass is held the last Sunday in August, weather permitting.

Where to Stay

$$–$$$ 🏨 **Rica Arctic Hotel.** In the center of Kirkenes, this hotel is the perfect choice for outdoor sports enthusiasts. It's at the edge of the world's largest forest, stretching all the way from Pasvikdalen to the Bering Strait. The spacious rooms are pleasant, with white-painted furniture and floral and light-color fabrics. ✉ *Kongensgt. 1–3, 9900* ☎ *78–99–29–29* 🖨 *78–99–11–59* ⊕ *www.rica.no* 🛏 *80 rooms* ⌂ *Restaurant, cable TV, in-room data ports, pool, gym, sauna, bar, convention center* ▭ *AE, DC, MC, V.*

Storskog

🟢 *About 15 km (9 mi) east of Kirkenes.*

Just east of Kirkenes is Storskog, for many years the only official land crossing between Norway and Russia. The tiny village of **Grense Jakob-**

selv, 50 km (30 mi) east of Kirkenes along the Russian border, is where King Oscar II built a chapel in 1869 as a protest against constant Russian encroachment in the area. Salmon river fishing is good and several beaches are popular.

off the
beaten
path

ØVRE PASVIK NATIONAL PARK – The southernmost part of Finnmark, about 118 km (73 mi) south of Kirkenes, is Øvre Pasvik national park, a narrow tongue of land tucked between Finland and Russia. This subarctic evergreen forest is the western end of Siberia's taiga and supports many unique varieties of flora.

Svalbard

⑤ *640 km (400 mi) north of the North Cape.*

The islands of the Svalbard archipelago, the largest of which is Spitsbergen, have only officially been part of Norway since 1920. This wild, fragile area lies halfway between the north pole and the mainland. Icelandic texts from 1194 contain the first known mention of Svalbard. After the Dutch navigator Willem Barents visited Svalbard in 1596, whaling and winter-long hunting and trapping were virtually the only human activities here for the next 300 years.

In 1906 John M. Longyear established the first coal mine and named the area Longyear City. Now called **Longyearbyen,** Svalbard's capital has a population of 1,200. With a local economy fueled by oil drilling, the town is a diverse community with excellent accommodations and restaurants. There's an abundance of organized exotic wilderness activities and tours such as dogsledding, snowmobiling, skiing, ice caving, igloo camping, and fossil hunting.

Svalbard has its share of sports and cultural events, too. Famous musicians and artists visit Svalbard for exhibitions and concerts. The Polar Jazz Festival takes place at the end of January, followed by the lively Sunfestival in early March. The Svalbard Ski Marathon is held late in April and early May, and the Spitsbergen Marathon in early June.

Sixty percent of Svalbard is covered by glaciers; plants and other vegetation cover only 6%; the rest of the surface is just rocks. Remote and isolated, the only way to fly in is from Tromsø. Only a few cruise ships and other boats land here, and no roads connect the communities on Svalbard—people travel between them with snowmobiles.

The archipelago's climate is surprisingly mild, with periods of summer fog. The small amount of precipitation makes Svalbard a sort of arctic desert. Permafrost covers all of Svalbard, which means only the top yard of earth thaws in summer. Because it's so far north, it has four months of the midnight sun (as well as four months of polar night).

Although they spend most of their time on ice floes, polar bears can be encountered anywhere on Svalbard because they give birth to their cubs on land. They are a genuine threat, so don't travel outside the settlements without an experienced guide.

TOURS IN SAMILAND & SVALBARD

Cruises

The **Hurtigruten** (☎ 810–30–000 ⊕ www.hurtigruten.com) coastal express boat cruises from Tromsø to Svalbard, dipping down to the North Cape afterward. Watching the midnight sun from the railing of a cruise ship is one of those incomparable Norwegian experiences.

Cavzo Safari (☎ 78–48–75–88) runs a riverboat excursion from Máze to Alta Dam that includes guided tours, listening to joik in a lavvu, and traditional dishes such as bidos, which is made with reindeer meat.

Tours Around Kirkenes

Several regional companies offer specialized tours in and around Kirkenes. **Grenseland AS** (☎ 815–36–900 or 78–99–25–01 ⊕ www.grenseland.no) focuses on the Barents Region, with nature, culture, and adventure tours in northwest Russia. **Kirkenes Opplevelser** (☎ 78–99–06–22 or 91–53–62–31 ⊕ www.kirkenesopplevelser.no) runs salmon- and crab-fishing boat expeditions spanning the region from the Kirkenes fjord to the Arctic Ocean.

Bugøynes Opplevelser AS (☎ 78–99–03–75 ⊕ www.bugoynes.no) visits a fishing community on the Arctic Ocean, where Kamchatka crab is served. Their tours include trying out an arctic sauna. **Neiden Fjellstue** (☎ 78–99–61–41 ⊕ www.samitour.no) plans deep-sea, ice fishing, and snowmobile trips; staying in mountain cabins; and dining and entertainment in a lavvu.

Tours in Svalbard

Svalbard's environment is fragile, and polar bears are dangerous as well as numerous (there are 2,000 to 3,000 in and around Svalbard). For these reasons, heading into the wilderness should only be done on an organized tour with an experienced guide.

Spitsbergen Travel (SPITRA) (☎ 79–02–61–00) organizes exciting activities and tours including glacier walks, horseback riding, dogsledding, and arctic barbecues. **Svalbard Polar Travel (SPOT)** (☎ 79–02–34–00) handles skiing, dogsledding, and snowmobile tours in winter and spring cruises around Spitsbergen and the northwest coast in spring and summer.

For winter camping trips, **Basecamp Spitsbergen** (☎ 79–02–46–00) sets you up with your very own Alaskan husky dogsledding team—or a snowmobile. In summer, the company operates hikes, trips with pack dogs or pack horses, charter boat tours, and camping excursions. **Svalbard Wildlife Service** (☎ 79–02–56–60) organizes tours into the arctic wilderness and day trips in the Longyearbyen area. The day trips may include mine visits, glacier walks, and boating.

Mine No. 3 (☎ 79–02–56–60), the last mine in Svalbard where coal was extracted using traditional methods, ended production in 1996. Guided visits can be arranged throughout the year. The mine is just outside of Longyearbyen. Contact **Svalbard Wildlife Service.**

Once a pig farm, the **Svalbard Museum** profiles the early trapper period, various Svalbard expeditions, the war years, and the biology of the islands. Learn about the history of mining on the first floor, where you can change into a miner's outfit and crawl into a copy of a mine tunnel. ✉ *Longyearbyen* ☎ *79–02–13–84* 🎟 *NKr 40* ⊙ *Daily 10–4.*

Where to Stay & Eat

$$$–$$$$ ✕ **Huset.** Considered one of Longyearbyen's best restaurants, Huset serves fine Norwegian food in an elegant but relaxed dining room. A wintery Kåre Tveter painting of Svalbard graces one wall. Dramatically covering another wall is the snowy skin of a polar bear that wandered into Longyearbyen in 1983 and was shot. Try tartare of arctic char, grouse, or reindeer dishes. Popular with locals as well as visitors, the restaurant is often fully booked. ✉ *Longyearbyen* ☎ *79–02–25–00* 🍴 *Reservations essential* 🖃 *AE, DC, MC, V.*

$$–$$$$ ✕🏨 **Spitsbergen Hotel.** This distinguished hotel is known for the relics that fill it as well as for the luxury and high level of service its staff provides. Each room is tastefully and elegantly decorated in dark woods and richly colored textiles. You can relax on a red burnished-leather couch by the library's roaring fireplace. At the Funktionærmessen Restaurant, dine on interpretations of local cuisine that include reindeer spring rolls. In cooperation with Spitsbergen Travel, the hotel offers such activities as snowmobiling, dogsledding, glacier walking, hiking, and boat trips. ✉ *9171 Longyearbyen* ☎ *79–02–62–00* 🖷 *79–02–62–01* ⊕ *www.spitra.no* ⇨ *83 rooms, 5 suites* ⚓ *Restaurant, cable TV, in-room data ports, sauna, bar, meeting rooms* 🖃 *AE, DC, MC, V.*

$$$ 🏨 **Radisson SAS Polar Hotel, Spitsbergen.** The world's northernmost Radisson SAS hotel excels in warm service and style. Every room is understated and elegant, with light walls, warm colors, and blond and dark woods. An enormous window in the dining and bar area provides a view of Mt. Hjorthavnfjellet across the waters of the Icefjord. In summer you can watch the sun cross from one side of the mountain at dusk to the other at dawn. Brasseri Nansen's menu includes seal and white grouse. Svalbard Polar Travel at the hotel can arrange tours and activities around the area. 🗀 *Box 544, 9171 Longyearbyen* ☎ *79–02–34–50* 🖷 *79–02–34–51* ⊕ *www.radissonsas.com* ⇨ *95 rooms, 6 suites* ⚓ *2 restaurants, hot tub, sauna, bar, meeting rooms, library* 🖃 *AE, DC, MC, V.*

Arts

To get a sense of frosty Svalbard during other times of the year, head to **Gallery Svalbard.** One of Norway's most admired artists, Kåre Tveter, donated 40 illustrations to the gallery. The "Arctic Light Over Svalbard" slide show is an eye-opening presentation of what makes this area special. Centuries-old Arctic maps and books fill an adjacent exhibition room. ✉ *9171 Longyearbyen* ☎ *79–02–23–40.*

Shopping

For such a remote and small town, Longyearbyen has a surprising number of spots for souvenir shopping, including the **Lompensenteret** (☎ 79–02–14–01) shopping center. Head to **Skandinavisk Høyfjellsutstyr** (☎ 79–02–32–90) for sportswear and clothes for the outdoors. **Svalbardbutikken** (79–02–25–20) is a group of stores selling groceries, wine and liquor, cameras, clothes, souvenirs, and other things you may need.

Samiland to Svalbard A to Z

To research prices, get advice from other travelers, and book travel arrangements, visit www.fodors.com.

AIR TRAVEL

SAS service the Longyearbyen Airport.

🛪 **Longyearbyen Airport** ☎ 79-02-38-00. **SAS** ☎ 79-02-16-50.

CAR TRAVEL

Most roads in northern Norway are quite good, although there are always narrow and winding stretches, especially along fjords. Distances between towns are often very great. Route E6 is the main highway that winds all the way to the north of the country, although getting to Tromsø and the North Cape involves additional driving on narrower roads off E6. Cars require specially studded tires for winter driving. In winter, near-blizzard conditions and icy roads sometimes make it necessary to drive in a convoy.

CRUISE TRAVEL

Hurtigruten, the coastal express boat, now cruises from Tromsø to Svalbard, dipping down to the North Cape afterward. Contact Norwegian Coastal Voyage for information.

🛪 **Norwegian Coastal Voyage** ✉ 405 Park Ave., New York, NY 10022 ☎ 212/319-1300.

TOURS

BOAT TOURS Cavzo Safari is a riverboat excursion from Máze to Alta Dam that includes guided tours, listening to joik in a lavvu, and traditional dishes such as *bidos,* which is made with reindeer meat.

🛪 **Fees & Schedules Cavzo Safari** ☎ 78-48-75-88.

TOURS AROUND   Several regional companies offer specialized tours in and around Kirkenes.
KIRKENES   Grenseland AS focuses on the Barents Region, with nature, culture, and adventure tours in northwest Russia. Kirkenes Opplevelser's salmon and crab fishing boat expeditions span the region from the Kirkenes fjord to the Arctic Ocean. Bugøynes Opplevelser A/S visits a fishing community on the Arctic Ocean, where Kamchatka crab is served. Their tours include trying out an arctic sauna. Neiden Fjellstue plans deep-sea, ice fishing, and snowmobile trips; staying in mountain cabins; and dining and entertainment in a lavvu.

🛪 **Fees & Schedules Bugøynes Opplevelser A/S** ☎ 78-99-03-75. **Destination Kirkenes** ☎78-99-80-69. **Grenseland AS** ☎78-99-25-01. **Kirkenes Opplevelser** ☎91/53-62-31. **Neiden Fjellstue** ☎ 78-99-61-41.

Svalbard's environment is fragile, and polar bears are dangerous as
well as numerous (there are 2,000 to 3,000 in and around Svalbard).
For these reasons, heading into the wilderness should only be done on
an organized tour with an experienced guide.

Spitsbergen Travel (SPITRA) organizes exciting activities and tours including glacier walks, horseback riding, dogsledding, and arctic barbecues. Svalbard Polar Travel (SPOT) handles skiing, dogsledding, and
snowmobile tours in winter and spring cruises around Spitsbergen and
the northwest coast in spring and summer.

For winter camping trips, Basecamp Spitsbergen sets you up with your
very own Alaskan husky dogsledding team—or a snowmobile. In summer the company operates hikes, trips with pack dogs or pack horses, charter boat tours, and camping excursions. Svalbard Wildlife Service organizes
tours into the arctic wilderness and day trips in the Longyearbyen area.
The day trips may include mine visits, glacier walks, and boating.

🄵 **Fees & Schedules Basecamp Spitsbergen** ☏ 79-02-46-00. **Spitsbergen Travel
(SPITRA)** ☏ 79-02-61-00. **Svalbard Polar Travel (SPOT)** ☏ 79-02-34-00. **Svalbard
Wildlife Service** ☏ 79-02-56-60.

VISITOR INFORMATION

🄵 **Tourist Information Info-Svalbard** ✉ 9171 Longyearbyen ☏ 79-02-55-50 ⊕ www.
svalbard.net. **Karasjok** ✉ 9730 Karasjok ☏ 78-46-88-10 ⊕ www.koas.no. **Kautokeino**
✉ 9520 Kautokeino ☏ 78-48-65-00. **Kirkenes** ✉ 9915 Kirkenes ☏ 78-99-25-44
⊕ www.kirkenesinfo.no.

UNDERSTANDING NORWAY

NORWAY AT A GLANCE

Fast Facts

Name in local language: Kongeriket Norge (long form); Norge (short form)
Capital: Oslo
National anthem: *Ja, Vi Elsker Dette Landet* (*Yes, We Love This Country*), by Bjørnstjerne Bjørnson
Type of government: Constitutional monarchy
Administrative divisions: 19 counties (*fylker,* singular: *fylke*)
Independence: June 7, 1905 (Norway declared its union with Sweden dissolved); October 26, 1905 (Sweden agreed to the repeal of the union)
Constitution: May 17, 1814 (modified in 1884)
Legal system: Mixture of customary law, civil law system, and common law traditions; Supreme Court renders advisory opinions to legislature when asked; accepts compulsory International Court of Justice (ICJ) jurisdiction, with reservations
Suffrage: 18 years of age; universal
Legislature: Modified unicameral Parliament or Storting (165 seats; members are elected by popular vote by proportional representation to serve four-year terms. For certain purposes, the parliament divides itself into two chambers and elects one-fourth of its membership to an upper house or Lagting.
Population: 4.6 million
Population density: 37 people per square mile
Median age: Male 37.3, female 39.1
Life expectancy: Male 76.8, female 82.2

Infant mortality rate: 3.7 deaths per 1,000 live births
Literacy: 100%
Language: Bokmal Norwegian (official), Nynorsk Norwegian (official), small Sami- and Finnish-speaking minorities
Ethnic groups: Norwegian; Sámi (fewer than 1%)
Religion: Church of Norway 85.7%; Pentecostal 1%; Roman Catholic 1%; other Christian 2.4%; Muslim 1.8%; other 8.1%
Discoveries & Inventions: The South Pole (1911); television (1924); the paper clip (1899); the cheese slicer (1925); first successful gas turbine (1884); spray can (aerosol forerunner, 1926); Jarlsberg (1815–32), Snøfrisk (1994), and Ridder (late 1960s) cheeses

"'Dark times' is what they call it in Norway when the sun remains below the horizon all day long: the temperature falls slowly but surely at such times. A nice metaphor for all those thinkers for whom the sun of mankind's future has temporarily disappeared."
— Friedrich Nietzsche

"No longer shall I paint interiors with men reading and women knitting. I will paint living people who breathe and feel and suffer and love."
— Edvard Munch

"The lazier a man is, the more he plans to do tomorrow."
— Norwegian proverb

Geography & Environment

Land area: 307,860 square km (118,865 square mi), about the size of Arizona
Coastline: 25,148 km (15,626 mi) along

Norwegian Sea, North Sea, and Barents Sea, including mainland, long fjords, numerous small islands, and minor

indentations. Extremely rugged, one of the longest coastlines in the world
Terrain: Glaciated; mostly high plateaus and rugged mountains broken by fertile valleys; small, scattered plains; coastline deeply indented by fjords; arctic tundra in north
Islands: Norway has some 50,000 islands off it's coast.

Natural resources: Copper, iron ore, lead, natural gas, petroleum, pyrites, titanium, zinc
Natural hazards: Avalanches, rock slides
Environmental issues: Acid rain damaging forests and adversely affecting lakes, threatening fish stocks; water pollution; air pollution from vehicle emissions

Economy

Currency: Norwegian krone
Exchange rate: 6.57 Norwegian kroner = $1
GDP: 1.2 trillion Norwegian kroner ($183 billion)
Per capita income: 262,824 Norwegian kroner ($40,000)
Inflation: 1%
Unemployment: 4.3%
Workforce: 2.38 million
Debt: 0
Economic aid: 7.9 billion Norwegian kroner ($1.4 billion)
Major industries: Chemicals, food processing, metals, petroleum and gas, pulp and paper products, shipbuilding
Agricultural products: Barley, beef, pork, potatoes, veal, wheat

Exports: 503.5 billion Norwegian kroner ($76.64 billion)
Major export products: Chemicals, fish, machinery and equipment, metals, petroleum and petroleum products, ships
Major export partners: U.K. 22.4%; Germany 12.9%; Netherlands 9.9%; France 9.6%; U.S. 8.4%; Sweden 6.7%
Imports: 303.85 billion Norwegian kroner ($45.96 billion)
Major import products: Chemicals, foodstuffs, machinery and equipment, metals
Major Import partners: Sweden 15.7%; Germany 13.6%; Denmark 7.3%; U.K. 6.5%; China 5%; U.S. 4.9%; Netherlands 4.4%; France 4.3%; Finland 4.1%

Political Climate

Norway's citizens voted down referenda to join the European Union (EU) in 1972 and in 1994, but Norway still contributes to the EU budget. The nation is a member of NATO. Two of Norway's hot-button political issues are the country's extensive welfare system and offshore oil and gas reserves. The petroleum reserves were discovered in the 1960s and were an economic boost, but the country is planning for the day

when they run out. Norway saves budget surpluses in a Government Petroleum Fund, currently valued at over $150 billion.

"I shall take all the troubles of the past, all the disappointments, all the headaches, and I shall pack them in a bag and throw them in the East River."
— Trygve Lie, U.N. Secretary-General

Did You Know?

• Norway has the highest newspaper circulation (per capita) in the world.

• Only Saudi Arabia and Russia export more oil than Norway.

• Norway scored highest on the Gender Empowerment Measure (GEM), which is an index based on UN data that measures gender equality based on economic participation and power over economic resources, and political participation and decision making.

• Norway is fourth in the world in milk consumption. On average, each person drinks 158 quarts a year.

• You can get a McLaks grilled salmon sandwich in McDonald's restaurants in Norway.

• The national cheese of Norway is Gjetost, which means "goat" and "cheese." Interestingly, it is usually made from cow's milk.

• Norway has won more Winter Olympics medals than any other nation.

• On Christmas Eve Norwegians hide all of the brooms in the house to prevent witches and mischievous spirits from stealing them.

NORWEGIAN LANDSCAPES

NORWEGIANS HAVE a strong attachment to the natural beauty of their mountainous homeland. Whether in the verdant dales of the interior, the brooding mountains of the north, or the fjords and archipelagoes of the coast, Norwegians' *hytter* (mountain cabins) dot even the harshest landscapes.

In almost any kind of weather, blasting or balmy, large numbers of Norwegians are outdoors, fishing, biking, skiing, hiking, or playing soccer. Everybody—from cherubic children to hardy, knapsack-toting senior citizens—bundles up for just one more ski trip or hike in the mountains. In one recent research poll, 70% of Norwegian respondents said that they wanted to spend even more time in nature. Although Norway is a modern, highly industrialized nation, vast areas of the country (up to 95%) remain forested or fallow. When discussing the size of their country, Norwegians like to say that if Oslo remained fixed and the northern part of the country were swung south, it would reach all the way to Rome. Perched at the very top of the globe, this northern land is long and rangy, 2,750 km (1,705 mi) in length, with only 4.5 million people scattered over it—making it the least densely populated country in Europe after Iceland.

Westerly winds carry moisture from the Gulf Stream, leaving the coastal regions with high precipitation, cool summers, and mild winters. The interior and east have a blend of clearer skies, hotter summers, and colder winters.

Norwegians are justifiably proud of their ability to survive the elements. The first people to appear on the land were reindeer hunters and fisherfolk who migrated north, following the path of the retreating ice. By the Bronze Age, settlements began to appear, and, as rock carvings show, Norwegians first began to ski—purely as a form of locomotion—some 4,000 years ago.

The Viking Age has perhaps left the most indelible mark on the country. The Vikings' travels and conquests took them west to Iceland, England, Ireland (they founded Dublin in the 840s), and North America, and east to Kiev and as far as the Black Sea. Though they were famed as plunderers, their craftsmanship, fearlessness, and ingenuity have always been respected by Norwegians.

Harald I, better known as Harald the Fairhaired, swore he would not cut his hair until he united Norway, and in the 9th century he succeeded in doing both. But a millennium passed between that great era and Norwegian independence. Between the Middle Ages and 1905, Norway remained under the rule of either Denmark or Sweden, even after the constitution was written in 1814.

The 19th century saw the establishment of the Norwegian identity and a blossoming of culture. This Romantic period produced some of the nation's most famous individuals, among them composer Edvard Grieg, dramatist Henrik Ibsen, expressionist painter Edvard Munch, polar explorer Roald Amundsen, and explorer-humanitarian Fridtjof Nansen. Vestiges of nationalist lyricism, including Viking dragon heads and scrollwork, spangle the buildings of the era, symbolizing the rebirth of the Viking spirit.

Faithful to their democratic nature, Norwegians held a referendum to choose a king in 1905, when independence from Sweden became reality. Prince Carl of Denmark became King Haakon VII. His baby's name was changed from Alexander to Olav, and he, and later his son, presided over the kingdom for more than 85 years. When King Olav V died in January 1991, normally reserved Norwegians stood in line for hours to write in the condolence book at the Royal Palace. Rather than simply sign their names, they wrote personal letters of devotion to the man they called "the people's king."

Harald V, Olav's son, is now king, with continuity assured by his popular son, Crown Prince Haakon Magnus, who married in August 2001. On January 21, 2004, Prince Haakon's wife Mette-Marit gave birth to daughter Princess Ingrid Alexandra, who became Norway's first-ever female heir to the throne. Norwegians continue to salute the royal family with flag-waving and parades on May 17, Constitution Day, a spirited holiday of independence that transforms Oslo's main boulevard, Karl Johans Gate, into a massive street party.

The 1968 discovery of oil in the North Sea dramatically changed Norway from an outpost for fishing, subsistence farming, and shipping to a highly developed industrial nation. Norway has emerged as a wealthy country, with a per capita income, standard of living, and life expectancy that are among the world's highest.

Domestically, great emphasis has been placed on social welfare programs. Internationally, Norway is known for the annual awarding of the Nobel Peace Prize and participating in peace talks about the Middle East and other areas.

Unlike its Nordic siblings, Norway has resisted the temptation to join the European Union (EU). In a referendum in November 1994, Norwegians rejected EU membership for the second time. However, Norwegians are warming to the EU as it expands its membership across Europe.

— Updated by Sonya Procenko

FOOD & DRINK

Food and the rituals of mealtimes are central to Norwegian culture. The Norwegians pride themselves on gracious entertaining and lavish dinner parties, for which they using their finest silver and glassware. Dining out in Norway is expensive, so many weekend nights are spent at the houses of friends and family, savoring long, candlelit dinners. (The BYOB—Bring Your Own Bottle—policy is common when you're invited to a dinner party, because alcohol is taxed heavily and tends to be very expensive.)

Dining Out

Despite the expense, eating out at restaurants is popular, especially in cosmopolitan centers like Bergen, Stavanger, and Oslo. In these large cities the restaurant scenes are vibrant and constantly evolving. Until the late 1990s, fine Norwegian restaurants were invariably inspired by French cuisine and based their menus around meat entrées. Today traditional Norwegian restaurants still serve the classic, national dishes. But there are many more restaurants specializing in crossover dishes or Asian, African, Latin American, and Mediterranean cuisine.

Chefs such as Terje Ness have been winning international cooking competitions and earning celebrity status back home. They're traveling and cooking widely, often inspired by their international colleagues and by stints abroad. Increasingly, they're taking pride in traditions, cooking Norwegian ingredients like lamb and wild game, and serving them with sauces made from the wild berries that make up the animals' diet. Celebrity chef Arne Brimi (⊕ www.brimi.no) has made the concept "Nature's Kitchen" famous and has a center for food culture in Lom. Arktisk Meny (Arctic Menu) (⊕ www.arktiskmeny.com) is a network of more than 30 northern eating establishments serving traditional and newer dishes based on northern Norwe-

gian ingredients. Norsk Sjømat (⊕ www.seafood.no) is an excellent source of information on Norwegian seafood. Many of Stavanger's famed festivals celebrate food, from chili peppers to garlic and the big summer festival is called Glad Mat, or "Happy Food."

Mealtimes

For centuries, Norwegians regarded food as fuel, and their dining habits still bear traces of this. *Frokost* (breakfast) is a fairly big meal, usually with a selection of crusty bread, jams, herring, cold meat, and cheese. Norway's famous brown goat cheese, *Geitost* (a sweet, caramel-flavored whey cheese made from goat and cow milk) and *Norvegia* (a Norwegian Gouda-like cheese) are on virtually every table. They are eaten in thin slices, cut with a cheese plane or slicer—a Norwegian invention—on buttered wheat or rye bread.

Lunsj (lunch) is simple and usually consists of *smørbrød* (open-face sandwiches). Most businesses have only a 30-minute lunch break, so unless there's a company cafeteria people bring their lunch from home.

Middag (dinner), the only hot meal of the day, is early—from 1 to 4 in the country, 3 to 7 in the city—so many cafeterias serving home-style food close by 6 or 7. In Oslo it's possible to get dinner as late as midnight, especially in summer. Most restaurants in Oslo stop serving dinner around 10.

Desserts often feature fruit and berries. Norwegian strawberries and raspberries ripen in the long, early summer days and are sweeter and more intense than those grown farther south. Red and black currants are also widely used in desserts. Two berries native to Norway are *tyttebær* (lingonberries), which taste similar to cranberries but are much smaller; and *molter* (cloudberries), which look like orange raspberries but whose taste has been compared to that of a mango or peach. Molter are often served as *moltekrem* (in whipped cream) as a dessert, whereas tyttebær preserves often accompany traditional meat dishes.

National & Regional Specialties

Traditional, home-style Norwegian food is stick-to-the-ribs fare, served in generous portions and smothered in gravy. One of the most popular dishes is *kjøttkaker* (meat cakes), which resemble small Salisbury steaks and are served with boiled potatoes, stewed cabbage, and brown gravy. Almost as popular are *medisterkaker* (mild pork sausage patties), served with brown gravy and caraway-seasoned sauerkraut, and *reinsdyrkaker* (reindeer meatballs), served with cream sauce and lingonberry jam. Other typical meat dishes include *fårikål,* a great-tasting lamb and cabbage stew, and *steik* (roast meat), always served well done. Fish dishes include poached *torsk* (cod) or *laks* (salmon), served with creamy sauce; *seibiff,* (pollack) fried with onions; and *fiskegrateng,* a fish soufflé, usually served with carrot slaw.

There are also regional specialties such as *smalahove* (sheep's head), common on the west coast, and *klippfisk* (also known as bacalao). This dried and salted fish is exported to Portugal, Italy, Spain, South America, and the Caribbean. *Pinnekjøtt,* (salted lamb ribs), and lutefisk (fish that's been soaked in lye and then simmered) are popular around Christmas.

Traditional desserts include *karamellpudding* (crème caramel), *rømmegrøt* (sour-cream porridge served with cinnamon sugar), and *saft* (drinks made from concentrated berry juices.). Rømmegrøt—a typical farm dish—tastes very much like warm cheesecake batter. It's often served with *fenalår* (dried leg of mutton) and *lefser*—a thin, tortillalike pancake made with sour cream and potatoes that's buttered and coated with sugar. Christmastime brings a delectable array of light, sweet, and buttery pastries. *Bløtkake* (layered cream cake with custard, fruit, and marzipan) is a favorite dessert for Christmas and special occasions, but can be purchased in bakeries year-round.

The Norwegians take their *kaffe* (coffee) black and bitter, and they typically drink it several times a day. The tradition of locally brewed *øl* (beer) dates back to Viking times, and most major cities have their signature brew. Wine is imported, since Norway is too far north to cultivate wine grapes. A special Norwegian liquor, however, is its *akevitt* or aquavit, which in this rendition is distilled from potatoes and usually flavored with caraway.

IN NORWAY AT CHRISTMAS

EVERY CULTURE REINVENTS the wheel. But every culture reinvents it slightly differently. In Norway a traditional dining table may rest not on four legs, as tables usually do elsewhere, but on a cubic frame, like an imaginary cage that imprisons your feet while you eat.

I am a Chinese who has fallen in love with Norway. I was invited by my good friends Ole and Else to spend Christmas and New Year's with them in Oslo. It turned out to be the most marvelous Christmas of my 52 years.

It was one long feast, moving from household to household. On Christmas Eve we held hands and sang carols and danced ring-around-the-Christmas-tree. We skied at night on an illuminated track, whose lights switched off at 10, plunging us into obscurity on the downward slope. We played squash on the Norsk Hydro court and afterward relaxed in the sauna. We ushered in the New Year with fireworks on Oslo's frozen streets.

I am probably one of the few Chinese in 2,000 years to have had such an intimate glimpse of Norwegian life. Of course, it is presumptuous of me to write about a people after an eight-day visit. Yet I have the feeling that Norwegians don't very much mind presumption (as long as it is straightforward and honest). Indeed, this exceptional tolerance of friendly rudeness bespeaks their generosity and is, to me, one of their most endearing qualities.

To begin with, to a Chinese who has seen something of the world, Norway is a most exotic country. Even ordinary, everyday things are done exotically here. For example, I saw my Norwegian friends drink aquavit at breakfast; eat breakfast in the afternoon; turn on an electric switch to heat the sidewalk in front of their house; get a thrill out of driving their car like a bobsled; leave the house lights on day and night, when they went out and when they slept; wash their dishes with soap without rinsing them.

Norwegians also love to give gifts and make philosophical speeches at festive dinners. They decorate their Christmas trees not with angels but with strings of Norwegian flags. They don't find it necessary to have curtains around their showers, because it's simpler to build a drain on the bathroom floor. Cold dishes are de rigueur in winter. There is a national horror of hot, spicy foods, and a national pact to ignore vegetables.

The Norwegians and the Chinese share certain cultural traits. The most striking is a fondness for rituals. Confucius insisted on the importance of rituals as a collective code of behavior that gives order to life. The Master said, "To suppress the self and submit to ritual is to engage in Humanity." This precept might just as well apply to the Norwegians as to the Chinese.

At Christmas, all the traditional rituals are performed, some older than Norwegian Christianity. A great deal of effort goes into making sure that they are done right. After each one—the baking of the gingerbread houses, the decorating of the tree—the excitement palpably mounts.

Christmas begins on the eve, with the hostess welcoming the guests to the dinner table. She assigns to each a specific seat according to a careful arrangement. The seating plan is the one touch of originality that marks the occasion. It is, in some ways, the hostess's signature for the evening. (You find seating charts of past banquets faithfully recorded in a family book.) It's quite touching to see a young hostess assign a seat to her own mother, who has undoubtedly done the same many times herself. It signals the passing of the torch from one generation of women to another.

Once the guests are seated and the candles lighted, the feast begins. It begins with dessert: rice pudding (reminiscent of the rice gruel that Chinese eat for breakfast and when ill, albeit without milk and butter). Toasts are offered, followed by a chorus of *skaals*.

Then comes raw fish of every kind—salmon, eel, herring, enough to send a sashimi-loving Japanese into ecstasy. From the sea, the food parade marches onto land. A whole side of roast pork, skin done to a golden crisp, is served with meatballs and sausage, and buried under potatoes. Throughout there is much toasting with aquavit.

Finally, after two hours the meal is done. You get up from the table and stagger into the living room. There, in a role reminiscent of her mother's, the little daughter of the house hands out the gifts with charming solemnity.

Great care is taken by each household to do everything the same way as it was done before, so that, as with the retelling of a familiar tale, all expectations are happily satisfied. Once in a while, one may introduce an oddity, such as a Chinese guest from afar, to liven up the routine. But in general, surprises tend to raise eyebrows.

If, for the Chinese, rituals recall the teachings of Confucius, for the Norwegians they go back to the pagans. In spite of the electric sidewalks, the past is very much alive in the modern Norwegian psyche. The feasting, the speech making, the gift giving, and especially the generous hospitality and the importance of friendship are all part of the Viking tradition. Yuletide was a pagan celebration of the winter solstice. The birth of Christ was a later liturgical imposition. In some families these days, it is celebrated almost as an afterthought.

The other thing that the Norwegians share with the Chinese is their strong attachment to the family. Like the Chinese, the Norwegians belong to extended families, practically clans. But what defines a family in Norway is not at all clear. The relations are so complex and intertwined that, rather than family trees, the Norwegians seem to have family bushes. To begin with, there is one's spouse and one's brothers and sisters and their spouses. And then there is one's former spouse and his or her present spouse. The children of the former spouse of one's spouse are somewhat like nephews and nieces. Beyond that, there are the living-together arrangements and the progeny thereof, who take on quasi-family status.

It's not unusual for people who are divorced to remain good friends. Their old pictures sometimes hang in each other's bedrooms; Christmastime finds them reunited with their old partners and all their children. At first, this kind of marital pluralism is slightly unsettling. What, no bad blood? No bitterness or jealousy?

I asked a young Norwegian if it upset him to be shuttling between his father's and mother's separate households. He looked at me with astonishment. "But that's normal," he said. "Every kid in my class is in the same situation."

His guileless reaction gave me food for thought. "And indeed what's wrong with that?" I asked myself. Why try to stay with an unhappy relationship when one feels the need to change? And once changed, why not try to reconcile the past with the present?

The Chinese family is a vertical structure. Like the society itself, it is hierarchical, ruled from the top down. Confucius said, "Let the prince be prince, the minister be minister, the father be father, the son be son." Patriarchy and gerontocracy are the order of things: old men will rule, and the young will obey. Repression is inevitable under such a hierarchy. The collective always takes precedence over the individual; order always takes precedence over freedom. This denial of the self is responsible for much of the envy, backbiting, and hypocrisy common in Chinese communities.

The Norwegian family, on the other hand—or perhaps I should say the *new* Norwegian family—is horizontal. Like a strawberry plant, it spreads in all directions. Wherever it touches soil, it sprouts a new shoot. An obvious sign of this strawberry-patch kinship is the diminished importance of the family name. These days people are known mostly by first names. Children, too, often address their parents by their first names. As more and more households are headed by women, the old nuclear family is giving way to a fluid tribalism.

One way to understand the difference between the vertical and the horizontal cultures is to compare their concepts of space. To the Chinese, any space must have a center. The Chinese name for China, Zhongguo, means Center Country. Every Chinese knows that the center of China is Beijing. Why? Because the vast expanse of China is not divided into time zones, and from the Pacific to Tibet every watch is set to Beijing time. Every Chinese also knows that the center of Beijing is the Forbidden City, the symbol of governmental power, and that inside the Forbidden City sits an old man whose word is law.

No one would dream of ordering Norway's space this way. Unlike elsewhere in Europe, you seldom see a square in a Norwegian town. People don't seem to feel the need to meet and sit in the sun and feed the pigeons. In some rural communities, the church stands not in the center of town but on a hill somewhere on the outskirts. The houses, in all forms and dispositions, are widely dispersed, disdaining to line up along a straight road. One gets the impression that zoning laws are not very strict in Norway.

The big question is, if the Norwegians are such confirmed individualists, why are they so conformist? It's voluntary, true, they choose it; but it's conformity all the

same. This is the question posed—but never answered—by Ibsen's plays.

For me, the key to understanding the Norwegians is to recognize that they are a nation of irreconcilable opposites. They have taken on the contradictions of their seasons: the long, happy summer days alternating with the gloomy nights of winter. They have inherited two pasts with totally different characters. For more than 200 years, from the 9th to the 11th century, they were the scourge of Europe. They raided Britain and discovered America; they ruled Kiev and besieged Paris; they served at the court of Byzantium, and—who knows?—maybe some of them even made it to China. Lusty, adventurous, destructive, and curious about the world, they were sea nomads, the maritime counterpart of the horsemen of Genghis Khan, who conquered Russia and China. Then, as suddenly as they burst upon the world in their splendid ships, they retreated to their home in the north. They were converted to Christianity and not heard from again.

Why the seafaring Vikings turned into God-fearing Christians is one of those mysteries that history doesn't explain very well. What made them turn their gaze inward? Why did they change from thinking big to thinking small? What finally made them give up violence for peaceful ways? There is no satisfactory answer.

In any case, as the final image of Ingmar Bergman's *Fanny and Alexander* so powerfully shows, there are two ghosts walking beside the Scandinavian soul: the ghost of the hard-drinking father and the ghost of the psalm-singing stepfather. They walk beside the boy, each with a hand on his shoulder, never exchanging a word.

So the Norwegian labors under a double identity. In one ear, the Viking ghost tells him to leave Norway, this cold, homogeneous, incurious community, and discover the world. Go! The center is elsewhere! There are wonderful places to see and fabulous riches to be had!

In his other ear, the Christian ghost tells him: Stay! Go back to your roots! Embrace the tradition and preserve the social order.

This ambivalence is at the heart of Norway itself. You see it reflected on canvas in the National Gallery in Oslo. Among the painters of the late 19th century one finds two divergent sensibilities: the naturalists, who took as their subject the Norwegian folk; and the cosmopolitans, who, having spent time in Paris or Rome, insisted that art was not sociology or geography but, simply and purely, a composition of color and light.

For eight centuries, Christian ethics held sway in Norway as in the rest of Europe. But since 1945 something important has changed. There is a gap between the values of the prewar and the postwar generations. Between the threat of nuclear destruction and the temptation of America, the influence of the church waned. More and more, people have stopped practicing their faith. As they do so, they are reverting to their ancestral Viking instincts.

One clue to this reemergence of pagan consciousness is the marital pluralism that I observed. Another clue, probably closely related, is women's push for equality, a push that has been more forceful and more widely accepted in Scandinavia than anywhere else. A third indication of this new pagan way, I believe—and here I'm sticking my neck out—is the nation's collective decision, in the 1970s, to turn Norway overnight into an oil economy.

There have been a lot of arguments about the reasoning behind this decision, but none of them address the Viking-versus-Christian dilemma. If Norway had listened to its Christian voice, it would have been content to remain a frugal, hard-working nation, tending the farm or the machine. Instead, after the oil crisis of 1973, Norway chose the Viking solution and went for broke. It decided to plunder the sea.

Agrarian people, like the Chinese, are naturally patient: it takes time to make things grow. The Vikings, on the other hand, never had patience. If they could survive by fishing and gathering berries, they would not care to cultivate. Whatever they could get by raiding, they would not care to make. It is still so today. Norwegians are willing to put all their ingenuity and technical skill into building gigantic derricks and drilling kilometers beneath the sea. They will do so in order to avoid making clothes and toys to compete with Hong Kong. This is the message I got from that magnificent Christmas feast: If it tastes good raw, *don't bother to cook it*. Take it raw. Don't transform. And nothing is rawer than oil.

In 1066, King Harald Hardråde left the shores of Norway to grab the big prize: the throne of England. At Stamford Bridge he was offered by his enemy 7 feet of English ground, "and more—if you are taller." Harald fought and lost. By nightfall, mortally wounded, he said, "I will accept that piece of kingdom that was offered me this morning."

I said to my friend Ole—who, as an oil engineer at Norsk Hydro, has staked his whole future on a challenge against the North Sea—"One day your oil will be depleted, and then where will you be?" He grinned and said, echoing King Harald's insouciance, "And then I will have nothing."

— by Chunglu Tsen

BOOKS & MOVIES

Books

A History of the Vikings (1984, 2001) recounts the story of the aggressive warriors and explorers who during the Middle Ages influenced a large portion of the world, extending from Constantinople to America. Gwyn Jones's lively account makes learning the history enjoyable.

One of the greatest influences on 20th-century drama and literature, Norwegian poet and dramatist Henrik Ibsen is best known for *Peer Gynt* (1867), *A Doll's House* (1879), and *Ghosts* (1881). His classic plays are still being performed in theaters from Berlin to Beijing.

Three Norwegian novelists were awarded the Nobel Prize for literature in the 20th century: Bjørnstjerne Bjørnson, Knut Hamsun, and Sigrid Undset. Bjørnson was renowned for his lyric poetry and authored the Norwegian national anthem, *Ja, Vi Elsker Dette Landet*. Hamsun grew up in Hamarøy on the Lofoten Islands; he described the coastal people in his novels, making northern Norway famous. His book *The Growth of the Soil* won the Nobel Prize in 1920. However, he is better known for his earlier work, *Hunger* (1890), which looks into the psyche of an alienated and poor young writer living in Oslo. Sigrid Undset was honored for her masterpiece *Kristin Lavransdatter* (1928).

More recently, Jostein Gaarder achieved international literary acclaim for his best seller *Sophie's World* (1997). Among Norwegian contemporary writers, you can find English translations of Erlend Loe's *Naiive Super*, Pernille Rygg's *The Golden Section*, Herbjørg Wassmo's *Dina's Son*, and Lars Saabye Christensen's *The Half Brother*.

For Norway's past, turn to *Norway: A History from the Vikings to Our Own Times* (1998), Karsten Alnaæs's *A History of Norway in Words and Pictures* (2001), and T. K. Derry's *A History of Scandinavia* (1996). Stunning images of the Norwegian landscape have been captured in the coffee-table books *The Magic of Fjord Norway* (2000), by Per Eide and Olav Grinde; *Panorama Norway* (1996), by Pål Hermansen; and Trym Ivar Bergsmo's *Lofoten* (2001).

Living in Norway (Abbeville Press, 1993) is a glossy depiction of Norwegian interior design.

Movies

In 1995 Liv Ullmann directed the epic film *Kristin Lavransdatter,* an adaptation of Sigrid Undset's trilogy set in 14th-century Norway.

In 2001 Herbjørg Wassmo's famous novel was made into the movie *I Am Dina.*

CHRONOLOGY

2,000 BC   Tribes from southern Europe migrate toward Denmark. The majority of early settlers in Scandinavia were of Germanic origin.

ca. AD 770   The Viking Age begins. For the next 250 years, Scandinavians set sail on frequent expeditions stretching from the Baltic to the Irish seas and even to the Mediterranean as far as Sicily, employing superior ships and weapons and efficient military organization.

ca. 870   The first permanent settlers arrive in Iceland from western Norway.

ca. 900   Norwegians unite under Harald I Hårfagre.

995   King Olaf I Tryggvasson introduces Christianity to Norway.

1000   Leif Eriksson visits America. Olaf I sends a mission to Christianize Iceland.

1016–1028   King Olaf II Haraldsson (St. Olaf) tries to complete conversion of Norway to Christianity. Killed at Stiklestad in a battle against the Danish king, he becomes the patron saint of Norway.

1028–1035   Canute (Knud) the Great is king of England, Denmark (1018), and Norway (1028).

1045–1066   King Harald III (Hardråde) fights a long war with Danes, then participates in and is killed during Norman invasion of England.

1217   Haakon IV becomes king of Norway, and its "Golden Age" begins. His many reforms modernize the Norwegian administration; under him, the Norwegian empire reaches its greatest extent when Greenland and Iceland form unions with Norway in 1261. The Norwegian Sagas are written during this time.

1319   Sweden and Norway form a union that lasts until 1335.

1349   The Black Death strikes Norway and kills two-thirds of the population.

1370   The Treaty of Stralsund gives the north German trading centers of the Hanseatic League free passage through Danish waters.

1397   The Kalmar Union is formed as a result of the dynastic ties between Sweden, Denmark, and Norway; the geographical position of the Scandinavian states; and the growing influence of Germans in the Baltic. Erik of Pomerania is crowned king of the Kalmar Union.

1520   Christian II, ruler of the Kalmar Union, executes 82 people who oppose the Scandinavian union, an event known as the "Stockholm bloodbath." Sweden secedes from the Union three years later. Norway remains tied to Denmark and becomes a Danish province in 1536.

1536   The Reformation reaches Scandinavia, as Lutheranism arrives at the Hanseatic port of Bergen.

1559–1648   Norwegian trade flourishes.

1660 Peace of Copenhagen establishes modern boundaries of Denmark, Sweden, and Norway.

1811 University of Oslo is established.

1814 Sweden, after Napoleon's defeat at the Battle of Leipzig, attacks Denmark and forces the Danish surrender of Norway. On May 17, Norwegians adopt constitution at Eidsvoll. On November 4, Norway is forced to accept Act of Union with Sweden.

1884 A parliamentary system is established in Norway.

1903 Bjørnstjerne Bjørnson awarded Nobel Prize for literature.

1905 Norway's union with Sweden is dissolved.

1914 At the outbreak of World War I, Norway declares neutrality but is effectively blockaded.

1918 Norwegian women gain the right to vote.

1920 Norway joins the League of Nations. Novelist Knut Hamsun receives Nobel Prize.

1928 Sigrid Undset receives Nobel Prize for literature.

1929–1937 Norway is ruled by a Labor government.

1939 Norway declares neutrality in World War II.

1940 Germany occupies Norway.

1945 Norway joins the United Nations.

1946–1954 Norwegian statesman Trygve Lie presides as first Secretary-General of UN.

1949 Norway becomes a member of NATO.

1952 The Nordic Council, which promotes cooperation among the Nordic parliaments, is founded.

1968 Norway discovers oil in the North Sea.

1971 North Sea oil extraction begins, transforming the Norwegian economy.

1972 Norway declines membership in the EU.

1981 Gro Harlem Brundtland, a member of the Labor Party, becomes Norway's first female prime minister.

1991 King Olav dies. King Harald V ascends the throne. His wife, Queen Sonja, becomes first queen since the death of Maud in 1938.

1993 Norway's Minister of Foreign Affairs, Thorvald Stoltenberg, is appointed peace negotiator to Bosnia and Herzegovina.

1994 Norway hosts the XVII Olympic Winter Games at Lillehammer.

1995 In a national referendum, Norwegians again decline membership in the EU.

2001 Crown Prince Haakon marries Mette-Marit Høiby.

2002 Princess Martha Louise marries writer Ari Behn.

2003 Princess Martha Louise gives birth to a baby girl, named Maud Angelica.

2004 Princess Mette-Marit gives birth to a daughter, named Ingrid Alexandra.

NORWEGIAN VOCABULARY

	English	Norwegian	Pronunciation
Basics			
	Yes/no	Ja/nei	yah/nay
	Please	Vær så snill	vehr soh snihl
	Thank you much.	Tusen takk	tews-sehn tahkvery
	You're welcome.	Vær så god	vehr soh goo
	Excuse me.	Unnskyld	ewn-shewl
	Hello	God dag	goo dahg
	Goodbye	Ha det	ha day
	Today	i dag	ee dahg
	Tomorrow	i morgen	ee moh-ern
	Yesterday	i går	ee gohr
	Morning	morgen	moh-ern
	Afternoon	ettermiddag	eh-terr-mid-dahg
	Night	natt	naht
Numbers			
	1	en	ehn
	2	to	too
	3	tre	treh
	4	fire	feer-eh
	5	fem	fehm
	6	seks	sehks
	7	syv, sju	shew
	8	åtte	oh-teh
	9	ni	nee
	10	ti	tee
Days of the Week			
	Monday	mandag	mahn-dahg
	Tuesday	tirsdag	teesh-dahg
	Wednesday	onsdag	oonss-dahg
	Thursday	torsdag	tohsh-dahg
	Friday	fredag	fray-dahg

Saturday	lørdag	loor-dahg
Sunday	søndag	suhn-dahg

Useful Phrases

Do you speak English?	Snakker De engelsk?	snahk-kerr dee ehng-ehlsk
I don't speak Norwegian.	Jeg snakker ikke norsk.	yay snahk-kerr ik-keh nohrshk
I don't understand.	Jeg forstår ikke.	yay fosh-tawr ik-keh
I don't know.	Jeg vet ikke.	yay veht ik-keh
I am American/ British.	Jeg er amerikansk/ engelsk.	yay ehr ah-mehr-ee-kahnsk/ehng-ehlsk
I am sick.	Jeg er dårlig.	yay ehr dohr-lee
Please call a doctor.	Vær så snill og ring etter en lege.	vehr soh snihl oh ring eht-ehr ehn lay-geh
Do you have vacant room?	Har du et rom som er ledig?	yay vil yehr-neh hah eht room
How much does it cost?	Hva koster det?	vah koss-terr deh
It's too expensive.	Det er for dyrt.	deh ehr for deert
Beautiful	vakker	vah-kehr
Help!	Hjelp!	yehlp
Stop!	Stopp!	stop
How do I get to . . .	Hvor er	voor ehr
the train station?	jernbanestasjonen	yehrn-bahn-eh sta-shoon-ern
the post office?	posthuset	pohsst-hewss
the tourist office?	turistkontoret	tew-reest-koon-toor-er
the hospital?	sykehuset	see-keh-hoo-seh
Does this bus go to . . . ?	Går denne bussen til . . . ?	gohr den-nah boos teel
Where is the W.C.?	Hvor er toalettene?	voor ehr too-ah-leht-te-ne
On the left	Til venstre	teel vehn-streh
On the right	Til høyre	teel hooy-reh
Straight ahead	Rett fram	reht frahm

Dining Out

menu	meny	meh-new
fork	gaffel	gahff-erl
knife	kniv	kneev

spoon	skje	shay
napkin	serviett	ssehr-vyeht
bread	brød	brur
butter	smør	smurr
milk	melk	mehlk
pepper	pepper	pehp-per
salt	salt	sahlt
sugar	sukker	sook-kerr
water/bottled water	vann	vahn
The check, please.	Jeg vil gjerne betale.	yay vil yehr-neh beh-tah-leh

INDEX

PHOTO CREDITS

NOTES

ABOUT OUR WRITERS

Australian **Daniel Cash** has lived in Oslo since 2001. He resides with his family in a former wheat silo converted into a modern apartment building with a view of the city. Daniel has contributed to previous editions of *Fodor's Norway* and *Fodor's Australia,* and during another stint in Oslo in 1998 he was co-editor of *Trade Winds,* the Norwegian shipping newspaper. Besides writing and editing, he runs a company to recruit Norwegian students to Australian universities. Daniel says that the best thing about living in Oslo is the variety of activities available due to the dramatic change in seasons. "In late summer you can swim in a beautiful lake, just 10 minutes' drive from Oslo's center, and only four months later skate or ski on top of the same lake. On the other hand, the most difficult thing about living in Norway for an Australian is the expensive beer prices."

Norman Renouf was born in London and educated at Charlton Secondary School, Greenwich. Always interested in travel, he started writing travel guides, articles, and newspaper contributions in the early 1990s and has covered destinations throughout Europe. Norman updated the Smart Travel Tips chapter for this edition of *Fodor's Norway.* Now living in Richmond, Virginia, he has also written several guides about Washington, D.C., and the mid-Atlantic region.

In the 12 years since he finished his political science degree at the University of Bergen, **Lars Ursin** has worked as a freelance journalist and translator. He has traveled extensively in Norway, partly for his journalistic assignments, but mainly to satisfy his addiction to everything mountain related, especially hiking, skiing, and snowboarding. Lars updated the Bergen and West Coast chapters.